D0982681

Legacies of Dachau
The Uses and Abuses of a Concentration Camp, 1933–2001

Auschwitz, Belsen, Dachau. Three generations later, these names still evoke the horrors of Nazi Germany around the world. What should be done with sites where hundreds of thousands of people were murdered and cremated? Punish Nazis? Tear down the buildings and plant trees? Build stores and apartments? Educate teenagers? All of these things happened at former concentration camps after 1945.

Marcuse's insightful narrative takes one of these sites, Dachau, and traces its history from the beginning of the twentieth century, through its twelve years as Nazi Germany's premier concentration camp, to the camp's postwar uses as a prison, residential neighborhood, and, finally, museum and memorial site.

With superbly chosen examples and an eye for telling detail, this absorbing book documents how Nazi perpetrators were quietly rehabilitated to become powerful elites, while survivors of the concentration camps were once again marginalized, criminalized, and silenced. The early postwar dodge "We didn't know!" became "We don't want to know," and German officials first rebuilt the camp as a huge housing project, then attempted to bulldoze it and the crematorium into oblivion. However, by 1965 camp survivors were able to ensure the preservation of some remains as a memorial site.

Always situating Dachau within the broader context of German history, Marcuse reveals the underlying dynamic of German memory debates from the 1968 rebellion to the *Holocaust* mini series in the 1970s, to Bitburg in the 1980s, to the Goldhagen and Berlin "murdered Jews" memorial controversies of the 1990s.

Combining meticulous archival research with an encyclopedic knowledge of the extensive literatures on Germany, the Holocaust, and historical memory, *Legacies of Dachau* unravels the intriguing relationship between historical events, individual memory, and political culture, enabling it to offer the first unifying interpretation of their interaction over the entire sweep of German history from the Nazi era into the twenty-first century.

HAROLD MARCUSE is Associate Professor of History at the University of California, Santa Barbara, where he teaches modern and contemporary German history. The grandson of the German émigré philosopher Herbert Marcuse, he returned to Germany in the 1970s to trace family roots. He soon became interested in West Germany's relationship to its Nazi past, and in 1985 he co-produced an exhibition about monuments and memorials commemorating events of the Nazi era. That exhibition was shown in nearly thirty German cities, including Dachau. Marcuse has since published numerous articles on Dachau, German history, and memorial culture.

PUBLISHED BY THE PRESS SYNDICATE OF THE UNIVERSITY OF CAMBRIDGE
The Pitt Building, Trumpington Street, Cambridge, United Kingdom

CAMBRIDGE UNIVERSITY PRESS
The Edinburgh Building, Cambridge CB2 2RU, UK
40 West 20th Street, New York, NY 10011–4211, USA
10 Stamford Road, Oakleigh, VIC 3166, Australia
Ruiz de Alarcón 13, 28014 Madrid, Spain
Dock House, The Waterfront, Cape Town 8001, South Africa

http://www.cambridge.org

First published 2001

Printed in the United Kingdom at the University Press, Cambridge

Typeface Utopia 8/11pt   *System* QuarkXPress™   [SE]

A catalogue record for this book is available from the British Library

ISBN 0 521 55204 4 hardback

Legacies of Dachau

The Uses and Abuses of a
Concentration Camp, 1933–2001

HAROLD MARCUSE

CAMBRIDGE
UNIVERSITY PRESS

Erinnern
das ist
vielleicht
die qualvollste Art
des Vergessens
und vielleicht
die freundlichste Art
der Linderung
dieser Qual

Remembering
that is
perhaps
the most painful way
of forgetting
and perhaps
the most gentle way
of soothing
that pain

Erich Fried

Contents

Contents

Contents

Illustrations

Illustrations can be found between pages 126 and 127 and pages 334 and 335

1 Regional map of Dachau showing the town, and the SS and concentration camps.
2 Plan of the Dachau concentration camp and memorial site.
3 Aerial view of the "residential settlement Dachau-East," 1956.
4 Aerial view of the KZ Dachau memorial site, ca. 1969.
5 The Dachau gas chamber–crematorium building, built in 1942, ca. 30 April 1945.
6 Sign in front of the Dachau crematorium, fall 1945.
7 The camp "service building" at the south end of the prisoners' compound, 1946.
8 Entrance to part A of the Dachau Prisoner of War Enclosure, ca. 1945–8.
9 US soldier showing crematorium to Dachau notables, 8 May 1945.
10 One of many posters displayed throughout Germany in the early summer of 1945.
11 Courtroom in the service building, November 1945.
12 Postcard commemorating the first anniversary of Dachau's liberation, April 1946.
13 Dachau mayor Josef Schwalber unveiling a plaque, April 1947.
14 Poster for the Dachau International Information Office, 1945–6.
15 Postcard of entry gatehouse, sold in the Dachau crematorium museum, ca. 1945–8.
16 Postcard of cremation process, sold in the Dachau crematorium museum, ca. 1945–8.
17 Exhibition in the Dachau crematorium undressing room, ca. 1945–9.
18 Exhibition in a room of the Dachau crematorium, 1950–3.

Tables

Preface

Like many young Americans, I first visited Dachau during a college vacation abroad. That visit, in 1977, had a powerful effect on me, probably because I realized that my Jewish grandfather might have ended up there if he had not presciently emigrated with his 4-year-old son in 1933. I have been back to the Dachau memorial site many times, but I still remember some impressions of that first visit. The camp seemed much larger than I had imagined, and the huge photographs in the museum left a lasting impression. I also remember seeing the film with footage of Dachau citizens leading horse-drawn carts laden with corpses after liberation.

My experience was roughly typical of that of most young American visitors. I did not know much about the concentration camps or the Holocaust, although I had seen films on the Nazi era, such as *The Diary of Anne Frank*, and *Night and Fog*. I remembered little of such films, except for the piercing tatu-tata of the German sirens at the end of the former, and the shocking concluding pictures of vintage bulldozers pushing piles of naked corpses into huge pits in the latter.

Much less typical was the role that my brief visit eventually came to play in my life. I did not return to Dachau again for six years, but in the intervening time other experiences resonated with the impulse I received during that visit. One such experience was meeting the war-generation parents of my German friends, who were uncomfortable when they learned I was Jewish. I still remember how one mother sat me down on the kitchen bench when we were alone. She drew up a chair opposite me and clasped her gnarled hands nervously on the table. "You know, Harald [she was speaking German], back then there was nothing we could do. I [or was it 'we'?] saw them at the train station, but what could we do? We were helpless." And so on. I was uncomfortable too, and I reassured her that those were hard times. It was like a scene in a bad movie.

While numerous similarly awkward encounters with other Germans from my generation on up made me much more conscious of the Holocaust and the presence of history in Germany, it was a meeting with

American Jewish friends that finally prompted me to return to Dachau in 1983. A friend of my parents, Anita S., had visited me in Freiburg, where I was studying, a year earlier, and I had given her a tour of the city's gothic cathedral. When I stopped by to see her at her home in the US, she took me to her studio to show me some works inspired by Freiburg's stained-glass windows: twisted barbed wire covered with smoky gray plaster was arranged on sheet metal cut to the shape of the gothic pointed-arch windows. Entwined in the barbed wire were attributes of Christian saints, such as a wheel for St. Catherine, and a tower for St. Barbara – the instruments of their martyrdom. I was impressed by both their aesthetic quality and their symbolism. A vague image of Dachau came back to me, a memory of Christian churches in the memorial site. I thought these reliefs would be ideal in such a church, and I promised to find out who might be in charge of the Dachau chapels. And that is what set me on a quest to find out how, and why, the former Dachau concentration camp came to have the rather improbable form it has today.

In the intervening years numerous individuals have helped me to research, conceptualize, and write this history. In addition to thanking all of the friends, colleagues, librarians, archivists, photographers, and artists who are too numerous to name here, I would like to express my gratitude explicitly to Barbara Distel, the director of the Dachau memorial site, for all of her help and support, and to my family, for their forbearance during the many years I have worked on this project. The Friedrich Ebert Foundation, the University of Michigan, the University of California, Santa Barbara, and the Center for German and European Studies at UC Berkeley provided financial support.

This book is dedicated to everyone who worked and is working to preserve the former concentration camp at Dachau as a place to remember the past and work towards a better future.

Abbreviations and glossary

AEMF   Archiv des Erzbistums München und Freising, Catholic episcopal archive in Munich

AP   Anton Pfeiffer papers, held by BayHsta

AvS   Arbeitsgemeinschaft verfolgter Sozialdemokraten, SPD organization of former persecutees

AWJD   *Allgemeine Wochenzeitung der Juden in Deutschland*, Jewish weekly newspaper in West Germany

BaKo   Bundesarchiv, Koblenz, West German national archive

BayHsta   Bayerisches Hauptstaatsarchiv, Bavarian Main State Archive, Munich

BayStaA   Bayerisches Staatsarchiv München, Bavarian State Archive, Munich

BJR   Bayerischer Jugendring, the Bavarian Youth Ring

BLA   Bayerisches Landtagsarchiv, Munich (archive of the Bavarian state parliament)

BVN   Bund der Verfolgten des Naziregimes, CDU/CSU organization of former persecutees

CDU   Christian Democratic Union

CID   Comité International de Dachau, umbrella organization of national associations of former KZ Dachau inmates

CSU   Bavarian Christian Socialist Union, political party

DaA   Archive of the Dachau Concentration Camp Memorial Site (Archiv der KZ-Gedenkstätte Dachau)

DDW   Dokumentationsarchiv des deutschen Widerstands, Frankfurt, archive with many VVN materials

DGB   Deutscher Gewerkschaftsbund, Association of German Trade Unions

DM   deutschmark (West German currency after June 1948)

DNZSZ   *Deutsche National-Zeitung und Soldaten-Zeitung*, right-wing weekly newspaper

dpa   Deutsche Presse-Agentur, (West) German newspaper wire service

DPs   Displaced persons, postwar jargon for liberated persecutees in foreign countries

Dulag   *Durchgangslager,* transit camp for refugees or forced laborers

EKD   Evangelische Kirche in Deutschland, German Protestant Church

EZB   Evangelisches Zentralarchiv, Berlin

FAZ   *Frankfurter Allgemeine Zeitung,* national newspaper

FDP   Freie Demokratische Partei, German liberal party

FIAPP   Fédération Internationale des Associations des (Anciens) Prisonniers Politiques

FIR   Fédération Internationale des Résistants, international umbrella organization of which the VVN is a member

FNDIRP   Fédération Nationale des Déportés et Internés Résistants et Patriotes, French national organization

FR   *Frankfurter Rundschau,* major West German newspaper

FstHH   Forschungsstelle für die Geschichte des Nationalsozialismus in Hamburg

Gedenkstätte   Memorial site

GSE   *Gesellschaft, Staat, Erziehung,* journal for educators, 1956–72

Hebertshausen   Small town northeast of Dachau where the SS had a shooting and execution range

HS   Hans Schwarz papers, held by FstHH

IfZ   Institut für Zeitgeschichte (Institute for Contemporary History), Munich

IIO   International Information Office, service organization for liberated Dachau inmates

IMT   Published trial records of the Nuremberg trials, officially: *Trial of the Major War Criminals before the International Military Tribunal, Nuremberg, 14 November 1945–1 October 1946*

IPC   International Prisoners' Committee, resistance organization in the Dachau concentration camp, predecessor of CID

Jourhaus   Entry gate building of Dachau concentration camp

JS   Joseph Schwalber papers (mayor of Dachau 1945–7, Bavarian politician), held by BayHsta.

Jusos   Jungsozialisten, youth organization of the SPD

KPD   Kommunistische Partei Deutschlands, German Communist Party

Kräutergarten   "Herbal Garden": Dachau concentration camp plantation

KZ   (prounounced "kah-tset"), common abbreviation for *Konzentrationslager,* concentration camp (KL was the official Nazi abbreviation)

KZler   Colloquial term for concentration camp inmates in the Nazi and postwar periods

Lager   camp

Landesverband   "regional association," used here as a short form for the Landesverband der israelitischen Kultusgemeinden in Bayern (Regional Association of Israelite Cultural Communities in Bavaria), the umbrella organization of post-1945 Jewish communities in Bavaria

LEA   Landesentschädigungsamt, Bavarian State Office of Restitution

Leiten   Hill near Dachau concentration camp where thousands of inmates are buried

LFR   Landesrat für Freiheit und Recht, anticommunist former KZ inmates' organization in Munich

LGD   Lagergemeinschaft Dachau, organization of the West German Dachau camp survivors

LRA   Landratsamt, County Governor's Office; in this case, of Dachau county

MArb   Staatsministerium für Arbeit und Soziales, Bavarian government ministry responsible for refugee camps

MFin   Bavarian Ministry of Finance (files in BayHsta)

MM/DN   *Münchner Merkur/Dachauer Nachrichten*, local edition of Munich newspaper

MSo   Bavarian Ministerium für Sonderaufgaben, responsible, *inter alia*, for denazification

NA   Archive of the Dokumentenhaus Neuengamme (former concentration camp near Hamburg)

NARA   National Archives and Records Administration, US national archive in Suitland, Maryland

NPD   Nationaldemokratische Partei Deutschlands, West German neo-Nazi party

NS   National Socialist (Nazi)

NYHT   *New York Herald-Tribune*

NYT   *New York Times*

NZ   *Neue Zeitung*, national newspaper 1946–50, published by former German émigrés for the US High Commissioner in Germany

Obb   Oberbayern, administrative district in Bavaria, includes Dachau

OK   Papers of Otto Kohlhofer (former Dachau inmate), held by DaA

OM   Papers of Oskar Müller (former Dachau inmate, leading prisoner functionary [*Lagerältester*] of the camp at liberation), held by DDW

OMGBy   Office of (United States) Military Government in Bavaria

OMGUS   Office of Military Government in Germany, United States

POW   (also PW) prisoner of war

Priestergemeinschaft   "priests' association": Organization of priests who survived imprisonment in KZ Dachau

RG   Record Group (call number of documents in NARA)

RM   Reichsmark (German currency prior to 1948)

RSHA   Reichssicherheitshauptamt, SS Main Office of Reich Security

SAPMo   Stiftung Archiv der Parteien und Massenorganisationen der DDR, Berlin (East German national archive)

SED   Sozialistische Einheitspartei Deutschlands, East German union of SPD and KPD

SPD   Sozialdemokratische Partei Deutschlands, German Social Democratic Party

Staatssekretär   Highest administrative post under a cabinet minister

StAHH   Staatsarchiv Hamburg

Stk   Staatskanzlei, Bavarian State Chancellory files in BayHsta

StMü   Stadtarchiv München, Munich city archive

SZ/DN *Süddeutsche Zeitung/Dachauer Neueste*, local edition of Munich newspaper

SZA   Archive of the *Süddeutsche Zeitung*

USHMM   United States Holocaust Memorial Museum, Washington, D.C.

Vergangenheitsbewältigung   "Mastery of the past," term commonly used in Germany since the early 1960s to denote attempts to come to terms with the Nazi past. It stands in contrast to *Aufarbeitung der Vergangenheit*, literally "working through the past."

VfZ   *Vierteljahrshefte für Zeitgeschichte*, journal of IfZ

VVN   Vereinigung der Verfolgten des Naziregimes, (West) German organization of former persecutees

VVNN   *VVN-Nachrichten*, bi-weekly newspaper of the VVN

WVHA   Wirtschaftsverwaltungshauptamt, SS "Main Office of Economic Administration," a branch of the SS created in February 1942 to coordinate SS business and construction ventures.

Dachau: past, present, future

Each of the three ways of dealing with the past is suited to one kind of
soil and one climate only: in every other context it turns into a
destructive weed. If the creators of great things need the past at all, they
will take control of it by means of monumental historiography.
Someone who, in contrast, likes to remain in familiar, venerable
settings will care for the past as an antiquarian historian. Only someone
who feels crushed by a present concern and wants to throw off the
burden at any cost has a need for critical, that is judging and
condemning historiography.

Friedrich Nietzsche, in *On the Uses and Abuses of History for the*
Present (1874)

Historians have long known that each age creates its own history out of the
raw material of the past, according to what it sees as its own present needs
and future goals. As the Nazi concentration camps were liberated in the
spring of 1945, they became part of that raw material of the past. Although
in many of the former concentration camps some efforts were made to
preserve a few remains as a record of what had happened there, most of
them were first devoted to other purposes, such as emergency housing for
liberated inmates and refugees, or internment camps for German suspects. Not until the 1950s did concerted efforts begin to preserve them for
educational purposes, and those efforts often did not bear fruit until the
1960s, and in some cases not until the 1970s or 1980s. Depending on the
political situation at the time, as well as on the influence and composition
of the groups and agencies vying for control of the sites, the end results
varied widely. Thus the history of each former concentration camp reflects
not only the political and cultural history of its host country, but also more
specifically the changing values and goals held by various groups in that
society.

From the outset, the Dachau concentration camp occupied an especially prominent place in the Nazi concentration camp system. It was the
first camp to be set up in 1933, and it was the first to be under the direct
supervision of Heinrich Himmler, who later controlled the entire concentration and extermination camp network. In April 1934, when Dachau's
commandant was appointed "Inspector of Concentration Camps," the

1

Dachau system became a model for all other Nazi concentration camps. The flagship concentration camp also served as a "school of violence" for concentration camp leaders, with eighteen of the top concentration camp commandants and *Lagerführer* (head of the prisoner area of the camp) receiving their initial training there, including Adolf Eichmann, the bureaucrat who masterminded the industrially organized extermination of the Jews, and Rudolf Höss, the infamous commandant of Auschwitz.[1]

Dachau was also the camp where the Nazi regime's most prominent prisoners, including chancellors and cabinet ministers from occupied countries, as well as high-ranking religious leaders, were incarcerated. Dachau's postwar notoriety was ensured by its liberation a week before the end of the war, before it could be destroyed or evacuated, and just after an intensive Allied media blitz to publicize the atrocities in the Nazi camps had begun. Finally, since Dachau was located on the western side of the postwar "Iron Curtain," it was accessible to tourists from all over the world, and susceptible to the lobbying efforts of local, regional, and international groups. (In Eastern Europe, governments held a monopoly on the forms of memorialization.) For all of these reasons, Dachau is especially suited to serve as a representative case study of broader Western and particularly West German uses and abuses of the Nazi past after 1945.

In the first fifty years since the Dachau concentration camp was liberated in April 1945, more than 21 million people visited the site, 19 million of them – 90 percent – since the former Nazi camp was designated as a memorial in 1965. Visitors go to Dachau to learn more about the history of the concentration camp, and they find a museum and terrain that have been designed to convey certain lessons about it. Few of them know how the site was used in the twenty years before it was turned into a memorial, nor are they aware of the many choices that were made in the creation and modification of the present memorial site. How did the Dachau memorial site come to be? What are the lessons it teaches, and who decided how to convey them? How are the site's messages received by visitors, and what short- and long-term effects does a visit to the site have upon them? This book was written to provide answers to those questions.

The Dachau camp, 1916–2000: A brief history

Before delving into the specifics of the Dachau memorial site's past, an overview of the history and layout of the site reveals important aspects of its reconstruction.

The origins of the Dachau concentration camp reach back to World War I, when the Bavarian government decided to locate a gunpowder and munitions factory on the outskirts of this town, on a railroad connection about 15 km from downtown Munich (see ill. 1). The factories, company housing, and workers' barracks were shut down under the disarmament terms of the Versailles Treaty, and they stood unused during the 1920s. When Hitler's Nazi Party was looking for facilities to locate camps to neutralize its opponents after it gained control of the national government in early 1933, the abandoned armaments works near the birthplace and headquarters of the party offered an ideal solution. Two years later Hitler and Himmler decided to make the concentration camp system a permanent feature of their new state. A number of new camps were constructed from scratch, beginning with Sachsenhausen and Buchenwald. In 1937–8 the Dachau prisoners' compound was completely rebuilt, and new barracks were added to the SS portion of the camp to house two divisions of SS military troops (ill. 3). Thus by the end of the war the Dachau concentration camp was a huge complex, more than one square kilometer in size.

The Dachau camp's postwar history can be divided into five main phases. The first was the shortest, lasting only three years, from July 1945 until the summer of 1948. During that time the US army used the concentration and SS camps to intern up to 30,000 officers from Nazi Party organizations and the German army (ill. 8). In the Dachau internment camp, the US army conducted a series of trials of the personnel of various concentration camps (ill. 11). In early 1948, as the wartime alliance between the Soviet Union and the Western powers broke down, the United States quickly brought its program of "denazification" to an end in order to increase German support for the West.

The second phase of the former concentration camp's history began when the US military government returned the compound to the Bavarian government in 1948. The Bavarian government first decided to use its portion of the former concentration camp as a "correctional institution," but soon changed its mind. Faced with a refugee crisis, as ethnic Germans were expelled and fled from the Soviet bloc, in April 1948 the Bavarian parliament decided instead to convert the prison camp into a residential settlement. Thus in the fall of 1948 the prisoners' barracks were transformed into apartments and stores for about 2,000 Germans from Czechoslovakia (ills. 3, 23–5). This settlement, officially named Dachau-East, remained in the former prison camp for fifteen years until 1964. Its infrastructure evolved gradually. The prison walls and barbed wire were replaced by storage sheds, and some of the watchtowers were torn down (ill. 26). The main camp street was paved and street lights installed (ill. 27). Only the crematorium compound remained accessible as a designated relic of the camp. However, Bavarian government officials removed an exhibition on display in the larger of the two crematorium buildings in 1953, and attempted – unsuccessfully – to have the building torn down in 1955 (ills. 5, 18).

Increasing public interest in the site during the late 1950s and early 1960s helped to facilitate the transition to the Dachau camp's third postwar function: a memorial site. In 1962, after the annual number of visitors had tripled from about 100,000 to over 300,000 (see ill. 73), the Bavarian government finally yielded to pressure from a lobby of surviving camp inmates and agreed to maintain the former camp as a memorial site. During the conversion, completed in 1965, the government had all of the prisoners' barracks and several other historical buildings torn down, and new monuments and buildings erected in their place. Only a few icons of the camp remained: the gatehouse and watchtowers, the service building with a tract of individual cells, two reconstructed barracks, and the crematorium–gas chamber building (ill. 4). With the dedication of Protestant and Jewish memorial buildings in 1967 and a large memorial sculpture in 1968, the memorial site and museum designed by survivors within constraints dictated by the Bavarian government reached their final form.

The decades from 1968 to 1998 build a fourth phase of Dachau's postwar history. It is characterized by stagnation in the physical appearance of the site, but by dramatic changes in the visitor demographics. During the 1970s the total number of visitors tripled again to nearly 1 million. At the same time, the average age dropped precipitously, with the age group under 25 – born long after the end of the war – comprising a majority of visitors. Except for the addition to the tiny administrative staff of nine secondary school teachers on a rotating basis in 1983, few changes were made to accommodate this group until 1996. By that time a sufficient number of members of the postwar generations had become established in local, state, and national political life. At the end of the 1990s a radical revision of the infrastructure at the site was begun. A visitors' center was planned, additional bus lines improved public access, an overnight youth center was chartered and built, and a new multimedia museum with supplementary exhibitions and classrooms was designed. This book concludes with a glimpse forward to a new, fifth phase of Dachau's postwar history: the memorial site as an experiential educational space for people increasingly distant from the events that transpired there.

A visit to Dachau, 2001

What will visitors find when they travel to the Dachau memorial site after the current construction is completed in 2001? (When this book went to press in 2001, bureaucratic and conceptual difficulties made the scheduled completion date of November 2001 increasingly unlikely. Readers should thus take "2001" to mean "when the renovations begun in 1998 are complete.") Especially for foreigners, who make up about two-thirds of Dachau's visitors, a trip to the memorial site begins with the discovery that the name Dachau signifies more than just a Nazi concentration camp. Dachau is also a city of about 35,000 residents that was established more than 1,000 years before it became home to one of Germany's most notorious concentration camps. (Its pre-camp history is briefly recounted in chapter 1.) This "other Dachau," as some of its residents call it, dominates the approach to the memorial site. Whether visitors take the S-Bahn from Munich (line 2 of the fast and efficient commuter train departs every twenty minutes for the twenty-minute trip) and arrive at Dachau station, or whether they drive from Munich on local roads or the autobahn, they find adequate signage directing their way (ill. 77).[2]

This was not always the case: for decades local and regional officials tried to make the former Dachau camp difficult to find (ill. 78). The local populace's changing opinions of the memorial site is one of the important narrative threads running through this book. For instance, in 1955 Dachau county's representative in the Bavarian parliament tried to have the crematorium torn down in order to discourage visitors. When his initiative failed, he had all directional signs to the former camp removed. Visitors in the 1950s and 1960s often reported receiving evasive answers to their requests for directions to the former Dachau camp. From the 1950s to the 1990s the single bus line traversing the three kilometers between Dachau's train station and the camp made only nine round trips between 9 a.m. and 5 p.m., with gaps of more than an hour during the peak midday period.[3]

After 2001 the new entrance to the memorial site will lead past the site of the commandant's villa, built in 1938 and torn down in 1987, to a visitors' reception center in one of the few remaining buildings from the World War I munitions factory that was converted to create the original Dachau camp in 1933. The relocation of the entrance reflects an important feature of what West Germans learned about Nazi atrocities after 1945: except for the first short period immediately after the war, the perpetrators of those atrocities were hidden or ignored until the 1990s. The Dachau concentration camp was originally four times larger than the prison compound that has become the memorial site (see ill. 1). The huge SS camp adjacent to the prisoners' compound included housing and facilities not only for hundreds of camp guards, but for many thousands of SS military troops as well. For example, a major SS hospital, the payroll office for more than a million SS men, and numerous production facilities were located there. (The SS, short for *Schutzstaffel* or "protective formation," was founded as Hitler's personal bodyguard detachment in the 1920s. In the 1940s it grew to an organization of over a million men. The two most notorious of its many branches were the "death's head" division – the concentration camp guards – and the *Waffen* or weapon SS – the fighting troops.)

For decades this SS section of the original concentration camp was concealed behind a cement wall and a high earthen barrier. From 1945 to 1971 the former SS camp served as the US army's Eastman Barracks. Since 1971 it has been the home of a detachment of the Bavarian state police. The original entrance to the prisoners' compound, which came through the SS camp, was accessible only from inside the memorial site. Since 1965 visitors have had to enter the memorial site through a breach in the wall on the opposite side of the camp (see ills. 2, 4, 80). The 1998 redesign plan recommended giving a corner of the Bavarian state police compound to the memorial site, so that the original concentration camp entrance route could be restored.

Even though the Bavarian police demolished a majority of the buildings between 1978 and 1992, the SS part of the camp still contains far more original buildings than the memorial site itself. The central SS pay-processing bunker, the dispensary, and several factory halls and warehouses are all still there, as is the triangular swimming pond that is now stocked for recreational fishing (ill. 1). What astonished me most, when a retired state policeman showed me around the complex in 1991, was the *Holländerhalle*, a large hall named for the Dutch rag-cutting machines used when the complex was a munitions plant during World War I. Inside, in neat rows angled to drive out of the wide doors in a hurry, were dozens of riot police vans and imposing trucks with water cannon (ill. 67). But this adjacent historical site is off limits to the visitors of the memorial site. Its presence is only revealed in rare incidents such as in 1981, when tear gas from a house-storming exercise drifted over to the museum (ill. 68).

From the reception center at the edge of the former SS camp visitors will go on to the *Jourhaus*, the entrance building of the prisoners' compound, through the iron gate inscribed "Arbeit macht frei": "Work makes free" (see ill. 15). This is one of the last surviving relics of what I call the "clean" concentration camp, a Nazi fiction that situated the concentration camps in their plan to create a pure Germanic master race by using hard labor to "educate" recalcitrant Aryans.

The guiding principle of the latest renovation was to re-create as closely as possible the path taken by inmates entering the camp. Traversing that same path is indeed a powerful way to help visitors to imagine and identify with the inmates' horrific experience, and thus be motivated to avoid the behaviors that made the atrocities of KZ Dachau possible. However, except for this entrance inscription, all traces of this Nazi fiction have been effaced, including the prison library and several didactic sayings painted on roofs and walls throughout the camp.

Entering visitors see a large expanse of barren, stony ground straight ahead, an angular black monument and the museum building on the right, and two drab gray barracks with more bare, gravelly ground on the left (ills. 2, 4). The impression of a barren, sanitized place predominates. A closer look to the left reveals two long rows of low concrete rectangles behind the two barracks. Between them two rows of poplar trees sway in the wind, and another couple of hundred meters further back rise the geometric shapes of Protestant, Catholic, and Jewish memorial buildings at the northern edge of the site.

After 2001 some of the concrete rectangles may carry black poles marking the outlines of a few barracks. The memorial site redesigners of 1998 deemed the functions of those particular barracks especially noteworthy: for example, the infirmary barrack where prisoners were used as guinea pigs in medical experiments. In the early 1960s the Dachau survivors designing the first memorial site wanted to leave all of the original barracks intact, but the Bavarian government demolished them in 1964 to save renovation and upkeep costs. In order to document some of the specific features of the site, in 1985 and again after 1999 a total of about thirty-five large signs and tablets with drawings, texts and historical photographs were placed around the camp (ill. 83). They are a feeble attempt to convey a sense of the original appearance of this barren expanse.

Dachau has changed a great deal since its concentration camp days. There are no corpses, no inmates, no dogs, no guards, no living relics at this site. Antiseptic gray with a few touches of green and black predominate. There are no smells – of sweat, excrement, or death, so prominent in the narratives of the liberators – and no sounds except the feet of other tourists treading on the gravel, or perhaps an occasional guide giving explanations to a tour group. Barely a handful of camp survivors still give tours, and their voices will fall silent soon. Survivors, local volunteers, and a few public school teachers on special assignment began giving regular tours in the early 1980s. By the end of the millennium, many hundreds of tours were offered each year, the vast majority of them by volunteers. Before that, individuals and groups were left to themselves to explore the terrain. After 2001 visitors should be able to rent tape-recorded tours in several languages at the reception center.

The tour of the site usually begins with the main museum in the former service building at this end of the camp. The almost 200 meter long C-shaped building, with its 70 meter long east and west wings, was built when the Dachau concentration camp was remade in 1937–8. Originally, on the gatehouse side it contained workshops and rooms for registering and shaving incoming prisoners (ill. 2). In the long middle tract were the boiler room, showers, kitchen, and laundry. Clothing and belongings taken from prisoners upon entry were stored in the east wing. The post-2001 exhibition will illustrate an important feature of Dachau's postwar history: as the past recedes in time, it becomes increasingly necessary to provide explicit re-creations of that past. When the first exhibition in this building was designed in 1965, experts deemed it sufficient to present enlargements of documents and photographs illustrating important characteristics of the concentration camp system as exemplified by Dachau. According to the 1996 recommendations, the original functions of the existing buildings and rooms should be explicitly marked and coordinated with the exhibitions they contain. By reversing the usual left-to-right direction of the museum, visitors will retrace the route traversed by inmates arriving at the camp.

Another planned 2001 innovation is the inclusion of information about hitherto marginalized groups of prisoners, such as Sinti and Roma (gypsies), homosexuals, Jews, Jehovah's Witnesses, and Christian clergy. Exemplary individual biographies help visitors to empathize with their values, fates, and the choices they made. Corresponding to the great public respect accorded to camp survivors since the 1990s (their status climbed steeply in the 1980s after a very slow ascent from rock bottom in the 1950s), an exhibit of artworks by camp survivors may be mounted as well. As a final 2001 innovation, in consideration of the decades that have passed since 1945, the museum is to include a section retracing the postwar history of the site.

A memorial site exists to document a specific period of history, but it also uses the power of authenticity and location to help its visitors form an emotional connection to that history. Unfortunately, most opportunities to document the postwar uses of the Dachau camp were lost. For instance, a church built by interned SS men in November 1945 stood in front of the entry gate until 1963 (ills. 3, 42). It was torn down because it had not been a part of the concentration camp, and probably also because it presented a potentially confusing aspect of the perpetrators' biographies: their rapid postwar conversion into pious men. If this church had been left standing, it might have helped future generations to understand their own relationship to the concentration camp. For Germans that relationship includes having parents and grandparents who grew up in a time when dedicated Nazi henchmen metamorphosed en masse to nominal West German democrats. In spite of the realization that original relics vastly increase the educational impact of the museum, in 2000 the policymakers were divided over whether to preserve some post-1945 murals discovered in a portion of the service building used as a mess hall by the US army. These paintings depict scenes such as a Hawaiian sunset and the Manhattan skyline (ill. 88). Although the murals would provide a powerful backdrop for the exhibit on the postwar uses of the camp, some German pedagogues advocate their demolition. They may fear that this postwar relic might detract from the experience of the former concentration camp they want future generations to have.

After exiting the museum and walking past the jagged black bronze international memorial, most visitors walk down the tree-lined central camp street to the back, where the religious memorials and the crematorium compound are. These poplar trees were planted along the central street in the 1980s to replace the aged camp-era originals that were felled in 1964 (ills. 27, 29). Visitors walk between thirty-two long, narrow, rock-filled concrete rectangles, often referred to as barrack foundations, although they were poured in 1965. The original barracks, built in 1937–8, were only designed to last fifteen years and had no foundations worth mentioning. By the early 1950s, according to SS chief Himmler's calculation, Nazi Germany would have won the war and "purified" its domain of unwanted people, making concentration camps unnecessary.

Until 2001, visitors were not to be given any information about the different functions and residents of the individual barracks (see ill. 2). The first four barracks at the end nearest the museum are not numbered. On the left was the camp canteen, where "privileged" prisoners could buy food and a few necessities, the camp office, where the index of inmates was kept, and the camp library, where privileged inmates could check out books. The canteen had a porchlike entrance in the front, which has not been reconstructed. For a time Kurt Schumacher, a Social Democratic politician who narrowly missed becoming West Germany's first Chancellor in 1949, was the prisoner librarian. On the east side were the two infirmary barracks; the last quarter section of the second one was the morgue where each day's harvest of dead was collected for transportation to the crematorium.

There was also a clear hierarchy among the barracks, depending on the distance to the service building. Germans were housed in "blocks" (as the barracks were called in camp jargon) 2 and 4, where the walk to the kitchen with the heavy vats of soup was not so long. On the right, block 15 was known as the "punishment block." Enclosed by a separate barbed wire cage, it was for the true unfortunates in the camp, mostly Jews. One used to see flowers left at some barrack numbers by survivors who had spent time in them. As the ranks of the survivors dwindled, so too did this living tradition. At the far (north) end of the prisoners' compound, blocks 26 and 28 were the priests' barracks. Block 26, with its own chapel (ill. 41), housed a few hundred German clergymen, block 28 about three times as many Polish priests.

Visitors arrive next at the ensemble of religious memorials at the north end of the memorial site. These buildings illustrate another important feature of the memorial site's history, which is also a fundamental principle of memorialization: memorials reflect the concerns of the living, not the history of the dead. The creation of this religious ensemble began with the dedication of a tall cylindrical Catholic chapel "of Christ's Mortal Agony" in 1960 and the opening of a Carmelite convent outside the north wall in 1964 (ills. 43, 45, 47). The ring of trees and grass around the chapel is a last testimony to the plan to turn the memorial site into a park (ill. 46). The two Catholic memorials were followed in 1967 by a half-underground concrete Protestant "Church of Reconciliation" and a cavernous, semisubterranean Jewish memorial (ills. 63, 64).

The towering Catholic chapel symbolizes the transcendence of earthly suffering through Christ's sacrifice, while the Protestant church seeks to foster reconciliation through spiritual and intellectual reflection (it contains a reading room staffed by volunteers). The Jewish building is not a house of God, but merely a place to mourn the dead. The international memorial in front of the museum, too, reflects the interpretation of its makers as much as or more than it does the history of the camp (ill. 59). The memorial sculpture is composed of sticklike figures stretched between the strands of a barbed wire fence. It embodies the camp as a site of senseless mass death, the way most of Dachau's predominantly non-German inmates experienced it in the 1940s. Non-Jewish German survivors, mostly political prisoners, wished to erect a tall but fragile spire of resistance, but they were overruled by survivors from other countries (ill. 60).

At the back of the memorial site on the left, a sign directs visitors to the "Crematorium, open 9–5." In 1970 artist Jochen Gerz took photographs of many such signs in the Dachau memorial site.[4] He used them to create an installation documenting the incongruity between their banal meaning today as part of a memorial site, and what they signify when read in the context of the concentration camp. Entitled "Exit: The Dachau Project," the name played on the multiple meanings of the "exit" signs in the memorial site: the direction to go in order to exit the site today, the frequent "exit" of death during the camp era, and the departure from civilized norms that made the murderous camp system possible.

A concrete path crosses a strip of grass and a stream flowing in a concrete channel to a gate in a barbed wire fence. This grassy band marks the former no-man's-land: the strip of ground in front of the electrified fence, barbed wire barriers, and ditch or moat (compare ill. 84). Nothing documents what transpired here, a site of suicides and lethal SS amusement. Guards are known to have tossed inmates' caps into the zone, so that the men would be shot when they retrieved them. At liberation in 1945, corpses of SS guards floated in this stream; during a protest sit-in in the hot summer of 1993 Sinti children frolicked in it (compare ill. 81).

The crematorium compound itself has been landscaped as a park since the 1940s. Its lush, well-kept vegetation stands in sharp contrast to the stony gray of the rest of the memorial site. The serenity of the surroundings of the murder installation highlights the tension between the two primary functions of the memorial site: commemoration of the victims, and documentation of the circumstances of their lives and deaths. Scattered throughout the park are various memorials: a diminutive statue of a shorn "unknown concentration camp inmate" on a high pedestal (ill. 38), and tablets with trilingual inscriptions such as "execution range with blood ditch," and "grave of thousands unknown." Another much smaller crematorium building with only one small oven and no morgue or ancillary rooms is hidden among the trees.

Since 1945 the large crematorium–gas chamber building, erected in 1942, has been a central attraction for most visitors (ills. 5, 15, 16). After the war it housed the first exhibitions about the concentration camp (ills. 17, 18, 50, 51). It contains more than a half-dozen different rooms: gassing chambers for infested clothing, an undressing room, a gas chamber for people, a morgue, a large incinerator room with four cremation chambers, and offices for the crematory personnel. From 1965 until after 2001, these rooms were bare except for the briefest of signs: in the gas chamber, for example, the cryptic "GAS CHAMBER / disguised as a 'shower room' / – never used as a gas chamber" (ills. 53, 54).[5] In this case the sanctity of the space was given priority over the site's educational mission. Didactic original murals in one of the back rooms were destroyed or painted over for the same reason. One depicted, for instance, a man riding on a pig. The inscription beneath it read: "Wash your hands, cleanliness is your duty."[6]

After completing this tour visitors are left to ponder the multitude of impressions and messages conveyed by the memorial site. This history is not easy to sort out. The memorial site focuses on the victim experience, with a strong emphasis on death, not day-to-day survival. The perpetrators remain in the background as the creators of the camp and authors of many of its documents and photographs. Visitors, however, enter as bystanders, a group that is essentially ignored. How can we heed the imperatives spelled out on the various monuments: "Remember those who died here," "Never again"? What significance does this place have for us, for our lives here and now? Should visitors go to Munich or Berlin tomorrow, or Rome or Paris instead?

This book is divided into four parts. The first recounts the history of Dachau from its beginnings as a market town and dynastic residence centuries ago through its repressive and genocidal phase, 1933 to 1945. Dachau's histories as a town, a camp, and a symbol of genocide are the basis for its reincarnations after the war.

Three phases of the camp's history after 1945 are examined in the following three parts. Part II focuses on the decade from 1945 to 1955. It begins with a portrayal of the three primary responses to the crimes symbolized by "Dachau": the myth that the German people had been victimized by "the Nazis," the myth that most Germans had been ignorant of the crimes their neighbors, friends, and relatives were committing, and the myth that most Germans had been upright citizens who resisted Nazism as much as possible without taking inordinate risks. From the early 1950s those myths of victimization, ignorance, and resistance were expressed by three inversions of historical fact (that do not correspond one-to-one with the myths, but amalgamate them). Those inversions are the subject of the three chapters in part II, which show the development and effects of the conception that Nazis had been "good," the consequences of the feeling that concentration camp survivors had been and still were "bad," and the transformation of Dachau and other former concentration camps into "clean" camps. These three historical myths and the resulting mythic inversions played an important role in the establishment of the West German state and the peculiar nature of its politics from the late 1940s until the turn of the millennium – they are thus referred to as the three founding myths.

Part III traces the images of Dachau embraced and propagated by the groups most involved in shaping its postwar history. It focuses on the period 1955–70, although it begins with a survey of the first impulses to memorialize the Dachau camp after the war. Subsequent chapters examine how the camp survivors – German Catholics, Jews, and Protestants – worked to represent their own present conceptions of the meaning of the concentration camp's past. The final chapter of part III introduces a theory of generational cohorts to demonstrate how, at the end of the 1960s, a generation of Germans born between roughly 1937 and 1953 began openly to challenge the veracity of the three founding myths. However, those children of the "generation of the perpetrators" were themselves enmeshed in the distortions of their parents' myths. While they denied their parents' claim of victimization, they saw themselves as victims. While they rejected their elders' professions of ignorance and sought knowledge about the Nazi past, their own understanding remained abstract, intangible, and unconnected to real life. And while they scoffed at claims of resistance during the Nazi years, their own resistance against present injustices was at times motivated more by a desire to compensate for past injustices than justified by the consistent application of moral principles.

Finally, part IV outlines the process of overcoming, since 1970, the mythically distorted collective images of the Nazi era. It examines how the perpetrator and first postwar generations' legacies of victim identification, historical ignorance, and overblown resistance have been challenged and even overcome by members of younger age cohorts. Taken together, the three founding myths had served to establish Germans' innocence of Nazi crimes. Overcoming them entailed recognizing guilt and accepting responsibility for those crimes, as well as correcting the inversions that emerged from the three founding myths during the 1950s. At the close of the twentieth century, Nazi-era Germans are once again becoming "bad" (or at least informed and accepting of horrendous crimes), Hitler's victims are regaining their "good" standing (additional groups are being compensated for their losses and persecution), and the former concentration camps are losing their "cleanliness" as recent historiography and renovations seek to re-create long-destroyed or ignored aspects of the past.

This book concludes with an examination of the renovation of Dachau originally slated for completion in 2001. It explores in detail some of the questions of commemoration, pedagogy, and meaning raised above. Specifically, it looks at ways in which the founding myths and their legacies have found expression in the current redesign plans, and suggests ways in which uses by a post-millennial generation might be considered, in order to avoid the distortions of past abuses.

13

Before we turn to the historical Dachau, a few remarks about the terminology of individual and group memories are in order. Historical icons such as "Dachau" are situated at the border between concrete individual experiences and broader public understandings. Of late much has been written about historical consciousness, collective memory, public commemoration, and the like.[7] I will not explicate these terms in detail here, but it is important to note that I distinguish between *remembering* as the *individual* act of recalling experiences and knowledge to the conscious mind, and *recollection* as the *group* process of collecting, creating, and propagating information about the past. Public commemorations are merely one way of practicing recollection (as are history teaching, historical films, historical tours, etc.).

While *historical consciousness* can be understood as a general awareness of the present as a product of the past, the popular but vague term *collective memory* can be used to refer to a set of more specific images of and opinions about the past held by members of what I call a *memory group*. Such groups usually share common experiences, values, and goals as well as images of the past. Jewish Holocaust survivors from Eastern Europe, German SS veterans, and members of the French resistance would be examples of memory groups. Other groups with common but unarticulated historical experiences, such as victims of forced sterilization, army deserters, or forced laborers, only become memory groups when they begin to share their memories. Individuals who accept the memories, values, and aspirations become part of a memory group; members who no longer share them, leave it. However, the term collective memory is sometimes used to denote the aggregate of historical images present in one place at a given time. Thus the collective memories held by German veterans, German refugees, German intellectuals, German concentration camp survivors, German Protestants, German Catholics, German Jews, etc. can be called *German collective memory*. I think it is better to avoid this usage and refer instead to *public recollection*.

When private memories are offered publicly, they often challenge the ideas about the past held by others, including members of memory groups. New groups can thus form, dissolve, and reconstitute themselves. This process of public negotiation of conflicting images of the past is recollection. It takes place simultaneously in the local and regional public spheres and in the broadest reaches of the national and international public arenas, wherever different images of the past vie for recognition and acceptance.

PART ONE

Dachau 1890–1945: a town, a camp, a symbol of genocide

Dear Guests!
You have come to Dachau to visit the memorial site in the former concentration camp. I should like to welcome you on behalf of the town of Dachau.

Innumerable crimes were committed in the Dachau concentration camp. Like you, deeply moved, the citizens of the town of Dachau bow their heads before the victims of the camp.

The horrors of the German concentration camps must never be repeated! After your visit you will be horror-stricken. But we sincerely hope you will not transfer your indignation to the ancient, 1,200-year-old Bavarian town of Dachau, which was not consulted when the camp was built and whose citizens voted quite decisively against the rise of National Socialism in 1933. The Dachau concentration camp is a part of the overall German responsibility for that time.

I extend a cordial invitation to you to visit the old town of Dachau only a few kilometers from here. We would be happy to greet you within our walls and to welcome you as friends.

Dr. Lorenz Reitmeier, mayor (1985)[1]

This brief statement is set in a full-color glossy pamphlet between photographs of Dachau's city hall, parks and baroque castle, and Bavarians in traditional costumes sitting in an outdoor beer garden (compare ill. 69). It seeks to attract to the nearby town the many hundreds of thousands of visitors who come to the Dachau concentration camp museum each year. Its wording reflects a delicate balance, the result of decades of wrangling over the primary meaning of the word "Dachau." While most outsiders connect the name with a Nazi concentration camp, or with a site of the genocide perpetrated by the Germans against the Jews, many Dachau city residents wish to view their home as a picturesque 1,200-year-old town in southern Germany with a rich cultural heritage.

The following two chapters retrace the history of both the town and the camp from their pre-concentration camp days to 1945. This excursion into the past reveals why some local residents see the concentration camp as an unfortunate blip in a long and illustrious history, while most foreigners (and many Germans) associate the name Dachau with a site of Nazi atrocities.

 1

Dachau: a town and a camp

Before 1933

Dachau, a town with about 35,000 residents since the 1970s, has roots reaching back beyond Roman times to the Celtic era.[1] The oldest surviving document mentioning the settlement "Dahauua," which meant "loamy soil surrounded by rivers," was written in the year 805, when Charlemagne was emperor of Europe. This medieval Bavarian market town was situated so picturesquely on a hill with a view of the Alps that the Wittelsbach kings built a summer residence there in the 1500s, but first marauding Swedes in the 1630s, and then Napoleon's armies in the early 1800s, reduced much of it to ruins. When painters discovered the outdoors as a theme in the late nineteenth century, they also discovered this picturesque bucolic village. By the 1890s Dachau was the home of a thriving artists' colony. This history is still one of the primary sources of local pride. As Hans-Gunter Richardi, the author of the town's leading tourist guidebook, wrote in 1979:[2]

> In 1890 Dachau's golden age as an artists' colony began . . . Painters of the highest quality came to the market town: Lovis Corinth [and] Max Liebermann . . . 1890 was the year Adolf Hölzl (1853–1934) came to Dachau, too. To him it owes its art historical significance. Together with his friends Ludwig Dill (1848–1940) and Arthur Langhammer (1855–1901), whom he brought to Dachau, he founded the "New Dachau School" in 1897, which received much attention in artists' circles and turned Dachau into an artists' Mecca . . .
>
> Finally so many artists lived in Dachau that in the years around 1900 people used to say that every tenth person one met on the street was an artist.

Painters came to Dachau from as far away as England and Scandinavia. Richardi's popular tourist guide continues with an anecdote by the Swedish writer Carl Olof Petersen (1880–1939), who came to Dachau in 1903 and made it his home of choice. In his book *Moosschwaige* ("Hut in the Moor"), Petersen described what prompted him to leave his job as a grocer in Sweden:

> I first heard the name Dachau from the Swedish painter and writer Ernst Norlind in Malmö. He was studying to be a sculptor in Munich. Suddenly, however, he switched to painting and moved out to Dachau, which had just become famous as a painters' colony. I always listened enthusiastically when Norlind described the venerable old market that dreamed of its former days of glory on a sunny hill on the Amper river, or when he told about the great wide expanse of the moor that stretched to the Alps on the distant horizon.

However, World War I brought the town's happy days to an end. As Richardi writes: "The young artists left the market town to follow the call of duty. Many of them never returned. Thus sank Dachau's star as an artists' colony. It would never again burn so brightly as in the glorious years between 1890 and 1914."

The town needed a new source of revenue, so when in 1916 the Great War began to drag on, the city fathers welcomed the establishment of a combined gunpowder and munitions factory to boost the local economy. War industries are notoriously dependent on the fortunes and tides of war, however. When Germany was resoundingly defeated in 1918, the Dachau "Powder and Munitions Factory," fondly called "Pumf" by the local residents, was closed down. Defeat in World War I came as a surprise to many Germans. They suddenly realized that their government had been misleading them, and that the deprivations of this first "total war" had been for naught. Thus, in the wake of war, revolution swept across the country. What began as a sailors' rebellion in a northern port triggered a series of urban uprisings that spread to Berlin and the south. Throughout Germany workers' and soldiers' councils replaced the imperial and local governments.

In Bavaria, Kurt Eisner, a Jewish journalist from Berlin, organized the most viable Socialist government in the country, but in February 1919 he was assassinated.[3] The lack of a dedicated leader left the Socialist movement easy prey to the counterrevolutionary "White" forces (named after the color of their armbands), who were mostly demobilized World War I soldiers disgruntled by what they saw as Germany's shameful capitulation. After reconquering the rest of Germany the Whites swept down into Bavaria towards Munich from the northwest. A pitched battle with the revolutionary "Reds" just outside of Dachau decided the fate of the last revolutionary republic in Germany: the loyalist Whites of the "Görlitz Free Corps" were victorious. They marched on to Munich, where they soaked the streets with the blood of hopeful democrats. Germany, presented with an ultimatum from the victors of World War I to accept the terms of the peace settlement they had worked out in Versailles, was in political turmoil.

One 30-year-old soldier in Munich at that time, in the summer of 1919, had hitherto supported the revolutionary movement behind Eisner as a Social Democrat. After the shock of the Versailles Treaty terms was added to the defeat of Eisner's cause, this soldier let himself be recruited by a new right-wing party that combined German nationalism with socialist populism. This "German Workers' Party" wanted him to drum up support and membership in Munich's beer halls, where the ex-soldier was a popular impromptu speaker. That 30-year-old was Adolf Hitler. Within a year he rose to a leadership position in the party, whose name was soon changed to the "National Socialist German Workers' Party." Since the Socialists were already known as "Sozis," from the German word *Sozialismus*, the National Socialists became known as the "Nazis."

Dachau did not have an easy time in those years. It was burdened with high unemployment in the 1920s, since many of the 7,000–8,000 demobilized armaments workers remained there with their families.[4] Attempts to convert the "German Works" (the new name of the former "Pumf") to peacetime production were unsuccessful, so that even before the Great Depression reached Germany in 1930, Dachau had the dubious honor of having the highest unemployment rate in the country – 6.6–9.2 percent in 1926–8, more than double the national average.[5] In June of 1931 local hopes were raised by the plan of a German–American investment consortium to build a gynecological clinic and recuperation center on the property, but that project was never realized. Just days before Adolf Hitler was named Chancellor of the German Republic on 30 January 1933, the town fathers abandoned their attempt to attract private industry to the buildings. Instead, they lobbied the Bavarian government to utilize the empty workers' barracks and halls of the German Works as a civilian labor or militia camp, should the rumors prove true that national conscription for either of those programs was imminent.[6]

The suddenly instated Nazi government did have plans to create a network of large camps. However, they were neither for public works projects nor for training secret paramilitary units prohibited by the Versailles Treaty. Instead, opponents of the new regime were to be incarcerated there. The idea of erecting special camps for large numbers of political opponents was not new.[7] Already in speeches in the early 1920s Hitler mentioned the "concentration camps" erected by the British in the Boer War. For example, in September 1920 he said: "In South Africa, England deported 76,000 Boer women and children to concentration camps, thus forcing the men to return to their homes."[8] He made clear that the Nazi Party could and would use such camps to ensure a quick takeover of power, but also to isolate Jewish Germans who purportedly endangered the Germanic racial collective he envisaged. In 1921 Hitler wrote: "The Jews are to be prevented from undermining our people, if necessary by securing their instigators in concentration camps." In preparation for Hitler's first attempt to seize power in November 1923, the Nazi Party conspirators drafted a dictatorial new constitution. Its sixteenth paragraph stated:[9]

> The regional administrators will immediately . . . take measures to purge and unburden the cities and resort towns, in particular they will remove all security risks and useless eaters. These people are, if necessary, to be put into collection camps, and if possible to be put to work on communal projects. Whoever resists or attempts to resist the transfer will be punished by death.

Although the Nazis' November 1923 *putsch* attempt failed, the plan to use concentration camps to secure power in the event of a takeover was not abandoned. In August 1932, as the Nazi Party reached a pinnacle of electoral support and its assumption of national leadership appeared within reach, its newspaper, the *Folkish Observer*, proclaimed quite publicly that, when the National Socialists took over the government, they would "immediately arrest and condemn all Communist and Social Democratic functionaries . . . [and] quarter all suspects and intellectual instigators in concentration camps."[10]

The National Socialists were true to their word. On 8 March 1933 Reich Interior Minister Frick announced that:[11]

> When the new Reichstag convenes on 21 March 1933 more important and more useful work will prevent the Communists from participating. They will have to get used to doing productive work again; they will be given an opportunity for that in the concentration camps. If they let themselves be educated to become useful members of the nation again, they will be welcomed as full national comrades. However, not only the Communists must disappear, but their red Social Democratic compatriots as well, since Social Democracy is the root that brought forth communism.

Even though concrete plans for such camps were just being drawn up, the Nazis made no secret about their intentions. Frick's statement also reveals an aspect of the camps that played a central role in post-1945 German recollections of the concentration camps: the idea of "education through work."

20

In Dachau, it may not have been the efforts of the city fathers in January 1933, but the intervention of Hans Behm, a demobilized World War I officer who lived in Dachau and was active in the Nazi stormtroopers (*Sturmabteilung*, SA), that brought one of these concentration camps to the former Pumf grounds.[12] Be that as it may, in March the higher-ups in the Nazi Party approved the site. A special "protective custody" ordinance, decreed after the torching of the Reichstag in Berlin on 27 February 1933, had been liberally applied by newly appointed Chancellor Hitler's henchmen. On 9 March, three days after Hitler had won a 44 percent plurality in the national election, his party assumed power in the state of Bavaria as well. A wave of "protective custody" arrests of Socialists and Communists followed: 5,400 Bavarian men were jailed by mid-April.[13] Dramatic overcrowding in the state prisons required a quick solution and on 20 March one of Hitler's closest associates, Heinrich Himmler, announced at a press conference that "a concentration camp for political prisoners" who endangered state security would be erected near Dachau. At that time Himmler was the head of Hitler's personal bodyguard, the SS, and chief of the Munich police.

The camp opens, March 1933

In Dachau things moved very quickly after the 9 March takeover in Bavaria.[14] On 13 March a commission of Himmler's Munich police spoke with the factory administration and toured the site to see if it could be used for quartering protective custody prisoners. The commission's architect identified a suitable portion of the complex, and the next day fifty volunteers from a Nazi work camp arrived to repair the electricity and water lines. Within a week, space had been made for 540 prisoners, with provisions for rapid expansion to a capacity of 2,700. With the physical set-up prepared, the next problem to be solved was obtaining guards. In a letter to the Bavarian government on 20 March, Himmler requested a detachment of regular police to guard a "collection camp for political prisoners" – the term "concentration camp" was apparently still too new to make clear what the men would be doing. The Dachau concentration camp was ready. On 22 March four large police trucks arrived with about 200 prisoners from Stadelheim prison in Munich and the Landsberg fortress, the same jail where Hitler had written *Mein Kampf* during his own imprisonment in 1924. Crowds of Dachau residents along the streets and at the factory gate waited hours to get a glimpse of the camp's first detainees.[15]

At this time Dachau was not yet the "hermetically sealed" camp Germans would recollect after 1945. In May 1933, for instance, a French journalist was able to snoop around and take a number of pictures of the camp and its inmates, which he published in a popular illustrated magazine in Paris.[16] However, in the fall new regulations governing the treatment of the prisoners singled out attempts to communicate with the outside world for especially draconian punishment, namely death by hanging. The infractions included:[17]

> collecting, receiving, burying, or passing on true or false information . . . about the concentration camp or its adjunct facilities to outside visitors or others; smuggling information out of the camp by means of secret letters, written or oral messages to released or transferred inmates, stones thrown over the camp wall . . . climbing on the barracks roofs or trees, making light signals or other signs to the outside world.

This regulation provides a comprehensive list of the ways in which communication could and most likely did take place, while the severity of the punishment indicates how serious the attempt to cut off the flow of information was.

In the early months of its rule the Nazi Party had to resort to numerous temporary measures, among them the use of regular state policemen to guard the protective custody prisoners in Dachau. During the first weeks of the camp's operation, the prisoners were not humiliated or mistreated, their heads were not shaved, they were not identified by numbers, and they were not forced to work. However, in early April Himmler gained authority over the "auxiliary political police," a branch of the state police that was actually part of the SS. He named the rough-and-ready SS officer Hilmar Wäckerle "commandant" and replaced the Dachau camp's regular police guards with his own SS men. On Himmler's orders Wäckerle devised a system of "special rules" for the treatment of prisoners. Already by May 1933 violence and terror were institutionalized as part of life in the camp.[18] By the end of the month twelve men had been tortured to death or murdered outright.[19]

Jews were already being singled out for the most brutal treatment. One example was the Jewish legal intern Wilhelm Aron from Bamberg, who arrived at the camp on 15 May. The tall, red-haired 26-year-old attracted the attention of the SS guards right away, and they beat him so severely that bones protruded from his buttocks. Each morning for the next three days the delirious young man was torn from his infirmary bed and whipped across his infected wounds. Only his death on 19 May spared him further agony.

22

Wäckerle's men did not take precautions to cover up their misdeeds, however. The day after the SS took over guard duty on 11 April, four men, all of them Jews, were led out of the camp and shot under the pretense that they were trying to escape. One of them survived his five gunshot wounds and was taken to a hospital in Munich. Before he died, he told the story of the shooting to his doctors. Munich public prosecutor Carl Wintersberger began an investigation of the camp. He uncovered so much evidence of criminal brutality that Himmler found it necessary to replace Wäckerle and mobilize his contacts to have Wintersberger taken off the case. The SS was not yet all-powerful and the civic rights guaranteed by the 1919 Weimar constitution, one of the most progressive in the world, were still being defended by a few courageous state officials.

At the end of June, Himmler named Theodor Eicke, a former army paymaster and private security guard, as the new commandant of Dachau. The 40-year-old Eicke had been a pioneering SS leader, organizing new formations of SS troops in the region near Heidelberg. By November 1931 he had become a battalion leader commanding more than 1,000 men. Himmler knew that Eicke was a fanatically dedicated Nazi and a gifted organizer, as well as a stubborn, ruthless, and brutal man. On 26 June 1933 Eicke arrived in the concentration camp. Himmler had given him the opportunity to get the Nazi Party out of a tight spot, and he was determined to prove himself.

During a visit to the Dachau camp on 4 August both SS chief Himmler and Himmler's superior, SA chief Röhm, praised Eicke's work highly.[20] In a 1936 self-assessment, Eicke summarized what he had accomplished since his appointment as commandant of Dachau:[21]

> The SS death's head formations were created from a corrupt guard detachment of about 120 men in Dachau in the fall of 1934. There were times when no uniforms, no boots and no socks were available. Without complaints the men wore their own clothing while on duty. We were generally thought of as a necessary evil that only cost money, as drab guards behind barbed wire . . . My men lived in drafty factory halls. Everywhere there was poverty and misery . . . I found disloyalty, embezzlement and corruption. For those reasons I had to dismiss 60 men in only four weeks.

This was a far cry from the snappy and self-assured SS guards we commonly hear about in portrayals of the concentration camps, but it is an accurate rendition both of the early phase of the camp system, and of how ambitious and opportunistic men used their energy to create the barbarous system that was firmly established by 1940.

Eicke's work to make Dachau a showcase of National Socialist ideology included a revised set of rules and regulations for the camp that he announced in October 1933. These rules soon became the blueprint for the treatment of prisoners in all of the concentration camps during the 1930s. Rudolf Höss, the builder and commandant of Auschwitz (whose 1946 memoir has become one of the most widely read sources about the gas chambers), worked in Dachau from 1934 to 1938. In his memoir he recalled the essence of his training under Eicke:[22]

> Eicke thought that every trace of pity showed the *enemies of the state* a vulnerable spot that they would immediately exploit. Any empathy with *enemies of the state* was unworthy of an SS man. There was no room for the soft-hearted in the ranks of the SS; they would do best to disappear into a monastery as soon as possible. He [Eicke] could only use hard and determined men who would obey every command without a second thought. Not for nothing did they wear the death's head and carry a loaded weapon at all times. *They were the only soldiers who, even in times of peace, had to face the enemy day and night, the enemy behind the fence* . . . Eicke drummed the concept of dangerous *enemies of the state* so vividly and convincingly into his SS men . . . that every one who did not know better was completely permeated with it. . . .
>
> Eicke's intention was to use his constant reprimands and the corresponding orders about criminal dangerousness to orient his SS men completely against the prisoners, to make them hate the prisoners, to suppress any feelings of pity right from the start (emphasis in original).

Höss, writing after being sentenced to death for the assembly-line genocide he had organized and supervised at Auschwitz, was at the time feeling quite sorry for himself. He wrote that his guilt began with the suppression of his sympathies for the prisoners – in accordance with Eicke's teaching. He was, in his own opinion, a victim of this fanatic's indoctrination.

The nazification of the town, 1933–1935

While the SS was establishing its inhuman regimen in the Dachau camp, the Nazi Party was making inroads in Dachau township. On the evening of 10 March 1933, the day after Hitler forced the Bavarian government to reconstitute itself under Nazi leadership according to the national election results (known as *Gleichschaltung*, "coordination"), a truck of armed SA stormtroopers occupied the Dachau town hall. Two of the town's newspapers were closed soon afterwards because they printed reports critical of the takeover. By the end of March twelve of twenty-one city council members had been relieved of their duties. Lord Mayor Georg Seufert, a member of the Catholic Bavarian People's Party, joined the Nazi

Party, enabling him to remain in office for another year, until conflicts with the local SS finally forced him to withdraw to another town.

At the end of April 1933 the Dachau city council was reconstituted. The total number of seats was reduced to fifteen, which were distributed equally among the three remaining parties in rough accordance to the proportion of votes each party had received locally in the 6 March national election: the Catholics (29 percent), the Social Democrats (28 percent), and the National Socialists (24 percent). Dachau, by the way, had by no means been a stronghold of Nazi support. Nationally the party had garnered about 44 percent of the vote, almost double the Dachau tally. Dachau did quickly gain the reputation of being a rural center of Nazism, but that was not because the populace supported the Nazis in any exceptional way. Instead, the reputation came from two important Nazi institutions established in the town in 1933: a model camp of the volunteer labor corps (the men who renovated the "Pumf" to receive the concentration camp prisoners, for example, came from that camp), and the first training school for Nazi Party leaders at the district level.[23]

It is important to note that two of the five new Nazi city council delegates, Hans Zauner and Karl Bergmann, were very recent converts from a Catholic–conservative local party. Zauner, who soon became second vice mayor, and whom we shall meet again as Dachau's lord mayor during the 1950s, later told a denazification court that he had only joined the Nazi Party because fellow turncoat Lord Mayor Seufert convinced him that his presence on the council would help to keep the unruly Nazi neophytes under control. This is not implausible, but it says nothing about the extent to which Zauner also served the Nazi cause.

The next phase of the purge of Dachau's non-Nazi politicians took place at the end of June 1933. On 24 June the Social Democratic Party was outlawed, so its members had to resign. On the 29th and 30th the five Catholic Party members were taken into "protective custody" – in the local jail, not in the Dachau camp. One councilor joined the Nazi Party and continued to serve, while the other four, including Josef Schwalber, whom we shall also meet again after the war as one of the early mayors appointed by the US army, resigned. By September, when the council was finally purged of all non-Nazis, six of its fifteen members had formerly belonged to other parties, allowing a measure of continuity and traditional control.[24]

During the months of the Nazi takeover in Dachau, local businessmen were optimistic about the economic impact of the new concentration camp. As the *Dachau News* editorialized on the day the camp opened, "For Dachau [township] the camp will be economically very advantageous, since the large number [of prisoners] there will require guards and administrators, who will bring a substantial increase in customers to the hard-pressed Dachau business community."[25] However, although local business did pick up somewhat during the first year, the camp did not bring the expected turnaround. At the end of 1934 Dachau still had the lowest per capita tax revenues in all of Bavaria, and a Bavarian Interior Ministry commission appointed to investigate the town reported that its situation was still "catastrophic" in March 1935. The ministry tried to help out by publishing a report in the journal of the Association of Bavarian Industrialists that praised Dachau's suitability for industrial development. In response, a single inquiry came from a Berlin entrepreneur, but Dachau's mayor had to inform him that the buildings suitable for industry were "already being used for other purposes."[26] Thus the concentration camp not only brought little short-term benefit to the local economy, it hindered long-term local economic development as well. Not until the prewar mobilization at the end of the 1930s did things begin to look better.

The image of the "clean" concentration camp

The absence of economic benefit to the town was due to the particular path of the entire German concentration camp system, beginning with its reorganization and regularization under Eicke in 1934. Within a year of his appointment as commandant in Dachau in June of 1933, Theodor Eicke was promoted to the new position of "Inspector of the Concentration Camps and SS Guard Units" for the whole German Reich. Soon the minute guidelines he had drawn up for Dachau were applied to other camps as well. One stipulation in Eicke's 1 October 1933 regulations for concentration camp prisoners was the obligation to work. He coined the motto "Arbeit macht frei" – "work makes free" – which was inscribed on the gates of Dachau and Auschwitz.[27] By 1934 the Dachau camp had its own bakery and meat-processing plants, in addition to workshops for machine building, carpentry, painting, tailoring, and shoemaking. Even though the vast majority of inmates were forced to perform senseless back- and spirit-breaking work such as pulling the huge cement "Jew and Bigshot Roller" around the camp, the various workshops did make the camp increasingly independent of the local economy.

Eicke's, Dachau's, and the entire concentration camp system's future took an important turn with the events of 30 June 1934, known as the "Night of Long Knives."[28] On that night Hitler was able to neutralize the SA, the only remaining Nazi Party formation not completely under his control, by having Himmler's SS murder its leader Ernst Röhm, as well as other dissident or potentially rival Nazi Party leaders. Röhm, who had increased the SA's size from 500,000 men to almost 4 million during 1933, aspired to take over the Reichswehr, the German army. His men, mostly rough-and-ready thugs, were growing increasingly restless in the relatively calm period in early 1934.

In order to gain the support of the army for Hitler's impending purge of Röhm, Himmler's security service, the SD (from *Sicherheitsdienst*), spread rumors that Röhm was preparing an army coup. Himmler's officers also drew up lists of dangerous and potentially dangerous elements within the party who were to be liquidated at the same time. The actual purge was to be carried out by Hitler's personal SS bodyguard regiment, but Eicke was instructed to have units of his guard troops from Dachau in readiness at a nearby junction, just in case. Although Eicke's men were not needed that night, they subsequently executed seventeen SA leaders in Dachau, and Eicke himself probably shot Röhm in a Munich prison cell the next day. An important consequence of Röhm's murder was that Himmler now had no superior between himself and Hitler, and the SS became an autonomous party formation that soon surpassed the SA in importance. Eicke was immediately promoted for his loyal role in the purge.

The "Night of Long Knives" was a surprising and disturbing event for the German public, which by 1934 had begun to accustom itself to a less violent political climate. Hitler was able to allay these fears by claiming that the purge had been necessary precisely to do away with the violent elements in the party. In his speech to the Reichstag on 13 July 1934, Hitler concluded his list of party misfits who had been liquidated with a remark that characterized the "harsh but honorable" concentration camps that many Germans claimed to have believed in after the war: "Finally, three members of the SS were shot, since they were guilty of shameful mistreatments of protective custody prisoners."[29] Whenever Hitler's regime mentioned the concentration camps in public, they were portrayed as "clean" camps.

The Nazi state devoted a great deal of effort to controlling the information available in the public sphere.[30] The mass media were very tightly controlled, and the utilization of prohibited sources of information (such as prohibited publications or foreign radio stations) was punishable by draconian measures, as was passing on rumors or information about forbidden topics – which explicitly included the concentration camps.[31] Under this threat a dual image of the concentration camps emerged:

leaked information that could only be passed on in private suggested that the camps were dreadful, dangerous places, while official sources portrayed them in a much more benign light.

It is important to examine this image of the "clean camp" more closely, because after the demise of the Nazi regime in 1945 most German citizens claimed to have known only that official image, completely denying the private one. The officially disseminated and tolerated image was one of orderly, spartanly efficient camps designed both to "educate" persons with "asocial" behavior to become productive members of the German racial collectivity, and to isolate incurable political, social, and racial "parasites" from the rest of society.[32] For instance, one of the earliest official stories about Dachau, a July 1933 article in the *Munich Illustrated News*, claimed that in the camp "members of the *Volk* who fell victim to foreign seducers ... are being educated to become useful members of the National Socialist state by the healing effects of productive work and tight discipline."[33] In 1935 a popular clandestine joke bestowed the surname "University of the Fourth Reich" on the town because it had complained to state authorities that its reputation and economy were suffering increasingly due to the concentration camp. The humor hinged upon the equation of the "educational camp" with the intellectual mission of higher education.[34] In December 1936 the *Illustrated Observer*, the official illustrated news weekly of the Nazi Party, published an article describing the Dachau concentration camp as "clean," "immaculate," "beautiful," and "orderly."[35]

At the same time, essentially all of these official descriptions of the camps referred implicitly or explicitly to the existence of a differing view, a critical anti-truth about the concentration camps.[36] The 1933 article mentioned above was entitled "The Truth about Dachau," and in 1934 the commander of the Oranienburg concentration camp near Berlin published a book about his camp entitled "*Anti*-Brown-Book," which was written to refute documentary evidence collected by anti-Nazis and published in a *Brown Book* in the late summer of 1933.[37] The Anti-Brown-Book admitted that "some of the arrestees received treatment that was not all too gentle," but reasoned that that was a "compelling necessity" because they had fought ruthlessly against the National Socialist vanguard. Between the glowing lines of the 1936 illustrated party news weekly report, forced castration in Dachau was mentioned (against which a prisoner could supposedly appeal!), as was the fact that "all legal means" were used against intractable persons. What "legal" meant in those years of arbitrary arrest and condoned police violence would have been quite clear to most readers – although it would have been risky to discuss such issues in public.

28

There is another interesting aspect to the propagation of this "clean" image. In a self-deceiving manner typical of Nazi Germany, even officials privy to the truth used only the official euphemisms – even when they were talking amongst themselves. In the early years of the camps much was done to promote this image. After touring the Dachau camp in March 1934, the Minister President of Bavaria wrote to Heinrich Himmler:[38]

> I congratulate you on the creation of this institution, which is as necessary as it is salutary for the protection of the new state and its citizens. I was especially pleased that the Economics Minister of [the German state of] Baden and the Minister President of Anhalt, who also took part in the tour, were as impressed as I was by what was going on. I hope that the education of the inmates of the concentration camp will be successful, so that they can soon be freed, ready to participate in public life.

In May of 1935 Himmler showed a carefully selected letter to Hitler, in which a released Dachau inmate thanked commandant Eicke for his experience in the camp. In flawed and simple language the letter began:[39]

> Excuse me if I bother you with these lines but I often think of you my dear Mr. Commandant. For you and Sister Pia [a former nun who had participated in Hitler's 1923 *putsch* attempt; as a reward a Dachau work detachment was put at her disposal] were the first two people who created both respect and admiration in me who in plain German got to know me as a human being and forced me to think. The result was that I especially became a german [sic] again secondly a German family man and 3 a free man again. Think often about the Nice Time as a prisoner . . .

Himmler's use of this letter indicates a substantial level of self-deception at the highest levels of the Nazi hierarchy, and, as far as the documentary record is concerned, leaves open such questions as how much Hitler personally knew of the atrocities committed under his authority in the mid-1930s, or how successful his underlings were at shielding him from that information.[40] At any rate, overwhelming evidence suggests that many Germans knew quite well what was going on in the camps.[41]

When the concentration camp system was revamped after 1936, the newly constructed camps were designed to project the clean counter-image, as evidenced not only by the inscription "Arbeit macht frei," but also by a slogan painted in large letters in prominent places in all of the camps, such as the roof of the main camp building in Dachau: "There is only one path to freedom. Its milestones are: Obedience, Diligence, Honesty, Orderliness, Cleanliness, Sobriety, Truthfulness, Self-Sacrifice, and Love of the Fatherland" (ills. 7, 86). Himmler, the mastermind of the concentration camp system, held fast to this "clean" image throughout the 1930s and 1940s until the very end of the war.

Numerous reports describe the tours of the Dachau concentration camp Himmler regularly offered to foreign dignitaries.[42] For example, in February 1941 he visited KZ Dachau with Oswald Pohl, the SS administrator in charge of the entire camp system, Anton Mussert, the head of the Dutch National Socialists who was looking for ideas on how to keep order in the newly conquered realm under his charge, and Hans Piorkowski, the commandant of the Dachau camp. The entourage first toured the camp kitchen, laundry, and infirmary, including the rooms where German doctors were conducting pseudoscientific experiments on human subjects. They then visited one of the barracks that housed German inmates, exchanged a few words with specially selected prisoners, and looked at some of the camp's special features, such as Himmler's angora rabbit breeding farm, and an experimental plantation that he hoped would make Germany independent of imported herbs and spices. In fact, Himmler often took his daughter Gudrun (b. 1929) to visit the camp, where she especially enjoyed the exotic plants in the gardens and the furry rabbits.[43]

Even at the very end of the war, as the Third Reich was rapidly collapsing, Himmler tried to convince foreign representatives that his concentration camps had been "clean." In the face of Germany's inevitable defeat in April 1945, after months of wavering between obedience to Hitler's "scorched earth" policy and a desire to save his own skin, Himmler met secretly with Norbert Masur, the director of the Swedish section of the World Jewish Congress, to negotiate the rescue of the surviving prisoners. As related by Himmler's doctor and confidant, Himmler responded to Masur's reproaches about the concentration camps as follows:[44]

> Actually they should have been called educational camps, for criminal elements were lodged there besides Jews and political prisoners. Thanks to their construction, Germany, in 1941, had the lowest criminal rate for many years. The prisoners had to work hard, but all Germans had to do that. The treatment was always just . . . I concede that [crimes were committed in the camps] occasionally, but I have also punished the persons responsible.

Himmler had indeed punished several of the most sadistic and corrupt concentration camp commandants. He replaced the sadist Piorkowski in Dachau, for instance, with the much more competent Martin Weiss in September 1942, and Buchenwald's infamous commandant Koch was tried in an SS court in December 1943 for his corruption in office. He was convicted and executed by the SS in early 1945. Himmler, who knew very precisely and firsthand what went on in the concentration camps and extermination centers, thus reduced factory-scale murder to "occasional crimes" committed by a few renegade SS. To Masur, he also tried to explain away the crematoria:

> These Eastern Jews aid the partisans and help the underground movements; they also . . . are the carriers of epidemics such as typhus. In order to control these epidemics, crematoriums were built for the countless corpses of the victims. And now we are threatened with hanging for that!

These delusional lies provided a convenient subterfuge for the citizens of Nazi Germany when the conquering Allied armies confronted them with evidence of the atrocities in 1945. As we will see, the German public held no less fast to them after the war than Himmler had done before.

The expansion of the camp system, 1936–1939

Let us return to the development of the concentration camp system.[45] In 1935 it was by no means clear that the institution would be permanent. "Protective custody" may have been necessary while the Nazis were consolidating their hold on power, but after the "Night of Long Knives" in 1934 that goal had been attained. Some high government officials, such as Reich Interior Minister Frick and the *Reichsstatthalter* (national executor) for Bavaria, Ritter von Epp, pushed Himmler to reduce the number of costly protective custody prisoners, which was disproportionately high in Bavaria.[46] In Dachau, their numbers had increased from about 2,000 in June 1933 to 2,600 in December, then fallen gradually to about 1,300 by November 1934. In a crucial meeting with Hitler in February 1935, Himmler gained the Führer's approval to maintain the camps at the current level, and in June Hitler approved Himmler's plan to increase the size of the guard detachments. Additionally, Hitler decided that, beginning in April 1936, the camps and their guard detachments would be financed out of the national budget.

The reasoning behind that decision reveals the Nazis' longer-range preparations for war, and it exemplifies the ad hoc process by which their strategies developed. Himmler's argumentation was two-pronged. On the one hand he showed Hitler how the camps helped to fulfill the Nazis' goal of improving the German people – he produced the laudatory letter quoted above as evidence of this. On the other hand, in the spring of 1935 Himmler also expounded the concentration camps' usefulness against potential civilian unrest. This argument hinged on plans that were being drawn up for what was code-named "Situation A": war.[47] At that time several events under consideration might have triggered Situation A: the illegal reoccupation of the demilitarized zone between Germany and Belgium and France by German troops (March 1936), the annexation of Austria (March 1938), the occupation of Czechoslovakia (March 1939), and the invasion of Poland (September 1939). Hitler's skillful diplomacy postponed the actual outbreak of Situation A until 1939, but the concentration camps proved their utility in the Austrian and Czechoslovakian takeovers, albeit more along the lines of their original function in 1933 – "neutralizing" opponents during the period of consolidation.

In order to be a reliable tool in such a serious situation, the camps had to be expanded and regularized. In February 1936 Gestapo (secret police) chief Reinhard Heydrich began compiling an "A list" of people who were to be arrested (put in "protective custody") in the event of Situation A. By 1937 he had compiled a list with 46,000 names. This was, by any measure, an enormous number, and it far exceeded the actual and planned capacities of the concentration camps at that time. Himmler, Eicke, and the head of SS administration Oswald Pohl set to work to realize expansion plans. The largest hurdle to be overcome was funding: although the national budget paid basic upkeep costs and guard salaries, the individual states were responsible for new construction, administrative costs, and food for the prisoners; most German states did not have any money to spare.

The three SS leaders came up with various solutions. For their first project, the construction of a new camp, "Sachsenhausen" near the capital Berlin, which would replace the Oranienburg (in an abandoned suburban brewery) and Columbia House (in the middle of the city) camps, they sold an existing camp in northern Germany, Esterwegen, to the National Labor Service, a branch of the Reich Ministry of Finance. The new owner had been working with its state-level counterpart, the Prussian Ministry of Finance, to keep the budget for the concentration camps as small as possible. These two government ministries were able to cut the demanded purchase price for Esterwegen of over 1 million Reichsmarks by about 25 percent, leaving Eicke with a deficit of about RM500,000 for building Sachsenhausen. It had to be paid out of Himmler's SS coffers. Another means to reduce costs, the use of camp inmates to draw the blueprints and perform much of the construction work, became Pohl's specialty. It added the production of income to the camps' previous functions of neutralizing political opposition and practicing "racial hygiene" in an unsystematic way.

For the next project, a new camp in the state of Thuringia southwest of Berlin, Eicke found a different solution: a loan from the national government.[48] Since negotiating with the Reich ministries had proven so fruitless in the past, he went straight to Hitler for authorization, which he received. In his justification Eicke pointed out that Thuringia would play a key role in "Situation A," since it was both in "the heart of Germany" and close to Czechoslovakia and Poland. Construction of Buchenwald concentration camp near Weimar began in June 1937.

By the time the SS was ready to begin the third major project, the reconstruction of Dachau in 1937–8, the costs were simply paid out of the national budget. During this phase Dachau concentration camp received its characteristic appearance of a 250 × 600 meter rectangular enclosure. About a dozen one- and two-story stone barracks were torn down and replaced by thirty-four long wooden barracks in two columns, with an expansive roll-call square and the large C-shaped service building at their south end (ills. 2, 3).

The Nazis were quite proud of these new camps and the role they played in the construction of the new racist state. Just as today groups of students and teachers are taken on tours of the concentration camp memorial sites, in 1938 it was suggested that whole groups of government officials be taken on tours of the concentration camps. After a visit to Dachau on 4 April 1938, Dr. Karl Doerner, an official of the Reich Ministry of Justice, was enthusiastic about what he saw:[49]

> The prisoners live in newly built, light and airy barracks . . . The prisoners work ten hours a day, including Sundays; if a prisoner doesn't complete his allotted amount of work, he has to continue working until he has finished it . . . The prisoners have abundant food. Every prisoner can purchase limited quantities of additional foodstuffs with his own money. In their leisure time the prisoners are not supervised and can do as they please.

Many of these claims were based on what Doerner had been told, not what he saw, since his short visit only provided a brief snapshot of events and contact with a few selected prisoners.[50] Doerner concluded:

> I think it is desirable that the head and experts of the department of corrections take the opportunity to visit such a KZ camp. In my opinion, knowledge of how protective custody [*Schutzhaft*] is implemented is important to consider when planning the implementation of preventative detention [*Sicherungsverwahrung*].

Doerner's superior, State Secretary Roland Freisler, an attendee of the notorious Wannsee Conference who later presided over the national People's Court (*Volksgerichtshof*), responded that he did not think regular visits to the camp would be feasible, but he had no objections to "occasional visits when officials were near a KZ camp on official business."[51] In fact, many German and foreign dignitaries were taken on tours of the camps throughout the 1930s and 1940s, including some "high American police officials," as SS General von Eberstein, who accompanied numerous tours, told the Nuremberg court in 1946.[52]

The three camps, Dachau, Buchenwald, and Sachsenhausen, were the mainstays of the concentration camp system at the end of the first phase of expansion and regularization in early 1938. Three more camps were added before Hitler triggered World War II in September 1939: Flossenbürg between Nuremberg and the Czech border in April 1938, Mauthausen in Austria in July 1938, shortly after Germany annexed that country, and Ravensbrück north of Berlin in May 1939, which was exclusively for female prisoners. Mauthausen and Flossenbürg were located at large granite quarries so that prisoner labor could be used for the economic benefit of the SS, which was branching out from police and military functions to economic activities. The stone was to be used in the Nazis' grandiose construction projects.

What effect did the expansion and reconstruction of the Dachau concentration camp in 1937–8 have on the town? Although the camp had more than doubled in design capacity by 1938, from 2,700 to 6,000 inmates, there was no immediate effect on the town. The first calculable economic benefit from the camp did not come until the eve of World War II in 1939. It resulted in the incorporation of the camp's territory within the town limits. That measure was initiated in 1937 by the commandant of the Dachau concentration camp, Hans Loritz. In order to reduce the number of civilian authorities with whom he had to deal, Loritz applied to the county office to have his camp incorporated into any one of the three communities on whose territory his camp lay.

Already in 1924 the "German Works" had applied for incorporation for the same reason, but then Dachau township had demurred because it was worried about complications associated with the potential dissolution of the Works, and it did not want to be responsible for welfare payments to the unemployed still living in the barracks there.[53] But in 1937 things looked quite different. The camp was in the midst of a massive reconstruction and expansion project that indicated a rosy future. The commandant's request jolted the town's mayor into action. He immediately talked with Oswald Pohl, the head of the SS administrative office, and received a promise of support for the selection of Dachau instead of one of the two other communities. On 22 March 1939, exactly six years after the opening of the camp, the document granting official approval was signed.

Dachau township thus included four major SS installations within the large camp complex (ill. 1): the "protective custody" prison (the concentration camp proper), the barracks of the SS camp guard regiment "Upper Bavaria," an SS training camp, and the barracks of the SS motorcycle battalion "N." The whole complex was four to five times as large as the prisoners' compound alone. During the war it was augmented to include a major regional SS hospital, clothing factories, and warehouses for the entire SS (numbering nearly 1 million men in 1944), as well as the personnel and pay office for the SS's death's head divisions.[54]

Increased tax revenues were the town's main benefit from the incorporation of the camp: 28,700 Reichsmarks that had previously been collected each year by the other two communities now went into Dachau's coffers. That was about 8 percent of the town's total tax revenue of 345,000 Reichsmarks in 1938. This sum was nothing to scoff at, but whether it alone would have been enough to turn Dachau's economic fortune around we will never know, for in September of 1939 Hitler began his effort to conquer Europe, and the war forged its own economic course.

Wartime changes, 1938–1942

Although the military conflagration of World War II did not begin until September of 1939, Germany's occupation of Austria in March 1938 and Czechoslovakia a year later, as well as the beginning of a major offensive against Jewish Germans in November 1938, meant that the war-related use of the camp had already begun in 1938. After 1933 the number of new prisoners brought to Dachau remained relatively constant at around 2,000 per year. If there were not enough political suspects, unemployed transients (so-called asocials) and convicted criminals were taken there as well.[55] Periodic releases kept the total number of inmates roughly constant. That changed dramatically in 1938, when more than 18,000 new prisoners arrived in Dachau. Many thousands of them were arrested in Austria for resisting the March 1938 Nazi takeover; exactly 10,911 more were brought to Dachau after the *Kristallnacht* pogroms of 10 and 11 November.[56] The majority of these men did not stay long, however. About one-third were released after a short period of brutal intimidation; another third within a few months after they signed papers promising to emigrate. By the summer of 1939 the total number of inmates had been reduced to about 5,000, leaving ample room for new additions. Well before the November 1938 pogrom, preparations were made to increase the capacity of the camp for a large influx of prisoners. Inmates reported, for instance, that in the weeks before the pogroms they had to make bedding by stuffing thousands of sacks with straw. This supports the claim that Nazi leaders were planning to take a large number of new prisoners at about that time.[57]

During the war the Dachau concentration camp became much more multinational, and economic interests played an increasing role in camp life. However, as far as the town was concerned, there were no dramatic changes for the first few years. The town post office still delivered the mail to its branch office in the camp, sorted according to the two destinations "concentration camp" and (SS) "training camp." City officials still filled out death certificates for the men who died in the camp, a total of 3,856 from April 1933 until May 1941, when a registry office was opened in the camp itself. During some months the city officials had registered well over 100 deaths, in others only a few. During the entire year 1935, for example, only twelve deaths were registered.[58] In November 1937 a city bus began operating along the three-kilometer stretch between the town and the camp, serving the SS and their families. About seventy-five civilian (that is, non-SS) families living in barracks directly adjacent to the camp (on the property where the "Roman Grove" condominiums were built in the late 1980s) were not forced to relocate until 1938, because the town repeatedly refused to build housing for them.

By the time the war began in 1939 the positive official portrayals of the concentration camps had tapered off. On the one hand the exceptional wartime mobilization made the implementation of extermination programs such as the systematic gassings of physically and mentally handicapped Germans possible; on the other hand more attention had to be paid to potential sources of popular discontent.[59] After 1941 propaganda regarding the concentration camps seldom focused on them directly. Instead, it vilified Allied camps, especially bygone turn-of-the century British camps in South Africa. In the postscript of a 1940 novel about British concentration camps during the Boer War, an explicit comparison was made with "our [German] camps."[60] The author claimed that in German concentration camps "criminals are living under conditions with which the 122,000 Boer women and children [in British camps] would love to switch." The statement misleadingly uses the present tense, implying that the British still kept civilians in the camps (they had left South Africa in 1907), and the number substantially inflates even the figure of 76,000 inmates that Hitler had used in his 1920 speech.[61]

As concentration camp labor was harnessed to meet increasing war needs in the 1940s, conditions improved somewhat. On 1 January 1940 Oswald Pohl consolidated all of the factories in the Dachau camp into the "German Equipment Works, Inc." (Deutsche Ausrüstungswerke, DAW).[62] They included not only the aforementioned carpentry and metalworking shops, but also a slaughterhouse and meat-processing plant that supplied meat for 25,000 prisoners and SS men, and a commercial bakery that produced 8,000 loaves of bread each day. After the military setbacks of 1942 and early 1943, the Nazi leadership decided to systematically exploit prisoner labor in armaments production. A reorganization at the top level of SS administration reflected this change of priorities.[63]

In February 1942 an SS "Main Office of Economic Administration" (known by its German abbreviation, WVHA) was created to coordinate all SS administrative, economic, and construction projects, in contrast to the police and secret service functions of the "Main Office of Reich Security" (RSHA). One month later, on 5 March 1942, the concentration camp system was placed under the authority of the WVHA. On the one hand this transfer ensured the continued control of the SS over the camps, which were being eyed by cabinet minister Albert Speer's Reich Armaments Ministry, and by Hitler's General Commissioner for Labor, both of whom were using every means at their disposal to obtain civilian workers in occupied Poland and the Soviet Union. On the other hand, the transfer brought about a temporary improvement of conditions in the camps.

The extermination of the Jews

For many years historians have debated whether the Nazi plan to systematically exterminate all of the Jews of Europe already existed in Hitler's mind in the 1920s, or whether it grew out of a radicalization of policy during the late 1930s and early 1940s.[64] Out of this debate an intermediate position has emerged that suggests that while *a* "final solution" to the "Jewish question" was indeed one of Hitler's intentions from the 1920s (hence the name "intentionalism" for this historiographical school), the particular solution of mass murder was arrived at only after several other possible "final solutions" had been attempted but abandoned because they were dysfunctional (hence the name "functionalism," which also stresses the various political functions of the persecution and annihilation of Jews).[65] The title of a book by historian Karl Schleunes, *The Twisted Road to Auschwitz* (1970), offers a succinct formulation of this position.[66] Still other historians have stressed the roles of top-echelon Nazis vying with each other to ingratiate themselves with Hitler by finding optimal solutions to the "Jewish question" that obsessed him. In this view, the nature of the power structure in Nazi Germany (hence the name "structuralism") was responsible for the radicalization of Nazi anti-Jewish policy, culminating in systematic mass murder. German historian Hans Mommsen has been one of the most outspoken proponents of this view. The development of the concentration camp system during the 1930s and early 1940s and its role in this process support a functionalist–structuralist position in which Hitler's thinking evolved through a variety of "solutions," proposed by opportunistic underlings vying for his favor, before settling on mass murder.

As we have seen, although Jews were singled out for especially brutal treatment in the concentration camps from the very start, it was not until the pogroms of November 1938 that the camps began to play a role in "solving" the "Jewish question." At that time the solution included intimidation, persecution, extortion, and forced emigration. Between March and October 1938, 50,000 Jews were persuaded or forced to emigrate from Nazi-controlled Austria: this was considered a major step towards solving the so-called Jewish question there.[67] Because Nazi planners thought that such high emigration figures would not be consistently attainable, alternatives to mere emigration from the German Reich were sought. When Hitler began the war in 1939, his plans for the Jews consisted of massive resettlement, first to the Lublin district in eastern Poland, then, after the defeat of France in June 1940, to the French colony of Madagascar. The large number of people who would have been involved in such population transfers, however, posed difficult logistical problems.[68] As an interim "solution," in 1940 Jews were concentrated in walled or fenced ghettos in several Polish cities. Many died of starvation and epidemic diseases while awaiting the further disposition of their fate.

A new "solution" began to emerge after December 1940, when Hitler began planning the invasion of the Soviet Union. For instance, in March 1941 various statements by Hitler lead some historians to believe that at that time mass murder emerged as one weapon that he planned to wield in his attack on the "Judeo-Bolshevik intelligentsia" in the Soviet Union.[69] When the German armies began their advance into Soviet territory in late June 1941, special "task forces" (*Einsatzgruppen,* made up of *Einsatzkommandos*) followed in their wake, rounding up real and imagined enemies in the captured towns and villages, and murdering them. According to Otto Ohlendorf, one of the task force commanders, Gestapo chief Reinhard Heydrich, transmitted an order from Hitler whereby all "Communist functionaries and activists, Jews, Gypsies, saboteurs and agents . . . are to be executed without further ado."[70]

In practice, this order resulted in marching the victims, who were primarily Jews, to somewhat secluded locations, forcing them to dig their own mass graves, and then executing them with rifles or machine guns. The task forces were heterogeneous groups, consisting of about 50 percent SS and Gestapo men, 15 percent German police, 10 percent local (non-German) personnel, and 25 percent technical and administrative personnel. Logistical and psychological problems (for the executioners) with mass shootings as a method of "finally solving" Germany's imagined racial problem led Nazi officials to consider other methods of mass murder. From November 1941 to the summer of 1942 specially retrofitted trucks whose exhausts were piped into the sealed cargo compartments were used, but this method was too inefficient for the large numbers of Jews who were falling into German hands.[71]

Since January 1940 carbon monoxide gas introduced from pressurized tanks into special gas chambers had been successfully used in a program to murder mentally and physically disabled Germans and Austrians living in institutional care.[72] With time, however, news of this so-called "euthanasia" program leaked out, provoking disquiet among the German population. For instance, there were fears that disabled war veterans and institutionalized senior citizens might be included in the program. In August 1941 this unrest reached a peak when Bishop von Galen in Münster condemned the program in public sermons. The large-scale program of gassing was quickly scuttled, although patients continued to be killed by lethal injection or slow starvation. The end of that program left a number of personnel trained in and inured to mass murder by gassing out of work. Many of these men were sent to eastern Poland to help design, supervise, and run gassing facilities using carbon monoxide from the exhaust fumes of diesel motors.

The first of these installations was constructed near the Polish village of Chelmno, about 45 miles from the Lodz ghetto. Deportees were ordered to strip at a manor house on a hill, then forced down a ramp into waiting trucks, in which they were gassed en route to a nearby forest, where they were dumped into mass graves. Chelmno began operating in December 1941.[73] Death factories at Belzec and Sobibor, with stationary gas chambers fueled by diesel exhaust, commenced operation in March 1942. Treblinka, set up specifically as a murder factory for the Jews in the Warsaw ghetto, began operation in July 1942.

These extermination centers were quite different from concentration camps. Historians now designate them as VL, for *Vernichtungslager* (extermination camps), in contrast to the official Nazi abbreviation KL, for *Konzentrationslager*. To emphasize that these facilities were quite different from concentration camps, historians sometimes call them "extermination *centers*." They were comparatively small facilities where arriving deportees were immediately stripped of their possessions and forced into gas chambers, then cremated or buried in large pits. There were warehouses to store the belongings the victims had brought with them, and accommodation for a small number of inmates and guards who staffed the facility.[74] Of close to 2 million victims who were murdered in these centers, it is estimated that only a few hundred Jews survived, essentially all of them "work Jews" whom the Germans used to help operate the camps.[75]

During this same period, other experiments with a different gassing agent at existing concentration camps led to the creation of a hybrid type of concentration–extermination camp. In September and October 1941 experiments were conducted at the Auschwitz concentration camp using cyanide gas from pellets saturated with prussic acid to kill Soviet prisoners of war and small groups of Jews.[76] The cyanide gas, trade-named Zyklon B, was widely used in concentration camps to fumigate barracks and clothing. Auschwitz near Cracow, and Maidanek on the outskirts of Lublin in eastern Poland, were the two chief hybrid camps. The combination of penal concentration camps and mass gassing programs at these hybrid concentration camp–extermination centers has contributed to popular confusion about the Nazi camp systems. Usually, and not incorrectly, all three types of camp are subsumed under the term "death camp." This imprecision has, however, provided a basis for the claims of people who deny that Nazi Germany ever implemented large-scale programs of mass murder. Such deniers take testimony about Dachau, for instance, which was one of the least horrifying of the camps, and claim that the testimony applies to all camps.[77]

Just as the mass gassings of Polish and western European Jews at Chelmno were getting underway in the late fall of 1941, the stupendous victories of the German army on the eastern front ended, bringing the *Blitzkrieg* against the Soviet Union to a preliminary halt. Nazi leaders began to take an interest in eliminating the mass graves as evidence of their genocide. In March 1942 Reinhard Heydrich met Paul Blobel, the commander of the task forces that had slaughtered Jews in Kiev and the Ukraine, to discuss the opening of the mass graves and destruction of the corpses.[78]

Since Blobel was ordered not to create any written record of the project, this gruesome program of eradicating evidence is one of the least-documented aspects of the Holocaust.[79] Blobel began experimenting with various methods at the Chelmno mass graves in the summer of 1942. At first the pits were opened and then exploded with incendiary bombs, but uncontrollable fires made this method impracticable. Blobel's men finally settled on the method of exhuming and burning the decomposing corpses on grates made of railroad track, then grinding the unburned bones. By late 1942 this program, code-named "Special Action 1005" (after its RSHA file number), was extended to encompass the mass graves filled by the task forces, as well as the burial pits in the other extermination centers.

In the winter of 1942–3 the German army suffered catastrophic losses on the eastern front, prompting Nazi leaders to mobilize all of Germany's resources for "total war," as Propaganda Minister Josef Goebbels called it in his infamous February 1943 speech in Berlin. One element of total war was the use of peoples slated for extermination as slave labor prior to their murder. This program, which historians call "extermination through work," granted Jews and other deportees a brief reprieve to contribute to the German war effort before they died from exhaustion or disease, or were murdered by gassing or other means. By 1943 the SS no longer buried the corpses of the victims of its extermination programs, but meticulously burned them and buried the ashes or dumped them in ponds and rivers. In Dachau, a large four-oven crematorium with a gas chamber was built in the camp complex in 1942, augmenting the small two-oven crematorium constructed in 1940 (see ill. 5).

When the extermination centers in occupied Poland had finished turning their living raw material into ashes and loot, the facilities were carefully dismantled and destroyed. In 1943–4 a pine forest was planted and a farmhouse built to conceal the site of the former Treblinka murder factory, and Sobibor and Belzec were completely effaced as well. Thus there are essentially no visible traces left of the extermination centers.

In contrast, the hybrid concentration–extermination camps Maidanek and Auschwitz-Birkenau continued to operate until shortly before they were captured by the advancing Red army in July 1944 and January 1945. Maidanek, which was situated at the eastern edge of Poland, was overrun so unexpectedly in July 1944 that none of the camp was destroyed or dismantled. The Soviet army found partially burned skeletons in the crematorium ovens, as well as tens of thousands of shoes and other booty taken from the victims of factory-scale murder. The dismantling and destruction of the huge Auschwitz and Auschwitz-Birkenau camps had begun in the late fall of 1944, so that when they were finally liberated in January 1945, some evidence had been destroyed. However, most of the physical plant, including the remains of the dynamited gas chamber–crematorium buildings in Birkenau, still stood. Protected by Polish law since 1946, these camps contain the largest amount of physical remains of any of the former concentration camps.

The Dachau camp during "total war"

During 1943, after the vast majority of Jews in Poland had been killed, the murder operations shifted from the extermination centers to the Auschwitz-Birkenau hybrid work–extermination camp. The slower pace of industrial murder necessitated by the greater distances from which the Jewish victims had to be brought, and the lower concentrations of Jews in those areas, made the newly increased murder capacity of Auschwitz alone sufficient. This shift also centralized and simplified the process of selecting some able-bodied workers for the war industries, where the pace of labor and the living conditions would kill them in a short period of time. As the demand for productive labor increased, considerations of efficiency brought with them a moderate improvement of living conditions in the camps. Gradually, another related shift took place as well. At first the SS attempted to bring private industry into the camps to take advantage of prisoner labor, but business interests preferred to have workers brought from the camps to their premises.

However, since the factories were not always located close to the camps, the long marches each morning and evening wasted precious working time. Soon "branch camps" subordinate to main concentration camps were set up at convenient locations near sites of production. One of the first – and largest – such camps served the I. G. Farben chemical conglomerate at Auschwitz. Beginning in November 1942 a separate camp, Monowitz (also known as Auschwitz III), was set up adjacent to the factory.[80] While there were only eighty-two such branch camps in the German Reich in December 1942 (twenty-nine of them were near Dachau), by January 1945 there were 662, making them a common feature in industrial regions throughout Germany, especially in the vicinity of main concentration camps.[81]

Prisoner labor was used at twelve places in the town of Dachau.[82] By far the largest employers were the Wülfert wurst factory (ills. 1, 20), which began using sixteen prisoners in August 1941 and was paying the SS for

350 by the end of the war, and the screw factory Präzifix, where up to 400 camp inmates worked making airplane parts. While a separate branch camp was set up at the Wülfert works in February 1943, Präzifix was located within the SS camp, so civilian workers from the town and detachments of inmates from the camp met there each day. Additionally, between ten and twenty prisoners worked at a couple of shoe factories; others worked at an SS tailor's shop set up in a town restaurant, in potato storage cellars, and at the municipal electricity works. The Dachau mayor even had a prisoner for his personal use. Prisoners under guard working in the town were not an uncommon sight by the end of the war.

Another major point of contact between inmates and townspeople was the camp plantation, a large agricultural complex on the far side of the concentration camp (ill. 1).[83] Work on the gardens began in 1935, and the project attained major proportions in 1939, when in the first six months of the year nearly 1 million Reichsmarks were invested in new construction. Its primary purpose was not to supply the camp, but to determine whether it would be feasible to make Germany independent of herb and spice imports. This plantation was commonly known as the "Herbal Garden" (*Kräutergarten*), the name its bus stop and access street still bear today, or simply as "the plantation." After being used by different private firms since 1945, this property is now used by the Dachau parks department. In the 1940s the sale of plants and agricultural products to the local populace provided many opportunities for contacts. The case of Imma Mack, a young woman from a nearby convent who regularly purchased products from the plantation and smuggled goods in and out during the last year of the war, documents the close connections between civilians and camp inmates.[84] In spite of all difficulties, dangers, and fears, Mack persisted in her regular clandestine aid to the prisoners up to the very end.

As we have seen, from the start Dachau served as a model for the whole concentration camp system. In later years this model camp served a number of special functions as well. Two of the most important, especially in light of developments after 1945, were its use as a special detainment facility for prominent public figures, and its use from 1940 on to consolidate all of the Christian clergymen being held in "protective custody" in the Reich.[85] In 1938 and 1939, forty-nine German and Austrian clergymen were imprisoned in Dachau, primarily for political reasons. After the consolidation in 1940 there were more than 1,000 priests in Dachau, about 4 percent of the 23,000 inmates in the camp that year. By the end of the war, a total of 2,762 clergymen had been imprisoned in KZ Dachau. The overwhelming majority, 2,579 (93 percent), were Catholic, while the rest (141, or 7 percent) were Protestant. The largest national contingent was from Poland (1,780, or 64 percent), with the Germans (447, or 16 percent), French (6 percent), Czechs (2 percent,) and other nationalities following far behind. Of the total number, 1,034 (37 percent) died in the camp.

The clergymen were housed in barracks nos. 26, 28, and 30 on the west side of the camp toward the back (away from the service building and roll-call square), and they were initially accorded some privileges such as supplementary rations and exemption from hard labor. The priests were allowed to convert one room of barrack 26 into a chapel, which was officially off limits to other camp inmates (ill. 41). After 1941 even the Polish priests in barrack 28 were barred from using it – a measure not too difficult to enforce, since barbed wire fencing separated some of the barracks in the camp.

In April 1942 all privileges for the priests except the use of the chapel were rescinded, and they were forced to do heavy agricultural work in the camp plantation. From the outbreak of a typhus epidemic in January 1943 until April 1944, when it was discovered that priests had been smuggling letters out of the camp, they were also allowed to work as prisoner orderlies responsible for maintaining discipline and order in the individual barracks. This enabled them to mitigate some of the harsher aspects of camp life. In 1944 priests were permitted to oversee their own barracks, thus eliminating the potential capriciousness of brutal overseers, who were sometimes chosen from common criminals being held in the camp.[86] In 1943 the priests were allowed to receive packages from their parishes, which helped to alleviate the worst tribulations of hunger. It also offered a means by which the local Dachau parish could channel foodstuffs into the camp.

The other special group of prisoners in the camp were prominent public figures. They were housed in a special tract of individual cells behind the service building.[87] Their cells were not locked, they were allowed to move freely within the courtyard separating their tract from the service building, their food came from the SS kitchen, and they were sometimes taken on walks in the surrounding area. Among them were Prince Frederick Leopold of Prussia, the former Austrian Chancellor Kurt von Schuschnigg (who later became a professor at Washington University in St. Louis), the former president of the Reichsbank, Hjalmar Schacht, a French general, and two German church leaders who played important roles in the postwar history of the camp: the Catholic episcopal canon Johannes Neuhäusler, and the head of the oppositional Protestant "Confessing Church," Martin Niemöller. Another of these special prisoners who later took an active role in shaping the memorial site, Munich lawyer Josef Müller, recalled that one of the worst aspects of their imprisonment was the use of some cells as torture chambers for ordinary inmates, and the use of the courtyard as an execution range. These "special" or "honorary" prisoners enjoyed special privileges. Müller, who later became the Bavarian Minister of Justice, was able to meet his personal secretary at the camp gate to receive parcels and exchange information.

During the war, even under normal circumstances, prisoners arriving at the camp may have been quite visible to the townspeople. One contemporary admitted having seen handcuffed Russian prisoners of war being brutally beaten as they were driven from the train station to the camp in the early years of the war.[88] A November 1941 directive from the chief of the SS's security service, Reinhard Heydrich, to the officers in charge of sending POWs to the concentration camps makes quite clear how public these transports were:[89]

> The commandants of the concentration camps complain that 5–10 percent of the Soviet Russians destined for execution arrive dead or half-dead in the camps. This gives the impression that the army POW camps are trying to get rid of such prisoners by these means.
>
> In particular it has been determined that on marches, for instance from the train station to the camp, a not inconsiderable number of POWs collapse dead or half-dead from exhaustion, and have to be picked up by a trailing wagon.
>
> It cannot be prevented that the German populace takes note of these things.
>
> Even if such transports to the concentration camps are usually conducted by the German army, the populace will nonetheless attribute these conditions to the SS.
>
> In order to preclude such situations as much as possible in the future I decree, effective immediately, that mortally ill Soviet Russian suspects . . . are absolutely prohibited from being transported to the concentration camps for execution.

This directive spotlights both the cynical attitude of the SS toward human life, and its effort to maintain the public façade of the "clean camp," even in the face of overwhelming evidence to the contrary.

There was also the camp crematorium, whose pungent smoke sometimes blew in the direction of the town. By late 1939 a small crematorium with one oven containing two incineration stretchers was in operation in the camp.[90] In May 1942 plans were completed for a much larger replacement building that included undressing rooms, disinfection chambers for clothing, an airtight gas chamber disguised as a shower, a morgue, and a four-oven crematorium with eight incineration chambers – all neatly lined up according to the dictates of streamlined industrial processing.[91] Although only trial gassings were conducted in the gas chamber (death by other causes supplied enough human raw material for the ovens), the furnaces reduced tens of thousands of corpses to ash between the summer of 1942 and the spring of 1945, when the death rate was so high that burials in nearby mass graves supplemented burning as a means of corpse disposal.

2
_____

Dachau: a symbol of genocide

Dissolution, 1944–1945

In 1943, when the prospect of a German victory in the war began to appear dubious, the Nazi leadership began a campaign to eradicate the physical evidence of its atrocities. Initially, as described above, this program was limited to digging up mass graves and burning the decaying human remains in them.[1] As Allied armies, especially the Soviet army in eastern Poland, approached the concentration and extermination camps in 1944, the cover-up of the atrocities was expanded to include the evacuation of the concentration camp inmates to camps closer to the heart of the Reich.[2] In July 1944 the inmates of Maidanek (near the present Polish–Ukrainian border) were forced to march west to Auschwitz, and at the end of August the last 7,000 inmates of Natzweiler (near the French–German border) were transported eastward to Dachau.

By the winter of 1944–5 material shortages and Allied bombing raids were taking their toll on the German transportation infrastructure. As the Allied advance accelerated, the SS was increasingly unable to cover its bloodstained tracks. Beginning in November 1944 Auschwitz was dismantled and the remaining prisoners sent to camps further west, primarily to Sachsenhausen (on the outskirts of Berlin), Buchenwald (south of Berlin near Weimar) and Mauthausen (in western Austria). By late January 1945 the last German military offensive of World War II had been repelled. The Americans occupied the city of Aachen on Germany's western border and the Soviets liberated Auschwitz in southern Poland. The slow but unrelenting conquest of Germany proper began. A new stage of deadly evacuation marches began in March 1945, with long treks of prisoners leaving Sachsenhausen and Buchenwald by cargo train and on foot for Bergen-Belsen and destinations near the Baltic Sea, or to Flossenbürg, Dachau, and their branch camps in southeastern Germany.

As Allied troops penetrated further into the heart of the Reich, the murderous chaos heightened to staggering proportions: death went out of control. Local SS officials could no longer deal with the results of their handiwork. On 1 March 1945 Commandant Kramer of Belsen wrote a long letter to his superiors at the SS Main Office of Financial Administration about the problems he faced:[3]

> You informed me by telegram of 23rd February, 1945, that I was to receive 2,500 female detainees as a first consignment from Ravensbrück. I have assured accommodation for this number. The reception of further consignments is impossible, not only from the point of view of accommodation due to lack of space, but particularly on account of the feeding question . . . [I]t was decided that the camp could not hold more than 35,000 detainees. In the meantime this number has been exceeded by 7,000 and a further 6,200 are now on their way. As a result all barracks are overcrowded by at least 30 percent . . . In addition to this question, a spotted fever and typhus epidemic has now begun, which is spreading every day. The daily mortality rate, which was still in the vicinity of 60–70 at the beginning of February, has now attained a daily average of 250–300 and will increase further in light of the prevailing conditions.

Kramer went on to describe problems of food supply, clothing, cooking machinery, illness, delousing, sewage, other epidemics, and cremation. He concluded obediently: "For my part it is a matter of course that these difficulties must be overcome. I am now asking you for your assistance as far as it lies in your power . . . I know that you have even greater difficulties to overcome and appreciate that you must send to this camp all internees discharged from that area; on the other hand, I implore your help in overcoming this situation."

At this time Himmler, very aware that Germany would lose the war and interested in gaining personal bargaining points with the Allies, began to allow the release of some inmates to foreign governments.[4] On 5 April 1945 he discussed the fate of the concentration camps about to be liberated by Allied forces with the head of the SS's foreign espionage service, Kurt Becher. Himmler offered Becher the position of "Reich Commissioner for All Concentration Camps," and sent him to inspect Bergen-Belsen, where he may have played a role in Commandant Kramer's decision to surrender the camp on 15 April.[5] On 14 April Himmler authorized Becher to negotiate the surrender of Dachau and other camps as well, but an outburst by Hitler compelled him to reverse that order the next day. Hitler's last-minute solution was either to evacuate or to murder all remaining inmates, a desire that resulted in a telegram from SS headquarters to the commanders of the concentration camps that "no prisoner shall be captured alive by the enemy."[6] This directive to murder all unevacuated survivors was obediently followed in many camps throughout the shrinking Nazi Reich, precipitating scenes of incomprehensible barbarity, in some places only hours before Allied troops arrived. Photographs of fields of charred corpses in Leipzig-Mochau, Gardelegen, and Landsberg shocked newspaper readers the world over.[7] The Dachau SS drew up a plan for the aerial bombardment of the camp.[8]

At the same time Dachau, because it was located in southern Germany farthest from the advancing Allied armies, was one of the final destinations for the evacuations from other camps. Pestilent freight cars filled with wretched, dying, and dead human beings came through the train station, and columns of starving men were driven by heavily armed guards from surrounding areas through the access streets to the camp. There are reports that Dachau townspeople heard them coming and left foodstuffs on the sidewalk for the men to grab before they entered the camp.[9] The townspeople disappeared inside to avoid confrontations with the guards. In this period the Dachau death rate skyrocketed.[10] From 1940 to 1943 the annual death toll ranged between 1,000 and 3,000 prisoners; it exceeded 400 per month only twice. In 1944 it climbed from 403 in October, to 997 in November, to 1,915 in December. In the first four months of 1945 it ranged from 2,625 to 3,977 *per month*, with fully half of all documented deaths in the camp occurring in the last six months before liberation. Put another way, during the eleven years prior to December 1944 there was an average of about four deaths per day – a statistic shocking enough in its own right. But in the first months of 1945 an average of over 100 people died *each day* in Dachau.

Since late fall of 1944 sufficient coal for the cremation of corpses had not been available in Dachau. Prisoners had been forced to haul corpses to a mass burial pit on a nearby hill. As the Allies closed in on upper Bavaria in late April, work details no longer left the concentration camp grounds. Literally thousands of corpses were stacked in and around the crematorium, and near the sick-bay. Approximately forty boxcars with circa 2,000 evacuees from Buchenwald were left unattended at the camp unloading platform for several days. It seems that at one point the camp SS went along the train asking for the survivors to come out. Anyone who moved was shot and left lying in the doorway or on the ground. When the Americans arrived, this train was one of the first things they saw. Only seventeen of its 2,000 occupants showed signs of life, all of them already beyond hope.[11]

49

Insurrection and liberation, 28–29 April 1945

All through the twelve years of Nazi rule the vast majority of Dachau citizens had shown either tacit acceptance or explicit support of the camp on the outskirts of their town. As the Nazi regime began to crumble, increasing numbers of Germans withdrew their support and began making plans for after the demise of the Nazi regime. By the end of April 1945, when the collapse of the regime was imminent, a few camp inmates escaped and joined forces with some town residents in an attempt to overthrow the Nazi town leaders and save the town from the suicidal defense and self-destruction Hitler had ordered.[12] The action was coordinated by Georg Scherer, a former concentration camp inmate who still worked at the Präzifix screw factory in the SS camp, and Walter Neff, another released inmate who still worked in the camp, in the laboratory for medical experimentation.

When a Bavarian resistance group in Munich issued a radio call for active resistance on 28 April, the Dachau group decided to launch its takeover bid, even though the liberating US army was still more than twenty-four hours away. These oppositionals stormed city hall and disarmed the police. To deceive the SS in the camp, the siren signaling a direct American tank attack was sounded. When a newly formed civilian militia of young boys and old men arrived to defend the town, they either joined the insurgents or were disarmed and sent home. An SS officer staying at a downtown hotel alerted the Dachau camp SS, however, which sent a combat unit to crush the rebellion. This overwhelming force quickly disarmed the insurgents. As a warning, the corpses of six men who had been killed or executed, three townsmen, and three camp inmates were displayed on the sidewalk in front of the savings bank in the center of town.

That night most of the camp guards and military SS withdrew, and the warehouses of the SS camp were opened to the local residents for plundering. At liberation some US soldiers watched in disbelief as German citizens unconcernedly walked and pushed their bicycles down the camp road alongside the railroad tracks with the train full of corpses, on their way to collect loot from the warehouses.[13]

The next day, 29 April, two different detachments of American troops arrived.[14] Members of the 45th "Thunderbird" Division came from the northwest, arriving first at the camp across fields from the plantation side. A squad from the 42nd "Rainbow" Division came from the east, skirting the northern edge of the town. The American soldiers were completely unprepared for what they saw when they first entered the Dachau concentration camp. They had, however, had substantial experience with fanatical German resistance in what was obviously a hopeless military situation. The 45th Division, for example, had been held up for nearly a week and sustained heavy casualties as the nearby cities of Aschaffenburg and Schweinheim were defended "to the last man."[15] And just before it reached the camp, the liberating unit of the 42nd Division had suffered a casualty in a skirmish with a small squad of *Waffen-SS* soldiers dispatched from the camp that morning to "hold up the American advance for as long as possible."[16] The US soldiers, prepared to expect the most irrational behavior from German fighting forces, were nevertheless sickened and outraged by the sights they saw in Dachau.

One of the first soldiers from the 45th Division to enter the camp in the early afternoon of 29 April 1945 was Colonel Bill Walsh.[17] Walsh led his company along the railway siding into the SS garrison, where they came upon a train of thirty-nine open boxcars, each filled with many dozens of contorted, emaciated corpses. Some corpses with bullet wounds were lying in front of the open doors. Some of Walsh's men became physically ill, many were distraught, still others were enraged. A lead scout described his entry into the Dachau camp complex:[18]

> I remember walking along a railroad track. The rest of the squad was about 100 feet behind me. Finally there came into view these boxcars, laden with dead bodies, piled on top of one another . . . I waved the squad forward. After viewing this situation we went further on, boiling mad, half out of our heads.
>
> We came across a German hospital. How comfy the patients were, lying between clean white sheets with no regard for what was going on a few yards away. We ordered everyone out, regardless of their condition. We pressed further on and came to the inner enclosure . . . We cleaned out the guard towers.

Events during and shortly before liberation explain why the American liberators met with such little resistance. Martin Gottfried Weiss, who had been commandant of Dachau in 1942–3 before he was sent to Maidanek in eastern Poland to bring order to that concentration camp, was ordered back to Dachau in March 1945 to take charge of the catastrophic and rapidly deteriorating situation. Weiss was a relatively benign commandant, in contrast both to his predecessor and to the men under him who were directly in charge of the protective custody compound.[19] Weiss was inclined to surrender the camp instead of evacuating it or murdering the remaining 35,000 inmates. To that end he sent several telegrams to SS headquarters, which, as mentioned above, answered unequivocally on

15 April that under no circumstances were any prisoners to fall alive into the hands of the enemy. Weiss thereupon began a halting evacuation of some groups of prisoners, but he also began negotiating conditions for a surrender of the camp with Victor Maurer, a representative of the International Red Cross.[20] Maurer was not allowed to inspect the camp, but he was allowed to distribute food packages to the inmates.

In the night after the insurgency, Weiss, the regular concentration camp guards, and the SS garrisons left the camp. SS officer Wicker was left in charge of the complex with about 560 troops, some of whom were Hungarian SS, and some of whom had been held in the SS's disciplinary prison within the camp. At 7 a.m. a white flag was raised on the main gate of the SS complex, but guards remained in the watchtowers to keep the prisoners in check. When the first unit of US soldiers arrived, Wicker did in fact surrender the camp. However, there was some sniper and machine-gun fire from within, and the American soldiers were not inclined to treat the camp personnel they found as normal POWs. At the slightest provocation or hint of provocation, captives and men in the process of surrendering were gunned down, perhaps forty to fifty of them, including Wicker.[21] In these first hours the Americans also refrained from intervening when survivors attacked the most brutal of their former tormentors and informants.

In the evening, after some semblance of order had been restored, the prisoners took Bill Walsh on a tour of the camp. He viewed the rows of corpses on the ground outside the sick-bay, then he was shown the interior of one of the filthy, overcrowded barracks, the kennels of the camp's bloodhounds (which had been shot by one of the liberators), and finally the crematorium with its heaps of corpses and its ash-laden ovens (ills. 5, 9, 10). Many US soldiers were taken on such tours during the first days after liberation, and the camp was explicitly left untouched so it could be viewed and documented by two particular groups of visitors: a delegation from the United States Congress, and an assemblage of the most prominent newspaper reporters and editors from the US.

The liberation of Dachau coincided with an effort mounted by Allied Supreme Commander Eisenhower after the liberation of Buchenwald to publicize the German atrocities in the United States and Britain.

The media blitz, May 1945

Beginning in early April 1945, army units accompanied by photographers and journalists overran camp after camp littered with smoldering and decomposing corpses, and in town after town the remains of hastily buried concentration camp evacuees were discovered.[22] On 12 April and 15 April Allied troops occupied the first two main concentration camps that had not been evacuated: Buchenwald and Bergen-Belsen.[23] Among the tens of thousands of sick and dying survivors there were literally tens of thousands of corpses. Scenes of incredible cruelty and carnage were subsequently discovered on 16 April at Gardelegen, on 17 April at Penig (in central Germany), and on 18 April at Thekla near Leipzig.[24] Reports about these atrocities began to make headlines in the international press.

Since 1933, a substantial amount of relatively detailed information had been available not only to Allied policymakers, but to foreign publics at large as well. The British *Manchester Guardian* was perhaps the most consistent and reliable reporter of conditions in the Nazi camps, but even readers of the *New York Times* had been exposed to dozens of reports of barbaric mistreatment of prisoners in the camps.[25] Although newspaper and magazine reports specifically about the concentration camps give an indication of what readers *could* have known, articles with indirect references to the German camps indicate how much contemporary journalists assumed was *actually* popularly known, because they implicitly presumed a certain level of knowledge among their readers. In a November 1941 series about theater in countries with repressive regimes, the journal *Theatre Arts* published an article about plays performed in German concentration camps that presupposed that its readers would be astonished that plays could be both legally and illicitly performed in the camps.[26] And in January 1942 the illustrated *American Magazine* began an article about US camps for Axis nationals stranded in the United States by the war in Europe with the words: "To most Americans, who regard concentration camps as devilish examples of Nazi sadism, it comes as a shock to learn that Uncle Sam himself operates a trio of them today."[27]

Further examples of articles and books published in the United States about the German concentration camps that assume a certain established negative image could be cited, but in spite of this readily available information, the camps were essentially ignored by public officials and never became a public issue abroad.[28] There were various reasons for this, perhaps including antisemitism in the US State Department, and, after the United States entered the war, fear of hurting public morale by raising concerns about the treatment of Allied POWs in German hands.[29] This stance changed dramatically on 12 April 1945, when Allied Supreme Commander Eisenhower viewed the remains of Buchenwald branch camp Ohrdruf (near Gotha in Thuringia) with Generals Patton and

Bradley.[30] Eisenhower was deeply shocked by what he saw. Afterward he ordered every nearby unit that was not on the front line to tour the camp. "We are told that the American soldier does not know what he is fighting for. Now, at least, he will know what he is fighting *against*," he reasoned.[31] On 19 April, after reports about the occupation of Buchenwald and Belsen had reached him, Eisenhower sent a telegram to United States Chief of Staff Marshall:[32]

> We are constantly finding German camps in which they have placed political prisoners where unspeakable conditions exist. From my own personal observation, I can state unequivocally that all written statements up to now do not paint the full horrors.
> In view of these facts, you may think it advisable to invite about 12 congressional leaders and 12 leading editors to see these camps. If so, I shall be glad to take these groups to one of these camps. Such a visit will show them without any trace of doubt the full evidence of the cruelty practiced by the Nazis in such places as normal procedure.
> A similar invitation is being sent to similar representative British groups.

Following that invitation from Eisenhower, ten members of the British parliament inspected Buchenwald on Saturday, 21 April.[33] On the same day three US congressional representatives who happened to be in the area were also given a tour of the camp.[34] Top US policymakers also responded quickly to Eisenhower's telegram. Within hours of receipt of the telegram Marshall telegraphed back that Secretary of War Stimson and President Truman had approved the suggestion. In spite of the organizational difficulties, the delegations were assembled over the weekend, leaving for Paris on Sunday, 22 April, and flying to Buchenwald the morning after their arrival in Europe.[35] The delegation of editors of prominent US newspapers and magazines was also quickly assembled. It toured Buchenwald with journalists from London, Switzerland, Denmark, and Sweden on 25 April, only one day after the congressional group.[36] Buchenwald, however, had been liberated on 12 April, and much of the devastation and evidence of atrocities had already been cleaned up.[37] Thus when news of Dachau's liberation on 29 April reached the high command, General Patch ordered that the evidence of German brutality be left untouched awaiting the inspections.

Four members of the congressional delegation toured Dachau on 1 May, within forty-eight hours of liberation.[38] The eighteen-member newspaper delegation arrived on 3 May. The stacks, piles, rows, rooms, and boxcars full of corpses were still untouched (see the pictures on ill. 10). The liberated inmates were still dying at a rate of over 125 per day, an average of one person every eleven minutes. The effect of this media blitz on the British and American publics can hardly be overestimated. Not only did the presence of the prominent visitors and editors signal to the reporters in the field that newly discovered atrocities were to be one of the top news items, the delegations' itineraries were themselves newsworthy. In the last week of April and in early May, as the number of camps discovered multiplied, the number and size of the articles and photographs increased dramatically. Starting on 1 May newsreel footage of German atrocities was distributed to movie theaters throughout the United States to be shown during the eight-minute pre-film newscasts.[39] A collection of the most shocking pictures, today still the most commonly reprinted, was published in *Life* magazine on 7 May.[40]

In a pre-tour briefing upon arrival in Paris, Eisenhower made clear to the delegation of journalists why the US government had brought them to Germany to tour the concentration camps. In the words of one of the editors, Eisenhower "realized that Americans, being a decent people, found it hard to believe that such depravity and sadism could exist. He told us frankly that, for the sake of the peace and security of the world, he hoped that some way would be found to blast this skepticism. He wanted somehow to make the American people understand what sort of savages we were dealing with."[41] Similarly, Eisenhower and other army commanders wanted to make sure that the German populace could not deny that such atrocities had been committed.

The German bystanders: "We didn't know!"

In the face of the atrocities, combat commanders in the field took matters into their own hands. A need to punish, coupled with the documentary impulse that prompted Eisenhower to call for high-level foreign witnesses, led them to bring in the local populace. Residents from nearby towns were brought to camp after camp and forced to view the horrifying scenes. The order "Hands down!" came into common use, as many townspeople instinctively covered their eyes.[42] As additional punishment, civilians were often put to work burying the corpses and cleaning the camps. One of the first documented civilian tours of a liberated concentration camp followed a 15 April order by General Patton to the mayor of Weimar that:[43]

> at least 1,000 inhabitants of the city, half of whom are to be women, are to view the camp at Buchenwald and the hospital attached to it *in order to be convinced of the conditions at the camp before they are altered.*[44] Those who

are required to make the trip include: men and women from 18 to 45,
particularly those who belonged to the NSDAP. Two-thirds of those are to be
of the more prosperous classes and one third the less. They must be strong
enough to endure the march and the inspection (it will last about 6 hours;
the distance is 25 kilometers). Food is to be brought and it is to be consumed
before viewing the camp. Nothing will happen to the participants. The
march will be accompanied by trucks of the German Red Cross and doctors
in order to give help should anyone need it (emphasis added).

This order shows that such tours had two primary purposes: to document
the atrocities by obtaining reliable German witnesses, and to "teach a
lesson" especially to the Nazi Party members singled out for participation.
Accordingly, a reporter for the *New York Herald-Tribune* called the
Buchenwald trip "a first step in the re-education of the German people,"[45]
and William Shirer editorialized in his column "Propaganda Front" that in
Buchenwald "the most effective kind of re-education of the Germans" had
begun.[46]

These public tours of atrocities, often coupled with burial or clean-up
work, soon became part of an unwritten policy,[47] and in dozens of towns
from the North Sea to the Alps German civilians were forced to view the
dead.[48] At Ludwigslust, a town about halfway between Berlin and
Hamburg, for example, all residents 10 years of age and older were compelled to view the nearby camp at Woebbelin, and then the able-bodied
had to bury the dead.[49] There was also a strong practical motivation for
these punitive–pedagogical measures. Once the initial shock of discovery
and the immediate danger of attack by German forces had subsided, the
liberating troops were faced with Herculean health and sanitation tasks.[50]
Literally thousands of corpses in various stages of decomposition had to
be removed in order to slow raging epidemics, and the accumulated and
accumulating refuse of tens of thousands of freed inmates disposed of.
Since the survivors were understandably disinclined or unable to do the
work, it was only natural for the occupation forces to press captured
German army or SS soldiers into service. Where that manpower was
insufficient or unavailable, various groups from the civilian population
were compelled to assist.

Such forced tours and work details may have been "educational" in the
sense that they informed people of something they might not have known,
but they were structured in such a way that they were more likely to arouse
feelings of bitterness and disgrace than impart a lesson in civic obligation
and democratic behavior to the conscripts. Pictures of such scenes often
show armed GIs overseeing the work of the natives, or even lecturing

them.[51] The most common German reaction was not to reflect on one's own responsibility, but to deny having had anything to do with the atrocities. In the words of *New York Herald-Tribune* reporter Marguerite Higgins, who observed several such tours firsthand: "As has been the case everywhere, the German spectators in the Buchenwald tour seemed sincerely horrified, yet maintained that they had been completely ignorant of events there, and thus were free of blame."[52]

Dachau was no exception to this pattern. On 7 May, after a warming trend made the immediate burial of the dead imperative, all farm wagons in the vicinity of Dachau were requisitioned. A group of townspeople selected by the local Antifascist Committee[53] was forced to load and transport 2,400 of the corpses found in the camp at liberation to mass graves shoveled by captured SS men.[54] For three days, columns of twelve horse-drawn carts each laden with about thirty emaciated corpses passed through the town to a nearby hill called the Leiten, where the SS had begun burying its Dachau victims in the fall of 1944. Afterwards, at least one soiled cart was left at a central point in town as a warning for the citizenry. It certainly made an impression on some of the younger residents, since it resurfaced prominently in their reminiscences in the 1970s and 1980s.[55]

While this burial work was taking place, an American officer decided to take a group of 25–30 responsible but not directly implicated Dachau notables on a tour of the Dachau concentration camp (ill. 9). They were followed by journalists and an army film crew.[56] In other pragmatic–punitive–pedagogic actions former Party members were forced to dig graves in the city cemetery for the over 2,000 camp inmates who died after liberation,[57] and the wives of high-ranking SS officers were forced to clean the aforementioned forty train cars in which circa 2,000 people had died after having been imprisoned in them for more than a week without food or water.[58] It seems that German women were often selected to do traditional "women's work," such as caring for the sick or cleaning, and that they were in no way spared the most abhorrent and sickening tasks.[59]

A first attempt on 10 May to have 30 of the 130 captured SS men do the daily garbage collection in the camp had to be stopped because of harassment by survivors. A few days later, however, thirty of the captured Germans were successfully assigned to clean-up details. Working double time, they cleared 1,033 truckloads of garbage in eight days.[60]

Patricia Lochridge, who had been an exchange student in Germany before the war and had accompanied the Dachau notables on their tour, sought out some of the involuntary participants a short time later and asked them about their reactions to what they had seen.[61] Their responses show that the tour hardened them against accepting responsibility for what had gone on in the camp. Doctor Robert Koschade told her that "This business at the camp was none of our affair . . . We were shamefully deceived, there was nothing we could do, the town was full of Gestapo and SS troops." A contradiction is apparent here: the physician asserts that he was ignorant of what was happening, while at the same time he claims that he was prevented from acting on what he knew. This is an example of one of the collective tropes of the following decades, which I will introduce as the "myth of ignorance" in part II.

A high school teacher who overheard Lochridge's interview of the SS camp barber and was "anxious to please," by saying what he thought she wanted to hear, told her: "Yes, the conditions at the camp are frightful, but you must understand we knew nothing of its horrors." After Lochridge expressed her disbelief at this professed ignorance, the teacher continued, "We understood a little, but it was dangerous to know too much. A man must live himself." As in the case of the doctor, the teacher hinted that he, too, was a potential victim of Nazi brutality. This individual ruse was repeated on a collective scale during the ensuing decades; we will meet it again in part II as the "myth of victimization."

A well-to-do property owner, who had been a faithful Nazi and at 62 the oldest woman who had been on the tour, said of the prisoners: "The state put them there. They weren't good Germans. Most of them weren't Aryan." This claim that the prisoners had deserved the horrifying treatment they received reflected the image of the "clean camps" projected by Nazi propaganda. As a consequence of the myth of victimization, would-be victims perceived the inmates of the concentration camps as criminals who had deserved their punishment. Some Germans even went so far as to exonerate Hitler. A housewife who had broken down in tears at the sight of the corpses in the crematorium told Lochridge: "Nothing more terrible could have been done than was done at Dachau. But most Germans weren't involved. Der Führer couldn't have known about it. He would not have permitted such suffering." In the twisted logic of these subterfuges the roots of a third myth can be found, the "myth of resistance": the Germans (including Hitler) did and would have resisted, inasmuch as they had known what was happening.

Lochridge reports that her notebook was full of similar statements from other women she approached in the town. Typical responses in this vein were: "We want to see it for ourselves." "We heard such horrors were committed by the Russians. How could such cruelties be done by Germans on our own people?"; "My son is a storm trooper but he could never have done such acts." So horrifying were the results of twelve years of Nazi rule that many Germans refused to accept even what they could not deny.

The post-liberation events that transpired in the microcosms of Dachau and similar places near concentration camps were echoed by a systematic campaign of "atrocity education" throughout Germany. Even though many field commanders who liberated concentration camps may have been acting spontaneously when they brought in local residents, planning for a systematic confrontation of the German populace with the atrocities goes back much further. It was commonly conceived as part of a program of "reeducation."

Atrocities and "reeducation"

"It is difficult to educate; it is more difficult to re-educate; it is well-nigh impossible to re-educate a foreign nation. To attempt to re-educate Germans by military government action is to attempt the impossible."[62] This 1947 assessment by one of the US State Department's leading experts on Germany summarizes the dilemma faced by those wishing to reconstruct Germany as a sound member of Western civilization. Nonetheless, if lasting peace were to be achieved, the impossible had to be undertaken.

The roots of the concept of reeducation go back to World War I.[63] During that war propaganda was viewed as an effective tool to demoralize the enemy, and "political warfare" divisions were created to manipulate enemy opinion.[64] With the standardization and institutionalization of public education in the early twentieth century, and with the widespread introduction of the new mass media, radio and film, in the 1920s and 1930s, the systematic manipulation of public opinion on a mass scale became a world-historical possibility. The role of nationalist German sentiment in triggering World War II implied that the economic and military constraints placed on Germany after World War I had not ensured lasting peace. It was logical for Allied planners to conclude that after World War II the minds of the German people would have to be changed as well.

In the summer of 1940, shortly after Germany attacked England, the term "reeducation" gained currency in the British discussion of what to do with Germany after its defeat.[65] In Britain, which took the lead in developing plans for the mental reorientation of the German population after the war, the proponents of such an educational approach to ensuring lasting peace tended to be "soft-liners" such as the British diplomat–historian E. H. Carr, who wrote in his 1942 book *Conditions of Peace*:[66]

> It will be necessary to give the German people not only a common interest
> in the building of the new Europe, but also the sense of a common moral
> purpose . . . The problem is sometimes described as that of the "re-
> education" of Germany; and the description is not a bad one if we realize the
> importance of applying the results of modern psychological science, which
> shows that neither penalty nor precept, but example and confidence are the
> most potent instruments of education.

The leading figure in the opposing camp was Robert Vansittart, a viru-
lently anti-German diplomatic adviser in the Foreign Office. Vansittart
adamantly opposed appeasement and advocated unconditional surrender and total occupation as war goals. A doctrine known as "Vansittartism"
attributed Germany's expansionist goals to the essentially immutable
nature of the German people and called for the complete dismemberment
of Germany as a military and industrial power.[67] However, even liberals
such as Carr believed that any conciliatory programs would have to be
preceded by military defeat and an occupation that included some coercive measures.

The various didactic and strategic considerations of policymakers such
as Carr and Vansittart crystallized in July 1944 in the US army's "Draft
Directive on the Re-education of Germany."[68] The directive outlined two
phases: a period of coercive and repressive measures immediately after the
end of hostilities, and a second, longer phase during which "interest in the
ideas of popular democracy, such as freedom of opinion, speech, the press
and religion" would be promoted. Due to the expectation of widespread
resistance to occupation after the defeat of Germany,[69] the first period was
given priority, and the planning of the second left to be pursued after the
war. By that time, however, although some uncoordinated attempts were
made to implement a democratic reeducation of Germany, the efforts were
thwarted first by the outrage over the atrocities and then by considerations
stemming from the Cold War, namely that it was expedient to enlist the aid
of former Nazis in the reconstruction of Germany. Thus in practice "reeducation" was centered around broad-based measures to confront the entire
German people with the atrocities.[70]

The first plans to show pictures of German atrocities to the German
public after the war date back to October 1944, when the German
Committee of the United States Office of War Information (OWI) discussed
using motion pictures of "German cruelties" to "reeducate" the German
people.[71] In February 1945 that committee initiated a film project about
atrocities committed by Germans because showing such films would
"explain why the Allies have to make sure that the Germans do not have

another chance to instigate a war."[72] In March, the Psychological Warfare Division of Eisenhower's headquarters (known as SHAEF: Supreme Headquarters, Allied Expeditionary Forces) began collecting material for a planned film *KZ* to be produced jointly by US and British teams under the supervision of the British Ministry of Information. This hastily realized film was shown at the founding conference of the United Nations in San Francisco at the end of April, and for some time in occupied Germany as well, although many considered it too superficial for showing to a broader and perhaps hostile or defensive German public. As one of the filmmakers put it, footage of atrocities could definitively show only that some members of a collectivity were unbelievably brutal and inhuman, but not that all individuals were partially responsible for the brutality of their collectivity.[73] In spite of this realization, the atrocity program was pursued systematically during the first days, weeks, and months of occupation.

All channels of the mass media were utilized in the campaign (ill. 10). Newspapers printed numerous articles and ran didactic series on the camps;[74] placards showing pictures of heaps of corpses with texts such as "YOU ARE GUILTY OF THIS" were posted in cities, towns, and Military Government offices everywhere;[75] picture exhibitions were displayed in storefronts;[76] pamphlets collecting the most shocking images were printed and distributed free and sold;[77] radio reports about the camps were broadcast at regular intervals;[78] and film footage of the liberated camps was included in the weekly newscasts at German movie theaters – for instance, the newsreel *Welt im Film* devoted its entire issue for the week of 15 June 1945 to "the most horrifying footage from the camps."[79] Camp inmates released prior to liberation, who had remained silent during the Third Reich, and survivors returning home also held public presentations and published articles and brochures about the camps.[80] An Allied intelligence officer who conducted a survey of German reactions to the information about the camps in June found that "Within four weeks after V-E Day, almost every German had had direct and repeated contact with our campaign to present the facts [about the atrocities]."[81]

The doubts of the program's critics were soon confirmed by practical experience. A Psychological Warfare Division (PWD) study investigated the reactions of German audiences to an early feature-length version of the "atrocity film" (as it was called in the PWD) shown to test audiences in Erlangen in July. The report concluded that the film "completely missed the mark of trying to arouse a feeling of individual or collective guilt. Except for a few cases, the members of the audience did not see any connection between themselves and the guilty."[82] Another more general survey of the reactions of the German populace to the entire publicity campaign about the atrocities brought similarly negative results.[83] It confirmed that during Nazi rule the majority of Germans, although cognizant of the existence of the camps, had in fact been unaware of the full extent of the brutality practiced in them. The study found a direct correlation between the (former) strength of Nazi allegiance, and skepticism about the veracity of the atrocities. It also revealed a general dearth of specific knowledge about the camps – even after the informational campaign. On the question of responsibility the survey found that "with automatic regularity . . . all types of personalities and social classes" claimed innocence because they had not known what was going on inside the camps, and even if they had known, ruthless Nazi terror would have prevented them from taking action.[84] Interviewed respondents pointed explicitly to the disjuncture of perception between themselves and their conqueror–liberators: "You Americans can hardly understand the conditions under which we were living. It was as if all of Germany were a concentration camp and we were occupied by a foreign power. We were unable to do anything to oppose them. What could one person do against that powerful organization?"

Even though it was quite clear that the media campaign was not having the desired effect, the program had developed its own momentum and was continued for almost a year. War Department officials worked out guidelines for a more sophisticated film about the atrocities by early May 1945. They detailed two reasons for the production of the film.[85] First, by showing "specific crimes committed by the Nazis in the name of the German people," the film was supposed to "turn the German people against the National Socialist Party," thereby undermining any attempts to organize a guerrilla resistance movement. Second, by "reminding the Germans of their tacit complicity in the crimes and making them aware that they could not evade responsibility," the film was supposed to convince the Germans to "accept Allied occupation measures." There were two major problems with this plan. Most obviously, the two objectives were mutually contradictory. On the one hand the film was to pinpoint the blame of the Nazi Party, on the other it was supposed to arouse a feeling of individual responsibility for the crimes. Additionally, the second goal was predicated on the achievement of the first. "*Reminding* the Germans of their tacit complicity" presumed that most Germans did indeed feel responsible for the atrocities, regardless of whether they had known about them, or whether they could have prevented them had they known. But the very fact that such films were deemed necessary presupposed that the

Germans did not know! Finally, Germans were much more likely to deny all complicity in the crimes when an admission of responsibility brought unpleasant consequences with it.

The flawed reasoning behind these films betrays a fundamental mis-conception of German society under Nazi rule. British and American planners did not realize that Nazi Germany was not a representative democracy similar to their own, where the accountability of elected officials to the electorate places ultimate responsibility on the populace. The predominance of this conception among Allied policymakers at the end of the war is reflected in the text of the film *Your Job in Germany*, which was shown to US soldiers on their way to Germany or already stationed there: "These Germans – the ones who said they didn't know – were responsible, too. They had put themselves – gladly – into the hands of criminals and lunatics."[86] That may have been an accurate assessment. However, in the war-ravished situation of 1945 only a few incorrigibles were willing to admit, to themselves or anyone else, that they had ever "gladly" supported the Nazis. The apparently overwhelming German self-identification with the Nazi state, as manifested in the suicidal resistance during the last months of the war,[87] vanished with astonishing rapidity once the Allies physically occupied the towns and cities of the Reich.[88] *Life* photographer Margaret Bourke-White summed up the Allied perception of this phenomenon concisely in a sentence she attributed to an American major: "The Germans act as though the Nazis were a strange race of Eskimos who came down from the North Pole and somehow invaded Germany."[89]

For their part, most Germans did not understand how the Allies could consider them responsible for the atrocities. Under National Socialism the ruling elite had nurtured authoritarian traditions and done its utmost to keep power concentrated at the top of the pyramid, so that most subjects of the state saw themselves solely as obedient executors of policy without responsibility for their actions. And the moral universe where the magni-tude of the wrongdoing precluded mere ignorance as a defense against responsibility was utterly foreign to most Germans.[90] Without any feelings of personal responsibility, most Germans could not accept that "the atroc-ities" called for any expiation or sacrifices on their part. Instead, they resented and felt humiliated by the penance forced upon them. Additionally, most Germans did not (or preferred not to) share the Allied conception of the camps as long-standing festering mills of death, so they perceived the informational campaign as a crude propaganda attempt that selected exceptional circumstances – the conditions of the concentration camps at liberation – to justify harsh and unjust policies. If most Germans could have been receptive to such ethically sophisticated reasoning after the war, they almost certainly would have behaved very differently during the Nazi period. As one German historian has argued, it was illusory to think that the caesura of defeat could or would completely reorient the mainstays of German self-identification.[91]

In spite of the overwhelming evidence that pictures of the atrocities would not achieve a reorientation of German moral consciousness, a Czech émigré who had become a Hollywood producer before joining the US army took over the film project in July and pursued it to completion with missionary zeal.[92] In response to criticism that his efforts would fall upon deaf German ears, producer Hanus Burger exclaimed, "But how else do you think that the Germans will realize what was happening in their midst and in their name?"[93] A 22-minute final version of the atrocity film entitled *Death Mills* was finally completed by late 1945 and distributed to movie theaters in Bavaria and Berlin in early 1946.[94] The average attendance rate in Bavaria was 12 percent, and especially young people and former POWs rejected the film's message.[95] Distribution of the film was finally officially discontinued in March 1948.[96]

This bungled "reeducation" with its combination of accusation and expectation of repentance thus not only reinforced the (preexisting) inclination to deny all responsibility, it perpetuated the absence of a sense of the absolute immorality of the concentration camps in the transition from historical event to remembered event. It is open to speculation whether Germans of that war generation would have developed a collective sense of the immorality of the concentration camps if they had been left to their own devices. In any case, the Allied policy of forced confrontation stifled that potential development from the outset, while fostering feelings of renewed victimization.

The survivors

The surviving 31,000 inmates of the liberated Dachau concentration camp were an immensely diverse population. They included about a thousand relatively privileged German and Austrian political prisoners who had survived many years in the camp in relatively good condition, several thousand western Europeans subject to somewhat less favorable conditions, well over ten thousand Poles, Russians and other eastern Europeans who had endured much harsher treatment and were considered suspect by their home governments, and several thousand Jews of various nationalities who hovered on the brink of death after suffering unspeakable tortures and deprivation.[97] Those Jews, among them several hundred women, had only arrived at the camp in deadly forced marches during the last weeks.

The needs of each group were correspondingly diverse, so that the Americans found it expedient to enlist the leaders of the national groups that had organized secretly during the final days before liberation in their effort to run the liberated camp.[98] The governing body was known as the International Prisoners' Committee, or IPC. The Jews presented a special problem, since the Americans did not want to break with the principle of national representation and recognize other interest groups. A solution was soon found, however, in that a "Jewish Information Office" with all of the rights of a national committee was created.[99] In an attempt to sort out the various categories, on 1 May a questionnaire was distributed. Some of the questions were designed to aid the IPC in identifying common criminals who had been serving time in the camp, as well as prisoners who had collaborated with the SS. On 2 May the Americans decided that health and safety concerns mandated a quarantine of the camp. They proceeded to create a tight structure of authority modeled after that of the concentration camp: the US commander became "camp commandant," the president of the IPC "camp leader" (corresponding to the SS's *Lagerführer*), and a "camp senior" and "capos" were named as well. Although this structure was efficient, it did not sit well with many of the survivors, who felt that they had not been liberated, but merely exchanged one set of overlords for another. As the newsletters of the national groups show, the IPC spent much time convincing the survivors of the necessity of these measures.

After liberation, alleviating the severe overcrowding was a top priority.[100] The American commandant and the IPC moved some national groups to areas within the SS camp, others to an SS installation in the nearby town of Schleissheim. After the unconditional surrender of the German army on 8 May, various national groups were repatriated, beginning with the Dutch, Belgians, and French. By the end of May many of the ca. forty self-identified national groups had returned home, and by late June all who wanted to go home had done so. That left about 2,000 Poles who did not want to return to a Poland under Communist rule, over a thousand Hungarians and Rumanians, a few hundred Russians who feared Stalin's wrath upon their return, and many Jews who had lost all family members and anticipated antisemitism in their homelands.[101]

To support the survivors of the Dachau concentration camp in particular, and survivors of Nazi persecution traveling through the area as well, an

"International Information Office" (IIO) was set up in early June upon orders of US Military Government by the city of Dachau (ill. 14).[102] It was located near the former branch camp at the Schuster cardboard factory on Schleissheimer Street (the factory is still located there today).[103] Similar to "KZ care centers" set up by cities and towns all across Germany to provide for the needs of local and traveling liberated inmates, the Dachau International Information Office distributed cards enabling survivors to receive double rations for eight weeks, and disbursed sums of money and items of clothing based on individual need.[104] The Dachau office also maintained the records of the camp inmates, and issued identification cards and certificates of proper conduct in the camp.[105] In Dachau, with its large number of liberated Poles, the IIO was first headed by the Pole Walter Cieslik.[106] From the beginning until its final dissolution in 1950, the German section of the IIO was led by Richard Titze, an activist from the German Communist resistance who settled in Dachau after the war and remained active in memorial site politics until his death in 1990.[107] One of the IIO's early "extracurricular" projects was the installation of an exhibition in the crematorium–gas chamber building, which is described in detail in chapter 5, below (ill. 17).[108]

By the end of June, none of the remaining liberated inmates were still living in the former "protective custody compound." It now housed about 1,000 German POWs who were being used "on an extensive program of cleaning up the premises," as an inspector from the Displaced Persons Branch of the US army reported on 2 July.[109] Although at that time camp commandant Colonel Paul Roy planned to burn down the prisoner barracks, within a week the Dachau complex was officially transformed into a "War Crimes Enclosure" with a capacity of 30,000 prisoners.[110] Thus began the second reuse of the concentration camp after liberation: it was converted from a makeshift camp for survivors who could not be repatriated (so-called "displaced persons") into an internment camp for Germans active at higher levels of the SS, Nazi Party, and army.

Many of the men who served on the IPC also played important roles in the creation of a memorial site after 1950. One of them was Albert Guérisse, a Belgian who had worked for the British secret service until his capture by the Germans. He was known in the camp under the pseudonym Pat O'Leary, and was elected president because, as the only "Canadian" (his assumed identity) in the camp, his nomination avoided the rivalries between other countries for the honor of the highest office. From 1962 until his death in 1989 Guérisse served as president of the Comité International de Dachau, or CID, which was founded in 1955 as the successor to the IPC in order to lobby more effectively for the use of the former concentration camp as a memorial site. A second key figure was Arthur Haulot, the head of the Belgian group, who became IPC president after Guérisse left for England on 7 May 1945. Haulot worked tirelessly on the repatriation of the inmates until early June, when he returned home. He was reelected president of the Belgian survivors' association (now called "Amicale de Dachau") and worked behind the scenes for decades to keep the international organization a viable force.

Another leading figure in the IPC was Oskar Müller, a German Communist who retained his position as camp senior. Müller, who became Labor Minister of the German state of Hesse shortly after the war, was also one of the leading members of the largest German organization of camp survivors, the Association of the Persecutees of the Nazi Regime, known by its German abbreviation VVN (for Vereinigung der Verfolgten des Nazi-regimes). Several members of the IPC returned to Dachau in November 1945 at the trial of the former camp personnel. At that time they planned to meet again in 1946 to maintain the international solidarity of the survivors, but pressing political problems in each of their homelands delayed the realization of that plan for almost a decade.[111]

Genocide on trial

According to a statement released by the "big three" Allied heads of state, Churchill, Roosevelt, and Stalin, after their meeting at Yalta in February 1945, the program to remove Nazi influence from German society was to have four foci: the destruction of Nazi institutions, the annulment of Nazi laws, the punishment of war criminals, and the removal of active Nazi supporters from all public and private positions of responsibility.[112] While the institutions and laws could be abolished by decree, the latter two goals concerned complex issues of legal guilt, moral responsibility, and personal involvement. They required cumbersome apparatuses and much more time to achieve. We turn first to the program of punishing war criminals, in which the former Dachau concentration camp played an important role.

As the eventual defeat of Germany became nearly certain in the summer of 1944, plans for the summary execution of German "arch criminals" circulated in Britain, the United States, and the Soviet Union.[113] However, various considerations gradually swayed Roosevelt and Churchill around to Stalin's position that the benefits of conducting brief trials of major perpetrators outweighed the costs (Stalin was no novice at conducting show trials).[114] For one thing, the leaders feared that if German commanders knew that summary execution awaited them, they would fight all the more tenaciously, increasing Allied casualties. Another advantage was suggested by US Secretary of War Stimson, one of the leading advocates of the judicial route. He argued that trials would expose the brutality of Nazism and shed positive light on the Allies as the victors over this scourge.[115] The discovery of the mass murders at Maidanek near Lublin in eastern Poland in July 1944, a mass shooting of unarmed US POWs in Malmédy (Belgium) in December 1944, and then the liberation of the concentration camps in 1945 provided decisive arguments for the proponents of trials over summary execution: here were clear-cut crimes whose prosecution would be short and simple.[116] As originally envisioned, the trials would not have granted the suspects full due process, although they would have given them an opportunity to testify on their own behalf and call in defense witnesses. It was only later, after the Potsdam Conference in August 1945, that legal experts met in London to hammer out in detail the principles according to which the trials would be conducted. Those August 1945 guidelines, developed by legal experts in peacetime, were very different than the vague vision embraced by the leaders during the war. They necessitated a vast bureaucratic apparatus to administer the trials.

First of all, if large numbers of Germans were to be tried in courts of law, large numbers of suspects would have to be detained. Various plans for the automatic arrest and internment of "security suspects," that is, members of incriminated organizations, accompanied the development of the trial program. Based on a directive known as Joint Chiefs of Staff 1067 (JCS 1067), automatic arrest found its first practical formulation in a 7 July 1945 list of 136 mandatory removal categories according to the principle of "guilt by virtue of office."[117] During the initial months of occupation, 400 to 700 persons were arrested each day, resulting in well over 100,000 German detainees in the US zone alone by December 1945.[118] (That figure did not include millions of captured German soldiers.[119]) There were substantial logistical problems associated with interning such large numbers of people, and in war-ravished Germany the reuse of Nazi detainment facilities such as concentration camps was an obvious solution. In addition to practical reasons, the symbolism of the sites was an added bonus, since they embodied the crimes of the internees.[120]

Thus in June and July 1945, after the majority of the liberated prisoners had been repatriated, major former concentration camps in all zones of occupation were reopened as internment camps. The Soviet secret service NKVD ran Buchenwald as "Special Camp No. 2" and Sachsenhausen as

"Special Camp No. 7";[121] the British converted KZ Neuengamme near Hamburg into "No. 6 Civil Internment Camp"[122] and KZ Esterwegen to "No. 9 CIC,"[123] while Dachau became the US Counterintelligence Corps' "War Crimes Enclosure No. 1" in early July.[124] The Nazi Party's national parade grounds in Nuremberg, the *Reichsparteitagsgelände*, became "Internment Camp Nuremberg-Langwasser."[125] Since these camps were run by secret service agencies whose records have not been made accessible to researchers, relatively little is known about actual conditions within them, especially during the early months.[126] However, scattered published reports and archival records of auxiliary authorities enable us to trace general developments in the case of Dachau.

Various parts of the Dachau camp were used for different categories of prisoners (ill. 8). The largest enclosure was the "protective custody" compound in which the KZ inmates had suffered, which became the "SS compound" for former concentration camp guards and members of the *Waffen-SS*. Within that enclosure there were barbed wire subdivisions: the east side (away from the SS complex) was called the "open camp" (*Freilager*), and another area was known as the "special camp" (*Sonderlager*).[127] The latter was a high security area with each barrack separately fenced in, and was reserved for persons suspected of committing particularly heinous crimes.[128] Within the larger SS complex two groups of eighteen barracks each were fenced in as containment centers for functionaries of the Nazi Party and its affiliated organizations falling under various automatic arrest categories, as well as for officers of the German army and so-called unfriendly witnesses at the Dachau trials.[129] Within these latter two enclosures there were also separate "cages" for women and younger men.[130]

Once World War II had finally ended with the surrender of Japan on 15 August 1945, the Allies began to put the perpetrators of atrocities on trial. The trial of the camp personnel of Bergen-Belsen by a British military court was first, followed by that of the euthanasia institution Hadamar, and several trials of residents of towns in which Allied pilots had been lynched after parachuting to safety. The famous "Nuremberg trial" conducted by an *inter*national military court against top-level representatives of the Nazi Party and its organizations, the German government, and the German army began on 14 November 1945; the first major trial at the Dachau tribunal, against forty members of the concentration camp staff who had been captured, began one day later.[131]

Just as the symbolic value of the former concentration camps had made them preferred sites for the internment of suspected Nazi criminals, so too did it make the Dachau camp a choice site for their trials (ill. 11). At least the first trial was conducted in the former prisoners' compound itself, in the large service building that now houses the library and museum. (Except for the trial transcripts, very little is known about these trials. Photographs of some buildings on the north side of the SS camp show that they also served as courthouses, possibly for denazification hearings as well. It is unclear whether the trials of other concentration camp personnel were conducted in the prisoner service building.)

To underscore the symbolism of the site of the Dachau trials, the crematorium was preserved as evidence of the atrocities. Before the first major Dachau trial began, a sign was mounted on a tree in front of the building, proclaiming: "This area is being retained as a shrine to the 238,000 individuals who were cremated here. Please do not destroy" (ill. 6).[132] The number 238,000 *cremated* was a gross error. It approximates the number of inmates who were "*processed* through Dachau," as the first official report about the camp, published in May 1945, phrased it.[133] One official estimate available in November 1945 was that 228,930 total prisoners had passed through the concentration camp, of whom 31,417 were known to have died.[134] Today the most reliable figures set the numbers at 206,206 total inmates, of whom at least 31,591 are documented to have died or been killed prior to liberation.[135] (The remaining ca. 175,000 inmates were released or transferred to other camps.)

The erroneous number of deaths on the sign gained a certain notoriety, because several prominent visitors to the site publicized it quite widely, long after the official death toll of ca. 32,000 had been established.[136] (See the story of Martin Niemöller's November 1945 visit in chapter 11, below.) As we will see, in the 1960s Holocaust deniers seized upon the figure as evidence for the inauthenticity of the crematorium itself.[137] In any case, the erroneous figure reflects the image of Dachau held by the Allies: it was a site of genocide, and no number could adequately reflect its horror. Germans, on the other hand, were apt to misquote the death tolls of the camps in the other direction: in 1965 German stonemasons inadvertently dropped a "0" from the number of dead in the Neuengamme concentration camp, making it 5,500 instead of 55,000.[138] Survivors coincidentally discovered the mistake on the day before the dedication; it was hastily repaired.

In contrast to the first Nuremberg trial, which lasted almost a year, the first Dachau trial was over in less than a month. On the morning of 13 December 1945 the Dachau sentences were announced: thirty-six men were to be executed by hanging, one was sentenced to life imprisonment, the remaining three to ten years in prison.[139] In three reviews in early 1946 a total of eight death sentences were commuted to life imprisonment. The twenty-eight remaining executions took place on 28 and 29 May at Landsberg prison, within sight of the cell where Hitler had been imprisoned in 1925. The hangman had two busy days: seven men were hanged each morning, and seven each afternoon.[140] To preclude the use of the graves in the prison cemetery for pilgrimages by old and new Nazis, they were only numbered. The severity of the sentences was typical of the trials held shortly after the end of the war, as was the relative swiftness with which the executions were carried out. In the years that followed, however, the Western Allies became markedly more lenient because they wanted to win the West Germans as allies in the emerging Cold War. And most Germans proved resistant to learning the "lesson" these trials were supposed to impart.

In January 1946 Eugen Kogon, a survivor of Buchenwald and the author of one of the first and in many respects still unsurpassed books about the concentration camp system, explained why:[141]

> A people that had seen the charred remains of its women and children in every last corner of its bomb-ravished cities could not be shaken by the amassed piles of naked corpses that were shown to it from the final phase of the concentration camps . . .
>
> The policy of "shock" awakened not the powers of the German conscience, but the powers of resistance against the accusation of complete co-responsibility for the shameful misdeeds of the National Socialists. The result is a fiasco.

Kogon points to two salient features of postwar public sentiment: a feeling of great victimization by the Allies on the one hand, and a strong will to resist perceived injustice. The role of the Cold War in transforming denazification into a "fiasco" of rehabilitation is intertwined with these feelings, which helped West German society come to terms with the Nazi past. In the following section I describe what I call the "three founding myths of West Germany," whose legacies still affect the political culture of the Federal Republic of Germany today.

PART TWO

Dachau 1945–1955: three myths and three inversions

Ladies and Gentlemen!

How peaceful life once was here! Dachau, once the epitome of rural stolidity and earthiness, closely bound to its artists and their noble cultural efforts for more than a century! To mention only a few of the names that carried Dachau's reputation into the world: Christian Morgenstern . . . Karl Spitzweg, Wilhelm Leibl, Lovis Corinth, [Max] Slevogt . . .

That was once our Dachau!

But then nonlocal sadists came and settled on the outskirts of our city, and with horror and fear we had to watch as they defiled the name Dachau in the eyes of the entire civilized world.

For twelve long years the concentration camp weighed like a nightmare upon us.

At the beginning sparse reports about the inmates of the camp leaked out to us. But after construction was complete the hermetic isolation left us with only dark premonitions about the fates and human suffering behind the concrete walls topped with barbed wire.

Dante's saying should have been written over the gate: "Lasciate ogni speranza, voi, ch'entrate!"

We know that since 1940 alone at least 28,000 people died a miserable death. The lists show that 220,000 passed through the camp. And the name of our beloved Dachau is associated with all of these cruelties!

But *the real Dachau was different!*

Today, with pure hearts and clean hands this "other Dachau" commemorates all of the victims whose blood has soaked our native soil and whose ash covers the paths within the camp.

You dead, however, who have been taken up by our native soil, rest there in peace! Your memory shall not only be honored by a monument of stone, but we will carry it in our hearts as long as the heavens allow us to breathe the air of freedom, and allow the sun of peace to shine.

And in the future Dachau shall once again become a center of true culture and respect for human rights, for the good of our city and all of humanity.

Josef Schwalber, 9 November 1945[1]

Josef Schwalber, a member of the Bavarian Catholic Party (BVP) who had been appointed mayor of Dachau because of his opposition to Nazi rule, spoke these words at a commemorative ceremony in Dachau castle on

9 November 1945, the anniversary of the 1938 *Kristallnacht* pogroms against Jewish Germans (Schwalber is depicted in ill. 13).[2] This first major public speech in commemoration of the victims of the Dachau concentration camp was attended by senior officers from Allied military detachments all over southern Germany, and prominent survivors of the camp were on hand as well. They had come to testify at the trial of Dachau's SS that began in the camp a few days later (ill. 11). The mayor's address was broadcast in all of Germany by Radios Munich, Hamburg, and Stuttgart, and throughout Europe by the BBC and Radio Luxembourg. It was recorded and flown to Washington for broadcast the next day.[3]

Let us examine this key document more closely. After effusively evoking a positive image of Dachau to which he can return at the end, Mayor Schwalber describes how the citizenry "had to watch," transfixed by "horror and fear," while outsiders created the camp that was to defile their reputation. Then began the town's twelve-year "nightmare." The phrases "sparse reports," "hermetic isolation," and "dark premonitions" conjure up a veil of ignorance about what was actually taking place in the camp. Finally, Schwalber returns to the image of a pure "other Dachau," the "real Dachau," as he puts it, which embodies the higher values of "rural stolidity" and "noble cultural efforts." He implies that only extraordinary circumstances, such as dictatorship (lack of the "air of freedom") or war (darkening of the "sun of peace"), will prevent the citizens of Dachau from fulfilling their moral obligations in the future.

Schwalber's schematic depiction of the relationship between the town and the concentration camp expresses three longings that, like a constellation of lodestars, guided the restoration of national politics in West Germany during the next decade, and that have remained influential in West German politics to the present day. They are: the desire to have collectively fallen victim to developments beyond "Germany's" control; the wish to have been ignorant of what was happening in the concentration camps and extermination centers; and the sanguine vision of an unsullied "other Germany" that had done its best to resist rioting and intruding barbarians, or at least rein in their excesses.

These three longings can be reformulated as what I will call the three founding myths of the Federal Republic.[4] These myths were suitable tools for effacing the memory of genocide and replacing it with a much more palatable history. They are, to use a convenient mnemonic, the myths of VIR: Victimization, Ignorance, and Resistance. *Vir* is the Latin word for "man," and these three myths form the plot of a stereotypically masculine drama.

To recapitulate Schwalber's scenario in a slightly more abstract form: Dachau, and by extension Germany, was the victim of "nonlocal sadists" (perhaps a "strange race of Eskimos from the North Pole," as the American major in the last chapter put it) who committed the atrocities, whatever they were. After this tacit admission of at least limited knowledge of what had transpired, ignorance of the true enormity of the crimes prevented the citizens from taking action. Once the barrier preventing contacts between the populace and the crimes began to crumble, however, long-standing higher values prevailed and the citizens did what they could to mitigate the brunt of the outside sadists' misdeeds.

Admittedly, the aspect of resistance does not appear very strongly in this first speech. In another of Schwalber's early speeches, at the dedication of a collective gravestone on the first anniversary of the 28 April 1945 uprising of escaped concentration camp inmates and townspeople, however, it was the primary motif. I quote this remarkable oration in full:[5]

> With the comrades of the fallen prisoners the city of Dachau stands in sadness and gratitude at this simple burial mound. Dachau has many prisoners' graves in its fields, but none that are so closely and immediately connected to the city as this one.
>
> The prisoners Dürr, Hackel, Hubmann not only died fighting for a free Germany, they also fell for the sake of our closest community, together with four additional victims from the civilian population.
>
> They fought for freedom out of idealism. They did have their lives to lose, but they did not need to fear for property and try to rescue it at the last moment, as did so many who are now trying to boast of having been antifascists of the final hour. Our fallen men [the escaped prisoners] had already regained their own personal freedom. They escaped from the camp henchmen and knew they were safe with trustworthy residents for the few hours that separated them from complete freedom. Only the burning impatience not to have to bear for another hour the yoke of bondage erected by the overpowerful tyrants led them to grasp the long-missed weapons.
>
> Together with the freedom fighters from Dachau itself they faced their tormentors with bared weapons and sealed this bond between the prisoners and the antifascist residents with their blood.
>
> A hard fate deprived them of that which they had dreamed in the long years of bondage. They sank down in the red dawn of the first day of coming freedom.
>
> In the chaos of the first days of occupation we could not give them the honorable burial they deserved. They had to be buried unceremoniously.
>
> Today, however, on the anniversary of their sacrificial death, the city of Dachau thanks them from the depths of its heart for the selfless use of their lives. Although the uprising was ultimately crushed by the advancing SS, the hopelessness of a defense had become an immutable fact and "Dachau" was

surrendered to the Americans on the next day without any noteworthy resistance.

Of course we ceremoniously erect a monument of stone for our fallen prisoners at the end of their efforts and at the end of their torment. But much more important is that which they have won in our hearts: a memorial for all future generations. Their names have entered the history of Dachau. The city will keep and care for their graves.

In this truly unique situation where concentration camp inmates and townsfolk had joined to resist the Nazi overlords, and on an occasion when many camp survivors had gathered to pay their respects to their comrades, Schwalber chided his fellow citizens for claiming to have resisted in the final hour. In 1946 it was already a boast that "so many" of his townsfolk were making. Remarkably, Schwalber revealed his ignorance of the real reason for the escaped prisoners' "burning impatience": they were desperately trying to prevent additional thousands of prisoners from being sent out on death marches. Not only did Schwalber not know specifics about what transpired in the camp before liberation, he had still not bothered to find them out. Schwalber's speech also reveals the preconceived notion that the "prisoners" were situated so low in society that they had nothing left to lose after regaining their freedom. Actually, most Dachau inmates had had steady jobs, families, and property, for which they had been fearing for years, not just "at the last moment."

The relationship between these fanciful images of the past and their realization in the present are often such perverse parodies of reality that the connection between them is not immediately apparent. I will describe this transmogrification for each of the founding myths in turn (see also table 2 on p. 328). The myth that "the Germans" had been victims of "the Nazis" mutated into the perception that they were victimized by, first, their Allied conquerors, who wrongfully held them accountable for crimes and atrocities they had not committed, expelled them from territories where they had lived for generations, and deprived them of the national unity for which the German lands had strived since the Napoleonic invasions. Many Germans also felt victimized by the survivors of the camps, who demanded compensation for sufferings for which those Germans felt no responsibility. Finally, many Germans – with some notable exceptions, especially since the 1980s – felt and feel victimized by anyone who reminds them of the crimes in their national history, especially other Germans interested in the crimes of the Nazi period, but also including visitors to concentration camp memorial sites, who they presume show no appreciation of the finer sides of German culture, but only harp on this distasteful past.[6]

Ignorance of what actually transpired in the concentration camps allows its professors to pretend that what presumptively happened, namely the propaganda lie of the "clean camps," was true. Thus the myth of ignorance resulted in the postwar perpetuation and realization of a Nazi propaganda lie. It manifested itself in the retroactive creation of "clean" camps for the rehabilitation of "dirty" elements in society. Concomitantly the survivors – in Germany they have been known as "former inmates" for decades (only in the 1980s did younger generations introduce the term *Zeitzeugen,* "historical witnesses") – came to be seen as common criminals, while the vast majority of SS henchmen and Nazi bureaucrats were reconceived as honorable men who had faithfully served the fatherland by containing such criminal elements. In consequence, the survivors were excluded from the guarantees and protections of civil society, while active Nazis were rewarded for their past service and allowed to participate in public life.

The consequences of the myth of resistance are more straightforward; they correspond to the causes of the perceived revictimization, against which resistance was mustered. To demonstrate the veracity of this myth, Germans doggedly battled to remove the evidence of the atrocities, took to the streets to demonstrate for the return of their kidnapped sons and husbands (POWs in Soviet labor camps) and stolen ancestral lands (Poland west of the Oder and Neisse rivers), and conspired to prevent the survivors from receiving compensation or even recognition for their suffering. Later, and still today, many Germans resist just as doggedly the creation, recognition, and maintenance of concentration camp memorial sites as educational institutions.

The three chapters of this section retrace the reenactment of the "VIR" story during the first postwar decade, during which West Germany regained its manhood. The founding myths were not realized in neat, chronological order, but in overlapping, parallel processes. Nonetheless, by 1955 present correlates of all three myths had been realized. And those correlates persevered well into the 1980s, some of them until today, albeit in modified forms. These chapters focus on three areas in which the realization of these myths is especially evident: the Germans' perceptions of themselves, the Germans' perceptions of the survivors, and the treatment of the physical remains of the camps.

3

"Good" Nazis

The paradox that Nazi collaborators and even perpetrators emerged in the 1950s as some of West Germany's leading citizens has political and psychological explanations. Before we turn to the international political situation in which this inversion was possible, an examination of two biographies illustrates how this process looked at an individual level.

Hans Zauner, mayor of Dachau 1933–1945, 1952–1960

Hans Zauner (1885–1973) was a member of one of the leading families in Dachau.[1] He was a printer and a bookbinder in a town dominated by paper mills, and he was elected to the town council in 1929 at age 42. In order to keep that seat, he joined the Nazi Party on 1 April 1933, only a week after the Nazis took control of the council. He was immediately named second vice mayor (the third-highest rank in the town administration), a position he held until the Allies conquered the town in 1945. In 1938 his Party superiors wrote in an evaluation that Zauner had "financially supported the Party even before it took over power. He has been head of the local Party Chamber of Commerce and Trades since [1 March] 1933 . . . He is industrious, level-headed, helpful, and self-sacrificing. Politically reliable in every respect."[2] During the Nazi years Zauner voiced no reservations when prisoners from the concentration camp were used in public works projects in the town.

Immediately after Dachau's occupation Zauner was appointed temporary mayor of Dachau by the town's US commandant, and was forced to oversee difficult tasks for the occupation forces. For instance, he was responsible for collecting foodstuffs to feed the ca. 30,000 freed inmates, and threatened with dire consequences if he did not fulfill the quotas.[3] In his memoirs Zauner described how on 1 May two soldiers, without a word of warning or explanation, pulled him out of his office, pushed him down the stairs and set him on the hood of their jeep, whereupon they took the

59-year-old for a "joy ride" around the hilly town. Eventually the GIs brought Zauner back to city hall and let him dismount. In 1960 he recalled:[4]

> Today I think that if that was supposed to have been a joke, it was a coarse, boorish wild-west joke, an insult to human dignity committed on a man who had nothing to do with the misdeeds and cruelties of the Nazis [sic!]. That afternoon I went back to work and registered a complaint with the [US] city commander. He reprimanded the two rowdies. From then on I was treated decently, and when I was discharged from office [on 12 May 1945] the commander thanked me for my manly behavior. After fulfilling my civic duties I returned to my workshop.

Retrospectively Zauner's outrage about his mistreatment has mutated into fondness for the new rulers. He proudly recounts how he, as an upright, law-abiding citizen, used proper channels to obtain satisfaction, and how successful he was, earning commendation and perhaps even respect from the (former) enemy for the obedient performance of his duties. It is also noteworthy that Zauner does not count himself among the "Nazis" responsible for the "cruelties" in the concentration camp. The memory of the concentration camp and the populace's tolerance of it is neatly superseded by a countermemory of personal victimization and successful resistance against that. In his memoir Zauner did not mention that he was among a group of the Dachau Nazi elite forced to tour the Dachau crematorium on 8 May 1945 (ill. 9). That event did not lend itself to recasting as a case of unjust victimization, and the horrific scenes Zauner witnessed there were something he preferred not to immortalize in print.

In 1952, when many former Nazi officials were being reinstated nationally, Zauner was elected head mayor, an office he held until 1960. He never relinquished his view that the camp had been a legitimate institution for keeping society "clean." On 10 November 1959, coincidentally the anniversary of the *Kristallnacht* pogroms against the Jews when nearly 11,000 Jews were brought to the Dachau camp, Zauner proposed to the city council that indigent apartment-seekers be housed in empty refugee apartments in the former concentration camp. And it was Zauner's opinions about the camp that finally forced him to end his term of public service. Shortly after Christmas 1959 the 74-year-old mayor told a British reporter interested in a wave of antisemitic incidents sweeping across West Germany that he should not "make the mistake of thinking that only heroes died in Dachau. Many inmates were . . . there because they illegally opposed the regime of the day . . . You must remember there were many criminals and homosexuals in Dachau."[5] When the regional news reported that these remarks had been published in London and Washington, the aging Zauner was induced to retract his candidacy for another term as mayor. Until his death in 1973 he remained a popular and highly respected figure in the town. Similarly, many highly compromised former Nazis rose to high positions in the local, state, and national governments. By means of various manipulations these former Nazis were able to reinterpret compromising behavior in their pasts and become good citizens of the new state.

German army general Gert Naumann

The image of the "good Nazi" was not restricted to civilian members of the Party. Even highly complicit members of the inner circle of leadership in the Nazi state came to see themselves as heroically resisting victims. The story of Colonel-General Gert Naumann, a member of Hitler's general staff, is based on the published version of the diary Naumann kept during his internment in Dachau in 1945–6.[6]

Although he had sworn loyalty to his supreme commander Adolf Hitler, Naumann claimed to have always felt that he had been fighting for his fatherland, Germany. As an honest man, he neither tried to conceal himself from the Americans after the war, nor did he attempt to escape once arrested, even though he had several opportunities. He arrived in Dachau with a transport of other arrestees on 8 October 1945 (see 190). They saw a tall crucifix on the roll-call square, and a sign "to the crematory" on the gatehouse (ills. 7, 15). The men were taken in groups of ten into a small wooden barrack, and returned reeling, some with bloody noses (139). When it was Naumann's turn he saw on one wall "huge pictures from the KZ, horrible pictures of starving KZ inmates, mountains of corpses, tortured creatures." The German internees had to stand right in front of the pictures, and an American soldier came by from behind and punched their heads so that their faces smashed against the pictures. After that initiation, however, the American soldiers outside behaved "correctly and almost politely" while searching the Germans' bags. Naumann's diary was taken away from him, but he managed to convince the searcher to let him keep a picture of his mother, and he smuggled some cigarettes and chocolate through the frisking as well.

Naumann and his compatriots were then led down the central camp street with its tall poplar trees to the "special camp" at the back (140). While separating out the SS men, a short, dark-haired American officer cursed them in perfect German. Naumann wondered whether the little man was "an Italian type, a Jew??" Later it turned out that this "Mr. Patterson" was actually Max Strauss, a famous German waltz dancer, and that he was very fair to the internees (185). The newly arriving internees asked the "old hands" if they knew what it had been like in the Dachau concentration camp (142). Those men claimed not to know, either, "because they were from the fighting SS," and not the death's head division of the SS that had guarded the camps. But they had already been taken to see the crematorium, where everything had been left "just as the Americans found it when they entered the camp, except that the corpses lying around had been replaced by wax figures" (ill. 17). In the fall of 1945 the legend that the Americans had forced German POWs to build the crematorium after the war was not yet in circulation.

Soon a daily routine set in. Naumann found the German-built Dachau "downright comfortable" in comparison to the camp built by the Americans at Aibling, from which he had come (141, 144, 162, 194). Dachau's barracks were, he wrote on a scrap of paper later entered into his diary, "well built and clean, its paths dry and covered with gravel, and then the sanitary facilities: washroom with large sinks! Flush toilets with seats!!" The barracks were crowded but tolerable. Annoying were the constant searches, during which contraband from chocolate to letters, from string to pocket knives was confiscated. One colonel broke down in tears when the chocolate he was saving for his children was confiscated. Soon these German army officers were so practiced that they were able to hide their contraband safely before the soldiers entered the barracks. As upstanding Germans they had set up a toilet-cleaning crew even before the Americans told them to. A whole cultural program was in operation, including a lecture series from a professor who was a Dante expert. Every two weeks the army men were led to the showers: 200 nozzles spraying "glorious hot water" (implying that gas did not emanate from them). In fact, for a time Naumann had to work heating the water in a barrack in a separate part of the "special camp" fenced off for the death's head SS concentration camp guards. Naumann noted that they looked like "real criminal types, who back then had been able to advance from concentration camp inmates to guards and capos" (145). He thus implied that the concentration camps had been "clean" until sullied by the inmates themselves.

The worst aspects of life were the steadily decreasing food rations as winter approached, and the lack of news from their families. Some inmates did receive packages, but the letters were removed beforehand, a victimization Naumann noted again and again (173, 190, 193, 194). Once, after the internees cut down some fenceposts to burn in their barracks stove, a whole jeepload of letters was dumped and burned before their very eyes. They were outraged at this unfathomable meanness – "Are we not in the KZ??" Naumann wrote, as if that location was likely to predispose the Americans to behave more sympathetically (174, 176). Another source of outrage among the internees were articles in German daily newspapers (167). One described the "unbelievably filthy" acts committed on thousands of "innocent victims" in the concentration camps. But, Naumann noted, he "had imagined all that as little as the people living outside today know how we are doing," thereby equating his position with that of the KZ inmates. As evidence he quoted from a second article about present internment camps such as Dachau, which described comfortable conditions. The camps were supposedly furnished with "lamps, flowers and curtains . . . fresh vegetables . . . a camp library and cabaret," as well as rich rations. "Why the fat lies?" he wondered, and suggested that the Americans did not honor the freedom of the press. Once, while waiting for the "SS dentist," he asked the dental receptionist, a survivor of Buchenwald concentration camp employed by the Americans, whether the stories about the Nazi camps were true (170). This insider told him that the newspapers could not possibly know so much about the concentration camps, when even he, as a former prisoner administrator, had not known about them. Here Naumann is constructing what I call the myth of ignorance, with its corollary implication that the atrocities were American fabrications.

In interviews and published testimonies I found this story repeated numerous times with slight variations.[7] For example, in a statement typical of former SS men, Ludwig H. told me how, in the spring of 1946, he and his fellow internees were shown documentary films of the conditions in the liberated concentration camps.[8] In the darkened auditorium tension mounted until finally someone shouted: "That's all despicable lies!" The lights went on, the heckler was identified and questioned. He claimed that there had never been "so many incineration ovens" in Dachau. The Americans agreed to check the story, and broke off the film showing. Ludwig H. never heard it mentioned again, so he concluded that the heckler must have been right. He also asked a fellow German internee, who had been briefly imprisoned in the Dachau concentration camp under Hitler, what had really happened there. The man had told him that a train full of corpses had indeed been discovered by the Americans – it had come from Buchenwald but had been delayed so many times due to the destruction of the rail lines by Allied bombers that its passengers had died before it arrived. There had also been a large number of deaths in the camp, but they were primarily caused by epidemics aggravated by the catastrophic supply situation brought about by the Allied advance at the end of the war.

To return to Naumann's story, the imprisoned members of the general staff celebrated Christmas, New Year and each other's birthdays to break the monotony of camp life, for they were not allowed to work. The Americans gave each of them four packets of tobacco and seven ounces of coffee for Christmas, which raised their spirits. But not for long. In a copy of the *New Zurich News* they read an article "The Land of Death" about the areas of German settlement now reoccupied by Poland (184). Plunder, rape, typhus, syphilis, and hunger were described by the respected Swiss newspaper. The German inmates were stunned at such "revenge" and "base sadism." They discussed the topic again and again, and when a new arrival who had trekked through those areas before his arrest confirmed the report, they could not understand why "world opinion" remained silent. In contrast to the rest of the world, the internees thought, as Naumann put it, inserting the stereotypical reproach in quotation marks, that "the comparison to the 'horrible deeds of the SS-bandits in the KZs' is quite apt" (186). A short time later Naumann wrote with satisfaction that a high official of the Protestant Church in Bavaria told them during his visit that "things have not really gotten better in comparison to the conditions in the Dachau concentration camp" (187). Apparently that official felt well informed about camp conditions during the Nazi era, belying the myth of ignorance.

Naumann was overjoyed when the American commandant returned his diary on 24 January 1946, and he immediately set to work recording the notes he had made on loose scraps of paper (190). Things were looking up, again, and he went to an impressive lecture on "Which Church is the Right One?" by the Jesuit [sic] Father Leonhard Roth, a survivor of the Dachau concentration camp now ministering to the spiritual needs of his former jailers (191). (Roth's story is told on pp. 246f, below.) When the camp was turned over to German hands, Naumann noted that the anti-Nazi Germans running it were so harsh that the Americans reversed their decisions (191, see also Naumann's references to the "little Pole," 192, and the "Communist denazification minister," 163). When he was released from Dachau in early February 1946, Naumann reflected on what he had learned in the internment camp (197):

> I learned a lot in this camp Dachau: practical things of daily life, but also
> deeper insights, which make one more mature. I think of the many hours of

close community with my fellow prisoners . . . It's not my fault that I'm here.
My conscience is clean . . . Of course I suffer from the illogic and hatefulness
of those spirits who need to take their overbearance out on us. And who gag
my hands [sic].

Naumann remained emotionally untouched by evidence of Nazi
Germany's inhuman practices, and did not consider that the postwar
plunder and rapes of Germans in Poland were a response to the Nazi
plunder and rape committed and made possible by his own German army.
He remained antisemitic, too. When he learned that German girls would
again have to serve a "household year," as they did under the Nazis, but
that former Nazis would not be eligible for such help, he noted wryly that
German girls will "once again be in the households of Jewish families"
(195). His racism survived intact as well. When he read that "in Bavaria a
servant girl has given birth to the first Negro baby," he was agitated about
that event's bleak implications for Germany's future (198).

I did not attempt to find Naumann, who would have been in his eight-
ies, and interview him today about how he now feels about his sojourn in
Dachau, although, since he published his diary in 1984, we can assume his
opinion has not changed much. But I did interview several other internees. In the Dachau memorial site archive I found a copy of the diary of
General Karl Schnell, who had donated the seven volumes of his privately
published *magnum opus* in 1993.[9] I called him at his home in Karlsruhe in
July 1993, and he was quite willing to talk. When I asked him whether he
had been taken to see the crematorium, he answered: "I couldn't have
done that. The crematorium wasn't built yet. The Americans had German
POWs build it after I left the camp [in 1946]." Even when I told him what
Naumann, a good friend of his, had written, he refused to concede the
point. Not wishing to listen to more, I ended the conversation.

The Cold War provided a backdrop against which this private inversion
could become a public phenomenon. The "sun of peace" that shone so
brightly in the first months after the war, as Mayor Schwalber lyrically
intoned at the end of his first speech, darkened behind the clouds of the
East–West conflict. As it did so, the memory of the victims slipped out of
the "hearts" of many West Germans.

The Cold War backdrop

From the start, the World War II alliance between the Western powers and
the Soviet Union had been a marriage of convenience. It was based on the

common need for defense against the onslaught of Hitler's armies. The uneasy relationship dated back to 1919, when Britain and the United States had supported the Czarist armies against the communist revolutionaries in the Russian Civil War. In the 1920s the young Soviet Union, an outcast from the League of Nations, had found an international ally in the similarly ostracized German Reich. The friendly relationship was formalized in the Rapallo Treaty of 1922. By the end of the decade the Soviet Union helped Germany to circumvent the Versailles Treaty by allowing German soldiers to train on its soil. In 1939 Stalin agreed to a pact with Hitler that allowed the two leaders to divide League of Nations member Poland up between themselves. That agreement immediately set the stage for World War II.

In June of 1941, however, Hitler turned the tables on Stalin and launched a surprise attack against the Soviet Union, drawing it into the war already raging in Western Europe. Even if Britain and France (the United States did not enter the war until December) at first mistrusted Hitler's newest victim, they were heavily dependent on its participation. Soon 200 German divisions were fighting on the eastern front, compared to only forty in all other theaters combined. Without Soviet involvement, the prospects for the Western powers would have looked much bleaker. Old suspicions were laid aside, and the Grand Alliance of Britain, the Soviet Union, and the United States was formed. Once Hitler's Germany was defeated in 1945, however, the old differences began to resurface.

At the first meeting of the "big three" after Germany's defeat, the conference at Potsdam near Berlin, a common proclamation could only be reached through vaguely formulated goals behind which each side envisaged something very different. The dual goals of eliminating Nazism and establishing democracy are a good example of this. The policymakers of the West conceived of Nazism as a political phenomenon that could be eradicated by removing Nazis from positions of power. The ideologues of the Soviet Union, in contrast, viewed Nazism as the political manifestation of an economic and social system based on monopoly capitalism. The eradication of fascism would require the destruction of that whole socioeconomic system. Similarly, the Soviets defined democracy in theory not merely as a method of ascertaining the popular will, but as a society free from exploitation, where the equality of citizens is not only legal and political, but economic as well. In practice that meant the expropriation of large landholdings and a state takeover of industry. It is easy to see why such tenets were anathema to the advocates of capitalism in the West. Coupled with Stalin's obvious willingness to disregard legal and political

rights in his ostensible quest to establish that economic equality, the ideological differences between the Western and Eastern Allies soon widened
into an unbridgeable chasm.

Only a year after that last common declaration at Potsdam, the Western
Allies began to seek the favor of the German populace. In the summer of
1946 there was unrest in Germany. Large numbers of people demonstrated for increased food rations, and for the collectivization of industry
in the Ruhr industrial region. There was also evidence that communism
was becoming more popular among the German people. These developments alarmed politicians in the West. In March 1946 Winston Churchill
spoke of an "Iron Curtain" descending between East and West, thus giving
an evocative name to the hardening front between the superpowers.
Western policymakers decided to support anticommunist forces in their
zones of occupation, which meant both constraining many left-wing anti-
Nazis, and supporting conservatives who may have been Nazi sympathiz-
ers, but were clearly anticommunist. The Western occupiers decided to try
to improve economic conditions, since material dissatisfaction led many
Germans to look to the Communists for solutions. The change in Western
Allied policy was announced in September 1946 by US Secretary of State
Byrnes in a famous speech in Stuttgart. He proclaimed: "The American
people will help the German people find their way back to an honorable
position among the free and peace-loving nations of the world."[10]

Concrete policy changes followed in 1947. The first measure was taken
in January, when the "bizone," a common economic region uniting the US
and British zones, was created. In March 1947 the Cold War became
official with US President Truman's congressional speech enunciating the
"Truman Doctrine": the containment of Communist expansion, wherever
it might occur. In early April 1947 the foreign ministers of the four occupying powers left a meeting in Moscow admitting that they had insurmountable differences. In June US Secretary of State George C. Marshall
announced that the United States would introduce a program of economic aid to put Europe back on its feet after the devastation of war. The
Soviet Union and its satellite socialist countries in Eastern Europe refused
the offer of American aid, since it was predicated on the existence of a
market economy.

Gradually the Western powers began to return control of domestic politics to German economic and political elites,[11] and in April 1948 the US
Congress approved George Marshall's European Recovery Program, so
that millions of dollars could begin to flow into the devastated economies
of (Western) Europe, including Germany.[12] Two prerequisites for this

massive influx of capital were hastily realized in the following months: the integration of France's zone into the British-American bizone, and the introduction of a new currency. The currency reform, which took place on 20 June in the new trizone, prompted the Soviet blockade of Berlin from 24 June 1948 to 12 May 1949. This was the first open battle of the Cold War, and the Germans were simply its victims. However, they did not see themselves as victims only of aggression from the East; the Western Allies had been conducting a threatening program as well.

Denazification and "brown-collar" criminals

"Denazification is like delousing: you get rid of the Nazis" was an early metaphor for the hard-line stance on how to deal with Germans in occupied Germany.[13] This complete exclusion of former members of the Nazi Party and its many affiliated organizations from social, political, and economic life contrasted sharply with the reeducators' view, according to which Nazism could simply be removed from the Nazis, leaving good, democratic German citizens.

Within a few years, Western Allied policy moved from a hard- to a soft-line stance. Denazification began, as did the war crimes trials, with a crackdown. As described above, on 7 July 1945 the "automatic arrest" of 136 categories of officeholders was decreed. In "Operation Tally-ho," a two-day raid beginning in the night of 21–22 July, 80,000 Nazis in the American zone were rounded up and put into internment camps.[14] Not a few Germans may have been reminded of Gestapo methods and the November 1938 mass arrests on *Kristallnacht*. On 26 September automatic arrest was extended to German elites from the economic and cultural realms as well, prohibiting continued employment and blocking the property of people who had held important positions in those areas under the Nazi regime.

By the end of 1945 there were full internment camps and a serious lack of trained German personnel to perform crucial functions. Approximately 13 million questionnaires about individual activities during the Nazi era had been turned in. (The number of questions in the first printing, 131, coincidentally became the number of the provision in the 1949 West German constitution that enabled the rehabilitation of Nazi officials.) It was clear that this mountain of paperwork could only be processed with the help of German personnel. To fulfill the Allied denazification goals German experts drafted a compromise law, which was promulgated on

5 March 1946. This "Law for the Liberation from National Socialism and Militarism" applied only to the German states in the American zone, but set the standard for the British and French zones as well.

Under this law special denazification and appeals chambers (*Spruch-kammern* and *Berufungskammern*) were created, where at the local level German anti-Nazis, not Allied personnel, conducted the hearings. All adults were to be classified into five categories based on the 1945 ques-tionnaire: "major offender" (what I call "brown-collar" criminals, see below), "offender" (active supporters of the Nazi Party), "lesser offender" (people who had collaborated, but in less serious ways), "followers" (opportunists who had joined Nazi organizations but not participated in their activities), and "exonerated." The "Liberation Law," as it was known in Germany, automatically imposed harsh restrictions on anyone whose Nazi organizational affiliation or rank placed them under suspicion of being in categories I or II, until and unless they were individually cleared in a denazification chamber. For example, a business manager or former mayor might only be allowed to work at menial labor until cleared at a denazification hearing. The number of cases ultimately registered by the hearing boards indicates the magnitude of the undertaking: in the US zone alone, 12,753,000 cases were processed.[15]

At this point it is necessary to define and explain my use of the term "brown-collar criminal" for the so-called major offenders. The crimes committed under Hitler, Himmler, Heydrich, and the coterie of top-echelon Nazis ranged from the white-collar organizing by men like prop-aganda chief Joseph Goebbels and bureaucratic mastermind Adolf Eichmann, to the grisly nine-to-five (this was quite literally the way the men worked) bloodletting by the policemen mobilized in the task forces. The crimes included the militarily disciplined stoicism of zealous National Socialists such as Auschwitz commandant Rudolf Höss, the cold rational-ity of the doctors who selected out the able-bodied on the ramps and administered lethal injections in the hospitals, the moral unscrupulous-ness of businessmen who ran their factories with inmate labor, and the technocratic ingenuity of the engineers who designed eight-chamber clean-as-you-burn crematorium ovens. Such crimes were unprecedented in human history, transcending all situations for which laws had been devised. They were extremely modern in their conception and administra-tion, and archaically barbarian in their day-to-day implementation.

We do not even have a word that adequately characterizes the unique-ness of factory-style mass murder.[16] The Greek word "holocaust" can be applied to any mass murder; the Hebrew "shoah" (meaning disaster, catastrophe) and the Latinate "judeocide" (Arno Mayer) focus on Jews, excluding other ethnic and social groups slated for extinction; "mass murder" and "atrocities" do not connote the centrality of bureaucratic and technological planning; "genocide" can take many forms that do not share the modern rationality of what was introduced into world history by Germans under the Nazi regime. This was an entirely new scale of criminality committed in a full-scale racial war against unarmed civilians. A German legal scholar, Jahrreis, testifying at Nuremberg described how inconceivable such crimes had been only a short time before:[17]

> I was once a judge myself. In our time the jury trial of a single murder case usually took two to three weeks and was an awful experience. Two murders by one person, that was horrifying; if someone had eight to ten murders on their conscience, the European press portrayed him as a mass murderer, and people asked themselves whether normal criminal justice was adequate to deal with such cases. Last year when I was in the courtroom of the main war crimes trial listening to the witness Höss from Auschwitz, he answered the question, how many people he murdered, by saying that he could not remember exactly whether it was two and one-half or three million. At that moment it became completely clear to me that this has absolutely nothing ... to do with legal considerations.

Among postwar West German legal specialists, these crimes have come to be known as "NS crimes," or "NSG crimes" (short for *nationalsozialistische Gewaltverbrechen*: "National Socialist crimes of violence").[18] That may be precise, but such dry bureaucratese cloaks rather than evokes the scope and the horror of industrial mass murder.

These were crimes perpetrated by human beings against the basic tenets of civilized coexistence, and the category "crimes against humanity" was created for the Nuremberg trials in order to include all crimes perpetrated by Nazi Germany. Incidentally, another indication of the German inability or unwillingness to conceive of what had transpired is the euphemistic mistranslation of this category in German.[19] From its first use at Nuremberg this English term was officially mistranslated into German as "crimes against humaneness" (*Verbrechen gegen die Menschlichkeit*, instead of *Menschheit*). This euphemism has been used ever since in essentially all German books on the subject, even critical works.[20]

In the term brown-collar, "collar" connotes the civilian and day-to-day work aspects of organizing and implementing systematic human extermination (as in the terms blue-collar, white-collar, and pink-collar), while "brown" characterizes both the military style and specifically Nazi aspects of the crimes. (In the 1930s Nazis were commonly known as "brown shirts" after the unofficial gang uniform of the SA stormtroopers.) Other possible identifying colors are not uniquely Nazi: the color black was associated with the Catholic clergy before it was worn by the SS, while the red of blood is not characteristic of the clean-handed managers and technocrats, and it is commonly associated with socialism and communism.

In spring 1946 the denazification chambers began the Herculean task of clearing the brown manure out of the German stables. In order to prevent functionaries preliminarily classified in groups I and II, who had in reality been petty collaborators, from receiving punishment incommensurate with their transgressions, the denazification chambers decided to begin with these easier cases. The chambers were soon overwhelmed by hundreds of thousands of cases of people who wanted to return to their professions. Two Allied amnesty programs attempted to prevent a complete collapse of the denazification apparatus: in August 1946 all persons aged 27 or less were exempted from hearings, and on Christmas 1946 all persons with disabilities or of low income were exempted, if there was no evidence suggesting a classification in groups I or II. In 1946 the delousing metaphor was no longer appropriate, and denazification came to be associated with laundering. It cleaned Nazis of their brown taint and turned them into gleaming white democrats.[21] A caricature in a June 1946 German satirical magazine gives an amusing portrayal of this (ill. 19).[22] At the top, black sheep in Nazi uniforms dive off a conveyor belt into a large vat. After going through the machinery they emerge on a conveyor belt as white lambs in white frocks with crosses around their necks and lilies of purity in their hands. The caption reads:

> Just jump in! What can happen to you,
> You black sheep from the brown family!
> You will be painlessly rehabilitated,
> As white lambs you come out below.
> Of course we know: You never did it!
> (The others are always to blame –)
> How quickly the bad can change to the good,
> Can be seen in this picture, black and white.

These wash associations became stronger over time. What was known as "Persil certification" (Persil is a best-selling brand of laundry detergent), became standard practice for exonerating Nazi offenders who had already been convicted in the first round of hearings. At appeals hearings sentenced offenders presented affidavits of good character from prominent citizens, such as the town priest, and letters attesting to good conduct from former colleagues, many of whom were convicted of similar or worse activity.[23] An average of ten affidavits per case were presented to the appeals boards; a researcher has determined that there was a direct numerical correlation between the magnitude of the crimes and the number of affidavits presented.[24]

The two 1946 amnesties reduced the case load by more than 70 percent, so that more individual attention could be given to the remaining hearings. From January to October 1947 about 50,000 cases were reviewed each month. Problems still beset the program, however. The former Nazi big shots, stripped of their uniforms and haggard in the lean years after the war, cut pitiable figures before the hearing boards. Even vehement anti-Nazis found themselves moved by the sight. On 9 November 1945, the day Dachau's mayor Schwalber gave his speech in Dachau castle, George Orwell published an article about his visit to an internment camp in Germany. He entitled his thoughts upon seeing the pitiable figure of a former top-ranked SS bureaucrat "Revenge is Sour," and described his feelings for the man as follows:[25]

> He could have been an unfrocked clergyman, an actor ruined by drink, or a spiritualist medium. I have seen very similar people in London common lodging houses, and also in the Reading Room of the British Museum . . . So the Nazi torturer of one's imagination, the monstrous figure against whom one had struggled for so many years, dwindled to this pitiful wretch, whose obvious need was not for punishment, but for some kind of psychological treatment.

Ralph Giordano, a young Jewish German whose family had been murdered by his countrymen, had similar feelings when he observed denazification hearings in Hamburg from 1946 to 1949:[26]

> But even though I was so close to the horrors of personal persecution I found it impossible, looking at these scenes, to repress feelings of pity, spontaneous caring, thoughts of extenuating circumstances, and the hope for a lenient sentence. There he stood, the Party Member of yesterday, humbly shrunk to about half of his former master race-itude, like a little sausage, personifying political harmlessness and "naive" seducibility; his individual behavior was like that of every other defendant before him and after: it implored innocence!

The brown Nazi wolf had become a meek lamb, and hunting him had lost its urgency.

In addition to the practical problems with denazification, Cold War maneuvering began to determine occupation policy in 1947.[27] The Office of Military Government for the United States (OMGUS), faced by increasing pressure from Washington and in Germany to end the program swiftly, accelerated its retreat from the hard-line policies of the first postwar months. In October 1947 OMGUS promulgated another amnesty that gave even more authority to the local denazification prosecutors. They could now, subject to Military Government approval, reclassify as a "follower" anyone previously preclassified as an "offender," unless he had been a member of one of the organizations declared criminal at Nuremberg (those men were being held in the internment camps). This essentially exempted the most heavily incriminated suspects from a hearing. Just as the chambers had finished fining tens of thousands of "little fish" and were turning to the "big fish," most of them were let off without so much as a verbal reprimand. In November 1947, 787,000 cases remained to be heard, whereby the vast majority (640,000, or 81 percent) were suspected of being at least formerly active Nazis. Two months later, in January 1948, 400,000 men and women had been amnestied and released with no blemish on their record.

With the wind blowing in the other direction, another problem became acute. Stripped of its political support, Nazi-hunting now became dangerous for the hunters. From the start the local-level denazification prosecutors had been under pressure not to classify their neighbors into categories that would vest them with serious penalties. In a 1948 petition automatic arrestees in the Dachau internment camp wrote that their cases were being delayed because not enough denazification jurors (*Beisitzer*) could be found. The incarcerated Nazis described the jurors' situation quite graphically: "We have heard that no one wants to do this work because they think that in a couple of years their necks will be stretched if they participate in convictions."[28] In Dachau, camp survivor Zola Philipp headed the denazification chamber. He was stubborn in his pursuit of his former tormentors and their intellectual and administrative backers, and for that he was often defamed in town. In April 1948 he placed a restraining order on a Catholic Party candidate for the county diet because of incriminatory material that had been found.[29] Immediately the candidate's friends complained to the Bavarian government that the communist Philipp had committed a "monstrous" injustice and should be removed from his office. It turned out that Philipp had not initiated the restraining order, but had received it from the Bavarian appeals chamber. The higher government official responded coolly to the complaint: "I would like to take the opportunity to point out that political motives are often suspected behind measures of the denazification chambers, while in reality the measures are justified by existing political documents."

Philipp, however, made himself even more unpopular by insisting on hearing the case of Dachau's senior priest, Pfanzelt, as well as that of Dachau's popular county governor Heinrich Junker (a man who, as we will see, attempted to have the Dachau concentration camp crematorium torn down in 1955).[30]

Although by late 1947 the denazification program was no longer taken seriously, in order to save face and preserve the appearance of fairness Allied policymakers wanted to pursue it to completion. In January 1948 denazification prosecutors were further empowered to downgrade suspected "offenders" without approval from Military Government. At the same time, Military Government received orders from Washington to end denazification and empty the internment camps by early May 1948. In a face-saving attempt to complete the denazification program by that date, the chambers began rubber-stamping the remaining cases, releasing thousands of the heavily suspect internees without hearings in early spring 1948.[31] Ultimately, an extension of the completion deadline was granted for the hearings of a few heavily incriminated individuals, so that by late June only about 300 internees were still in Dachau, where the last cases in Bavaria had been collected.[32]

If denazification began with waves of sweeping arrests that included many innocent people, it ended with the wholesale release of heavily compromised Nazi activists. The Cold War and denazification interacted with many Germans' self-centered feelings of victimization, self-exonerating claims of ignorance, and self-glorifying visions of resistance to produce the specific political constellation of West Germany in its founding years. Some examples illustrate the interconnections.

"Brown-collars" in the denazification laundry

In the German populace hard-line denazification policies such as automatic arrest and placing the burden of proof on the accused gave rise to a feeling of victimization at the hands of the Western Allies very soon after the war.[33] Once the responsibility for denazification had been turned over to German authorities, the ostensible act of victimization slid backwards into the Nazi period, and an image of the Nazi "followers" as "victims of fascism" established itself in the public sphere. In a January 1947 parliamentary debate about the program, even the Bavarian Minister of Denazification applauded a deputy who called these accused "poor victims of fascism."[34]

For the sake of simplicity let us assume that there were four types of Germans in the postwar years:

- a small but not insubstantial group of true brown-collar criminals;
- a substantial group of convinced supporters and opportunistic collaborators, who may have been swept up by the Nazi movement, but were now willing to go along with the new regime;
- a third, also quite substantial group of people who had not been associated with the Nazi Party in any important way, but had behaved neutrally, as opposed to offering any resistance; and
- a fourth, relative handful of active anti-Nazi survivors.

The examples in this section are drawn from the first and second groups of brown-collar criminals, activists, and opportunists. A typical example from the third group of "neutrals" is Dachau's early postwar mayor Josef Schwalber, the author of the commemorative speeches discussed at the beginning of this section, while the fourth group of active anti-Nazis, most of whom ended up dead or in concentration camps, is the subject of the next chapter. First, however, one telling example from the first group illustrates the cleaning power of the denazification laundry.

In 1948 the case of trade school teacher Otto Friedrich Braun was heard in a Munich denazification chamber.[35] Herr Braun was not just any Mr. Brown, but the father of the late Eva Braun, and the father-in-law of Eva's deceased husband Adolf. Before levying a denazification fine, the Munich chamber had to determine Mr. Braun's net worth, which was in turn dependent on how much he would inherit from his daughter and her husband, who had been childless when they committed suicide in their bunker shortly before the fall of Berlin. Thus the Munich chamber had to have some idea of how much of the children's fortune would be confiscated by the state, and how much divided among the heirs: it was necessary to "denazify" the dead. The posthumous defense lawyer for Eva Hitler-Braun and her husband argued that Eva should be classified in denazification group V, "exonerated," while the Führer would have received, in his estimation, ten years in a work camp. After all, the evidence linking him to the brown-collar crimes was circumstantial, and his subordinates had actually designed and implemented the mass murder schemes.[36] This argument illustrates the dilemma inherent in applying normal judicial standards to brown-collar criminality.[37]

A Dachau example from the second group illustrates how the development of denazification policy helped to turn less prominent Nazi activists from socially stigmatized perpetrators to self-styled victims, then to self-righteous heroes in the years from 1947 to 1949. Hans Wülfert and Bernhard Huber were co-owners of a sausage factory in Dachau (ills. 1, 20). Already in 1923, when the local Nazi organization found itself in desperate financial straits after Hitler's failed coup, they became its main sponsors. In 1930 Wülfert was one of the three founding members of the local Nazi Party branch.[38] In the depression years that followed, the firm teetered on the brink of bankruptcy, but it remained Dachau's fourth largest employer with fifty workers. In 1933 it was awarded the title "First National Socialist Company in Dachau." From 1937 to the end of the war, the firm sold nearly half a million Reichsmarks worth of meat and meat products to the Dachau SS camp. The owners shared a close relationship with some of the camp's commandants. For example, in August 1938 the company was allowed to use two SS camp buses with drivers for a workers' outing.

The advent of the war in 1939 brought huge commissions from the German army and the SS to the Wülfert factory, bringing total sales from RM2.9 million in 1941 to RM8.1 million in 1943. The war also created a shortage of workers, for which Wülfert and Huber compensated by using inmates from the nearby concentration camp. By the end of the war, the number of prisoners working for Wülfert had increased from 16 to 350. In February 1943 a branch concentration camp was opened adjacent to the factory. The inmates received no pay, but the SS was paid, depending on prior training, RM4 or 6 per inmate per day. This was 25–40 percent less than normal civilian laborers' wages, which averaged RM6.60 to RM8.[39] In spite of drastic punishments imposed when the factory owners and overseers reported misconduct to the SS, work at the meat products factory was one of the most sought-after jobs available to Dachau inmates because it presented the opportunity to steal food and thus increase one's chances of surviving.

Wülfert and Huber were arrested in the summer of 1945, interned in the Dachau camp, and tried in March 1947 by one of the US military courts.[40] They were found guilty of "intentional and illegal participation in mass cruelty and mass mistreatment," as well as support of the Dachau concentration camp, and sentenced to two years imprisonment, with credit for time served, so that their sentences were already essentially over. Because of the US military court's verdict, in their March 1948 denazification hearings Wülfert and Huber were automatically classified as "major offenders" with accompanying mandatory imprisonment and loss of civil rights. They appealed the decision and were heard by the appeals chamber in November.[41]

For the appeals hearing the factory owners' lawyer procured a number of Persil certificates. He produced a sworn statement by Wülfert's brutal overseer Palme, who was imprisoned in Landsberg, which contradicted one of the more serious charges in the original trial. Testimony from a witness who had been beaten at Wülfert's behest was discounted because, it was argued, his work at the Wülfert factory had saved his life: the inmate probably would not have been able to survive without the extra food he received at work. Two "independent" specialists evaluated the firm's accounts and came to the conclusion that Wülfert and Huber had *lost* money by using inmate labor, because they had had to pay the SS for them. Finally, the two owners produced a number of former inmates now reemployed at their factory who testified that work in Wülfert's plant had been far more desirable than most other labor details. The appeals chamber came to the conclusion that Wülfert and Huber were "lesser offenders" and sentenced them to fines of DM20,000 and DM15,000 respectively.[42] (These fines went into a fund for the restitution of losses suffered by survivors.)

When their probation was over in March 1949, Wülfert and Huber returned triumphantly to their factory, where they were hailed as victims of terrible injustice.[43] A sign "Welcome Back" hung over the Wülfert factory gate for the rest of the year – a French survivor saw it there in November.[44] Those words symbolized the return to power of the former German elites and the final return to normality in German daily life.[45] Wülfert enjoyed great respect well into the 1970s. The local newspaper congratulated him on his eightieth and eighty-first birthdays, without mentioning this potential blemish on his past.

How had this radical turnabout become possible? A look at the war crimes trial program, which faced the same problems as denazification, albeit in a magnified form, provides some clues.

The end of the "war crimes" trials

At the International Military Tribunal in Nuremberg a total of thirteen trials were conducted.[46] At the first trial, which is the best known, all four Allied powers sat in judgment over top representatives of the state and Nazi organizations and army leaders. In the so-called successor trials, businessmen, professionals such as doctors, and hands-on murderers such as members of the task forces were subjected to the scrutiny of the court. There were four charges: war crimes (the mistreatment of POWs and civilians in occupied countries, including deportation and murder, and plundering), crimes against humanity (the same as war crimes, but by Germans against Germans), crimes against peace (starting a war), and conspiracy to commit the first three. The entire series of trials is commonly grouped together under the title "war crimes trials," but I prefer the term "brown-collar trials" because it does not conceal the genocide practiced by Germans at places far from the theaters of the war, such as Auschwitz, and at the "euthanasia" institutes in Germany itself. In fact, Germans used this terminological vagueness in the early 1950s to conceal the crimes that were at issue. In official communications and publications in the fall of 1948 the term "war criminals" was first set in quotation marks and then progressively euphemized from "war condemnees" to "military condemnees" to "condemned soldiers" to "war-imprisoned Germans" to "Landsberger" (after the prison where they were being held).[47]

The program for dealing with suspected group I brown-collar criminals went through a development similar to that of the denazification laundry, and it similarly left a host of people, mostly men, with deeply criminal pasts feeling that they had been victimized. Some statistics about the numbers of potential and actual trials reveal the scope of the Allied brown-collar trial program beyond the Nuremberg group trials.[48] From November 1945 to the time the program was ended in June 1948, investigations into 3,887 cases had been initiated, for which 12½ tons of records were amassed. However, by February 1947 close to 2,000 cases had been dropped for various reasons, such as the insignificance of the crime, or the difficulty in obtaining sufficient evidence for conviction. In the end, only 489 cases, 13 percent of the total, came to trial. The other 3,400 were dropped.[49]

The cases that did come to trial, however, included the most heinous perpetrators of the most despicable crimes, as evidenced by the high proportion of guilty verdicts and the severity of the sentences.[50] In the 489 cases, a total of 1,672 people were tried and 1,416 (85 percent) found guilty as charged. Of the guilty, 297 (21 percent) were sentenced to death and 279 (20 percent) to life in prison. However, with the passage of time the sentences were substantially reduced. By September 1948, only 158 (53 percent) of the death sentences had been carried out; further executions in 1948 and 1951 brought the final percentage up to about 65 percent. Of the ca. 350 war criminals sentenced to life imprisonment or who had their death sentences commuted, only forty were still in prison in August 1955. All of the ca. 120 who had been sentenced to twenty years or more had been released, amnestied, or let out on parole within ten years. Finally, in

December 1957, the last four "lifers" still serving time in Landsberg were granted clemency and released, because, the clemency committee reasoned, none of the German brown-collar criminals sentenced by British or French military courts were still serving time either.

The case of one of the brown-collared doctors whose multiple death sentences were successively commuted illustrates how such statistics look at an individual level.[51] Dr. Hans Eisele served as SS camp doctor successively in Natzweiler, Buchenwald, Mauthausen, and Dachau from August 1941 (he was 29 years old) until liberation in 1945. He routinely administered lethal injections, practiced surgical operations with an extremely high post-operative mortality rate, and performed other experimental techniques on prisoners. In November 1945 he was sentenced to death for his participation in the operation of the Dachau concentration camp. That sentence was commuted because he had been at the camp for only 2½ months at the very end in 1945 and had attempted to improve the catastrophic medical care for prisoners in the camp, and because he was not personally accused of any mistreatments. However, in the trial of Buchenwald personnel in August 1947 he was sentenced to death a second time for murdering by injection and improper surgery. That sentence was confirmed in March and again in early June of 1948.

By then, however, the political wind had changed direction, and on 28 June a new War Crimes Board of Review recommended reducing the second death sentence to life imprisonment, because the Board had doubts about one crucial bit of testimony. In August another commission sent to Germany to ensure consistency of sentences across all of the trials recommended commuting Eisele's Buchenwald sentence further to ten years, but in December it was confirmed as life imprisonment. Two years later, in October 1950, another commission recommended remitting the Dachau sentence entirely, and reducing the Buchenwald sentence to ten years, with ten days off for each month of good conduct. The recommendation was approved, and on 19 February 1952 Eisele was released from Landsberg. As far as the new West German government was concerned, Eisele had been captured and imprisoned by the enemy, so that he was eligible for compensation payments (*Heimkehrerentschädigung*).

Eisele used his government award to open a licensed family practice in Munich, where he lived untroubled by his past until 1958, when testimony in the trial of a sadistic Buchenwald guard before a West German court heavily incriminated him.[52] Warned by sympathetic officials that he would be arrested, he personally dropped off a letter to the editor of the Munich *Evening News*, in which he defended his reputation, and boarded an airplane to Egypt, where he was employed within a network of former Nazis in an army hospital. Later he was promoted to head doctor of the rocket center in Heluan, where at least 200 other fugitive German and Austrian specialists were working (they were developing missiles to be used against Israel). Eisele died at age 55 in 1967, untroubled by further investigations into his past.

Eisele's sentencing, amnesty, and successful new career – as well as his sudden reconfrontation with his crimes at the end of the 1950s – mirrors the trajectory of memory in West Germany during that same period. But that is another story, to which we will return later.

Brown-collar criminals as victims

When one sorts through the statements brown-collar criminals made in their own defense, their feelings of victimization are unmistakable. It seems that the more heinous their crimes, the more victimized the perpetrators felt. At the Nuremberg trial of the "task forces," groups of Germans organized to hunt down Polish and Soviet Jews and shoot them into mass graves, the commander of one group answered under cross-examination as follows:[53]

Q: How did the victims behave?
Blobel: It was like this with them, a human life was worth nothing, sort of. Either the people had already had some kinds of experiences themselves, or they didn't recognize their inner value.
Q: In other words: They went to their deaths happily?
Blobel: Whether they were happy I'm not able to say. They knew what was in store for them, they were told that, and they accepted their fate. That is the nature of these people there in the East.
Q: And was your task easier because they didn't resist?
Blobel: Yes, of course . . . Everything went very calmly, it didn't take much time. I have to say that our men who participated had more problems with their nerves than those who had to be shot.
Q: In other words, you felt more sympathy for your men who had to shoot the victims, than for the victims themselves?
Blobel: Yes, well, our men had to be taken care of.
Q: Did you feel very sorry for them?
Blobel: Some of them really experienced the utmost there.

In the Belsen trial the head of the female SS guards testified as follows:[54]

I, Elisabeth Volkenrath, was the senior SS guard. I am 26 years old. My husband is also in the SS. I know that it was really awful in these camps, but

100

it was awful for us, too, and we couldn't do anything about it. We were
punished just like the prisoners, in that our pay was kept from us, up to RM5
by Commandant Kramer, and we were also imprisoned in the camp, on
orders from Berlin, and we were treated almost exactly as if we were
prisoners.

Volkenrath's "just like" and "almost exactly" reveal both a staggering lack
of empathy and a surfeit of self-pity. Her subordinate Irma Greese, a
simple but fanatical Nazi who had joined the Party to spite her left-wing
father, felt victimized by her work in the camps as well:

The conditions in the concentration camps were bad for everyone, including
the SS. The only time that I was allowed to go home for five days was after I
had finished my training in Ravensbrück. I told my father about the
concentration camp and he hit me and told me never to enter the house
again.

And Rudolf Höss, the model commandant of Auschwitz, described in his
memoir how he suffered under the acts he forced others to commit. One
day he "had to" order one of his men to drag two playing children into the
gas chamber. He wrote:[55]

Believe me, I felt like shrinking into the ground out of pity, but I was not
allowed to show the slightest emotion. Hour upon hour I had to witness all
that happened. I had to watch day and night, whether it was the dragging
and burning of the bodies, the teeth being ripped out, the cutting of the hair;
I had to watch all this horror. For hours I had to stand in the horrible,
haunting stench while the mass graves were dug open, and the bodies
dragged out and burned. I also had to watch the process of death itself
through the peephole of the gas chamber because the doctors called my
attention to it. I had to do all of this because I was the one to whom
everyone looked, and because I had to show everybody that I was not only
the one who gave the orders and issued the directives, but that I was also
willing to be present at whatever task I ordered my men to perform . . . Today
I deeply regret that I didn't spend more time with my family. I always
believed that I had to be constantly on duty. Through this exaggerated sense
of duty I always made my life more difficult than it actually was.

Höss's regrets have nothing to do with his victims, only with his own
suffering.

In Dachau, too, the SS men interned after the war felt they were victims
of treatment worse than that in the concentration camps. As the mass
amnesties in the spring of 1948 began, the remaining internees – the men
suspected of the most heinous crimes – began writing letters in an attempt
to hasten their release. They drew up petitions to the Bavarian Minister
President, the Minister for Denazification, and the Parliamentary

Commission on Denazification, and they sent copies to public figures such as Church and party leaders.[56] In these letters, as in the magazines that the inmates of the larger internment camps had produced over the years, they attempted to paint a vivid picture of the injustice they felt they were suffering.[57] In a February 1948 Dachau petition the internees first made a statistical argument that hardly any of them could be group I war criminals.[58] They calculated that since only fourteen of the 1,600 cases heard thus far had been classified as Major Offenders, it stood to reason that "only 27" (sic!) of the remaining 3,100 would be classified the same way. Thus they were "unjustly" being held. They then complained that they were receiving a "slave wage" of 30 to 50 pfennigs per day for the work they performed, and they were being prevented from helping their families, who were living in poverty. Because they did not want to "make ourselves guilty in the eyes of history or our families, in that we silently bear the injustice of the present situation," they demanded that the Liberation Law be rescinded, and if that was not possible right away, that measures be taken to ensure their quick release.

At the end of February 1948, when writer Carl Zuckmayer, author of the era's most-performed play *The Devil's General*, visited the camp, the inmates went so far as to accuse the denazification boards of the same brown-collar crimes they themselves were suspected of having committed.[59] They explained to Zuckmayer that "because revenge- and hate-filled antifascists run the denazification chambers, the decisions are not expressions of a will to justice, but an attempt to exterminate [*vernichten*] National Socialists as people with differing political opinions." We will hear several other examples of the use of Holocaust terminology in postwar Germany, but it never describes the Holocaust itself. Rather, it is used to highlight the perceived postwar "victimization" of German civilians, *excluding* concentration camp and Holocaust survivors.[60]

In a third letter in June 1948 the remaining 300 Dachau internees reiterated that they were the victims of "screaming injustice."[61] They argued that they had been imprisoned under the "dictate of a foreign power" that had been passed after their purported transgression (violating the judicial principle *nulla poena sine lege*, "no punishment without a law"). Alluding to the Nazi law that had been the basis for committal to a concentration camp (protective custody law), they argued that they had been imprisoned based on mere suspicion, and had never been told when their detainment might end. Finally, with open reference to the Nazi practice of imprisoning the family members of a suspect at large (*Sippenhaft*, "family arrest," a kind of hostage-taking by the police), the internees complained that their families were "suffering from three years of family arrest." Because of such mockery of law and justice, the internees concluded, they were "forced not to ask for, but to demand" their immediate release. They concluded: "We are determined to do everything in our power to do away with the defamation and violation of rights that result from a law that is immoral in content and enforcement." This strident self-righteousness indicates that the nonresisters of the past were becoming the resisters of the present.

It was quite clear to most contemporaries that postwar conditions in Dachau and other Bavarian internment camps were harsh, but that they were in no way comparable to those in the German concentration camps.[62] In the words of historian Lutz Niethammer, "In comparison to the fates of many victims of the National Socialist regime and of the war in all countries, and relative to the general living conditions at that time, internment in the US zone was in general a relatively tolerable experience."[63] The Western Allied and Ally-controlled German press was quick to point out how much better the US internment camps were than the Nazi KZs, but the German internees, drawing on the image of the "clean" concentration camps, saw the relationship quite differently.

In response to several articles in the Regensburg internment camp magazine that emphasized how much better the internment camps were than the concentration camps had been, an internee wrote a letter to the magazine's editor in September 1947.[64] It was published under the heading "KZ – Internment Camp." For that internee, the previous articles had avoided the "essentials," which were, in his opinion, the similarities between the two types of camp. He thought the inhuman treatment of the KZ inmates had not been a fundamental part of the system, but the result of a development that no one had foreseen in 1933. In conclusion, the internee expressed his exasperation at the lack of due process and legal recourse: "Compared to the concentration camps, the internment camps are 'humane' only if being hanged is the measure . . . Concentration camp inmates had – if they could avoid the cruelties – at least hope for the future, but we are without hope." This image of victimization views the concentration camps as merely severe correctional institutions where a few too many hangings had been carried out.

Brown-collar ignorance

Brown-collar criminals on trial had no qualms about claiming ignorance in the most improbable of situations. For instance, at the first Nuremberg trial former Nazi Economics Minister and Reichsbank president Funk was asked where he thought the huge quantities of eyeglasses, wedding rings, and gold teeth in the vaults of the Reichsbank came from. He answered: "How could I even imagine that the SS had obtained these valuables by desecrating corpses!" An even more crass example from the same trial, which even his own brown-collared cronies found outrageous, was offered by Ernst Kaltenbrunner, the man in the SS main office in charge of the racial war against the Jews.[65] When he claimed that he did not know about the murders in the concentration camps until March 1944, behind him in the dock Göring leaned over to Admiral Dönitz and whispered: "Listen to that!" Dönitz, Hitler's hand-picked successor, replied "He ought to be ashamed of himself." Dönitz himself later denied having known where the 12,000 shipbuilding workers he had ordered from the concentration camps had come from.

Businessmen were equally prone not to have known anything. In the trial of the I. G. Farben chemical conglomerate, the head engineer of I. G. Farben's "Interest Group" I. G. Auschwitz, Walter Dürrfeld, made the following statements under cross-examination:[66]

> Q: Did you never speak to any SS men who could have told you, or didn't you ever hear anything from your own co-workers about the extermination measures, or rumors about them?
>
> Dürrfeld: No. From no one. That is why I cannot understand how people can say that the extermination of human beings was generally well known.
>
> Q: Some witnesses have argued that a strange smell was noticeable near Auschwitz. Did you notice that yourself?
>
> Dürrfeld: Yes, I remember that once or twice, when I drove out of the city of Auschwitz to the west – that I smelled a particular smell that I couldn't identify. My driver, that was in the summer of 44, said that it came from the crematorium, where corpses were burnt, as they say. When I came back from the trip I coincidentally met SS Major Schwarz. I asked him whether that was right, and he admitted freely that the smell came from burning corpses. He explained that with the high death rate in the camp, because of a typhus epidemic that came from the east.

Not knowing was as simple as that.[67] In I. G. Auschwitz's own camp Auschwitz-Monowitz, directly adjacent to Dürrfeld's factory complex, 25,000 prisoners had died while Dürrfeld went about his business.

Brown-collar criminals as rescuers

By the end of the 1940s a completely new conception of criminal guilt for activities during the Nazi regime was developing in West Germany. In the

1945 Dachau trial of the comparatively benevolent commandant Martin Weiss the court explicitly discounted the defense argument that Weiss should be treated less severely because he had improved conditions in the camp. His punishment might be reduced because of that, but his guilt was in no way affected. The Allied tribunal at Nuremberg reiterated this principle unmistakably in the celebrated case of Baron Ernst von Weizsäcker, a high-ranking Foreign Office official who had served as ambassador to the Vatican (and whose son Richard later became West Germany's president). Von Weizsäcker was able to document that he had prevented the Gestapo from deporting 185 Jews hidden in a convent in Rome to Auschwitz, thereby saving their lives. On the other hand, von Weizsäcker had personally signed dozens of deportation lists. The Allied court argued:[68]

> We reject the opinion that . . . someone might go unpunished for committing grave crimes because he hoped thereby to prevent worse crimes from being committed. Or that general positive behavior towards individual persons can excuse or justify crimes committed against anonymous masses.

The prosecutor had formulated it even more clearly: only someone who sent thousands to their deaths had been in a position to save a few. No one else had had that opportunity.

West German courts saw this very differently. The question arose in the trial of a doctor whose job had been to make lists of mentally disabled persons to be sent to the extermination centers. He was also able to cross names off the lists, which he sometimes did. The German court acquitted him, with the following argument:[69]

> If one assumes that the accused knew that about 1,000 people went to their deaths, while by measures of sabotage another 250 were able to be saved, there results a proportion of at least 20 percent, or, expressed another way, through the activity of the accused at least every fifth man was able to be saved.

The West German Supreme Court confirmed this reasoning in a later case: no longer were Nazi doctors to be judged by how many people they had killed, but by how many they had allowed to live. The murderers had become rescuers. Historian Jörg Friedrich summed up the result of the West German brown-collar crimes trial program as follows: "It certified the politeness of the Gestapo, the mercy of the euthanasia doctors, and the legal impeccability of the hanging judges."[70]

Rescuing brown-collared "victims"

Two developments followed the rapid conclusion of the Allied war crimes trials in 1948. First, in accordance with the myth of resistance, members of the West German elite began an intensive lobbying effort to oppose the Allied courts' convictions and save the men and women on death row, and then to free the other convicts. Second, the myth of victimization was used to justify the rehabilitation of former high-ranking Nazis into positions of power and influence. We will look at each development in turn.

The slew of petitions and letters sent off by the inmates of Dachau internment camp in the spring of 1948 had little direct effect, but the plight of the heinous brown-collar convicts in Landsberg penitentiary did prompt leading members of the German Catholic and Protestant Churches to take action.[71] Two prominent churchmen, both of whom had spent a few years in Dachau as "special prisoners" in the tract of individual cells behind the service building, expended much energy lobbying Allied authorities especially for the commutation of death penalties, but also for the release of the convicts.

German Protestant Church president and former Dachau "special prisoner" Martin Niemöller may have thrown himself so wholeheartedly into this "resistance" effort in an attempt to compensate for the "too little, too late" of which he had accused himself under Hitler. Along with Bishop Wurm and Prelate Hartenstein, Niemöller assembled hundreds of pages of documents, analyses of trial records, "Persil" affidavits, and biblical quotations into memoranda that they sent to US General Handy, who was empowered to grant clemency to the convicted men.[72] In one letter Niemöller and his Protestant colleagues compared the Allied trials to Hitler's show trials of the resisters who had conspired to assassinate him on 20 July 1944.[73] This comparison not only equated mass murderers with Hitler's opponents, but implied that the Allied courts were as criminal as Hitler's. Ultimately, however, these self-serving arguments led to the creation of several investigatory commissions, as well as to the granting of clemency to most of the brown-collar convicts. After a revision on 31 January 1951, only seven of the twenty-eight "red jackets" on death row in Landsberg had not been pardoned.

Immediately prior to that 1951 revision, Niemöller and the German bishops mounted a final effort to save men such as Oswald Pohl, the head of the SS administrative office for concentration camps; Paul Blobel, the organizer of the Babi Yar massacre of 35,000 Jews in two days; Erich Naumann, the commander of daily massacres of 500 Jews in Lithuania;

and Werner Braune, the head of a special commando that worked over-time to slaughter 10,000 Jews so that the German army could celebrate Christmas in a Jew-free zone. Niemöller wrote to Handy that: "hovering between life and death [for five years] is an experience of extreme terror." Thus, he concluded, the convicts had already suffered enough and should be pardoned.

Catholic bishop and fellow former Dachau special prisoner Johannes Neuhäusler was also extremely energetic in resisting the "injustice" being committed against the mass murderers. Beginning in 1948 he worked together with the Nuremberg defense lawyers Aschenauer and Froeschmann, tirelessly writing letters to Generals Clay and Handy, to the US ambassador, President Truman, various United States congressmen (including Joseph McCarthy, who was quite sympathetic) and US bishops, and to the Vatican. At one point he complained to General Clay because the prison director denied the Landsberg convicts permission to have an advent wreath with candles at Christmas. Neuhäusler wrote that he had never experienced such "brutal treatment" in his four years in Dachau, where he was "never once denied an advent wreath or Christmas tree." Handy checked into the matter at Landsberg: it turned out that candles were prohibited in the prison, and the infuriated director had thrown the four advent candles the length of the mess hall.

Neuhäusler recommended that Clay follow in his, Neuhäusler's, foot-steps: "I forget the unjust persecution in the 3rd Reich that lies behind me and aspire to the fine ideal clothed by the Apostle into the words: 'Oversee the evil by the good.'"[74] Neuhäusler did not limit himself to the bible, he also pulled the anticommunist register, reminding Clay not to disappoint the German people: "The Soviet Union is committing the worst postwar crime by keeping German soldiers as prisoners . . . and torturing them to death . . . The Federal Republic of Germany is called upon to join the Western powers in creating a strong defensive bloc against the Bolshevism of the East."[75]

In January 1951 John McCloy, Clay's successor as the highest US official in charge in Germany, wrote in response to one of Neuhäusler's innumer-able letters:[76]

My dear Bishop Dr. Neuhäusler,
I would like to point out that crimes for which these defendants were tried rank . . . among the most atrocious known in history. They include mass murder . . . [T]he testimony of reliable witnesses, as well as their own statements, established that the defendants were guilty of the torture and death of hundreds, and in many cases thousands, of helpless human beings.

Hundreds of petitions from "common people" were mailed in, some claiming that they could not sleep at night because they thought of the hangings. On 7 January 1951, 3,000 Germans demonstrated in Landsberg for the release of the brown-collar criminals.[77] Shortly thereafter 300 Jews living in a nearby camp arrived to counterprotest. When they chanted "Down with the murderers!" the Germans answered "Juden raus" ("Jews get out," a Nazi slogan). In a letter to the Minister President a member of the Bavarian parliament summed up the keynote speeches at the pro-Nazi rally: "Representatives of all parties in parliament and high church officials spoke. They rejected the execution of people because of their religion, race and political views as well as the extermination [*Vernichtung*] of 4.5 million Germans in the East in 1945–46."[78] The use of the term "extermination" in this context is another example of Germans' use of Holocaust imagery to present themselves as victims of horrific Allied or Soviet crimes.

The remaining seven Landsberger inmates, including Pohl and Blobel, were hanged on 7 June 1951. Those were the last legal executions carried out in West Germany. Parallel efforts to free brown-collar convicts being held in the French and British zones continued for several more years. They, too, were ultimately successful. Once they were out of prison, the way was clear to rehabilitate these men into their former positions of responsibility and influence.

Brown-collar criminals as leading citizens

In the section on the Nazi takeover in Dachau we met the town's mayor Hans Zauner, who opportunistically joined the Nazi Party in March 1933, either to prevent the old Nazis from having a completely free hand in government, or to further his own career. While it is hard to judge whether he did the former, he certainly managed the latter. The master bookbinder was second vice mayor, the third-highest post in the town council, for most of the Nazi period. Soon after his "denazification," in 1952, he was elected lord mayor, a position he held until 1960, when incautious remarks he made about the inmates of the concentration camp provoked an international scandal (see pp. 80f). Zauner's career in 1950s' West Germany was by no means exceptional. We will examine two cases from the highest level of national politics, one that shows how denazification was manipulated to whitewash even the brownest of collars, and one that demonstrates how the redefinition of brown-collar criminals as rescuers opened the doors of rehabilitation to even the most compromised Nazis.

Kurt-Georg Kiesinger was a 29-year-old lawyer when he joined the Nazi Party on 1 March 1933, the morning after the Reichstag burned.[79] At a press conference in 1968 Kiesinger claimed that he had joined neither out of opportunism, nor out of conviction, but that by 1934 he had already seen "where that was leading" and did not involve himself further in Party activities. For a time he maintained a small law practice in Berlin, tutoring law students on the side. With World War II came new opportunities, and former students helped him get a job at the Foreign Office in April 1940. Although his position was entitled "Academic Assistant," as the head of the Reich radio department he was the Foreign Office's main liaison to Goebbels' Ministry of Propaganda. His department was responsible for summarizing the "enormous amount" of information relevant for foreign policy broadcast by all foreign stations, and for "influencing and manipulating" foreign broadcasters (especially, but not solely, in occupied countries) according to the wishes of Foreign Minister Ribbentrop. In January 1943 Kiesinger's department submitted an analysis of an article entitled "Hitler's Short-Wave Rumor Factory" in the 21 November 1942 *Saturday Evening Post*. The *Post* had given a detailed summary of the means Kiesinger's department employed to reach "its two main goals – mistrust and racial hate." This 1942 insight had been lost by the 1950s.

Kiesinger had advanced exceptionally quickly to a position of extreme confidence. The Gestapo simply ignored claims by two rivals who tried to denounce him, and in January 1945 he was recommended to Goebbels as one of the few men "who, on the basis of their experience at the front lines of foreign radio, is most likely to know what should be done" to delay the fall of the collapsing Nazi Reich for as long as possible.

In the spring of 1945 Kiesinger had himself transferred from Berlin, which was endangered by the rapidly advancing Soviet army, to southern Germany, where he was arrested by the US army in March. He spent the next 1½ years, until September 1946, in the "3rd Army Internment Camp 74" in Ludwigsburg with other members of his department. For his first denazification hearing in March 1947 he went to the northern Bavarian village where his father-in-law presided over the denazification chamber. He was classified in group IV, "follower." However, even "followers" were not allowed to hold elected office. Kiesinger appealed, presented a number of Persil affidavits at his hearing in August 1948, and was reclassified as "exonerated." In the meantime he had become regional leader (*Landesgeschäftsführer*) for the Christian Democratic Party (CDU), and he was elected as a representative to the first national parliament in the fall of 1949. As a talented speaker he served as the CDU's star orator in parliament on many occasions, but his goal of a cabinet position eluded him. Finally in 1958 he accepted the position of Minister President of the south German state of Baden-Württemberg, which he held until 1966. In that year the CDU selected him as its candidate for Chancellor of the Bonn republic. Thus a former ranking Nazi was able to accede to the highest office in the country.

Although there were other brown-collared members of the West German cabinet in the 1950s, Hans Globke's collar had the darkest hue. Globke was a department head in Chancellor Adenauer's cabinet from 1949 to 1963. One of his early and most lasting achievements was the creation of the Office of the Federal Chancellor (*Bundeskanzleramt*), the executive office that runs the nation.[80] However, shadows loomed in this gifted bureaucrat's past. Back in 1932, weeks before the Nazi takeover, legal expert Globke drew up guidelines on approving name changes for the Prussian Interior Ministry. In the antisemitic climate of the times, some Jewish Germans thought that it might make their lives easier if they were not called, for example, Cohen or Goldberg, but, well, perhaps Kiesinger or Globke. Just before Christmas, on 23 December 1932, Globke wrote:

> Existing law presumes that surnames characterize the origins of a certain family. Every change . . . masks the racial origins [*blutmässige Abstammung*] and makes it easier to conceal one's status . . . Attempts by Jewish persons to conceal their ancestry by changing their names can therefore not be supported. The conversion to Christianity gives no cause to change a name. Just as little can a change of name be justified by reference to antisemitic tendencies.

In 1937 it was Globke's idea (he drafted the law) to give all current and future Jewish Germans the names Israel and Sarah. (Later he claimed that this suggestion preempted Bormann's plan to give all Jews the uglier name "Jud." Bormann was the head of Hitler's Chancellory, just as Globke later led Adenauer's.) Globke also wrote a 300-page commentary on how to apply the Nuremberg racial laws of September 1935. One provision prohibited new marriages between non-Jewish and Jewish Germans. Globke argued for the broadest possible interpretation, also prohibiting, for instance, marriages concluded abroad. Such was the case of Berlin Communist Party member Karl, who had met the Russian x-ray technician Rebekka in Berlin in 1932. After the law was passed Karl went to Leningrad with Rebekka, where they married, but the Russians soon deported him back to Germany as a possible spy. The German court found that although the Law for the Protection of German Blood said nothing about "mixed" marriages concluded abroad, Globke's commentary stipulated that such marriages were prohibited and punishable as well.

Globke even gave the judges the broadest possible interpretation of sexual intercourse. In a 1937 article in the *Journal of the Academy of German Law*, Globke wrote that while one expert defined sexual intercourse narrowly as intercourse with penetration (*Beischlaf*), most relevant commentaries (including his own, which he cited) included "similar and surrogate activities" (*beischlafähnliche und Ersatzhandlungen*) as well. The court welcomed this clarification, because "it will serve to make undesired sexual relations between Jews and Germans more difficult and prevent circumventions of the Law for the Protection of German Blood." For Jewish men, the punishment for violations of this law was, by the way, death.

After the war Globke was able to obtain Persil statements from various sources. He did not need real affidavits because his application to become a Nazi Party member had been turned down (the reasons are not known). As a government official with no formal affiliation to the Nazi Party he did not need to be denazified. In one supporting letter the bishop of Berlin told the press that Globke had kept the episcopal office informed of the Interior Ministry's plans regarding the Jews. This did not compromise the Church for taking no action, but exonerated Globke. The bishop argued:

> We have primarily his [Globke's] intelligent and brave collaboration with the Episcopal office to thank that the two draft laws calling for the forcible divorce of all racially mixed marriages were never passed, due to the threatening attitude of the German bishops. Since this sabotage [*Zersetzungarbeiten*] had to be kept secret from all participants in order to be effective, no nonparticipants ever learned what the Jews in Germany have to thank Mr. Globke for.

Indeed. The bishops' "threatening attitude" had not been able to rescue any of the Jews who had converted to Catholicism, or even the priests and nuns in concentration camps, and it is unlikely that it saved any Jews in this case. Instead, the draft forcible divorce laws were not implemented because many of the 30,000 non-Jewish partners in such German mixed marriages stood by their spouses in spite of official sanctions. Their courage created some difficult situations for the government, including a mass public protest in Berlin in 1943.[81] Nonetheless, just as the handicapped had to thank the list-making doctors, the Jews had to thank Globke for his benevolence.

Article 131 and the "renazification" of West Germany

The list of brown-collared bureaucrats such as Kiesinger and Globke, who were defended by the government against all odds and all critics, can be extended to all levels of state administration. Former Nazi Party members came to comprise the majority of the employees in many government institutions: for example in the Bonn Foreign Office in 1952, 85 percent of the leading officials had been in the Nazi Party, a higher proportion than under Hitler.[82] A US study of West German political elites in 1956 found that at least 24 percent of all West German politicians had been active supporters of the Nazi regime, while at most 19 percent had opposed it.[83] Because the study relied solely on published information, which probably revealed support of Nazism only if that was unavoidable, while emphasizing oppositional attitudes whenever possible, the study's results can be taken as a minimum baseline of "renazification," as it was called at the time. (The term "renazification" was already in use in 1948, when an essay entitled "Denazification or Renazification?" was published in a book about postwar Germany.[84])

Like denazification, "renazification" has two meanings: the physical return of compromised Nazis into positions of power (to use the old metaphor, a kind of reinfestation with lice), or the return to Nazi attitudes and behaviors by the holders of power. Although the reinfestation clearly took place, the return of antidemocratic and militarist behaviors was not extensive. How were these Nazi elites able to return to their offices so soon after their removal? One prerequisite was the removal of the brown stains from their past by the denazification laundry. Another factor was the need for their technical expertise under the exigencies of the Cold War. And a third was a number of government programs that actively promoted the return of former Nazis to positions of power. The first step for this third prerequisite was taken by the brand new West German parliament in December 1949. One of the first laws it passed was a blanket amnesty for all brown-collar crimes whose *minimum* punishment was less than six months.[85]

This first politically approved amnesty protected crimes such as those committed during the November 1938 pogroms, "wrongful deprivation of personal liberty," and "grievous bodily harm (even if resulting in death)," unless it could be proved that they had been committed out of "cruelty, dishonorable motives, or greed." Believing in Nazi ideology was considered an honorable motive. Other amnestied crimes were: denunciation and the public use of firearms resulting in death – a common crime in the final phase of the war when uptight Nazis tried to force their faltering neighbors to fight to the bitter end. Especially these latter crimes were fresh in the memories of many Germans, and the amnesty was intended to help restore social peace. Another crime falling under the amnesty was the use of a false identity. Around 100,000 Germans had gone underground at the end of the war because they feared that their past work for the Gestapo, SS, or other brown-collar organizations would land them in prison. They had jettisoned their careers, pensions, and academic credentials. Some were able to remarry their purported widows, but they had to break off contacts with friends and neighbors for fear of recognition. Under this new law any former SS officer could now register his address with the proper authorities, pick up his denazification certificate, and pick up where he had left off without further ado. There would be no investigation of his past unless, coincidentally, he was recognized and charges were pressed by a survivor of his master-racist ministrations.[86]

The most important springboard for former Nazi officials was a provision of the new West German constitution, Article 131, governing the rights of state officials.[87] The article merely stipulated that laws governing the rights of officials tenured by the Nazi regime would have to be passed. The West German parliament passed the first such law in 1951. That so-called "131 law" made the reinstatement of all Nazi officials dismissed during denazification *possible*, and practice soon showed that essentially no one who applied was refused reemployment.[88] The law was modified several times, so that by 1954 a quota system was in place, according to which each public authority was required to hire a certain proportion of "131ers."[89]

The question arises: why did the Bonn government conclude this "great peace with the perpetrators," as political novelist Ralph Giordano has called it? Chancellor and Foreign Minister Adenauer, called upon by a parliamentary investigative committee to explain the "nazification" of the Foreign Office, put it quite concisely: "Ladies and gentlemen, one cannot create a foreign office if one does not have, for the beginning at least, in the key positions, people who have some understanding of the preceding history."[90] In other words, the technical expertise of these former Nazi officials was necessary. But the real reason lay deeper than that. Nazi Germany had been run by active Party members, opportunists, and collaborators. To begin the enormous task of rebuilding Germany as quickly as possible, it was essential to integrate these, literally, millions and millions of people into the new democratic state. Did they pose a danger to the development of democracy? Not necessarily. As long as the new leadership gave them the right direction, they would most likely follow. After all, if the great mass of Nazi personnel had obeyed their brown-collared superiors even as their cities and towns sank into ruins, they would most likely obey them – brown-collared or not – again when new cities arose from the ruins.

It may sound appalling that a large proportion of West Germany's key personnel was heavily complicit in brown-collar criminality, but before we pass judgment it is important to know what effect that renazification actually had on the nature of the new state. It turned out that, with the major exception of the quality of life for the survivors of Nazi persecution, renazification accelerated economic recovery, thus endearing West Germany's democratic system to many of its skeptical citizens.

Denazification: a fiasco?

German historian Jörg Friedrich, to whom I am indebted for many of the examples cited above, passes harsh judgment on the German populace's reactions to denazification, which he describes as follows:[91]

> No matter what measures were tried by the Americans or the Germans to establish a serious feeling of responsibility for National Socialism, they ended up serving Bolshevism, hitting precisely the wrong people, putting off the good-willed, discrediting democracy, encouraging antisemitism, adding coal to the fires of the Nazis, ruining the middle class, driving the elites to depression and suicide, inciting denunciation and mistrust, ruining families, ruining the economy, destroying religious faith and mercy, hindering every insight and leading to stubbornness, undermining the rule of law, threatening international understanding, driving the just into the arms of wrongdoers, inciting the wrongdoers to uprisings and revolts, [and] preventing a genuine new start.

After compiling case after unbelievable case of perverted denazification, however, Friedrich is forced to concede that allowing the former Nazis to plead victimization was beneficial to the initial establishment of democracy in Germany.[92] As we will see, its negative effects did not manifest themselves until the 1960s with the rise of revanchists and deniers.

In any case, regardless of this farcical denazification's role in the process, West Germany as a whole, including some of the most despicable brown-collar perpetrators, took leave of Hitler's racist utopia and only glanced back wistfully every now and then.[93] Even if most Germans had flooded into the Nazi Party out of self-serving opportunism, and even if they streamed to democracy for the same reason, they did behave democratically. Denazification forced hundreds of thousands of individuals to create possible (although seldom plausible) humanitarian versions of their personal behavior during the Nazi period. These fabrications served as artificial memories on which democratic identities, including a heightened sensitivity to injustice and an increasing willingness to protest against it, were based. The myth became reality, or, to use the words of philosopher Martin Heidegger, *Schein* (appearance) became *Sein* (reality). Mary Fulbrook, the author of a widely used textbook on postwar Germany, summarizes the development as follows:[94]

> while former Nazis gained relatively easy re-entry into political life under Adenauer, this was paradoxically a stabilizing rather than destabilizing phenomenon. Sufficiently constrained by the system not to be able to attack it openly, former Nazis were also sufficiently accepted by and incorporated into the new system not to want to attack it. Since the system appeared to be delivering the goods . . . these potential dissenters were in fact quite willing to accord the system a certain passive support.

Two examples illustrate this paradoxical development. The first is the so-called Naumann Affair.

In his final testament Hitler named Werner Naumann, a department head in Goebbels' Ministry of Propaganda, to succeed Goebbels as Reich Minister. Naumann was a National Socialist of deep conviction. In the early 1950s he was proud that his former Party comrades were rising to positions of responsibility and power in the new Federal Republic of Germany. In 1952, in a newsletter distributed to former Nazis, he wrote a remarkable defense of former Nazis mistrusted by the West German government, which I quote at length:[95]

> The system that we serve today is certainly not ideal. But we, too, live in this state. It is in none of our interests to endanger the state, because its disruption would also hit our people, our families and our future . . . Although Hitler's followers are being persecuted and tormented [sic!] as has never happened before under the rule of law, although they have been debased and banished from society, they have nonetheless proved themselves to be model elements of order, reliability and the will to work. In these years there have been no underground movements, no assassination attempts, and no acts of sabotage. A comparison with the years after 1918 helps us especially to appreciate this behavior . . . An underground movement in Germany did not arise not because it was impossible. It did not develop solely because of self-controlled and responsible personalities [I think of commandant Rudolf Höss, quoted on p. 101], who continued to be respected by their compatriots, who did not want that development and resisted every attempt to initiate it . . . Whoever opens their eyes can see that they have quite openly distanced themselves from the political Bohemians who everywhere today are trying to establish organizations based on the past. Does Bonn not know anything about these forces supporting the state?

Goebbels' rhetorically gifted department head advised his fellow ex-Nazis to take what the 1968 generation would later call the "long march through the institutions." His own march began in 1950, when he started advising a leading official of the West German liberal party (Free Democratic Party, FDP, the political home of many former Nazi Party members), who had once been in charge of "Jewish questions" for the German embassy in occupied France. Together with a number of Naumann's former subordinates from the Propaganda Ministry they began to infiltrate the FDP in North Rhine-Westphalia. Soon they had installed several former Nazi *Gauleiter* (provincial Party governors), and high SS officers in key party offices.

New York Times correspondent Drew Middleton broke the story on 29 November 1952. The British Foreign Ministry began to investigate, releasing its report at a press conference on 15 January 1953. On 28 January British Foreign Minister Eden reported to the House of Commons that although there was a "conspiracy of National Socialists," it did not present any acute danger to the democratic order in Germany.[96] The group's first concrete goal was German national unity and a sovereign German army (the latter was already being planned under the European Defense Community anyway),[97] but some of its less "self-controlled" members had made high-spirited comments in tapped telephone conversations, such as "the next parliament is a transitional parliament, hopefully the last one." Another remark compared Chancellor Adenauer's politics to Gustav Stresemann's politics of fulfillment of the Versailles Treaty in the 1920s, implying that Germany might change the terms of peace once it regained its sovereignty.

Chancellor Adenauer claimed that the vision of a "March on Bonn" (a reference to Mussolini's March on Rome in 1922) was absurd, but he did have the men removed from their FDP offices. The West German press, however, rose in almost unanimous outrage at this meddling in German affairs by foreign powers. A lone critical voice in the progressive *Frankfurter Rundschau* wrote, "A nationalistic press campaign set in that did not spare the British a single word of reproach from the vocabulary of outraged neodemocrats." The story of the Naumann Affair ended unspectacularly. The West German courts decided that Naumann could not be charged with any criminal offenses and released him. He then ran for election to parliament in a district that had voted 69 percent Nazi in 1933, but was disqualified when a specially modified article of the denazification code automatically classified him as an "offender" without voting rights. He did not play an important role in public life after that.

What does this example show? For one thing, it demonstrates that, even if they did not say it openly, most former Nazis had clearly realized that some of Hitler's policies had not been good for Germany. Secondly, most former Nazis realized that the best way to ensure Germany's recovery was to link it to the leading Western power, the United States. If they privately entertained hopes that the pomp of Hitler's authoritarian Germany in the 1930s might some day be restored, they did so more because that would have vindicated their past efforts than because they thought that it was a more promising way. The brown-collared democrats of patriotic circumstance may not have been ideal democrats, but they did not endanger democracy either.

A comparison with East Germany is instructive here. In the east denazification of the highest levels was more thorough and lasting (there was clearly no comparable renazification), but the authoritarian socialist state offered a multitude of nondemocratic opportunities to its Nazi-experienced citizens. Those lower echelons showed themselves to be willing wielders of surveillance, mistrust, manipulation, denunciation, intimidation, and a host of other measures not congenial to creating a democratic society. The guiding socialist ideals played less of a role in shaping political culture than the behaviors the Stalinist leaders called on to achieve them.

Because known former Nazis in the West were under constant scrutiny by the domestic and foreign press as well as by several governments and (mostly Jewish) organizations, the recycling of known brown-collar experts in new government positions was less threatening to the development of West German democracy than the antidemocratic behavior of former Nazis who succeeded in concealing their pasts. German author Bernt Engelmann (a survivor of Dachau and other camps) coined the term "compelled democrat" (*Zwangsdemokrat*) for this type of nominal democrat. If such forced democrats were not known to be linked to the Nazi government, they had relative freedom to behave undemocratically in postwar Germany. In sharp contrast, former high-ranking Nazis in Adenauer's cabinet had to be careful not to poke into old wounds. An example for each case is instructive.

Theodor Oberländer, for example, was carefully watched for any signs of Nazi revivalism. Oberländer had been the brown-collared expert on Eastern European affairs under Hitler who had developed "resettlement" plans for Nazi-occupied Eastern countries. He held the analogous position as Minister for Refugee Affairs first in the Bavarian, then in 1953 in the West German national cabinet. When he was under fire for his past, even Adenauer was not willing to claim that he had been a "decent" Nazi, only that he had been "more decent" than some others.[98] When Federal

Minister for Refugee Affairs Oberländer planned to visit the last handful of his former cronies still serving time in Landsberg prison in December 1956, the Foreign Minister vetoed the idea with reference to foreign sensitivities.[99] In the early 1960s public pressure forced Oberländer to drop a defamation suit against a left-wing newspaper. Thus this former Nazi had to tread carefully, and his attempts to support right-wing groups or hinder left-wing organizations were not always successful.

The classic example of the unconstrained "compelled democrat" whose Nazi complicity was never widely known is Franz Josef Strauss. Strauss's disregard of democratic procedures became almost legendary. He was an early member and organizer of the conservative Bavarian Christian Socialist Union (CSU) in 1946, and deputy in the federal parliament since it first convened in 1949.[100] He became Federal Minister for Special Tasks in 1955, for Nuclear Affairs in 1955–6, and for Defense from 1956 to 1962, when he was forced to resign after having used his army and government connections to carry out a vendetta against the news magazine *Der Spiegel*, which had repeatedly reported his nepotistic transgressions.[101] By 1962 he had a string of "affairs" under his belt, including squandering huge sums of money for 10,860 Swiss tanks, commissioning Lockheed to add so many bells and whistles to its F104 Starfighter that it had to develop a new jet without many of the original's advantages, the government tank tracks commission that propelled his wife's "Uncle Aloys" from rags to riches overnight, and the "Finance Building" (FIBAG) housing construction scam, among others.[102] Strauss, however, did not have to lie low for long; he rejoined the federal cabinet again as Minister of Finance from 1966 to 1969; from 1978 until his death in 1988 he was Minister President of Bavaria.

Who was this Franz Strauss? He had not been involved in politics during the early Nazi years.[103] In the early 1930s he was valedictorian at the elite Max Gymnasium, excelling especially in Latin and Greek. In 1935 the 19-year-old was the southern German champion in bicycle racing. He began studying ancient languages and history at Munich University, completing the qualifying examination for state service in 1940. Army service prevented him from completing his dissertation in ancient history. He fought on the eastern front and was one of the few men who were flown out of Stalingrad before the German army capitulated there in February 1943. A few months later he received a permanent appointment as Nazi indoctrinator ("officer for protective leadership spirit," *wehrgeistige Führung*). He was a member of two Nazi organizations, one for students (which was not necessarily incriminating), but also a motorized squad that admitted only "thoroughly reliable National Socialists."

Strauss was captured by the Americans at the end of the war. Because of his excellent knowledge of English, however, he served as an interpreter instead of serving time as an internee. The Americans never found out that he had been a Nazi official with security of employment, so he did not have to be denazified. His efforts as aide–interpreter for the US commander of Schongau county, First Lieutenant Ernest Hauser, to soften that Austrian émigré's dictatorial rule, helped him to win the confidence of the populace and become Schongau's first elected county governor in 1946. He probably learned a thing or two from Hauser, who remained Strauss's close personal friend and was his contact at Lockheed during the 1960s' scandal about the F104 Starfighter jets. Strauss's ascent up the political ladder from local to Bavarian to national politics was astonishingly rapid; the patronage of CSU Party leader Josef "Ochsensepp" Müller, a one-time special prisoner in Dachau and thus above reproach from the left, contributed in no small measure.[104]

Thus the white-vested ex-Nazi Strauss was able to give his antidemocratic leanings relatively free rein, and he managed to bridge the gap between younger pre-1945 Nazi activists and a postwar generation of neo-Nazis who had little or no firsthand experience with the Third Reich. Strauss's support of the extreme right spans the history of the Federal Republic from the 1950s to the 1980s. In January 1953 Strauss agreed to be the featured speaker at a meeting of the "Circle of Former Members of the General- and Waffen-SS" in Munich;[105] in 1983 he was a supporter of the neofascist Turkish Hitlerist "Gray Wolves."[106] In his book *Second Guilt* Ralph Giordano analyzes in detail Strauss's antidemocratic preachings and the role they played in West German politics.[107] Strauss, in a celebrated outburst in 1969, gave West Germany's founding myths a classic formulation: "A people with these [great] economic achievements has a right not to want to hear any more about Auschwitz."[108] In the minds of such compelled democrats, the three myths live on: they see Germans as victims of the continuing public recollection of Auschwitz, they wish to remain ignorant about Auschwitz and all that it symbolizes, and they claim a "right" to resist such victimization.[109]

The victims of the 1950s: German POWs and expellees

The three founding myths were adapted to fit new circumstances and fulfill new needs over the coming decades. Strauss's victimization by the memory of Auschwitz was far less injurious than being locked up in an internment camp for years. A number of steps reach from one to the other. The first adaptation was already necessary in the early 1950s, when the victimization attributable to the Western Allies was drawing to a close. Denazification was, for all practical purposes, concluded during the year 1948,[110] the last trial at Nuremberg ended on 14 April 1949, direct military government ended with the establishment of the Federal Republic of Germany in the summer of 1949, and most of the convicted war criminals had been taken off death row or released by early 1951. Simultaneously, however, the Cold War offered another source of victimization: the Soviet Union, the generations-old Communist threat. The public West German self-identification as victims of Soviet injustice grew sharply when the Soviets closed all trade routes between Berlin and the western occupied zones from June 1948 to May 1949.

Thus in the early 1950s Germans were no longer victims of the Western conquerors, and two new groups of "victims" emerged: the German prisoners of war still being held by the Soviet Union, and the Germans who had been expelled or fled from their eastern homelands after 1945.[111]

Two commemorative speeches given in April 1951 in the Bavarian diet by Parliamentary President Georg Stang and Minister President Ehard indicate clearly that two groups ranked far higher in public consciousness than the victims of National Socialism: the military and civilian casualties of World War II, and the victims and refugees of the population displacements in the aftermath of World War II. Stang, now a member of the conservative Christian Socialist Party (CSU), had been the foreman of the committee that had investigated Hitler's *putsch* attempt of 1923, so that he was held in "protective custody" in 1933 and in KZ Dachau in 1944.[112] One might expect that he would have been less prone to make apologetic pronouncements about the victims of the concentration camps than other politicians. He conceded in his commemorative speech that the victims of racial, religious and political persecution under the Nazis were "admittedly . . . due to the date [of the liberation of the concentration camps] . . . at the forefront of today's ceremony. But," he continued,[113]

> we want to extend this hour of commemoration of the victims of fascism to include the memory of the armies of millions who breathed their last on the battlefields . . . In sadness on this day we also call to memory the thousands and millions of people who were buried in a hail of bombs . . . and we remember also the injustice that has been forced upon those expelled from their homelands.

The latter group, commonly known in German as *Heimatvertriebene*, referred to a very specific group of Germans and persons of German

120

ancestry who, after the war, had been forced to leave territories formerly occupied by Nazi Germany. In contemporary discourse the term did not include people deported or forcibly relocated by the Nazis, who were referred to by the Allied term "DPs" (for "displaced persons"). Stang went on to mention "sporadic" complaints that

> under the influence of our fight for daily life some segments of our people are again gradually beginning to become apathetic and disinterested, even callous towards the events [a euphemism for crimes during the Third Reich]
> ...
> But how much inhumanity, how much violence and terror, how much unfreedom and force has the world seen since 1945 as well! Was it not glaring injustice, for which the victorious powers are accountable, that with brutal force German human beings, members of the German Volk were torn from the native soil of their homelands ... Thousands of German brothers and sisters languish once again in concentration camps in the Eastern Zone today!

After Stang's speech, Minister President Ehard also underlined the "injustice caused by terror and naked violence ... after 1945," but he went into greater detail about the West Germans' relationship to their past.[114] He spoke explicitly of "our wish to eradicate the accusing reality of the concentration camps from the sorrow-afflicted history of our people," but warned that "hate and revenge" should not be allowed to fuel the attempt to "liquidate an ill-fated past." Instead, he suggested, the restitution program, although "inadequate," was the proper way to achieve that goal. For about half an hour he then described the services performed and aggregate amounts of money paid out to various groups under Bavarian *Wiedergutmachung* (making good again), as the program was known. Ehard's efforts to cast the compensation and restitution program in a more positive light were an implicit answer to the devastating criticism leveled at that state authority a few days earlier by Dachau survivor Alfred Haag in a meeting of 400–500 former persecutees in the Munich Collosseum (compare ill. 21).[115] Haag criticized the endless delays and bureaucratic hurdles raised by the Finance Ministry.

As this discourse of victimization reached its peak in the early 1950s, the blurring of the categories of victims even penetrated into the commemorative ceremonies of the former KZ inmates. The second Sunday in September had been celebrated as the "Day of the Victims of Fascism" in several German states since 1946. In 1951, the September date was celebrated in Bavaria as the "Day of the Victims of the War and Nazism," and a Protestant clergyman told a gathering of 800–1,000 persons that the organizers were not, as the populace thought, "exclusively Communists," but also people who wanted to commemorate "soldiers who had to lose their lives for Hitler's regime, as well as persons annihilated in their homeland by the aerial bombardment."[116]

This leveling of differences between types of victim had its counterpart in the federal government's effort to merge explicitly anti-Nazi commemoration with the more neutral commemoration of all dead. On the national level, in November 1952 the unpolitical, semi-religious "People's Day of Mourning" (*Volkstrauertag*) of the Weimar period was reintroduced. It replaced both the "Day of the Victims of Fascism" and the official "Heroes' Day" introduced by the Nazis in the 1930s.[117] While fallen soldiers and civilian war dead may legitimately be considered victims, their victimization was more or less coincidental, whereas racial, religious, and political persecutees were specifically and intentionally targeted, and their political goals were at the opposite end of the moral spectrum. However, this blurring of the qualitatively different categories of victimization served to mask the mythic redefinition of brown-collar criminals into victims. How and with what consequences did the creation of this homogeneous "victim soup" take place?

We will examine the German prisoners of war (POWs) first. In early October 1950, the West German government declared 26 October to be a national "Day of German POWs."[118] At noon all church bells in the country were to be rung and all traffic halted for two minutes. State governments were to organize and sponsor protest rallies. In Bavaria the government hurriedly made the necessary preparations (three weeks is not much lead time), and encouraged the entire cabinet to attend the central rally in Munich.[119] In 1951 the memorial day was expanded to a memorial week and moved up to the end of April, in fact to 28 April – 5 May, precisely the week in which the anniversaries of the liberation of the concentration camps were celebrated. Although negative publicity prompted the relocation of the "POW memorial week" back to late October in 1952, it remained one of only two national commemorative ceremonies with official government sponsorship from 1952 to 1957.[120] (The other was the anniversary of the 17 June 1953 workers' uprising in East Germany, a celebration of postwar German resistance!) Flags were flown at half-mast and traffic halted for a short time each year until 1955, when Chancellor Adenauer made West Germany's first official visit to Moscow and obtained the release of all remaining POWs.

Adenauer's September 1955 trip to Moscow was the culmination of a fascinating and unexpected turn in West German history.[121] As we will see, some of the brown-collar criminals among the prisoners Adenauer brought back with him provided one hinge between the forgetting of genocide in the early 1950s and the recovery of memories of the concentration camps in the second half of the decade.

How did the visit come about? There is some justification for the statement that West German sovereignty was born in Korea in June 1950, when Kim Il Sung's troops marched on the southern capital Seoul.[122] A year earlier Mao Tse-tung and the Communist revolution had gained the upper hand in China, and the future of Truman's policy of "rolling back" communism looked grim. Realizing that Germany would be one of the next battlefields if the Cold War turned hot, Western leaders wanted to be able to have West Germany's active military support in case of a conflict. Although French and British mistrust of Germany prevented the creation of a joint army in the European Defense Community, a path was cleared for Germany to join the North Atlantic Treaty Organization (NATO), which had been founded in 1949.

In 1950 Adenauer and US High Commissioner McCloy began discussing various scenarios of what could happen if armed East German police marched into West Germany.[123] First steps towards the rearmament of West Germany soon followed. In March 1951 the Western Allies revised the Occupation Statute that still limited full German sovereignty, and in July they declared the state of war with Germany to be at an end. (There could be no peace treaty since there was no all-German government that could sign it.) In the summer of 1951 veterans' organizations all over Germany sprang up and rejoiced in a literal flood of celebrations. At the largest such gathering, when 5,000 demobilized paratroopers met in Braunschweig, their former division commander stated the conditions for rearmament unmistakably in his keynote speech:[124]

> There will be no rearmament as long as (1) the defamation of German soldiers continues, and (2) comrades are held in Allied jails as prisoners of war. Under such circumstances the front-line soldiers of World War II will not be available as advisors, as experts, or as cannon fodder.

Such potentially revanchist convocations of veterans provided some strange commemorative bedfellows in November 1951. Three commemorative ceremonies in Berlin in early November 1951 illustrate the tension between German anti-Nazis commemorating the 1938 pogrom, unreconstructed German Nazis commemorating Hitler's 1923 *putsch* attempt, and Americans commemorating the armistice that ended World War I in 1918.[125] At the first event trade union leader Christian Fette appealed to the political leaders in West Germany to put an end to the "neofascist spook in West Germany," since former Nazis were becoming increasingly brazen on all fronts. Berlin mayor Ernst Reuter and author Luise Rinser echoed his warning. That same day in Berlin former SA and SS leaders donned their old uniforms to celebrate the anniversary of Hitler's *putsch* attempt and to renew their pledge of allegiance to the Führer, whom they called the "primordial foe of Communism." Two days later General Handy, the supreme commander of US troops in Europe, recalled the end of World War I in 1918. He told the US soldiers that they were now being called upon to put a stop to the Soviet Union, "that threat to the peace-loving world." Although Handy's sympathies lay with the anti-Nazis, his message supported the anticommunist Nazis. This constellation of events reflected the dilemma of Western policy in Cold War Germany: it was difficult to be antifascist democratically if you needed the help of fascist anticommunists.[126]

Re-creating the German army was fraught with difficulties for Adenauer, too. He was attacked by Christian pacifists ranging from Protestant Church leader Martin Niemöller to Gustav Heinemann in his own CDU Party, as well as by the traditional left-wing working-class rank and file and those workers organized in the German Communist Party.[127] The Social Democrats under the leadership of the cantankerous Kurt Schumacher (the inmate-librarian of the Dachau concentration camp) were not much help either, because even though they agreed to a defensive army and rejected the Communist bloc, they were not willing to pay for those objectives with the division of Germany.

At the same time, Adenauer was under fire from the far right, which found him far too accepting of the Allied judgments against German war criminals. His critics were resolute militarists such as General Guderian, a leader of West Germany's largest veterans' organization, the Association of German Soldiers (Verband deutscher Soldaten), which included the *Waffen-SS*, and even the not negligible number of incorrigible Nazis who were organized in the "Socialist Reich Party."[128]

In this difficult situation, Adenauer found a way to conciliate both sides. The Allied penalties against Nazi criminals were unpopular in West Germany, especially on the right, but also among mainstream figures such as Niemöller. The Western Allies wanted West Germany to accept the new occupation statute, so that West German rearmament could begin. Adenauer convinced the Allies that a large-scale release of convicted war criminals would help him gain the support needed for the ratification of the treaty. Over a hundred brown-collar convicts were released, and the

parliament promptly voted with Adenauer. Schumacher was angry and
called the treaty "a plump victory of the Allied-Christian coalition over the
German people," and anyone who voted for it "no longer a good German,"
but the course was now set. The mills of rehabilitation and government
strategizing churned on, and in the fall of 1954 full West German sovereignty was ratified in the Paris Treaties, taking effect on 5 May 1955. By
then the first recruits to the new German army had already finished their
training under the watchful eyes of officers, every one of whom had once
sworn unconditional loyalty to Hitler.

The Soviet Union, meanwhile, attempted to hinder this development.[129]
Before his death in February 1953, Stalin tried to avert West German rearmament and integration into the Western military alliance by sending his
famous three "notes" offering German unification, the first one on 10
March 1952. (The later overtures are generally believed to have been propaganda ploys to make clear to West Germany what the cost of its new alliance would be.) Stalin's successor Khrushchev took a more conciliatory
course and found the German POWs – the Soviet Union called them war
criminals, which many of them were – to be a useful bargaining chip. At
the Berlin four-power conference preceding the Paris Treaties, for
example, Khrushchev hinted about their release to improve his negotiating position. In January 1955 it was rumored that Khrushchev was negotiating the release with the leftist opposition parties in Bonn in an attempt
to weaken Adenauer's government. The West German government was
falling victim to its own overinflated POW propaganda, which made the
issue appear much more important than it was: in April 1953 Adenauer
gave the official number as 300,000 POWs; in August West Germany told a
United Nations commission on POWs that there were 102,958; by early
1955 Adenauer only spoke of 40–50,000 men, and finally, right before the
Moscow trip, the Bonn Foreign Office admitted that there were actually
only "about 9,000" men still being held.

At the end of September 1955 the Supreme Soviet announced the
release of all 9,626 Germans still in its custody. All were granted amnesty
except 749, who were to be transferred directly to the German (East and
West, according to place of origin) penal authorities. At first the West
German authorities let all of the men go free (as did East Germany, which
officially announced a full amnesty), but outrage by German Jews and in
the German press about Carl Clauberg, an Auschwitz doctor who had performed excruciating and lethal experiments on prisoners in an attempt to
develop a practicable method of mass sterilization, prompted the Bonn
government to reexamine the releases. It wavered and procrastinated in

the cases of two guards from KZ Sachsenhausen, Gustav Sorge and Wilhelm Schubert, but they were eventually arrested, tried, and found guilty of sixty-seven and forty-six murders, respectively, each of which was proven by witnesses in court to the satisfaction of the German judges. KZ doctor Hans Eisele's flight to Egypt in 1958 was prompted by the trial of another returnee, Buchenwald guard Gerhard Martin Sommer.[130]

These examples suggest how, in 1955–6, the positive political valuation of former Nazis slowly began to change: we will examine this process in chapter 7. First we return to some other consequences of the three founding myths in the first postwar decade: the criminalization of survivors, and the "cleaning up" of the former concentration camps.

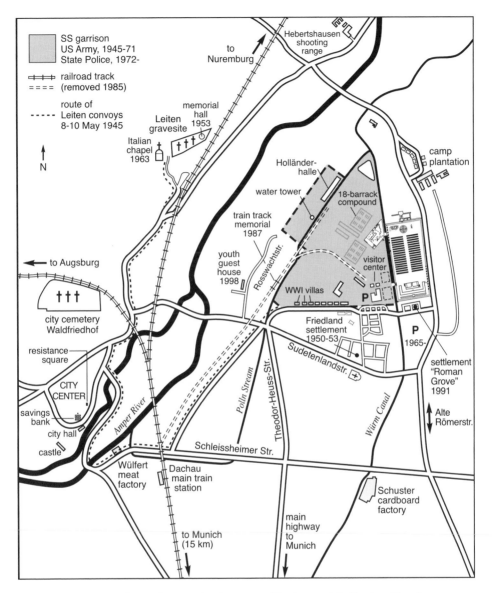

1   Regional map showing the city center of Dachau and the Dachau SS and concentration camp complex, about 3 km away. Among the twelve places in the community where Dachau concentration camp inmates worked during the 1940s were the Wülfert meat factory and the Schuster cardboard factory (drawing by Steve Brown and the author).

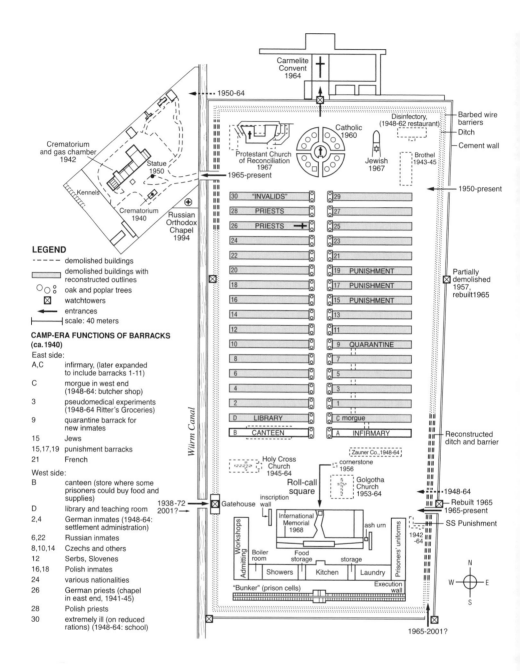

2   Plan of the Dachau concentration camp memorial site, showing original features and postwar changes, 1945–2001 (drawing by Steve Brown and the author).

3 Aerial view of the "residential settlement Dachau-East," 1956. About 2,000 people lived in the settlement at this time. Note the postwar factory buildings and churches on the roll-call square. The building that is cut off on the lower left side was torn down in 1985 (see ill. 75). The World War I *Holländerhalle* shown in ill. 67 is to the right of the water tower just above center on the left edge. The houses and buildings of the camp plantation are visible at the right edge, just beyond the camp. The missing and partially demolished watchtowers are visible in the camp wall at right. Note also the storage sheds that have replaced the barrier and fences between the watchtowers (Deutsches Luftbild, Hamburg).

4 *(above)* Aerial view of the KZ Dachau memorial site, ca. 1969. Note the memorial site entrance at bottom right, the reconstructed watchtowers on the right, and the ring of grass and trees around the cylindrical Catholic chapel at the far end (courtesy of Dachau memorial site).

5 *(above right)* The Dachau gas chamber–crematorium building, built in 1942, ca. 30 April 1945. The US soldiers are viewing the corpses stacked there during the final days of the camp. Note the smoke-blackened crematorium chimney (courtesy of Dachau memorial site).

6 *(below right)* Sign in front of the Dachau crematorium, fall 1945. The figure 238,000 "cremated" is incorrect. It was one of the early estimates of the total number of inmates registered in the camp (now thought to be about 202,000). About 35,000 deaths in KZ Dachau have been documented; additionally an estimated 4,000–6,000 Soviet prisoners of war were executed at Hebertshausen (see ill. 55) (courtesy of Dachau memorial site).

THIS AREA IS BEING
RETAINED AS A SHRINE
TO THE 238.000
INDIVIDUALS WHO
WERE CREMATED HERE
PLEASE DON'T DESTROY

7 *(above left)* The camp kitchen, shower, and storage building ("service building") at the south end of the prisoners' compound, 1946. The Nazi-era inscription on the roof translates as: "There is only one path to freedom. Its milestones are: Obedience, Diligence, Honesty, Orderliness, Cleanliness, Sobriety, Truthfulness, Self-Sacrifice, and Love of the Fatherland." Within a few years it was allowed to fade or was painted over. The cross in the foreground was erected by Polish survivors after liberation (courtesy of Paul Wasmer).

8 *(below left)* Sign marking the entrance to part A of the Dachau Prisoner of War Enclosure, run by the US army, 1945–8 (courtesy of Dachau memorial site).

9 *(below)* US soldier showing corpses found in the crematorium morgue to notables from Dachau, 8 May 1945 (courtesy of Dachau memorial site).

10   One of many posters displayed throughout Germany in the early summer of
          1945. The headline translates as "These disgraceful deeds: Your fault!" The
          text below: "You quietly watched and tolerated in silence … That is your
          greatest guilt – You are co-responsible for these atrocious crimes!" In
          German, the word *Schuld* means both fault and guilt. Germans thus
          understood such posters as accusations of "collective guilt." The first three
          pictures are from Dachau, the last two from Dachau branch camps (BaKo,
          Plak 4/5/5).

11 *(above right)* Courtroom in the service building, November 1945. A witness is
          identifying Franz Böttcher, one of the more brutal SS guards. Seated at front
          left is Martin Weiss, one of the camp commandants (who was known for
          having improved living conditions slightly); next to him with beard and
          glasses is Dr. Schilling, a professor who performed malaria experiments on
          inmates (courtesy of Dachau memorial site).

12 Postcard commemorating the first anniversary of Dachau's liberation, April 1946 (courtesy DDW).

13   Dachau mayor Josef Schwalber at the unveiling of a plaque on the savings bank commemorating the victims of the 28 April 1945 Dachau uprising, April 1947 (courtesy of Dachau city archive).

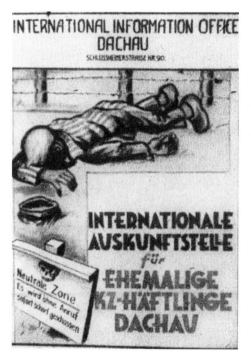

14

Poster for the Dachau International Information Office, 1945–6. The office was run by survivors who kept track of and gave identity cards and ration coupons to liberated inmates ("Album Dachau," ca. 1946, courtesy of Dachau memorial site).

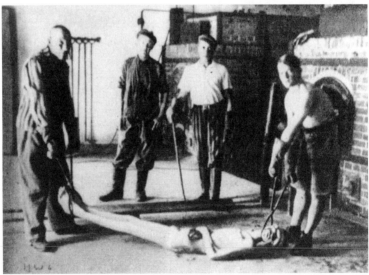

15, 16   Postcards sold in the Dachau crematorium museum, ca. 1945–8. The first depicts the entry gatehouse of the prisoners' compound, as seen from outside. Note that the inscription *Arbeit macht frei* ("Work makes free") has been removed from the iron gate (courtesy of Dachau memorial site). In the second postcard liberated prisoners who worked in the crematorium demonstrate how a corpse was placed on a crematorium stretcher. In early May 1945 about 800 of the decomposing corpses found at liberation were cremated under US auspices. The men who did the work were the same ones who had performed that task for the SS (courtesy of Dachau memorial site).

17   Exhibition in the Dachau crematorium undressing room, ca. 1945–9. Note how graphically the whipping horse punishment is presented (compare ills. 50, 51) (courtesy of Dachau memorial site).

18   Exhibition in a room of the Dachau crematorium, 1950–3. Note the less dramatic presentation of the whipping horse in front of the window, the preponderance of documents, also the urn of human ash and the prisoner uniform on the right (Preuss, *Remember That*, 1950 edn, 53).

SCHWARZ WIRD WEISS oder MECHANISCHE ENTNAZIFIZIERUNG

M. Radler

Springt immer rein! Was kann euch schon passieren,
Ihr schwarzen Böcke aus dem braunen Haus!
Man wird euch schmerzlos rehabilitieren.
Als weiße Lämmer kommt ihr unten raus.

Wir wissen schon: Ihr seid es nie gewesen!
(Die andern sind ja immer schuld daran — —)
Wie schnell zum Guten wandeln sich die Bösen,
Man schwarz auf weiß im Bild hier sehen kann.

J. Menter

19   This contemporary cartoon lampoons what was known as the
        "denazification laundry," 1946. The title reads "Black becomes white or
        mechanical denazification." The banner: "For one repentant sinner there is
        more joy than for ten just people." The vat: "denazificator, patent H.
        Schmitt" (the Minister for Denazification in the Bavarian cabinet who
        drafted a lax denazification law). Black sheep with weapons and Nazi
        uniforms jump in at the top and emerge below as white sheep with lilies of
        purity and crosses (*Simpl*, no. 6, 1946).

20   Letterhead of the Wülfert meat products factory in Dachau, 1940. Wülfert's
        factory used concentration camp labor. Although the prisoners were
        sometimes beaten, they liked to work for Wülfert because they had access to
        food. During denazification Wülfert was first classed as an "Offender," but
        then completely exonerated in 1949 (after Richardi et al., *Dachauer
        Zeitgeschichtsführer*, 238)

21   Concentration camp survivors demonstrate in Munich for speedier
        processing of compensation payments, 1950. The slogan asks Bavarian
        Minister of Finance Zietsch: "Should we wait for our compensation until we
        are dead?" (courtesy of Dachau memorial site).

22   Head of the Bavarian Commissionership for Racial, Religious, and Political
        Persecutees, Phillip Auerbach, at the unveiling of a monument at a rural
        mass grave site, May/June 1950 (courtesy of Dachau memorial site).

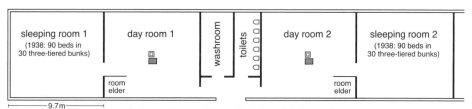

Schematic rendition of interior divisions of
concentration camp barracks,1938-45 (1/2 barrack)

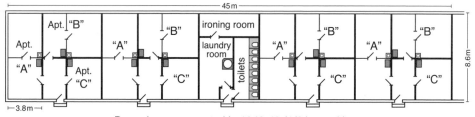

■ stove ▣ chimney   Barracks as renovated in 1948-49 (1/2 barrack)

23   Schematic floor plans of concentration camp barracks built in 1938 and
        subdivided as apartments in 1948 (Steve Brown and author after blueprints
        in DaA and BayHsta).

24   View of one of the streets between the barrack apartments in the "residential settlement Dachau-East" in the late 1950s (courtesy of Dachau memorial site).

25   Restaurant in the former disinfectory building in the northeast corner of the prisoners' compound, ca. 1960. A new owner renamed the restaurant "At the Crematorium" in 1961, and it was closed and torn down in November 1963 (courtesy of Dachau memorial site).

26   Partially demolished watchtower, September 1957. The sign reads "We want to get out of the KZ barracks into apartments fit for human habitation at prices that we can afford!" (courtesy *Dachauer Nachrichten*).

27   View down the central settlement street, ca. 1954, before street lights were installed. Note the Protestant church from 1953 at the end of the street on the left. In 1965 the church was moved to Ludwigsfeld, where it still stands today (courtesy of Dachau memorial site).

28   Demolition of the barracks with apartment subdivisions from 1948, 1964. The Bavarian government persuaded the survivors that it would be too costly, too dangerous, and not worthwhile to preserve the camp-era barracks because they had been modified so much (Photo Pröhl, courtesy of Dachau memorial site).

29   View down the central memorial site street as it has appeared since 1965, April 1983. Note the poplar trees that were replanted in the early 1980s (author).

30   One of the two barracks being reconstructed at the south end of the memorial site, 1965. Although the original barracks were constructed very simply with a life expectancy of ten to fifteen years, the new ones had cast concrete foundations and supports (courtesy of Dachau memorial site).

31
Sketch of artist Karl Knappe's proposed "Temple of Liberation," rear view. The semicircular rear wall of the memorial resembled the huge German octagonal national monuments erected since the late nineteenth century (*Süddeutsche Zeitung*, 26 Oct. 1945).

32 *(below)*
Model of "Temple of Liberation" for Leiten gravesite, November 1945. This monumental building was to be 35 m wide, and the 7 m disk atop the 28 m tall pylon was to be covered with gold mosaic tiles (LRA).

33 *(above)* Third-place entry in the 1950 Leiten competition, by Roth and Hiller. A simplified version of this design, without the arching cupola, interior columns or cryptlike substructure, was later constructed (*Baumeister*, Jan. 1951, 23).

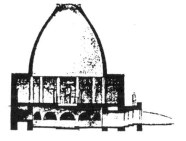

34 *(right)* Cross-section of the design for the Leiten memorial by Roth and Hiller (*Baumeister*, Jan. 1951, 23).

35 The 10.5 m tall memorial hall actually erected on Leiten hill in 1951–2. Today it is shrouded by trees (*Baumeister*, Dec. 1954, 796).

36 *(right)*
One of the temporary memorials erected at the rediscovered and provisionally marked mass graves on the Leiten hill, December 1949. This attempt to make the grave site appear respectable was part of the Bavarian government's effort to prevent further damage to its reputation after the accidental unearthing of some unmarked graves in the vicinity (courtesy Dachau memorial site).

37 *(above left)* Prisoner "pietà" by Fritz Koelle. This was the first design selected by State Commissioner Auerbach for a memorial at the crematorium in 1948 (courtesy of Dachau memorial site).

38 *(above right)* Statue of "unknown concentration camp inmate" (1.4 m), by Fritz Koelle, dedicated April 1950 (author).

39 *(above)*
Exhumation of the Leiten mass graves by a French medical commission, 1955–6. A French doctor devised a new system of forensic identification as part of the French effort to bring all French victims back to French soil (Georges Fully, "L'identification de squelettes des déportés morts dans les camps de concentration allemands" [MD thesis, Paris, 1955]).

40 *(right)*
Italian chapel Maria Regina Pacis (Mary, Queen of Peace), at its dedication in July 1964. West German President Lübke and Italian President Segni are descending the stairs (dpa).

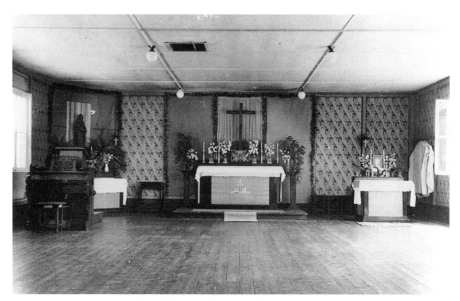

41   Concentration-camp-era Catholic chapel at the west end of barrack 26, ca. 1946. Note the Madonna on the left, which is now in the church of the Dachau Carmelite convent, as is the altar block (courtesy of Dachau memorial site).

42   Catholic church constructed on the roll-call square by interned SS men in November 1945. Note the gatehouse on the left, and the US-era watchtower on the right. The church featured an organ made of US army K-ration cans. The building was torn down in 1964 (courtesy of Dachau memorial site).

4

"Bad" inmates

For the overwhelming majority of the German populace in 1945, it was not pleasant to be confronted with pictures of the concentration camps. Encounters with survivors of the camps, if they were recognizable as such, often proved to be just as discomfiting. The survivors were living, speaking proof of the utter inhumanity and criminality of the regime that so many Germans had willingly served. In the psychological process of coming to grips with this evidence of their own complicity, many Germans followed the path of least resistance. As the Nazi horrors receded in time, most Germans did not question their own behavior, but simply reversed the postwar moral valuation of Nazism and its consequences. As we have seen, in public life barbarous Nazi perpetrators came to be viewed as "good Nazis" who had done their best in trying circumstances. Conversely, the survivors of Nazi persecution were reconceived as "bad concentration camp inmates" who deserved their fate. Just as denazification and the brown-collar trials had inadvertently fostered the perception that most Nazi Party members had been victims of circumstance, occupation policies intended to compensate for the injustices suffered by the survivors unintentionally fostered Nazi-era stereotypes of camp inmates as asocial parasites harming society and the state.

This negative stereotype has a linguistic reflection. In West Germany, survivors of the concentration camps (*KZ-Häftlinge*) were even in the 1990s sometimes still called "former prisoners" (*"ehemalige Häftlinge"*).[1] This term, although formally correct, reflects the notion that the concentration camps were basically prison camps, leaving open the possibility that some inmates were legitimately imprisoned. The less precise English term "survivor," in contrast, implies solely that the camps were death traps, while making no moral prejudgment of the inmates. (In France, by way of comparison, the survivors are known as "deportees" and "political internees," terms that are both accurate and morally neutral.) The German survivors called themselves "persecutees of the Nazi regime" or "victims of Nazi persecution," or, because they perceived the need to distinguish themselves from the small minority of common criminals who had been in the camps, "former political prisoners." The primary national organization of German survivors in the 1940s was the "Association of Persecutees of the Nazi Regime" (Vereinigung der Verfolgten des Naziregimes), known by its acronym VVN. In the early 1950s VVN members joked bitterly that it was now better to have been a "WWN," a *wirtschaftlich wichtiger Nazi* ("economically important Nazi"), than to be a member of their organization.

In fact, similar to the way in which Cold War politics paved the way for the rehabilitation of former Nazis, economic considerations played an important role in the renewed stigmatization, marginalization, and ultimate criminalization of the survivors of Nazi persecution. The stereotype of the "bad" survivor had two embodiments: surviving Jews came to be seen as flesh-and-blood incarnations of antisemitic stereotypes such as greedy black marketeers, while liberated political prisoners opposed to the renazification and remilitarization of West Germany were once again seen as "illegal opponents" threatening the new state's political and economic recovery.

This chapter retraces how, within a few years, the status of survivors in West Germany, the majority of whom were Jews or Communists, sank to the point where they were considered common criminals. We will look first at how government policy fostered the reestablishment of negative Nazi stereotypes. One of the most pressing problems for local authorities immediately after liberation was providing for the welfare of the survivors. Corresponding to denazification, the program developed to remove Nazis from the political realm, there was an inverse program designed to aid surviving victims – I use this vague term intentionally – in their reentry into normal social life. It was known as *Wiedergutmachung* (pronounced veederGOOTmakoong), which literally means "making good again."[2]

Helping the survivors: compulsion or compassion?

The Germans' first postwar encounters with survivors of the concentration camps took place in the context of liberation, when many civilians were forced to view the horrific conditions in the liberated camps, bury decomposing corpses, and even exhume mass graves. In the initial chaos after the very first camps were liberated, a small fraction of the survivors went on vengeful looting sprees in the surrounding countryside. In a remarkable collection of interviews conducted in 1946 in the vicinity of Bergen-Belsen by a Nazi journalist barred from her job, local residents reported stolen livestock as well as wanton theft and destruction of household furnishings.[3] In some cases, even rapes and murder were reported.[4] However, the Allied armies soon adopted a policy of confining the survivors to the camps until after the war when they could be repatriated, so that by late April 1945 German civilians had little to fear by way of spontaneous retribution. Nonetheless, reports of such incidents fueled fears in the populace at large, and as the events receded in time, such incidents were blown out of proportion to provide a retrospective justification for the original imprisonment of the camp inmates by the Nazi regime.[5] This phenomenon went so far that by the 1960s one author could characterize the survivors as "hungry animals let out of their cages; half-crazed by their newly won freedom, they thought that as persecutees of National Socialism they had the right to murder, rape and plunder."[6]

In reality, German civilians had less to worry about from marauding survivors than from outraged occupying soldiers who required them to supply clothing and foodstuffs for the liberated inmates.[7] In Dachau the liberating US forces installed Hans Zauner, who later claimed to have joined the Nazi Party in 1933 in order to remain on the town council, as acting mayor of Dachau immediately after liberation. Zauner described in his memoirs how in the first days the occupation authorities forced him to supply food for the camp survivors:[8]

> Shivers ran down my spine when I went at 9 a.m. to receive my daily orders and hear the new demands. For example, once I had to supply 30,000 eggs and 10 tons of potatoes immediately. The military government laid claim to all kinds of furnishings, among them a piano, eight radios, twelve armchairs, couches. They constantly threatened me with execution if I did not fulfill the demands.

He went on to describe how he distributed coupons for suits of civilian clothing to survivors, which exhausted the stocks of Dachau's two largest clothing suppliers. There are some indications that a feeling of obligation to aid survivors did exist among the German populace, at least for a time. Zauner, for instance, prefaced his description of the Allied demands by noting that citizens of Dachau and all neighboring towns, as well as private companies and local banks, all joined in to help care for the survivors by fulfilling the Allied demands. However, this behavior can also be explained as solidarity against a common enemy, for many local citizens reported having heard rumors that the Allies would shell the town in case of nonfulfillment.

Other evidence of voluntary assistance to liberated inmates is equally ambivalent. In late May 1945 the official Hamburg newspaper described under the heading "Small Gestures of Compensation" how in 113 towns voluntary relief groups had been established to collect food and clothing for survivors.[9] This claim of voluntarism cannot be taken at face value, however, since in the very next issue, the newspaper printed an official notice that in Hamburg every German male over 17 had to turn over to occupation authorities: "1 suit and vest, 2 pairs of socks, 1 set of underwear, 1 handkerchief, 1 blanket and pillow."[10] Such "donations" were required or ration cards would not be validated.

There is in fact strong evidence that especially in situations where Germans were personally required to make sacrifices to help survivors, the old negative stereotypes resurfaced. Some examples of this are shocking in their bald prejudice. At the Belsen trial in September 1945, one defense lawyer tried to excuse his client's brutality by explaining to the judge that KZ guards had to deal with "the scum of the ghettoes of Eastern Europe."[11] That same autumn a German Red Cross nurse who was directed to care for sick Buchenwald survivors complained, "Why should I care for criminals with tuberculosis?"[12] Former local Nazi journalist Hanna Fuess's interviews in the Belsen area in 1945–9 offer many further examples of such resentment.[13]

During the Third Reich millions of people had been deported and murdered at the whim of the government, and their personal funds and property had been confiscated. Hundreds of thousands of others had suffered physical disabilities and loss of livelihood due to hard labor, mistreatment, malnutrition, and atrocious working conditions; most of them received little or no remuneration for the work they had been forced to perform for the SS and private industry. They became "displaced persons," commonly known as "DPs." Many of these former KZler noted wryly that liberation had merely changed their acronym, but little else. There were an estimated 6.5–7 million DPs in Germany at war's end; by September 1945 about 1 million remained.[14]

Regardless of the extent of the sense of obligation towards liberated concentration camp inmates and slave laborers in postwar Germany, literally hundreds of thousands of them had to be fed, clothed, housed, and nurtured back to health. It was necessary to set certain standards of care and create structures that would ensure their implementation.

Institutionalizing aid: the origins of *Wiedergutmachung*

The first step in institutionalizing a program of assistance for survivors was to survey the existing ad hoc programs. Hans Schwarz, a political prisoner who had been inmate secretary of Dachau before his punitive transfer to Neuengamme, traveled through Germany in July 1945 to collect information about the local programs of assistance in various German cities. His report details how cities such as Berlin, Bremen, Frankfurt, Munich, Vienna, and many others, including Dachau, were distributing cash, clothing, double and triple rations, and housing to survivors.[15] Several cities also offered free medical care and assistance in finding work. Schwarz's report sounds guardedly optimistic and includes examples of cooperation between municipal authorities and committees of survivors. This honeymoon arising out of necessity did not last very long, however. As living conditions returned to a more normal state, and as the Allied rage over the conditions in the liberated camps faded, German authorities began to look out more for the interests of civilians like themselves than for the needs of the victims of Nazi persecution.

There were three different types of claims facing German authorities. Some of them were relatively straightforward, such as the *restitution* of property unjustly taken by the Nazi regime (known in German as *Rückerstattung*). This was governed by laws drafted by the Allied military governments, discussed with German authorities, and implemented in 1947.[16] *Reparations* to indemnify Allied governments for the costs of war were also stipulated by Allied decrees; they were circumscribed at a Paris conference in 1948. In contrast, the Allies left *compensation* for immaterial losses by individuals (in German *Entschädigung*) to be negotiated between the surviving claimants and German authorities.

The issues to be settled in the compensation program were quite complex. For instance, guidelines had to be set up to determine the monetary value of loss of livelihood and wages, education and opportunity, health and well-being, as well as compensatory sums for various periods of imprisonment or unremunerated labor. In cases of physical impairment, not only did the percentage disability have to be determined, but also the amount of it attributable to treatment by the Nazi government or its agents. Still other issues that needed to be considered were: was the injury permanent or temporary, and was it to be compensated in a lump sum or over time? How were families to be compensated for the murder of one of their members? How much was a human life worth? Was a man worth more than a woman? A doctor more than a laborer? A laborer more than a child? In many cases, entire families had been exterminated, leaving no heirs. What was to be done in such cases? Did it matter whether or not the crime had been committed on German soil, or where the claimant was now living?

The body of laws that evolved to regulate these thorny issues is exceed-ingly complex. In German, the programs of compensation devised to deal with such problems are commonly called *Wiedergutmachung*. This term has come to be associated primarily with payments that the West German government made to the Jewish Claims Conference and Israel in the 1950s and 1960s, but, as the titles of all major German books about these pro-grams indicate, it is commonly used to encompass all of the various pay-ments made to survivors of Nazi persecution (and their heirs).[17] It is important to bear in mind the euphemistic connotations of the word (in fact, the word was coined in 1919 as a euphemistic translation of "repara-tions," in order to sweeten the sound of the Versailles Treaty to the German people).[18] But monetary payments will never suffice to "make good again" the loss of one's health, loved ones, or community.

In the first postwar years even the institutional programs to settle the claims of the victims of Nazism were implemented on an ad hoc basis.[19] The attempt to standardize these programs in Bavaria was very serious and fairly comprehensive, but several intractable problems, first and fore-most the source of funds for such an entitlement program, postponed its implementation until the West German state was established in 1949.[20] At that time the Bavarian model was the one that was actually implemented nationwide. While the fiscal concerns of the German bureaucrats are understandable, they underscore the fact that in the minds of most German authorities financial matters weighed more heavily than moral obligations to victims of Nazi persecution. In fact, as the drawn-out debates about compensation payments to the state of Israel in the early 1950s show, conservative fiscal policy was far and away the most impor-tant reason opponents of the plan resisted it so tenaciously.[21] In the follow-ing we will examine some of the consequences the lack of firmly anchored institutional programs entailed for Dachau survivors. This debate reveals a great deal about the status of the survivors in German society.

The first Bavarian ordinance concerning compensation came not from a desire to right former wrongs, but was a by-product of the program to punish Nazi wrongdoers. On 5 March 1946 a law was adopted in Bavaria according to which assets of persons who had profited from unjust Nazi laws were to be confiscated.[22] When such confiscated monies began to accumulate in the summer of 1946, another law was drawn up by the Bavarian Ministry of Finance which created a "special fund for the purpose of compensation."[23] This was a convenient way to satisfy the obviously legit-imate demands of surviving persecutees without further burdening already overextended municipal budgets. This new fund was to be administered by two state agencies that had been established by cabinet order on 7 January 1946: a "State Commissionership for the Political Persecutees in Bavaria," and another commissionership "for the Care of the Liberated Jews."[24] The transition from the postwar ad hoc organizations to an official government institution was not unproblematical, however, as the conflict over the use of the first Bavarian convalescent facility for former camp inmates (*KZ-Erholungsheim*) in early 1946 shows.[25]

The facility was created by former political prisoners in a house donated by the Garmisch City Persecutees' Bureau and financed by donations. In his opening speech in February 1946 a representative of the Garmisch Bureau declared that through the donation of the house,

> the Bavarian people are paying off part of the debt of thanks that they owe to those people who, in clear recognition of the situation and out of idealism, opposed National Socialism, thereby often risking their lives and always forfeiting their health.

This must have been more an exhortation addressed to the general public to recognize that they owed a "debt of thanks" than a statement of accepted fact, because the representative went on to discount rumors (*Flüsterpropaganda*) spread by former Nazis that survivors were living off public funds. He explained that sojourns at the facility were financed by donations, hitherto primarily from former KZ inmates, although anyone could make a contribution. The former political persecutees, by calling on the German public to support them actively, were trying to improve not only their own material situation, but their status in society as well.

Most Jewish survivors, however, had no such idealistic desire to reform the attitudes of the German public. They had borne the brunt of the regime's oppression without so much as a hint of public (or even private) solidarity. Now some of their leaders saw no reason to be considerate of German public opinion, and they frankly stated their legitimate demands. Hermann Aumer, the first head of the Bavarian Commissionership for the Liberated Jews, was one such outspoken leader. He felt that Jews had just as much right to use the convalescent facility in Garmisch as the political persecutees who had set it up. In contrast, some of the former political prisoners felt overwhelmed by the enormous task of having to provide for the Jewish victims as well.[26] By the summer of 1946 considerable friction had developed between Aumer's office and the Commissionership for Political Persecutees, headed by Otto Aster, so that Minister President Hoegner considered dissolving the two agencies and having the social welfare authority take over their functions.[27]

However, events took a different turn because irregularities were discovered in Aumer's distribution of funds, and he was forced to resign on 13 August.[28] He was replaced by Philipp Auerbach, a businessman from Dusseldorf who had survived Auschwitz and the evacuation to Buchenwald (ill. 22).[29] On 15 September 1946 the two offices were combined into one "Commissionership for Racial, Religious and Political Persecutees" with Auerbach as commissioner and political commissioner Aster as his deputy.[30] Auerbach soon gained the confidence of survivor organizations across the political spectrum, including all of the major parties (CSU, SPD, FDP, and KPD) and an organization of Jewish Germans.[31] Under his leadership a certain regularization in the administration of the compensation programs took place.

In early December 1946 various representatives of racial, religious, and political persecutees from the US, British, and French zones met to discuss the necessity of supplementing relief efforts with a comprehensive program of restitution of property, compensation for unjust imprisonment, and remuneration for forced labor.[32] They recognized the need for a nationwide organization based on regional groups in order to lobby effectively for such a program. On 26 January 1947 Auerbach and Ludwig Schmitt, a medical doctor who had opposed the Nazis, called together various groups of German survivors in Munich to establish the Bavarian chapter of the "Association of Persecutees of the Nazi Regime" (VVN);[33] the next day a large congress of liberated Jews in Bavaria was held.[34] German public opinion with respect to the former persecutees had changed little in the year since the opening of the recreational facility in Garmisch. In his opening speech at the VVN meeting, entitled "What We Want," Schmitt decried the common misconception that concentration camp survivors were "criminals and welfare recipients" and declared that they only wanted "what we are entitled to."[35] But entitlement was precisely the issue that had to be settled, and it has remained a subject of heated debate right down to the present, when the end of the Cold War has given previously excluded Eastern European survivors the opportunity to voice their claims in West Germany.[36]

The separate congress of liberated Jews on the day after the founding meeting of the Bavarian VVN is indicative of their separate status as persecutees. While at first the political persecutees were subject mainly to guarded hostility or indifference, the Jewish victims were openly stereotyped and marginalized. The vast majority of surviving Jews in Germany were not Germans, and most of them did not wish to return to their native countries, such as Poland, both because their families and communities had been wiped out, and because they rightfully feared indigenous anti-semitism. In contemporary parlance they were classified as DPs and were quartered in camps run by Allied military authorities or the United Nations Relief and Rehabilitation Authority, UNRRA. In July 1945 US President Truman sent a commission to Germany to report on the situation of DPs in general and Jewish DPs in particular. The commission's verdict was damning: it compared conditions in the Allied-run camps to those in Nazi camps.[37] This celebrated "Harrison Report" brought an immediate improvement to conditions in the DP camps, but the negative stereotypes, both in the German populace and among some US army personnel, persisted.[38] The new American occupation troops arriving in the fall contrasted the neat, friendly German populace with the unkempt, sullen Jews in camps, while German civilians were preoccupied with black market activity that they attributed primarily to Jewish DPs. As it turns out, Jews participated in black market trading no more, and perhaps much less, than German civilians.[39]

The former camp plantation, 1947–1948

There are innumerable examples of such negative stereotyping and marginalization, but one particular confrontation between government officials and concentration camp survivors illustrates best both the mindset of most German civilians, and the process by which camp survivors first successfully combated their sinking status, but then were overtaken by economic and political developments and pushed to the margins of public life. That confrontation began in 1947 and centered around the former concentration camp plantation, the large agricultural complex carved out of the peat-rich Dachau moor in an attempt to make Germany independent of foreign herb imports.[40]

In Bavaria, all former property of the Reich that had been confiscated by the Allies was, upon return to German authorities, to be administered by the State Office for the Administration of Assets and Wiedergutmachung (Landesamt für Vermögensverwaltung und Wiedergutmachung, hereafter "State Holding Authority").[41] The camp survivors, however, wanted direct control over the assets they had created as slave laborers under National Socialist rule. In the spring of 1947 the Bavarian VVN, led by Ludwig Schmitt and Philipp Auerbach, selected the Dachau plantation to set a precedent that would establish the principle that all assets created by prisoners under the Nazis should become the property of the survivors.[42] The

plantation had been created after 1939 by imprisoned agricultural specialists and laborers, and in 1942, when all arrested clergy were centrally relocated to Dachau and their work exemption rescinded, it was worked by a
high proportion of priests. It was thus a clear-cut case where survivors
could stake a legitimate claim.

Since July 1945 several survivors of Dachau had been running the plantation, supplying farms growing medicinal herbs with seedlings. Since the
war the plantation had been administered under the trusteeship of Josef
Huber, who ran it with Richard Titze, a Dachau survivor active in the
Dachau chapter of the VVN.[43] The Bavarian VVN planned to incorporate a
business whose profits would go into a fund for the surviving relatives of
people who had died in the camps. In close cooperation with the VVN, in
June 1947 the Bavarian Union of Businesses for the Handicapped
(Landesverband der Versehrtenbetriebe, e.V.) petitioned the State Holding
Authority to have the plantation leased to a new corporation "Dachau
Medicinal Herbs, Inc." (Heilkräuter Dachau, GmbH). The State Holding
Authority refused, citing a letter from Military Government according to
which the "exceptionally valuable" scientific inventory of the complex
required that "the University of Munich or a similar institute of the
Ministry of Culture be given preference over private enterprises when
negotiating a lease."[44] Minister of Culture and Education Alois Hundhammer, however, was not satisfied by the prospect of a lease; he wanted
Munich University to gain sole possession of the entire plantation. This
was the point of contention between him and the VVN in the subsequent
debate.

In a barrage of letters to the Minister President of Bavaria in early
August, members and representatives of KZ care centers and regional VVN
offices (in 1947 the two were closely linked) contested Hundhammer's
plan with moral arguments.[45] They stated that because the complex had
been built by the "sweat and blood" of concentration camp inmates, they
had a "moral and material right" to the land and its proceeds. Because
many had died while building the plantation, the orphans of victims of
Nazi persecution were entitled to the benefits drawn from it. As an added
advantage of their plan, handicapped survivors of the camps would be
employed there. In a supporting letter, State Commissioner Auerbach
explained that the former persecutees would make the scientific laborato-
ries available to the university by lease, and he demanded in return that
"public proof of long-promised but never delivered *Wiedergutmachung*
finally be given." His letter in the name of 64,000 persecutees was co-
signed by representatives of the Bavarian Union of Jewish Communities,

the Bayerisches Hilfswerk (an organization of persons affected by the 1935 Nuremberg racial laws) and the political parties from the left (KPD, SPD) across the spectrum to the conservative CSU and FDP.[46]

In a memorandum to the Minister President in August 1947, Minister Hundhammer stated his case for the return of the complex to state possession.[47] Hundhammer ignored the moral claims of the camp survivors and limited himself to pragmatic issues. First he made short work of the supposed advantages of the former prisoners' proposal. It would never be possible to employ a substantial proportion of handicapped, he argued, because 95 percent of the plantation's present workers drew ration cards for workers or heavy laborers, and full mechanization would never be possible. Besides, a "universal" supply of medicinal herbs from the Dachau farm would never be possible – at best the complex could provide regional growers of medicinal herbs with seedlings. In the opinion of experts from the Ministry of the Interior and the university institute that was to receive the facility, Hundhammer wrote, the best use of the complex could be obtained by the university's Institute of Pharmacology, founded in 1935. As a fringe benefit, he continued, citing a professor of pharmacology, "the scientific utilization of the plantation should contribute to the rehabilitation of the name Dachau in a most objective manner." In closing, Hundhammer emphasized that if his ministry were given custody of the plantation, then "60 hectares [148 acres] of land would remain property of the State, instead of being given to a private corporation."

This letter is noteworthy in several respects. First of all, Hundhammer had himself been imprisoned in Dachau during the early months of the Third Reich. He had been a member of the Catholic Bavarian People's Party (BVP) and leader of a Catholic farmer's organization before the Nazi accession to power in 1933. Because of his anti-Nazi stance he was one of the first politicians to be imprisoned in Dachau, albeit only for a brief time. A staunchly conservative anticommunist after the war, he was one of the co-founders of the Christian Socialist Party (CSU) in Bavaria.[48] At that time Hundhammer did not see himself as a camp survivor. (However, as we will see, a decade later he became a leading figure in the survivors' struggle to establish a memorial site in Dachau.)

Second, each one of Hundhammer's arguments was deceptive. The ration cards did not imply that only laborers could work the plantation, because survivors, who comprised the majority of plantation workers at that time, were still entitled to workers' or heavy laborers' rations, whether they were handicapped or not.[49] No one had claimed that the plantation would be a "universal" supplier of seedlings, but it had been a very successful regional supplier since 1945. In fact, as Hundhammer indirectly admitted in his letter, earlier in 1947 a specialist from Munich's Technical University had given Huber and Titze's management his highest praise.[50] The self-serving plan of the university's Institute of Pharmacology to take over the plantation was later discredited when it was revealed that the institute was Nazi to the core, as was the professor cited by Hundhammer. Finally, Hundhammer's remark that Dachau's reputation would be rehabilitated belies the view that, with a few small adjustments, a model rehabilitation institution, the "clean camp" touted by the Nazis, might be created after all.

Once the hollowness of Hundhammer's arguments had been exposed, he was forced to address the VVN's moral claim directly.[51] He attempted to refute their claim based on the deaths and suffering of prisoners during the plantation's construction by quoting "Church sources" who asserted that the complex had been built primarily by imprisoned Catholic clergymen, and that the Church – to which he had excellent connections – had no reservations about his own plan to give the plantation to the university. Hundhammer now emphasized the moral advantage of his solution, arguing that as a university institute it would guarantee that "the use of the plantation . . . would benefit the general public and not serve the private interests of a few persons." This conception of the camp survivors as a small minority whose interests ran counter to those of the general public is indicative of prevailing public opinion at that time.

In December 1947 Auerbach tried to reach a mutually acceptable solution in a personal meeting with Hundhammer. While arguing reasons of principle (to set a precedent in the question of ownership) and ethics (the prisoners' suffering), he also appealed to Hundhammer's solidarity as a former prisoner, and enthusiastically agreed to lease the complex to the university.[52] Hundhammer remained unmoved. Immediately after the cabinet meeting of Saturday, 17 January 1948, Hundhammer personally called up the news agency DENA with the announcement that the cabinet had decided to give the plantation to his Ministry of Education. To confirm the report, DENA called up Auerbach, who knew nothing of the matter. Auerbach contacted another cabinet member, Minister of Justice and Deputy Minister President Josef Müller, who had served time in Flossenbürg and then Dachau among the "special prisoners," to find out what had really been said at the cabinet meeting. Müller immediately called up DENA and retracted Hundhammer's report. In a letter of protest to the Minister President, Auerbach first refuted Hundhammer's untrue claim that the plantation had been built by clergymen. In closing, Auerbach added one potentially explosive anecdote that the Minister

President underlined in red: Hundhammer planned to install Professor Ludwig Hörhammer, formerly a very active Nazi, as head of the university's future institute in Dachau.[53] Minister President Ehard also noted that Auerbach's offer to lease the facility to the university should be discussed at the next cabinet meeting.[54]

Hundhammer mustered his best arguments in the cabinet meeting of 11 February 1948. He tried to save face by conceding that the plantation had not been built by clergymen "in the beginning," but "afterwards almost exclusively." In fact, the gardens were begun in 1935 and the construction of the buildings in 1939, when nearly 1 million Reichsmarks were invested in the first six months of the year. Clergymen were not put to work in the complex until late April 1942.[55] Hundhammer related that Suffragan Bishop Neuhäusler, another of the former Dachau "special prisoners," had come to him (an improbable coincidence) to say that he, too, wanted the complex to go to the university. Neuhäusler had also told him that the present trustees and workers at the Dachau plantation were almost exclusively members or supporters of the German Communist Party. He claimed that they had already run up a deficit of 100,000 Reichsmarks by illegally distributing wagonloads of goods. Hundhammer then read aloud an unfavorable confidential evaluation of VVN chairman Schmitt that had been part of a review of Schmitt's application for a professorship at Munich University. To clinch his case Hundhammer concluded that it would be impossible for the cabinet to revoke a decision already published in the press. Minister President Ehard indicated his acceptance of the gist of Hundhammer's arguments, replying simply that the only problem would be to find a suitable means of satisfying "the legitimate interests of the KZ prisoners." Ensuring that, he thought, should be the task of the state, not the VVN. Minister Müller rebuked Hundhammer for playing groups of survivors against one another, but agreed with Ehard that "private" ownership by the VVN was not desirable.

Given this top-level consensus, ensuing protests by the survivors were ignored.[56] Hundhammer proceeded to draw up a lease between the State Holding Authority, which had finally obtained the complex from Military Government on 3 November 1947,[57] and his Ministry of Education.[58] Notably, proceeds from the lease were to be put into a fund "for the children of the victims of 20 July 1944" (the *putsch* attempt against Hitler by high military and secret service officials). This was Hundhammer's way of satisfying "the legitimate claims of the KZ inmates," even though the benefactors would have been the family members of a well-to-do elite that had occupied prominent positions in the Nazi regime. In May 1948, after discussion with Müller, Hundhammer changed that provision "in consideration of expected protest" to a fund for "surviving family members of victims of National Socialism." But at the same time he attempted to ensure that the survivors themselves would not be able to determine who received the funds: the proceeds were to be administered by, he suggested, an advisory council consisting of one member each from his own Ministry of Culture, the Ministry of Finance, the State Chancellory, the State Holding Authority, and, finally, Auerbach's commissionership. Aside from Auerbach's office, there was to be no representative of the potential recipients.

At the end of May 1948 Minister President Ehard replied that everything in the contract met with his approval and appeared "legally faultless and expedient" (implying between the lines that it was not morally impeccable); Hundhammer should appoint the advisory council as soon as possible. On 5 July Professor Hörhammer was called to the Chancellory, and it was decided that since Auerbach had not officially applied for a revision of the cabinet decision, the contract should go into effect. But Auerbach did find out about this attempt to present him with a *fait accompli*. He requested and received the help of Justice Minister Müller.[59] Two high officials in the Ministry of Finance, Ringelmann (a former persecutee) and Kiefer, called a meeting of all concerned parties at the plantation on 28 July 1948.[60] Ringelmann explained that due to some of its provisions, the Ministry of Education's contract could not go into effect. In recognition of the fact that the plantation and the two annexed estates were built by the forced labor of KZ inmates, the majority of the representatives concluded, "the whole complex should be put to use to compensate former persecutees." Josef Mayer, an assistant department head in Hundhammer's Ministry of Education, noted that he had tried to "get as much as I could for our ministry," but that he had been vastly outnumbered. Although "the entire former concentration camp Dachau" would soon be turned over to the state of Bavaria in accordance with Allied Joint Control Council Directive 50, an impartial legal entity (*Rechtsträger*) would be created to administer it. Beyond that, everyone received what they had wanted: Auerbach was given a credit of DM200,000 to cover costs arising from the currency reform and the need to modernize the complex (he wanted to set up a factory for the German condiment manufacturer Maggi),[61] and the university would be allowed to do research, teach, and rent the villas as dwellings for its employees. To keep formerly active Nazis out of the complex, Auerbach's office was given power of veto over the university employees working there.

This victory by Dachau survivors was short-lived, however. Broader political and economic developments in 1948–9, especially the US-funded European Recovery Program (commonly known as the Marshall Plan), made the enterprise unprofitable. As wages rose dramatically in other sectors, the former slave-labor plantation did not generate enough revenue to remain competitive.[62] It was closed on 1 April 1949 and the 400 remaining workers were dismissed.[63] The complex was later leased to the city of Dachau for use by its parks department; in the 1980s and 1990s the town has also used the buildings to house foreigners seeking asylum in Germany – the same use to which the former concentration camp itself was put in 1948, as we will see.

The founding of West Germany, 1948–1949

The period 1948–9 was a time of momentous changes in Germany. As the differences between the Western Allied powers and the Soviet Union became increasingly insurmountable, leading politicians made decisions that led to the creation of two German states in 1949.[64] In February 1948 the Western Allies initiated the process of drafting a constitution for their part of Germany. In July 1948 a parliamentary council was formed to draw up a "Basic Law" upon which a sovereign government could be based. (It was deliberately not called a constituent assembly to emphasize that its product would be temporary, and not a constitution for all of Germany.) At the same time, in April 1948, the US Congress appropriated funds for the European Recovery Program, which US Secretary of State George Marshall had announced a year earlier. Under that program, the lion's share of which went to Great Britain, France, and Italy, western Germany received $1.4 billion in aid from 1948 to 1952. Before that aid could begin flowing, however, a hard currency had to be introduced in Germany. The currency reform, substituting new Deutschmarks for the old Reichsmarks, took place in June 1948. It brought an immediate, enormous increase in the amount of goods available in western German stores, and it is a mark-stone in most people's memories of the period.

This western currency reform, which was essentially simultaneous with a monetary reform in the eastern zone of occupation, prompted Stalin to seal off all trade with Berlin, which was an island administered by all four Allied powers in the midst of his eastern zone. The Western Allies responded with an unprecedented eleven-month airlift, in which an average of over twenty-five flights per hour brought more than 1.5 million tons of goods into West Berlin. In the memorable words of French historian Alfred Grosser, in Western eyes Berlin was transformed from a bastion of Nazism and Prussian militarism to a symbolic last outpost of freedom and Western democracy in the midst of a Stalinist sea. Just four days before secret top-level negotiations brought this dramatic support effort to a successful close on 12 May 1949, the western Parliamentary Council presented its draft for the Basic Law. The western Allied military governors approved the draft the same month, and on 14 August 1949 the first national parliamentary elections were held. The new parliament, the Bundestag (federal diet), convened for the first time on 7 September, and on 15 September the delegates elected the conservative Christian Democratic politician Konrad Adenauer (1876–1967) to serve as the new Federal Republic of Germany's first Chancellor. The 73-year-old Adenauer received just one vote more than his left-wing competitor, the Social Democrat Kurt Schumacher (1895–1952), who was a generation younger and had been imprisoned for ten years in the Dachau concentration camp.[65] The selection of a conservative father-figure over a cantankerous concentration camp survivor parallels the choice West Germans made in ignoring the "dirty" Nazi interlude during the years from 1947 to 1955.

Skeletons resurface: antisemitic stereotypes and the Leiten Affair

In the summer of 1949, at the same time as these dramatic political developments were unfolding at the national level, figurative and literal skeletons from the past emerged in quite unsettling ways in Munich and Dachau. Their reappearance highlights the continuing processes of projection, unconscious repetition, and distortion of the past that had characterized the myths of victimization, ignorance, and resistance since 1945. Deep-seated stereotypes based on Nazi racial doctrines, forgetfulness of the barbarity of National Socialist rule, self-identification as victims of conspiracies perpetrated by camp survivors (especially Communists and Jews), a preoccupation with questions of guilt, repeated attempts of self-exoneration, and the unconscious use of specifically Nazi terminology in inappropriate contexts are some of the symptoms that came to light. Through all of this the image of the "bad" concentration camp inmate became more firmly entrenched in many West German minds.

At the end of July 1949 US High Commissioner McCloy said in a Heidelberg speech that the "Jewish question" would be "one of the real touchstones and the test of Germany's progress" towards democracy.[66] A commentator for Munich's *Süddeutsche Zeitung*, in anti-antisemitic intent, called on his readers to show "special consideration" for Jews living in Germany: Germans should not judge Jews based on the faults of individuals, nor on those faults which "that people might have in their over-cultivated breeding [*Durchgezüchtetheit*]."[67] It was not the antisemitic stereotypes manifest in this editorial that catapulted Germany onto the front pages of the international press, but the riots triggered by a viciously antisemitic letter to the editor that the *Süddeutsche* printed several days later along with a number of positive responses to the editorial.[68] When a spontaneous gathering of about 1,000 Jewish displaced persons began a protest march towards the *Süddeutsche Zeitung* that day, mounted German police tried to disperse them with batons.[69] The Jews responded with a hail of paving stones, and several police cars were set on fire or smashed. The incident did not end until US military police forced the German police to retreat.[70] The confrontation created quite a stir in the international public sphere, as *Time* magazine reported in late August.[71] The Bavarian government, the US Land Commissioner for Bavaria, and the US High Commission for Germany kept themselves busy during the next weeks writing reassuring letters to public figures and international organizations.[72]

When that controversy in Munich was at its height, the next scandal was already brewing. A sand-mining operation set up in March 1949 near the former Dachau concentration camp uncovered a communal grave in the early days of August, while the citizens of Dachau were celebrating their annual summer beer festival under the motto "The Other Dachau."[73] René Simon, a survivor of the Dachau camp who settled in the town after liberation, saw some skulls and human bones in the mining pit while taking a walk at a solitary hill near Dachau known as the Leiten (or Leitenberg), where the SS had buried several thousand KZ inmates in the winter of 1944–5, and where the US army had buried most of the approximately 2,000 corpses found in the camp at liberation. Simon took pictures of the skulls and skeletons he found and reported his discovery to the local VVN group, which informed the county governor (*Landrat*) and the Munich VVN headquarters.[74] The Dachau mayor, city architect, and cemetery director visited the site and decided that the newly discovered bones should be collected and reburied in the city cemetery, and that a fence be put up around the site.[75] Remarkably, the officials were not able to determine the exact location of the mass graves containing the corpses of the thousands of victims. The bones were removed and the site superficially cleaned up in expectation of a visit by 140 Austrian Dachau survivors in early September, but nothing else was done.[76] Even an inquiry from US Military Government's department for refugees was not taken seriously,[77] so that US Commissioner Bolds reprimanded Minister President Ehard.[78]

The Dachau VVN began to mobilize public opinion for a commemorative ceremony planned for 11 September, the "Day of the Victims of Fascism." It was clear to them that "the Bavarian government" will not take any action unless we push it energetically with help from the outside."[79] A press release brought immediate results.[80] On 9 September the *New York Times* and Germany's émigré-controlled national newspaper, the *Neue Zeitung*, printed large illustrated reports about the discovery of the bones.[81] Even though both were skeptical that the newly uncovered mass grave contained the remains of concentration camp inmates, both reported that the camp graves on top of the hill were neglected and forgotten; only a white cross and a yellow star of David marked the site.[82]

Commissioner of Restitution Auerbach pointed out in his commemorative speech in parliament on 11 September that the Bavarian government had spent RM720,000 prior to the currency reform and DM120,000 thereafter on the maintenance of KZ graves in Bavaria, and that workers were now digging trenches on the Leitenberg to determine the exact size and location of the mass graves containing the corpses of camp inmates.[83] The results of those excavations were followed closely by the international press, a fact that was in turn noted in the Munich newspapers.[84] Rumors spread as former SS men testified that up to 15,100 corpses had been buried on the Leiten during the concentration camp era, and an additional estimated 5,380 under American auspices after liberation.[85] At the end of September County Governor Junker discovered plans showing the exact locations of the graves – in his desk drawer.[86] For a time thereafter no more sensational discoveries were made and press interest diminished.[87]

The Bavarian government was planning to plant a commemorative grove and forget about past omissions when the French government, in response to public concern that the Germans were not treating graves of foreigners on German soil with proper respect,[88] sent an official inquiry about the Leitenberg to the German national government.[89] When an official French delegation visited the site in mid-November to prepare a report for a French parliamentary interpellation on 22 November, US Land Commissioner Bolds persuaded the delegates to postpone the discussion for two weeks to give the Bavarians a chance to remedy the situation.[90] Bolds then personally delivered a strongly worded letter to Minister President Ehard on 21 November. He pointed out that the "truly deplorable" condition of the graves was a clear violation of Military Government regulations, and continued:

> I cannot believe, Mr. Minister President, that the Bavarian government wishes merely to abide by *minimum* requirements in the maintenance of these graves but that it rather desires to do full honor to the dead of the Leitenberg, thus disassociating itself completely from the evil of the Hitler regime. Such a gesture, I feel, must come spontaneously and sincerely, and not through requests expressed by another agency.[91]

That same afternoon Ehard called an emergency cabinet meeting where it was decided that the three KZ survivors in the cabinet, Ankermüller (Interior), Hundhammer (Education and Culture), and Müller (Justice), would form a committee to take over responsibility for remedying the situation.[92]

One of the committee's first duties was to greet a second (unofficial) French delegation of parliamentary representatives who had also been imprisoned in KZ Dachau.[93] On 26 November 1949 Deputy Minister President Müller accompanied the group to the Leitenberg, where they interviewed, among others, some workers from the sand-mining firm, Zola Philipp from the Dachau VVN, Hans Schwarz, the general secretary of the German VVN, and Leonhard Roth, a Dachau survivor who had worked in the camp as a priest since liberation.[94] The delegation's report was even more strongly worded than Commissioner Bolds' letter to Ehard. The French Dachau survivors found that the graves were still not in a dignified condition. For instance, the only signs at the site read: "Entry prohibited – infested area," and "No trespassing – danger of infection"; no signs or memorials indicated the significance of the cemetery. The report concluded that Auerbach, as the responsible state official, had indeed allowed the "commercial exploitation" of the site, and it demanded that the former Dachau concentration camp and the Leitenberg be maintained as "commemorative sanctuaries . . . giving testimony to the crimes of the Nazis."

Auerbach responded to the accusation by denouncing the group as "communist." In an interpellation in the Bavarian state parliament on 30 November, Minister President Ehard called the communiqué "scandalous" and "a crime against the whole European cultural world," a formulation that echoes the condemnation of Nazi barbarity as "a crime against Western civilization," a term common at the time of the Nuremberg trials.[95] Whereas the communiqué mentioned only the "industrial exploitation" of the site,[96] Ehard polemically distorted the text and claimed it spoke of the "industrial exploitation *of the bones*," and when the press and Land Commissioner Bolds extrapolated this into "the bones of the deportees,"[97] they succeeded in turning the tables of public opinion against the French group. The negligent Germans now became the victims of an international conspiracy perpetrated by vicious communists who were perhaps even Jews – one newspaper described one of the more prominent members of the delegation in stereotypically antisemitic terms as "a small, hunched man with . . . shifty eyes."[98]

Although a visit to the site by Ehard, Bolds, Ankermüller, Hundhammer, and Müller on 2 December 1949 confirmed the findings of the French delegation and even reiterated some of its recommendations,[99] the US Land Commissioner, the Bavarian government, and high-level French government officials united to discredit the delegation. A third French delegation of survivors, headed by one of the most prominent French survivors of Dachau, Minister of Justice Edmond Michelet, arrived in Munich on 6 December.[100] According to the German press, the delegation's sole purpose was to present an "anticommunist counter-report" to the French National Assembly. The group inspected the site immediately after its arrival in Munich, asked Auerbach what measures would be taken against the responsible Dachau mayors, met with Minister President Ehard, and left.[101] Although the delegation emphasized that no one believed in the "industrial use" of the bones, it made quite clear that it considered the Bavarian or Dachau authorities guilty of gross negligence. When the largest Munich newspaper titled its report: "Bavarian Authorities without Guilt," the French protested energetically, and a new scandal threatened to break out.[102] The State Chancellory was, however, able to convince the editor of the Munich *Merkur* to print a retraction before the French parliamentary debate.[103]

The interpellation in the Assemblée Nationale on 13 December 1949 had far-reaching consequences for the future of all former concentration camps and gravesites of concentration camp victims in Germany.[104] Members of Parliament not only reported deplorable conditions in Dachau, but in Bergen-Belsen, Neuengamme, Mauthausen, and Hartheim (in Austria, where Dachau inmates had been taken to be gassed) as well. They also mentioned the discovery of another mass grave containing French corpses near Lübeck, and a neglected cemetery in Bremen.[105] Minister Michelet expressly confirmed the report of the second ("communist") delegation, although he reproached its members for not having been more unambiguous in the wording of their communiqué. Michelet made a strong impression when he read aloud a letter he had received from the daughter of a French politician who died in Dachau in the winter of 1944–5. The young woman deplored the condition of the Leitenberg and criticized the inaccessibility of the Dachau crematory and camp complex. The entire assembly was outraged because Minister President Ehard had publicly said that he would have "chased them [the survivor delegates] out of his office" if he had known what they were going to report about their inspection. When a delegate suggested that the most important concern of the assembly should be to preserve the dignified memory of the French victims and the good reputation of the survivors, he received applause from all sides.

The French National Assembly unanimously passed a resolution calling on Foreign Minister Robert Schuman to "indignantly protest the sacrilegious incidents relating to the Dachau camp," and to implement measures ensuring the conservation as memorial sanctuaries of the crematoria in Dachau and all sites where the remains of victims of Nazi barbarism are discovered. Schuman included the latter demand as a supplement to the "Protocol on the Termination of the Occupation Regime in the Federal Republic of Germany," signed in Paris in October 1954 (just in time to prevent the demolition of the crematorium in the summer of 1955, as we will see below).[106] In a press release immediately following the French debate Minister President Ehard, in his eagerness to exonerate his officials, claimed that Schuman had determined that bones of KZ victims had *not* been "shamelessly profaned"; in fact, Schuman had stated precisely the opposite.[107]

The French parliamentary interpellation forced the Bavarian government finally to realize that it would have to take serious action. On 9 December it was decided that the Leitenberg gravesite was to be landscaped and rededicated in a ceremony on 16 December (ill. 36).[108] The entire cabinet was invited, as were all members of both houses of parliament, all foreign diplomats and representatives of the Allies in Munich, the mayors and deputy mayors of Munich and Dachau, the rectors of both Munich universities, chiefs and deputy chiefs of the city and state police, representatives of more than twelve private organizations, forty-one photographers, radio and newspaper journalists – a total of 149 personal invitations were sent out.[109] The announcement of the invitation in the lower house of the Bavarian parliament triggered a discussion in which a conservative representative who had seen the concentration camp for the first time a week earlier called for the creation of an educational memorial site open to all Germans. He confessed:[110]

> I would not have believed it if someone had [merely] told me about what I saw with my own eyes. Thus the gentlemen of the Landtag and the Senate, and later the entire population should look and see . . . These places must be made accessible for viewing by the German and Bavarian peoples.

By 1963 similar sentiments in a majority of Bavarian parliamentary delegates would ensure passage of a bill calling for state support of school classes wishing to visit the newly created Dachau museum. However, much still had to happen in the intervening thirteen years.

The ceremony itself, with speeches by Bishop Neuhäusler, Protestant Bishop Daumiller, and Rabbi Ohrenstein,[111] served to quiet the waves of international publicity until mid-January, when the report of the official US–Bavarian joint investigation was published.[112] The primary question remained not one of responsibility, but, as the contemporaries phrased it, guilt – an indication that the rediscovery of the mass graves on the Leitenberg reopened traumatic wounds in the German psyche. On the morning of the dedication ceremony in December, the Dachau town newspaper printed a report about a discussion in the county chamber (*Kreisrat*) under the headline: "County Governor and Mayor Are Not Guilty!"[113] The quote was taken from a resolution passed by the council two days earlier, based solely on the county governor's and mayor's own testimony. In that discussion council members had found others to blame: the VVN was "also guilty," claimed Councilman Wittmann, a former supporting member of the SS and owner of property on the Leiten, because it could have approached the responsible authorities long ago.[114] Councilman Weiss declared that the "primary guilt" (*Hauptschuld*) rested on the shoulders of "certain KZ inmates who were still sitting in Dachau and who dealt on the black market from 1945 to 1949 instead of commemorating their dead."

This language reveals what the council members did not want to admit: their own feelings of guilt (the VVN was "also" guilty);[115] their rejection of denazification (*Hauptschuldige* was the German translation of the category "major offenders" in denazification); their antisemitic prejudice (the black market was firmly identified with Jews); and their subconscious preoccupation with the systematic genocide practiced by Germany – County Governor Junker used the term "final solution," the Nazi euphemism for the systematic murder of the Jews, when he referred to resolving the Leiten problem.[116]

Senate President Walter finished the Bavarian governmental investigation of the Leiten Affair in early January 1950. After parts of his report were leaked to the press, the State Chancellory decided that it would be better to make the whole document public, and distributed it to the press on 18 January.[117] The three Munich newspapers noted with great relief that no one was guilty of intentional negligence, and under the heading "The Examination of the Question of Guilt," the Dachau newspaper emphasized that the town had done almost everything possible to maintain the graves, although it conceded that the local authorities should not have "waited idly for years" for the state government to erect a monument.[118] Both Dietrich Sattler, the official in the Ministry of Culture responsible for the Leiten monument, and Auerbach, whose office oversaw the care of KZ and Jewish cemeteries, sent long but unconvincing letters to the Minister President explaining why they had remained inactive in the Leiten matter for so long.[119] In the final analysis it was quite clear that none of the state or local officials had cared enough to do anything when opportunities had presented themselves.[120]

As the creation of a new Leiten graveyard progressed during the first half of 1950, other "forgotten" mass graves of KZ victims continued to be uncovered, for example near Hersbruck in Franconia in late January.[121] When on 1 February the Bavarian cabinet decided to hold a design competition for a "memorial hall representing the religious and national idea of sacrifice on behalf of peace," the *Süddeutsche Zeitung* reported with a telling Freudian slip that the government was planning to erect a "crematorium" over the graves.[122] But that was not all. When the results of a US investigation of the age of the few skeletons discovered in August were made public in March, the announcement that they had no connection whatsoever to the concentration camp immediately gave rise to rumors that the entire Leitenberg would no longer be preserved as a memorial site. The rumors were so widespread that the press felt compelled to formally discount them – even though in the intervening months dozens of official reports, proclamations, and newspaper articles had presented incontrovertible evidence that there were also thousands of victims of the camp buried on the Leiten.[123] Since the German press interpreted the report about the original human bones to mean that the whole incident had been a lot of to-do about nothing, US Land Commissioner Bolds issued a supplementary press release stating that, as far as the other mass graves on the Leiten were concerned, "not enough attention had been paid to the careful burial of the mortal remains of KZ inmates."[124] Still dissatisfied with the complacent attitude of the authorities, Bolds reiterated his reproach in an open letter to Ehard in April 1950.[125]

Sensing that another scandal was brewing, the Bavarian authorities redoubled their efforts to make the cornerstone-laying of the new memorial hall a public relations success. The ceremony itself was planned for 30 April, with a special program on the state radio station and a reception for Dachau survivors from abroad the evening before.[126] During the week preceding the events, 500 posters announcing the event were put up on billboards and in public buildings in Munich, and five movie theaters in Munich and one in Dachau displayed a slide of the poster during the pre-film advertisements. The list of invitations was similar to that for the dedication ceremony on 16 December, except that this time the national government and representatives of German and foreign organizations of survivors were included.[127] The composition of the audience in April, however, differed markedly from that in December: whereas the members of the Bavarian government and parliament had been more numerous at the earlier dedication, delegations of foreign survivors were in the vast majority in the spring. Among the approximately 3,000 Dachau survivors who attended were groups from Austria (with Federal Chancellor Figl), Belgium (fifty-eight persons including Albert Guérisse, head of the International Prisoners' Committee), France (twenty-five with Minister of Justice Michelet), Luxembourg, the Netherlands, England, Norway, and Sweden.[128] The event itself was similar to the dedication in December, with the speeches by the same three clergymen at the Leiten cemetery, and a ceremony at the Dachau camp crematorium afterwards, where Auerbach, Land Commissioner Bolds, Eugen Kogon, and Michelet spoke after Ehard unveiled the statue of the "unknown concentration camp inmate" (ill. 38).[129]

The efforts of the Bavarian state to salvage its tarnished reputation were not limited to these commemorative ceremonies. For the landscaping of the Leitenberg and the construction of the planned memorial hall the Bavarian parliament set aside the enormous sum of DM600,000.[130] Most of the 493 gravesites of KZ victims in Bavaria were inspected, and the vast majority of them required extensive work.[131] In a logistical *tour de force* in mid-June Auerbach dedicated thirty-five of these sites in a two-day marathon with speeches and ceremonies in each village (ill. 22).[132] A somewhat more serious event was the opening of a new museum in the Dachau crematorium on 10 September 1950, the "Day of the Victims of Fascism."[133] This new exhibition was far less graphic than its predecessor in 1945 had been (ill. 18). Bavarian officials spared no costs to improve their image: a car was purchased to take visitors from the crematorium to the Leiten;[134] the Bavarian state built a street from the Römerstrasse (near the plantation) to the crematorium so that visitors would no longer have to enter the US military camp in the former SS complex;[135] and DM12,000 from state funds was given to noncommunist Dachau survivors to support their activities.[136]

These measures successfully banished the unpleasant resurfacing of the past from public awareness, for only a few months later state and local officials began a clandestine but then increasingly open dismantling of the Dachau memorial sites that had so hastily been created. As we will see, this dismantling took place against a background of marginalization and even criminalization of concentration camp survivors that had begun some years earlier.

Anticommunism and the criminalization of the survivors, 1949–1953

In 1947–8, during the struggle over control of the Dachau plantation, the status of concentration camp survivors in the West German public sphere was already beginning to wane. In January 1947 the VVN had been organized so that the survivors could be proactive in their struggle for social recognition; by 1948 the organization was clearly on the defensive. In January of 1948, for instance, the Bavarian parliament passed a law concerning household items that entitled former Nazis to enlist police aid when reclaiming goods confiscated from them and given to camp survivors.[137] In December 1948 former Bavarian Minister President Wilhelm Hoegner, who had escaped the Nazis by emigrating to Switzerland,[138] warned in parliament that concentration camp survivors were experiencing "a new persecution" because most of the measures implemented for their rehabilitation immediately after the war had since been reversed.[139] In July 1949 emergency motions by the SPD in the Bavarian parliament called for concrete measures to "curb neo-National Socialist activities," as well as for laws to finally establish specific guidelines for the *"Wiedergutmachung* of National Socialist injustice."[140] In that same July 1949 debate, a report on the rehiring of denazified officials was discussed. As of 31 December 1947, there had been 105,000 state officials and employees in Bavaria. At that time, nearly one-third (33,000) were former members of the Nazi Party, while just over 1 percent (1,092) were former political persecutees or Jews. It was assumed that since then, because of maneuvering by ex-Nazi colleagues made uncomfortable by the presence of survivors, only a fraction of this already tiny proportion were still employed in 1949.[141] Since former Nazis felt most comfortable amongst themselves, they tended to be concentrated in certain departments – the smaller, the more concentrated. According to another statistic, in March 1950 84 percent of the 924 Bavarian judges and public prosecutors were former Nazis, 77 percent of the 1,918 employees of the Ministry of Agriculture, and 60 percent of the 5,000 employees of the Ministry of Finance.[142] In contrast, at that time 60 percent of all former persecutees in Bavaria were unemployed.

For German politicians who were primarily concerned with the material reconstruction of society and the state within the framework staked out by the Cold War, the survivors organized in the VVN represented a bothersome force. Not only did the VVN support policies advocated by the German Communist Party (KPD), such as the unification of all four zones of occupation into a new German state and the rejection of the remilitarization of West Germany, but VVN members had a moral authority that could penetrate the mantle of legitimacy cloaking the old–new political elite, especially in the eyes of the international public. The latent enmity between the two groups became public as soon as Western Allied policy shifted from the punishment of compromised German elites to their recruitment as allies against the Soviet Union. Thus the shift in Allied priorities facilitated the German tendency to perceive concentration camp survivors as "bad" inmates.

In 1948 the established political parties began to ostracize the VVN. On 6 May 1948 the executive committee of the German Social Democratic Party (SPD) resolved that no SPD member could also be a member of the VVN.[143] For about a year, the SPD had difficulty enforcing this decree because at the grass roots former persecutees continued to work together in spite of the organizational separation,[144] and because some more visible SPD members (such as Philipp Auerbach) preferred to resign from the SPD and remain members of the VVN.[145] But by the time the concrete preparations for the establishment of the West German Federal Republic had begun in the spring of 1949, many of these stalwart VVN supporters had resigned from the VVN to join the SPD's newly established surrogate organization for former persecutees, the "Association of Persecuted Social Democrats" (Arbeitsgemeinschaft verfolgter Sozialdemokraten, AvS). The Christian Democratic parties CDU/CSU followed suit in February 1950 by requiring their members who were also in the VVN to quit that organization and join their own newly founded group, the "Union of Persecutees of the Nazi Regime" (Bund der Verfolgten des Naziregimes, BVN).[146]

In September 1950 the federal government decreed that members of the VVN could not be employed by the state (known as *Berufsverbot*, "prohibition of employment"), and in April 1951 it prohibited a national referendum on the question of remilitarization – an action carried out by the KPD and a number of grass roots organizations, including the VVN. From that decree it was only a short step for regional governments to outlaw the VVN for carrying out unconstitutional activities,[147] or to place it and suspected co- or successor organizations under the surveillance of police spies, as the Munich police had begun to do in February 1951.[148] In November 1951 the federal government applied to the Federal Constitutional Court to rule on the constitutionality of the activities of the KPD. After a series of aggressive measures, such as the confiscation of all KPD files in January 1952, the proceedings began in November 1954. The court ruled against the KPD in July 1955, resulting in an executive prohibition of the party in August 1956.[149] After the loss of its SPD and CDU members to the AvS and BVN in 1949–50, primarily members of the KPD were left in the VVN. The West German government thus imposed the same sanction against the primary organization of German concentration camp survivors that the Allies had imposed on activists of the Nazi Party and some of its organizations.

With time, the anticommunist government propaganda began to affect the solidarity of camp survivors. The first signs of a split between communist and noncommunist members of the VVN became visible in 1949. In May, Bavarian Commissioner of *Wiedergutmachung* Auerbach resigned from the VVN at a major commemorative ceremony in Hamburg because VVN members from the Soviet zone had criticized Hamburg's SPD mayor Max Brauer for attempting to prohibit the VVN's ceremony. Auerbach, who had resigned from the SPD when given an ultimatum by the regional SPD leadership in December 1948, thus reversed his decision and rejoined the Social Democrats in May 1949.[150] During the entire Leiten Affair in the fall of 1949 he and the VVN obstructed each other's work, even though they had several common goals. For example, Auerbach worked very hard to discredit the VVN commemorative ceremony on 15 April 1950 as "communist competition,"[151] and to exclude VVN members from the state commemoration he organized on 30 April.[152] In 1949 and 1950 commemorative ceremonies for the victims of fascism in other West German cities were also marred by anticommunist activities.[153]

Once the bad international publicity due to the Leiten scandal had been dispelled by massive public relations efforts in 1950,[154] the Bavarian state began to harass oppositional groups of former persecutees systematically. Early in 1951 Dachau survivors organized in the "Dachau Association" (Arbeitsgemeinschaft Dachau, AG Dachau) began planning a ceremony on 15 April in Munich and Dachau to commemorate the liberation of the concentration camps. To raise funds for that event, on the anniversary of the mass arrests of 10 March 1933 the AG Dachau planned to show a film entitled *War on War* that had been produced by the Vatican. Based on a decision by the Bavarian Ministry of the Interior of 1 February 1951, the AG Dachau was considered a "surrogate organization" of the VVN, and was thus *per se* not allowed to exercise the constitutionally guaranteed right of freedom of assembly.[155] After several futile attempts to contact higher

police authorities who could annul the prohibition, the AG Dachau persuaded the 300 persons who had come to see the film to disperse without
incident.[156]

As the prohibitions of the KPD and VVN spread to other West German
states, the Munich police became bolder and dispersed several events
organized by former persecutees, for instance a Christmas celebration
sponsored by the "Interest Group of the Survivors of Victims of the Nazi
Regime" (Interessengemeinschaft der Hinterbliebenen der Opfer des
Naziregimes) that was co-organized by several VVN members on 22
December 1951.[157] The police reasoned contortedly that they finally "had
to" disperse the meeting,

> because up to that point no Christmas song had been sung as is usually
> practiced in German Christmas celebrations, and because the celebration
> rather conveyed the sad image of Christmas as it is celebrated in Russia, it
> had to be judged as a purely political event.

A girls' choir had sung "The Little White Dove of Peace" (a popular children's song) and recited poems on the theme of peace, and a political
spoof about the behavior of Eastern and Western bloc statesmen at a
United Nations conference emphasized peaceful international relations
as well. World peace was apparently not an appropriate Christmas theme,
so shortly after the distribution of gifts the police ordered the 300 people
participating in the gathering, including fifty children, to go home.

In 1951 even skillful organization and the fresh memory of the Leiten
Affair could not overcome the mass media's disregard of events organized
by survivors of the concentration camps. Hans Schwarz, an Austrian who
had been imprisoned in Dachau for political reasons and transferred to KZ
Neuengamme near the end of the war because of oppositional activities
within the Dachau camp (he had been the *Lagerschreiber*, one of the
highest prisoner functionaries), appealed to Bavarian Minister of Justice
Josef Müller to use his influence in the cabinet to support the commemoration of the sixth anniversary of Dachau's liberation on 15 April
1951. Schwarz, who was both secretary of the VVN national council and
president of the AG Dachau, began by thanking Müller for his help against
defamation attempts during the Leiten Affair.[158] Müller, one of the co-
founders of the Bavarian CSU, was an arch-rival of his CSU compatriot,
the anticommunist Hundhammer. Müller publicly maintained contacts
with his communist friends.[159] Schwarz pointed out that a number of
foreign visitors were expected at the planned event, so that a prohibition
would be an "unbelievable shame" for Bavaria.[160]

Schwarz was able to gain Müller's support, and the ceremony was well attended, at least by Dachau survivors. Eight hundred survivors were in attendance at the ceremony in the conference hall of the German Museum in Munich on 15 April 1951.[161] West and East German, Dutch, French, and Austrian speakers emphasized the solidarity of concentration camp survivors from all countries and renewed their commitment to the fight for "peace, freedom, and understanding among peoples." They also unanimously condemned the remilitarization of West Germany and Western Europe under NATO. The public, however, took little notice of the event. The main Munich newspaper printed a brief report that characterized the meeting as a "poorly attended" gathering of Communists; liberal use of quotation marks around central concepts mentioned at the event (e.g. "communist fighters for peace," "the readiness for peace of the Eastern countries") tinged the report with irony. Finally, the concluding sentence underlined the unimportance of the gathering by degrading it to a prelude of the government's ceremony: "The official celebration of Liberation Day by the State Government will take place on 29 April."[162] That "official" ceremony consisted solely of a performance of Mozart's *Magic Flute* with free admission for all persons registered with the State Commissionership for Racial, Religious, and Political Persecutees.[163] Parliament had already decided not to hold a special memorial session on 29 April 1951, but to have a short commemorative ceremony prior to the regular session on 24 April instead.[164]

The survivors disappear from public view, 1950–1953

The effect of the reconceptualization of the concentration camp survivors as criminals and threats to the state, and of the rise of former Nazis to positions of power in government was the increasing disregard of the survivors by both governmental authorities and the general public. At the first major commemorative ceremony held by former persecutees in Munich and Dachau after the Leiten scandal, the aforementioned VVN ceremony on 15–16 April 1950, Munich head mayor Thomas Wimmer greeted the Dachau survivors in Munich, and Bavarian Minister of Justice Josef Müller spoke at the Leiten cemetery, but there was no official governmental support of the various events, and public officials with no personal connections to camp survivors, such as Dachau's Mayor Zauner and County Governor Junker, were conspicuous in their absence, which was noted by the participants, the speakers, and the state police. The latter reported that among the 700–800 participants, "noted persons of public life and representatives of state authorities were not to be seen. The populace of Dachau took very little note of this commemorative ceremony."[165]

The state-sponsored commemorative events in April 1950 in the wake of the Leiten Affair were but a brief interlude in the tacit policy of official disregard in the early 1950s, and even in those cases interest from the broader populace was not forthcoming. The Bavarian government's commemorative ceremony at the Leiten graves on 30 April 1950 was attended almost exclusively by the prominent persons personally invited by Minister President Ehard.[166] In order to avoid such an embarrassing situation, Philipp Auerbach devised a new strategy for his marathon two-day dedication tour of thirteen newly landscaped Bavarian KZ cemeteries in early June 1950 (ill. 22). In each town Auerbach instructed the local mayor or county governor to organize a public reception and attend the ceremony himself; in two cases the local authority simply brought along a group of children from the town school. Thus Auerbach was able to report to Minister President Ehard that "Everywhere there was a favorable and friendly attitude among the populace, sometimes it was even cordial, which gave me the satisfaction that the idea of a moral *Wiedergutmachung* for the dead of the Nazi regime is present in a large portion of our people."[167]

However, if Auerbach believed this, he was deceiving himself. Even when public officials participated in commemorative ceremonies, the populace showed no interest. The opening sentences of a report about a ceremony on the September 1950 "Day of the Victims of National Socialism" in Munich reflect the typical attendance at commemorative events that day:[168]

> On the morning of 10 September a memorial ceremony took place in the chapel of the Perlach Forst cemetery. It was attended by representatives of the Bavarian government and the city administration, and a large number of persecutees and surviving family members of victims.

The lack of public and media interest that day was a signal for politicians that the anger over the Leiten scandal had subsided, and they quickly withdrew their public support. A survey of ceremonies organized by former persecutees during the ensuing four years brings monotonously similar results: harassment and disregard. In September 1950 the city of Munich refused to reimburse decorating costs for the Day of the Victims of National Socialism as it had in the past. The personal intervention by Mayor Wimmer reversed the decision that year, but for the last time.[169] In April 1951 the state again officially boycotted the persecutees' commemorative ceremony, and the only state employees present at the ceremonies on 9 September 1951 and 17 September 1952 were the police.[170] At a mammoth combined May Day, liberation day, and VE Day ceremony on 4 May 1952 in Munich, the only state-affiliated persons among the 1,700 participants were one Communist Munich city councillor and a former persecutee from the Bavarian Senate.[171] That ceremony was overshadowed by the police occupation of the offices of the Restitution Authority on 10 March and the subsequent arrest and trial of Philipp Auerbach for various infractions, including the embezzlement of funds.[172]

On 1 May 1953 the *Süddeutsche Zeitung* entitled a short notice "For the First Time No Liberation Ceremony." This was a rather tendentious interpretation since the article reported that two organizations of Dachau survivors had commemorated the victims of the camp at the Dachau crematory and the Leiten mass graves.[173] The headline was probably meant to convey that there had been no official commemorative ceremony.[174] After the brutal suppression of workers' strikes in East Germany in June 1953, concentration camps were the subject of Bavarian parliamentary commemoration, but they were "Communist," not Nazi concentration camps. Deputies stood for a minute of silence for all those "languishing in prisons and concentration camps ... in the eastern part of Germany."[175]

In the weeks between the Bavarian parliament's noncommemoration of the Nazi camps and its moment of silence for imagined Soviet camps, the Bavarian Castle and Gardens Administration took a major step in the effacement of the historical record of the Nazi camps: it had the Dachau exhibition removed from the crematorium, and the building itself closed to the public. This was a first step in the third inversion accorded by the three myths: the creation of "clean" concentration camps. This inversion was a retroactive attempt to realize the Nazi propaganda image of the concentration camps.

5

"Clean" camps

For its eighth edition in 1939, the most popular German encyclopedia, *Meyers Lexikon*, revised the 1920s' definition of "concentration camp."[1] It no longer mentioned the British camps set up in South Africa during the Boer War (1899–1902), in which "women and children died in masses." Instead, in order not to raise any unpleasant associations, it began with the short definition:

> Better [called] containment and correctional camps. Since 1933 they have the purposes a) to hold . . . hardened criminals, and b) to temporarily neutralize Communists and other enemies of the state . . . and educate them to be useful national comrades.

As noted in chapter 2, during the Allied media blitz confronting the German populace with the horrors of the camps at liberation, most Germans responded by claiming that they had not known that the conditions in the camps were so atrocious. As soon as German authorities were given responsibility for the former concentration camps, the first thing they did was to attempt to refashion them in the image of the official Nazi definition. Thus their first plans were not to create memorials where the victims could be commemorated, or educational institutions where people could learn about Nazism, but to turn the concentration camps into model holding and correctional institutions for social groups they deemed undesirable. When this proved impractical or impossible, the sites of the camps were "cleaned" as much as possible of traces of the barbaric system that had been implemented there.

Concentration camps as model prisons

In November 1947 the Bavarian parliamentary Committee on Social Policy discussed a proposal from the Christian Socialist Party (CSU) that former Nazi camps be cleared for reuse as work camps, because a new

"Law to Combat Work-Shyness [*Arbeitsscheu*] and Loafing" was being drawn up that called for the committal of wayward women and lazy men to "educational work camps."[2] The matter was discussed in the full Bavarian House on 16 January 1948, and the representatives unanimously passed a resolution that called on the Bavarian government to

> immediately begin negotiations with Military Government for the soonest possible release of camp facilities (Dachau) in order to establish work camps for asocial elements . . .
> The importance of work camps as places for the reeducation [*Umerziehung*] of work-shy elements to productive citizens should be emphasized.[3]

Right down to the choice of words and the explicit reference to Dachau, this reasoning testifies to the postwar pervasiveness in the German public sphere of the image propagated by the Nazis of the concentration camps as disciplinary educational institutions.[4] The use of the term "*re*educa-tion" – uncommon during the Nazi period – also reveals that the Allied use of the camps as part of their "reeducation" program had become conflated in German public consciousness with the very traditions that program was trying to eradicate.

The Bavarian parliament's decision with respect to the conversion of the Dachau camp was not an exception in West Germany.[5] In October 1947 the Hamburg prison authority appealed to the Hamburg Senate to request from the responsible Allied authority the release of the former Neuengamme concentration camp for use as a prison in the Hamburg penal system.[6] In both cases pragmatic reasons were put forward first, but the psychological value of reversing the negative image of the camp played a crucial role, as a closer look at the documents reveals.

Prison officials from the entire British zone met in Hamburg in December 1946 to discuss penal reform. Herbert Blank, an anti-Nazi who had been convicted of high treason and spent essentially the entire Nazi period in various penitentiaries, argued that an entirely new kind of "camp" should replace conventional penal institutions. He reasoned:[7]

> One should not be put off by the fact that during the Hitler years the term "camp" was corrupted. That says everything against Hitler, but nothing against camps, against the opportunity to turn the morally ailing . . . back into productive and healthy members of society.

The actual conversion of Neuengamme began with a suggestion from the director of the Hamburg prison authority in October 1947. The official made his eradicatory intent quite explicit:[8]

> Neuengamme concentration camp weighs like a curse on Hamburg's
> conscience, its honor and its reputation. Neuengamme's reputation of
> inhumanity and cruel horrors must be eradicated from the memories about
> our times. Now the opportunity presents itself to build a model penal
> institution which will restore Neuengamme's and thereby Hamburg's
> reputation. This mark of past shame should be obliterated, and
> Neuengamme should signify an obligation to recompense past wrongs that
> we willingly take upon ourselves in that this institution is made into a model
> facility of humanity renowned the world over.

Hamburg's first postwar mayor Edgar Koch, an uncompromised liberal
politician from the Weimar years,[9] included this suggestion in his program
of penal reform in the summer of 1948.[10] Neuengamme was to become the
flagship of his reform, with up to 2,500 prisoners beginning their reintegration into society under "half-open" conditions.[11]

The intention of erasing Neuengamme's bad name succeeded, as
press reports praising the new prison during the following decade
repeatedly confirmed.[12] In fact, the realization of the "clean" Neuengamme
was so successful that there was still no noteworthy public opposition
to the addition of a high security facility in the late 1960s. Not until the
1980s was a sufficiently large sector of the German public outraged by
the myth of the clean concentration camp to lobby for the dissolution of
the prison – but that is the subject of a later chapter.[13] In Dachau the parliament's plan to convert the former KZ into a correctional work camp
was not implemented, perhaps because the Minister President dragged
his feet until the situation changed, or perhaps because the Allied
authorities in charge were unwilling to approve the request.[14] In the
months following the prison resolution, a new problem was arising in
Bavaria.

German refugees from the East, 1948

Germany's occupation policies in World War II made the mass expulsion
of long-standing German populations from Eastern European countries
after Germany's defeat a foregone conclusion. Article 13 of the Potsdam
Protocol of 2 August 1945 attempted to ameliorate the brunt of this population displacement by stipulating that any population transfers that took
place from Poland, Czechoslovakia, and Hungary to Germany "*should be
effected in an orderly and humane manner*," and that the expelling countries would be instructed "to *submit an estimate* of the time and rate at

which . . . transfers could be carried out, having regard to the present situation in Germany."[15] The wording of this mandate makes clear that in actuality the Allied powers had little influence over the course of events. By April 1947 an estimated 3.3 million evacuees had entered the Western zones of Germany.[16] As the gap between the superpowers the USA and the Soviet Union, and the ensuing division of Germany became increasingly obvious in 1947, a growing stream of refugees fleeing the countries in the Soviet sphere of influence for economic and political reasons entered the western zones, amounting to nearly 7.5 million persons by July 1949.[17] By the end of 1947 more than 1.6 million refugees (18 percent of the total population) had to be accommodated in Bavaria alone.[18] In November 1947 Dachau county had the highest occupation rate in all of Bavaria with an average of 2.9 occupants per dwelling room, as compared to 1.8 for Bavaria as a whole.[19]

Thus in 1948 the parliament decided to abandon its work camp plan and use former Nazi camps to house another problem group: refugees migrating to Bavaria from the East. On 29 April 1948 (coincidentally the anniversary of the liberation of KZ Dachau), the Bavarian parliament amended a resolution requesting that the state government put "all vacant accommodations of internees with all inventory at the disposal of the State Office for Refugees." The representatives wished to include a passage specifying that: "when people are assigned to newly vacated quarters the most effective means of putting them to work and the principle of proper familial accommodation shall be taken into account to the greatest possible extent."[20]

This amended resolution, which the Bavarian parliament passed unanimously, determined the fate of the former Dachau concentration camp until the mid-1960s. Parts of the Dachau internment camp had already been turned over to the Bavarian Ministry for Special Tasks in the fall of 1946[21] and in October 1947.[22] Dachau was the one internment camp selected to hold all of the Bavarian internees not released in the mass amnesty of April 1948.[23] However, in early July Allied Control Council directive no. 50 determined that it would be closed completely by 31 August.[24] This directive was so unexpected that notices of termination of contract to firms carrying out construction work in the camp had to be distributed by courier.[25] This hasty decision may have been triggered by the currency reforms of June 1948, after which the Soviets sealed off the Western sectors of Berlin, triggering another wave of migrants into western Germany. American officials were willing to do all they could to help West German authorities cope with the refugee problem.

A "residential camp" for refugees

In August 1948 an international summer course was held at the University of Munich. One of its main events was a visit to the Allach refugee camp (one of the larger Dachau branch camps in the immediate vicinity of the main camp) on 4 August, with a presentation by a representative of the State Commissionership for Refugee Affairs.[26] The students were so shocked by the deplorable conditions they saw that they drew up a memorandum and sent it to several Bavarian cabinet members, the president of the parliament, and top officials of the Catholic and Protestant churches.[27] On 11 August State Commissioner for Refugee Affairs Wolfgang Jaenicke addressed the students about their concerns and was soundly criticized.[28] While the students began to lobby Military Government and Bavarian politicians to improve conditions in the refugee camps, the refugees in the Allach governmental transit camp (*Regierungs-Durchgangslager*, Reg. Dulag) took matters into their own hands. On 18 August they formed a steering committee, drew up a list of demands, and sent them to the press as well as to the responsible government officials.[29]

The spokesperson at that first meeting was Egon Herrmann, a refugee from Czechoslovakia. Herrmann remained a decisive figure in the creation and dissolution of the housing project in the former Dachau concentration camp throughout the 1950s.[30] He was quartered in the nearby "Dulag" Dachau-Rothschwaige, a transit camp distinct from the concentration camp, which became the center of a refugee protest movement under his leadership.[31] The accommodation in Dulags was more primitive than in concentration camps and their major branch camps, because they had been and still were facilities for transients. The barracks in Rothschwaige, for instance, had floors of dirt, not wood, only one water faucet per 200 people, and "toilets that beggared description" (as opposed to two whole rooms each of communal sinks and toilets per barrack in the Dachau main camp; compare ill. 23, top). In Rothschwaige people of all ages and both sexes slept on cots in the primitive barracks.[32] All of the Dulags were still surrounded by walls and/or barbed wire, and refugees who were caught outside without passes were forcibly returned by the police, so that it was difficult not to conceive of the Dulags as detention centers.

Under Herrmann's leadership the situation escalated rapidly. At a meeting on 26 August 1948 Herrmann declared that he would use "revolutionary tactics" to press for a solution to the refugee problem – he had already contacted other refugee camps in Bavaria and begun preparations for a hunger strike.[33] The refugee authority realized the seriousness of the situation and immediately began working towards a solution. On 28 August it gained possession of a large branch camp of KZ Dachau in Karlsfeld (a neighboring town between Dachau and Allach) that had been empty since October 1947, and it was negotiating to take over the "former internees' camp" (i.e., the former concentration camp) in Dachau as well.[34] The authority planned to "remodel and expand both camps as residential camps [*Wohnlager*]." When the refugee authority announced that the Dulag would be only "thinned out" when the two new camps were finished, the Rothschwaige refugees decided to begin a hunger strike on 3 September.[35] Refugee camps Augsburg I, II, and III, Berchtesgaden, and Rosenheim sent telegrams to the Minister President in support of Dachau and Allach, implying that they, too, would begin hunger strikes if the demands were not met.[36]

Before the seven-day strike was over, 72,000 refugees had joined the fast in solidarity.[37] The action received considerable media attention (reporters from, among others, UPI, Radio Munich and a Swiss newspaper covered the story),[38] and the government quickly compromised on most demands. Rations were raised to 2,150 Kcal/day (i.e., those for heavy laborers), a monthly monetary allowance was granted (DM8 for men, DM6 for nonworking women, and DM3.75 for children up to 16 years), and identity cards with work permits were promised, as were immediate repairs on the barracks. But the refugees did not want to remain in those camps, and they had asked for a DM10 per person per month allowance regardless of sex or age, as well as immunity from reprisals for the organizers, so the strike continued. Representatives of all Bavarian refugee camps met in Dachau-Rothschwaige on 8 September to discuss the further course of action. Herrmann renewed his refusal to negotiate with Jaenicke, demanding that the Minister President or the Minister of the Interior be present.[39] The next day, as a compromise, Commissioner Auerbach accompanied Jaenicke to Rothschwaige, and within hours the strike was ended.[40] State Secretary Jaenicke found a euphemistic, face-saving formulation for the most important point of the compromise: "The transformation of the Government Transit Camp Dachau[-Rothschwaige] into a residential camp will be effected by the takeover of the former internees' camp [*Internierten-Lager*, i.e., the concentration camp] Dachau and the transfer of the camp inmates [*Lagerinsassen*] into that camp."

The conspicuous avoidance of references to the Dachau camp's primary history as a concentration camp ("former internees' camp") in all administrative correspondence indicates that German officials at that time preferred not to mention the camp's origins in the Third Reich.[41] It appears that at that time no one had second thoughts about the long-term reoccupancy of the former KZ. Even Auerbach, who as a member of the administrative council of the State Holding Authority and as the official governmental advocate of the survivors had the legal and moral authority to reject the reuse of the former concentration camp, had no reservations.[42]

An exception that confirms this rule can be found in a letter by one of the Catholic priests ministering to the Dachau internees, Neubauer. On 29 September 1948, the day the last German internee left the former con-centration camp, Neubauer wrote to Secretary Jaenicke, Minister President Ehard, and the chairperson of the CSU suggesting that instead of renovating the KZ barracks, one could use the funds to build perma-nent apartments on the adjacent grounds of the so-called release camp (*Entlassungslager*, presumably for processing internees about to be released). He wrote:[43]

> Anyone who knows about Dachau has to say: renovating and expanding the KZ barracks is like giving birth to a dead child. And if the barracks could be dismantled and sold as building materials, one more disgrace will have disappeared from the face of the earth and the proceeds would have some positive significance.

Ehard and the CSU forwarded their copies to Jaenicke, requesting that he investigate and report on the suggestion. In an accompanying letter Ehard's administrative secretary wrote that the Minister President "doesn't know whether the suggestions can be realized, but he thinks that the matter deserves consideration and would appreciate it if you could have someone evaluate the plan."[44]

The building control office replied a week later that for the projected camp renovation cost of DM 1 million, apartments for only 200 of the 500–600 families in the Dulag could be created, whereby the remaining 400 families would hardly be willing to wait an indeterminate amount of time for new quarters.[45] Additionally, according to the specialist, wood, iron, and clay roofing tiles for permanent apartments were in short supply, whereas the insulation and tar paper needed for the renovation were readily available. Finally, the proceeds from selling the barracks as build-ing material would be negligible because of unavoidable damage during dismantling.

When Jaenicke forwarded this answer to the Minister President, the CSU, and Pastor Neubauer at the end of October, however, he was seriously misleading them.[46] The figure of DM 1 million represented only part of the renovation costs. In parliament on 22 September Jaenicke had requested and received DM 3 million for the "winterization" of the barracks in KZ Dachau.[47] At that time Jaenicke's assistant's estimate of the total cost of renovation was DM 5 million (i.e., enough for 750 apartments), as Jaenicke told the parliament in December when applying for an additional DM 2.26 million to finish the job.[48] Workers had been working at the site since mid-September, so these higher costs were not due to unforeseen problems.[49] Since by 6 November 60 percent of the work had been completed,[50] contractually fixed prices must have been known for most construction firms by the time of the building control office's letter in mid-October. Also, the shortage of building materials was not as serious as it sounded, since German houses are built almost entirely out of bricks and cement, which were indeed available, if in short supply. Additionally, the estimate of DM10,000 per unit was high.[51] Actual building prices for residential dwellings were DM37 per m^3 of actual living space, or only DM7,500 for a generous four-room town house.[52] Finally, the argument that speed of relocation was an important factor in the decision to re-create the concentration camp as a residential camp was not conclusive. Although many of the occupants of the Dulag had been living there for more than two years,[53] the majority found Herrmann's demands excessive[54] and, in light of the fact that many of them had illegally entered Bavaria from the Soviet zone,[55] and given the general conditions in Germany at that time, the refugees would probably have been willing to wait the ca. six months needed to construct permanent housing if they had known that construction was actually underway.[56]

Although the Minister President's and the CSU chief's eager reactions to Neubauer's plan indicate that alternatives were considered, the conclusion seems justified that in the minds of officials such as Auerbach and Jaenicke, as well as the minds of the refugees, the remnants of the concentration camp could be recast as a residential settlement without the negative connotations of the camp's past. A brief description of the construction measures illustrates how permanent the settlement was expected to be.[57] Seventy percent of the exterior paneling was replaced; 67,000 m^2 of interior walls were put up to divide each barrack (90 × 10m) into twenty-four apartments (sixteen two-room and eight one-room); 1,800 interior doors were hung, and 500 toilets were put into individual stalls with new plumbing (ills. 23, 28, 48). Not all of the thirty-two barracks were converted into family dwelling units. One was converted into a school and department store, another into four workshops, two others into dormitories for single men and women, one into an office and communal kitchen, and a quarter of a barrack into a public bathing facility (using preexisting facilities installed by the Americans for the internees). The former delousing facility at the north end of the camp was turned into a restaurant with a meeting hall for up to 600 persons (ill. 25), and several of the apartment barracks also contained small shops. The two barracks of the former KZ infirmary were slated to be converted into a kindergarten, and offices for doctors and the future municipal administration. In the following seven years, the camp street was paved, street lights installed, flower beds planted, and more stores and factories granted concessions in the old camp buildings.[58]

Refugees as inmates of "clean camps"

These German-speaking refugees from Eastern Europe were officially accepted as full German citizens because of their German ancestry. However, many native West Germans resented their full access to welfare and other support programs. They were often seen as outsiders, in the extreme as rabble that belonged in concentration camps. For residents of the town of Dachau, the fact that the refugees' new "residential settlement" (Wohnsiedlung) was still surrounded by the original concentration camp walls and barbed wire fences at least until June 1950 certainly fostered that impression.[59] The authorities made an effort to refer to the refugees in the former concentration camp as Lagerbewohner, "camp residents," instead of the previously used term Lagerinsassen, which can mean camp occupants or inmates, but connotes the latter when used in conjunction with "camp."[60] However, from the very beginning the struggle between refugee representative Egon Herrmann and State Secretary Wolfgang Jaenicke shows that there was a widespread predisposition toward the identification of refugees with concentration camp inmates – as they had been portrayed by Nazi propaganda, namely as Communists and other "pests" harming the German nation (Volksschädlinge).

For example, after the first meeting in Allach in August 1948, a German informant for US intelligence suspected that the unrest among the refugees was the result of infiltration by Soviet agents working for the Socialist Unity Party (Sozialistische Einheitspartei Deutschlands, SED) in the Soviet zone.[61] The SED had been established as a union of Social Democrats and Communists in April 1946, but by 1948 the party had been transformed into a Communist-dominated party modeled after the Soviet CP, and was viewed with great suspicion in the West.[62] The students who visited Allach, too, if unwittingly, helped to promulgate this image. In their lobbying efforts to alleviate the situation in the refugee camps they pointed out that the deplorable conditions were "breeding-grounds for communist and anarchist elements."[63] As an indication of the students' confidence that their assessment represented majority opinion, they also sent this letter to US intelligence, the president of the Bavarian parliament, the Minister President, Secretary Jaenicke, the main organization of refugees, Radio Munich, DENA wire service, the *Neue Zeitung*, and Bertolt Brecht. While the students' letter implied that the refugees were not yet Communists, it played on the fear that they might become them.[64]

There were indeed many attempts to link the refugees to the KPD. On 9 September 1948, US military intelligence in Dachau reported at a briefing that "We have tried in some way to connect this committee with the KPD in Dachau or Munich with absolutely no success whatever."[65] None the less, the local press carried headlines such as "Communist Functionaries Disguise Themselves as Refugees," and Minister President Ehard denounced the hunger strikers as "agitators and rowdies in Moscow's service."[66] The refugees did their best to disprove such claims – Herrmann, for instance, turned over communist flyers distributed in Rothschwaige directly to the US Counterintelligence Corps (CIC) – but these Nazi-inspired Cold War fears were so powerful that they were used again and again by both sides.

Jaenicke had tried to exculpate himself in parliament by claiming that he "had not known" how bad conditions in the camps were, because he had not been able to visit all 680 of them personally. Herrmann pointed out the obvious parallel to the myth of ignorance about the brown-collar crimes, when he told a meeting of refugee camp delegates: "This explanation that one didn't know did not even count in the Nuremberg courts, since the accused who tried to use that excuse were hanged."[67]

The situation escalated once again in October 1948 because Secretary Jaenicke reneged on his oral promise to allow the refugees to participate in the writing of new camp rules.[68] Additionally, Herrmann revealed that Bernhard Reiter, a fellow member of the Control Committee, had embezzled several hundred marks from the camp cashbox. Reiter retaliated by trying to convince the CIC and Jaenicke's refugee authority that Herrmann was a Soviet agent.[69]

The climax was reached on 12 November when a Munich newspaper erroneously reported that Military Government would not release the concentration camp service building that was to house factories where the refugees could work, so that the whole project would have to be scrapped.[70] The next day the refugees began a second hunger strike, and Secretary Jaenicke announced that all negotiations with the refugees were officially prohibited, implying that as far as he was concerned, they could starve to death. The refugees immediately passed a resolution stating:[71]

> the refugee camp Dachau finds itself forced in its desperation to request that the proper authorities come at long last to the conclusion that is consistent with the attitude of State Secretary Jaenicke toward the refugees, and to apply instead of the slow death [by starvation] that is intended, a more rapid and less painful method of annihilation such as gassing [*Vergasung*] or other well-known methods of liquidation . . . to all men, women and children who are in the camp.

In the oral discussion of that resolution during the meeting Herrmann had been even more explicit. Now that the money from parliament for the renovation of the former KZ had been wasted, he suggested polemically that "the remaining building materials should be used to build gas chambers and crematoria to annihilate us, preferably quickly and painlessly, rather than letting us starve to death slowly."[72]

The aura of the Nazi camps also permeated Jaenicke's strategy to silence Herrmann. Jaenicke had a standing order to his employees to report any and all potential infractions so that he could have Herrmann jailed and thereby prevent him from organizing further demonstrations.[73] Jaenicke's plans were ultimately thwarted by Military Government when US Land Director van Wagoner told Minister President Ehard that in spite of the Military Government directive "the activities of committees may not be limited because of protests . . . Freedom of speech and assembly may not be restricted in any way."[74] Jaenicke did have Herrmann arrested on 28 November, but after two judges refused to sign the arrest warrant for reasons of insufficient cause, Herrmann had to be released pending his trial.[75]

In 1949 it became clear that in spite of the efforts of the authorities to turn the former concentration camp into a residential community, the future of the settlement remained bleak. Herrmann turned his energies to organizing a cooperative construction company that used the credits the refugees received from the new national government to build townhouses that would enable the occupants of "Residential Settlement Dachau-East" (Wohnsiedlung Dachau-Ost) to move out of the former KZ. Herrmann's enterprise was so successful that in 1950 the national organization of trade unions (Deutscher Gewerkschaftsbund) adopted it as a model for its own housing projects.[76] The "East Dachau Social Building Cooperative," as it was called, constructed seventy-two units from June to November 1950. By 1953 a total of 250 units, enough for 50 percent of the original Dulag occupants, had been completed.[77] This does not mean, however, that the population of the settlement diminished. New refugees were assigned to the settlement until 1957, so that the population remained fairly constant at around 2,000, i.e. ca. 1,800 registered residents and several hundred "illegals."[78]

The stigma of the former concentration camp that had been attached to the refugee-residents of the camp remained even after Herrmann's new housing project, called "Friedland" (roughly: "Peaceful Haven"), had developed into a thriving community no different in appearance than thousands of other reconstruction-era settlements all over West Germany. From the very beginning, the refugees had to cope with the prejudices of the "native" Dachau citizens. Leonhard Roth, a Dachau survivor who had remained as a priest for the SS internees and then the refugees, and who at that time was well connected to influential figures in the city such as Prelate Friedrich Pfanzelt, helped the project by convincing local landowners to sell the requisite plots.[79] His benediction at the groundbreaking ceremony helped gain publicity and legitimacy for the project. Nonetheless, the preexisting local building cooperative, disgruntled by the loss of potential members, agitated so vehemently against Herrmann's organization that Bavarian Minister President Ehard had to warn the state authorities to deal fairly with Herrmann, and to give him the loan securities he needed.[80]

The local situation was exacerbated by the left-wing press, which highlighted the problems of the refugee community and recalled the problematical relationship between the city and the KZ before 1945. In January 1949 an illustrated magazine ran an article "For the Second Time: Dachau," which began with the words:[81]

> First it was a concentration camp. That cost the little city of Dachau, not far from Munich, its good reputation. Later, after the war, the notoriety did not dissipate in the least. Now the refugee camp was guilty. It is just one of several camps maintained by the Bavarian government, but it is probably the most dismal one . . . A parliamentary commission once ascertained unambiguously that the conditions in the camp were a cultural disgrace and not fit for human habitation.

Other articles carried headlines such as "Dachau: Today a Prison of Poverty" (May 1950),[82] and "Does the KZ Still Exist in Dachau?" (March 1951).[83] The city itself struggled to prevent the incorporation of the state-run refugee camp into the city. Dachau city council filed briefs and petitions arguing that it would not take over responsibility for a camp that had been created without any input from local authorities.[84] After a visit by Bavarian State Secretary Oberländer (the former Nazi discussed on pp. 117f), the Dachau town council threatened to resign if the Bavarian government's decision to transfer responsibility was carried out. The city elders were now determined to resist what they had failed to resist in 1933: the violation of their reputation by a "cultural disgrace." This was one of the most obvious early manifestations of the myth of resistance.

The town's postponement tactics succeeded over the long run, for just as the final transfer of authority from the Bavarian state to the town was about to take place in 1957, the organization of Dachau survivors reached an agreement with the government that the settlement was to be dissolved.[85] That, however, did not prevent the town from making another attempt to finally realize the "clean camp" envisaged by Himmler and the Nazi leadership. In November 1959 the town council tried to gain permission to quarter homeless persons in the refugee settlement, whose population was beginning to dwindle.[86] For decades after the settlement in the concentration camp was dissolved – until the 1990s – the residents of that area of town were referred to locally as "KZler," and the bus running through East Dachau with the final destination Kräutergarten was known as the "KZ-Bus."[87] This lasting image of a "clean" concentration camp and its "dirty" inmates was just one consequence of the myth of ignorance.

The exhibitions in the crematorium, 1946–1950

The various exhibitions documenting the "dirty" history of the concentration camp contradicted the establishment of its "clean" image in local memory. The first such exhibition was set up in the crematorium–gas chamber building by Dachau survivors working in the International Information Office in the fall of 1945.[88] It was presumably supported by the US occupation authorities because of its public relations value during the Dachau trials of concentration camp personnel that began in November 1945. One postcard-sized picture pamphlet and a handful of existing photographs show that it emphasized the crass brutality of the concentration camp (ill. 17).[89] Life-size mannequins in SS and prisoners' uniforms were set up to demonstrate the use of the "whipping block" and the practice of "pole hanging": suspending prisoners from a tall pole by their hands bound behind their backs. A third group portrayed a recidivist prisoner "standing punishment" (*Strafstehen*) near the entry gate with a sign around his neck "I am back again." A series of postcards sold at that time depicted the process of taking a corpse from the morgue, dragging it to the ovens, and stuffing it in (ill. 16). (These scenes were reenacted after liberation, when the Allies had camp personnel restoke the crematoria in an attempt to deal with the huge number of corpses.) From what we know, the exhibition documented only the criminal nature of the camps, but not their history or political functions.

The immediacy of the reenactments of common camp tortures illustrates this focus on atrocities, as does the selection of pictures in the accompanying pamphlet. More than half of its twenty-three illustrations depict the most gruesome scenes in the camp at liberation: there are four pictures of the corpses in the death train, several pictures of the heaped and stacked corpses in front of the crematorium, and a series of five pictures in which liberated prisoners demonstrate how corpses were dragged from the morgue to the ovens with huge tongs and then pushed inside with a hooked metal pole.[90] Three illustrations are photographs of the mannequins in the exhibition, and the final photograph shows a dead SS man with a huge chunk blown out of his forehead. The caption comments: "The greater portion of the tormentors received just punishment. Here are dead SS men who could not escape in time. Many others have already been sentenced by the military court."

Although we do not know how this exhibition was changed after 1945, we can see how the accompanying pamphlet evolved.[91] A second edition of the brochure was published early in 1946, shortly after the end of the trial.[92] The total number of pictures increased from twenty-three to thirty-six, while the captions were now quadrilingual in English, French, and Polish as well as the original German. This second version still contained the same four pictures of the death train, but they were now interspersed between views of the camp buildings, and the shocking cremation sequence was reduced from five pictures to two. New were twelve pictures showing scenes from the proceedings of the first Dachau trial, as were the final two pages, which, instead of showing an SS man with his head blown open, replicate postcards and placards published by the Dachau International Information Office. One of them, depicting the New York Statue of Liberty framed with stylized barbed wire, and with the text "29.IV.1945 / Dachau," celebrates the Americans as liberators of the camp (ill. 12).[93] The other, a KZ prisoner with his right hand raised in salutation and an emaciated corpse draped over his left arm, bears an appeal to the German populace to support the survivors: "Their Sacrifice, Our Guilt / MAKE GOOD THROUGH COMPENSATION."[94]

Such messages were out of favor by 1947, and it is likely that the Dachau exhibition was largely ignored during the following years.[95] The next brochure accompanying the exhibition in Dachau was not published until late in 1949, after the neglect of the Leiten gravesite had attracted international attention.[96] Four slightly different versions of this brochure exist, indicating the haste with which it was prepared during the Leiten scandal. The first version, published under the title *Never Again / Jamais Plus*, contained even fewer pictures of the corpses found at liberation than the 1945–6 editions.[97] Instead, it included contemporary views of the various gravesites in Dachau, graphics portraying camp statistics, and a number of charcoal sketches of life in the camp, as well as a photograph of an Allied commission viewing an exploratory trench on the Leiten in the fall of 1949, and a bird's-eye view of a model of the entire Dachau camp complex. The shift from pictures of corpses to pictures of cemeteries illustrates the tendency to literally "bury" the horrors of the Nazi past and preserve kinder memories. A slightly revised version with the title *Remember That / Pensez-Y* was published shortly afterward.[98] The text, responding to reproaches that documents about the KZ stirred up bad feelings, emphasized that "This booklet was written without any thought of hatred or revenge."

When the revised exhibition was opened in the crematory on 10 September 1950, a sixty-four-page, larger-format (6″ × 6″) trilingual edition of the brochure was published. Its title reverted to *Never Again*, emphasizing a view towards the future, in contrast to the retrospective *Remember That*.[99] The brochure still highlighted its nonhostile purpose, concluding with the wish: "May all those who turn the pages of this booklet, which was compiled without any thoughts of hatred or revenge, take it with them as a reminder to value and uphold the dignity of humanity above all else." The pictures it contained of the new exhibition reveal that the mannequins demonstrating punishment scenes had been removed and that some efforts were made to show the genesis and development of the concentration camp system. New were a series of photographs of the Leiten cemetery, as well as pictures of the dedication of the statue of the "unknown concentration camp inmate" in front of the crematorium on 29 April 1950. An even later edition with eighty pages was almost identical, although the title *Remember That* was once again found more appropriate. Additional pictures of the relandscaped crematory park and Leiten cemetery, as well as of the nearly completed Leiten memorial hall, were included.[100]

Dachau survivor Erich Preuss, who worked in Auerbach's Commissionership, used a quotation after Schiller as the motto: "The worthiness of humanity is in your hands / Preserve it! / It falls with you! / With you it will rise!"[101] He included an area for the ritual commemoration of the dead: an urn flanked by candles on a high pedestal covered with a black drape (ill. 18). Existing photographs of the exhibition show that a chart illustrating how colored cloth triangles were used to categorize prisoners was on display, as were a map of concentration camps in Europe and a graph of the number of incoming inmates each year. This exhibition seems to have satisfied most groups at that time, but within a few years it received increasing criticism. That criticism began with a skeptical article by a Dachau survivor.

Removing the exhibition, 1951–1953

While international attention had prompted the creation of the 1950 Dachau exhibition, it was also the cause of its removal in 1953. A German newspaper editor who read the published description of a Jewish survivor's return to the Dachau site in August 1951 set the wheels of eradication in motion.

The survivor–author was Alfred Werner (1911–79), a Viennese Jew who had emigrated to the United States.[102] During the *Kristallnacht* pogrom in November 1938 Werner was one of nearly 11,000 Jews deported to Dachau, where he became prisoner no. 27,660. Early in 1939, when his visa to the United States was approved, he was released from Dachau and left Germany immediately. In the United States Werner published several articles about his experience in the concentration camp. In the summer of 1951 he returned to travel in Germany. Although he had not planned to visit his former prison, he was "magnetically drawn to it," to see, as he put it, "whether the fires were really out." In Munich his inquiries about the camp met with hostile reactions from Munich citizens, but once Werner was on his way to Dachau in a bus, talkative Dachau natives addressed him and told their version of what life near a concentration camp had been like. As his taxi from the Dachau bus station passed through a large US army installation, Werner mused about the riotous lives of the SS officers who had previously occupied the buildings.

Once inside the former prisoners' compound, Werner discovered a kind of shanty town, "a German version of a Hooverville," as he wrote. The barracks were now covered with "Eternite" asbestos cement paneling and inhabited by "DPs" from Eastern Europe. As the taxi cruised down the central camp/settlement street, Werner noted that the original barbed wire fence and moat still surrounded the compound. He resisted the urge to stop and inspect the barrack in which he had lived because he did not want to disturb the playing children. Finally the taxi drove into a walled enclosure surrounding what appeared to him to be a "tastefully land-scaped American state park." The park featured a statue, several plaques and two crematoria, the larger of which included a gas chamber bearing the inscription "shower room," a morgue, and four ovens. Werner com-mented positively on the graffiti on the walls, much of it from survivors like himself.

He contemplated the perfunctory manner in which his driver–guide explained the ovens and gas chamber to him, namely "with a certain cal-lousness . . . common to all guides who show visitors through cemeteries, battlefields, and the like." He reasoned that the memorial site was prob-ably designed as it should be: soothing for those who had suffered in the camp, a documentary warning for those who had not experienced Nazi Germany, and not so graphic as to disturb present-day life in the city of Dachau and in Germany. He suddenly felt deeply unsettled by what remained of the concentration camp's past, so he left Dachau "perhaps a bit too brusquely," wanting to shake the "cursed soil" of Dachau's past from his shoes.

Once back in the United States, where he was a successful art historian, Werner wrote up his experience for the Jewish political magazine *Commentary*.[103] His December 1951 article came to the attention of the Munich *Süddeutsche Zeitung*, which sent a member of its editorial board to retrace the Austrian-American visitor's tracks and prepare a report for German readers.[104]

In contrast to the returning Jew, the German newspaperman Joachim Steinmayr made no mention of the refugee settlement in his account of his visit. Nor did he reflect about his own impressions, or about what other German visitors might learn from seeing the preserved remains. His primary concern was the impression that a visit to the former camp made on foreigners. He found the small exhibition of photographs, models, posters, maps, relics, and explanatory tables "unattractive." In his article he repeatedly mentioned the groups of American soldiers gaping at the whipping horse, entering their "countless" names in the visitors' book, "heatedly" but "unconcernedly" discussing something near the former kennels of the SS's bloodhounds, and all the while taking pictures of sights such as the old crematory, the execution range, and the "gallows tree."

Steinmayr concluded his report with a series of quotations. A refugee farmer living in the former concentration camp barracks said: "Something must be done." The mayor of Dachau commented: "We Dachauer don't like this collection of curiosities at all, but we keep our hands off." A taxi driver told him: "Whether we like it or not, it attracts foreigners, and they would be disappointed if there were nothing to see." A Dachau survivor explained: "These deeds have to be kept alive as memories and supported by facts so that no one will one day be able to call us prisoners liars." Finally, a representative of the State Restitution Office told Steinmayr that he personally was dissatisfied with the exhibition, but explained that the German authorities were at the mercy of the Dachau survivors:

> If we change any part, foreigners would storm the barricades. They will say: the Germans want to cover up their guilt . . . Many of the foreigners who were once imprisoned in Dachau are completely justified in denying us Germans the right to have any say in what happens to the crematorium in Dachau.

Steinmayr did not explicitly interpret these quotes, but the uncommented barrage strongly implied that only foreign interests supported the exhibition. Steinmayr concluded his article with the simple demand that "something must be done." Steinmayr never said explicitly that the exhibition should be removed, but the article's title: "When Horrors Become a Tourist Attraction," and an accompanying editorial made it quite clear that the "horrors" drew the tourists, and it would be best if both disappeared. The editorial pointed out that the US government planned to build internment camps in the United States for use in domestic emergencies. The anonymous editorial concluded that even as "a kind of museum" former KZ Dachau was not a "deterrent [against setting up internment camps]."[105]

Steinmayr proceeded to do something himself: he made his opinion known to the broadest possible public. His article was reprinted two weeks later in the *Ruhr Nachrichten*, a newspaper in the most populous industrial region of Germany,[106] and then distributed by the news agency Nordpress in February.[107] Steinmayr's report did not remain completely uncontradicted, however. In April a popular illustrated weekend magazine ran a series of pictures that closely followed Steinmayr's narrative, but with a very different "spin": since so many publications were "serving the memory of those who served Hitler," the magazine editorialized, "we must and want to commemorate once again those who were his victims."[108] The last caption of the article, which was clipped for Steinmayr's newspaper archive at the *Süddeutsche Zeitung*, concluded with the contention that the crematory ovens "have become one of the most impressive memorial sites, a memorial site in two senses: an eternal accusation against the executioners, and an eternal commemoration of the unfortunate executees."

That was precisely what Steinmayr did not want, and he did not leave that contention standing for long. On 15 July 1952 he distributed a modified version of his article through the Munich *Nordpress* bureau.[109] This time he did not limit himself to suggestive description, but argued explicitly. After describing the museum he wrote:

> Thus this place that was supposed to stimulate introspection . . . turned into a site of curiosity and lust for sensations . . . Additionally, the visitors of the grounds, especially the conspicuously large number of American soldiers, show not the least trace of piety. They take pictures . . . and talk as if they were in a zoological garden or in a wax museum, not at a site of remembrance for the suffering and death of innocent people. Thus one has the impression that the gas chamber and the crematory ovens and the two mass graves . . . were never horrible reality. One leaves KZ Dachau in spite of all of the commemorative plaques . . . with the feeling that this place that was intended to be a fiery appeal to humanity does not or only poorly fulfills that mission.

In contrast to the explicit praise and emphasis on commemoration in the April illustrated magazine's report, phrases such as "in spite of all of the commemorative plaques" again made clear that the exhibition should be removed, without spelling out the demand.

The Bavarian authorities were not slow to respond to such expressions of dissatisfaction. The first step in the process was to regain control of the memorial site from Auerbach's Commissionership, which had been placed in charge to quell the adverse Leiten publicity. The process by which Auerbach's office had been selected to take responsibility for the memorial reveals how unpopular concentration camp memorial sites were in the early 1950s.

In the spring of 1950 the Minister President asked his cabinet secretaries to suggest who they thought should take charge of the grave sites. The Economics Ministry thought the Minister of the Interior should be responsible; the Justice Minister suggested the Ministry of Culture; the Minister of Culture passed the buck to the Finance Minister; the Finance Minister and the Labor Minister thought that, if possible, surviving relatives should take charge, although they conceded that that might prove difficult in the case of Jewish graves. If no family members had survived, Finance Minister Zietsch suggested, the local Jewish community should take charge; if no local Jewish community existed, the Bavarian Union of Jewish Communities should be responsible. And if that organization should not feel obligated in certain cases, his Office of Restitution would bear the burden of costs.[110] In fact, by October 1950, responsibility was centralized with the State Office of Restitution under Auerbach.[111]

At that time and again in January 1951, when the US Land Commissioner for Bavaria suggested that the State Chancellory take responsibility for the sites, the cabinet reconfirmed the decision that the Office of Restitution should remain in charge for the time being, while the government would "wait and see how things developed."[112] A year later, in February 1952, the question of responsibility was again discussed in the cabinet. The Minister of Finance was now anxious to transfer charge of the Dachau sites to the Minister of Education and Culture, who protested energetically.[113] Minister of Education and Culture Schwalber (the mayor of Dachau in 1945–6) argued that he had no funds for the upkeep of cemeteries, which were, according to a Bavarian ordinance, the obligation of the local communities. Awkwardly avoiding the Nazi euphemism for murder, "special treatment" (*Sonderbehandlung*), Schwalber said that "a separated treatment [*gesonderte Behandlung*] of the KZ cemeteries differing from that of the other cemeteries is totally unfounded."

The beginning of the end of the Office of Restitution's tenure as caretaker of the KZ sites was marked by the occupation of its offices and the arrest of top official Auerbach by the state police in March 1951.[114] When Auerbach's trial finally began in April 1952, the Restitution Office's reputation had been irreparably damaged by the year-long police occupation. In a widely criticized judgment, Auerbach was convicted and sentenced to a jail term, although he was guilty of relatively minor infractions, such as having perjured himself to obtain a "Dr." title (which he thought he deserved because the Nazis had prevented him from completing his Ph.D.). It appears that he had embezzled funds by nominally disbursing compensation to survivors who had left Bavaria. However, he had used those funds to support other victims of the Nazi regime who did not qualify for compensation or restitution under existing Bavarian law. His conviction was widely criticized in the German and international press.[115] The judges in the case, like the vast majority of West German judicial officials at that time, had served under the Nazis. Stunned by his second victimization at the hands of Nazi bureaucrats, Auerbach committed suicide in jail in August 1952. Without a strong figure at the helm, the Bavarian Office of Restitution never recovered its former importance. In the fall of 1952 charge of the concentration camp memorial sites was quietly transferred to the "Bavarian Administration of State Castles, Parks and Lakes," another branch of the Finance Ministry that was in charge of the upkeep of other state properties.[116] (It remained there until 1994, when responsibility was transferred to the Ministry of Culture.)

Almost immediately after the survivors' memorial ceremony on 30 April 1953, which, as mentioned above, was boycotted by state representatives, the Bavarian government took action. On 5 May 1953 the cabinet decided to remove the exhibition from the crematorium and close the doors to the public.[117] The executive order was carried out by the Castle Administration without prior notification of the exhibition's curator Erich Preuss, an employee of the Restitution Office, on 12 May.[118] The aggressive manner in which the exhibited objects were removed indicates how confident the Castle Administration was that it could deal with the survivors at will. At 10:30 a.m. a letter was delivered to Preuss's apartment informing him that the Finance Ministry had decided to close the museum, prohibit the sale of printed matter within the crematory complex and at the Leiten cemetery, halt all guided tours of individuals and groups, and disallow all commercial and public relations activity (*Werbetätigkeit*) at the memorial sites. Preuss, who did not receive the notice until he returned home in the evening, was told to come to the crematory to receive the exhibited objects. No time was specified. When Preuss arrived at the site early the next morning, officials in the US camp informed him that the exhibition had already been removed. Preuss immediately sent a letter of protest to the Minister of Finance and other politicians and survivors' organizations. The Finance Minister announced to the press that it had been necessary to clear out the exhibition in order to "counter uncontrollable propaganda" being spread by the curator, Mr. Preuss. He added several negative characterizations of Preuss's motives and behavior for good measure.[119] These were reprinted uncritically by the press.

The Bavarian government, however, did not realize that an "international pilgrimage" of Dachau survivors from France was planned for 7 June.[120] French survivors and family members of inmates who had perished had been coming to Dachau annually in June for a number of years; they had attracted little attention because the French never stayed overnight on German soil.[121] A short time after the pilgrimage Dachau survivor French Minister of Justice Michelet published articles condemning the removal of the exhibition in the French newspapers *Figaro* and *Le Monde*, prompting the French General Consulate to send an inquiry to the Bavarian government.[122]

The correspondence between the Ministry of Finance and the State Chancellory reveals the motives of the Bavarian government for removing the exhibition.[123] The State Chancellory suggested that the Finance

Ministry might mention that Preuss had set up the exhibition "without a permit"; that the type of presentation was, "in the unanimous opinion of the responsible authorities . . . not commensurate with the sacrifices of the camp prisoners" (sic!); and that Mr. Preuss had made substantial personal profits through the sale of brochures and postcards. The clinching argument was that "A broad spectrum of the public [*weite Kreise der Öffentlichkeit*], in particular also groups of former prisoners, felt that this was, for obvious reasons, an unworthy situation that was to be terminated." That suggested rationale was later used in the official answer to the French inquiry. The State Chancellory's accompanying explanatory letter to the Bavarian Finance Ministry, however, offers a glimpse of the real motivation: "For political reasons we strongly advise that especially no reference be made to the climate of opinion *vis-à-vis* the exhibition which obviously dominated certain circles in the city of Dachau."

The official rationale, which was duly sent to the French on 10 September 1953, was at best seriously misleading. When Preuss set up the exhibition in the summer of 1950, no one even considered the necessity of a permit, since Preuss was an employee of the State Restitution Office under Auerbach, who was explicitly empowered by the Minister President to take all necessary measures to limit the public relations damage done by the Leiten scandal.[124] That authorization included renovating the exhibition, which, prior to Steinmayr's first article, does not seem to have been publicly criticized.[125] The opinions of Bavarian authorities about the merits of the exhibition and the KZ inmates' "sacrifice," as they put it, were at best marginally relevant, given the world-historical significance of the events that had transpired in Dachau. It is telling that they considered an empty, locked and off-limits crematorium more commensurate with the prisoners' suffering. Other means of controlling Mr. Preuss's profits than physically removing him from the premises could surely have been devised. Finally, no record of protest against the exhibition voiced by survivors has been preserved in accessible government files, nor is any such protest ascertainable in the print media or in the files of the organizations themselves. On the contrary, both German and foreign survivors were very vocal in their protest *against* the removal of the exhibition.[126] As the Chancellory's confidential advice to the Ministry of Finance suggests, the protest originated in the town of Dachau; the reprints of Steinmayr's article indicate that the removal was also supported by regional and national published opinion.

Since they stood on such weak ground, it is not surprising that Bavarian journalists and state authorities resorted to a defamation campaign against Preuss in order to retain control of the public reaction to the removal of the exhibition. In late May 1953 the Munich *Merkur* published a pathos-filled description of a Swiss family's visit to Dachau.[127] The family members, according to the article, had felt quite at ease in the town until they decided to visit the former KZ. That evening they returned to their hotel completely distraught, and the "aging lady" suffered an "actual" heart attack. The family fled the town two hours later. "What happened in this 'symptomatic' case?" the journalist asked rhetorically, and indignantly answered his own question: "The former KZ prisoner Erich Preuss, employed for many years by the US camp [sic[128]], had described the tragic past with great authenticity."

The journalist apparently thought that Preuss should have been less authentic. A week later a Heidelberg paper characterized Preuss as someone who "could not forget what he had experienced as a KZ inmate."[129] The article also claimed that, after 1945, Preuss had been a "notorious" chair of a denazification court whose "judgments later had to be [sic!] reversed by an appeals court." We have already seen how misleading this was, since denazification appeals courts tended to repeal even the mildest sentences. The article, which suggested that "Dachau be turned into a memorial of reconciliation, just as the dilapidated barracks of the former KZ have turned into a blossoming city of expellees [*blühende Vertriebenenstadt*]," then fired its lowest shot at Preuss. In its most powerful invective it claimed that:

> He preferred to lead the columns of visitors, after they had completed their travels through the gorgeous landscapes of the [German] south, into *his* KZ memorial site, where [their impression of?] the reconstruction of the new Germany was destroyed by "parting impressions" and intentionally fostered feelings of resentment (emphasis added).

While that article made the brazen claim that the exhibition was Preuss's "private" project, the Finance Ministry's answer to the French inquiry, while implying the same, was more carefully (and correctly) worded: "A majority of the exhibits are in the *possession* of Mr. Preuss." In fact, many of them had been loaned to him from other survivors. In the fall, the Bavarian Auditor-General's Office conducted a grueling investigation of all financial transactions relating to the renovation of the exhibition, the landscaping of the crematory grounds, the use of the car purchased by the state to drive visitors to the mile-distant Leiten gravesite, the brochures sold and donations collected at the site, and the construction of the bronze statue of the unknown KZ inmate.[130] Even though all persons associated with Preuss (e.g. Walter Neff), and all firms who had carried out work at the memorial site were also audited, no incriminating misappropriations of funds were found.

In their replies to public outcry from groups of French survivors, French government officials sympathetic to West Germany endorsed the opinion disseminated by the Bavarian government. A French official in Munich, relaying to the French ambassador the lies circulated by Bavarian authorities, claimed that Preuss was a "dubious" person who had been in Dachau as a common criminal, not as a political prisoner.[131] Additionally, the French diplomat alleged that Preuss had sold earth mixed with ashes to visitors of the site, pursued commercial interests in showing the exhibits, and encouraged macabre sensationalism to make money. In March 1954, the French ambassador in Germany reiterated those allegations in response to an inquiry from the president of the French National Association of Families of Resistance Fighters.[132] While the claim that Preuss was a criminal was unfounded, the origins of the ash-selling rumor are easy to trace.

This was not the first time that French authorities friendly with the Bavarian government had vilified the caretakers of the Dachau exhibition. In the summer of 1950, while Preuss was preparing the new exhibition, the French observer in Bavaria, Captain Bonenfant (who had denounced the first French delegation of inquiry into the Leiten Affair in the preceding fall as "communist"), repeatedly sent con men into the crematorium to try to bribe an employee into selling them human ashes.[133] Nothing ever came of the affair, however, and Preuss's record was so clean that a high official in the Ministry of Culture recommended that he be given security of employment.[134] In the context of the Cold War some French government officials preferred sullying a survivor's reputation rather than preventing German officials from retroactively turning Dachau into a "clean" camp.

Closing the crematorium, 1953–1955

The success of these first measures to "clean up" the Dachau camp emboldened local officials. In September 1953 a Dachau city councillor found out that in spite of Preuss's dismissal and the removal of the exhibition, his booklet *Remember That* was still being sold by a restaurant and a news stand in the Dachau refugee settlement. The Dachau city council then formally applied to the Bavarian state prosecutor to prohibit the distribution of the publication, or at least to issue an injunction against its sale until "the responsible authority determines whether the continued sale of the booklet is in keeping with the preservation of the reputation of the German people."[135] The irony of this formulation – the continuing stream of foreign visitors to the former concentration camp indicates that the brochure was very much in keeping with Germany's reputation abroad – was probably lost on the letter's authors.[136]

Not wishing to depend solely on the state prosecutor, the council noted in its letter that it reserved "the right to press civil charges against the authors of the brochure for continued public injury to the good name of Dachau." The Bavarian Ministry of Finance was indeed very restrained in its answer to this brazen request. The ministry said that it had taken action against Preuss, not the brochure, and that it had no control over the sale of publications except on state properties.[137] The town never did press charges, although one restaurant owner was persuaded to stop selling Preuss's brochure.[138]

At this time, in 1952–3, national politicians began to pay more attention to public opinion with respect to the former concentration camps. The newspaper archives of the federal parliament (Bundestag) and the federal government (Bundesregierung) set up newspaper clippings files to monitor domestic and foreign public opinion about the former Dachau camp.[139] Articles began appearing in the international press again. For instance, in early March 1954 the *New York Herald-Tribune* published a front-page article about the memorial site.[140] The article, written in a cool, objective style, showed understanding for the removal of the old exhibition, but also criticized German attempts to sanitize remains of the Nazi past. The author described how the SS complex was being used by the "Dachau Detachment" of the US army to process food and rations for army units throughout central Europe, while the Bavarian government had refurbished the prisoners' compound to accommodate 5,000 "expellees" from the East. The directional sign at the entrance to the US installation listed eclectically "laundry and dry cleaning, chapel, crematory and motor pool." In the crematorium itself the author found no historical documentation, only hundreds of signatures on the walls. He explained that the exhibition, which had been removed nine months before, had been "offensive to good taste and . . . harmful to an improvement in international relations." He concluded with a critical note: the German caretaker had tried to convince him that the larger crematorium had been built by the US army after the war for propaganda purposes.

Another article, published in 1954 by the *Manchester Guardian Weekly*, was more critical of the German clean-up efforts.[141] Author Terence Prittie first contrasted the "raggety refugee-children" and old women peering out of the concentration camp barracks windows with the "perfectly preserved" garden around the crematoriums. Then he described the gruesome murder apparatus in straightforward terms, noting that the walls were covered with "scribbled messages." In conclusion he quoted a story in a German newspaper that repeated the claim that the US had built the crematorium to "pin guilt" on Germany. Prittie prophesied that in a year's time there would be neither a sentry nor directional signs.

He was almost right, since local officials did remove the directional signs, but their attempt to tear down the building failed. At the same time, foreign interest in Dachau was increasing. In April 1954 the federal government asked Dachau authorities for specific information about the Dachau camp so that it could answer foreign inquiries.[142] In Bavaria too, politicians became increasingly sensitive to foreign political opinion. Shortly after the exhibition had been cleared out in 1953, the Bavarian Minister of Finance applied for DM115,000 from parliament for the upkeep of KZ cemeteries.[143] He explained to the elected representatives that that budget amounted to the token sum of DM328 for each of the 350 Bavarian cemeteries. He concluded: "God knows that it is not necessary to start scrimping here, where *for political reasons* we have to behave in such a way that we can answer for our actions" (emphasis added). This was probably a reaction to the outcry after the exhibition had been removed.

Dachau County Governor Heinrich Junker and the Dachau city council, however, were not daunted by the more cautious stance at the state and national levels. Their attempts to blot out the local reminders of the camp predated the Leiten Affair, and they continued for decades afterwards. Junker, an engineer who had not become a Nazi Party member (although he had applied for membership and been refused),[144] was a longtime adversary of the camp survivors in Dachau county. His opposition can be documented as far back as the summer of 1948, when he tried to relieve his office of the obligation imposed by the Allies to finance the Dachau KZ care center (the International Information Office).[145] First Junker wrote to State Commissioner Auerbach to determine whether the center was a legally established public service (*öffentlich-rechtliche Institution*) or an administrative authority (*behördliche Einrichtung*) set up by executive fiat. Only in the latter case would the county have been obligated to pay, and that obligation could easily be rescinded. When Junker found out that the care center was technically a combination of the two, namely an administrative service department (*Dienststelle*), he requested clarification from Auerbach's superior, arguing that the Dachau center was neither a public nor a state service. Junker's initiative dead-ended when the superior routed the second letter back to Auerbach to be answered.

Junker continued his efforts to harass and marginalize the survivors in the ensuing years. For instance, he confiscated the proceeds of a collection to send VVN members to a meeting in Hamburg in April 1949.[146] In 1955, after the 1954 effort to prohibit the sale of literature about the Dachau KZ failed, Junker spearheaded a new initiative. In May 1955 the Dachau city council discussed the possibility of closing the crematory to the public.[147] But that was in the purview of the Bavarian state, not of the town. Junker, who as county governor was also Dachau's representative in the Bavarian House of Representatives, introduced a motion in parliament to completely block public access to the crematorium, and perhaps to tear it down.[148]

Junker released his proposal to the press and submitted it to the Bavarian parliament in July 1955.[149] It was immediately met by a barrage of vehement protest from camp survivors, from the news media, and even from high Bavarian government officials.[150] As we will see in part III, by 1955 the wind was blowing in a very different direction than during the 1952–3 anti-exhibition climate. The "economic miracle" was in full swing, West Germany had just been accepted into NATO and had begun rebuilding its army, and Chancellor Adenauer was about to leave for a visit to Moscow, where he would negotiate the release of the last POWs and convicted war criminals still being held there. Thus major causes of feelings of present victimization were disappearing. State officials were now turning their attention outwards and trying to establish an unblemished image in international politics, rather than catering to local concerns. The same Bavarian Minister of Finance who ordered the removal of the exhibition in 1953 told the press in 1955:[151]

> I think that the former concentration camp Dachau is so well known and so notorious the world over, and so many people died and were murdered there, that it would give the world a very false impression if one were to prohibit visitors. Landrat Junker was very poorly advised to have submitted this bill.

As the summer wore on, Junker's motion drew protest from ever widening circles at the regional, national, and international levels.[152] With one exception, an article in a regional newspaper in Essen, support for the motion was forthcoming only in the town of Dachau itself.[153] For example, on 10 August 1955, Bavarian Minister of Agriculture Josef Baumgartner, a native of Dachau county, gave a speech at a gathering of area farmers at the annual Dachau *Volksfest*, one of the rural Bavarian fairs similar to the Munich *Oktoberfest*.[154] At the climax of his speech Baumgartner declared:

> I was imprisoned by the Nazis myself, thus as a former prisoner I have the right to state my opinion. The crimes of the unfortunate [*unselig*] Nazi years cannot be made good again by looking at the crematory, so I take the position: the crematory has got to go! At some point we must put an end to the defamation of the Dachau region and its populace because it is impossible that . . . due to an unfortunate past a region can continually be burdened by the concentration camp crime [*das KZ-Verbrechen*, a euphemistic singular].

According to the press reports, the applause lasted several minutes.

Several weeks later it was discovered that an international treaty obligated West Germany to "maintain the original condition and ensure unhindered access" to a number of memorial sites, including Dachau.[155] This requirement had been added to the October 1954 Paris Treaty as a result of the December 1949 debate in the French National Assembly about the Leiten graves. County Governor Junker retracted his motion and attempted to recoup his losses. He proposed that a new cross and a star of David be erected on the Leiten to replace the weather-beaten originals,[156] but he also obtained permission to efface "misleading" inscriptions in the crematory building. These were, however, original signs put up by the SS, such as the word "Showers" (*Brausebad*) over the door of the gas chamber (ill. 51), and the text "Gassing time____ / Closed____ / Open____" (the times could be chalked in) on the doors of the clothing disinfection chambers at the far end of the building.[157] Whereas the former had been designed to deceive prisoners about to be gassed, the latter confused visitors because there was no information explaining that those chambers had been used to delouse clothing. As journalist Terence Prittie had predicted in December 1954, the signs directing visitors to the memorial sites were removed as well.[158]

These measures were, however, a futile attempt to stop a suddenly rising interest in the history of Nazi crimes. They may even have acted as a catalyst for that development.

PART THREE

Dachau 1955–1970: groups and their memories

The Dachau concentration camp memorial site – indeed, all concentration camp memorial sites created in West Germany before the 1970s – was initiated by the survivors of the camp. Without their dedicated work, documentation about the camp system would be very scant. The survivors, however, were a very heterogeneous group. They ranged from high-ranking foreign politicians and leading religious officials, to Communist and Social Democratic Party functionaries, to members of foreign resistance networks and religious sects, to so-called "asocials," prostitutes, and homosexuals, and finally to Jews at the rock bottom of the Nazi-imposed camp hierarchy. It was a difficult undertaking to forge an alliance between staunchly conservative Catholic politicians and committed working-class Communists, bourgeois Jewish émigrés and devout Polish priests, or Soviet Red army veterans and Gaullist French resistance fighters. Nonetheless, for the decade from 1958 to 1968 these groups worked together to create the memorial site that existed for the next thirty years.

However, the Dachau memorial site was not only a compromise between the widely diverging images of National Socialism held by various groups of survivors: because the site was controlled by German authorities, the survivors could realize their amalgamated vision only around and against the mythic German memories described in the preceding chapters. Various traces of both the survivors' varying visions and the Germans' mythic images are visible in the memorial site today.

The chapters that follow examine how various groups created symbolic representations of Dachau in Dachau. Before beginning the analysis of these memorials, it is important to realize a fundamental principle of such recollective monuments: commemorative markers generally reveal far more about the groups that create them than about the history they purport to represent.[1] The remains of the concentration camps themselves, however, present a special case. As historical documents they limit the freedom of shapers of recollection to represent themselves. Thus discordant remains are subject to removal. As Volkhard Knigge, director of the

Buchenwald memorial site in the 1990s, phrased it: "The minimization of remains is a prerequisite for the maximization of possibilities for creating new meanings."[2] As we will see, historical sites such as Dachau have continually been effaced and reshaped to reflect present conceptions of the past, not the past itself.

6

The first representations of Dachau, 1945–1952

The story of Dachau's postwar representations begins immediately after liberation in 1945, when the US army ordered local officials to create a memorial. The Germans responded with a project of staggering proportions. However, that project was difficult to realize in the war-torn context of the mid-1940s. By 1949 it was still unrealized and essentially forgotten, when the international scandal triggered by the coincidental rediscovery of the Leiten mass graves catapulted its completion to the top of the priorities list. In the early 1950s' context of renazification, marginalization of survivors, and effacement of remains, however, the initial grandiose scheme was reduced to modest proportions.

The first Leiten temple, 1945–1946

Six weeks after Dachau's liberation, on 14 June 1945, the Associated Press reported:[1]

> Two stone columns fifty feet high, one topped by a cross and the other by the Star of David, are being erected here [in Dachau] by German civilians under the direction of the Allied Military Government to mark the mass grave of 3,500 Dachau concentration camp victims.
>
> The grave will be covered with roses blooming from April through November and before it will be the columns and a spacious plaza. Almost a quarter-mile of broad stone steps will lead to the site, located on a hill north of the city.
>
> The memorial will cost 500,000 marks – $50,000 at the military exchange rate – which will be drawn from German funds. The labor is being performed by 150 German civilians. The stone is coming from the great Nuremberg stadium.
>
> Capt. Malcolm Vendig . . . military governor of Dachau, planned the project with the help of Brig. Gen. Paul Adams . . . Prof. Georg Buechner, Munich landscape artist, submitted plans. Captain Vendig expects the memorial to be finished by August.

At the end of the war the German populace at large would probably not have erected any memorials for the concentration camps if it had not been compelled by outside interests. In early June an "Anti-Fascist Action Committee" (Antifaschistischer Aktions-Ausschuss, AFA) with representatives from seventeen regions of Dachau was formed to govern the city.[2] This governing body, which included some Dachau survivors, oversaw the work on the two four-story tall columns with their religious symbols, which was begun on 8 June 1945.[3] On 27 July, however, when the AFA met for the first time as the Dachau "city council," the work was halted because Buechner had been affiliated with the Nazi Party.[4] Instead, an architect, Seidl, and a sculptor, Salmann, were commissioned with the artistic direction of a new project, which was to cost RM500,000 ($350,000 in 1998 dollars), and garden architect Seifert was to relandscape the Leiten hill for RM60,000 ($42,000 in 1998). These were staggering sums of money in war-ravaged Germany.[5]

Although the two towering columns were never erected as planned, this first proposal had a long afterlife in the memorial history of Dachau. A tall wooden cross erected shortly after liberation by Polish survivors did adorn the roll-call square for a year or more in 1945–6 (ill. 7).[6] In 1949 a wooden cross and a star of David were erected at the mass grave on the Leiten hill.[7] In 1956 they were replaced by the more permanent versions in bronze and stone that still stand today.[8] In 1960 the two columns appeared in yet another project: former special prisoner Suffragan Bishop Neuhäusler, who had just spearheaded the construction of a Catholic chapel at the end of the central camp street, suggested that columns crowned by a star and a cross flank his chapel to represent what he referred to as "the other two major world religions": Judaism and Protestantism (ill. 46).[9] The continued use of these abstract columns indicates that minimal, unhistorical commemoration remained the norm until the early 1960s.

We do not know whether the work by Seidl, Salmann, and Seifert was carried out. The next public mention of the Leiten project was in late October 1945, when a design by Professor Karl Knappe, a well-known Munich sculptor,[10] was published in the Munich newspaper (ill. 31).[11] This 35 meter tall and 20 meter wide "monument of liberation," as it was called,[12] had a massive semicircular base above which rose a 15 meter tall obelisk crowned by a gold mosaic "sun" (ill. 32). Concrete containing rubble from bomb-torn Munich was to give the "rugged mass an elemental naturalness." In the lower story, rooms 20 meters high were to house memorial plaques, pictures, and frescoes, while a steep staircase leading to the roof would open onto a wide panorama with the concentration camp in the foreground and the peaks of the Alps in the distance. No mention was made of any artifacts from the camp or any attempt to document or explain its history. The architect later explained his conception as follows:[13]

> My idea . . . was to point to the gravity of the events only in the lower rooms, and then to guide the visitors of this memorial site up onto the walls, which were to be built out of the ruins of Munich. Visitors would have climbed onto these walls and found . . . a "liberating" view of the Alps. I think it would have been sufficient to allude to the horrors in the large lower rooms, and not eternally block the road to freedom and salvation with remembrance.

The candid formulation "block the road to freedom . . . with remembrance" expresses the predominant anti-recollective sentiments of the broader German populace after the war. However, the temple of liberation was not realized.

As soon as the design was published, the monument and its designer drew heavy criticism. The extreme pathos reminiscent of huge National Socialist projects was not lost on the public,[14] and Knappe was accused of having designed a monument to commemorate the Nazi accession to power in 1933.[15] First the Union of Munich Architects protested in an open letter to the mayor of Dachau, comparing the planned Dachau monument's "lack of all sense of proportion" to the "misshapen" Battle of Nations monument in Leipzig.[16] The architects criticized the lack of "any sign of atonement," and suggested that a residential settlement, a hospital, or an orphanage for the survivors, coupled with a memorial grove and a simple monument might be a more positive way of honoring the dead. The letter was distributed by the German wire service DANA, and it received supporting editorials.[17] Following Mayor Schwalber's suggestion, Dachau city council decided to halt construction. The firm Sager and Woerner, which had already performed RM54,108 worth of landscaping, was requested first to secure and then to vacate the construction site, while the Bavarian executor for Dachau county (*Regierungspräsident*) evaluated the merits of the design.[18] In January 1946 the director of the Office of Military Government in Dachau said that he "would be glad to see the thing stopped" because the design was "unsuitable."[19]

Knappe's monumental project was finally abandoned, and a commission was formed by Minister President Hoegner to find a new solution.[20] The commission's recommendation, released in March 1946, closely followed the Munich architects' November 1945 suggestion:[21]

at the gravesite an architectonically framed sculptural group should be set in a memorial grove as a monument of remembrance and warning. Such a solution would have the advantages that it would, on the one hand, be free of false and exaggerated pathos, and, on the other hand, would require only a very moderate quantity of material.

The recommendation also suggested that qualifying artists should be "Bavarian," and "politically incontestable" – that is, they were to have had no Nazi affiliations. In late April 1946 the recommendation was approved by Military Government, and in June a competition publicly announced.[22] At that time there was a parking lot at the base of the hill and a road leading to the top, where each mass grave was encircled by a ring of pebbles. By September 1946 twenty-one designs had been submitted. Two were rejected outright because of the political histories of their creators, while none of the others was deemed aesthetically acceptable.[23] At its second meeting the jury decided to purchase four designs and solicit new projects from those artists and several others, including one of the critics of Knappe's design.[24] The prize committee now recommended that these invited artists submit projects having "the character of a cemetery." More precisely, they should "resemble neither a museum nor a place for an outing." A room for ritual activities and individual commemorative markers was to be included, as was a "living and meaningful connection to the surrounding landscape," such as a bell tower.

Bavarian officials waited nine months before they paid for the four designs selected from the first competition, which had already been destroyed by a fire in the Ministry of Culture in January 1947. The recommendation was then "forgotten" by the bureaucracy until the "Leiten Affair" catapulted its neglect into the headlines in September 1949.[25]

The statue of the "unknown concentration camp inmate," 1949–1950

Independent of this Allied-initiated, Bavarian government-led project, Dachau survivors pursued plans to create a permanent museum at the concentration camp site.[26] However, they had to overcome numerous organizational and political obstacles before they could begin effective work. First, in June 1946 representatives of survivor groups throughout Germany met in Frankfurt and resolved to establish regional chapters with common statutes as the basis for a new national organization. This was accomplished – in Munich by Philipp Auerbach and Ludwig Schmitt

– in early 1947.²⁷ In March 1947, at the first national meeting of delegates, the new Association of Persecutees of the Nazi Regime (VVN) decided to hold a large public meeting of its membership in Dachau in mid-May 1947.²⁸ At that Dachau meeting regional historical "research groups" were constituted. These research groups convened again on 30 January 1948 in Herford to draw up a program of activities.²⁹ The keynote address about "the political importance and effectiveness of research about the German resistance movement against the Nazi regime" shows that from the start concentration camp survivors were interested in disseminating knowledge about resistance against Nazism in order to influence the development of political culture in Germany. Researching and disseminating information about atrocities was not one of their priorities.

The division of the VVN into regional chapters was not advantageous for historical research about particular places, however, since survivors of a single concentration camp or prison, for example, were now widely dispersed. Thus trans-chapter working groups for several former concentration camps were constituted in April 1948 at a large liberation celebration in Buchenwald, where plans to install a permanent exhibition there were also discussed.³⁰ Now political barriers began to thwart the group's efforts as well. The currency reform in June 1948 made interzonal travel within Germany difficult and expensive. The Dachau group was not able to convene in its entirety that year, although a partial meeting was held in September.³¹ Mounting political difficulties under the combined pressure of Cold War political differences and increasing West German efforts to gain control of and eradicate certain aspects of memory hindered another major convocation planned for late August 1949 in Munich.³² A rash of resignations from the VVN in the spring of 1949³³ left the association in a weak position to defend itself from the accusations of negligence leveled at it after the Leiten scandal that fall.³⁴ Although the Leiten Affair temporarily eclipsed the VVN's historical work, it did help to strengthen the association's international contacts. In the mid-1950s those international contacts proved crucial in the push for a memorial site, just as they had been decisive in the Leiten Affair itself.³⁵

Just as the VVN was running into political obstacles in 1949, Munich VVN co-founder Philipp Auerbach used his position as State Commissioner for Persecutees to erect a memorial sculpture in front of the Dachau crematorium.³⁶ Auerbach selected a bronze sculpture created in 1946 by a well-known Bavarian sculptor of the 1920s, Fritz Koelle. Koelle was a working-class sculptor with an expressionistic style. His smaller than life-sized statue depicted a clothed concentration camp inmate supporting a naked, emaciated comrade with his left arm (ill. 37). Although the two figures are standing, they resemble the centuries-old motif of the pietà (the seated Virgin Mary mourning her dead son). Koelle added unsettling new features to this familiar icon: symbols of the camps such as emaciation, a shorn head, pajama-like uniform, and a sallow face with sunken eyes. Additionally, the clothed inmate has his free hand raised and pointing towards his dead or dying comrade in an accusatory gesture.[37] This statue is not inwardly directed and meditative, but outward and aggressive. Thus the figure adds accusation to the traditional meanings of the pietà: mourning, sacrifice for the greater good, and the close interpersonal bond.[38]

Auerbach printed this concentration camp pietà on an invitation to a September 1949 commemoration, at which he hoped to raise funds for the monument. However, he received negative feedback from other survivors.[39] Auerbach then selected another of Koelle's sculptures: a solitary, shorn inmate in a long, drooping coat (ill. 38). This "unknown concentration camp inmate," as the sculpture has come to be known, is fully clothed, so that only his gaunt face betrays emaciation. The accusatory right hand of the earlier statue is now buried in the coat pocket; the knit brows and focused gaze of the earlier work have been raised in a dreamy, undirected look. This second sculpture without the dying comrade expresses radically different meanings. The accusatory presentation of the inhumanity that reigned in the Nazi camps and the solidarity among the prisoners have been replaced by a vague and palatable representation of a victim of a relatively "clean" camp. It appears that Auerbach, in his desire to appeal to a wider audience, chose a statue more in keeping with the anti-recollective mood of the late 1940s. Although this sculpture was already in place on its high pedestal in front of the Dachau crematorium in April 1950, it was not officially dedicated until September, when the parklike relandscaping was completed and the new, historically objectified exhibition unveiled. The "unknown inmate," which still blankly stares over the heads of visitors today, is thus less a representation of the camps themselves than a monument to the predominant "clean camp" image of the 1950s. Its high pedestal bears the simple inscription "To honor the dead, to admonish the living."

The "home-baked" Leiten temple, 1950–1952

The Leiten Affair in 1949 sent Bavarian bureaucrats scrambling to explain why the second artistic competition had never been initiated in 1947.

They found no responsibility in their own offices, attributing it instead to "unfortunate circumstances" such as the 1947 fire in the Ministry of Culture, and financial difficulties after the 1948 currency reform. The bureaucrats' report even blamed the victims, the VVN, and Auerbach's Commissionership – for not having reminded the government of its own neglect. Finally, in February 1950, a new competition was hastily initiated so that a cornerstone could be laid on 29 April, the fifth anniversary of liberation.[40] The guidelines prescribed a design symbolizing "the religious and national idea of sacrifice on behalf of peace."[41] This conception, although it may have overlapped with the ideas of some camp survivors, clearly excluded the hallmarks of the Nazi camps: barbarity and exploitation, suffering and senselessness. It was "home-grown," so to speak, and very much in tune with the ahistorical, apolitical, religious conception put forth by one of the leading local anti-memory advocates: County Governor Junker. In the fall of 1949 Junker had been charged with finding a design.[42] In December he announced that "a kind of trans-denominational pantheon with several altars for the various religions" was to be erected. His cost estimate of DM 1–2 million, at the highpoint of international attention, when compared with the DM600,000 cap six months later, indicates the extent to which the project was driven by public relations concerns.

On 25 April 1950, four days before the dedication ceremony, the prize commission convened to examine the 175 entries that had been submitted. They were a motley and ultimately unsatisfying collection ranging from, as one journalist put it, "modified churches of every age, Roman forts, Gothic citadels and neo-German colonial forts . . . [to] shows of strength in *Heimat* style and transparent industrial halls, and even idyllic Biedermeier garden pavilions, [to] constructions reminiscent of the Leipzig Battle of Nations monument, and neoclassical theaters and halls of fame."[43] Trying to be diplomatic, the prize commission announced that although it did not find any of the submissions acceptable, it did find the following characteristics most appealing because they were "home-grown" (*heimatverbunden*): octagonal ground plan, stained glass windows, and sophisticated landscaping.[44] Based on this reasoning, the commission selected three designs to be returned to the artists for modification before a final selection would be made.

Although no design had been selected, a cornerstone was laid at the 29 April 1950 ceremony. The concluding exhortations of the document sealed inside confirms that the German public, when watched from abroad, was willing to admit that the victims of the Nazis had been honorable people,

not "bad" inmates. However, it also reveals an unspoken feeling that recollection of the "dirty" camps promoted hatred against Germans:[45]

> May this place, in memory of the dead of many nations and denominations
> who died for their belief in honor, freedom and justice become not only a
> site of reverence, but a sign of warning to all humanity.
>   May this place of hatred become a place of love, serving to promote
> understanding and peace in the world!

The use of "hatred" as the one adjective to describe the Leiten site (as
opposed to, for instance, inhumanity, sadness, horror, brutality, or
suffering), while manifestly referring to the bygone behavior of the SS,
reflects the hatred to which most West Germans felt themselves exposed
due to their circumstantial complicity in the Nazi atrocities. Egocentrically,
the German public wished that commemoration on the Leiten would
convert this sentiment into a feeling of international affection for the
Germans.

Considerations of cost – by May 1950 DM400,000 had already been
spent for landscaping and related work – dictated a relatively simple
solution whose realization was not to exceed DM200,000. Thus the prize
commission ultimately selected the simplest, third-place entry by architect Prof. Harald Roth and sculptor Anton Hiller, subject to some reduc-
tions (ills. 33, 34).[46] Their design featured a high twelve-sided building
crowned by a beehive-like cupola supported by twelve interior columns.
Prismatic glass vaulting at the apex of the dome brightened the interior.
A "solemn" bronze sculpture was positioned in the axis of the entrance
and plaques with the coats of arms of forty nations were mounted under
bronze candleholders in the colonnade. Although the requisite
simplifications had been made by late August 1950,[47] construction was
delayed until April 1951 because the funds had still not been allocated.[48]
This is another example of bureaucratic foot-dragging similar to the
delays between 1946 and 1949, and those that were to come in the winter
of 1951–2.

The lack of sensitivity for the meaning of the Leiten gravesite was especially manifest at a topping-off ceremony (a dedication of the structural
shell) in September 1951, after five months of construction.[49] According to
the customary practice, a mason standing on the scaffolding, dressed in a
traditional mason's suit with a top hat, recited a ditty, then said three
cheers, each time downing a glass of wine and smashing the empty glass
against the building. In childish rhyme the following two-verse sample
from an eighteen-verse poem, probably penned by one of the masons,[50]

likens some designs submitted to the competition to "lime ovens" (*Kalköfen*), perhaps a subconscious association with ovens used to burn bones. (In an article about the new competition in February 1950 the *Süddeutsche Zeitung* had reported that the government was planning to erect a "crematorium" over the graves.[51]) The ditty then pokes fun at the evasive tactics of the authorities, who waited to pay for the memorial "until the files were yellowed":[52]

> Thus the designs ranged, alas,
> From lime kilns to national colossuses.
> The right combination, found by Mr. Roth's power,
> Resulted in this model, resembling a water tower.
>
> But now everyone asked, who'll pay, who'll give money?
> So the files yellowed and the trees colored like honey,
> Until finally in 1950, in autumn
> Into winter, construction began from the bottom.

The next speaker, Auerbach's successor as president of the State Restitution Office, Dr. Zdralek, tried to return the ceremony to a more appropriate tone, as did the third orator, county executor and former county governor Kneuer. Although the German newspapers emphasized Zdralek and Kneuer's speeches in their reports, the leftist French paper *Combat* printed a scathing criticism of the whole affair, which included a reception with beer and an oversized cake modeled after the eight-sided monument.[53]

The completed building, 10.5 meters high and 9 meters in diameter, was made of dark, rough-hewn basalt (ill. 35).[54] Its massive bronze doors, interior torch mounts, baptismal font, and thirty-three heraldic crests are reminiscent both of the 1945 Knappe project, and of more traditional heroic monuments such as the eight-sided Tannenberg (1924–7 for the decisive World War I victory) and Annaberg (1938 for the victory of the reactionary forces in the 1918–19 revolution) monuments, or the German soldiers' memorial erected at the World War II battlefield El Alamein in Egypt in the early 1950s.[55] Today the Leiten's neo-Germanic hall is concealed by enshrouding trees, hidden from public attention like the graves of the concentration camp victims themselves.

Even before those trees were planted, the relatively small Leiten hall – it was only two-thirds as tall as the cross- and star-topped columns first proposed in June 1945 – slipped from public view: it was never formally dedicated. On 19 August 1952 the Bavarian cabinet decided to dedicate it on 5 October, but the Restitution Office's extensive plans, which included inviting representatives of the thirty-three countries whose citizens had been murdered in Dachau (some of them, such as Estonia and Latvia, were no longer independent countries) required more lead time, so the ceremony was first postponed until 2 November and then abandoned altogether.[56]

The Leiten gravesite was augmented several times in the next decade. In 1955 the French War Graves Commission embarked upon a mammoth exhumation project in which it attempted to identify the skeletons of all French war victims and transport them back to France (ill. 39).[57] At the end of the French project the Bavarian parliament commissioned a 4–5 meter high cross with bronze reliefs depicting the apostles at the central promontory of the new cemetery, and a small stone sculpture (ca. 1.5 meters high) with a star of David placed in a concealed area nearby.[58] Two other memorial projects, an Italian Catholic chapel and stelae with depictions of the stations of the cross, were completed in the early 1960s. They are discussed in chapter 8, pp. 225–8, below.

In keeping with the principle that memorials represent the present better than the past, the history of the Leiten temple project from 1945 to 1952 better represents the postwar realization of the three founding myths than the origin of the Leiten gravesite. First, in 1945, Bavarian authorities were "victimized" by Allied demands, which they then "resisted" by forgetting to complete the project. They reacted similarly to the renewed foreign "victimization" when the graves were rediscovered in 1949. They briefly accommodated foreign demands before battling the horrors of the Nazi past back into oblivion in 1952–3. By that time, however, changes of another sort were already in the offing.

Rising public interest, 1955–1965

In the early 1950s we can find several roots of a changing assessment of the historical significance of the Nazi concentration camps. First, there are signs that a younger generation with different concerns and a different agenda than the molders of the first postwar decade was staking a claim in the public arena. For example, whereas in the summer of 1947 students demonstrated for higher food rations and better housing for refugees, but did not support Jewish DPs protesting antisemitism in Munich in 1949, in 1952 young Germans congregated on the anniversary of the *Kristallnacht* pogrom to draw attention to antisemitic outbreaks.[1] Over the course of the 1950s these young Germans began to play a more active role in public life. In the words of a West German historian summarizing the results of a major sociological study of the attitudes of German youth at that time, "by the late 1950s the [West German] public sphere split into a group of those who were asking questions, and a group of those who were embarrassed for lack of answers but who made up the bulk of the electorate."[2] As we will see, this younger generation, born in the later 1920s and early 1930s, was more skeptical toward some aspects of the three founding myths, even if the challenge was not voiced loudly at first.

Second, and equally important, the political situation had changed. West Germany attained national sovereignty and became a member of the Western military alliance NATO in 1954. The "economic miracle" had begun and living conditions were on the fast track to reaching Western European standards. After Stalin's death in 1953 there was an easing of immediate Cold War tensions in Europe. For instance, in 1955 West German Chancellor Adenauer visited Moscow and secured the return of the last German POWs from the Soviet Union. Thus the public was freer to focus on moral issues than at any other time since 1945.

A third factor contributing to change in the 1950s was the activity of camp survivors. By 1955 survivors of Dachau and other camps had recovered from their early 1950s' West German marginalization to establish an effective international organization, and their lobbying efforts found supporters among the new generation of Germans. The monolithic domestic front against government support for the survivors' work thus began to crack. Finally, a fourth factor contributing to the shift was renewed media attention to Nazi crimes. This attention was based both on the resolution of war-related political problems, and on the openness to new interests among the younger generation. Among other things, the trials of hitherto concealed and surreptitiously rehabilitated perpetrators of brown-collar crimes provided occasions for media attention.

Early media events: Anne Frank and *Night and Fog*

The year 1955 marks a clear caesura in the public consciousness of widespread Nazi injustice. The results of my examination of five major West German newspaper clippings collections (*Süddeutsche Zeitung, Bayerischer Rundfunk, Presse- und Informationsamt der Bundesregierung, Deutscher Bundestag, Norddeutscher Rundfunk*) revealed that clippings about Nazi crimes became sparser and sparser from 1951 until 1954, when there were almost no reports whatsoever.[3] The reporting of the *New York Times* confirms this finding without being subject to the vagaries of various collecting agencies:[4] each year from 1952 to 1956 there were: 5, 0, 0, 5, and 4 articles about former concentration camps.[5]

Thereafter (between ca. 1957 and 1964) this situation changed even more dramatically. In media discussions the history of brown-collar crimes was gradually broadened from the vague conception of the concentration camps as nebulous places where awful things had taken place, to include anecdotes about repression, deportation, exploitation, and finally murder in extermination camps. The popular reception of the diary of Anne Frank in the 1950s is a prime illustration of this change.[6] The diary was first published in the Netherlands in 1947, then in German translation by a specialized publisher in an edition of 4,500 copies in 1950. But not until 1955, with the publication of a popular German paperback edition, was the book available to a wide audience.[7] That edition went through eighteen German printings with over 700,000 copies within five years, making it, according to a February 1960 West German government memorandum, the best-selling paperback in West German history.[8] That statistic did not even include the concurrent East German paperback edition. The Pulitzer Prize-winning 1955 American stage dramatization by Goodrich and Hackett was translated for German audiences in 1957.[9] By 1960 it had been performed 2,150 times for 1.75 million viewers. A 1959 film version of the play was seen by an estimated 4–4.5 million people within a year.

What effect did the Anne Frank wave have on public attention to concentration camp memorial sites? Its impact was especially strong on the younger generation. In the summer of 1956 West German newspaper reports about critical remarks regarding the neglected condition of Bergen-Belsen made by Winston Churchill and British journalists who had visited the site went virtually unnoticed.[10] That same year Erich Lüth, a left-wing West German politician, was only able to recruit two or three school classes to visit Bergen-Belsen. Less than a year later that situation had changed dramatically. As Lüth wrote in his memoirs:[11]

> Earlier attempts that I had made to bring Hamburg school classes to the mass graves of the former concentration camp [Bergen-Belsen] had failed. Instead of one or two hundred classes going to the memorial site, only two or three classes followed my invitation . . .

> But then [in October 1956] the play "The Diary of Anne Frank" opened on the same day in Hamburg . . . and sixteen [actually: six] other German cities. The effect was by no means smaller than that of the TV miniseries "Holocaust" twenty years later.

On 17 March 1957, about 800 schoolchildren went with Lüth to lay flowers on the graves in Belsen. In the group were Axel Springer Sr., at that time already one of the mightiest barons of the West German press (*Hamburger Abendblatt, Bild, Die Welt*), and his son Axel Jr. Springer senior gave the Belsen event good coverage, and a snowball effect set in.[12] A month later another 1,000 teenagers attended a Belsen ceremony organized by the Lower Saxony Union of Jewish Communities,[13] and in early June 500 more young people organized and financed their own buses to Belsen to commemorate Anne Frank.[14] At the main ceremony in April 1958 the number of participants climbed to 3,000,[15] then mushroomed to 10,000 in 1959.[16] Contemporary reports noted that this was clearly an interest of a younger generation. As one journalist wrote, older Germans preferred to use "reconstruction and the economic miracle to 'escape forwards' from the mirror of the past."[17]

Anne Frank's diary made it easy for young Germans to identify with the intended victims of Nazi policies. Anne's story is about life in hiding, not about concentration camps or the Holocaust. The published diary softened Anne's references to Jews being murdered, and the German translation omitted several of her references to "the Germans" as perpetrators.[18] And of course the diary ends abruptly just before Anne and her family were arrested and deported to Auschwitz in August 1944. Additionally, the play, and especially the 1959 film version of the diary based on it (which had reached the largest audience of all), were decidedly melodramatic.[19]

However, once the younger generation's interest had been awakened, additional media products appeared which included the story of the Holocaust. In 1958 German journalist Ernst Schnabel published a popular documentary narrative tracing Anne Frank's story beyond Amsterdam to the camps at Westerbork, Auschwitz, and Bergen-Belsen, where she died of typhus in March 1945.[20] This best-selling documentary was immediately adapted as a radio play, which was broadcast nationally and reached an even larger audience.

At the same time as Anne Frank's story was touching the hearts of millions of young Germans, they began to view a powerful and graphic film about the concentration camps: Alain Resnais's stark documentary *Night and Fog*. This film contains a great deal of documentary material about the concentration camps, most notably the unforgettable closing scenes of bulldozers pushing naked corpses into mass graves after the liberation of Bergen-Belsen. When this French film was first released in 1956, the West German Foreign Office successfully pressured the French government not to show it at the Cannes Festival, but several screenings for special German audiences received considerable media attention.[21] Public pressure obliged the National Office for Educational Materials (Bundeszentrale für Heimatdienst, renamed Bundeszentrale für politische Bildung in 1963) to commission a German synchronization.[22] By the spring of 1957 the film was being shown in commercial movie theaters throughout Germany, excerpts were broadcast on the TV discussion program *Panorama*, and distribution to educational film suppliers had begun.[23] In contrast to the public rejection of atrocity films during the media blitz at the end of the war, Germans were now lining up and paying to see a comparable film. A contemporary study noted that it was shown in "almost all adult education centers [*Volkshochschulen*]" in West Germany, where it was sometimes screened several times.[24] Although *Night and Fog* itself does not explicitly name the Jews as victims of Nazi barbarity, a contemporary guide for teachers contained accurate and comprehensive information about the development and inner workings of the concentration camps and the various programs of mass murder.[25]

How did these audiences' conception of the concentration camps differ from that of the older generation? Their interest in the former camps themselves implicitly rejected the notion of "clean camps" spawned by the myth of ignorance. However, the nature of some of the young groups' commemorations shows that they were still heavily influenced by the myths of resistance and victimization. On 20 July 1956, for example, the student government of the University of Hamburg laid a wreath with the inscription: "The students of the University of Hamburg honor the men and women of the other Germany," referring to the military elite's attempt to assassinate Hitler on 20 July 1944. In September 1956 nearby trade union youth organizations went to Belsen to commemorate the "victims of the National Socialist and communist dictatorships," and resolved to hold a ceremony each year on 17 June, the anniversary of massive workers' uprisings in East Germany in 1953. These working-class youths thus expressed their self-identification with both the anti-Nazi resistance and the victimization of the workers' movement in East Germany by the Soviet Union. As we will see, when this generation began to attack the myths of victimization and resistance at the end of the 1960s, this legacy of the myth of ignorance, namely knowledge devoid of emotional content, was to contribute significantly to the unfeeling radicalism characteristic of the far left (see pp. 312–19).

Youth groups in Dachau

In Dachau, which had no direct connection to Anne Frank's story, the convergence of a slightly different constellation of factors led to a similar sharp rise in the interest of young visitors. Already in 1952 a wave of anti-semitic outbreaks prompted the youth organization of the German trade union association (Deutscher Gewerkschaftsbund, DGB) to hold a memorial ceremony at one of Munich's Jewish cemeteries on the anniversary of the November 1938 pogroms.[26] A year later, in December 1953, on the fifth anniversary of the signing of the United Nations Charter of Human Rights, the trade union youth organization held the ceremony at the crematorium in Dachau with the noteworthy participation of 5,000 people.[27] Since 1954, the trade union youth has organized annual commemorative ceremonies in Dachau every November on the anniversary of *Kristallnacht.* The dramatic increase in media attention given to those events over the course of the 1950s is typical of the change in public memory of Nazi genocide and repression: there were essentially no media reports about the ceremonies prior to 1956, but an ever-increasing number thereafter.[28]

By the mid-1950s public awareness of neo-Nazi and militant right-wing organizations also increased sharply. In October 1954, two years after the trade union organization's first warning about increasing neo-Nazi activity, the steering committee of the state-sponsored Bavarian Youth Ring (Bayerischer Jugendring, BJR) passed a resolution warning the public, the press, the government, and the schools about a reawakening of nationalist and militarist sentiment among youth groups.[29] Two years later, in April 1956, the Bavarian parliament debated a bill calling for more political education to combat rising (right-)extremist tendencies among youth groups.[30] Detailed studies indicate that there was no quantitative increase in right-wing youth activity during the 1950s, so that we may read the advancement up the hierarchy from the trade union youth to the state youth ring to the Bavarian parliament as an increasing sensitivity to neo-fascist tendencies in public consciousness.[31]

The trade union youth's annual November commemorative ceremony in Dachau was finally reported in the pages of a Munich newspaper in 1956, albeit only marginally in the local Dachau edition.[32] In 1957 Heinrich Stöhr, a charismatic Bavarian parliamentary representative and highly respected Dachau survivor, addressed the gathering, which was now reported in the main Munich edition.[33] This increased media attention is not attributable to the size of the ceremony: the 2,000 participants and wreaths from sixty groups in 1957 were actually fewer than in years past. On the twentieth anniversary of *Kristallnacht* in 1958 the Bavarian and Munich Youth Rings co-sponsored the trade union event.[34] There was much more media attention, and several prominent political figures attended the ceremonies in Dachau and Flossenbürg.[35]

The trade union youth organization was not the only group interested in publicizing Dachau's Nazi history. In September 1956 West Germany's largest and oldest student magazine, *Colloquium*, printed a long article about the former KZ at Dachau and the results of the older generation's eradicatory efforts.[36] The journal's south German office in Munich wrote to the recently reestablished Dachau survivors' organization Comité International de Dachau (CID) to ask if it knew any sponsors who might fund the free distribution of that issue in student dormitories.[37] While this might be interpreted as an opportunistic attempt to receive outside funding for promotional efforts, the fact that the magazine thought that it would gain readers by publishing articles about concentration camps shows how interested student-age Germans were in the topic.

Even youth groups from the town of Dachau were becoming interested in the town's Nazi history: on Confessor's Day (*Bekenntnistag*) in June 1957 Catholic youth groups from the town sponsored a commemorative ceremony in the former camp.[38] A couple of weeks earlier Bavarian Radio broadcast a program entitled "Is Grass Growing over It? The German Past in the Eyes of Young People." The report's claim that most teenagers were not interested in the Nazi past provoked spontaneous letters of protest from teenagers.[39]

The year 1960 marks a clear watershed in the size and nature of commemorative events in Dachau. A wave of antisemitic vandalism that swept across West Germany in January 1960, and the trial of Adolf Eichmann in Jerusalem in 1961 (both are discussed in the next sections) sensitized the German public to the consequences of forgetting Germany's legacy of victimizing Jews. In Dachau, the dedication of a Catholic chapel within the camp during the Eucharistic World Congress in August 1960 (discussed in the next chapter) brought tens of thousands of visitors and dozens of celebrities into the former camp (ill. 47). That event highlighted Dachau's positive international symbolic power, which a variety of groups sought to use in the following years.

The heightened sensitivity after 1960 is evident in the Bavarian reaction to critical remarks in the foreign press about the construction of the Catholic chapel in April 1960. A London reporter noted that Dachau schools did not teach about the former concentration camp at all.[40] In contrast to its nonreactions to similar reports in the 1950s, this article immediately prompted the Bavarian parliament to take positive action. On 12 May 1960 the Committee on Cultural Policy unanimously endorsed a motion by the SPD fraction, headed by representative Wilhelm Hoegner, to ensure that the financial and didactic prerequisites for visits to KZ memorial sites by all Bavarian school classes before graduation were given.[41] The motion was adopted by the State parliament with one sole opposing vote.[42] Shortly thereafter the parliament investigated the adequacy of school textbook treatments of the Nazi period as well.[43] In November 400 Bavarian teachers were taken on a tour of the site, where they listened to historical texts and survivors' stories.[44]

After the 1960 watershed, attendance of commemorative events in the former Dachau concentration camp by young Germans consistently numbered in the thousands. For example 3,000 young Catholics marched to Dachau prior to the dedication of the Catholic chapel in August 1960,[45] and 2,000 teenagers attended the trade union/youth ring ceremony in November 1960.[46] Attendance at that annual event, which usually included an impressive torchlight parade, rose to 3,000 in 1962 and 5,000 in 1963 (ill. 71).[47] The highlight of the 1963 ceremony was a dramatic reading of a skit by writer Carl Meyer-Amery. In 1964 between 6,000 and 7,000 young people attended the November ceremony in Dachau, and another 5,000 in Flossenbürg.[48]

After 1960 the character of the annual November events changed as well. Whereas in the 1950s keynote speeches were given by prominent survivors, in the 1960s presentations by contemporary political authors and activists formed the focal point of the ceremonies. Renewed Cold War concerns – construction of the Berlin Wall, for instance, began in August 1961 – may have been responsible for the change, since many survivors had Communist leanings. At any rate, the "hinge" between these two modes of commemoration appears to have been a June 1961 meeting of German young people and international representatives of anti-Nazi resistance groups in Munich.[49] The Bavarian government and the youth ring initially joined with the international Dachau survivors' organization CID to co-sponsor the congress "Youth and Resistance." At the last minute, however, the Bavarian government organizations withdrew their support and announced that the congress was canceled (it was not). Their sudden about-face was prompted by media reports that groups from East Germany would turn the event into a propaganda maneuver directed against West Germany. Since many Eastern and Western European Communists were members of the CID, which did not consider excluding them, the organizers of the November event looked to other sources of speakers.[50]

Brown-collar crimes and the Ludwigsburg "Central Office"

By the mid-1950s the public tolerance towards renazification was showing signs of change as well. In order to publicize the influence of former Nazis, in 1956 a number of public figures founded a group called the Grünwalder Circle.[51] Its members included left-wing writers such as Heinrich Böll, Erich Kuby, and Hans-Werner Richter, and a young lawyer, Hans-Jochen Vogel, who became mayor of Munich in the 1960s and Federal Minister of Justice in 1974. However, it was the trials of brown-collar criminals that attracted the most media attention by the late 1950s and in the early 1960s.

The first major milestone in this respect was a 1958 trial in Ulm. In 1956 former SS Brigadier General (*Oberführer*) Bernhard Fischer-Schweder (1895–1960) sued for his reemployment as a state official after his position as head of a refugee camp was terminated.[52] A reader of a tiny press announcement of that lawsuit remembered that Fischer-Schweder had participated in mass executions of Lithuanian Jews as police director of the Baltic port of Memel (Klaipeda), and reported him to the authorities. The ensuing investigation by the Ulm prosecutor revealed that a large number of men who had carried out mass executions in German-occupied territories were still at large. State prosecutor Erwin Schüle in Stuttgart joined forces with the Ulm authority and began a systematic search for all members of the "State Police and Security Service Task Force Tilsit" (Einsatzkommando Stapo und SD Tilsit, an ad hoc group formed on the initiative of local authorities), for whom Fischer-Schweder's men had worked as executioners. Schüle and his investigators succeeded in finding some of the murderers, including the head of the task force, Hans Joachim Böhme. In the summer of 1958 ten of them stood trial.

The so-called "Ulm Task Force Trial" created a sensation in the West German public sphere.[53] The well-researched indictment revealed the bestiality of the systematically organized murder of 4,000 men, women, and children.[54] The cynical behavior of some of the culprits and the suicide of a witness fueled public interest in the case. It became obvious that the "work" of this task force had been but a minuscule portion of a huge program of systematic mass executions throughout Eastern Europe and the Soviet Union – and that a large number of perpetrators had never been brought to justice.[55] Many people had previously assumed that the Nuremberg courts had tried all Germans who had committed crimes abroad, and there was no delegated responsibility in the West German legal system for prosecuting citizens who had committed crimes outside of the country.[56] Schüle's recognition that only through centralized, systematic investigation would it be possible to investigate and expose the perpetrators so that they could be prosecuted by the responsible local authorities led to the speedy creation of a "Central Office of State Judicial Authorities for the Prosecution of National Socialist Crimes of Violence" in Ludwigsburg in December 1958.[57]

That Ulm trial marks the beginning of a series of trials which, in spite of their rather narrow judicial scope, made a major contribution to the public and historical knowledge of the Nazi camps. In 1958 and early 1959 the Bonn trial of two extremely sadistic SS sergeants who had operated primarily in KZ Sachsenhausen, Gustav Sorge and Wilhelm Schubert, kept the macabre brutality of Nazi criminals in the news.[58] The two men were convicted of sixty-seven and forty-six individual murders and numerous counts of manslaughter, respectively, each of which was proven beyond doubt by documentary evidence and witnesses under cross-examination. A film about the trial was made available to school classes in some parts of Germany.[59] In the following years prosecutions of members of execution commandos alone resulted in trials in Dortmund, Bielefeld, Tübingen, and Aurich (Schleswig-Holstein).[60]

Such trials exposed a division within West German society with respect to brown-collar crimes. Although a certain sector of the public sphere supported the prosecution of the criminals, there was much reticence on the part of the responsible authorities. Many government agencies were still laced with brown-collar perpetrators in key positions.[61] The police, for instance, could not be trusted with the investigations, searches, and interrogations of suspected brown-collar criminals because numerous high West German police officials belonged to that group. To give just one example, the chief of the Rheinland-Pfalz state police, Georg Heuser, was arrested under suspicion of having committed mass murder in Minsk.[62] Four years later he was convicted of being an "accessory to murder" in 30,000 cases – for which he was sentenced to a mere fifteen years imprisonment. That disproportionately mild sentence points to a second bastion of pro-amnesia sentiment in 1950s and 1960s West German society: the judicial system.

A cohort of judges, not one of whom was convicted after 1945 because of his partisan rulings under Nazi law, passed extremely mild rulings on even the most heinous brown-collar murderers.[63] Only one single person in the task force trials prior to the spring of 1963 was convicted as a murderer, although the vast majority had executed thousands of defenseless civilians.[64] Later a few of these lower-court exonerations were reversed by the supreme federal appellate court (Bundesgerichtshof), probably because of public attention. A good example of unpleasant publicity is the exhibition "Unrepentant Nazi Justice," organized in November 1959 by Reinhard Strecker (b. 1930) and students in Karlsruhe and Berlin.[65] Once the West German federal prosecutor confirmed the authenticity of the documents in that exhibition, the mainstream media took up the issue as well, with critical editorials appearing in newspapers such as *Die Zeit* and *Die Welt*.

One of the best indicators of the changing public assessment of brown-collar crimes are the parliamentary debates about the statute of limitations for manslaughter and murder that were held in 1960, 1965, 1969, and 1979.[66] (These parliamentary debates are commonly known as *Verjährung* debates, after the German term for "statute of limitations.") According to existing law, after fifteen years judicial authorities could no longer prosecute crimes of manslaughter, and after twenty years murder was no longer legally prosecutable. Thus unless the statute were changed, after 1960 many brown-collar criminals who had merely "followed orders" when slaughtering their victims (one of the criteria distinguishing "murder" and "manslaughter" is the presence of base motives) would be protected from prosecution.[67]

The 1960 parliamentary discussion started with a brief discussion about whether the fifteen-year clock started ticking in 1945 or 1949, when West Germany became a sovereign state. They decided on the earlier date, and a majority quickly emerged for allowing the crimes to lapse. The advocates of keeping the old lapse clause argued that a lengthening of the limitation would amount to the retroactive application of a new law, which would weaken people's confidence in the rule of law. In contrast to the debate in 1965 (which is discussed below), in 1960 neither key public figures nor the German public took any interest in the debate. As one delegate put it, the majority of the public "does not want to hear, see or know anything" about the brown-collar crimes.[68]

Interestingly, the percentage of West Germans who thought that brown-collar criminals should be allowed to escape punishment rose steadily throughout the 1960s, from 34 percent in 1958 to 67 percent in 1969.[69] When contrasted with the clearly rising interest in learning about the history of Nazism over the same period, these statistics indicate a shift in the focus of younger Germans' interest in the Nazi era: away from the individual crimes and towards the workings of the system as a whole. This interpretation is confirmed by the concurrent interest in the phenomenon of "fascism," and by the emergence of the so-called structuralist and functionalist explanations for Nazi policy towards Jews.[70]

One event that may have strengthened the desire of many older West German politicians to "close the books" on brown-collar crimes was a wave of antisemitic vandalism that swept across Germany from Christmas 1959 to late January 1960.[71] At the time the West German government had been fighting a low-grade battle to maintain a positive image abroad in spite of recurring smaller antisemitic incidents and exposures of high government officials with unsavory if not criminal Nazi backgrounds, such as Globke, Oberländer, and Schröder. With this wave of antisemitic incidents the public relations problem suddenly became acute. National and international attention focused on West Germany's relationship to its Nazi past. Given widespread skepticism of the claim that East German agitators were behind the incidents,[72] West German politicians adopted a "mea culpa" stance and initiated a number of measures to improve political education, especially historical education, in the schools. The immediate efforts at damage control included a 2 February 1960 statement delivered in Bergen-Belsen by Chancellor Adenauer and an 11 February resolution by the Conference of Ministers of Culture that it would examine "the treatment of the most recent past in history instruction." The resolution included a statement of intent to act upon the results of an examination of school history textbooks that had already been conducted in 1959.[73]

National Socialism in West German schoolbooks

Already in the late 1950s progressive educators had begun to study and theorize about Holocaust education.[74] They studied the prior knowledge and attitudes of boys and girls at various age levels, attempted to assess the effects of education about Nazism on political attitudes, and examined the various tools (such as films and textbooks) available to teachers. After the wave of antisemitic incidents the West German educational establishment began to take a keen interest in this research.[75] A 30 January 1960 directive from the National Conference of Ministers of Culture, coupled with critical reports in the press about the obvious inadequacy of didactic materials about the Holocaust, prompted a number of official and unofficial analyses of history textbooks.[76] These studies confirmed the results of previous research suggesting that the treatment of Nazism was woefully inadequate.

This problem was partially remedied in 1961 with the publication of several school textbooks about the Nazi period, foremost among them Hannah Vogt's *The Burden of Guilt: A Short History of Germany, 1914–1945*.[77] This was the first West German textbook since the late 1940s to deal openly and comprehensively with the Nazi period,[78] and it quickly found wide distribution.[79] Also indicative of the change was the attention pedagogues now devoted to examining the process of "coping" or "coming to terms" with the past (*Bewältigung der Vergangenheit*).[80] A justly famous presentation on that subject by Theodor Adorno at a conference of educators in Wiesbaden in November 1959 was published in the wake of the antisemitic incidents in the educators' journal *Gesellschaft, Staat, Erziehung*.[81] Adorno used the term *Aufarbeitung*, meaning "to work through," instead of the ambiguous *Bewältigung*, which can also mean "mastery," in order to emphasize that he meant an open-ended process, not a limited task that might soon be accomplished.[82] As we will see, his term did not catch on, and the concept of *Vergangenheitsbewältigung* ("mastery of the past"), with precisely the connotation he wished to avoid, has dominated the discussion since the late 1960s.

Changes in school history textbooks alone do not necessarily represent changes in present or future consciousness. As many participants in the discussions about the treatment of the Nazi period in postwar West

German schoolbooks have pointed out, formal history instruction was and is but a tiny fraction of the exposure of youngsters to the Nazi past in the home and through the mass media, so that it is not the dominant influence.[83] As one educator wrote in 1959:[84]

> In recent years the persecution of the Jews has been repeatedly thrust into public consciousness through the newspapers, court cases, films, radio and books, and we may assume that there is no ninth grade schoolboy who is unfamiliar with the basic facts about the extermination of the Jews.

The most important television series about the Nazi period was a fourteen-part documentary entitled *The Third Reich*, which was broadcast in 1960–61, and again in 1963.[85] The twelve-hour documentary was so popular that it was published in book form in 1964.[86] As the introduction to the book explained, it was aimed at the "millions of German citizens who grew into consumer society [*Wohlstandsgesellschaft*] without 'mastering' their most recent 'unfortunate [*unselige*] past,'" and it provided a first opportunity for the younger generation to see sounds and moving images from the period about which their parents had told them so little. In her memoir of what it was like to grow up in postwar Germany, Sabine Reichel devotes a whole chapter to a discussion of her viewing of the film with her father in 1963, when she was 17.[87]

Watching TV in the early 1960s was a family-centered event, and many families may not have been as open as the Reichels to allowing children to watch a documentary on the Nazi era. However, illustrated magazines have always been a source of information on taboo subjects for young people. Around 1960 there was a fundamental shift in the portrayal of Nazi history in such magazines, which studies indeed found to be one of the primary sources of knowledge about Nazism at that time. In his examination of the treatment of the Holocaust in the mass-circulation illustrated magazines *Stern* and *Quick*, Michael Schornstheimer found that by early 1960 *Stern* was describing the central characteristics of the German neo-Nazi world view in terms that described its own reporting on topics relating to Nazism only a short time before: downplaying of Nazi atrocities, attempting to portray the good in Nazi leaders, and discrediting any efforts to learn from the transgressions of the Nazi era.[88] Needless to say, *Stern*'s own message regarding Nazism itself had changed dramatically as well.[89]

However, this increasing knowledge of Nazi history does not mean that these youngsters were gaining an emotional connection to the historical events. Several studies conducted in the early and mid-1960s confirm this finding. For example, a study of history teaching in 1964 found that young Germans conceived of National Socialism as a period dominated by "omnipotent subjects, personalized collectives [the Jew, the Russian], stereotypical organizational criteria, and anthropomorphic referential categories [e.g. Hitlerism]."[90] A 1965 study characterized the attitudes of young people who evinced interest in the Nazi era as "cool, rational, upstanding . . . and without historical imagination."[91] As we will see below, this unfeeling relationship to the Nazi past had significant consequences. It gave rise to what mainstream and conservative critics were to call "left-wing fascism" in the late 1960s.[92]

Media attention: from the Eichmann trial to the Auschwitz trial, 1960–1964

While the repercussions of the wave of antisemitic incidents in 1959–60 were largely limited to the West German educational establishment, the trial of Adolf Eichmann in Jerusalem from April to August 1961 had a much greater impact on public knowledge of Nazi atrocities, both in West Germany and abroad.[93] Eichmann, head of the "Jewish Section" of the SS Main Office of Reich Security since 1939, had been the bureaucratic mastermind of the Holocaust. He had managed to escape Allied capture by fleeing to South America after the war. Finally discovered and abducted by the Israeli secret service in May 1960, he became the highest-ranking SS bureaucrat to be tried after the conclusion of the Nuremberg successor trials in 1948. In order to avert the danger that the international public would view a judgment against Eichmann as an exoneration of the tens of thousands of other cogs in the moloch of mass extermination, the Israeli prosecutor focused on exposing Eichmann's role within the complicated system of the Nazi state, thus turning the trial into what historian Peter Steinbach has called "a lesson in contemporary history."[94]

Especially in West Germany the Eichmann trial was received as such a lesson. It was accompanied by the publication of numerous biographies and collections of documents.[95] The trial also facilitated another qualitative step in the process of public recollection of the Holocaust: for the first time, that process of learning from past mistakes itself became a focus of broader public attention. In Munich, an exhibition of documents about Eichmann included panels about former brown-collar workers in the West German government, such as Hans Globke.[96] Summaries and analyses of the public reactions to the trial were published in the countries most interested in them: West Germany,[97] Israel,[98] and the United States.[99] In Germany, publications such as *We Sons of Eichmann* emphasized the enduring cultural legacies of the brown-collar crimes.[100] Additionally, the Eichmann trial, in contrast to the textbooks and magazines mentioned above, focused on the system and details of the National Socialist plan to exterminate all Jews within its sphere of influence. In other words, information about the complicity of the brown-collar bureaucrats was added to the knowledge of the direct physical brutality of many Nazi criminals.

Less than a year after the Eichmann episode ended with Eichmann's execution in June 1962, Rolf Hochhuth's play *The Deputy* opened in Germany in February 1963. Suddenly the Holocaust spotlight was trained on the Vatican.[101] The German and international publics reacted furiously to this well-documented indictment of Pope Pius XII's inaction in the face of detailed knowledge about the extermination of the Jews of Europe.[102] The published text of the play went through six German editions within the first three months, with about 200,000 copies within a year. It was soon translated into twelve languages. *The Deputy* sparked more than a dozen monographs in response, eight of which appeared within two years.[103] Whether or not one accepted Hochhuth's portrayal or the awkward excuses put forward by the Pope's defenders, the issue of taking a strong moral stand in the face of injustice was publicly debated for months. A work of high literary quality, *The Deputy* soon became part of the canon studied by West German high school classes.

During those same years of the early 1960s the Central Prosecutor's Office in Ludwigsburg initiated four major trials of members of execution squads.[104] As revealing as each of those trials were, they were overshadowed by the Frankfurt trial of Auschwitz personnel, which began in December 1963 and ended in August 1965.[105] Typical of the haphazard nature of work in Ludwigsburg, the trial was initiated by a chance occurrence.[106] A journalist noticed some charred files in the home of a survivor he was interviewing for an article on *Wiedergutmachung*. The survivor had taken the papers from police headquarters in Breslau after it was set on fire by the fleeing SS in 1945. The papers turned out to be forms closing cases brought against guards at Auschwitz for shooting "fleeing" inmates. The journalist showed them to state prosecutor Fritz Bauer in Frankfurt, who realized their importance and set the mills of justice in motion.

Bauer was an exceptional man, a postwar returnee to Germany, from which he had fled after concentration camp imprisonment.[107] Through his precise work and his office's meticulous preparation, the German and international publics learned about the shocking reality of daily life in

Auschwitz. Although in polls 40 percent of West Germans claimed never to have heard of the trial, more than half of the 60 percent who did know about it actively wanted to learn more about the Nazi past.[108]

The visitors at the Auschwitz trial were given an opportunity to learn more about Auschwitz at a concurrent documentary exhibition in Frankfurt's St. Paul's Church, a site of symbolic national importance because the first democratic parliament in Germany had convened there in 1848.[109] The trial itself spawned not only some of the most important historiographical works on the systematic nature of Nazi criminality (these are discussed below), it sparked a number of essayistic and literary reflections on Germany and its relationship to the Nazi past as well. These included contributions by well-known German intellectual and cultural figures such as Karl Jaspers,[110] Ulrich Sonnemann,[111] Kurt Sontheimer,[112] Martin Walser,[113] and Peter Weiss.[114] Weiss's oratorium *The Inquiry* was a stylized rendition of Bernd Naumann's trial reports in the *Frankfurter Allgemeine Zeitung*, which were also published in book form.[115]

The statute of limitations revisited, 1965–1979

The Frankfurt Auschwitz trial was just finishing as the twenty-year statute of limitations on the prosecution of murder approached in 1965. The West German public sphere was highly sensitized by the spectacular and horrifying testimony in Frankfurt, and this time, in contrast to the *Verjährung* nondebate of 1960, the parliament debated the difficult moral issues exhaustively, going back to first principles.[116] The 1965 debate also differed in that it was accompanied by broad-based efforts to educate the public and influence public opinion. Rudolf Augstein, editor of the news magazine *Der Spiegel*, interviewed Karl Jaspers and published his essay "There Can Be No Statute of Limitations on Genocide."[117] Simon Wiesenthal's publication of 200 opinions he solicited from public figures offers another example of broad public outreach.[118]

In the 1965 debate there were three basic positions. The cabinet, including the Minister of Justice but not Chancellor Erhard, argued that the statute should take effect because the Ludwigsburg Central Office had had ample time to prosecute all of the brown-collar murderers. We now know that this was not at all the case: a number of large and important cases were still being prosecuted until the 1980s. The Free Democratic Party, led by representative Thomas Dehler (1897–1967), argued that the statute should go into effect on schedule because otherwise Germans' trust in the rule of law would be shaken. This was the old 1960 argument that an extension would mean the prosecution of crimes under retroactively amended laws.

Ernst Benda (b. 1925) of the ruling Christian Democratic Party, who was too young to have been complicit in brown-collar crimes, joined forces with the Social Democratic opposition party, led by Adolf Arndt (1904–72), a member of the older generation, to contradict the majority desire to close the books on brown-collar murderers. He argued that an intuitive "feeling of justice" (*Rechtsgefühl*) was more important than trust in a manifestly unjust "rule of law" (*Rechtssicherheit*). The former would be corrupted, with all of the negative consequences, if horrific murders that could be prosecuted were not prosecuted.

Dehler, a member of the older generation, drew on the myth of victimization to support his claim that extending the statute would allow the prosecution of mistakes made in a situation of compulsion. Arndt, however, broke with the mythic triad and admitted his own complicity for "not having done enough." Thereby, and with his precise description of the crimes that were at issue, Arndt gained respect among the increasingly politicized younger generation, which was already moving toward the rebellious year 1968. The parliament, however, settled on a compromise. It reset the clock to begin with the establishment of the West German state in 1949, giving the Ludwigsburg prosecutors four more years to do their work.

Taking a brief look ahead on this issue, the *Verjährung* debate in 1969 was anticlimactic. The positions were basically the same as in 1965, but the balance of power had shifted in favor of those wishing to extend the limitation. This was visible in the inversion of a common German analogy, that of a bird "soiling its nest" (*Nestbeschmutzung*). No longer were people who recalled Nazi crimes soiling Germany's reputation; the criminals themselves were now seen as dirt that needed to be cleaned out. The issue of brown-collar criminals living freely in society had received an additional twist in 1968 when a law was passed to enable judges to pass light sentences on the many practitioners of civil disobedience at that time.

The new law stipulated that judges would have to consider the motivation for committing a crime, and to pass lighter sentences when base motivations were not present. As a putatively unintended consequence, all brown-collar criminals who were "only" accessories to murder (for instance, those who had acted under orders) were subject to a maximum sentence of fifteen years, and thus fell under the manslaughter limitation that had lapsed in 1960.[119] This "amnesty through the back door" embittered many members of parliament wishing to clean the brown dirt out of West Germany's nest. However, instead of drawing the most logical conclusion and removing the limitation completely, the majority of members of parliament followed the lead of Justice Minister Ehmke, who wanted to avoid any "special justice" (*Sonderrecht*) for brown-collar murderers. He still followed the 1965 argument that such a differentiation would shake the confidence of the populace in the legal consistency of the rule of law. Thus the limitation on prosecution of *all* murders was extended to thirty years.

In 1979, when the issue arose again, the situation had once again changed dramatically. Minister of Justice Maihofer now argued: "At some point grass will grow over murders, usually after one generation. But no grass grows over Auschwitz, not even in 100 generations." He wanted to remove completely the limitation for brown-collar murders, but keep that for other murders at thirty years. In contrast to the earlier debates, the majority of members of parliament now felt that instead of giving priority to the protection of murderers from potential injustice, they wanted to underscore that protecting human lives from physical harm is one of the highest values in a democratic society. Thus they voted to remove the limitation on prosecution for murder. However, in order not to appear to be singling out brown-collar criminals for special punishment, they removed it for every kind of murder, not just murder committed before 1945.

The use of trials of Nazi perpetrators as a means of collective moral education in the late 1970s was in essence a return to the didactic program conceived by the Allies at the end of World War II, and implemented in the Nuremberg and Dachau trials. In the words of historian Peter Steinbach, one of the foremost experts on West Germany's dealings with its National Socialist past, the progression in the statute of limitations debates "emphasizes the commitment to [develop] a moral–political consciousness of history as well as a sense of ethical–political responsibility."[120] The decisive difference between the didactics of the Allied and later German trials is that the first, carried out by the victors over the vanquished, was conducted in the postwar context of the myth of victimization. By the mid-1960s a large sector of the populace had either never subscribed to that myth, or, in the face of the events early in the decade, actively repudiated it. Before we return to Dachau we will examine one last area in which the rising public interest of the 1960s is evident: scholarly history, the discipline devoted to debunking myths.

German historiography of Nazi crimes

Several authors examining the historiography of the Holocaust note that the study of Nazi crimes by West German scholars began in the early 1960s.[121] If we look back to 1945 we can see why this took so long. The mammoth documentary project of the first trial at Nuremberg – the forty-two volumes were first published in 1947 – was rooted in the initial punitive mode of "reeducation" under Allied auspices. Tainted as it was by this origin, in the context of the late 1940s and early 1950s it was categorically ignored by German scholars, who had more interest in bolstering than in debunking the three founding myths. Instead of examining the documents, German legal scholars concentrated their efforts on demonstrating why the Nuremberg trial had been inconsistent with the "rule of law."[122] Shortly after the war, there had also been a large outpouring of survivor memoirs and shorter works about the Nazi regime.[123] However, within a short time, the market for this literature had dried up as well.[124] Thus for the first decade after its initial publication in 1946, Eugen Kogon's *The SS-State* remained the sole German publication that attempted a systematic portrayal of the concentration camp system.[125] Another paperback, Günther Weisenborn's collection of reports about various German resistance efforts, *The Silent Rebellion*, documented how Germans had been persecuted by the Nazis for oppositional activities.[126]

After Kogon, the next comprehensive treatment of a concentration camp was Hans-Günther Adler's *Theresienstadt 1941 to 1945*, first published in 1955.[127] This massive volume was one of the first publications marking the beginning of the mid-1950s' resurgence of interest in the history of National Socialist genocide in West Germany. That same year one of the major studies of National Socialist judeocide, Léon Poliakov and Josef Wulf's *The Third Reich and the Jews*, was translated into German.[128] In 1956 these works were followed by German translations of Lord Russell of Liverpool's *Scourge of the Swastika*,[129] and Gerald Reitlinger's *The Final Solution.*[130] With Reitlinger's book the first comprehensive portrayal of the Nazi mass extermination programs based on archival research (as opposed to lived experience) became available to West German readers. Two substantial collections of documents intended for wide audiences soon followed: Poliakov and Wulf's *The Third Reich and its Servants* (1956),[131] and Swiss historian Walther Hofer's *National Socialism: Documents 1933–1945* (1957).[132] German authors are conspicuously absent from this list of early works.[133]

The first overview of the Nazi period written by German historians, Hermann Mau and Helmut Krausnick's *German History of the Most Recent*

Past, first published in a German history series in 1953, was republished in a more accessible edition in 1956.[134] Those two members of the Munich Institute for Contemporary History, however, treated the brown-collar crimes only cursorily, barely mentioning the concentration camps or the "final solution," and conveying only the most abstract picture of the dimensions of Nazi genocide. At the same time, resistance to Hitler was given broad coverage. For example, nineteen pages were devoted to Hitler's neutralization of the potentially renegade SA under Ernst Röhm in 1934, and sixteen pages to the military resistance that planned the 20 July 1944 coup attempt. In contrast, only eleven pages are devoted to the entire topic of "persecution."[135] And even that short section was used to exonerate the German army. In conjunction with the "task force" operations, the smoothly organized shooting of hundreds of thousands of civilians in newly conquered territories, Krausnick wrote that the military, "resisting by its very nature" ("*von Haus aus widerstrebend*"), opposed the actions.[136] He concluded: "When . . . the worst excesses of some SS units against Jews began, army commanders took decisive steps against this riotous activity" (167).

Such claims were quite in keeping with the myth of resistance. In fact, military leaders were heavily implicated in brown-collar crimes. Krausnick himself admitted on a later page that "the opportunity [to attempt a *putsch*] presented by the SS excesses in Poland" passed without any action by Wehrmacht leaders (177). But even this was far from the truth. A short quotation from an October 1941 report conveys a quite different impression of the behavior of the German army: "At the outset it can be said emphatically that the cooperation with the Wehrmacht was, in general, good, and in individual instances . . . very close, even cordial."[137] Mau and Krausnick's book also contains lapses into unreconstructed Nazi jargon, such as the use of the collective singular "the Russian" to refer to the Red army (e.g. 192, 194), revealing the linguistic difficulty some West German historians had when attempting to portray the Nazi period.

By 1960 a few indigenous portrayals of the Nazi regime were available to West German readers. They included Wolfgang Scheffler's *The Persecution of the Jews in the Third Reich* (1960),[138] Martin Broszat's *The National Socialist World View* (1960),[139] and Karl-Dietrich Bracher's *The National Socialist Seizure of Power* (1960).[140] The first, a slim brochure later distributed by the Federal Center for Political Education, was more of an overview for history teachers, while the other two focused on explaining how the Nazis were able to attain and maintain their power for so long. Typical of the vast majority of publications about the Third Reich until well into the 1970s, all three devoted more space to opposition to Nazi crimes than to the crimes themselves.[141]

This focus on resistance – especially military resistance – to Hitler, and the concomitant lack of attention to the brown-collar criminality of the Nazi regime, indicate that the myth of resistance retained its interpretative power until the late 1970s.[142] Concomitantly, the persecuted victims and opponents of the Nazi regime were ignored as much as possible. The first West German academic history of a concentration camp was a study of Bergen-Belsen commissioned by the Lower Saxony state government – after Bergen-Belsen had received so much international attention during the Anne Frank wave. It was published by Eberhard Kolb in 1962.[143] The next historical examination of Nazi concentration camps by professional West German historians was not published until 1970, when a collection of studies about six camps, prepared for a colloquium at the Munich Institute for Contemporary History, was printed in an Institute series.[144] In the introduction to that volume, Martin Broszat speaks of an "overtaxing" of the topic in the public sphere on the one hand, and the "completely inadequate" basic knowledge about the camps on the other. The defensiveness of his opening sentence reveals the difficulties broaching the topic posed in West German society during the 1960s: "The National Socialist concentration camps, many readers will think, are a topic of contemporary history that has already been worn out by too much discussion, so that another treatment will not be able to attract especial attention." A decade later, the opposite would be true: German readers demanded more information about brown-collar crimes than German historiography could deliver.

Although the Munich Institute for Contemporary History had published some important documents of Nazi crimes in the 1950s, such as the eyewitness "Gerstein report" about the procedure of gassing in gas chambers (1953),[145] its main focus prior to the 1970s was on a more standard political history of the Third Reich.[146] However, the need for historical background information in order to assess the charges and defense arguments in trials of brown-collar criminals led, in the late 1950s, to a number of narrow investigations by researchers at the Institute commissioned by West German courts.[147] The magnitude of these reports changed dramatically with the advent of the Frankfurt Auschwitz trial. The meticulously researched reports prepared for it by Hans Buchheim, Martin Broszat, Hans-Adolf Jacobsen, and Helmut Krausnick were published in hardcover and paperback soon after the trial was over.[148] Until the mid-1980s they were unsurpassed in detail, and they still rank among the best works about the SS and the systematic criminality of the Nazi state.[149]

We now return to Dachau to see how, against this background of a rising public awareness of and knowledge about Nazi crimes, concrete representations of these events were fashioned in the West German public realm. We will look at the Dachau survivors and the three major religious groups that became involved in postwar commemoration in Dachau.

Catholics celebrate at Dachau

The 2,579 Catholic clergymen imprisoned in the Dachau concentration camp had been a special group among the camp inmates. We recall that in 1940 all of the Christian clergymen being held in "protective custody" in the Reich – about 1,000 at that time – were consolidated in Dachau.[1] They were housed in barracks nos. 26, 28, and 30 in the northwest corner of the camp. The priests were allowed to convert one room of barrack 26 into a chapel, which was officially off limits to other camp inmates (ill. 41). Depending on the whims of the various commandants, they were sometimes accorded and sometimes refused other privileges, such as exemption from hard labor, or permission to receive packages. About 450 of the final number were German or Austrian (the Poles with 1,780 were the largest national group), and they had a relatively high survival rate. With their common background, and ample time and opportunity in the camp, these German priests formed a tightly knit group that lasted long into the postwar era. The KZ Priests' Association (KZ-Priestergemeinschaft), as they called themselves, met regularly in Dachau and in the home districts of some of the more prominent and more active members.

Not surprisingly, Catholic clergymen were among the first to erect commemorative markers at the site. In accordance with the principle of memorials outlined on p. 187, their recollective efforts reflected Catholic belief more than the Nazi persecution of Catholics.

The crematorium–monastery plan, 1945

The basic conception of Catholic commemoration in KZ Dachau is already clearly visible in a monastery project proposed shortly after liberation. In May or June 1945 Otto Pies, a Jesuit priest liberated in Dachau, and Friedrich Pfanzelt, the priest of the main Catholic church in the city of Dachau, convinced US General Patton to allow them to convert the crematory into a monastery, with the church placed in a second story over the ovens.[2] It was to be named "Eternal Worship" (*Ewige Anbetung*). Pfanzelt's parish in Dachau was responsible for conducting an architectural competition to obtain plans for the structure, which was to cost 2 million Reichsmarks, four times the amount budgeted for the Leiten gravesite later that summer.[3] In July Munich Cardinal Faulhaber requested permission for the project from US Supreme Commander Eisenhower.[4] Faulhaber explained that the monastery was intended to "turn the site of godless human aberration into a place of prayer and atonement for the edification and emulation of all visitors to the camp, and for peace in the world."[5]

I was not able to find any response by Eisenhower. According to one of the priests who devised the plan, the Americans lost interest in the project after Patton, its advocate on the Allied side, was killed in a car accident in December 1945.[6]

How does this project reflect a Catholic conception of the concentration camps? We can infer the role of the crematory in the monastery from similar Catholic cult buildings. A Catholic tradition dating back to the original St. Peter's basilica in Rome and to the temple in Jerusalem integrates relics in a crypt or sub-church into the religious ritual performed above.[7] The church gains its legitimacy from the power attributed to the relics. The cult performed with the relics serves primarily to reaffirm religious dogma, and only secondarily to recollect the historical events represented by the relic. At the grave of a Christian martyr, for instance, the cult celebrates the martyr primarily as a reflection of Christ's sacrifice and an indication of the glory of God, while the physical destruction of that human's life plays at most a subsidiary role.

As we will also see in the camp and Leiten chapels, as well as the convent that was actually built, religion is the focal point, not history. The historical events are taken from their historical context and reinterpreted as elements of a path to salvation through the suffering of Christ.

The KZ barracks chapel and the postwar SS church

One of the distinguishing features of the Dachau concentration camp was that all priests imprisoned in the Nazi Reich were relocated there after 1940. They lived together in barracks 26 and 28. Additionally, a substantial number of the Italian and French political prisoners were devout Catholics. The German priests had been allowed to set up a chapel in their barrack (no. 26), where they regularly celebrated mass, clandestinely ministered to the religious needs of the other inmates, and even secretly ordained a priest. Thus there was an authentic religious site with an active Catholic community within the camp. However, Catholic groups and institutions in Bavaria showed little interest in preserving (or reconstructing) these authentic sites in the camp. Instead, they erected religious monuments at especially prominent places.

After liberation Catholics were the first survivors to erect commemorative markers in the camp. Photographs taken shortly after liberation show a high cross at the center of the roll-call square (ill. 7). Polish Catholics and German-descended Czechs who did not wish to return to their home countries erected another memorial in front of the crematorium building for All Saints' Day (31 October) 1945. It consisted of a catafalque (a symbolic coffin) on a raised platform crowned by a cross. This altar-like monument remained in front of the crematorium for at least a year.[8]

Also in the fall of 1945, a Catholic church was built by the former SS men interned in the camp (ills. 2, 3, 42).[9] It stood on one side of the roll-call square, between the entry gate and the canteen barrack. Dachau survivor Leonhard Roth, a priest who had been imprisoned in the concentration camp for two years, initiated the project. Roth had remained in the camp after liberation at the request of the Munich Cardinal Faulhaber in order to minister to the religious needs of the internees. Roth needed a church because the chapel in the priests' barrack had been dismantled by the Americans when they converted the concentration camp into an internment camp. Construction on this new "Church of the Holy Cross" began in November 1945 and was completed in early 1946, when it was dedicated by Cardinal Faulhaber.[10] This new postwar church was built by SS internees out of an unused barrack. It had a masonry tower, could seat 1,500, and featured an organ made of US army "k-ration" cans.[11]

The church's location near the entrance to the inner compound of the internment camp gave it a checkered history. When the US army turned the internment camp over to the Bavarian authorities in October 1947, the church was part of the transferred inventory.[12] At that time all concerned parties were of the opinion that it belonged to the Catholic archbishopric. When the German internment camp administration fenced off its offices at the south end of the camp a short time later, the church also became off limits to the internees, except on Sundays.[13] That situation was rectified with a special fence in spring 1948.[14] The church was repainted and its roof repaired in August, shortly before the internment camp was closed and converted into a refugee settlement.[15] It did not remain part of the refugee settlement for long, however. Because of its proximity to the US military complex, the US army confiscated it again in December 1949 as part of an annex within the former prisoners' compound.[16]

Father Roth, who remained in Dachau to serve as the refugees' priest after the internment camp was closed, was thus forced to set up another church in refugee barrack 32 at the northeast side of the camp – it had once been concentration camp barrack 27 for the "punishment detail," opposite the clerics' barrack 28.[17] The SS church on the roll-call square was presumably unused until it was relinquished by the Americans in 1956.[18] As part of the expansion of the refugee settlement, a Protestant "Golgotha" church was built on the roll-call square near the former infirmary barrack in 1951.[19] When the CID and the Bavarian government began planning a new memorial site in 1956, they decided to tear down all buildings constructed within the camp after the war. Roth, however, persuaded them to preserve the two churches on the roll-call square.[20] Although the CID incorporated the preservation of the churches in its official list of demands,[21] some members may still have hoped to remove them sooner or later, as internal documents from 1958 show.[22] In any case, late in 1959 the organization of surviving concentration camp priests joined the proponents of the demolition of the old internees' church.[23] Instead of the rickety old SS barrack church, they were planning to erect a large new stone chapel at the far end of the central camp street. The dedication of the tall new chapel was to provide a focal point for the Eucharistic World Congress the next summer. When Roth committed suicide in 1960, the only outspoken advocate of the church's preservation disappeared from the scene. In 1962 the plan to demolish the "temporary church" (*Notkirche*), as Catholic officials began to call it, was confirmed by all groups involved in the planning of the new memorial site.[24] The actual demolition took place late in 1964 (ill. 28).[25]

The KZ priests' approval of the demolition of the postwar church does not mean that they were opposed to preserving all historical remnants. In March 1959 they drew up a petition calling for the re-creation of the KZ chapel in block 26 as part of the memorial site.[26] Later that same year, when it was clear that it would be very costly to preserve all of the camp barracks, the KZ priests still called for the preservation of the two priests' blocks (barracks 26 and 28) and the end walls of the other barracks along the central camp street.[27] Soon, however, this plan was dropped as well. It was easier to remove those traces of life and history in the camp that did not fit into the message that the memorial site was to convey.

Both the KZ barrack chapel in block 26 and the 1945 SS church would have been discordant remains in a memorial site documenting the brutality of concentration camp life. The KZ chapel – especially if it were the only barrack in the vicinity left standing – would have overemphasized the presence of clerics in the concentration camp. The SS church would have conveyed the impression that the interned former Nazis had been hard-working, religious men, and it would have been a reminder of the drawn-out and ultimately unsuccessful attempt to bring them to justice after the war. The Dachau survivors conceived of the camp as a place to commemorate and learn about the victims; why should they preserve a relic casting the victimizers in a favorable light? What could its role have been in the memorial site? In the 1950s the likelihood was great that many Germans would have seen the SS church as evidence of their own "victimization."

Thus it was logical that, in the 1950s, when even the preservation of remains of the Nazi-era camp was hotly contested, little thought was given to documenting its postwar uses. Only the SS church's initiator, priest-survivor Leonhard Roth, advocated its preservation.[28] After his suicide in 1960 it was demolished unopposed. Not until the late 1990s, in the wake of a heated debate about the creation of a museum in Buchenwald to document the postwar use of that concentration camp as a Soviet internment camp, did public support for preserving postwar modifications within the camps develop. And even then, this support was limited to traces left by the occupying powers, not by the interned Germans. The murals in the Dachau service/museum building (discussed in chapter 15, below), the Soviet insignia in Ravensbrück, and the camp for British POWs in Sachsenhausen are examples of this. In contrast, I would argue that future generations, whose primary interest is to learn about how they inherited the conditions that made the camps possible, would benefit from concrete evidence of that process of modification. Perhaps some day the foundation of the postwar church will be marked, or even a building constructed to exhibit documents of the German internees.

The Italian chapel "Mary, Queen of Peace"

The German drive to create a new chapel in 1960 was most likely sparked by a mid-1950s initiative by Italian survivors to create a Catholic chapel at the Leiten cemetery. In 1955 the Ferneries chapter of the "Democratic Resistance- and Freedom-Fighters of Italy" initiated the project, which was later taken up by the Italian committee in the CID.[29] By February 1957, when Pope Pius XII donated a chalice to help raise funds for the building, a design by architect Ehea Ronca modeled after the Pantheon in Rome had been completed.[30] Other prominent Italians supported the effort. Pope John XXIII donated chasubles, and the archbishop of Milan (later Pope Paul VI) contributed the marble for the altar. The Bavarian government joined these illustrious donors and released the Leiten plot on which the votive chapel was to be built. Locally, however, the votive chapel was not greeted as warmly. After all, it was only a short time after Dachau natives had cheered the Minister of Agriculture for calling for the demolition of the crematorium (see pp. 184f).

When pictures of the model were published in Dachau in 1958, the classical Roman style of the church was sharply criticized as "inappropriate" for the Bavarian landscape (ill. 40). Revealing the Dachauers' self-confident self-image as a city with an international reputation for its artistic merits, the local newspaper editorialized: "The purely Italian taste does not fit in here at all. What would the Italians say if someone built . . . a Bavarian baroque church on the Via Appia or one of the hills of Rome?"[31] As an alternative the newspaper suggested a copy of the Bavarian pilgrimage churches Mariabrunn or Maria-Birnbaum, or at least planting a group of trees around the building. In any case, neither the Italian design nor the Dachau suggestion had any symbols or forms connoting the concentration camp.

The votive chapel was given the name "Mary, Queen of Peace" (Maria Regina Pacis) because, as a newspaper reported in 1958, "it is to be visible testimony of the will to peace and the brotherhood between the Italian and the German peoples."[32] This dedication, while drawing on the image of solidarity between Italian and German antifascists in the concentration camp, is completely oblivious to the historically much stronger and more important "brotherhood" between Italian and German fascists as the Axis powers in World War II.

In spite of the support from prominent people, the Italian chapel took until 1963 to complete. During the August 1960 Eucharistic World Congress in Munich, when tens of thousands of Catholics came to the former Dachau camp, the Italian Union of Catholic Freedom Fighters laid their cornerstone on the Leiten. It was blessed by Veronese Bishop Giuseppe Carraro in the presence of the Patriarch of Venice, Cardinal Urbani, and General Cantaluppi, the president of the construction committee.[33] The general said that the chapel was to commemorate 38,000 Italians who died in German camps.[34] Of the 8,900 Italians imprisoned in Dachau alone, 1,735 had been killed and 2,184 liberated, the remaining 4,880 transferred or released.

The 1960 evocation of democratic brotherhood by the successor states of the fascist "Axis" powers was repeated when the Italian chapel was dedicated three years later, on 31 July 1963. That ceremony included the highest-ranking politicians and religious leaders who were ever to visit any of the Dachau KZ memorial sites. After the archbishop of Bologna, Cardinal Lercaro, dedicated the chapel, Italian President Antonio Segni invoked the German romantic poet Novalis's (1772–1801) image of a "peaceful, united and free Europe" and spoke of "an important event in German–Italian relations" before an audience that included Bavarian Minister President Alfons Goppel and several members of his cabinet, Archbishop Bafile, the papal nuncio in Bonn, Suffragan Bishop Neuhäusler, Italian Foreign Minister Piccioni and other members of the government, 800 German and 300 Italian resistance fighters, and banner-toting delegations from Italian cities, organizations, and police units.[35] Twenty-five journalists from Italy's leading newspapers were flown in, and German TV Channel Two broadcast the speeches to Italy for RAI.

The character of the ceremony itself revealed that political bonding was more important than reverence to the dead. A critical journalist noted that some Bavarian "gentlemen" had come in their leather shorts, and some Italian students in blue jeans. Italian workers drank beer they had brought, women in light summer dresses took off their shoes and discussed the weekend itinerary, the band played a march from Richard Wagner's *Tannhäuser*, and Segni and German President Lübke sat in leather armchairs viewing the colorful banners.[36] Finally, the acoustics were bad because of the many people crowding into the area around the microphone, prompting the conductor of the famous Roman military orchestra Banda dei Carabinieri to burst out in tears of frustration.

In that atmosphere the only reference to the past, a powerful and politically charged speech by Lübke, received little or no response. Foreshadowing words he was to repeat in a celebrated speech in Bergen-Belsen two years later, Lübke spoke of "horrible crimes on innocent people," which, he said, "we admit in sadness were committed by Germans." With reference to his predecessor Theodor Heuss's speech in 1957 at the Ardeatine Caves near Rome, where Germans executed 335 Italian Jews in 1944, Lübke recalled the leaders of the 20 July 1944 *putsch* attempt as proof that "even in those years there was a different, a better Germany."[37] He concluded with a clear formulation of the myth of resistance:

> May this chapel always remind all good-willed people of their obligation to fight for the truth, the dignity of humankind and its freedom and justice. Thus we can pay off our debt of guilt to the cherished dead, to whom this chapel is dedicated, and we honor the many martyrs of European peoples and of our own people who had to give their lives in the fight for these ideals.

Minister President Goppel, too, drew on elements of the myth of resistance in his effort to dispel negative associations with Germany's past. In his speech at a subsequent lunch reception for the Italian journalists, he tacitly abandoned the myth of victimization by saying that Germans felt "sadness, pain and deep shame for the past." He then employed the image of the "good German" in his appeal to the journalists to take with them the conviction that "the German populace has the honest will to rectify [*wiedergutmachen*]" the past.

The ahistoricity of Catholic commemoration is reflected in the iconography of this three meter diameter marble copy of the Pantheon, which emphasizes its role as an Italian memorial site, but contains no references to concentration camps. The stained glass windows picture Mark, the patron saint of Venice, and Zeno, the first African bishop of Verona; frescoes depict Francis of Assisi and Catherine of Siena, the patron saints of Italy. The entrance is framed by thorny vines weaving around Christ's ascension, while scenes of homage to the mother of God surround the base of the gilded dome, and a 2.5 meter tall "Mary, Queen of Peace" decorates the wall behind the altar. On the floor next to the iron gate across the entrance stands a votive lamp on a Roman capital donated by President Segni. Even the approach to the chapel from the parking lot was functionalized for Catholic religious ritual: in the fall of 1962 fourteen large stone tablets bearing reliefs of the stations of the cross were placed along the path.[38]

Thus Catholic visitors could retrace the events of Christ's Passion as they approached the chapel. Although much of the religious symbolism and ritual in the former concentration camp was profoundly ahistorical, there are parallels between the torture and execution of Christ for his challenge to the established political order, and the torture and murder in the KZs of people who were perceived as threatening by the Nazi regime. We will return to this point later in the discussion of ritual commemoration at the Mortal Agony of Christ chapel, especially the speeches held at its dedication.

Bishop Johannes Neuhäusler (1888–1973)

Johannes Neuhäusler was one of the single most influential figures in the conversion of the former Dachau concentration camp into a site of recollection. Reacting to numerous impulses in the late 1950s, in 1960 he single-handedly pursued the construction of a Catholic chapel on the site. In turn, his suggestion that German Jewish and Protestant organizations construct their own monuments prompted those communities to action.

He also guided the initiative to create a Carmelite convent at the site. Before we examine these efforts, let us acquaint ourselves with the man himself.

In 1932, at age 44, Neuhäusler became a canon of the Munich Catholic Cathedral Fathers (*Domkapitel*).[39] In 1941 he was sent to Sachsenhausen concentration camp for disobeying a governmental order prohibiting the public reading of a critical pastoral written by Munich Cardinal Faulhaber. In July of that year he was transferred to Dachau with other religious leaders (among them Martin Niemöller, see below), with whom he spent the next four years as a "special prisoner," semi-isolated from most of the inmates in the camp. After the war he interceded for Germany with Pope Pius XII, whom he had known as Cardinal Pacelli, former papal nuncio in Munich,[40] and he wrote a book, *Cross and Swastika* (*Kreuz und Hakenkreuz*), documenting oppositional activities of the German Catholic Church against the Nazi regime.[41] In 1947 Neuhäusler became a suffragan bishop in Munich. From 1948 to 1951 he expended enormous energy and financial resources leading an initiative to obtain pardons for Nazi war criminals convicted by Allied courts.[42]

Prior to 1959 Neuhäusler had little to do with the former concentration camp, although in 1949–50 he gave several commemorative speeches there during the Leiten mass grave scandal. However, he preferred not to think about his awful experiences in KZ Dachau. As he said himself: "I prefer to speak about the nice memories associated with the name Dachau," such as the ecumenical bible readings in the camp, and the Christmas tree the SS set up for prisoners in 1941.[43] After a prominent Briton visiting Dachau with a group of priests in 1959 expressed his shock at the neglected condition of the former concentration camp, Neuhäusler used his office to spearhead a campaign to improve Dachau's image abroad. Within a year he had a monumental cylindrical chapel "of Christ's Mortal Agony" (*Todesangst Christi*) built at the end of the camp street, and he published a book about the history of the concentration camp to help combat rumors and incorrect information about the camp.[44] In 1963–4 Neuhäusler also spearheaded the construction of a convent for Carmel nuns adjoining the camp wall (see ills. 44, 45). His plans to break a gate into the camp wall, and to use the adjoining watchtower to display relics from the camp-era chapel in barrack 26, were vetoed by other groups in the CID. In spite of concerted lobbying by other CID groups, Neuhäusler refused to allow the removal of the ring of grass and oak trees around "his" Catholic chapel, where they remain to this day. When he died in 1973, Neuhäusler was buried in the convent chapel.

The Chapel of Christ's Mortal Fear, 1960: a turning point

Although Bishop Neuhäusler never admitted it, the planning of the Italian chapel on the Leiten was probably one of the events that finally prompted him, in 1959, to take up a suggestion made at the KZ priests' meetings in September 1950 and September 1955 and initiate the construction of a Catholic chapel in the camp itself.[45] In a pre-Christmas editorial in the Dachau newspaper in 1958, Leonhard Roth responded to the criticism that had been leveled at the Italian chapel with the observation:[46]

> For years I have been asking myself simply: Where are the Germans hiding? Where are the German episcopate and the German Catholics . . .? I note: Until now the German bishops have shown no initiative . . . to build a memorial church in Dachau – thirteen years have passed since the downfall of Hitler's . . . empire! And where are Dachau's Catholics? I think it is shameful that a small minority of Italians . . . build a chapel on the Leiten while the German Catholics still have not done the least little bit.

This reproachful article was reprinted in the March 1959 issue of the KZ priests' newsletter, where it was sure to have drawn Neuhäusler's attention, if he had not already seen it in the local press. By April 1960, when Neuhäusler publicly explained what prompted him to initiate the memorial church, Roth's outspokenness had alienated him from Neuhäusler and the church establishment, which manifested itself most concretely in a November 1959 prohibition forbidding Roth to publish articles or grant interviews.[47]

In April 1960 Neuhäusler claimed that a September 1959 visit to Dachau by Captain Leonard Cheshire, the British observer in the bombing of Nagasaki, and thirty priests and lay persons on the twentieth anniversary of the outbreak of the war made clear to him that the former concentration camp would need to be put in a more dignified condition if it were not to be perceived as an international disgrace during the Eucharistic World Congress in 1960.[48] Neuhäusler's belated insight was confirmed often enough in the following months. In November 1959 the youth groups of the Bavarian Youth Ring criticized the older generation for its neglect of the site.[49] And early in 1960, after the wave of antisemitic vandalism had focused foreign attention on Germany, newspapers from as far away as Australia criticized the "carnival atmosphere" in the camp cum refugee settlement.[50] Shortly before the dedication ceremony, in July 1960, Neuhäusler mentioned two incidents preceding Leonard Cheshire's visit that supposedly prompted him to take action.[51] In 1959 the widow of a

Dachau KZ inmate came to Dachau and found no suitable place to pray for her husband. She later wrote Neuhäusler a letter with a donation, requesting that he help to build a dignified memorial site. Neuhäusler also said that he had received DM5,000 from an Italian count because he, Neuhäusler, had been confined to his cell for a week after having been caught hearing the man's confession.

All of these anecdotal causes should not obscure the fact that pressure from outside Germany was the primary, if not sole, motivating force behind the construction of the Catholic Dachau chapel. As Neuhäusler put it in the closing words of his call for donations in May 1960:

> The world is positively waiting for the right words to be found [by us Germans] about the past and present, about guilt and atonement, freedom and peace, conscience, obedience, God's commandments and human dignity. The world will watch what we create, listen to what we say, interpret what we do.[52]

Within this context of moral supervision from outside, Neuhäusler's chapel-building initiative significantly modified the local and regional German discourse about the Dachau concentration camps.

Throughout the 1950s criticism of the condition of the former KZ Dachau in foreign newspapers had triggered outrage and defensive reactions in the local press. We have already seen how the removal of the Dachau exhibition in 1953 had been prompted by an article in 1951, and how the popular 1955 initiative to tear down the crematorium had been thwarted by foreign attention and intervention. In January 1960 local feelings about the memorial site were especially bitter because a British journalist had reported Mayor Hans Zauner's derogatory remarks about the camp inmates. He said they had been mostly homosexuals – a very dirty word in those days – and common criminals, and that even the political prisoners had behaved illegally. A bitter battle ensued between Zauner and Leonhard Roth, the priest–survivor living in the refugee settlement.

Leonhard Roth (1904–60) was a Catholic priest who had been imprisoned in Dachau with the black triangle badge of the "asocials."[53] Roth is an extremely interesting figure who played an important role in the postwar history of the Dachau camp. His case illustrates the complex relationship between individual biography and memory, and public recollection.

After studying German literature and philosophy in Berlin, Roth decided to become a priest. In 1931, at the age of 27, he was ordained as a Dominican monk in a monastery near Cologne. Probably because of sexually improper behavior towards boys under his tutelage (since Roth's homosexuality is still a taboo subject, most biographies claim that he was arrested because of the anti-Nazi orientation of his sermons),[54] the

Gestapo issued a warrant for his arrest in January 1937, but he was able to flee to Switzerland. He was captured by Swiss police in March 1941 and extradited to Germany, where he served a two-year prison sentence. At the end of his term in 1943 the Gestapo committed him to the Dachau concentration camp instead of releasing him. He was the only known priest in the camp who was forced to wear the black triangle of the "asocials," as opposed to the red triangle of the political prisoners.

Roth's self-sacrifice in helping his fellow prisoners bordered on masochism, and he soon won recognition for his almost superhuman altruism. In November 1944 he was among fourteen priests who volunteered to care for the prisoners afflicted by a typhus epidemic. At liberation six months later, he was one of only two priest–caregivers who had survived that ordeal. Roth was still caring for convalescent survivors when the US army converted the Dachau KZ into an internment camp in July 1945. At Roth's own request, Munich Cardinal Faulhaber appointed him priest for the SS internees. From 1945 to 1947 Roth found a large following among his former tormentors, and with them he built a church on the Dachau roll-call square in November 1945. In his sermons Roth tried to lead his SS "flock" back to Christianity by leaving out references to the atrocities in their past, and by showing understanding for some aspects of Hitler's world view.[55]

That strategy proved to be his undoing, however. In October 1947 the press reported on Roth's use of elements of Nazi ideology in a sermon he delivered in a Nuremberg internment camp. The Bavarian ministry responsible for administering internal affairs in the US internment camps promptly prohibited Roth from speaking in public. Finally in January 1948, at his own request, Roth was relieved of his duties in the Dachau internment camp. However, when the former concentration camp was converted to a refugee settlement in 1948–9, Roth became the curate for the new parish. After several years' service in which he was an active leader in the refugee community and an outspoken lobbyist for the settlement's needs, Roth, naming the continual strain of his work, requested a transfer to a different position. His appeals to the archbishop in 1953, 1955, and 1957 were, however, all denied. Even when he was accused of having a homosexual relationship with an orphaned tenant who worked with him, the affair was hushed up and Roth continued his work in the refugee settlement. In 1956 he began working with the newly established international organization of Dachau survivors, which was lobbying to relocate the refugee settlement and preserve the former concentration camp as a memorial site. That created another plane of friction between him and Bavarian authorities.

The 1960 conflict between Roth and Zauner climaxed in a public meeting in Dachau on 18 March 1960, to which Roth and German survivor Otto Kohlhofer had invited the mayor (who, by the way, did not attend).[56] After the meeting, before the Monday paper was published, Roth wrote elatedly to his friend and KZ comrade Oskar Müller that the meeting had gone "beautifully." But the local paper came down heavily in favor of Zauner. After several days of massive criticism of Roth in the *Dachauer Nachrichten*, the dejected curate sent Müller a letter with the bitter conclusion: "The protest meeting on 18 March in Dachau broke my neck. The entire hate of the Dachau citizenry has turned against me. They demanded my dismissal, which was granted by the bishop's office."[57] Because of continuing criticism of his own position, however, the aging Zauner also felt compelled to resign as mayor, which he did on 1 May.[58]

In the battle to silence Roth, Bishop Neuhäusler sent a "secret" letter to Catholic institutions around the state. In it he used information from Roth's Gestapo file to imply that Roth had a criminal background.[59] In June 1960, alienated by his isolation from the Church and the Dachau mainstream, Roth took his own life with an overdose of sleeping pills on an isolated mountainside in Austria.[60] He is still remembered and revered by many of his former Dachau parishioners.[61]

In the midst of this acrimonious battle the town of Dachau began to respond positively towards the memory of the camp. The city council announced that Dachau would participate in a program in which communities collected money to pay for the transportation of a particular delegate to the Eucharistic World Congress.[62] At a well-attended town gathering, city priest Johann Jäger suggested that Dachau invite a KZ priest, and Adam Kozlowiecki, a Jesuit who had become a bishop in Northern Rhodesia (since 1963 Zambia/Malawi), was selected. It was decided that Kozlowiecki would stay in Dachau as an official guest of the city during the entire congress.

Dachau officials then began to apply their energies to the construction of the Catholic chapel in the camp and the preparations for the commemorative ceremony in the former KZ during the World Congress. A commission consisting of County Governor Schwalber, Mayor Böck (Zauner having resigned), and city priest Jäger was formed to oversee the fundraising.[63] Individual donations poured in from all corners of the city.[64] When another British reporter interviewed Zauner in late May, it was again reported in the local news.[65] The British article itself was no less critical than the January report, since the journalist noted the "official apathy and local obstruction" of the efforts to create a memorial site. He wrote that he had been "shocked" by the neglected condition of the camp and the lack of information available to visitors, and "appalled" by the ignorance and apathy towards the camp that he had encountered in the town. He quoted survivor Alfred Haag as having said that "the Dachau town council has shown as much concern about the concentration camp as the kitchenmaid of the Australian Prime Minister!" This time the *Dachauer Nachrichten* did not reprint the article, however, but noted only that the report's "agreeable . . . objectivity" (!) set it apart from previous articles in the foreign press.[66]

As the date of the World Congress celebration in Dachau on 5 August neared, the local press published glowing reports about the chapel and the contributions to its construction with increasing frequency. Drivers-in-training from the West German army transported 700 truckloads of stones more than 200 miles from the Isar river to Dachau;[67] Munich city council voted to donate DM50,000 to the fund;[68] the West German cement industry donated 150 tons of its product, which the national railroad transported for free.[69] A pre-climax was reached with the announcement on 23 July that DM15,000 had been collected in Dachau city and county, above and beyond the DM5,000 appropriated by the city council.[70] When the architect of the 1945 Leitenberg temple donated his model to the county governor, the *Dachauer Nachrichten* printed a picture of it as evidence that "already in 1945 the city made a serious effort to establish a dignified monument to the victims of National Socialism."[71]

This sudden (and temporary) change in local opinion about the concentration camp memorial site was possible because in Catholic recollection religious elements predominate over historical references. Only among the KZ priests was tension between the religious and historical poles manifest. The content and organization of the commemorative speeches at the Dachau ceremony during the Eucharistic World Congress exemplify this. On 5 August 1960 an estimated 30–60,000 people came to the former Dachau concentration camp to attend the dedication of the new Catholic chapel in an official ceremony during the World Congress (ill. 47).[72] That number was thus probably greater than the ca. 30,000 prisoners in the camp at liberation. Two specially chartered trains from Munich brought some of the visitors directly into the camp on the railroad tracks where the "death train" with 2,000 corpses had stood at liberation. The most prominent Catholic Dachau survivors spoke the introductory words (Canon Reinhold Friedrichs), gave the keynote speeches (president of the Austrian National Council Leopold Figl, Bishop Kozlowiecki, and French Minister of Justice Edmond Michelet), and held the concluding sermon (Bishop Franz Hengsbach).[73]

While the historical references in some of these addresses – especially Friedrichs' and Kozlowiecki's – make them some of the most imposing recollective speeches ever held in Dachau, others barely refer to the concentration camp at all. Additionally, the speeches were interleaved with readings from the Passion of Christ. The local press predictably abstained from reporting the contents of the historical speeches. Under the back-slapping headline "10,000 More Cars Could Have Parked / KZ Memorial Service Superbly Organized – 'Dachauers Are Friendly People,'" the *Dachauer Nachrichten* reported that:[74] "Everywhere people think that with the construction of the chapel and the museum something fundamental in the way of a memorial site was created, and that thereby the defamation of Dachau's populace in the entire world will finally have to stop."

In accordance with the official Catholic conception of the construction of the chapel as an act of expiation, in the local press it was persistently referred to as the "Chapel of Atonement" (*Sühnekapelle*), even though Cardinal Wendel had selected the official name "Mortal Agony of Christ" in May.[75] Local articles called the dedication ceremony an "act of expiation and consecration" (*Sühne- und Weiheakt*). This conception of freeing oneself of guilt, reminiscent of the sale of indulgences, explains not only the enthusiasm with which the Dachau natives supported the construction of the chapel, but also their renewed resentment when criticism of the relationship between the city and the camp did not desist after the dedication.

The oscillation of Catholic memory between the unpleasant push of historical experience and the reconciliatory pull of religious zeal created at least one stridently discordant note at the dedication ceremony during the World Congress: the participation of Hjalmar Schacht (1877–1970). Schacht had been president of the Reichsbank from 1923 to 1930, and again from 1933 to 1939 – after the candidate he supported assumed the office of Reich Chancellor. As Reich Minister of Finance he masterminded the financing of the German armaments program, but was dismissed from Hitler's cabinet in January 1939 because he disagreed with Hitler's war aims. After the July 1944 *putsch* attempt he was arrested and imprisoned in Dachau as a "special prisoner" in the separate tract with Neuhäusler and others.[76] After liberation he was interned by the Allies, but released in 1946 when he had been found innocent of the charges at the first Nuremberg trial. In the 1950s Schacht became an influential figure in the reconstruction of West Germany, serving on the boards of directors of several large firms. In May of 1960 he made headlines by speaking out against school classes visiting the KZ Dachau memorial site at a parent–teacher meeting.[77]

Neuhäusler personally invited the 83-year-old to attend the dedication of the chapel as an honored guest. Schacht sat in the front row, where he was the only one wearing an irreverent light-colored suit among the black-suited VIPs. Criticism of Schacht's attendance was noted in some (but by no means all) of the press reports,[78] but after Schacht's indignant response to a critical letter to the editor in the *Süddeutsche Zeitung* was published on 19 August,[79] Bavarian Minister of Agriculture Hundhammer and Federal Minister of Justice Fritz Schäffer joined the critics of Schacht's attendance.[80] Neuhäusler, however, true to the Christian doctrine of forgiveness that had motivated him to work so hard to obtain pardons for the worst of the convicted brown-collar criminals in the early 1950s, justified his invitation of Schacht as if the latter had distanced himself from his former crucial support of Hitler. Neuhäusler, who refused to admit that Schacht's attendance had been inappropriate, defended Schacht with a quote after the poet Friedrich Rückert: "They are wise who travel to truth through error / They who persist in error are fools."[81] As far as Neuhäusler was concerned, the brown-collar crimes had been an "error," and now it was time to adopt a new position and move on.

The chapel itself, whose name translates literally as "Christ's Mortal Fear" (*Todesangst Christi*; officially translated as "Mortal Agony of Christ"), also illustrates the predominance of religious symbolism over historical references. It stands at the north end of the central camp axis as a striking counterpoint to the international memorial on the roll-call square, which was dedicated eight years later. The 14 meter high cylindrical chapel, with a wide, full-height opening on the side facing the camp, is also 14 meters in diameter (ill. 43). The building was financed by donations and built within a span of about four months, so that narrow limits were set on the types of material that could be used. In the final design a thin wall of reinforced concrete was covered on both sides with a layer of rounded stones from the Isar river (instead of costly rough-hewn basalt, as originally planned), which were cemented in a herringbone pattern.

A high wrought-iron sliding gate and a conical metal roof recessed within the cylinder close off the building's front and top openings, leaving a view of a suspended triumphal cross below a ring of twisted iron rails forming a stylized crown of thorns. An artist's conception by Josef Wiedemann, an architecture professor at Munich's Technical University, shows a large, broad-armed cross with a very small figure of Christ in its center as the dominant motif in the interior.[82] (Later, a much larger figure was mounted on the cross.) A large altar for religious services stands on a slightly raised platform in the center of the chapel.

The chapel, by far the tallest building in the memorial site, occupies a commanding position. Its unusual architecture and material stood out against the barracks of the refugee settlement at that time; now the rounded stones blend in with the gravel and light-colored pebbles covering the whole terrain. Today the ring of scrub oak trees and the grassy area surrounding the chapel strike a dissonant note at the barren end of the camp, even though they complete the rows of poplar trees, which in the Nazi period, as today, lined the camp street (ill. 4). This bit of greenery around the chapel is a last reminder that Bishop Neuhäusler had originally planned to landscape the entire former prisoners' compound as a park with trees and grass, although the CID vetoed that idea (ill. 46).[83]

This building symbolizes the group memory of the Nazi concentration camps typical of organized Catholicism. Except for the iron T-beam crown of thorns at the top, which might connote the heat-twisted truck chassis used as grills to incinerate huge piles of exhumed corpses, the chapel contains no historical references to the Nazi past. Its symbolism is limited to the salvation of humanity through Christ's sacrifice. Its 14 meter height makes an uplifting impression in contrast to the Jewish and Protestant memorials flanking it, which are buried in the ground and rise only a few meters high.

Another even more elaborate Catholic cult site in Dachau illustrates the Catholic emphasis on salvation over history even more clearly: a convent adjoining the north wall.

The Carmelite convent

The prioress of the West German Carmelite convent in Bonn became aware of the squalid conditions in the Dachau KZ memorial site after the Eucharistic World Congress. Late in 1961 she wrote to Munich Cardinal Döpfner to suggest the establishment of a Carmelite convent at the former camp. She thought that a documentary memorial site would be too "neutral"; that only through religious ritual could the significance of the site be maintained:[84]

> In the whole world Dachau is seen as the prototypical concentration camp. Its name will always be associated with the most horrible atrocities of humanity. A place where such sins were perpetrated, where so many people suffered unspeakable tortures, should not be allowed to be degraded to a neutral memorial site or even a place for sight-seeing.

In early January 1962 Cardinal Döpfner assented to the prioress's proposal and commissioned Bishop Neuhäusler with the realization of the project.

In August 1961 the Carmelite mother convent in Rome gave its approval as well.[85] In March 1963, on the thirtieth anniversary of the opening of the concentration camp, Neuhäusler inaugurated a fundraising drive. His supplicatory brochure portrayed prayer as the highest form of commemoration and revived the idea of purchasing exoneration:[86]

> Help to turn this place of godless human error into a place of prayer and atonement for the education and emulation of all visitors to the camp and for the promotion of peace in the world . . . Even if you know yourself to be free of all cheering-along, following-along, joining in and helping to cause [*Mitschreien, Mitlaufen, Mittun und Mitverschulden*] – as a part of the German people and even more a part of the "body of Christ" you are still called upon to co-atone [*mit Sühne zu leisten*] for the sins that were committed in Dachau and at countless places by German citizens . . . I have no right to play prosecutor or judge. It goes against my nature to claim that the German people are collectively guilty. But everyone who went through those years – whether as a voting citizen or as a politically courted boy – should put themselves on trial.

It is conspicuous and worthy of note that this thinly veiled accusation of collective responsibility (if not guilt) received no hostile public response whatsoever. Apparently the moral authority of the Catholic Church, and the coupling of the claim with a procedure and the prospect of expiation were sufficient to silence those who rejected any notion of trans-individual accountability. This stands in sharp contrast to other public professions of German guilt, from that proclaimed by leaders of the German Protestant Church in October 1945 (see p. 277, below), to that implicit in a 1995 exhibition documenting the brown-collar crimes of the German army (the exhibition is discussed on pp. 380f, below).

Neuhäusler's forceful proclamation of collective responsibility, however, exonerated the officials of the Catholic Church, especially Pope Pius XII, who had refrained from condemning Hitler's regime for fear of endangering Catholic priests in Germany. At a large ceremony for the cornerstone-laying of the convent on liberation day 1963, Neuhäusler phrased his collective reproach on the German people very clearly:[87]

> Our faces should redden with shame, our hearts burn with repentance . . . Anyone who believes that he or she has contributed even the smallest pebble to this mountain of guilt – perhaps only by silently casting their vote, by occasionally marching along or celebrating along or even by remaining silent with their fist in their pocket – may not now wash their hands in innocence.

Then, explicitly referring to Rolf Hochhuth's highly controversial play *The Deputy* about the complicity of Pope Pius XII, who had been a close friend of Neuhäusler's, Neuhäusler exonerated the Pope for remaining silent because speaking out would have been futile: "If the Pope had known an avenue of help for the Jews without opening the doors and floodgates of even greater disaster, he would have pursued it immediately." It is hard to imagine what greater disaster than the "final solution" might have ensued. In this speech Neuhäusler has tacitly abandoned the myth of ignorance, because only through knowledge of brown-collar crimes would Germans assume "co-responsibility." However, in his words the myth of victimization is alive and well. He was clearly thinking only of the negative consequences that the Pope's open condemnation of Hitler's politics might have had for the comparatively minuscule group of the German Catholic clergy.

The cornerstones of Carmelite convents are dedicated with taps of a special ceremonial hammer by future patrons and advocates of the cloister, and each tap is accompanied by a wish (ill. 44). When the cornerstone of the Dachau convent was dedicated on 28 April 1963, the wishes of its patrons reflected the attitudes of the various groups towards commemoration in Dachau concentration camp.[88] Both the regional leader of the Carmelites in Bavaria and Bavarian Minister President Goppel implicitly recognized the noninnocence of Germans, although they looked toward the future, not the past. The Carmelite wished: "May the convent be a monument of atonement, a warning sign for all coming generations, and a pledge of reconciliation," while Goppel said: "May the Carmelites some day pray here that in our people love will grow instead of hate, humility instead of self-righteousness, shame instead of arrogance." In contrast, County Governor Schwalber and Mayor Böck of Dachau focused on the long-held local feeling of victimization. They wished that "the blood innocently shed in Dachau not be burdened upon the Dachau citizens." Even the local newspapers were obsessed with expiation – every report about the convent had the word "atonement" in its headline. Only the clergyman who spoke for the commander of the US forces in Europe was not burdened with feelings of guilt or victimization. He expressed the "prayers and wishes of the American people for peace in the world."

Construction of the convent could not begin immediately because it was discovered that the site had previously been a pond that had been filled with gravel in 1937 in order to expand the concentration camp. Building finally began in August of 1963, and the shell of the 10,000-square-meter facility was completed in July 1964.[89] The nuns began moving in in September, and on 22 November 1964 the Carmelite convent in Dachau was dedicated.[90] It now houses some two dozen nuns who raise money by selling handmade candles and other crafts, and by renting rooms to visitors to the memorial site. The convent is also devoted to the memory of Bishop Neuhäusler. His purple bishop's robe is displayed in a glass case in the courtyard, and his grave is next to the altar in the chapel.

The unanimous local, national, and international public acceptance of Dachau's Carmel convent in the early 1960s stands in marked contrast to the bitter criticism and stiff resistance sparked by the Carmelite convent established in Auschwitz in the late 1980s. Why were the two cases so different? First, let us examine the situation in Auschwitz.[91]

Inspired by the success of the Dachau convent, in 1984 Carmelite nuns, supported by the Metropolitan of Cracow, were granted permission to rent a warehouse bordering on the outer fence in Auschwitz, where canisters of the lethal insecticide Zyklon B had been stored in the Nazi era.[92] (Plans to convert the building into a casino for the SS had never been realized.) Ten nuns moved into the severely deteriorated building. In order to raise funds for renovations, they appealed to the organization "Church in Need," which decided to call for donations during Pope John Paul II's visit to Belgium in 1985. That call introduced the project to the wider public in the worst way: its "triumphant" language was considered "tactless," revealing, among other things, an extreme lack of sensitivity towards the survivors of the National Socialist judeocide. This insensitivity touched a raw nerve: although the vast majority of murder victims in Auschwitz had been Jews, official Polish ritual and institutional memory had all but written them out of the site's history. A physical battle for memorial terrain ensued when the nuns erected a large cross within the camp perimeter. The nuns were staking out a Catholic claim to Oświęcim as a symbol of Christian death and suffering under Nazi rule, while Jewish groups were struggling to gain recognition of the singular magnitude of the Nazi murder of the Jews, which for them was symbolized by KZ Auschwitz. (Jewish groups were particularly sensitive at that time, because US President Reagan had paid an official visit to a German army and SS cemetery in May 1985.) Ultimately, in 1993, the nuns vacated the warehouse and moved to a newly erected building a small distance from the camp.[93]

In Dachau, the situation was quite different. First of all, even though many thousands of Jews had died in Dachau, the camp had not been an extermination factory and was not as closely associated with Hitler's plan to annihilate all Jews. Thus Dachau had never been a central symbol of judeocide for Jews – it was more a symbol of brown-collar crimes in general than of the Holocaust in particular. In contrast, by the 1980s there was a long tradition of Israeli youth groups visiting Auschwitz and Birkenau to commemorate the Holocaust. The first Israeli groups did not visit Dachau until years after the convent had been erected. Additionally, Catholic Bavaria did not have the same history of antisemitism as did Poland, so Jews were not nearly as likely to see the convent as an attempt by Catholics to "take over" the site. Also, since thousands of priests had been imprisoned in Dachau, it was much more natural to have Christian cult sites there. Last but not least, in the 1980s there was much more public attention to commemorations of brown-collar crimes than there had been in the 1960s.

However, at one point in the summer of 1964 the Dachau Carmelite convent did spark some dissent. The Catholic tendency to superimpose religious meanings on nonreligious historical relics was the cause. When Bishop Neuhäusler announced that "the concentration camp past would consciously be integrated into the convent" by using the guard tower in the north wall not only as an entrance gate, but as a museum for relics from the KZ chapel as well, German survivors voiced their concern about what was perceived as an ecclesiastical takeover. German CID co-founder Otto Kohlhofer wrote to the CID executive committee: "If the site immediately adjacent [to the former camp] was already pushing the limits of tolerance, this new plan [to install a museum in the watchtower] is indefensible."[94] Kohlhofer was especially worried that the other religious communities would want to expand their projects in a similar way – in 1960 Neuhäusler had suggested that Jews and Protestants erect memorials as well – and that the preservation of the "historical context" of the camp would be endangered. Neuhäusler and other KZ priests subsequently dropped that plan, and the artifacts – an altar, a Madonna, and a monstrance – were installed in the convent chapel instead.[95]

The survivors of Dachau, represented by the Comité International de Dachau, were the only force behind the establishment of a memorial site in the 1950s. Without their efforts, there would not have been any memorial sites in West Germany before the 1970s, and perhaps never any at all. The next chapter examines how the survivors overcame the resistance of Dachau and Bavarian officials in the 1950s to disband the refugee settlement and create a permanently chartered memorial site with a large museum, library, and archive.

The survivors negotiate a memorial site

Establishing an international organization, 1950–1955

In the section on the statue of the "unknown concentration camp inmate" we heard about the early organizational efforts of the Dachau survivors, and about the setbacks due to the split between the German Communist and Social Democratic parties in 1948–9, compounded by the general marginalization of survivors in the early 1950s and the recriminations against them during the Leiten Affair (see pp. 192ff). As the dust from the Leiten Affair was just beginning to settle in January 1950, a number of prominent German survivors of Dachau met in Munich to formally establish a group that had been meeting for several years, the "Dachau Working Group" (Arbeitsgemeinschaft Dachau, AG Dachau).[1]

Dachau survivor Hans Kaltenbacher presided over that meeting of 400 survivors, many of whom were to maintain close ties to the memorial site until their deaths in the 1970s, 1980s, and 1990s. Denazification and *Wiedergutmachung* were among the topics discussed at the meeting, but setting an agenda for documenting the history of the camp was an important priority. Committees were formed to collect material on resistance in the camp, testimony about Nazi criminals, and documents about the administration and organization of the concentration camps.

Because of the obstacles placed in their way by Bavarian authorities convinced that they were "bad" inmates, the AG Dachau was not able to organize a large international gathering of Dachau survivors in Dachau until June 1953.[2] Representatives of Belgian, French, Dutch, and Austrian Dachau survivors' organizations came together with the West Germans for a two-day program of commemoration and discussion.[3] The West Germans answered questions about the reestablishment of a German army, the resurgence of the radical right, and restitution policies. The foreign participants resolved to have their home governments protest against the removal of the exhibition from the crematorium only four weeks before. Over the longer term the survivors decided to hold a meeting of all Dachau survivors on the tenth anniversary of liberation in April 1955. The next months saw an increasing exchange of information between the various national groups.[4] In December 1954 the Fédération Internationale des Résistants (FIR; the international umbrella organization of the VVN) resolved to hold its next international congress in Dachau on liberation day 1955.[5] Also, many Dachau survivors were among the 40–50,000 participants at Buchenwald's tenth anniversary celebration on 11 April 1955. The museum opened at that event became a model for the future design of the Dachau site.[6]

Otto Kohlhofer, a Communist Dachau survivor who had been the West Germans' representative to the FIR, assumed responsibility for organizing the 1955 Dachau event. His first hurdle was to overcome the division in the ranks of the survivors themselves: the "State Council for Freedom and Justice" (Landesrat für Freiheit und Recht, LFR), a survivors' organization founded by Auerbach and other disgruntled former VVN members in 1950, had already won the sponsorship of Minister President Hoegner for its commemorative ceremony on 23 April in Munich. The LFR enjoyed the support of the SPD (Hoegner), the CSU (Hundhammer), the FDP, the Munich Jewish community, and the Catholic Church (Neuhäusler). It was Kohlhofer's task to convince them to join the new association of Dachau survivors.[7]

Although it proved impossible to combine the two 1955 ceremonies on such short notice, there are indications that momentum towards unity across ideological and national lines was increasing. In his imposing speech to the LFR, Minister President Hoegner emphasized the need to overcome divisions and work together to preserve the memory of those who had died in the Nazi camps.[8] Also, to demonstrate solidarity in spite of political differences, a representative of the LFR spoke during the Dachau Association's celebration on 8 May.[9] Prior to the ceremony itself, a network of local "Dachau camp associations" (*Lagergemeinschaften*) was created throughout West Germany to contact other survivors and begin public relations work.[10] In Hesse, for instance, the Dachau organization sent an invitation to Protestant Church President Martin Niemöller. However, since Niemöller had been expelled from the Hesse VVN in 1947, he was not won over right away.[11] Two years later, however, Niemöller became an important supporter of the initiative to establish a permanent memorial site.

The large convocations of concentration camp survivors in the anniversary year 1955 provided a basis for a future network to lobby for a memorial site in Dachau. On 8 March 1955, 10,000 survivors met in Mauthausen,

40–50,000 in Buchenwald on 11 April, and at least 3,000 in Dachau on 8 May.[12] The organization of former Dachau prisoners that had been informally constituted at that May 1955 gathering was formally chartered as the Comité International de Dachau (International Dachau Committee, CID) in Brussels in November 1955.[13]

In 1955, when over 2,000 ethnic Germans from Eastern Europe were living in the converted Dachau barracks and local officials were calling for the demolition of the crematorium, the physical preservation of the remaining relics of the camp had to be the survivors' first priority. At the Brussels meeting they listed the following five goals: (1) the preservation of the crematorium, (2) the restoration to the original condition of the entry gate building, the service building, the roll-call square, the bunker and its courtyard (which had been an execution range), and one or two barracks, (3) the preservation of the Leiten as a memorial site, (4) the transfer of the whole area to international governance, and (5) the erection of a central commemorative monument on a site the committee would choose.[14] The survivors did not mention the possibility of displaying artifacts and documents at the site.

However, in June 1955 the West German government was given partial custody of the enormous collection of documents from the concentration camps kept by the Tracing Service of the International Red Cross in West German Arolsen.[15] The survivors were skeptical of this development and called for a transfer of responsibility to an international survivors' organization instead. Oddly, at the November meeting the CID did not demand that documents pertaining to Dachau be placed in an archive in the former camp, but rather that "all archives in Arolsen and those containing relevant information . . . in other places should be transferred to a neutral country, for example Austria." It was not until nearly a year later that the CID decided to collect material for a Dachau archive.[16] Crucial to that decision, and instrumental in the creation of a research library at Dachau, was the Dutch journalist Nico Rost, a survivor of the camp.

I Returned to Dachau: Nico Rost, 1955

Nico Rost (1896–1967) was a journalist and member of the Dutch Communist Party. In 1942 he was deported to a concentration camp in Holland, and in 1944 transferred to Dachau because of his contacts with the Dutch resistance movement. With the help of inmate-functionaries in the camp he obtained a position working in the prisoners' infirmary and survived until liberation in 1945. After liberation he published the diary he had secretly kept in Dachau under the title "Goethe in Dachau," to emphasize that upstanding people had been imprisoned in the camp, not barbaric criminals. In 1955 Nico Rost returned to Dachau to visit the former concentration camp and the town.[17] He walked through the residential settlement, where he discovered a kindergarten in the former infirmary, a tannery in the erstwhile shower building, a butcher's shop where prisoners had been used as living guinea pigs for malaria, ice water and high altitude experiments, a food store in the former sick-bay morgue, and a restaurant in the old delousing building (see ill. 25). He noted that there were no signs or documents explaining the history of the concentration camp, and that the parklike ambiance around the crematorium created a false impression about what had transpired there. In town, he found that there were no signs in the city directing visitors to the memorial site. Instead, he saw the wedding procession of Mayor Hans Zauner's son, who had been a member of the SS.

Rost published a scathing critique of the situation in Dachau, *I Returned to Dachau*, which he sent to a number of prominent persons in West Germany. Many of those who wrote back to him were later asked to join a "curatorium" to aid the lobby for a memorial site. Rost played an active role in the CID, which was established a few months after his 1955 visit. In 1957 Rost became head of the library committee in charge of collecting books about Dachau. He was also invited to speak at commemorative ceremonies for young people, and he helped to design the new documentary exhibition that opened in 1960, for which he wrote a guidebook. His own private collection of books became the core of the Dachau memorial site library.

The "Spirit of the Camp Street": Otto Kohlhofer and Leonhard Roth

The survivors of Dachau ranged from Communists such as Rost to staunch conservatives such as Bavarian Christian Party co-founder Alois Hundhammer, and Munich Suffragan Bishop Neuhäusler. Another survivor played a central role in bridging the ideological differences between the survivors: Otto Kohlhofer (1915–89).[18] In a February 1955 letter to Bavarian Minister President Hoegner, Kohlhofer evoked what he called the "Spirit of the Camp Street," which became the motto of his work during the next three decades:[19]

> Our dead comrades would not have wanted us to celebrate the tenth
> anniversary of our liberation without the old unanimity of spirit that was
> present in the camp. It would be regrettable if, ten years after our liberation
> from the concentration camps, in which we formed a community
> transcending differences of political opinion, religious beliefs and
> nationality, whose spirit each of us still carries in his heart, we were to
> separately commemorate our dead.
>   This community, which developed in times of deepest human abasement
> where each comrade was judged only according to his human characteristics,
> should not retrospectively be divided into certain organizations or groups.
> On the camp street no one asked about family or national origins or
> political beliefs, but [looked to see] whether someone was good or bad at
> heart.

This spirit of solidarity has since become an important element of the collective memory of the concentration camp propagated by Dachau survivors. It is the functional equivalent of the civilian "myth of resistance," although it has a more extensive basis in fact. Nonetheless, there were many inmates at lower levels of the camp hierarchy who felt that the solidarity of the upper levels did not extend far enough.[20] This was inevitable in a situation of such extreme privation and repression as in the concentration camps.

One of the most important allies won over by Kohlhofer was Leonhard Roth, the Dominican monk imprisoned in Dachau with the black triangle of the "asocials" (see pp. 231f). Roth, who had stayed on in the Dachau camp after liberation to work with the SS internees, had gradually distanced himself from the other survivors. In May 1947 he resigned from his post at the Dachau International Information Office, which provided administrative assistance to concentration camp survivors, because the Association of Former Persecutees refused to include a church service in its annual commemorative ceremony.

Roth had participated in commemorative activities since the early postwar years and had often guided visitors through the camp and crematory area.[21] He was also involved in meetings of the KZ Priests' Association, one of the oldest groups of survivors that had met continuously since liberation.[22] In the mid-1950s Roth stood firmly on the side of the anticommunist "Council for Freedom and Justice" (LFR), and he rejected plans to preserve the entire former camp as a memorial site (the crematorium and Leiten graves were enough, in his opinion).[23] When in April 1956 the CID publicized its goals for the future of the site, which included the demolition of the church Roth had built with the internees in 1945 as part of the restoration of the former KZ to its original state, Roth protested energetically.[24]

At this point Kohlhofer intervened. He immediately contacted Roth and the two agreed that the SS internees' church could be left standing. Roth proved to be an extremely valuable ally. He was generally one of the first to know when Bavarian officials were attempting to restrict recollection of the concentration camp. For instance, he immediately registered protest with government authorities against the proposed closing of the crematory in 1955, and he prevented bulldozers from razing the watchtowers in 1957. After Roth joined the reestablished international organization of Dachau survivors (CID), he served as the official representative of the KZ priests in the CID executive committee until late 1959, when his critical remarks about Bavaria and Dachau's relationship with the former camp prompted Bishop Neuhäusler's office to prohibit him from speaking to the press or making public statements about the camp.

The coalition between priest and Communist was emphasized in a widely read article by Ursula von Kardorff, a leading figure on the editorial board of the Munich *Süddeutsche Zeitung*. She concluded her article with the words:[25]

> The chairman of the German department of the International Dachau Committee . . . agrees with the priest: "No hatred shall be sown here, but the truth must not be concealed." – "This is a holy place for us," says the priest. "It must become a place of pilgrimage," says the communist.

Roth became the delegate of the KZ Priests' Association in the CID. As a community leader in the East Dachau settlement, he also represented and served as a contact person for the current residents of the former camp. The advantage – and necessity – of having a contact person at the site soon became apparent: in July 1957 Roth ran out just in time to stop the Bavarian Construction Authority from demolishing the KZ watchtowers.[26]

With Roth's guidance the residents of East Dachau supported the Dachau survivors in their effort to force the Bavarian government to close down the settlement. In the summer of 1957 the residents hung a banner across the camp street and on one of the watchtowers proclaiming "We want to get out of the KZ barracks into apartments fit for human habitation at prices we can afford!" (ill. 26).[27]

Government foot-dragging, 1956–1964

Camp survivors found it was very difficult to persuade the Bavarian government to relocate the new residents of the former camp. State officials first met with representatives of the CID on 7 April 1956.[28] The representative of the Ministry of Finance, Josef Panholzer, himself a former persecutee, conceded that the state had an obligation to preserve and make the complex accessible to the public (that was required by the 1954 Paris Treaties anyway), but he explained that the state could not assume the financial burden of building new apartments to house the residents of the "East Dachau settlement." Thus, he argued, it would not be possible to evacuate the settlement, the first prerequisite for the creation of a memorial site. However, a month earlier Minister President Hoegner – also a victim of Nazi persecution (he had fled to Switzerland) – had already orally promised the evacuation of the settlement to the CID.[29] Thus the Bavarian Ministry of Finance was obligated to find a solution.

Meanwhile the CID mounted a public relations campaign to increase the international pressure on the Bavarian government. First, in September 1956 it organized an international pilgrimage to Dachau. A cornerstone for the planned international memorial was lain on the former roll-call square.[30] Panholzer from the Finance Ministry was called upon to unveil the inscribed block, and Curate Roth gave a moving speech (ill. 57).[31]

The stone, which today is encased in Plexiglas at the top of the ramp to the international memorial (ill. 58), bears the simple Latin text: "This first stone of a monument to be erected in memory of the victims of Nazism who died in the Dachau prisons in the years 1933–1945 was set here on 9 September 1956."[32] The date on the stone is one of the few remaining traces documenting the survivors' long struggle to preserve the former concentration camp as a memorial site. However, there is no indication that the memorial was not completed until 1968.

But even such publicity measures did not prompt the Bavarian government to hasten the evacuation of the settlement. A polemical editorial in the *Tat*, a Frankfurt weekly newspaper close to the VVN, noted that if the Ministry of Defense had needed the barracks for the new West German army, they would have been cleared out within a month.[33] However, the international Dachau survivors' committee was not the Ministry of Defense, and the evacuation timetable was excruciatingly slow. At a meeting in Dachau in May 1957 Bavarian Labor Minister Stain announced that sixty-one apartments would be built that year for 400 of the ca. 2,000 settlement residents.[34] If his "firm hope" that no new settlers would be quartered there held true, Stain's most optimistic forecast was that the KZ barracks would be empty in "two or three years." In fact, in spite of support from the federal government for new construction,[35] postponement followed postponement, and the last residents did not move out of the former concentration camp until April 1965, only days before the new memorial site was dedicated.[36] The barracks were torn down on their heels, ostensibly to prevent squatters from moving in.

During this period the survivors' conception of the memorial site developed from a relatively straightforward relic of the past to an elaborate complex of reconstructions, monuments, and didactic facilities. In other words, it moved from a kind of lowest common denominator of collective memory to an institution that could preserve, propagate, and produce images of the past. This can be seen both in the design of the memorial site as a whole and in the specific meanings represented in the museum.

The new memorial site, 1955–1965

The CID's first goal in 1955 was the restoration of the roll-call square end of the camp to its "original" condition. However, for various reasons this was not practicable. First, the postwar modifications of the service building – it had been converted to a courtroom – and the barracks had been so drastic that restoration would have amounted to new construction. Without public support for such an undertaking the costs were clearly prohibitive. There had also been substantial construction during the concentration camp era as well, so that there was no clear-cut "original" condition. By 1945 the roll-call square included a number of additional buildings made necessary by the intensive use of prisoner labor in local industry. Although an eclectic solution would have solved that problem, at the time financial considerations were paramount, so the CID scaled down its project to the reconstruction of the ensemble around the roll-call square. This smaller solution presented problems as well: the immediately adjacent barracks had housed the infirmary and the prisoners' canteen, so that their reconstruction would not have represented the typical living quarters in the camp. And it would still have been extremely expensive to refurbish the interior of the service building, now a leather factory, with the original clothing storeroom, showers, kitchen, administrative rooms and workshops. There was also the problem of postwar construction – Leonhard Roth had persuaded the CID to preserve the church built by the interned SS in 1945 as testimony to the atonement of the perpetrators.[37]

Over the course of the next five years the present solution evolved in various rounds of negotiation with the Bavarian authorities. All buildings on the roll-call square were razed or removed (ill. 4). Roth met a sad end in 1960, and so did the church he had built with the SS internees in

November 1945. After the aforementioned conflict between Roth and Dachau Mayor Zauner in March 1960 (see pp. 232f), Bishop Neuhäusler used information from Roth's Gestapo file to imply that Roth had a criminal background. Defamed, depressed, and isolated, Roth took his own life in June 1960. After the death of its only advocate, the SS church was torn down, as were all of the barracks in the camp.

The service building was redesigned to accommodate an archive, library, and museum, with apartments for the caretakers in the attic. The two barracks immediately bordering the roll-call square were rebuilt according to modern standards, with cement floors, tightly fitting windows, locking doors, etc. (The concentration camp barracks from 1937 had had a life expectancy of ten to fifteen years – after that time Himmler predicted the Nazis would be able to dispense with concentration camps.[38]) One barrack was left empty, the other furnished to show the three chronologically successive interior bunk designs in spatial succession in the central section of the 90 m length of the building. One day room, washroom, and communal toilet room were reconstructed as well (ills. 23, 30). The more comfortable rooms for the barrack elders were not reconstructed. The locations of the other thirty barracks were marked by low cement curbs filled with pebbles. Small cement markers indicated the original block numbers, but not the special functions that the various barracks had (see. ill. 2).

The original roll-call square had been subdivided by raised curbs, which were also not reconstructed. Instead, the international monument with its broad substructure was placed within the wings of the service building. This left the vast expanse of the original assembly grounds completely empty. The roll-call square itself, and the entire camp including the areas where the barracks had stood, were strewn with gravel and small, light-colored pebbles instead of the original grass, dirt, gravel, and cement. The SS inscription on the roof of the service building, mockingly proclaiming Prussian virtues such as obedience, sobriety, cleanliness, and hard work as the "milestones to freedom," was not reconstructed, nor were a number of other SS signs and pictures throughout the camp, such as the mural behind the crematorium ovens depicting a man riding on a pig reminding workers "Wash hands before touching corpses, any one who does not wash is a pig," and the saying "One louse – means death."[39]

Almost all of the special function buildings in the camp were demolished and not replaced: the aforementioned canteen and infirmary barracks, the inmates' library, the punishment barracks, the priests' chapel, the disinfection building for clothing, the brothel, the greenhouses, the kennels, the rabbit hutches, and the SS prison. Only the entry gate, the watchtowers, the "special prisoners" bunker behind the service building, and the two crematoria were left standing (or, in the case of the watchtowers, reconstructed). Taken together, these changes reduce the multifaceted and contradictory hell of KZ Dachau to a rather sterile, unidimensional image: a barren, gray-white expanse surrounded by a high cement wall and watchtowers, a museum that looks like it might have housed offices, and two dormitory barracks at one end, and a crematorium with a gas chamber at the other. Thus the former Dachau concentration camp was reduced to a stream-lined symbol: it had all of the stereotypical attributes of a Nazi camp – near the entrance a section of the ditch and barbed wire barrier was reconstructed as well – but otherwise it had been reduced to a representation of the spotlessly "clean camp" of Nazi propaganda and its postwar mythic adherents. And that seems to have been the goal of Bavarian officials.

Already in 1959 former camp senior Oskar Müller noted that the Bavarian authorities were constantly trying to destroy as many relics of the camp as they could. In a letter to Roth he wrote:[40]

> We aren't making any progress in the creation of a warning and memorial site in Dachau. It is quite obvious: The motivation for this stance [of the Bavarian authorities] is the intention to spread the cloak of silence and oblivion over the last period of German history. The persecutors of yesterday who are once again setting the tone fear the presentation of historical truth, they fear those documents that reveal their shameful deeds.

In 1966, after the memorial site was completed, a critical reviewer wrote that Dachau was "made up like a witch who wants to appear harmless."[41] He noted the fresh paint on the service building, the clean gravel on the roll-call square, the absence of barracks, the trim "chapel of atonement" at the end of a beautiful tree-lined lane, and the cypress trees and well-trimmed hedges surrounding the crematoria. And in 1968, after the international memorial was dedicated, a reporter for the London *Times* described a similar impression for his readers.[42] Noting that "much of the camp does not . . . act as an effective reminder of the past," he offered the following description:

> The watchtowers and barbed-wire fences remain, but all the barracks are gone save two, which are renovated and clean, almost clinical . . . the barrack areas are now neatly marked off and numbered . . . The crematorium – complete with ovens, a stretcher in the mouth of each – is a chilling sight, but it is hidden behind trees in a beautifully kept garden and it is outside the camp itself.

The journalist also quoted several survivors who felt that the concentration camp should have been left in its original state. "It means nothing as it is," one said.

The new museum, 1960–1965

Once the decision had been made to strip the camp of remains, a museum became more important as a means of documenting the past. Since 1953 there had been no museum in the former camp, and in April 1956 the CID did not even include the creation of a historical museum in its list of primary goals.[43] At that time they conceived rather vaguely that, as in the Auschwitz memorial site in Poland, different barracks would house different exhibitions, sponsored by the countries that had lost citizens in Dachau:

> The barracks should be fitted with old furniture, objects of remembrance [*Erinnerungsstücke*], and documentary photographs. The national groups will decide on the arrangement of the objects, but the state castle and garden authority will care for the memorial site.

Over the next two years, the plans for the memorial site and the museum became much more specific. The publication in June 1956 of a comprehensive plan for a museum in Buchenwald in East Germany, which was to include a library and archive, and for which research groups were to be constituted at the University of Leipzig, may have played a role in the CID's decision to prioritize the collecting of documents and to include a historical museum in its plans.[44] In the official statutes of the CID, written in 1958, a preservative museum and a didactic exhibition ranked high in its program. The eight goals were:[45]

1. cultivation of memory (*Erinnerungspflege*);
2. protection of the respectful commemoration of the dead;
3. restoration of the condition in 1945, with a documentation center and a museum;
4. construction of a monument;
5. defense of the rights of the victims and their successors;
6. to fight against everything that could lead to a recurrence of Nazism;
7. active participation in the understanding and friendship between peoples;
8. mediation between the major organizations of former persecutees and maintenance of regular contacts to them.

In the first plans drawn up by the Belgian architect René Vander Auvera for the CID, the original conception of the museum is laid out.[46] In the former infirmary barrack visitors were to proceed through rooms dedicated to specific aspects of concentration camp life. They began with the "origins of the camp," continued with "administration," "work," "hygiene and diseases," "medical experiments," and ended with "extermination," "cremation," "liberation," "balance sheet of death," and "literature." The canteen barrack was to contain a "room of flags," a "room of reunion," a film projection room, a barrack room from 1933, a washroom, and a barrack room from 1943. Each room or group of rooms was to be designed by a specific national committee of the CID. The Germans and Austrians were to be responsible for the first two museum rooms, the Poles for "work," the Luxembourgers for "hygiene" and "medical experiments," the Soviets for "extermination," and so on.[47] After an initial design phase, the conceptions were to be collected and internationally coordinated and discussed. This plan was never realized because by 1963, when the relocation of the residents began in earnest, it had already been decided to raze the barracks and use the former service building for the museum.

In the meantime a temporary exhibition was installed in the crematorium building in 1960, in anticipation of the expected tens of thousands of participants at the dedication of the Catholic chapel during the Eucharistic World Congress in August. That exhibition was constructed with extreme haste – only three weeks lay between the granting of permission to set it up and the official opening on 30 July – but it contained many of the elements of the permanent exhibition that opened in 1965 (ill. 50).[48] In one room a model of the prisoners' compound of the concentration camp, which had already been commissioned by the CID in 1957 for the permanent museum, was displayed.[49] The rest was a collection of artifacts, charts, photographs, and facsimile documents. It made the following impression on a contemporary German reporter:[50]

> Statistics, blueprints, and documents aid one's memory: arrest warrants from the Gestapo; orders to send the prisoners' tooth-gold directly to the medical office, to make women's hair into felt and yarn, and to bring the low temperature experiments "to a good conclusion"; clemency petitions, reports about autopsies, police investigations; photocopies of orders of the day and liquidation squad lists; pictures, graphs. In their midst stained gray-blue striped prisoners' uniforms, bull whip, whipping horse, and other instruments of torture. A "profitability calculation" makes a ghastly impression: for an average life span a net profit of 1631 Reichsmarks per prisoner is calculated, "not including the proceeds from the utilization of the bones and ash," says the panel. Under it the terse preprinted forms: "exit due to death" – sent to the families of dead prisoners. The last room of the exhibition is dominated by the headlines in the international press – about the liberation of the Dachau KZ prisoners on 29 April 1945, and about the subsequent trials of the SS thugs and henchmen. In one glass case lie nearly fifty books and brochures – memoirs of liberated prisoners. At the exit a placard warns: "Never Again!"

It is interesting to examine the differences between this exhibition and the one installed in the service building in 1965 (see ill. 54). Most notably, the earlier documentation did not contain any reference to the systematic extermination of the Jews. Of course there was little room in the crematorium to display such documentation, but since it was missing from the early conceptions of the 1965 museum as well, considerations of space do not appear to have been the reason for its exclusion. Rather, in 1960 there was very little public awareness of the Holocaust *per se*. Only after the Eichmann trial in 1961 did the enormity of the Holocaust – and its links to their own camp – become clear to the survivors of Dachau.[51]

Interestingly, the 1960 exhibition gave more prominence to two sites of mass murder associated with Dachau than the 1965 exhibition would. The former "euthanasia" gassing facility at Hartheim in Austria, where almost 3,200 Dachau inmates were sent to be murdered in 1942, and the shooting range at nearby Hebertshausen, where an estimated 4,000–6,000 Soviet POWs were executed in 1941–2 (ill. 55), were represented by three-dimensional models. In the 1965 museum, only three nondescript photographs and several facsimile documents referred to these atrocities.[52] Instead of augmenting the models with documents, as Dutch survivor Nico Rost, one of the leading figures in the movement to create a museum, had suggested, they were replaced by "flatware." This reduction in the 1965 museum follows the trend toward sanitizing the memorial site to reflect the image of the "clean camp."[53]

The 1960 exhibition also showed evidence of an *over*sensitivity to recent claims that the gas chamber in Dachau had been built by German POWs under American command after the war. Next to the original stenciled sign "Shower Baths" over the entrance to the gas chamber an explanatory text commented: "*This room would have been used as an undressing and waiting room if the gas chamber had worked. The sign 'shower baths' served to deceive the prisoners*" (ill. 51). In fact, the gas chamber was in good working order long before the war was over, and it was even tested on at least two groups of prisoners. It was indeed never used for systematic gassings, probably because the death rate in Dachau was high enough to keep the crematorium ovens running at capacity anyway. The explanatory sign thus inadvertently supported the myth of the "clean camp," by implying that the gas chamber had been some sort of nonfunctional sham.

The permanent museum's conception, developed in conjunction with German specialists sympathetic to the survivors' cause, was presented to the public in May 1963. It claimed programmatically that it would serve to "transmit to the widest possible audience a realistic and in every respect truthful picture of all events that occurred in this camp. Beyond that the exhibition has to show how this murderous system could develop and expand."[54] In keeping with this second goal, the 1965 exhibition included an introductory section on antisemitism and the Nazi rise to power, and another section on the program to exterminate the Jews.[55] The four main sections are entitled:

"The Prehistory up to the Takeover of Power"
"The Dachau Concentration Camp"
"Extermination" and
"The End of the Concentration Camps."

The first goal of being "realistic and truthful in every respect," however, proved more difficult. Almost exclusive use of documents and photographs, for instance, was less realistic than the mannequins used to reenact punishment scenes in the 1945 exhibition. Instead, realism was achieved primarily by huge enlargements of very graphic photographs of scenes in KZ Dachau and other concentration camps (ill. 54). For example, one series depicts the death of a human subject during "high altitude" experiments in a decompression chamber; another shows an SS man standing among corpses in a mass grave after the liberation of Bergen-Belsen.

And while everything was truthful, it may not have been the whole truth. Excluded were "cultural" activities not related to bare physical survival or suffering and death, so that the exhibition does not convey the aspects of the daily routine that helped to make life remotely livable under the extreme SS repression. Reading, writing, dramatic productions, and political discussions, for example, were important to many of the long-term inmates. Another example would be the role of religion in the daily life of some inmates, to which one case of the 1960 exhibition was devoted, but which was dropped from the 1965 exhibition. Or the clandestinely tolerated use of forbidden "bed smoothers": polished sticks that helped to make the perfectly smooth beds needed to avoid punishment. In fact, given the importance of the photographs in the exhibition, the overall impression is exclusively of repression, horror, and inhumanity. The decision to rely solely on official documents made it much easier to document exploitation, torture, murder, suicide, and emaciation than to portray solidarity and resistance among the inmates. A graduate student studying memorial site exhibitions concluded in 1990:[56]

> Those who leave the memorial site [museum] take shocking pictures of
> horrors with them. These pictures do not serve only as sources of historical
> information. The greatly enlarged photographs reproduce especially the fear

and terror that the prisoners experienced, presented from the perspective with which perpetrators view their victims. Almost all pictures are contextualized by explanatory texts and historical documents, but the emotional shock that they are able to trigger predominates nonetheless . . . Consciousness of one's own [distancing] reactions when confronted by photographs of horror is not made possible by the primarily emotional appeal of the pictures in Dachau, but rather only by intellectual reflection about historical reality. The pictures in Dachau, especially the ones in the section about the medical experiments performed on prisoners, are detrimental to this approach [of fostering intellectual reflection].

In 1960 the general secretary of the CID, Georges Walraeve, explained why the museum focused on barbarity:[57]

As a monument of inhumanity it should teach the coming generations love of their neighbors, fraternity and respect of human rights . . . [It] should not arouse feelings of hatred towards the German people, although the public, especially the younger generations, must be informed about the past without making things seem better than they were.

In the concluding chapter of this book we will return to the contradiction inherent in using horrifying images to teach solidarity and respect.

In the final analysis the West German government's unwillingness to preserve relics of daily life in the camp, coupled with the survivors' need to document the barbarity of the SS under which they suffered, gave rise to a memorial site and museum that were not conducive to fostering the survivors' goals. The next two examples, a monument for Soviet victims, erected at the height of the Cold War, and the central camp monument on the roll-call square, also illustrate how memorials better reflect contemporary politics than past history.

A monument for the Soviet POWs executed at Hebertshausen, 1964

In June 1941 Hitler broke his treaty with Stalin and attacked the Soviet Union. The German army seemed unstoppable through the summer and early fall. Beginning in October 1941, thousands of prisoners of war were shipped to Dachau, marched directly to an SS shooting range at Hebertshausen (about one mile from the camp, see ills. 1, 55), and executed. This was a secret program, and the POWs were never registered in the camp, so that we do not know precisely how many were murdered. Prisoners who washed the bullet-riddled uniforms in the camp laundry estimated about 6,000 executions.[58] Since so little was known about this "action," and because Soviet survivors had no access to Dachau during the 1950s, this potentially important commemorative site did not figure at all in the recollective events of that decade. Not until 1961 was Hebertshausen included in a memorial ceremony.[59] A suggestion at that ceremony to dedicate a plaque on 29 April 1962 soon grew into a plan to create a memorial. When the West German survivors took the initiative and commissioned a monument without first consulting the CID, the international organization was somewhat disgruntled, but nonetheless contributed DM1,500, over one-fifth of the total cost, indicating that it approved of the commemoration.[60]

At the dedication ceremony on 3 May 1964, Erich Braun of the West German camp association spoke first, then Martin Niemöller, and finally Wadim Sobkow from Kiev for the Soviet Association of War and Nazi Victims. Braun explained that the West German camp association was erecting the monument to express its "sadness for the humiliation, pain and damages" inflicted on the soldiers who had only been doing their duty when their motherland was attacked. Niemöller emphasized the need to pass memories on to the generation that had no personal experience of the Nazi "insanity of power," and demanded punishment of the guilty. Finally Sobkow invoked the Dachau concentration camp as a symbol of international unity and world peace: "Here Germans and Russians, Poles and Italians, sons of the most different nations fought side by side against fascist terror. The common fight for peace shall not be disrupted by a new war. Long live German–Soviet friendship! Long live peace in the whole world!"

This ideal conception of international brotherhood, however, had to remain vague in order not to provoke Cold War sensibilities in the West German populace at large, and perhaps among some groups of Dachau survivors as well. The inscription on the completely abstract, billboard-like upright concrete slab is very specific in some respects, but does not tell the whole truth (ill. 56). It reads: "Thousands of PRISONERS OF WAR were MURDERED here by the SS." This names both the deed and the perpetrators in precise terms, but it is silent about the most significant fact differentiating this atrocity from all others committed in Dachau: the Soviet citizenship of the victims. This silence testifies to the tension between the Western and Eastern blocs shortly after the construction of the Berlin Wall in 1961 and the Cuban missile crisis of 1963.

The genesis of the international memorial on the former roll-call square also illustrates how different present images of the past gave rise to the particular artistic form.

The international memorial, 1959–1968

Because of the different implications for their present status in society, the German survivors did not completely agree with the non-Germans about what the central monument in the planned memorial site should symbolize. In the 1950s the West German survivors were severely marginalized by a society of self-proclaimed victims. Thus the German survivors wished to emphasize the solidarity, resistance, and heroism of their struggle against National Socialism. That would portray them positively, but not provoke German society by reminding it of the heinous crimes committed in its name by many of its members. The non-German survivors, in contrast, were well recognized in their home countries (in May 1956, for example, Charles de Gaulle presided over a meeting of the French Dachau Association).[61] In those countries, in keeping with the media blitz at the end of the war, the concentration camps were still associated with pestilent mills of inhumanity and death. Therefore a representation of the horrors of the camps was more natural for them. Additionally, these opposing conceptions of the past accorded with the different groups' status in the camp hierarchy. The Germans had been situated at the top with a comparably tolerable life and many more opportunities to show solidarity; the foreigners always ranged below them with much greater privation, harsher penalties, fewer contacts with the outside, and far fewer resources available for sharing.

After the symbolic cornerstone for the central camp memorial had been laid in September 1956, details of the memorial's size and location were worked out. On 1 January 1959 the CID announced an artists' competition for a memorial that would "show future generations the courage of the political prisoners during their incarceration and their love for their fellow human beings."[62] The call for submissions from artists who had survived Nazi persecution brought in sixty-three entries from eighteen countries by mid-August.[63] In November 1959, forty-five of the projects were exhibited in the Brussels Ministry for Health and Family, where CID president Albert Guérisse worked (Guérisse is seen on ill. 65).[64] Delegates from seven major organizations of Dachau survivors attended the opening, as did nine foreign diplomats, and reporters from six major newspapers, radio and television. The CID newsletter described the six favored entries: a tall, winged iron sculpture; a pyramid with 238,000 pipes symbolizing the number of "dead" of KZ Dachau (actually, that was the total number of inmates: there still seems to have been confusion on that issue); a massive, cryptlike, open-roofed "descent into hell," a "very expressive sculpture" on a zigzagging ramplike base; a 15–18 meter tall crystalline "cathedral," against which some delegates expressed reservations; and a tall, thin, thorny tower that was "not worked out enough."[65]

In March 1960 the prize committee decided to ask the creators of four of the prize-winning projects to submit designs for sculptures to be placed on the ramplike foundation of the "very expressive sculpture" submitted by Yugoslavian sculptor Nandor Glid. Apparently the prize committee did not find Glid's original sculpture, a tall, skeletal humanoid form made of bonelike bronze bars, completely satisfactory.

In the following years the CID focused its energies on the realization of the museum and memorial site, so the formal invitation to the four artists was not sent until January 1965.[66] In June of that year the prize committee deliberated about the four new sculptures, and chose Nandor Glid's. The German delegate, Otto Kohlhofer, reported dissension and dissatisfaction with the choice among some of the committee members, who yielded to the opinion of Guérisse.[67] In particular, the Germans did not like the sculpture's overwhelming emphasis on the horrors of the camp. In Glid's dark bronze sculpture sticklike stylized emaciated bodies with small heads and barblike hands are interwoven and mounted on high bronze fenceposts with angled tops (ills. 58, 59). Short, thick segments of barbed wire within the sculpture, and flanking cement fenceposts on both sides strengthen the impression of a mangled mass of humanity tangled into a barbed wire fence. The dark, sprawling sculpture is predominantly horizontal: 16 meters wide and 6.3 meters tall. It is also well over a meter deep, but viewers only realize this if they walk down the angular ramplike foundation that serves as the base of the sculpture, and view it from underneath. From below, the filigree structure of the piece shows the true weight of the bronze: a crushing burden of nameless, faceless mass death.

The West German committee in the CID did not like this evocation of mass misery, mass death, and complicity in the machinery of death. The Germans preferred a model by Hamburg architect Hansdietmar Klug in which a slender, 35 meter tall column of jagged, interlaced strands towered over a large and a smaller stone prism thrusting in opposite directions (ill. 60).[68] While the jagged edges of the ladderlike tower connote the pain of camp life, the verticality of the piece signifies honor and resistance. The thrusting triangles are reminiscent of a famous 1923 monument in Weimar designed by Bauhaus architect Walter Gropius to commemorate the trade unionists who died defending the new German republic in the 1918–19 revolution.[69] That monument had been blown up by the Nazis and restored after the war.

Glid's original design did contain a symbol of resistance, which was included in the final project. A second sculpture concealed within the ramplike base was composed of three large stylized links of a chain adorned with triangles glazed in the colors of the cloth badges that the SS used to categorize the various groups in the prisoner hierarchy (ill. 61). This bas relief symbolizes the international solidarity of the prisoners within the camp. However, two of the colors used in the camps are not included in the sculpture: the green of the "professional criminals" and the pink of the homosexuals. Whereas the absence of multiple criminal offenders who usually collaborated with the camp SS is not without logic, the exclusion of the persecuted homosexuals reveals prejudices in the survivors' organization at that time. Homosexuals were victims as innocent as Jews, whose yellow triangles are amply represented in the sculpture. As we will see, only in 1994 did the CID finally allow a plaque commemorating the persecution of homosexuals in Dachau to be officially displayed in the memorial site (see pp. 354f).

The memorial's quadrilingual inscription also bears witness to the conflicting conceptions and goals of its creators (ill. 62). Its English text reads:

> May the example of those *who were exterminated here* between 1933–1945
> because they resisted Nazism help to unite the living for the defense of
> peace and freedom and in respect for their fellow men (emphasis added).

The German text renders their "extermination" more euphemistically: "May the example of those who *lost their lives* here from 1933 to 1945 because of *their* fight against National Socialism unite the living." Whereas the English text stresses the "extermination" of people resisting an oppressive regime (as do the French and Russian texts), the German version emphasizes the "loss of life" of political idealists who chose to fight for their own cause.

After the new museum in the service building was completed and the final design selected, fundraising for the international memorial began. In August 1965 the CID solicited public donations to cover the construction costs.[70] When construction began in the fall of 1967 approximately 60 percent of the DM1.2 million costs had been received. This amount included DM300,000 (25 percent) from the West German federal government, DM200,000 from the CID (17 percent), DM50,000 (4 percent) from the city of Munich, DM1,500 (0.13 percent) from Dachau, and DM644 from the employees of the Bavarian Restitution Authority.[71] An additional DM165,000 (14 percent) was contributed by groups in France, Belgium, the Netherlands, and the United States, bringing the total secured funding to DM717,000. I presume that the Bavarian government ultimately contributed most of the remaining 40 percent.

The international memorial on the roll-call square was finally dedicated on 9 September 1968, in a ceremony marred by a conflict between representatives of the West German government and members of the generation of 1968 rebels, as we will see below. Before its completion, however, two other large memorials were constructed at the opposite end of the memorial site: a Jewish and a Protestant memorial completed the religious "ensemble" envisioned by Neuhäusler around his Catholic chapel.[72]

10

Jews represent the Holocaust at Dachau

There are two fundamentally different groups of Jewish survivors of Dachau. The first are the German and Austrian Jews who were arrested during the *Kristallnacht* pogroms in November 1938. Some of them were released after a short time, while others were allowed to go once they had secured emigration papers. Most of these Jews had been assimilated into German culture and had experienced Dachau for a relatively short time in the prewar years before conditions became absolutely untenable. This group's feelings toward Dachau often resembled those of non-Jewish Germans: it was an aberration of German culture that should be allowed to fade into oblivion.[1] In the chapter on the "clean camps" we met a member of this group: Alfred Werner, whose article about his 1951 visit prompted Bavarian authorities to remove the exhibition in the crematorium in 1953 (see pp. 173f). The famous psychologist Bruno Bettelheim, who returned to Germany to visit the camp in 1955, is another example.[2]

The other group is composed of Jews from various Eastern European countries, especially Hungary and Poland, who were either brought to Dachau in 1944 to serve as slave laborers at Dachau branch camps such as Landsberg, Mühldorf, or Allach, or who were evacuated to Dachau in 1945 during the last chaotic months before Germany's defeat. Most members of this group emigrated from Germany as soon as possible and had little interest in ever returning. For them, Dachau was a murderous hell-hole in a country populated by genocidal antisemites, one of many sites where Nazi Germany's maniacal program to murder all Jews had been implemented.[3] These survivors' conception of Dachau is shared by many Jews the world over – and by younger cohorts including non-Jews in Germany and abroad.

Jewish commemoration in the former Dachau concentration camp during the first years after the war was dominated by this latter group of Eastern European Jews. Two notions held by this group influenced the nature of the Jewish memorial built in Dachau in the 1960s. They were perceived and perceived themselves as a foreign body within Germany. They did not wish to interact with Germans, and they wanted to leave the country as soon as possible. Thus their monuments are not addressed to Germans and make no attempt to be understandable to them. Also, for these Jews who had been situated squarely at the bottom of the concentration camp hierarchy, the concentration camps were sites only of death. Other categories of prisoners, priests in particular, had been able to practice cultural pursuits such as religion or writing (albeit in a severely limited way) in the camps. The emotional boost from preserving such small remnants of "normal" life was crucial to physical survival in the Nazi concentration camps – an often noted but never systematically studied aspect of the Nazi camps.[4]

In any case, for the overwhelming majority of Jews religious practice played no role in the camps. After the war they could not draw on a tradition of clandestine practice, and they did not think that a "house of God" could or should be erected on the "Godless" soil of a former concentration camp. Thus the Jewish memorial completed in 1967 is *not* a synagogue, and only the Kaddish, the Jewish prayer for the dead, is recited in the memorial site. In contrast, regular church services with Communion are held in the Protestant church and masses are celebrated in the Catholic chapel.

Both the importance of cultural practice for longer-term survival and the isolation of the postwar Jews from German society are evident in the early postwar Jewish commemorations in concentration camps.

Early Jewish commemoration after 1945

Immediately after liberation the practice of religious ritual had especial significance for Jews, although it was important for all groups with a religious identity. One of the most moving events during the liberation of Dachau was a short biblical benediction given by US army rabbi Leland Loy from the tower of the gatehouse: "Comfort ye my people, saith the Lord your God."[5] That public profession of Jewish culture more than any other symbolized the end of SS rule. This symbolic reclaiming of Jewish identity was repeated on an individual level by Yoel (Joel) Sack, who soon became the head of the Dachau committee of liberated Jews. He had survived the evacuation of Flossenbürg by posing as "Yulian Sakowski," a Polish Catholic.[6] One of his first acts after liberation, while he was still hovering on the brink of death, was to have his correct name and religion entered in the barrack register.

For the liberated Jews in Dachau the return of organized religion was one of the first concrete signs of their new freedom. US military rabbi David Eichhorn arrived in Dachau on 30 April 1945, the day after liberation, but the situation was still so chaotic that he could do little more than survey the scene.[7] A day later in the nearby branch camp Allach, however, Eichhorn held a moving religious service for 3,300 Jewish survivors and gave them a torah from Treuchtlingen. The torah had been hidden in the town hall during the November 1938 pogrom and turned over to him as a liberator by the German city official who had hidden it. Eichhorn returned to the Dachau main camp again on 3 May, where he held a Sabbath service on Friday afternoon, 4 May, for Jewish women who had been liberated in the camp. The main Sabbath service for all of the Jews in the camp was planned for the next morning.

It is characteristic of the situation of the Jews in the camp that that Sabbath service had to be held in the camp laundry instead of on the roll-call square. Although the International Prisoners' Committee announced that it would support the service by sending an honorary delegation from each national group, non-Jewish Poles, the largest group of survivors in the camp, threatened to break up the service by force.[8] After US officials were informed of what had happened, they provided an "honor guard," and the ceremony was repeated in public the next day. The service in the Dachau laundry was not the only case in which liberated Jews feared repression at the hands of antisemitic Poles. A large group of liberated Polish Jews in the Heidelberg–Mannheim area feared for their lives when they heard that they were to be transferred to a Polish DP camp, and another group feared to board a train full of Christian Poles.[9]

Jewish commemorations after the immediate postwar phase were characterized by exclusion of the Germans on the part of the Jews, and philosemitic behavior on the part of the Germans, at least as long as they were under the watchful eyes of the Allies. As an example of Jews excluding Germans, on 15 April 1946, the first anniversary of the liberation of KZ Belsen, the Jewish committee of Belsen dedicated a monument carrying the following inscription in Hebrew and English:[10] "Israel and the world shall remember / Thirty thousand Jews / Exterminated in the concentration camp / of Bergen-Belsen / at the hands of the murderous Nazis. / Earth conceal not the blood / Shed on thee! / First anniversary of liberation / 15th April 1946 / 14th Nissan 5706." The monument claims to speak for "Israel and the world," not the Germans, who are bitterly rejected as "murderous Nazis."

The dedication of a newly constructed synagogue in Munich in May 1947 is an example of philosemitic German support of Jewish commemoration under Allied scrutiny. Bavarian Minister President Ehard took the opportunity to express the German will to materially and morally compensate Jewish victims of Nazism to US military governor General Clay and other Allied representatives.[11] We have already seen how little came of this *Wiedergutmachung* in spite of such public pronouncements. When the Allies were not present, Jews often found themselves on the defensive.[12] At the first large VVN commemoration in Dachau in May 1947, Auerbach chastised the German populace for begrudging the Jews the extra rations they were receiving. According to a report, Auerbach "condemned the flood of [German] protest that broke loose because of a few scant bonus rations for the persecutees, while not a voice had been heard when only 500 calories were given out in the concentration camp, or when for years Jewish citizens were given no meat, sugar, etc."[13]

After two weeks of reflection about Auerbach's reproach, one of the leading figures in the KZ priests' association, since he considered himself "not to be an antisemite," took the liberty (as he put it) to publish the following advice to the "full Jews" (he used the Nazi term) living in Germany:[14]

> Everywhere one hears complaints that individual [Jews] disagreeably push themselves to the front of the line and state their claims. They demand apartments, furniture, offices. In Bavaria the East-Jews even inundate the countryside and thus provoke the displeasure of the Bavarian people. Wouldn't it be more in the interest of Jewry to exercise [i.e. if the Jews exercised] genteel restraint? . . . It would be better for them not to be so prominent in the field of vision of the public. The aversion of the broadest circles against us KZ inmates is already great enough.

With advice like this from a sympathetic and well-meaning fellow survivor, Jews in West Germany were indeed well advised to keep a low profile to avoid provoking antisemitic reactions from the German populace. And that they did.

As Cold War considerations made the Western Allies less critical of German activities, antisemitic incidents began to occur with greater frequency.[15] In the spring of 1948 a rash of desecrations of Jewish cemeteries in Bavaria prompted a parliamentary inquiry.[16] In August 1949, as detailed on p. 143 above, the printing of a rabidly antisemitic letter to the editor in the *Süddeutsche Zeitung* sparked a riot in Munich. It is not surprising that when, at the dedication of the Leiten cemetery in April 1950, a representative from the Berlin Jewish community merely quoted from the Old Testament and mentioned the "murder" of 6 million Jews, the police reported that "His words were poorly received by the participants, some of whom did not approve of them because they were strongly attuned to the Israelite people."[17] In other words, the Jews were not catering to the Germans.

The problem essentially solved itself because this group of Jews dwindled substantially through emigration. And those Jews who remained in Germany, if they did not follow the KZ priest's advice and keep a low profile, were sometimes forcibly removed from the public sphere. For example Auerbach and the rabbi of the postwar Munich Jewish community, Aaron Ohrenstein, were arrested and effectively silenced in 1952.[18] There followed a period of scant Jewish interest in the camp – except for sporadic visits by returning émigrés such as Alfred Werner and Bruno Bettelheim.

The new Jewish memorial building, 1960–1967

When Bishop Neuhäusler suggested in 1960 that a Jewish monument be set up near his Catholic chapel, Munich Rabbi Blumenthal first answered that the Jewish community would be content with the construction of a "modest star of David" in the camp.[19] This response must be seen against the background of a lack of Jewish interest in commemorating the Holocaust in the 1950s. As a number of historians have noted, the Holocaust in the narrower sense of the extermination of the Jews was not even a concept in Jewish historiography and *public* Jewish memory until the 1960s.[20] However, as the May 1960 abduction of Adolf Eichmann brought the Holocaust to Germany's attention – polls revealed that 95 percent of the populace had heard of his 1961 trial, and 90 percent knew what it was about – the other Jewish leaders in Bavaria realized the need for a symbolic focal point of ritual memory in KZ Dachau.[21] The Jewish community decided to erect a more elaborate memorial structure.

The Bavarian Association of Jewish Communities (Landesverband der israelitischen Kultusgemeinden in Bayern, hereafter "Landesverband") sent Munich engineer Stefan Schwarz to Israel to solicit advice and support for the Bavarian project in December 1960.[22] He went to the Israeli national museum and memorial for the Jewish victims of Nazi genocide, Yad Vashem, which had been established by an act of the Israeli parliament in 1953.[23] When Yad Vashem officials told Schwarz that they would not be able to support the building financially, but only with artifacts and religious objects, Schwarz approached the Jewish Committee for

Persecutees and Deportees in France. By March 1961 the Bavarian Landesverband had published a call for donations addressed to other Jewish associations in Germany and Jewish institutions abroad, and had decided to commission the architect of the postwar synagogues in Dusseldorf and Hanover, Hermann Guttmann, to design the building.[24]

In June 1961 Guttmann visited the former concentration camp with Schwarz to look at the proposed site 40 meters east of the Mortal Agony of Christ Chapel. At that time the KZ clothing disinfection building still stood nearby – it had been converted to a restaurant (ill. 25).[25] In fact, shortly after Schwarz's and Guttmann's visit, a new restaurant leaseholder renamed that largest gastronomic establishment in the residential settlement "Restaurant at the Crematorium" ("Gaststätte zum Krematorium"), presumably because he thought the name would bring additional business. The name was changed in November after a group of visitors lodged a complaint with Bavarian authorities, who now recognized it as a nuisance.[26] At a meeting of the three religious organizations and CID representatives in March 1962 the demolition of the disinfection/restaurant was slated for the fall.[27] However, it was not carried out until a full year later, after three appeal courts had rejected the restaurant owner's suit to stop the eviction.[28] Finally, in November 1963, on the day before the ceremonies commemorating the twenty-fifth anniversary of the 1938 pogroms, a unit of the National Border Guard was brought in to "tear down the building and everything around it, and take it away."

The haste with which the building, a remnant of the concentration camp, was torn down can be attributed to the offense caused by the restaurant, but it also reveals the lack of concern for documenting aspects of the concentration camp's past that did not fit into a simple scheme of evil perpetrators and anonymous victims. Protest against the demolition of the crematorium or watchtowers, for example, had been immediate and successful. On the other hand, no protest was forthcoming when the former camp brothel, which had also been near the site of the Jewish memorial, was demolished.[29]

By 1963 Jews began to take a more active role in commemoration in Dachau. In April 1963, for the first time since 1950, an official representative of a Jewish victims' organization spoke at the liberation ceremony.[30] (Even at the *Kristallnacht* ceremonies in Dachau organized by German youth groups since 1956, no representatives of Jewish organizations participated in an official capacity.[31]) Also in 1963, the return of Werner Cahnman[n], the Bavarian syndic of the Central Association of German Jews from 1930 to 1934, who had spent two months in Dachau in 1939, gave more visibility to the Bavarian Jews.[32] Cahnman[n], who had become a noted sociology professor in the United States, founded a United States organization of Dachau survivors in 1964.[33]

On liberation day in April 1964 the Association of Jewish Persecutees and KZ Invalids in Munich dedicated a monument it had commissioned for the Dachau city cemetery.[34] It stands near a field of graves for about 2,200 primarily Jewish KZ inmates who died after Dachau was liberated. The monument, designed by the sculptor–painter Dieter Aldinger from Cologne, is a 5 meter tall tower segmented into four stories of three-sided stone blocks. The top and bottom corners of the blocks are blunted, giving them six-sided faces. The second story carries the text in Hebrew, English, and German: "Remember the Victims." A star of David is inscribed on the third story, a menorah on the top.[35]

The location of this Jewish "monument of choice" – the memorial building in the camp was erected only after Neuhäusler's suggestion – is more typical of Jewish commemoration: it takes place at the actual location of the corpses (or ashes) of the victims. Thus in Dachau the first Jewish markers were erected at the Leiten mass graves, over the pits of human ash in the crematory garden, and at the city cemetery. In Belsen and Auschwitz, to name other examples, according to this Jewish perception, the whole camp area was a cemetery because blood had been shed and corpses strewn everywhere. Thus the German Protestant Church was requested not to erect a chapel in the former Belsen camp in 1963, and that was also one reason why the Carmelite convent in Auschwitz provoked such conflict in 1986.[36] Additionally, orthodox Jewish tradition dictates that the dead be left in their original graves with their original markers until the coming of the Messiah. Thus Bavarian Jews protested when the scattered graves of KZ prisoners murdered along the routes of evacuation treks were consolidated into a few large cemeteries in the early 1960s.[37] Only after the National Socialist judeocide became a central element of Jewish identity in the 1960s were autonomous "Holocaust" monuments established in cities all over the world.[38] They are thus evidence of a radical secularization of Jewish identity in recent decades.

The funds for the Jewish building were, like those for all major memorials in Dachau except the 1952 Leiten hall, raised by soliciting donations. Financing memorials in this way implies that they express recollective desires "from below," as opposed to state-imposed commemoration "from above." When excavation work began in September 1964 DM50,000 had already been pledged by the Bavarian Jewish Community Fund, and DM30,000 by the city of Munich.[39] For the rest of the projected DM250,000 building costs a mailing was sent out to all Jews registered to pay religious taxes in West Germany, and to French, Belgian, and Dutch Jewish organizations. Construction proceeded slowly as funds came in. Some changes were made along the way. For instance, the planners decided to leave the surface of the outer walls roughly hewn instead of smooth. This contrasted with the river-rounded stones of the Catholic chapel and the smooth concrete of the Protestant church: for Jews, commemoration of brown-collar crimes was painful, not soothing.

By May 1965 the outer shell of the building was complete and the selection of the inscriptions and symbolic fittings began.[40] One discussion centered around whether a menorah should crown a white marble strip protruding from the apex of the roof, or whether a nonsacred symbol would be more appropriate.[41] In the end, the familiar seven-armed candelabrum was chosen. Although this holy relic from the ancient temple in Jerusalem was not the nine-armed Hanukah version, some viewers probably associate it with that symbol of victory over an overpowering enemy and of God's favor after the destruction of the first temple, and not merely as a symbol of Judaism.

Architect Guttmann suggested a quote from Psalm 9:21 as the primary inscription above the main opening: "Give them a sign of warning, eternal one! The peoples should learn that they are mortals."[42] Werner Cahnman, the German émigré survivor, felt that it was inappropriate because the ninth psalm was a "psalm of vengeance," but Dr. Ophir from Yad Vashem agreed with Guttmann's reasoning, namely that the Dachau monument was addressed to all peoples, not only to Jews. Ophir, however, thought that the monument should also specify that it commemorated the exceptional fate of the Jews.[43] Thus an additional inscription was selected for the interior wall:[44]

> Monument of warning to commemorate the Jewish martyrs who died in the years of the National Socialist rule of terror 1933–1945.
>
> Their death is a warning and obligation for us.
> Erected by the Regional Association of Israelite Cultural Communities in Bavaria in the year 1966/5727.

These two inscriptions reflect the differences between the two groups of Jews, and the shifting emphasis of Jewish Holocaust commemoration in the 1960s. On the one hand, the thoroughly Germanized Cahnman wished to avoid anything accusatory towards Germans. On the other hand, the German Jews of the 1960s, who were still relatively isolated within German society, wished to address "all peoples," although they revealed their inner-directedness by proclaiming – albeit in a less prominent place – that the Jewish deaths were warning and obligation "for us," and then signing their names. The elevation of senseless victims to "martyrs" who had died for their beliefs or some cause is typical of most memorials. After all, for outsiders recollection is logical if it achieves a positive goal, as opposed to memory solely for memory's sake. And commemorative art is not *l'art pour l'art*, but *l'art pour le souvenir*.

The Jewish memorial in Dachau was finally dedicated on 7 May 1967. It is wedge-shaped in both the horizontal and vertical planes, making it a three-dimensional trapezoid (ill. 63).[45] Its perimeter is parabolic with the entrance on the open side of the parabola. An 18 meter long ramp, bordered above ground on both sides by a railing supported by wide, stylized barbed wire pickets, leads downward from ground level to the interior floor 1.8 meters (six feet – the depth of a grave) below. The slightly vaulted roof of the building, which begins above the bottom edge of the ramp, slopes upward towards the apex of the parabola. The 10 meter wide subterranean opening of the building is blocked by a gate of barbed iron bars. The door handles, in contrast, are olive twigs, signs of God's reconciliation with Noah after the biblical flood. The rough-hewn interior walls of the 9 meter tall interior are adorned by seventy candleholders representing the seventy elders of Moses. A symbolic lectern bearing the Hebrew inscription "Yiskor" ("commemorate") and a ritual washing basin complete the furnishings. For some visitors the dark underground room at the end of the ramp might connote the lightless gas chambers, although it was intended to symbolize the underground hiding places many Jews used to escape the Nazis. At the back of the dark interior a vertical strip of light marble ascends the apex of the parabola and extends through a small round opening at the highest point of the roof, where light beams in. On the outside the strip ends with a menorah.

The column of light entering from the hole in the roof, even if it might connote the Zyklon B portals of the Birkenau gas chambers, or the crematorium chimneys that were the only exit for Jews in the extermination camps, is supposed to symbolize hope, salvation, and liberation. The marble strip at the back was hewn at Peki'in in Israel, a place where at least one Jew is supposed to have been living at all times in biblical history. It thus symbolizes the continuity of Judaism and Judaism's connection with Israel. The menorah represents the salvation that is the goal of the continuing Jewish hope. Of course, such hopefulness contrasts starkly with the absolute hopelessness of the vast majority of Jews in the concentration and extermination camps, in the ghettoes and at the mass execution sites.

Thus the Jewish Dachau memorial, too, emphasizes aspects relevant to contemporary Jewish identity that have little to do with Jewish life in the camps. It does, however, include more unmistakable historical icons than the religious memorials of the other religious denominations: the barbed wire enclosure, the ramp, the underground gas chamber, the chimney.

The message of hope expressed by most concentration camp memorials since the 1960s is indicative of a broader tendency to integrate younger generations into the recollection of Nazism. Central to that undertaking is historical education. With the traditional Jewish emphasis on learning, it is not surprising that Jewish groups were among the first to call for didactic facilities in Dachau. In September 1955, in response to County Governor Heinrich Junker's initiative to close the Dachau crematorium to the public, the vice president of the Bavarian Jewish Landesverband suggested building an "international student or youth hostel with an associated library of documents and pictures from the Hitler period" adjacent to the memorial site, instead of demolishing the crematorium.[46] This prophetic idea, which was finally realized in 1998, went well beyond the CID's contemporary plan for a memorial site with a museum.[47]

The emphasis on education was reflected at the dedication ceremony for the Jewish memorial building in May 1967. All three keynote speakers, cabinet minister Hundhammer, Bavarian senator Jean Mandel, and Israeli ambassador Asher Ben-Nathan, focused on the use of concentration camp memorial sites to educate Germany's youth.[48] The Israeli ambassador's words were spoken in a period of high tension in his country's history: Egypt was threatening to wipe the Jewish state off the map. Ben-Nathan thus concluded with a warning: "Many monuments to this memory have been erected, but the forests and fields of Israel are a living monument for us. Now we are able to defend ourselves without outside help because we have become independent!" Just four weeks later, on 10 June 1967, the Six Day War began with Israel's lightning preventive strike against Egypt. As I have shown elsewhere, Holocaust imagery was brandished by both Egypt and Israel in that war.[49] The Israeli victory was widely viewed as the final proof that Jews had overcome the legacy of the victimhood that had reached its nadir in the Holocaust.

Tragedy at the 1972 Munich Olympics

Several years later the triumphalist Jewish vision of having overcome the Holocaust through the founding and defense of the state of Israel suffered a tragic setback. In 1972 the Olympics were held in Munich – the first time they had been in Germany since 1936, when Hitler had exploited the Games to boost his domestic and international prestige. Many people in Israel, where the anti-German recollection of the Eastern European Jewish survivors predominated, viewed the participation of Israeli athletes in 1972 with grave reservations. To show that they had not forgotten German culpability, the Israeli government planned a special commemorative ceremony for its athletes in Dachau on 1 September, the anniversary of the German attack on Poland that started World War II.

The West German government, itself acutely conscious of international skepticism about its relationship to the Nazi past, also planned a major gathering in former KZ Dachau.[50] It was held on 25 August 1972, prior to the opening of the Games. Probably because they were to have their own ceremony a few days later, only five of twenty-eight Israeli athletes attended the German event.[51] In fact, very few athletes from any countries went to the ceremony, which was packed with VIPs and extensively reported by the media. The Israeli press was outraged by its country's athletes' apparently casual attitude, and printed vicious indictments. The Israeli government's ceremony on 1 September was accordingly well attended.

Four days later, on 5 September, just as German newspapers were reporting the outrage in Israel over the low participation of its athletes in the first ceremony, eight heavily armed Palestinian terrorists broke into the quarters of the Israeli athletes. Two Israelis were murdered on the spot and nine taken hostage. In dramatic negotiations the Palestinians rejected Munich mayor and member of parliament-elect Hans-Jochen Vogel's offer to be substituted for some of the athletes.[52] The nine Israeli hostages were killed when the helicopters they were in blew up during a failed rescue attempt. Also unfulfilled was the agenda of the Palestinian terrorists: to liberate 200 Arabs in Israeli prisons and to draw attention to the repression of Palestinians by an Israel that used the Nazi judeocide to legitimate its aggressive politics of "self-preservation."

Foreign Jewish tourists, 1960s to the present

Incidents like the kidnapping at the 1972 Olympic Games had little effect on the longer-term trend of Jewish recollections of the Holocaust in Dachau and Germany. An examination of visits by foreign Jews shows a remarkable consistency during the 1960s, 1970s, and even 1980s. However, it was only in the late 1970s, and increasingly during the 1980s, that foreign Jews visiting Dachau no longer saw it as a site of the Jewish Holocaust, but as a fixture of German history. Most of this group of Jewish visitors (I myself am an example) had been born well after 1945, had not received an emotionally wrenching education about the Holocaust prior to their visit, and did not have parents who had shown strong feelings about the Holocaust. Some examples illustrate this point.

Midge Decter was a writer and critic who published in *Harper's*, *Partisan Review*, and other periodicals.[53] She was married to Norman Podhoretz, the editor of *Commentary*, the magazine in which Alfred Werner had published his account of his visit to Dachau in 1951 (see Werner's story in chapter 5). In 1967 Decter traveled with a group of academics and writers invited to tour Germany by the Ford Foundation and the "Atlantic Bridge," an organization of German businessmen and industrialists interested in fostering foreign contacts. As an adolescent during the war she had learned about the Nazi atrocities, and she had some misgivings about accepting an invitation to Germany. When filling out a checklist of places they would like to see, she and her husband spontaneously put down "Dachau and Buchenwald" in the space marked "other." Before she arrived in Dachau, Midge Decter was worried about how the visit would affect her. Afterwards she summed up:

> But the visit turned out to be easy. You could feel nothing (and in truth one felt very little) and still get the message. Let me describe the place, what is left of it. Dachau, like, I suppose, all the other camps in West Germany, has been "cleaned up"; its barracks taken down; a chapel of each of the three major faiths constructed on the grounds; its mass graves marked with tasteful memorial plaques, planted with good lawn, and bordered with neat flower beds; its gallows replaced with a marker; its administration building converted into a modern, well-lighted museum of horrors; and everywhere the memorial wreaths with ribbons identifying their donors.

Her impression was thus similar to Alfred Werner's sixteen years earlier: the former camp was much "cleaner" than she had expected, but it still got across its "message." The main difference to earlier visits was that the residential settlement had now been evacuated and the camp barracks razed, making the site that much cleaner. Decter wrote that all six members of her group "were offended by the way the camp had been fixed up, prettified." The new museum, opened in the large service building in 1965, was much more respectable than the previous provisional exhibition in the crematorium–gas chamber building, but Decter still wrote it off as a "modern, well-lighted museum of horrors." She concluded her tour with a visit to the crematorium, where she spent her time trying to imagine how, concretely, human beings treated fellow human "material."

The comparison between Decter's preconceptions and the present reality of "Dachau" is the dominant theme of her description of her visit. That same motif predominated in Alfred Werner's 1951 narrative, and in that of Irving Halperin, a Fulbright exchange professor who spent a year in West Germany in 1963–4.[54] Silvia Tennenbaum, a Jewish-American writer who visited Dachau in May 1975 and published a description of her experience and impressions, reacted similarly, although her narrative included much more reflection about Dachau as an educational site.[55] Tennenbaum recorded every detail with minute accuracy, including the "great expanse of . . . empty graveled space," the "spiky black sculpture," and the museum "filled with grisly artifacts and photos," which she found particularly disconcerting. Tennenbaum mused:

> Did I really think I would learn something in the museum at Dachau? Like any other museum it exists to collect objects; to sift information and classify statistics. The glass cases preserve the striped uniforms worn by the inmates, their wooden clogs, the whips used to flog them.

She converged on the crematorium building with many other visitors, noticed the clicking cameras and the German schoolchildren uneasily eyeing the foreigners while their teacher lectured. As she walked to the parking lot, she asked herself, "What's the good of three chapels set down in a field of stone and a museum . . . if they offer no explanation from the well of a more sensitive experience and do nothing to transform our lives?" But she immediately conceded, "how *can* they?" Realizing that some American acquaintances she made at the crematorium were getting into their nearby cars to tour the Olympic Village and watch a soccer game, she was overcome by a strong urge:

> I want (suddenly, desperately) to run after them, grab them, tell them what *happened* here. But there is already a great distance separating us – they are getting on their buses, going for lunch, touring the Olympic Village, watching a soccer game.

Tennenbaum repressed the impulse to confront them. That afternoon she went to the Alte Pinakothek, one of the famous Munich art museums, where she was enraptured by its collection. In the evening she realized with a start, "how *German* of me, to swoon over Beauty and to revere Art on the very day I have gazed at the gas chambers and the crematoria." In that she was far more sensitive than most visitors, who may be shocked but are not affected deeply enough by the memorial site to perceive the thin line that separated and separates the horrors from more "normal" daily existence.

By the 1980s the typical experience of young Jews visiting Dachau was changing: it depended less on age than on historical education. It is difficult to date the transition exactly, because it is highly dependent on the personal background of the individual visitor. The more visitors know about the Holocaust before they come to Dachau, the more concrete are their expectations. My own experience in 1977, described at the beginning of this book, was typical of the more naïve visitors, who have few preconceptions. In contrast, Stanford student Carolyn Bronstein, who visited Dachau in 1987 while participating in a German–American exchange program, had such concrete expectations of what she would experience that she broke out in tears in the bus on the way to the site.[56] Another well-prepared visitor, Belinda Davis, was 20 when she visited Dachau during a year studying abroad in 1979.[57] Davis had visited a Holocaust museum in Israel on a family trip when she was about 13 years old, and she remembered her mother breaking out in tears, a reaction she did not fully understand at the time. While describing her own experience in Dachau seven years later, Davis constantly measured what she saw against her expectation. For example, she explained her emotional response to the pictures in the museum – she began to cry – as the triggering of "what I already knew at the gut level," although the depictions of the horrors were "not as strong as I wanted." She described a feeling of "gratification" upon finding certain icons of the camp, such as the inscription "Work makes free" on the gate.

With the passage of time an increasing number of Jews with less foreknowledge of the brown-collar crimes were visiting Dachau. They were less critical of the Dachau memorial site's clean appearance, since it still contained the icons they expected: the watchtowers and barbed wire, the mocking inscription on the gate, the photographs of atrocities, and the crematorium. For them, Dachau was not so much the physical embodiment of the Holocaust and thus the culmination of their education about it. Rather, it was a concrete starting point of an educational odyssey about the brown-collar crimes.

11

Protestants make amends at Dachau

In many respects German Protestants were even more complicit in Nazi rule than most other groups. They had flocked to support the Nazi Party in disproportionate numbers, making up a majority of its members, and many low and high Protestant Church officials had been active brown-collar criminals. The deep complicity of the German Protestant Church (Evangelische Kirche in Deutschland, EKD)[1] in brown-collar crimes was barely known until fairly recently.[2] There are several reasons for this. For one, the connection was hidden by Nazi-era euphemisms. Hitler wanted National Socialism to be devoid of visible connections to Christianity, so when his Protestant supporters wanted to name themselves "Christian National Socialists," he suggested the name "German Christians" instead.[3]

Secondly, after 1945 most German Protestants kept silent about their collaboration, in keeping with the myth of ignorance. Thirdly, there had been a small but strong oppositional movement within the ranks of the Protestant Church, known as the Confessing Church (Bekennende Kirche). After the war, German Protestants invoked the activities of the pastors involved in that group as a factual basis for the more generalized myth of resistance.

Martin Niemöller, one of the founders of the Confessing Church, was imprisoned in Sachsenhausen and Dachau from 1938 to 1945. As a staunch German nationalist and decorated veteran of World War I, he had initially supported Hitler, but soon changed his position. In November 1933 he formed the "Pastors' Emergency League," which founded the Confessing Church at a synod in Barmen the following year. That organization soon became an island of resistance to Nazism.

Although Niemöller was not typical of mainstream Protestant commemoration in Germany, his example bridges the gap of silence between one exceptional early postwar initiative and the 1960s' revival of recollective interest among a younger generation. His case thus illustrates some of the important features of Protestant recollection.

Martin Niemöller (1892–1984)

After his arrest in 1937 because of his oppositional activities, Niemöller spent the rest of the Nazi period in prisons and concentration camps. In Dachau he was kept as a "special prisoner" in an individual cell in the bunker behind the service building, where he could converse with other "special prisoners" such as Neuhäusler.[4]

After liberation Niemöller resumed his critical work within the mainstream of the German Protestant Church. With other leading figures from the Confessing Church, Niemöller lobbied the EKD leadership intensively for a public statement of the Church's complicity. This statement, known as the Stuttgart Declaration of Guilt (*Stuttgarter Schuldbekenntnis*), was accepted and published by the executive council of the EKD in October 1945.[5]

This statement should be seen in connection with Niemöller's first return visit to Dachau after his liberation. In early November 1945, on his way home to Munich from a speaking engagement in Stuttgart, Niemöller drove past Dachau. He wanted to show his wife the place of his imprisonment, so they sought out the former concentration camp.[6] A US army officer showed them Niemöller's former cell, then led the couple to the crematory, where they saw a sign reading "In the years from 1933 to 1945 238,756 people were cremated here" (ill. 6).[7]

According to an anecdote he included in numerous sermons in 1946 and 1947, this sign disturbed Niemöller deeply. Prior to his arrest in 1937, he told many audiences in Germany and the United States he had done nothing to defend the communists and other regime opponents who were sent to concentration camps. "From that moment on," Niemöller said, "for me the question of guilt was no longer theoretical."[8]

Niemöller probably used the anecdote so often in 1946–7 because the Stuttgart Declaration had unleashed a storm of protest from officials of the German Protestant Church. They mobilized the three myths in defense of their denial.[9] First, they claimed that National Socialism had been brought about by the victimization of Germany in the Versailles Treaty after World War I. Second, they said that even if some Protestants were guilty, others had indeed resisted. Finally, they turned around and attacked their detractors, claiming that since wars were made by elites, not common people, whoever claimed otherwise was only interested in victimizing the common people.

Later in 1947, however, Niemöller ceased to mention German responsibility for the brown-collar crimes. He was under attack from other camp survivors because he was accused of having CARE packages from the United States sent to privileged elites who had suffered minor losses under the Nazis, but not to camp survivors who had lost far more. In that controversy Niemöller's testimony during Gestapo interrogation in 1937 surfaced. Niemöller had tried – unsuccessfully – to portray himself as an antisemite in order to ingratiate himself with the Nazis and thus avoid arrest. At the end of the 1940s he became an activist in the movement to grant clemency to the brown-collar criminals on death row. That engagement, too, was incompatible with the public proclamation of German responsibility. Thus for almost a decade beginning in the late 1940s, there was no one in the EKD leadership to endorse the 1945 declaration of guilt, and it was temporarily expunged from official Protestant memory.[10]

In the late 1950s, after initial hesitation, Niemöller responded positively to Otto Kohlhofer's request to support the creation of a documentary memorial site in Dachau. At that time a younger cohort of Protestants was rediscovering the burden of responsibility they had inherited. One indication that things were changing was the establishment of a Protestant youth group, the "Action Sign of Atonement" (Aktion Sühnezeichen, AS) in 1958. It was committed to performing volunteer work abroad and at home in order to make amends for Germany's past misdeeds. In fact, in 1966 volunteers from the Action Sign of Atonement helped to build a Protestant church in the Dachau memorial site.

Even in the broader EKD establishment, things were beginning to change, as a commemorative ceremony during the annual convocation of Protestant groups (Evangelischer Kirchentag) in Dachau in August 1959 indicates.[11] In the 1960s Niemöller returned to Dachau several times to hold commemorative speeches. He exhorted his listeners to look inside themselves, recognize the ways in which they had avoided responsibility for others, and work towards promoting peace and brotherhood in the world.[12]

The need for a Protestant church in Dachau

When Catholic bishop Neuhäusler proposed the construction of Jewish and Protestant monuments to flank his Catholic chapel in Dachau in November 1960, the EKD council responded by commissioning a survey of existing Protestant memorial sites in West Germany.[13] None of the Church districts in the country reported any Protestant monuments at sites of former concentration camps in their area. In fact, Rhineland and

Westphalia reported that they were not even aware that concentration camps had existed in their districts. Of course there had been many "branch" concentration camps in both districts. Osthofen, for example, one of the larger early camps, and the subject of Anna Seghers' celebrated novel *The Seventh Cross* (1942), was among those in the Rhineland. But just as Seghers' widely read novel was not in print between 1951 and 1962, Osthofen slipped from Protestant awareness in that period as well.

In spite of the complete lack of Protestant memorials for the victims of Nazism, in May 1961 the EKD's executive council resolved "that in Dachau the construction of a Protestant chapel is out of the question."[14] It reasoned that it would be inappropriate to erect a Protestant memorial in Bavaria, a primarily Catholic region of Germany. Also, the council thought, since the Catholic chapel did not have any explicitly denominational attributes, it could serve Protestants as well. The council concluded with a – in light of the church's past involvement in furnishing concentration camps with Jews to be martyred – noteworthy Freudian slip: "At most it might be considered whether our district church might donate a crucifix or something of that nature for the final furnishing of the concentration camp."[15]

The council then considered whether or not it should erect a chapel in a district with a predominantly Protestant population, but did not reach a decision. Shortly thereafter, however, an impulse from abroad finally prompted the council to take action. In the summer of 1961 a Dutch pastor whose brother had died in Dachau approached German EKD *Präses* Ernst Wilm to request a memorial chapel where he could commemorate his brother.[16] Wilm, himself a survivor of Dachau, contacted Bishop Kurt Scharf, another former persecutee who was chairman of the EKD's executive committee.[17] "The way things appear," Wilm wrote, "it looks as if only the Roman Catholic church had martyred priests and members. It is not a good thing if three religious memorials are built in Dachau, but the EKD has to do something and has to be willing to pay for it."

Wilm and Scharf formed a committee to work out a proposal for the Protestant memorial. In September 1962 Wilm outlined the results of the committee's deliberations in a letter to Bishop Lilje in Hanover.[18] A church with regular services should be erected, he argued, because

> we need a sign of warning, commemoration and atonement where and with
> which we put ourselves on the side of the dead, and humble ourselves
> before the murders under God, and where we can honestly tell our children
> and our children's children what happened and exhort them to do what is
> commanded by God so that such events do not occur again.

Stripped of its religious trappings, this was a very comprehensive memorial conception that included education of the next generations. Wilm went on to detail the reasons for the construction of a chapel not in Dachau, but rather in Bergen-Belsen:

1) after Dachau, the most victims are buried there;[19]
2) the populace of the region is mostly Protestant;
3) it has a relatively central location;
4) in the past fifteen years the federal government has used it as a central memorial;[20] and
5) many foreigners and Jews are buried there, who could, analogous to the "unknown soldier," represent all victims.

The basics of this plan for a "Church of Atonement" (*Sühnekirche*), as Wilm called it, were approved by Lilje and a Church conference in Berlin. The only concern they raised was that Belsen was too isolated.[21] Instead, the church might be erected in Frankfurt, the critics suggested, "because it was the home of many Jews, who were deported from there, and because many foreigners traveling through Germany also go through Frankfurt." I would like to point out two implications of this rather surprising suggestion. First, the concern for Jews and foreigners reveals that these German Protestants had little interest in commemorating the victims of Nazism, but did so primarily for public relations purposes. Second, the idea of removing the memorial from a historical site reveals the persistent desire to strip recollection of concrete referents, to "clean up" the past. The EKD commission decided to stick with Belsen, however.

The Protestant Dachau survivors were still not satisfied with the Belsen solution. At a meeting of the executive committee of the Conference of European Churches in January 1963, a representative of the CID and a member of the Dutch Protestant Church (probably de Loos) explained the plans for the memorial site in Dachau to Wilm.[22] They informed Wilm that the EKD wanted to erect only a simple cross, and they suggested that a church would be more appropriate. A short time later the Ministry of the Interior of Lower Saxony (in which Bergen-Belsen is located) told the EKD central office that "important Jewish representatives" had requested that the Belsen memorial site be kept free of religious buildings because a large number of Jews were buried there, and any construction would disturb the rest of the dead as defined by Jewish tradition.[23] The council of the EKD thus ultimately decided to erect the central Protestant memorial church in Dachau. It also decided that the public announcement of the project would be made at a dedication ceremony in November 1963, on the twenty-fifth anniversary of the *Kristallnacht* pogroms. This date was considered "advantageous" because of heightened recent interest in the concentration camps due to the Eichmann trial (1961) and the preparations for the Auschwitz trial in Frankfurt, which was slated to begin in December 1963, and also because Probst Grüber could pre-announce the plan during his trip to Israel at the end of October.[24] In contrast to the Stuttgart Declaration of Guilt in 1945, which had been a bold attempt to lead public opinion, this second Protestant initiative to recognize the victims belatedly followed existing trends, and was still driven by foreign pressure.

The naming of the planned church was a particularly knotty problem. The original suggestion, "Church of Atonement" (*Sühnekirche*; *sühnen* can mean both to atone for specific sins, and to free from general guilt), was rejected because it was inappropriate for foreign Protestants and KZ survivors participating in the project – who needed neither to atone nor be freed of guilt – but also because is was misleading, since, as Wilm phrased it, "the crimes were so horrible that no expiation is possible."[25] The next solution, "Church of the Expiation of Christ" (*Sühne-Christi Kirche*), which was used in the official announcement of the project in November 1963, was later deemed unsatisfactory because it resembled the name of the Catholic chapel, "Church of the Mortal Agony of Christ," too closely, and because it implied that Christ's sacrifice had already expiated the guilt, so that people did not need to atone actively themselves.[26] Finding a suitable name to express the relationship between commemorative activity and Nazi crimes proved to be quite difficult. Still other names were suggested but rejected: "Church of Penance and Pleading" (*Buss- und Bittkirche*) was too soft, "Church of Judgment and Mercy" (*Gericht- und Gnadekirche*) too hard. Finally the name "Church of Reconciliation" (*Versöhnungskirche*) was chosen. It avoided the problem of prescribing what was to take place at the site by expressing the goal of commemoration, not the process by which it was to be reached.

As with the other main memorials in the camp, the Protestant church was to be financed by donations in order both to indicate widespread support of the project, and to raise awareness of and commitment to it. At the 9 November 1963 ceremony Kurt Scharf read a call for donations addressed to all Protestant Christians in Germany.[27] He explained that the purpose of the church in Dachau was to commemorate all sites of Nazi horrors and to honor all victims of Nazi persecution. He emphasized the central role that this symbol of commemoration was to play for German Protestants:

> With the construction of this church we want not only to honor the sacrifice of our Protestant brothers and sisters, but also to attest our solidarity with all victims of the National Socialist regime of violence. There, where people were scorned, insulted, humiliated and tortured, and where life was exterminated, Jesus Christ shall be preached, He who is the brother of the miserable and the persecuted, and He who calls upon us to show solidarity with them. He exhorts us to change our ways and offers us forgiveness for all of our guilt; He gives us His peace and shows us the way to reconciliation among ourselves, and to works of peace among other peoples.

In May 1964, when the church districts were commissioned to collect funds, the text they were given specified the reasons even more precisely:[28]

> 1) cleansing of actual personally committed crimes, 2) keeping the memory of these events and of the victims of that time alive, 3) understanding these events through the cross and the resurrection of Christ, whereby the sign of reconciliation would point the way into the future.

Why should Protestants want a church in Dachau? In the early 1960s, the answer was because they could expiate their guilt and achieve reconciliation among themselves and with others.

The "Church of Reconciliation"

The design of the Protestant building was found in 1964 through a limited competition in which seven architects were invited to submit plans.[29] At a 20 January 1964 meeting the working committee for Dachau decided on the minimum requirements of the building.[30] It was to have a chapel and a meeting room, as well as a sacristy, an office, a kitchenette, and a storage room. The chapel was to have 100 seats, with room for 50 more inside and 200–300 outside, while the meeting room was to seat 75. The furnishings included a pulpit, an altar, an organ, and two bells, but no baptismal or gallery. In July the prize committee went to the memorial site to discuss the advantages and disadvantages of the designs it had received. In the end they favored a project by the Mannheim architect Helmut Striffler.[31]

Striffler's project sought to break the orthogonal symmetry of the camp with a curving outer wall of unfinished concrete, which was also intended to join the church, a public meeting room, and an intervening courtyard into one enclosed, protective space.[32] Unlike the upright Catholic chapel, which was built near a number of other buildings in a camp full of barracks, the low-lying Church of Reconciliation was designed with a varying contour "in complete contrast to the pathetic flatness of the camp" (that is, the memorial site). While the Catholic chapel had to tower above the rag-tag barracks of the residential settlement, the architectural form of the Protestant church was already adapted to the sanitized memorial site around it.

The elongated church building is recessed one story below ground level (ill. 64).[33] It is made of gray concrete and thus blends into the monotone of the memorial site terrain. It can be entered from either end: visitors coming from the central Catholic chapel descend a broad, open stairway that narrows as it leads down to an enclosed courtyard. At the bottom, visible through glass walls on the left, is a reading room with benches and book niches that can be used for meetings and exhibitions, and a sparsely furnished chapel straight ahead. All surfaces except the carpeted floor of the meeting room are left in unfinished cement, creating an impression of barrenness. Several cement cubes serve as seats in the courtyard. The path continues up a ramp at the side of the sanctuary, past the organ at the top left, to a heavy bronze portal bearing the biblical inscription: "Refuge is in the shadow of Your wings" in German, Polish, Dutch, and French.[34] This biblical quotation was chosen by the architect to reflect his idea that the church should "afford a short breathing space, a gesture of help, to visitors to the camp as they make their way through it."[35]

A tall cement wall along the narrow ramp shields exiting visitors from the view towards the crematorium just beyond the camp wall – which is usually the next stop on a tour of the camp for those who have come down the central street. Visitors who begin their tour of the memorial site in the museum – probably the majority – usually proceed from its exit to the main concentration camp entrance gate ("Work makes free"). Once they are at the edge of the camp enclosure they continue down to the crematorium instead of returning to the central street. Upon exiting the crematorium area they look directly at the high naked concrete wall of the Protestant church from its most intimidating side. The bronze door with its offer of refuge is angled out of view, a mere slit in a forbidding cement façade. Only as visitors pass by the church do they see the narrow cement passageway leading down into the sanctuary. Given the associations of narrow cement enclosures with gas chambers, this highly uninviting perspective runs counter to the architect's intention. He probably did not consider this typical visitor route because in the 1960s – until 1967 – the US army still held the gatehouse as part of its "Eastman Barracks" in the former SS camp, so that it was off limits to visitors. (The inscription "Work makes free" was only reconstructed in 1972. It had been removed in the first years after the war; see ill. 15.) Thus when the church was built the only access to the crematorium was via the central camp street, with the "correct" approach to the Protestant chapel.

The size of the Protestant church was controversial from the very start. When the prize committee examined the various designs in July 1964, it already noted that the height of the outer wall on Striffler's model was "somewhat exaggerated."[36] When the construction committee for all three religious memorial sites met a month later, Neuhäusler expressed his concern about the "weight and size" of the Protestant church.[37] Faced with criticism about intrusive aspects of his Carmelite convent, however, Neuhäusler assented to the plan. The next day, when the committee visited the construction site, the Catholic bishop complained again, prompting the other committee members to state explicitly that they approved of the size of the church. Only Otto Kohlhofer said that he would have to consult with the CID at its next meeting before he could give final confirmation. In fact, the CID was also concerned about the size of the project, because it disturbed both the "original condition [appearance]" of the camp and the "aesthetic balance" of the three religious memorials.[38] Striffler thereupon reduced the height of the wall and church by one half meter, which satisfied CID president Guérisse.[39] In order to preserve the aesthetic unity of the religious memorials, the size of the Jewish memorial was reduced by 25 percent as well, and it was moved 8 meters closer to the Catholic chapel.[40]

One difference of opinion regarding the aesthetic unity of the three religious memorials proved to be insurmountable: whether greenery could be used to bind them together. Neuhäusler's original conception was to convert the entire barracks area into a grove of trees, and he wished to group the religious sites together in a grassy, parklike area with axial paths (ill. 46).[41] Even after the firm opposition of the CID forced him to drop his plan of greening the entire memorial site, Neuhäusler was not persuaded to change his plans for the religious area. At a meeting with the three architects in March 1965, Guttmann, the architect of the Jewish memorial, demanded a 30 meter "tree-free" zone around his chapel, and Neuhäusler's own architect Wiedemann said that a "pebbled surface with sparse natural plantings" was best suited to his design.[42] All of those present assented to Wiedemann's conciliatory suggestion that it might be possible to plant a "few tall trees" in the memorial site, if it were done with the necessary reserve. Nonetheless, Neuhäusler remained adamant. Finally, shortly before the dedication in

May 1967, "in consideration of the personality and age of the suffragan bishop," as the Protestant negotiator put it, the grassy area was reduced to a small ring around the Catholic chapel, and the circle of oak trees was left standing (ill. 4).[43] This ring of green thus testifies not only to the soothing Catholic conception of memory, but to the incompatibility of various groups' ideas about how to recollect the crimes of the Nazi past.

The funding of the Protestant chapel, which ultimately cost DM1,200,000, provides an interesting look into the politics of establishing memorials.[44] In keeping with the idea that financing by grass roots donations both documents support and creates a vested interest on the part of the donors, this amount was to be collected at the local level from all West German Protestant churches.[45] Pentecost (the seventh Sunday after Easter, when the Holy Spirit came to the apostles), 17 May 1964, was chosen as the day to begin the collection because it was a national holiday that symbolized reconciliation. EKD leader and Dachau survivor Kurt Scharf wrote the text to be included in the sermon.[46] Although building the church would "honor the sacrifices made by our Protestant brothers and sisters" (he did not spell out *for what* they had made those sacrifices), he wrote, it would also "testify to our connection with all victims of the violent rule of National Socialism." Given the widespread Protestant collaboration with Nazism, and the continuing lack of concern for Nazism's victims in the 1960s, both claims were historically wide of the mark. Scharf concluded with a message that reveals the deep chasm separating Protestant (and Catholic) from Jewish recollection:

> There, where human beings were ignored, insulted, humiliated and tortured and where life was annihilated, Jesus Christ shall be preached, He who is the brother of the miserable and the persecuted, and who calls upon us to show solidarity with them. He admonishes us to change our ways and offers us forgiveness for all guilt, He gives us His peace and shows us the path to reconciliation among one another and the way to works of peace among all peoples.

Here the purging of guilt and the prospect of reconciliation with one's own victims were to be the motivating factors.

As things turned out, in spite of the repeated mobilization of the entire Protestant infrastructure in Germany, the willingness to donate was not enough to cover the costs. Almost a year later only about DM325,000, 27 percent of the total cost, had come in, so a detailed proportional table was calculated, according to which each Protestant church district was given a fundraising quota commensurate to its membership.[47] Donations continued to trickle in, so that by September 1965 32 percent of the total had been raised, and in March 1966 the DM1,000,000 mark was reached.[48] Finally, in March 1967, most church districts that had not met their proportion simply transferred funds from their operating budgets.[49]

While the broad mass of Protestants apparently tired of making donations for the Dachau church, one small Protestant group took it upon itself to help in every way it could: the youth group "Action Sign of Atonement."

The "Action Sign of Atonement"

The origins of the group can be dated back to 1952, when a leading EKD official called for concrete activities to reduce some of the world's animosities towards Germany.[50] In reality, however, it took until 1958, after Berlin students became interested in this suggestion, before the organization was formally established. In March 1959 the first groups left for work in Norway and Holland.[51] Work in England and France followed a short time later, and by the early 1960s Israel had become a favored place to do atonement work. In 1962, when church leader Wilm still wanted to have the Protestant church erected in Belsen, he immediately thought of the group, suggesting that AS volunteers could build it themselves.[52] In accordance with its foreign image-related mission, AS had hitherto been active primarily in foreign countries, but there were advantages to having sites in Germany as well. For one thing, project work at home helped to prepare the individuals for project work abroad, and it publicized AS's work in Germany as well. One of the first Dachau volunteers explained that such work at home raised the credibility of the group during its foreign missions by showing that the group was acting in the name of all Germans.[53]

That was clearly wishful thinking. The first AS group worked in Dachau from mid-September 1965 to the end of January 1966.[54] At first, the Bavarian Castle Administration would not approve even their temporary accommodation in a barrack on the site.[55] The five young men and four young women lived in private houses in the local Protestant community until the EKD renovated a barrack at the site in late October. During that sojourn in the community the group reported that it sensed feelings of distrust from most Dachau citizens. As one of them told a local journalist, "One can almost speak of a 'Dachau-complex' because most residents take it personally when one mentions the concentration camp."[56] The strongest confirmation of this local attitude of rejection came near the end of the group's stay, when group leader Vicar Klaus Heienbrok and two other volunteers visited high schools in Dachau and Munich to show slides about Israel, the group's next station after their five months in Dachau.

In the Dachau high school they found that the 18- and 19-year-olds were unanimously against the construction of any monuments or museums in the former camp because, as the AS diarist wrote, "that would only evoke the past again. The students said the past was past and should be left in peace."[57] These Dachau students were probably reproducing stereotypical attitudes they had learned at home. A show of hands revealed that only one student in two classes had ever visited the memorial site. The Dachau students also said that they were "against too close friendship with the Jews because that would only annoy the Arabs, and because philosemitism would only produce new antisemitism in Germany." Except for the last aspect, namely that preferential treatment of Jews (for that is what was meant by philosemitism) would lead to antisemitism, the students were probably not speaking from firsthand experience either.

The Munich students were somewhat more open. While willing to recognize a specific German guilt for the Nazi crimes, however, they were divided over whether the younger generation had to concern itself with that guilt. And the AS participants were again warned that their "philosemitism" was counterproductive. It would only produce an unfavorable atmosphere in West Germany, where Jews would officially be given preferential treatment, but unofficially be discriminated against.

If there were some differences between the AS volunteers and members of their own generation, it was much smaller than the gap between their understanding of AS work and that of the EKD leadership. In his concluding report, AS Dachau group leader Heienbrok noted wryly that with the three new memorials "the new powers are immortalizing themselves" in Dachau, while excluding the socialists, communists, and atheists who made up the majority of victims in the camps.[58] Heienbrok was merely restating the basic principle of memorial art: it reflects the present more than the past.

The dedication ceremony, 1967

The cornerstone of the Church of Reconciliation had been laid in May 1965 during the large twentieth anniversary celebration with the opening of the new museum.[59] Construction was completed for a dedication service on 30 April 1967.[60] The speeches given by the Dachau survivors Bishop Scharf and Church President Niemöller at that ceremony illustrate paradigmatically the split between "mainstream" West German Protestant memory and the more critically inclined recollective work being performed by a young generation of West Germans. (Niemöller, although an aged man, was very popular with young people, and his unconventional opinions were frequently at odds with the official EKD stance.) Scharf began his address by praising God for manifesting Himself in the concentration camp. He quoted from Psalm 66, which had just been sung for the live TV and radio broadcast: "Praised be the Lord, who did not reject my prayer nor rescind His goodness from me. God heard me and noticed my pleading."[61] Scharf continued:

> This church on this site and in this form . . . calls our generation and coming generations to God the master of history, to the God who redeems and forgives . . . Here God was beseeched incessantly, in horrible pain, in cries of death. He was also cursed in utmost desperation. God responded to this pleading. He miraculously helped many individuals in this hell of human brutality! He also understood the cursing and accepted it . . . God does not reject prayer. God even forgives horrifying guilt. God's goodness is universal.

Scharf was clearly not thinking of the millions of people whose prayers had been answered with Zyklon B or a bullet through the skull, or of the 2,000 men who had starved to death in the train shortly before Dachau's liberation. While this rather thoughtless treatment of the unimaginable suffering in the concentration camp was approved in advance by the top echelons of the EKD, Niemöller's spontaneous, activist conception of commemoration was branded a "scandal" by Church leaders.[62] What did Niemöller say?

He first politicized his remarks by criticizing United States' aggression in Vietnam: "What is happening in Vietnam today can well be compared in every respect with what happened in our days here [in Dachau]," he remarked caustically.[63] Niemöller then criticized all Christians for their inaction. If Christians had lived according to Christ's example for the past 2,000 years, he continued, the concentration camps would not have been possible: "The circle of violence would have been broken." Niemöller went on to criticize the self-serving desire of the perpetrators to expect reconciliation instead of earning it: "Church of Reconciliation – but where is the reconciliation, where is the peace for which our souls are thirsting and crying? Nothing has changed since then – we must take the first step."

Even if some EKD leaders were outraged by such a stance, Niemöller's speech was very much in tune with the views of the politicized youth of what we now call the 1968 generation. Many politically active members of this age cohort were acutely sensitive to injustice and refused to tolerate it.

12

The 1968 generation: new legacies of old myths

The history recounted in the preceding chapter shows that by the end of the 1960s a younger generation of Germans was becoming increasingly important in shaping the nature of recollection at Dachau. The natural process of history dictates that at some point people who experienced certain historical events will no longer predominate in the recollective political and cultural institutions of their society. Instead, younger generations move into those positions and begin to shape the character of public recollection. In our case, these younger generations' attitudes toward the past were determined primarily by two factors: their learned knowledge of that past, and their emotional feelings towards the people who experienced it.

Let us look at the hypothetical case of someone born in 1940, whose parents were born around 1915. That person might have learned of the brown-collar crimes in the late 1950s through films such as *Night and Fog* and *The Diary of Anne Frank*. She or he would not have had much formal instruction about the Nazi period in school, but would have heard about the trials of brown-collar criminals in the late 1950s and early 1960s. This person's parents would in all likelihood have participated in Nazi organizations and worked for the "totalitarian" Nazi regime, so they are likely only to have portrayed the Nazi past in terms of the three myths. Of course, the older the parent, the less convincing these exoneratory myths would appear. Without convincing, empathetic explanations, the horrifying, uncontextualized images of Nazi atrocities would remain emotionally isolated for the young adult, who might react in one of three ways: embrace, ignore, or reject the explanations of her or his elders.

As it turns out, although each of those three reactions did occur, the postwar Germans who rejected the mythic explanations of their Nazi-era parents were the most outspoken. In the late 1960s and 1970s they dominated the public discussion of the Nazi past. If we want to examine the interrelationships between Nazi-era and postwar generations systematically, we must first differentiate between age cohorts with different formative experiences of Nazism. Then we can see whether the postwar generations of their children exhibit certain common attitudes and behaviors.

Sociologists have observed that pivotal experiences between the ages of 16 and 26, in certain circumstances from 14 to 30, are critical in shaping lifetime political attitudes.[1] Certain momentous political events such as wars and economic crises may overshadow important events in individual biographies and affect most people born during a range of years.[2] For the cohorts maturing under Nazism, the critical events were the formation of the Nazi state in 1933–4, and the tangible turning point in the war in 1943. These cohorts would have been born between approximately 1904 (age 26 in 1930, when Nazism's popularity skyrocketed) and 1927 (age 16 in 1943, when military service became probable death).

Let us take the midpoint of 1915–16 as the transition between these two experiential cohorts (these dates are somewhat arbitrary and must be confirmed based on actual cases). The older group (born ca. 1904–15) would have had children born ca. 1926–37, who would have been shaped by events after 1943, such as the end of World War II, the beginning of the Cold War, and the economic recovery after the currency reform of 1948. The group born between 1916 and 1926 would have had children beginning roughly in 1937 and trailing off by the mid-1950s.

Before we turn to actual members of the age cohort born after 1937, a systematic terminology will help track the interrelationships (see table 1). The actual ranges of the birth years are approximate and depend heavily on the eccentricities of individual biography. The biographies of the people in the "examples" column help to draw the dividing lines, but even some of these cases can be characterized in different ways.

A theory of age cohorts

The first politically relevant cohort in the twentieth century, which I will call the *1918ers*, is important in this context only inasmuch as its members created the pivotal event that set the whole dynamic to be outlined here in motion: the Nazi accession to unprecedented political and cultural power after 1930. This cohort, born at the end of the nineteenth century (ca. 1890–1902), contributed most of *Nazism's founding fathers*.[3] These activist visionaries were branded by what they saw as the betrayal of the revolutionaries of 1918 and the shameful injustice of the Versailles Treaty.[4] Those who came to support the Nazi Party never felt comfortable with the democratic government that signed that treaty. This cohort included, to name

Table 1: *West German political cohorts, 1890–1976*

Birth years (approx.)	Pivotal events ages 16–26 or parental attitudes that shaped political behavior	Shorthand name; descriptive names	Examples with birthdates
1890–1902	1916–1919: World War I experienced as a profound, disorienting rupture; no loyalty to postwar state	1918ers (includes the founders of Nazism; generation of 1914	Hitler (1889) Göring (1893) Goebbels (1897) Himmler (1900) Höss (1900)
1903–1915	1920–1938: formed no strong relationship to Weimar republic; experienced Nazism as a positive turning point	1933ers careerist Nazis; reviled generation, generation of the perpetrators (parents of 1948ers)	Oberländer (1905) Speer (1905) Eichmann (1906) Filbinger (1913) F. J. Strauss (1915)
1916–1925	1939–1943: grew up under Nazism, fought for it during World War II; experienced both elation and devastation of war; most decimated by war	1943ers World War II cohort; younger careerist Nazis; Stalingraders; deceived generation (children of 1918ers, parents of 1968ers)	M. Maschmann (1918) H. Schmidt (1918) R. v. Weizsäcker (1920)
1926–1936	1944–1957 (currency reform): end of Nazism in 1945, economic upturn after 1948 and "economic miracle" of 1950s	1948ers 1945ers; skeptical, Hitler Youth, betrayed, flak helper, white, reconstruction generation (children of 1933ers, parents of 1979ers)	M. Broszat (1926) G. Tempel (1926) Chr. Geissler (1928) W. Scheffler (1929) H. Kohl (1930)

1937–1953	1958–1969: 1943er parents' failure to admit Nazi past in early 60s; Vietnam War, Grand Coalition and political weakness of democratic political system	1968ers first postwar cohort (children of 1943ers)	Ursula Duba (1939) Niklas Frank (1939) Ursula Hegi (1939) B. Klarsfeld (1939) Detlef Hoffmann (1940) S. Reichel (1946) G.v. Arnim (1946)
1954–1966	1970–1980 (Holocaust film): interest in Nazi background of 1933er grandparents; grew up under more historically open Brandt/Heinemann and Schmidt governments of 1969–82	1979ers *Alltagshistoriker* (began to research Nazi history in 1980s); second postwar cohort; (children of 1948ers, grandchildren of 1933ers)	(see part IV) Norbert Frei (1955) Jürgen Z. (1958) A. Rosmus (1960) Stefanie (1960) M. Brenner (1964) M. Heyl (1965) Sybille S. (1966)
1967–1976	1983–1993 (post-Bitburg): learned of Nazi past through media and school; no close relationship with 1933ers	1989ers (1990ers) third postwar cohort; (children of 1968ers, grandchildren of 1943ers)	(see pp. 402ff) Klaudia K. (1970) Tanja K. (1970) Mathias F. (1970)

only the most infamous examples, Hitler (b. 1889), Göring (b. 1893), Hess (b. 1894), Goebbels (b. 1897), Bormann (b. 1900), Hans Frank (b. 1900), and Himmler (b. 1900).

Given the close succession of formative events in early twentieth-century German history, new cohorts emerged every five to fifteen years, and the generational links between parents and children tend to leapfrog cohorts.

The next cohort, the *1933ers* or *careerist Nazi cohort*, was born roughly from 1903 to 1915.[5] Recent German authors refer to this cohort as the *Tätergeneration* – the generation of perpetrators.[6] The members of this cohort had developed loyalty neither to the pre-World War I monarchy nor to the German republic of the 1920s. For many of them, Hitler's assumption of power in 1933 was a vindication of Germany's national pride. They immediately took the opportunity to make careers building and consolidating his state. Examples include Leni Riefenstahl (b. 1902), Werner Best (b. 1903), Reinhard Heydrich (b. 1904), Theodor Oberländer (b. 1905), Albert Speer (b. 1905), Adolf Eichmann (b. 1906), Baldur von Schirach (b. 1907), and Hans Filbinger (b. 1913). Rudolf Höss (b. 1900) is an example who exhibits elements of both the founding and careerist Nazi cohorts.

The cohort born between 1916 and 1925 also contributed to the "generation of perpetrators," but this age group did not have the opportunity to rise to the prominence of the above examples during the Nazi period. Their experience of the elation of the prewar Nazi years was overshadowed by the hopelessness of the situation after 1943 and the defeat at Stalingrad. Thus I refer to them as *1943ers*.[7] These 1943ers staffed the offices, schools, and institutions – including the army and concentration camps – of the Nazi Reich during Nazism's stable phase after 1935. This cohort was also the most decimated in World War II. At the end of the war many of them were able to distance themselves from Nazism.[8] The budding Nazi careers of older members such as Franz Josef Strauss (b. 1915) and pollster Elizabeth Noelle-Neumann (b. 1916) were suddenly cut off in 1945, but they were able to reestablish themselves as solid democrats.[9] They were young enough to have had only limited complicity in constructing the Nazi regime, even if their work for Nazism had left its stamp, positively or negatively, on their values.

Richard von Weizsäcker (b. 1920) is an example from this cohort who overcame his incipient Nazi complicity.[10] (Weizsäcker, who defended his converted Nazi father Ernst at Nuremberg in 1947, later became one of West Germany's most honest, open, and respected democrats (see chapter 14). We will meet him again in 1985 as a president of the Federal Republic who catalyzed the process of coming to terms with Nazism.) Irma Greese (b. 1921), a notorious Auschwitz and Belsen guard, is an example of a younger woman in this group who was so complicit (and intellectually limited) that she never renounced her allegiance to Nazism.[11]

The next cohort, the *1948ers*, born from the mid-1920s to the late 1930s (ca. 1926 to 1936), grew up within the Nazi system, but was branded by that system's depravity, which could no longer be ignored after 1943.[12] These Germans were young enough for any positive experiences of Nazism's best years prior to 1942–3 to be overshadowed by their conscious experience of the devastating phase of the war and its aftermath. They were not complicit, even by apathy or inaction, in Nazi crimes. Although they were thoroughly disabused of any positive attitudes towards Nazism, they had still worn the uniforms of the Hitler Youth and the League of German Girls (membership was compulsory after 1936), some had served in combat, and they were educated by careerist Nazi teachers right into the 1950s. This created a dissonance within each individual biography, an ambivalence between understanding for those who had been complicit in Nazism, and rejection of all that Nazism stood for.[13]

While other scholars call this cohort the "1945ers," I prefer to refer to them as 1948ers, since Marshall Plan aid and the currency reform of 1948 gave them their first positive political orientation, as opposed to the total disorientation in 1945.[14] In a phrase made memorable by West German Chancellor Helmut Kohl (b. 1930) in 1984, this cohort was thus blessed by the "grace of late birth."[15] For some, their unhesitating embrace of the new democratic state prevented them from recognizing its flaws.[16] For instance, many harbored fears of noninstitutional politics, and thus overlooked the state's attempts to repress grass roots activism. The first German historians to investigate brown-collar crimes belong to this cohort – for example Martin Broszat (1926–89) and Wolfgang Scheffler (b. 1929).[17] As we have seen in the above discussion of the historiography of the brown-collar crimes, in the early 1960s members of this cohort initiated an implicit challenge to the public silence about Germany's Nazi past. Authors such as Siegfried Lenz (b. 1926), Günther Grass (b. 1927), and Martin Walser (b. 1927), whose writings attempt to force a public engagement with the Nazi past, are also 1948ers.[18]

The next cohort, the *1968ers*, was the first not to have consciously experienced 1948 as a defining moment for the future. Instead, its members came of age in the prosperous years of the late 1950s and early 1960s. This first postwar cohort was born from the late 1930s to the early 1950s (ca. 1937 to 1953).[19] In rebellions culminating in the watershed year 1968, some members of this cohort stridently rebelled against their presumptively complicit 1943er parents. On the other hand, other members of this cohort aligned themselves with the conventional obedience-and-order mentality of their Nazi-socialized parents and boosted the neo-Nazi party NPD into several state parliaments in the late 1960s. The political attitudes of most members of this postwar cohort lay somewhere in between these extremes but, as individual biographies show, their confrontation with their parents' Nazi past decisively influenced their identity. This first postwar cohort is commonly referred to as the 1968ers, because the anti-establishment movement culminating that year left a lasting stamp on their political attitudes, positively or negatively.

In 1964 the returned German–Jewish émigré philosopher Günther Anders coined the phrase "we sons of Eichmann" to express the 68er cohort's legacy of upbringing by careerist Nazi 1933ers.[20] They did not begin to articulate this until the 1980s.[21] Physically leaving Germany helped some of them put pen to paper. German–American writers Sabine Reichel (b. 1946, *What Did You Do in the War, Daddy?*, 1989), Ursula Duba (b. 1939, *Tales from a Child of the Enemy*, 1995), and Ursula Hegi (b.1939, *Tearing the Silence*, 1997) offer examples of this phenomenon.[22]

Let us look more closely at a member of this first postwar cohort.

The story of Detlef Hoffmann, b. 1940

Detlef Hoffmann was 20 years old when he first saw the former Dachau concentration camp in 1960.[23] In 1956 he had been deeply moved by the story of Anne Frank, which became very popular in Germany after 1955 (he had seen the stage version of the *Diary* and heard Ernst Schnabel's sequel *Portrait of Courage* as a radio play).[24] Detlef Hoffmann was active in the Catholic youth movement in Hamburg in the mid-1950s, among other things as the Catholic representative in the national youth organization "German Youth Ring." As a Youth Ring delegate he participated in one of the commemorative Anne Frank trips to Bergen-Belsen. Still underage in 1956, he sneaked into Alain Resnais's documentary film *Night and Fog* about the concentration camps, which was rated for adult audiences. He also read a copy of Alexander Mitscherlich and Fred Mielke's *Doctors of Infamy* about the crimes of Nazi doctors, which he had found in his parent's closed bookcase.[25] (The German Association of Doctors distributed free copies to its members in 1947; Hoffmann's father, a psychiatrist during the Nazi period, may have received his copy that way.)

When Detlef Hoffmann went to the huge international Eucharistic World Congress organized by Suffragan Bishop Neuhäusler in Munich in August 1960, he did not go to the memorial service in the Dachau camp because he was angry that Bishop Neuhäusler had excluded Curate Roth, the outspoken survivor priest who had worked in the camp refugee settlement. Instead, Hoffmann attended a memorial service for the Scholl siblings, two Munich University students who were executed in 1943 for distributing anti-Nazi leaflets. He sought out the Dachau memorial site later with his girlfriend in their new VW bug. He vividly remembers how, once they were in the vicinity – there were no signs – they searched, "like archaeologists," through high grass and bushes before they located an entrance to the former concentration camp.

Years later, Hoffmann became a frequent visitor of the memorial site. He was not present in Dachau when socialist students heckled conservative government speakers at a memorial service in September 1968, but he followed the press reports closely and strongly sympathized with the students' point of view. As an art history professor at a smaller German university in the 1980s, Hoffmann fought against the tendency to "sterilize" concentration camp memorial sites by removing original artifacts and buildings that are difficult to maintain. In professional presentations he argued for the "preservation of traces," namely the creation of memorial sites that not only preserved as much original material as possible, but also the traces of their postwar uses.[26] Hoffmann's various encounters with Dachau (and other former concentration camps) have made him a kind of crusader for remembrance. He spearheaded a large research project that compared the iconography of various concentration camp monuments and memorials. Detlef Hoffmann is not typical in the extent of his recollective work about the concentration camps, but his biography and relationship to the Nazi past is typical of many Germans who participated in the cultural opening of the 1960s.

Generational conflict

We have already seen that Germans of this first postwar "68er" cohort began taking an interest in the Nazi past in the mid-1950s. Although the Anne Frank wave, for instance, included older Germans as well, those whose interest went beyond the diary to its sequel by journalist Ernst Schnabel and those who were motivated to participate in the commemorative pilgrimages to the site of Anne Frank's death in Bergen-Belsen were primarily from this younger age cohort. It was also younger Germans who worked for the German release of Alain Resnais's 1955 film *Night and Fog* about the concentration camps and atrocities committed in them. West German students were also the prime movers in the protest movements against the reinstated Nazis in Adenauer's government, and the West German judicial and university systems (see the discussion in chapter 7, above). In the publishing world this cohort was beginning to define itself in opposition to its presumably complicit parents in the careerist Nazi cohort.

In the early 1960s, a literature in the manner of *J'accuse* began to emerge, authored by 1948ers who were themselves too young to have been responsible for brown-collar crimes.[27] Examples, with titles of the English editions, include Christian Geissler's (b. 1928) *Sins of the Fathers* (1960) and Gudrun Tempel's (b. 1926) *Germany: An Indictment of My People* (1963).[28] Notably, in consideration of the sensibilities of older German potential purchasers of these books, the German originals bore the innocuous titles *Inquiry*, and *Germany, But Where Is It?* Even William Shirer's 1,600-page paperback *The Rise and Fall of the Third Reich*, a thick history book based on a "Luther-to-Hitler" indictment of German history, made the German bestseller list in November 1961 and remained there for six months.[29] The popularity of Shirer's accusatory portrayal is attributable to its resonance with the feelings of the younger 1948ers and 1968ers. Such books, which spared no reproaches, stood in sharp contrast to similar reflections by members of the Nazified 1933er and 1943er cohorts.

Illustrative of the lack of reflection even among more thoughtful 1933ers is Hermann Eich (b. 1913). Eich had been editor of major Düsseldorf newspapers from 1933 until 1939, when he took a position in the foreign press office of the Nazi government. In 1963 he wrote a self-pitying exoneration of Germany entitled *The Unloved Germans*.[30] Especially his chapter on "The Tragedy of the Jews" pulls every register of the three founding myths. Eich even equated Germans with Jews, at one point citing playwright Carl Zuckmayer's lament that "We Germans share with the Jews a certain unpopularity in the world that always distorts other people's views of us." Still, this statement illustrates a small but significant change in the discourse of victimization among the careerist Nazis. There was now room to accept that Jews were victims "too," a noteworthy step away from the image of the "bad" survivors of the early 1950s.[31]

A rare example of a member of the 1943er cohort who was able to overcome her investment in Nazism and contribute to the early 1960s' airing of the past is Melita Maschmann (b. 1918). She had been swept away by

Nazism's appeal in the 1930s and became a leader in the "League of German Girls." She remained totally committed to Nazism until after the war, when experiences in an internment camp and an empathetic priest helped her to come to terms with what she had done. Her autobiography, whose title translates as *Taking Stock: Not an Attempt to Justify* (1963), was written in the form of a letter to a lost Jewish schoolmate.[32] Maschmann attempted to explain her and her cohort's naïve dedication to Nazism. As the *J'accuse* literature written by 1948ers made the rounds, 1933ers and especially 1943ers asked themselves, to quote the title of a collection of their biographies, "Was I a Nazi?"[33] Their answer was overwhelmingly negative. Reversing the actual burden of historical responsibility, the 1968ers rejected this response from their 1943er parents far more strongly than the 1948ers did from their 1933er parents. The 1948ers, who had experienced the fear and chaos at the end of the war, were far better able to empathize with their parents' feeling of victimization than the postwar-born 1968ers.[34]

What role did the three founding myths play for those postwar 1968ers? First, most of them categorically rejected the myth of ignorance. Even if their parents denied and offered long explanations for their lack of knowledge about brown-collar crimes, the children never accepted them. If the parents had not known everything, they had certainly known enough that they should have wanted to find out more. Nonetheless, the silence spawned by the myth of ignorance had a rather ironic consequence. The public and private silence about Nazism had in fact left this cohort ignorant of the nature of life under the Nazi dictatorship. In spite of the consciousness-raising events of the early 1960s that publicized brown-collar crimes, these babes of the war and its desolate aftermath still had no concrete notion of what daily life had been like under Hitler or during the war, nor did they have any personalized idea of who the victims were and how inhuman *their* victimization had been. These people in their teens and twenties during the 1960s had been spellbound by Anne Frank's diary, but it was a story about eluding hunters, not about the chase, the kill, or the hunters themselves. Even Ernst Schnabel's sequel said little about the horrors Anne faced after her deportation.

In the surety of their rejection of their elders' professed ignorance, the 1968ers did not realize how their own actions might unintentionally reproduce the lack of empathy their 1933er and 1943er parents had exhibited. As A. D. Moses has written, the 1968ers "reflected rather than solved West Germany's problems with the Nazi past."[35] The careerist Nazis' silence thus left the 1968ers not only without an empathetic understanding of life under

Nazism, it blinded them to fascist aspects of violence and uncritical self-righteousness.[36] That legacy played an important role in the late 1960s and in the 1970s, as we will see.

Since the first postwar cohort of 1968ers felt that their parents must have known enough about brown-collar crimes, in their eyes the myth of victimization by the exogenous Eskimo-Nazis (see chapter 2) was unconvincing. Many parents thus gradually shifted their tack. No longer did they bemoan their victimization in Hitler's society. Instead, in the late 1960s especially the 1943ers began to complain that they were being victimized by what they called professional "masterers of the past" (*Vergangenheitsbewältiger*). In a memorable phrase by Franz Josef Strauss, they claimed a "right not to want to hear any more about Auschwitz."[37]

However, although the postwar youngsters rejected the myth of victimization, they inherited a legacy from it as well: a strong feeling of solidarity with victims of persecution the world over. Thus for those in their teens and twenties victimization was not an excuse to deny responsibility, but a compelling reason to accept it. In the mid-1960s it was commonplace to hear West German students state: "We are the Jews of today."[38] However, when Israel defeated Egypt in 1967, many of those same students shifted their sympathies to the subjugated Palestinians forced to live under Israeli occupation. This legacy of the myth of victimization explains why causes such as the Vietnam War, the Greek Civil War, and the Palestinian liberation movements resonated more strongly with younger West Germans than with their peers in other countries.

Given their rejection of their parents' professed ignorance and purported victimization, it goes almost without saying that the 1968ers rejected the 1933ers' myth of resistance as well. They realized that without mass acquiescence and dedicated support National Socialism could not have had such success in executing its agenda down to the bitter end. This rejection had different consequences for each age cohort. Many 1933ers and 1943ers redoubled their efforts to portray anything short of complete compliance as resistance, and they denounced attempts to deal publicly with the Nazi past – such as the ongoing brown-collar trials – with renewed vigor. For their part, many 1968ers were determined to right the wrongs of the past by speaking and acting against repression and injustice in the present, wherever they might occur. Whereas their parents had spinelessly come and gone with the surge of the Nazi tide, they would work to root out injustice in the world. Thus among the 1968er cohort the myth of resistance persisted in a determination to make up for the resistance they missed in their parents' past behavior.

Among a radical fringe of the 1968ers this self-righteousness and blind solidarity with oppressed peoples yielded a grotesque historical perversion that rivaled the "good Nazis" and "bad survivors" inversions of the 1950s. As we will see, some young German leftists routinely referred to Israeli policy with respect to Palestinians as the "Israeli final solution."[39] In fact, on the anniversary of *Kristallnacht* in 1969, a left-extremist newspaper wrote:[40]

> Every memorial ceremony in West Berlin and West Germany conceals the fact that the *Kristallnacht* of 1938 is now being repeated every day by the Zionists in the occupied territories, in refugee camps and in Israeli prisons. The Jews expelled by fascism have become fascists themselves, who, in collaboration with American capital, want to eradicate the Palestinian people. We must smash the direct support of Israel.

However, in contrast to the "bad survivor" trope of the 1950s, in the late 1960s such sentiments remained limited to a small, marginalized minority of 1968ers in a society that vociferously supported Israel.

The national political context

In the early 1960s there was a synergistic effect between the increasing historical curiosity of the 1968er cohort and certain issues in contemporary politics. One such issue was the exposure of the Nazi complicity of prominent members of West German government and society. These revelations often originated in East Germany, but they also emerged from trials in West Germany.[41] In contrast to the 1950s, when revelations about the Nazi complicity of government officials did not spark sustained public outcry, in the 1960s public interest often kept such cases in the headlines.[42] The East German origins of some of these revelations were used in attempts to discredit them, but most of them were documented well enough for Adenauer's Bonn government to feel obliged to respond officially.[43] As we have seen, Rolf Hochhuth's 1963 exposé of the Vatican's inaction in spite of detailed knowledge of the Holocaust had a galvanizing effect on young Germans.

Another politicizing event was the so-called Spiegel Affair of 1962, in which high West German government officials ordered a night raid on the news weekly *Der Spiegel* in an attempt to censor the magazine. That raid and the ensuing cover-up provoked the first major domestic political crisis of the West German government. On 9 October 1962 *Der Spiegel* published material revealing the sorry state of the West German army's military preparedness. This report proved especially embarrassing a few days later, on 15 October 1962, when the existence of Soviet missiles in Cuba was confirmed and the United States notified West Germany that a military showdown might take place. In such a situation documentation of its lack of military readiness was the last thing the West German military establishment needed. The Defense Ministry decided that the article was a breach of the Official Secrets Act and ordered the news magazine's production halted.[44] In a night raid on 26 October a detachment of riot police stormed the building, stopped the current print run, confiscated a large amount of material, and sealed the magazine's offices. The parallels between this search and seizure raid and Nazi methods were not lost on the domestic and international press, nor on thousands of Germans who took to the streets to protest against this blatant violation of the freedom of the press.[45]

Coincidentally, the *Spiegel* editor responsible for the article had gone to Spain on vacation. Defense Minister Franz Josef Strauss used high-level channels to contact the Spanish government and have the editor arrested by Spanish authorities. Not only was the Defense Minister's meddling a breach of West German law, but Strauss also lied to parliament about his involvement. When the truth came out, not only was Strauss forced to resign, but 87-year-old Chancellor Adenauer, who had vouched for him in parliament, was hurried into retirement as well. This marked the beginning of a sea change in West German politics, which had been dominated by the aging Adenauer since 1949.[46]

In the 1961 and 1965 parliamentary elections the left-wing Social Democrats gained ground on Adenauer's conservative CDU. Adenauer's successor in 1963, Ludwig Erhard, had proved his mettle in the 1950s as the engineer of West Germany's "economic miracle." In the 1960s, however, his politics of austerity proved less popular. When Erhard called for a tax increase in October 1966 to help West Germany combat a recession, the small, economically liberal FDP withdrew from the ruling coalition. In November 1966 a remarkable thing happened: a "Grand Coalition" of the two major parties CDU and SPD was formed. It was led by CDU Chancellor Kurt Kiesinger (1904–88), whom we met earlier as the Foreign Office liaison to Goebbels' Ministry of Propaganda, and by Willy Brandt (1913–92) from the SPD as Foreign Minister. Brandt had emigrated to Norway in 1933 to escape Nazi persecution. As a foreign correspondent during the war he had wielded his pen against the Nazi regime. This unlikely coalition of former Nazi and anti-Nazi held the government together until 1969, when a continuing leftward shift enabled Brandt to form a coalition with the liberals, unseating the conservative CDU for the first time in the twenty-year history of West Germany.

Historians consider the Grand Coalition of 1966–9 to be a construction of responsible politicians desiring to form a stable government and banish the specter of rising neo-Nazi parties from the political arena. Since 1965, when the economic boom upon which Adenauer's support had been based turned into a recession, the extreme right began gaining support.[47] The NPD unexpectedly won enough votes in the November 1966 elections to place representatives in the state parliaments in Bavaria and Hesse.[48] Within a year NPD delegates were in six state parliaments. Their greatest support was in Baden-Württemberg, where they garnered 9.8 percent of the vote. By 1969, however, their support had withered, and they did not pass the 5 percent threshold in the national elections. By 1972 they had failed to repeat their success at the state level as well, and that year they received only 0.6 percent of the vote in the national elections. It is difficult to say whether the demise of the radical right was due more to the success of established party politics, or to the improving economy, or both.

During the Grand Coalition, with the major left- and right-wing parties cooperating in parliament and the small liberal party situated comfortably between them, there was no effective voice of dissent in the legislature. This unanimity had positive and negative consequences. On the positive side (for the government), it enabled the ruling coalition, on 30 May 1968, finally to pass emergency laws governing police powers in situations of national crisis. These laws, which had been debated since 1958, allowed the government to suspend various constitutional rights, just as the Nazis had done before the March 1933 elections.[49] West German politicians desired such laws because until West Germany could guarantee the safety of Allied troops stationed on German soil, the victors of World War II retained the right to intervene in German domestic affairs.

On the negative side, the parliamentary unanimity worried those (primarily younger) Germans who feared that the government was granting itself too much power. Already in 1967, prior to the emergency laws, the Grand Coalition government had passed a Law for Promoting Stability and Growth, which granted the government broad powers to intervene in the economy. In order publicly to voice dissent against such parliamentary railroading, what became known as the Extraparliamentary Opposition (Ausserparlamentarische Opposition, APO) was formed on the streets and in the universities of West Germany.[50] The Nazi past was one of the weapons the APO movement brandished in its resistance against increases in government power.

The target of one of the most celebrated of those attacks was Kurt Kiesinger, who had been elected Chancellor in December 1966.[51] For some time Beate Klarsfeld (b. 1939), the 29-year-old German wife of a French Jewish lawyer, had been trying to draw public attention to Kiesinger's Nazi past, but with little success. When the emergency laws were passed, Klarsfeld finally decided to publicly slap Kiesinger in the name of her generation. Her opportunity came on 7 November 1968, the last day of the congress of Kiesinger's CDU party in Berlin (and coincidentally shortly before the thirtieth anniversary of the 1938 anti-Jewish pogroms). Posing as a journalist, Klarsfeld walked up behind the Chancellor before he delivered his speech, and slapped him as she screamed "Nazi, Nazi!" She was arrested but immediately given a suspended sentence in order to avoid the embarrassment of lengthy court proceedings. Klarsfeld's prepared statement explaining the slap argued that it was aimed more broadly at the members of the older generations of Germans who supported and tolerated Kiesinger: "I slapped Chancellor Kiesinger to prove that part of the German people, especially its youth, is enraged that a Nazi who was the vice-director of Hitler's Office of Foreign Propaganda can today be chancellor."[52]

Klarsfeld tirelessly disrupted Kiesinger's reelection campaign in the summer of 1969, heckling him with leaflets and calls of "Sieg Heil" at public rallies. Her efforts and those of her compatriots paid off. After the September 1969 elections Willy Brandt acceded to the chancellorship of West Germany, ending the Grand Coalition. As a former anti-Nazi, Brandt embodied the resistance against the Nazi past so sorely missed by the 1968ers. When he visited Warsaw in December 1970, Brandt went to the site of the Warsaw ghetto and paid homage to the Jewish resistance by falling to his knees in front of the monument there.[53] Such a gesture by a West German politician would have been unthinkable just a few years earlier; in 1970 it still provoked controversy in West Germany.

Given the myth of resistance, celebrating anti-Nazi resistance was comparatively easy. Understanding the brown-collar crimes and finding an appropriate relationship to them would take decades. The process of working through the past began with the difficult task of overcoming ignorance about it.

"Mastering the past": education or defamation?

Examinations of schoolchildren's knowledge of Nazism in the early 1960s found that, as a 1963 report put it, "for the younger generation (born between 1940 and 1950 [i.e. the 1968ers]), the time span between the present and the concentration camps is, subjectively, as long . . . as the one between the present and the medieval witch-trials."[54] This emotional distance persisted throughout the decade. Another study, prompted by the outbreak of left-wing violence following the Easter 1968 assassination attempt on student leader Rudi Dutschke (1940–79), found that students recited knowledge of the National Socialist period "by rote as ancient history might be," and that "the horrors of the concentration camps are reported in a disconcertingly sober and detached way."[55] In 1970, when a 1964 study of the historical consciousness of young Germans was republished, its authors justified the unchanged reprint in a new preface with the claim: "As impressively as political sensibilities and the readiness to become politically involved have grown in the 1968ers, their ahistorical relationship to the past has not changed."[56]

This detached relationship to the Nazi past had less to do with the postwar children, however, than with their 1943er teachers, who were uncomfortable with the material.[57] Still in 1970, one of the best curricular guides on teaching National Socialism drew a blank when it came to the concentration camps. It recommended that teachers should show the film *One Day*, a disturbing depiction of one day in a concentration camp, and then send the children home afterwards, "unless they express a desire to stay and talk about it."[58] Sabine Reichel (b. 1946) described how her teachers treated the National Socialist period in the early 1960s:[59]

> As it happened, Hitler and the Third Reich were the subjects under discussion when we were about fourteen years old, which is not to say that we discussed anything at all . . . .
>
> Teaching this particular period was a thankless, though unavoidable, task. It was accompanied by sudden speech impediments, hoarse voices, uncontrollable coughs, and sweaty upper lips. A shift of mood would creep into the expansive lectures about kings and conquerors from the old ages, and once the Weimar Republic came to an end our teachers lost their proud diction.
>
> We knew what it meant. We could feel the impending disaster. Only a few more pages in the history book, one last nervous swallowing, and then in a casual but controlled voice, maybe a touch too loud, Fräulein Lange would ask, "We are now getting to a dark chapter in German history. I'm sure you all know what I mean?" . . .
>
> We knew that she was referring to the terrible time between 1933 and 1945 when Germany fell prey to a devil in brown disguise. There were fifteen pages devoted to the Third Reich, and . . . then there was an extra chapter, about three-quarters of a page long. It was titled "The Extermination of the

Jews," and I had read it in my room at home many times. I always locked the door because I didn't want anybody to know what I was reading . . .

There was no explanation for my unspoken questions, no answers in Fräulein Lange's helpless face. She seemed embarrassed and distraught, biting her lip and looking down at her orthopedic shoes while trying to summarize the Third Reich in fifty minutes . . .

We never read that particular chapter aloud with our teacher as we did with so many other ones. It was the untouchable subject . . . There was a subtle, unspoken agreement between teacher and student not to dig into something that would cause discomfort on all sides.

Two years later, the subject was again on the curriculum. This time Reichel's teacher, Herr Stock, gave the pupils a "highly entertaining performance," including a theatrical rendition of a Hitler speech. However, when the war and brown-collar crimes came up,

everything went downhill. His hands stopped moving, his voice became reproachful . . . His saddest expression was reserved for the tragic end of "Germany under National Socialist dictatorship." It was time for the untouchable chapter again, the chapter that made Herr Stock nervously run his hands over his bald head, clear his throat, and mumble something about "six million Jews." It was the chapter that made him close the book with a clap, turn his back to the class, and announce with a palpable sigh of relief, "Recess."

Reichel notes that it was impossible for her 1968er cohort to relate to this type of portrayal. "Understanding is always personal," she writes. "Only stories that humanized the numbers might have reached us. Had we been allowed to draw a connection between ourselves and the lives of other people, we might have been able to identify and feel compassion."[60]

In fact, with very few exceptions, emotionally stirring memoirs of concentration camp life were not widely available in 1960s' West Germany.[61] The only major book specifically about brown-collar crimes that can be found on reading lists for schools is Gerhard Schoenberner's *The Yellow Star* (1960), which contains some of the most graphic images of Holocaust atrocities in existence.[62] It went though numerous editions and remained in print throughout the 1960s. However, the horrors depicted in full-page photographs were more likely to provoke shock and shame than discussion.

Of the other emotionally evocative books that deal with the victims' experience of Nazi persecution, two stand out – neither of which were included on the school lists.[63] Bruno Apitz's novel *Naked among Wolves*, based on a true story of how Buchenwald inmates saved a toddler from the clutches of the SS, was published in East Germany in 1958 and soon became a worldwide bestseller.[64] It may not have made the West German school reading lists because it was fictionalized, or because it was published in East Germany.[65] Primo Levi's famous Auschwitz memoir *If This Is a Man* (better known under the title *Survival in Auschwitz*), after becoming successful in Italy and the US in the late 1950s, was published in West Germany in 1961.[66] Although the German edition reached forty thousand copies, the book was not included on lists of recommended texts for use in schools, either. An examination of its reception reveals the difficulties such moving, empathetic portrayals posed for the 1933er and 1943er cohorts.

Primo Levi himself later published an analysis of the letters he received from West Germans in response to his Auschwitz memoir.[67] They clearly show the generational divide between those who claimed not to have known, and those thankful finally to be finding out. The one side was represented by Dr. T. H. in Hamburg, who was insensitive enough to instruct Levi on mythic German ignorance ("Who could suspect that we were riding [sic] a criminal and a traitor?"), victimization ("there remained only the choice between Hitler and . . . communism"), and resistance ("on July 20, 1944, just on one day, thousands and thousands of officers were executed"). The 1968er cohort was represented by student H. L., with whom Levi corresponded over an extended period. As an "heir and accomplice" to Nazism, she wrote, she was "fully conscious of . . . yesterday's horrors and sufferings," which she would work to alleviate, "so as to avoid their being repeated tomorrow." In response to Levi's query for more information about what people in Germany thought about National Socialism, H. L. responded with a twenty-three page letter, in which she noted that her professors did not avoid the subject. On the contrary, they had used contemporary newspapers to document how they had fallen victim to the Nazi misinformation campaign – which, as Levi notes, corresponded quite exactly to Dr. T. H.'s exculpatory litany. Levi also mentions his correspondence with an official in the Hessian Ministry of Culture who tried, unsuccessfully, to have Levi's out-of-print memoir republished after 1966.

As we have seen, even without many empathetic accounts of the atrocities, the public visibility of brown-collar crimes increased substantially in the early 1960s. For example, references to the Nazi past were used in political discussions with growing frequency. Soon a counterreaction set in, with public demands that the past had been "mastered" enough.[68] The first voice to propose "closing the book" (or "drawing a bottom line" – *einen Schlussstrich ziehen* – as the German metaphor went) was the Hamburg psychology professor Peter R. Hofstätter (b. 1913).[69] In three articles in the weekly newspaper *Die Zeit*, Hofstätter suggested that too much attention to the Nazi past – specifically, too many trials of brown-collar perpetrators – was detrimental to Germany's political culture. A debate on the editorial pages of *Die Zeit* ensued, as did a tumultuous discussion forum at the University of Hamburg. By September the debate had played itself out, with Hofstätter essentially conceding defeat to the more progressive cultural circles represented by the university students and the readers of *Die Zeit*.

The 1964 Auschwitz trial, and especially the 1965 debate about the statute of limitations for prosecuting mass murderers, triggered the next round of claims that Germans should not dwell on the Nazi past.[70] Karl Jaspers' important rebuttal in that debate was noted on p. 214, above. In 1966 Jaspers published a retrospective critique of the parliamentary debates on the statute in his influential book *The Future of Germany*.[71] Jaspers argued that brown-collar trials were an absolute necessity for forging West Germany's path into the future, and he took those Germans to task who felt that they had no need to subject themselves to personal moral scrutiny. In the following years two of Jaspers' students published significant works on the issue of West Germany's need to learn lessons from its Nazi past.

Another contributor to the later 1960s debates was literary scholar Gert Kalow (b. 1921). Kalow actually began writing his book, *The Shadow of Hitler: A Critique of Political Consciousness* (1967), after the trials of concentration camp sadists Sorge and Schubert in 1958.[72] At that time, however, the audience for his analysis was too small. Supporting his mentor Jaspers' legalistically argued conclusions, but traversing a humanistic path to make the same point, Kalow argued for a need to confront the past in order to "clean the nest." He rejected the notion of collective guilt as a "typically fascist mode of thinking," but he still concluded that the Nazi experience obliged West Germany to take an active role in working for a peaceful and just "world domestic policy."

Another of Jaspers' students, political commentator Armin Mohler, also joined the debate about the role of the Nazi past in present West German politics because he felt that Germany's future was at stake. In contrast to Jaspers and Kalow, however, he argued that Germany was being victimized by both domestic and foreign actors. They were, he argued, using Germany's past to constrain the state's responses to what he saw as an antidemocratic threat from the left. Mohler, born in Switzerland in 1920, had been so taken by Hitler's strong state that he went to Germany and tried to join the SS in 1942.[73] That attempt, although unsuccessful, firmly established Mohler's love for things German. The media blitz at the end of the war made him despise Nazism, but it did not dampen his nationalist German fervor. In 1949 he completed his dissertation under Jaspers on "The Conservative Revolution in Germany, 1918–1932." In the 1950s he worked as personal secretary to the nationalist German novelist Ernst Jünger, then for a number of years as a journalist in France, before he became the head of the conservative Carl Friedrich von Siemens Foundation in Munich.

At the heart of his book, *Mastery of the Past: From Purification to Manipulation,* are fifty theses, divided into four groups.[74] The first group briefly outlines some of the misuses of the past in the present; the second exposes some of the worst excesses drawn from the three postwar myths. In the third, main section, Mohler shows his colors. He attempts to establish exactly how, where, and why the use of the Nazi past in the present leads to negative consequences. Finally, the last few theses argue for a "closing of the book" on the Nazi past and an amnesty for all brown-collar criminals.

Mohler's book was one of the first explicit formulations of the neoconservative counterreaction against the attempt to use the Nazi past to create a moral dimension in contemporary politics. Although Mohler offers some valid observations on the use of the past in the present, he adopts faulty logic when he concludes from an anomalous misuse of an argument, that the argument itself is faulty. For instance, he gives a scathing analysis of the myth of resistance, noting that many "once again prominent" former Nazis "enumerate a series of hard-to-confirm acts of civil disobedience against totalitarianism between 1933 and 1945," even though they also "convincingly represented the Third Reich in important areas."[75] From there, however, Mohler argues that the media brings the pro-Nazi activities of these persons to public attention only when they "do not conform" – to what, Mohler does not say, although he implies that it is to the opinion of the monolithic mass media. From there he derives the "forced mediocrity" of West German politics, which is constrained by so many taboos that West Germany cannot pursue its "national interests."

Although Mohler's publishers kept his book in print for over a decade, his demand for "closing the book" on the Nazi past never found much following.[76] In the 1970s the agendas of public discussion were set by the left, not the right. Thus a 1967 study of the political implications of West Germany's collective relationship to the Nazi past by the left-wing psychoanalysts Alexander and Margarete Mitscherlich became what one former activist called the "bible" of left-wing political activists.[77]

Political taboos and undemocratic structures also prompted the Mitscherlichs to formulate their *The Inability to Mourn* in the mid-1960s.[78]

In contrast to Mohler, they called for a vigorous recollection of the Nazi past, and their arguments still figure prominently today in the discussion of how West Germany should deal with the atrocities in its past.[79] In fact, as we will see below, their analysis provides a key to understanding developments in the public reception of the brown-collar crimes in the 1970s and 1980s. In spite of its theoretical problems, this book marked a step forward in the discussion because it did not merely call for inner recognition of the losses incurred through brown-collar crimes, but also offered an explanation why that past had been rejected, and what consequences that rejection had for the present.

The Mitscherlichs' criticism of the "immobilism" of the West German political establishment resonated with the APO protest movement in ways that Jaspers' legalistic analysis did not. The Mitscherlichs were concerned, to list some of the ills of 1960s' West German society they name, about: political and social rigidity, apathy, indifference, detachment, provincialism, political illusionism, authoritarian bureaucratic structures, a culture of obedience and subordination, cultural prejudice, inhumanity, and more.

The Mitscherlichs' point of departure is the traumatic juncture of 1945.[80] Most Germans, they argue, had strongly believed in (or at least unquestioningly accepted) Hitler and his megalomaniac claim that they were members of a master race. This hyperinflated self-valuation ended in a massive, collective deflation of personal value when the incontrovertible evidence of German criminality was rubbed into the collective face of the populace at the end of the war. At first guilt and fear prevented the German populace from accepting or even recognizing this essentially unbearable loss. Soon what the Mitscherlichs called a "derealization" of the Nazi past set in, with the founding myths providing a convenient alternative to the psychic realization of the loss. That loss was then covered over in a "manic making undone" during the economic miracle of the 1950s.

The Mitscherlichs called for recognition of two types of loss. First, they argued, it was necessary to recognize that the national collective had erred in its faith in its own superiority. The Germans had loved Hitler narcissistically as the realization of a heroic dream, but now they needed to realize that they had always been ordinary mortals.[81] That would enable them to interact socially in a more humane way and to run their polity more rationally. In order to recover more future-oriented creative powers, however, a second recognition was also necessary. The Germans would have to recognize and mourn for people most of them had never valued: communists, Jews, Roma, homosexuals, and other victims of their super-racial delusions.

Implicit in the analysis, and perhaps typical for psychoanalysis at the time, was the expectation that recognition of the causes of psychic deformations was tantamount to curing them. The authors themselves, as well as other scholars, have since pointed out the need to offer "appropriate psychological understanding," and to open up a supportive "therapeutic space" if Germany is to be able to take control of the unintentional and undesired consequences of its past.[82] In a 1987 essay Margarete Mitscherlich described the process necessary to become capable of mourning, which she called *Trauerarbeit*, labor of mourning. The labor of mourning "requires a labor of remembering," she wrote, "but not so much the remembering of facts and topics as the remembering of behaviors, values, feelings and fantasies." This repeated painful remembering would bring about a slowly progressing internalization of the loss, which would in turn lead to changes in a person's spiritual constitution.[83] This theoretical insight was proposed as a key to overcoming the failure of teaching about National Socialism described by Sabine Reichel and many others.

Of course the debate about coping with the past was not limited to the extremes represented by Mohler, who condemned working through the Nazi past, and the Mitscherlichs, who advocated its thorough examination. An intermediate stance was taken by 1943er Hans Buchheim (b. 1922), a researcher at the Munich Institute for Contemporary History and the author of one of the historical reports for the 1964 Auschwitz trial. Buchheim, who unequivocally rejected Nazism but did not condemn its adherents, attempted to mediate between the clashing generations.[84]

In a 1967 essay entitled "The Federal Republic and the Third Reich," Buchheim chastised the 1968ers for their accusatory criticism of the Nazi-complicit 1933ers. Invoking the myth of resistance, Buchheim claimed that criticism such as Hochhuth's (b. 1932) indictment of papal inaction was historically inappropriate. It was unfair to criticize the Pope without considering the reasons he had for keeping silent. Additionally, Buchheim argued that it was false for the 1968ers to think, based on actions such as those of the Munich "White Rose" students (who had been executed for distributing anti-Nazi materials in 1942 and 1943), that it had been possible for normal citizens to resist the regime. Balance and political realism, he concluded, were what West Germany now needed, not political irrationalism based on moral arguments. This appeal to moderation was the "lesson of Weimar" that was soon to be invoked by members of the 1948er cohort in response to the militant civil disobedience practiced by the young social protest movement.[85]

Fascistoid antifascists? Mythic resistance in the postwar cohort

By the mid-1960s German universities were populated exclusively by students from the first postwar 1968er cohort, born between ca. 1937 and 1953. Many of these students were keenly interested in the Nazi period and committed to vaguely formulated antifascist ideals, but they lacked a deeper understanding of the human component of fascist systems. For instance, students closely followed the scandals about the Nazi backgrounds of their government and judicial officials, as the Oberländer and Globke affairs attest. They also began to investigate the backgrounds of their own professors.[86] In 1963 the first in a series of books documenting what became known as the "brown university" – the Nazi connections of older professors – was published.[87] There were also more conciliatory initiatives. In 1964, prompted by students, the University of Tübingen organized an interdisciplinary lecture series about the academy during the Nazi era.[88] This series inspired similar programs at several other universities, most notably the Free University of Berlin and the University of Munich.[89]

Even though some of the lectures provided revealing analyses of the Nazi era, in the majority of them the members of the 1933er and 1943er cohorts employed various combinations of the three myths in order to excuse complicity with National Socialism.[90] The more committed fringe of the audience remained critical. In 1967 Wolfgang Fritz Haug (b. 1936), an editor of the left-wing journal *Das Argument*, analyzed the texts of the individual lectures. He argued that the unconscious apologetics in many of the lectures revealed links between fascism and liberalism.[91] He published his results under the celebrated title *Helpless Antifascism*, which expressed his opinion of the professors' version of the myth of resistance: whatever they may have attempted to do to resist Nazism, it had been completely ineffective. In meticulous detail Haug argued that since members of the 1933er cohort who had advanced their careers under Nazism lacked insight into their own pasts, they perpetuated "fascistoid" behaviors in the present (that is, behaviors resembling fascism and thus potentially fascist). Margarete Mitscherlich later described the postwar behavior of these unreflective members of the careerist Nazi cohorts as "striving for success, persevering in the face of adversity, repressing pain and feelings, adapting and obeying, rejecting guilt, and looking for scapegoats."[92]

Haug's recognition of the role of the three myths in perpetuating potentially fascist behaviors did not mean that the "antifascism" of his 1968er cohort would be any less "helpless." Its lack of success when teaching about brown-collar crimes is one example of its own mythically incurred helplessness. Still unaware of the mythic legacies it had inherited, the 1968er cohort's overly moralizing and humanly empty instruction about National Socialism may have differed in content and delivery from what Sabine Reichel had received in the early 1960s, but it was no better at promoting understanding of the human causes and consequences of the genocidal juggernaut. In the mid-1980s Stefanie, the 19-year-old granddaughter of a brown-collar criminal executed after the war, told an interviewer how she had learned about brown-collar crimes in the late 1970s:[93]

> We once had a history teacher. Long hair, beard, ski sweater, jeans – the works. Boy, did he carry on about everything. For hours he'd talk about the Jews, the Communists, the Gypsies, the Russians – victims, nothing but victims . . .
>
> Once someone asked him in class: "Tell us, where was the madness? Why did all those people shout hurrah and Heil? . . . There must have been something to it." He just looked stupid, our dear teacher. He called the boy who'd asked the question a neo-Nazi, asked him whether he had no respect for the victims, and so on . . . then he let loose. He screamed at us. Gone was that left-wing softy of the sixties. All hell broke loose. At last we had broken through the façade of this all-understanding, all-knowing, all-explaining puppet.

Such extreme pedagogical rigidity may not have been typical of the 1968ers, but it was fairly widespread. Lea Fleischmann (b. 1947), a child of Holocaust survivors who abandoned a successful career as a German high school teacher for precisely that reason in 1978, published a scathing critique of her 1968er peers' focus on technical problems as opposed to human issues. She wrote that they had replaced empathetic teaching by what she called a "pull yourself together" and "don't let yourself go" pedagogy.[94] As we will see, it was not until the early 1980s, when students in the next, "1979er" cohort began to unearth the "history of everyday life" under National Socialism for themselves, that a more humanly empathetic picture of life under Nazism began to emerge. And not until the 1990s did the pedagogical discussion face this challenge head on. However, let us first return to the 1960s and see how brown-collar crimes came to inform the emerging political consciousness of the 1968ers.

In the political conflicts of the late 1960s analogies to the National Socialist past were brandished on both sides of the generational divide. In 1965 the 1968ers, for example, compared US tactics in Vietnam, such as the use of napalm and poison gas, with genocidal Nazi methods.[95] And in

November 1966 in Dachau banners with the following texts were surreptitiously posted at the memorial site entrance: "Vietnam is the Auschwitz of America," and "American leathernecks are inhuman murderers like the SS."[96] The 1933er and 1943er cohorts did not take such comparisons sitting down, but responded in kind.

The careerist Nazi 1933er cohort (born ca. 1903–15), which had clear memories of the street violence of the early 1930s, was determined to quell public protests in the 1960s. In 1967 conservative publisher Axel Springer, who controlled 80 percent of the total daily newspaper circulation in West Germany, began to equate left-wing civil disobedience with the tactics of Nazi stormtroopers. One incident occurred on 2 June 1967, when the Berlin police brutally broke up a demonstration against the Shah of Iran's visit.[97] The police used water cannon to force the protesters into a narrow street, then moved in from both ends and began clubbing the trapped students. The students responded by throwing stones and bottles. In the heat of the battle a young policeman shot bystander Benno Ohnesorg in the back of the head. The next day Springer's *Die Welt* made up a story according to which Ohnesorg was in a group that had attacked the police with knives.[98] (It was a complete fabrication.) Springer's tabloid *Bild* editorialized (in reference to the behavior of the protesters, not the police): "We do not like SA methods. The Germans do not want a brown or a red SA. We want peace, not gangs of thugs."[99]

The use of Nazi vocabulary in invectives against the young demonstrators was not uncommon among 1933ers. After the anti-Shah protest, the student government of Berlin's Free University received letters with statements such as the following: "Starting now my colleagues and relatives are prepared with dog whips and sticks," and "Vermin should be doused with gasoline and set on fire. Death to the red student plague!"[100] The students had no doubts about the Nazi origins of such verbiage. At a meeting following Ohnesorg's death, one of the student activists, Gudrun Ensslin, called out: "They'll kill us all – you know what kind of pigs we're up against – that is the generation of Auschwitz we've got against us – you can't argue with the people who made Auschwitz. They have weapons and we haven't. We must arm ourselves."[101]

The Israeli Six Day War began only days after the shooting of Benno Ohnesorg in June 1967. References to the Holocaust and World War II were abundant.[102] Egypt's President Nasser, who threatened to "exterminate" the Israelis, was compared to Hitler; Israeli Defense Minister Moshe Dayan, the one-eyed military leader who would save the Jews, was likened to would-be Hitler assassin Claus von Stauffenberg; conciliatory Israeli Prime

Minister Levi Eshkol was compared to "appeaser" Neville Chamberlain. The victorious Israeli *Blitzkrieg* drew an enormous outpouring of support from all sectors of German society.[103] Within weeks, however, the ideological congruence with the "establishment" on this issue made the radical fringe of the leftist 1968ers uncomfortable.

In July 1967 left-wing columnist Ulrike Meinhof (1934–76) linked the 1933ers' and 1943ers' jubilance over Israel's victory to the mythic unworked-through past. Using Springer's *Bild* tabloid as a symbol of the careerist Nazi cohorts, Meinhof wrote:[104]

> In Sinai *Bild* won, finally, after 25 years, the battle of Stalingrad. Anticommunist grudges fit seamlessly with the destruction of Soviet MIG fighters . . . If we had taken the Jews, instead of gassing them, to the Urals, the Second World War would have ended differently . . .
>
> Not the recognition of the humanity of the Jews, but the hardness of their combat, not the recognition of their rights as citizens, but their use of Napalm, not the acceptance of our own crimes, but the Israeli *Blitzkrieg*, our solidarity with the brutality, the expulsion, the conquest led to this questionable reconciliation. The spirit of "I will determine who is a Jew" links Israel and the killers of Berlin at the same time. If Israel were a socialist country these sympathies would certainly not exist. Then there would only be the sympathies of the European left, unwavering, rational, honest.

However, those "unwavering" left-wing sympathies could cut against the Jews as well. Some members of the left were able to repress completely their human empathy for the benefit of abstract ideals. For instance, the national leadership of the left-wing student organization SDS (in Germany, this stood for "Socialist German Students' League," not "Students for a Democratic Society," as in the US) prefaced a 5 June 1967 press release with the words:[105]

> We socialists in the FRG, who from the beginning have fought antisemitism not only for moral, humanitarian or even anti-racist reasons, cannot confuse our feelings for the Israeli people . . . with the rational, economic and political analysis of the position of the Israeli state in the international conflict between the highly industrialized countries and the countries of the Third World.

This "inhuman" dimension of radical left-wing German politics had tragic consequences, which are discussed in the next section.

As the extreme left of the 1968ers drifted towards such inhuman thinking, the older cohorts' dislike of grass roots activism began to surface. Ohnesorg's death by a police bullet was the first shot in an escalating spiral of violence. In February 1968 the SDS staged a mock trial of Springer, and again, as in 1962, tried to halt delivery of his bestselling tabloid, *Bild*.

Springer's newspapers responded by equating student leader Rudi Dutschke with Hitler.[106] In one of the pre-1968er cohorts' more bizarre realizations of the myth of resistance, the Berlin populace responded, more than thirty years too late, by trying to lynch this new putative Hitler. On 21 February, hundreds of people attending a city-sponsored counter-demonstration to a planned anti-Vietnam demonstration tried to kill an office worker whom they mistook for student leader Dutschke.[107] The man barely escaped with his life. A month later Dutschke himself was not so lucky. On 11 April 1968, inspired by the assassination of Martin Luther King, Jr. on 4 April, and probably incited by the reporting of Springer's newspapers, an anticommunist apprentice plumber shot Dutschke four times at point blank range.

The SDS responded by issuing a bulletin proclaiming: "Irrespective of whether Rudi was the victim of a political conspiracy, one can now positively assert that this crime was plainly the consequence of systematic incitement, mounted by the Springer company."[108] *Der Spiegel* reported that protests against what were seen as West Germany's fascist tendencies were erupting "in almost all western European countries."[109] In London, for example, 800 people gathered in front of the Springer affiliate *Daily Mirror* and taunted the newspaper with the Nazi acclamation "Sieg Heil." At the end of May the West German Grand Coalition of CDU and SPD, galvanized by what it thought was increasing anarchy in West Germany, passed the so-called emergency laws. The main protest demonstration against the laws drew up to 70,000 protesters to Bonn on 11 May, with as many again protesting in other cities.[110]

Almost drowned out in the heat of these invectives were the more moderate voices, which came primarily from the 1948ers.[111] They, too, applied terms linked to the Nazi past to the present debate, albeit in a far more nuanced way. Jürgen Habermas (b. 1929) was a critical sociologist at the University of Frankfurt who had long been interested in student political activism.[112] In a discussion after the shooting of Ohnesorg in June 1967, Habermas used the term "left-wing fascism" (*Linksfaschismus*) to characterize the violently activist tactics of the most radical protesters.[113] Although Habermas soon retracted that epithet because he realized that he had misunderstood the circumstances of Ohnesorg's death, the term was picked up by the media and remained in use for some time.[114] For example, in October 1967 Richard Löwenthal (b. 1908), a returned Jewish émigré who had become a political science professor at the Free University of Berlin, suggested that the radicals were both reacting to fascist behavior and unconsciously reproducing it:[115]

The present radicalization in the engagement of the leftist intellectuals is thus not *only* a conscious counterattack against the ideas of National Socialism and the horrors of its rule, which still permeate the critics as they do all of us. It is *also* the unconscious continuation of some of the intellectual currents that helped to make those horrors possible (emphasis in original).

That was the double legacy of the myths of ignorance and resistance for the 1968er cohort: the replication of certain elements of fascism in the attempt to resist others. While this legacy was recognized and overcome by the vast majority of the activist youth, in the following decade a radical fringe drifted into increasingly inhuman behaviors.

Left-wing terrorism, 1968–1977

The young German radicals took a first concrete step towards antihuman violence one week before the attempted assassination of Dutschke.[116] On 2 April 1968 four left-wing activists left incendiary devices in two Frankfurt department stores shortly before closing time.[117] Andreas Baader (1943–77), Gudrun Ensslin (1940–77), Thorwald Proll (b. 1941), and Horst Söhnlein (b. 1942) proclaimed that the fires, which broke out around mid-night, were intended as "a beacon for Vietnam."[118] At his sentencing, Proll read a prepared statement in which he accused the judicial system of being "fascist" and predisposed to favoring the right, as well as to letting "big murderers of Jews" (that is, brown-collar bureaucrats) off the hook while convicting "little murderers of Jews" (the sadistic murderers of the concentration camps).[119] Such references indicate that the arsonists had been following the mid-1960s trials of brown-collar criminals very closely.

As West Germany moved into the next decade, this complex mix of legacies gave rise to the specific nature of West German radical politics in the 1970s. In the United States, the radical movements of the late 1960s were more clearly bifurcated into a "soft" flower-power counterculture on the one hand, and a militant subculture of concretely repressed minorities such as the Weathermen and Black Panthers on the other. In West Germany, the Berlin equivalent of Haight-Ashbury, "Kommune I" and "Kommune II," were not only more insular than their US counterparts, but much more politicized and less hedonistic as well. In the 1970s and 1980s, when the radicalism in the US largely subsided, increasingly isolated West German ultra-radicals became increasingly violent. The German terrorists were recruited primarily from the middle class, and they saw themselves resisting a theoretically conceived victimization. The myth of ignorance informed their rationale for the lack of popular support for their activities: they were saving the ignorant German masses in spite of themselves.[120]

The four arsonists were soon arrested, tried, and sentenced to three years in prison. They were temporarily released in June 1969 while their appeal was pending, because the authorities felt that they were neither dangerous nor likely to flee.[121] When their appeal was rejected in November, the four went underground. In April 1970 Baader was coincidentally arrested because he was driving a stolen car. Once the police realized who he was, they jailed him, but granted him permission to visit a library to research a book he was writing about the "organization of young people on the margins of society." On 14 May his compatriots, under the leadership of Ulrike Meinhof, freed him from the reading room in a hail of bullets, one of which seriously wounded a guard. On 2 June 1970, the third anniversary of the shooting of Benno Ohnesorg, the group sent a letter to the German Press Agency, in which they called for armed resistance to state authority and the formation of a "Red army." That was the beginning of what has become known as the "Red Army Faction," or RAF. At the time it was known as the "Baader–Meinhof" group.

The increasingly antihuman and violent activities of the RAF in the 1970s are extreme legacies of the myths of victimization and resistance. They were a pathological outgrowth of a vanguard that had lost touch with its base in the extraparliamentary opposition after the summer of 1968.[122] The APO's pro-Communist members were discredited when the Communist bloc countries crushed the Prague Spring movement in August 1968. Increasing feminist consciousness further divided the patriarchically structured movement, and the collapse of the Grand Coalition and accession of the left-leaning SPD to power in 1969 took further impetus away from the APO. Many of its members decided that what was called the "long march through the institutions" was now the best way to achieve social change.

Without a popular movement behind them, the Red Army Faction resorted to increasingly violent tactics. Several incidents reveal how the legacies of the three founding myths shaped the RAF's political assessments and activities. Their hollow understanding of brown-collar victimization led them to embrace the "bad survivor" image and conceive of Jews as perpetrators. For instance, when Arab terrorists murdered eleven Israeli athletes at the Munich Olympics in September 1972, Ulrike Meinhof, from her prison cell, announced her approval of the deaths of what she called "Zionist soldiers masquerading as athletes."[123] The

318

terrorists' ironclad self-identification as victims allowed them to unconsciously replicate the behavior of brown-collar murderers. The crassest example of such brown-collar echoes occurred in 1976, when German terrorist Wilfried Böse (1949–76) "selected" Jews for execution from the rest of the passengers on a hijacked jetliner in Entebbe, Uganda.[124] The exact parallel between Böse's selection and Nazi actions shocked the German left and initiated what one former terrorist later called "the return to humanity."[125]

However, that hijacking was not the last terrorist battle echoing the Nazi past. In September 1977 RAF activists gunned down four bodyguards and kidnapped Hanns-Martin Schleyer, the president of the German Employers' Association. The RAF targeted Schleyer because he had already been a member of the Nazi Party before 1933, and had later joined the SS. The terrorists felt that he should not have been allowed to hold such a high position in postwar society. The RAF hoped to use Schleyer to bargain for the freedom of Baader, Ensslin, and Jan-Carl Raspe (1944–77), who were serving life sentences in a specially built ultra-high-security prison in Stuttgart-Stammheim.

In a statement indicating how much the terrorists identified themselves with concentration camp victims, Ensslin compared the difference between the Stammheim conditions and "normal" prison isolation to "the difference between Auschwitz and Buchenwald."[126] The three terrorists did not have to bear those conditions for very long, however. In early October 1977 they were found shot dead in their prison cells. They probably committed suicide, but at the time many people assumed that they had been executed because of the presumed impossibility of smuggling guns into their cells. The day after their deaths were announced, the RAF strangled Schleyer with a piano wire and left his corpse in the trunk of a car on the German–French border. That cold-blooded murder was the culmination of the "hot fall" of 1977, which had seen two other political assassinations and an airline hijacking. It was a new highpoint of disregard for human lives by left-wing terrorists, who had committed another thirty political murders by the early 1990s. (The RAF officially announced its dissolution on 20 April 1998.[127])

However, this increasingly marginalized and desperate group should not be seen as representative of mainstream developments in West German society in the late 1960s and early 1970s. Rather, from 1969 on, progressive activists began to attempt what newly elected Chancellor Willy Brandt called "daring to practice more democracy." Several incidents in Dachau in 1968–9 are indicative of the shift.

Dachau, September 1968

On 8 September 1968, twelve years to the day after the symbolic corner-stone of the international memorial was consecrated in 1956, the memorial itself was dedicated. For almost a year the international committee of Dachau survivors' organizations, the CID, was preparing for the crowning ceremony to mark the completion of the last element of the program it had announced a dozen years earlier. Since 1956 Otto Kohlhofer had performed yeoman service in mediating the differences among the various member organizations of the CID to forge a united front working for the creation of the memorial site. Now, as the achievement of the common goal was finally in sight, some of the old divisions began to resurface.

The 1968 dedication ceremony was conceived primarily by the Belgian and French members of the CID, who had long led the organization. Many of the Belgian and French survivors had come from the resistance and made careers as military men after the war, and they decided to give the ceremony a military flavor, with honorary detachments from the countries that had lost citizens in Dachau. Since it was unthinkable that members of the Communist bloc countries of eastern Europe should send military formations to West Germany, participation was *de facto* limited to armies from NATO countries.

Whereas the Western European Dachau survivors wanted to celebrate the military might that had ultimately defeated Nazism, the German survivors, many of whom were Communists, drew a different lesson from the Nazi era. They saw Hitler's militarism as the core of Nazism's evil, and wished to emphasize pacifism and solidarity among peoples, not military prowess. The West German survivors' association, headed by Otto Kohlhofer, was put in charge of local arrangements for the ceremony. This placed Kohlhofer in an awkward situation. Should he follow his inner convictions and withdraw his support for the military ceremony, or should he conceal his reservations to preserve the solidarity he had worked so hard to create?

The open conflict began in June 1968, when the CID met with representatives of the Bavarian Youth Ring (BJR), including its president, Hermann Kumpfmüller.[128] The Youth Ring was asked to reschedule its annual November ceremony in Dachau to September, but it was not allowed to take any active role in the ceremony. The BJR was taken aback that young people were to be no more than "props" for a ceremony that Kohlhofer feared would be "more a military ceremony for war veterans than an admonishing commemorative ceremony in a concentration camp." The

BJR set three absolute conditions for its participation: (1) it would have to be a full member of the planning committee; (2) a speaker for the youth group would have to have an appropriate amount of time; and (3) there would be no military participation.[129] While some of the CID member organizations were open to the conditions, they did not like the "authoritarian" tone of the "ultimatum." On 18 July the planning committee decided to accept Kohlhofer's suggestion that preparations would continue without the youth group in spite of the problems and reservations.[130] Kohlhofer and the Germans would be responsible for local arrangements, but they would not assist with the preparations for the military formations.

This compromise was not a very satisfactory solution, however, and soon difficulties began to appear. In August 1968 the left-wing newspaper *Die Tat*, which was close to the VVN and probably received funding from East Germany, published an article entitled "NATO Military on the Roll-call Square in Dachau?," in which it criticized not only the army formations, but also the lack of interest in including the younger generation, as well as the participation of Bavarian Minister Hundhammer (whom Kohlhofer had won as a member of the curatorium for the memorial site in the late 1950s).[131] Hundhammer, it reported, had recently given the Adenauer Prize of the German Foundation to Emil Franzel, who had made a name for himself by saying that protesting students were "vermin" who should be "combated with appropriate chemical agents."[132] It was quite obvious that his words harked back to the "combating" of Jews at Auschwitz with the insecticide Zyklon B.

Such newspaper reporting gave a clear signal to young West German radicals that the Dachau ceremony would celebrate "the establishment." The German anti-establishment protest movement was at its peak in 1968. It had gained impetus from the successful North Vietnamese Tet Offensive against US troops in January, and was outraged because NATO was supporting the Greek military junta under Papadopoulos that had seized power in 1967. West German activism had reached highpoints in April and May 1968 after the shooting of Rudi Dutschke and prior to the parliamentary vote on the emergency laws. In 1968 the promise of "socialism with a human face" symbolized by the Prague Spring had given further momentum to the movement – until 21 August, when troops from the socialist bloc countries invaded Czechoslovakia and crushed the reforms. In this charged atmosphere young activists did not need to be invited by concentration camp survivors to confront top-level representatives of an "establishment" they considered fascist.

The 9 September 1968 ceremony featured marches and music by honorary formations of the Belgian, French, and US armies and the British air force, and a fly-over in cross formation by US and Dutch military jets. The young protesters' particular focus, however, was the keynote address by West Berlin Mayor Klaus Schütz, who as head of the Parliamentary Council substituted for the West German President.[133] The demonstrators found Schütz's participation in the Dachau ceremony especially offensive because he was a hard-liner who replaced Berlin Mayor Heinrich Albertz when Albertz had expressed his sympathies for Benno Ohnesorg in the summer of 1967. More recently, in April 1968, Schütz had ordered the suppression of the mass protests and attacks on the Springer press buildings after the assassination attempt on Rudi Dutschke.[134]

When Mayor Schütz approached the podium in Dachau to begin his remarks, a group of about forty university-age people ducked under the cordon and began to unfurl banners. Some of the texts branded present government officials as brown-collar perpetrators: "Today Pogrom and Propaganda, Tomorrow the Final Solution, Herr Schütz," and "They commemorate today and exterminate tomorrow." In other chants, such as "Where did Benno Ohnesorg die?" and "Today Dutschke, tomorrow us!," the demonstrators expressed their own real and potential victimization. In contrast, the slogans "We fight against Fascism, NATO, and Imperialism," and "Dachau greets Hitler's successors" reveal the demonstrators' self-identification with the anti-Nazi resistance. Finally, still other chants indicate that the protesters were concerned about present injustice: "Ho, Ho, Ho Chi Minh!" expressed support for the North Vietnamese leader, while "Ena, ena, tessera!" (Greek for "1–1–4") invoked the article of the Greek constitution that protected the right to resist unjust rule.[135] The legacies of the myths of victimization and resistance were alive and well among this cohort.

Most of the banners and slogans were incomprehensible to the primarily francophone Dachau survivors present that day. Almost immediately someone called out "C'est les fascistes!" ("It's the fascists!"), and a physical struggle ensued between concentration camp survivors and the demonstrators (ill. 66). West German police quickly pushed the young people into a corner near the camp gate, where they remained, too far away from the ceremony for their chants "Schütz – Fascist!" and "Down with Schütz!" to be disruptive, until the end of the ceremony. However, as soon as the former victims of the Nazis realized what the protest was about, they tried to express their support for the demonstrators. One protester recalled:[136]

Five cops grabbed my Vietnam flag, but I didn't let go. They dragged me away with the flag. When we went past the VIP seating an old antifascist jumped down and punched me in the face. I lost my flag. A half an hour later the old man came running up to me, hugged me, stroked my cheek again and again and repeated probably about ten times "Pardon, mon Camerade."

At a reception for the CID member organizations that afternoon the young demonstrators discussed their concerns with the Dachau survivors. The survivors unanimously felt that the protest during the commemorative ceremony was "out of place," but some, including especially the East and West Germans, but also the Czechs and Cahnman for the Americans, expressed their disapproval of the "NATO parade."[137] Kohlhofer went so far as to send a press release to twenty-six newspapers, Bavarian radio, and the German wire service in which he wrote that the military displays "grossly distorted the meaning of the ceremony."[138] Kumpfmüller from the Youth Ring wrote to the CID to express his regrets for the disruption of the ceremony, but noted that his fears regarding the military display had been justified.[139] He added that it was especially regrettable that no mention had been made of Dachau's legacies for the younger generation.

In the late 1960s and early 1970s some young Germans embarked on a quest to find out just what those legacies might be.

New ways of using the past

The controversy at the September 1968 Dachau commemoration is situated in a period of transition to a more sensitive, less instrumental understanding of human behavior under fascism. This development is visible in several subsequent events in Dachau.[140] In the wake of the street violence in 1968, conservative legislators had proposed a "protective custody" law that would have allowed police arrests without charges or a warrant in order to ensure the public safety. That was precisely the same justification the Nazis had used for their initial waves of arrests in 1933. Instead of organizing potentially confrontational demonstrations, in January 1969 the satirical magazine *Pardon* staged a symbolic reopening of the Nazi Dachau concentration camp to draw attention to the parallels between the proposed law and its Nazi-era predecessor.[141] In contrast to the September 1968 protest, Dachau survivors were informed beforehand, and they were present to lend their support.

At the fall 1969 *Kristallnacht* ceremony in Dachau a radically different format for the participation of the younger generation was tried out.

Instead of having the participants passively listen to speakers, three parallel "working groups" were organized, in which the following topics were discussed: (1) "the goals and tactics of nonviolent resistance"; (2) "the roots of National Socialism and right-wing extremism today"; and (3) "democracy in industrial society."[142] With historical experts such as Gerhard Schoenberner (author of the first comprehensive pictorial documentary of the Holocaust in 1960) leading the workshops, this was a concerted effort to gain historical insights into present concerns, as opposed to merely instrumentalizing historical analogies to score political points.

In the 1970s the leftist 1968ers entered the political mainstream and began what they called "the long march through the institutions." As high school teachers, for example, they took their classes to concentration camp memorial sites in unprecedented numbers. In 1969 the number of school groups visiting the Dachau museum nearly doubled from 471 to 922.[143] In the early 1970s that number climbed to over 1,000 groups per year, and by the end of the decade it had surpassed 5,000 annually. (After reaching a highpoint of 5,900 in 1985, the number has stabilized at about 5,600 since the mid-1990s.)

The year 1969 marked the beginning of a major transition in West German national politics. After twenty years of conservative rule, a coalition of the leftist SPD and centrist FDP assumed power and began implementing a number of radical changes in government policy. One of those changes was the reversal of the "official" attitude of silence about the Nazi past. No longer were the skeletons in the national closet to be ignored and preferably forgotten, but rather, as newly elected Federal President Gustav Heinemann proclaimed in his acceptance speech in July 1969: "Our own history still needs be clarified in the best interests of the future."[144] This call was taken seriously by the Dachau chapter of the Social Democratic youth organization Jusos (Jungsozialisten – "Young Socialists"). At a press conference in March 1970 Meinolf Kalthoff, the group's speaker, presented a list of seven demands that were to be discussed at a public meeting in April:[145]

1. the city council will draw up a comprehensive official statement on the relationship between the city and the concentration camp;
2. the city will commission a scholarly documentation of the concentration camp;
3. the city will build a center for youth encounters with space for informational material, discussions, and seminars, and for overnight accommodation;
4. the city will appoint a director of the youth center;

5. the city will organize an annual commemorative event and lay an official wreath at the memorial;
6. the city will make the film shown at the memorial site available to Dachau schools;
7. the text in the city's tourist brochure will be changed.

As the twenty-fifth anniversary of Dachau's liberation in April approached, an animated public discussion of this proposed program of active local participation in recollection began.[146] Although interest in the program waned once the major anniversary had passed, its elements were revived time and again over the next three decades.

Apparently another generation had to pass before the brown-collar past could become an integral part of mainstream West German historical consciousness. As the 1933ers died off and the 1948ers gradually relinquished the reins of power in the 1970s and 1980s, the 1968ers created an institutional infrastructure for recollecting the Nazi past. That infrastructure included new memorial sites, some scholarly and serial publications, and school curricular guidelines. This recollective framework was filled with content by members of a second postwar cohort, born between the mid-1950s and the mid-1960s. These "1979ers" were the children of younger 1948ers and older 1968ers; their grandparents had been 1933ers and 1943ers.

PART FOUR

Dachau 1970–2000: new age cohorts challenge mythic legacies

In part II of this book we saw how the three founding myths of victimization, ignorance and resistance emerged at the end of the war to help Germans to come, emotionally and morally, to terms with the Nazi past. These three myths produced three pervasive distorted collective images of that past, namely of "good" Nazis, "bad" survivors, and "clean" concentration camps. At the end of part III we saw how, in the 1960s, these three collective images persisted in modified form despite the efforts of the 1968ers to overcome them. Their 1933er parents' putative ignorance left this younger generation with a derealized picture of the Nazi past, and ignorant of everyday fascist behaviors. The parents' claims of victimization led the children to self-identify with victims of oppression in other parts of the world, and the parents' unlikely avowals of resistance against Nazism reemerged among their children as hyper-sensitive and overblown political opposition.

As we will see in the final three chapters of the book, both the original myths and their legacies among the 1968ers lost their power as persuasive public paradigms in the decades after 1970. I impute these developments to three factors. First, there was a maturing and learning process among the 1968ers: they became less self-righteously confrontational, and they unearthed a wealth of information about life – and death – during the Nazi period. Second, the 1948ers changed as well. As the 1933ers died off and the 1943ers retired from public life, the 1948ers were increasingly able to accept the less mythic relationship to the past demanded by the 1968ers. Finally, the entry into public life of an even younger generational cohort, the 1979ers (born roughly 1954–66), allowed the mythic legacies of the 1968er cohort to die out.[1] Although these were uneven processes that were still incomplete at the end of the millennium, we can say roughly that mythic ignorance lost its hold on the mainstream in the 1970s, mythic victimization lost its predominance in the 1980s, and mythic resistance began to lose its persuasiveness in the 1990s.

Table 2 summarizes the three myths and some of their legacies for the different age cohorts.

Table 2: *The three founding myths and their legacies*

Post-1945 myths among 1933ers and 1943ers	Myths and mythic legacies among 1933ers, 1943ers, and 1948ers	Mythic legacies among 1968ers	Mythic and post-mythic tendencies among 1979ers
Victimization by Nazis	Victimization by Allies by tourists	Victimization by 43er parents Powerful, unquestioning solidarity with oppressed peoples (esp. third world)	Recognition of survivors as "historical witnesses" Willingness to accept historical responsibility
Ignorance of genocide	Ignorance of renazification Silence about Nazi past	Ignorance about Nazi past (abstract conception of life under Nazism)	Quest for knowledge about Nazi past Tendency to emphasize cognitive learning over empathetic portrayals
Resistance against Nazis	Resistance against learning more	Resistance to/intolerance of perceived fascist tendencies Dedication to teaching about Nazism (Over)eager acceptance of counter-mythic works	Resistance to three myths and their legacies Dedication to finding out more Reflective or critical acceptance of countermythic works

Before we examine the process of exposure, challenge, and abandonment of each of the three original myths and their legacies, we will look at the biography of an individual whose personal story embodies aspects of the broader transformation of public remembrance. Lorenz Reitmeier was a 1948er who, as mayor of Dachau from 1966 to 1996, left his mark on local politics throughout this period. The defense of the three myths that he mounted in 1970 was gradually overtaken by shifts in commemorative activity beginning at the end of that decade. By the time Reitmeier left office in 1996, his position with regard to Dachau's past was so out of touch with local public opinion that his successor, a 1979er, was able to take a diametrically opposite course. Mayor Kurt Piller, whose story is told at the end of chapter 14, saw the town and the former camp as inextricably linked, and he worked hard to present that unity to the outside world.

Lorenz Reitmeier (b. 1931), mayor of Dachau, 1966–1996

Lorenz Reitmeier was born of a well-to-do family in Dachau in 1931.[2] (See ill. 69.) He experienced the occupation of Dachau and the liberation of the concentration camp as a 14-year-old without great fears, although the US army confiscated his parents' house and set up its headquarters at his grandparents' farm. In the first days after liberation, a liberated Polish priest took the curious youngster into the KZ and showed him some of the horrifying sights, including the train full of corpses. More than two decades later, in 1966, Reitmeier was elected mayor of Dachau as an independent candidate, an office he held for thirty years – proof of his great popularity and ability to mediate between the majority conservative Catholic CSU and the more moderate Social Democrats. In May 1966, and at several commemorative celebrations in the KZ memorial site thereafter, Reitmeier represented the city of Dachau, but he never gave a speech in the memorial site.[3] A man of the center, he also participated in anniversary celebrations of the "other" side, too: for instance in May 1969 at the graves of the "White guard" that had crushed the revolutionary "Red guard" in a crucial battle near Dachau in 1919. At that ceremony Reitmeier stood comfortably among representatives of veterans' organizations and the neo-Nazi NPD.[4]

After taking office, Reitmeier became a crusader for the "other Dachau," which in his opinion underwent a change from a "charming artists' retreat to the site of horrifying cruelties" through no fault of its own.[5] For example,

Reitmeier reacted quickly to reproaches by the Social Democratic youth group Jusos in 1970 that the city had done too little to define its relationship to the camp.

It is worth examining Reitmeier's impressive 1970 speech at a special session of the city council on the twenty-fifth anniversary of liberation more closely, because it reveals how the 1948ers adapted the three postwar myths inherited from their careerist Nazi 1933er elders.[6] Throughout the 1970s it was quoted in news reports and publications, and it remained in circulation well into the 1980s – I received a copy from city hall in 1985.[7] Thus it can be taken as a benchmark of change in the three founding myths a quarter-century after the end of the Nazi era.

Reitmeier began his speech with a narrative about how he had personally experienced Dachau's liberation in 1945 at age 14, which he embedded in the standard disclaimers of the myth of ignorance. One of his strongest memories was the change in the attitude of the occupation soldiers after they had seen the camp (4). Two or three days later, when a liberated Polish priest took him inside, Reitmeier saw what the Americans had seen:

> Instantaneously I realized what feelings had overcome the . . . American officers during their trip through the camp . . . I could not hold it against them that they, in the face of such massive horrors, simply could not believe that we Dachau citizens knew *almost* nothing about it (emphasis added).

After softening the claim to ignorance, Reitmeier narrated a long anecdote about the origin of the train full of corpses standing on the camp rail spur at liberation. He described with particular detail how, in the village of Namring, a local priest had collected 200 kilograms of potatoes and hundreds of kilograms of bread for the surviving prisoners while the train was held up in the village for four days (6). After portraying this example of "resistance" to the murderous policies of the Nazi regime, Reitmeier backtracked to 1933 to describe the initial victimization of Dachau, which he described with outrage:

> with no consideration of our over one thousand year history, without consideration of the centuries-old . . . good reputation of Dachau, without asking the Dachau populace and quite contrary to their majority will, this first KZ was set up on the grounds of the former gunpowder factory.

Reitmeier noted that the camp should not have been named "Dachau" at all, because at that time the property belonged to the community of Prittlbach; not until 1939 was it incorporated into Dachau township.[8] Reitmeier then listed Dachau's famous writers and artists, adding a few names to Schwalber's 1945 list (8f).[9] After a long and imposingly detailed description of life in the camp, the mayor explicitly rejected the use of the myth of victimization to relativize the brown-collar crimes – they could not be diminished by comparing them to other atrocities and injustices. He then returned to the issues of guilt and resistance (12). Repeating his claim that the city of Dachau had no part in the decision to set up the concentration camp, he continued with an image of amelioration as resistance:

> The many proofs of assistance, even under personal risk, have often been mentioned. I still remember very well with what persistence and willingness to help, even the children of the old city center tried all possible ways, in spite of prohibitions and the watchful SS guards, to give bread to the emaciated prisoners working outside the camp.

Reitmeier then returned to the lament of victimization, but now in an updated, 1970s' version – victimization by foreigners interested in the Nazi past. No longer did he use it in conjunction with the myth of ignorance for self-exoneration, however. Now he combined it, as his crematorium-closing predecessors had done in the 1950s, with the myth of resistance to establish a "right" to resist continuing victimization in the present:

> In spite of this undeniable historical situation we Dachauers *still suffer today as we did in 1945* because the city and its inhabitants are, again and again, thoughtlessly identified with the horrors and crimes of the KZ. Also, the attempt is continually made to burden our city with a special responsibility above and beyond the general guilt for the crimes of a whole state . . .
> To burden Dachauers with a special responsibility for these events would be *genuine* [sic!] injustice: injustice even for those citizens who lived in Dachau from 1933 to 1945. But still greater injustice for the younger generation that came of age after the war, and for the thousands of expellees and other new citizens who did not move into our city until after the war (13f; emphasis added).

The final sentence indicates another change in the use of the three myths attributable to the generational shift during the 1960s. For the Germans born after the late 1920s, having been too young to have been guilty was a better reason for rejecting responsibility than not having known about the crimes. Thus the myth of ignorance was jettisoned by this cohort of 1948ers, to be replaced by what Federal Chancellor Helmut Kohl (born in 1930, a year before Reitmeier) called, in a classic formulation during his 1984 visit to Israel, the "grace of late birth."[10] But as the *J'accuse* authors had argued in the 1960s, young age did not mean that Germans were free of the behaviors and attitudes which enabled the perpetration of the brown-collar murders.[11] In fact, the claim implies that this cohort might have behaved just like its careerist Nazi 1933er and 1943er predecessors, if Nazism had still held sway over Germany when it reached maturity.

Reitmeier continued with a call to resistance that characterized official city policy until the mid-1990s: "We must do everything we can to oppose those unjust prejudices [against town residents] as well." Reitmeier himself worked tirelessly to promote the "other Dachau's" good image. In 1975 he was presented with a medal by the international committee of Dachau survivors for his assistance with the thirtieth anniversary liberation celebration. He thereby gained permission to distribute, in the concentration camp museum, a color brochure extolling the picturesque attractions of the city.

Reitmeier also tried diligently (albeit unsuccessfully) to find a "sister city" for Dachau,[12] and he collected and published a multivolume edition of all known paintings painted in and of Dachau, when it had been a popular artists' colony earlier in the century.[13] In the preface to the final volume of the trilogy, Reitmeier pithily formulated the purpose of his project:[14]

> Friends of art and the world will be shown that Dachau is and was more than the lamentable name of twelve years of horrors. The name Dachau, which was misused so inhumanely and without asking shall be restored to at least some of its old glory as one of the most important and largest German artists' colonies outside of the metropolitan centers of artistic production.

He presented the boxed set to foreign dignitaries who came to visit the memorial site, for instance East German head of state Erich Honnecker in 1987 (ill. 70).[15]

Reitmeier suffered humiliating setbacks when he attempted to introduce leading foreign personalities to Dachau's more charming side. For instance when the British journalist Hugh Carleton Greene, who had been a BBC correspondent in Berlin before the war, and whose reports on the liberation of Belsen had electrified the British public, visited the camp in the 1980s, he brusquely pushed away the proffered three volumes of Dachau art with the words "That doesn't interest me."[16] And when Ronald Reagan was looking for a concentration camp site to visit during his 1985 trip to Germany, Reitmeier invited him to the city as well.[17] Reagan, as it turned out, decided to go to Belsen instead, because the parklike memorial site there was not as "grisly" as Dachau, as his press secretary Deaver put it. Reitmeier retired in 1996 and was succeeded by a mayor who made it his policy to integrate the history of the camp into that of the town.

Before we turn to the events of the 1970s, a look at statistical evidence suggests that it is appropriate to generalize based on the impressionistic evidence of individual biographies.

Visitors' statistics: the post-1970 boom

There is some "hard" evidence that fundamental changes began in the 1970s, reached a highpoint in the 1980s, and moved towards a resolution in the 1990s. Dachau visitors' statistics suggest that this was a generational phenomenon. A look at the aggregate number of visitors to the memorial site shows a jump around 1960 from roughly 160,000 visitors per year to about 360,000 visitors per year (ill. 73). Then from 1975 the curve of total visitors climbs steeply to about 900,000 per year in the early 1980s, where it oscillates sharply before falling off slightly to a new plateau of about 700,000 in the mid-1990s.[18] The sharp oscillations of the 1980s are due to events such as the closing of the memorial site on Mondays for maintenance since 1983; the upsurge of interest during the anniversary years 1985 and 1990, and a falling off of foreign (especially American) visitors at the time of the Gulf War in 1991. Nonetheless, the plateaus of the 1950s, 1960s, later 1980s, and later 1990s are clearly visible, as are the periods of change in the early 1960s and later 1970s.

A closer look at the breakdown between German and foreign visitors allows a more precise dating of transitions. The two curves do not begin to diverge until after 1965, when the number of German visitors falls off slightly and does not begin to pick up again until 1974, five years later than the climb in the number of foreign visitors. Thereafter the number of Germans climbs more steeply until 1979, when it again begins to level off in comparison to the more constantly rising number of foreign visitors. Looking at yet another level of detail within the German visitors, we can see that the proportion of Germans coming to the Dachau memorial site in organized youth and school groups increased dramatically during the 1960s and 1970s, from ca. 2.5 percent in 1965 to 14 percent in 1970, to 21 percent in 1975 and 42 percent in 1980.[19] The curve rose much more gradually to 50 percent in 1990, after which it jumped to and then oscillated around ca. 60 percent through the middle of the decade. The steep rise from the late 1960s to 1980 reflects the generational transition in interest in the Nazi past during the 1970s. Even if most of these groups of young Germans came to Dachau at the initiative of their 1968er teachers, the subsequent plateau indicates that interest in the memorial site was strong enough to be self-sustaining.

It is difficult to assess the effects of other factors on the number of visitors to Dachau, such as the rising standard of living, which increased leisure and travel time, and the role of improved transportation infrastructure (availability of school buses, quality of autobahns, construction of a commuter railway to Dachau, etc.). A comparison with two other Bavarian tourist attractions, the Deutsches Museum of Science and Technology in Munich, frequented primarily by Germans, including especially school groups, and Neuschwanstein castle, equally popular among foreigners, can help to answer this question (ill. 74). The relatively steady upward climbs (with a slight steepening in the late 1960s) in these curves indicate that the sharp climbs and plateaus for Dachau are not attributable to external factors of accessibility. The bar graphs of youth groups going to Dachau and the Deutsches Museum also show that there is a clear lag for Dachau, which can be explained by the willingness of younger teachers to organize visits to the former concentration camp.

Against this background of generational change in the 1970s, the following chapters outline how the original three myths were challenged and eventually overcome first at the local, then at the national level. This was by no means a smooth process. Especially during the 1980s proponents of the three myths commanded substantial media attention. Nonetheless, in the so-called Historians' Debate and in the attempt to establish a national victims' memorial in Bonn in the mid-1980s, counterattacks from "incorrigibles" whose personal identity had become too deeply vested in the three myths were successfully warded off. The 1990s were a period of searching for appropriate ways to develop nonmythic images of the Nazi past in the youngest German generations. A concluding examination of the current plans to revise the Dachau memorial site shows that vestiges of the three postwar myths are still present in the process of historical education. Explicit consideration of these mythic legacies suggests ways to improve the pedagogy of the Nazi past for the coming millennium.

Like the late 1950s, the 1970s were a decade of gradual, subterranean changes in West Germany's collective valuation of its Nazi past.

43   Catholic "Chapel of the Mortal
Agony of Christ" by Josef
Wiedemann, 1960. The bell
tower was donated by Austrian
survivors in 1961. Rounded
stones from the Isar river were
patterned around a concrete
shell. A crown of thorns made of
rail-like steel girders hovers over
the entrance. Note the ring of
dwarf oak trees and grass
surrounding the building
(author).

44   Suffragan Bishop Neuhäusler
striking the cornerstone of the
Carmelite convent with a
symbolic hammer, April 1963
(Richardi [ed.], *Dachauer
Dokumente*, vol. II, 78).

45   Aerial view of the Carmelite
convent and Catholic chapel.
Note how the entrance to the
convent passes through the
watchtower (courtesy Carmelite
convent).

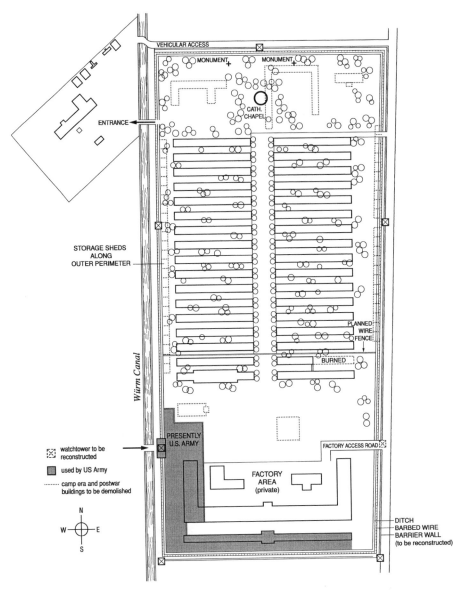

VEHICULAR ACCESS

MONUMENT

MONUMENT

CATH.
CHAPEL

ENTRANCE

STORAGE SHEDS
ALONG
OUTER PERIMETER

PLANNED
WIRE
FENCE

BURNED

Würm Canal

⊠ watchtower to be
reconstructed

■ used by US Army

...... camp era and postwar
buildings to be demolished

PRESENTLY
U.S. ARMY

FACTORY ACCESS ROAD

FACTORY
AREA
(private)

N
W ⊕ E
S

DITCH
BARBED WIRE
BARRIER WALL
(to be reconstructed)

46   Enhanced redrawing of a January 1960 plan by Josef Wiedemann, the
      architect of the Catholic chapel, "for the reconstruction of the fencing and
      watchtowers, and for the construction of the Catholic chapel." Wiedemann's
      design represented the idea of Bishop Neuhäusler, who wanted to plant trees
      among the barracks. The Bavarian Ministry of Finance approved the plan in
      March 1960, the city of Dachau in April (drawing by Steve Brown and author,
      after original plan reproduced in Hoffmann, *Gedächtnis der Dinge*, 78).

47   Aerial view of the dedication of the Catholic "Chapel of the Mortal Agony of Christ," August 1960. About 60,000 people attended the ceremony, probably more than had ever been in the site at one time. Note the camp-era greenhouses at top left and disinfectory cum restaurant at top right (see ill. 25). The 1953 Protestant Golgotha church that was moved to Ludwigsfeld is visible at the bottom edge (courtesy Carmelite convent).

48   Postcard of the "residential settlement Dachau-East," ca. 1955–60. The
individual pictures are captioned "square with church" (compare ill. 42),
"main altar of barrack church," "stone building," barracks store," and "camp
street" (courtesy of Dachau memorial site).

49   Postcard sold in the crematorium after 1960. The individual pictures show
"new incineration ovens," "old incineration ovens," and "monument of
warning" (courtesy of Dachau memorial site).

50   Third exhibition in the crematorium, 1960–4, in its provisional state in 1960. Note how the whipping horse is displayed (compare ills. 22, 23, 54) (courtesy of Dachau memorial site).

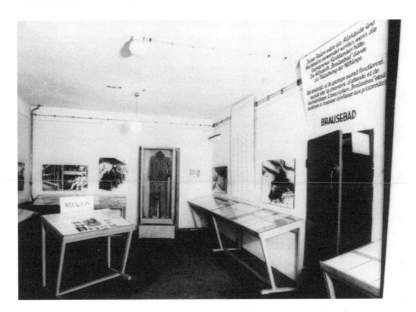

51   Third exhibition in crematorium, 1960–4, after 1961 renovation. Note the sign "Brausebad" (showers) with the erroneous explanation that the gas chamber was never functional (courtesy of Dachau memorial site).

GASKAMMER
getarnt als „Brausebad"
– war nicht in Betrieb

GAS CHAMBER
disguised as a „shower room"
– never used as a gas chamber

CHAMBRE A GAZ
„chambre de douche" camouflée
– ne fut jamais utilisée

CAMERA A GAS
camuffata da „bagno a doccia"
– non fu messa in funzione

Камера для газа
маскированная как „душ"
– не был в действии

52, 53   Gas chamber in the 1942 crematorium building, as it appeared after 1965, when the exhibition was moved to the service building. In German, English, French, Italian, and Russian the sign reads: "Gas chamber / disguised as a 'shower room' / – never used as a gas chamber" (author).

54   Exhibition in the central tract of the service building after 1965. Note the use of large photographs and the display of the whipping horse in an enclosure (courtesy of Dachau memorial site).

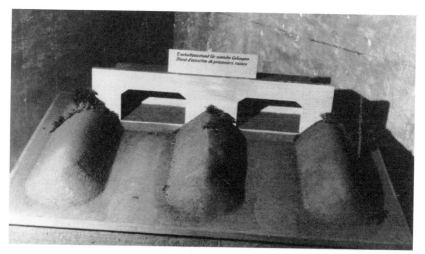

55   Model of the Hebertshausen shooting range displayed in the 1960–4 museum in the crematorium. Approximately 4,000–6,000 Soviet prisoners of war were executed at the shooting range in 1941 (courtesy of Dachau memorial site).

56   Monument by Will Elfers unveiled at the Hebertshausen shooting site on 3 May 1964. The inscription reads "Thousands of PRISONERS OF WAR were MURDERED here by the SS." In this period of high tension during the Cold War, no mention was made that the prisoners had been *Soviet* soldiers (author).

57

Leonard Roth speaking at the dedication of a cornerstone for the planned international memorial, September 1956. The stone's Latin inscription reads: "This first stone of a monument to be erected in memory of the victims of Nazism who died in the Dachau prisons in the years 1933–1945 was set here on 9 September 1956." This event marks the beginning to the public campaign to create a memorial site. The memorial itself was not begun until more than a decade later (courtesy DDW).

58

The 1968 international memorial with the 1956 cornerstone encased in Plexiglas, 1995 (author).

59   View through the international memorial (designed 1959, dedicated 1968),
      between the two reconstructed barracks, down the camp street to the
      Catholic chapel. The emaciated, twisted limbs of the blackened bronze
      figures are entwined like barbed wire to symbolize the suffering of the
      inmates (author).

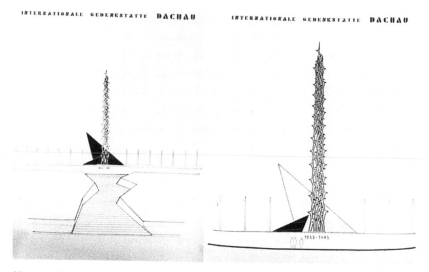

60   Design for an international memorial by Hansdietmar Klug, 1959. The 35 m
      tall towering forms glorify the resistance of the camp inmates. The German
      survivors favored this design, but survivors from other countries did not
      (courtesy of Dachau memorial site).

61   Chain link sculpture in the base of the international memorial, 1968. This
        sculpture was included in the monument to portray the solidarity among the
        inmates. However, the triangle badges are filled with enamel in the colors
        denoting all prisoner groups except "asocials" (black), "habitual criminals"
        (green), and homosexuals (pink). When this picture was taken in the late
        1970s, the World-War-I-era munitions factory buildings that became part of
        the Dachau SS training camp were still visible behind the trees (at center
        right) (author).

62   The quadrilingual inscription wall for the international memorial in Dachau,
        1968. The English inscription reads: "May the example of those who were
        exterminated here between 1933–1945 because they resisted Nazism help to
        unite the living for the defence of peace and freedom and in respect for their
        fellow men." The German text renders the murders more euphemistically:
        "… those who left their lives …" (author).

63   Jewish memorial building in Dachau, by Hermann Guttmann, built 1964–7.
A ramp descends between two jagged, stylized barbed-wire fences to the
barred entrance of this wedge-shaped building. A strip of white marble
extends through a hole in the roof to emerge as a menorah, a symbol of
Jewish resistance (author).

64   Protestant "Church of Reconciliation," by Helmut Striffler, built 1964–7.
Most of the naked concrete buildings, including the reading room, are
underground; only the chapel rises above ground level (author).

65   From left, Bavarian State Secretary Hugo Fink, former Bavarian cabinet minister and Dachau survivor Alois Hundhammer (with beard), Federal Minister Egon Franke, International Dachau Committee President Albert Guérisse (with hat and gloves), and Bavarian Youth League President Hermann Kumpfmüller walk down the camp street during the May 1970 memorial ceremony. Munich mayor Hans-Jochen Vogel (with chain pendant) is visible behind Hundhammer (dpa).

66   Dachau survivors try to prevent young Germans, who are protesting against the participation of NATO military formations, from disrupting a commemorative ceremony, 9 September 1968 (courtesy of Dachau memorial site).

67 Bavarian state police vans in the Holländerhalle, a World War I munitions factory building that was reused as part of the Dachau SS camp, ca. 1990. The US army used the complex from 1945 until 1971; since then four 100-man detachments of Bavarian state police have been stationed there (courtesy of Dachau memorial site).

68 Bavarian state police practicing the forcible evacuation of a building in the former Dachau SS camp, 1981. This exercise made headlines because megaphone announcements could be heard in the memorial site. This World War I munitions factory building was demolished in 1985 (see ill. 75) (Reinhard Papenfuss, *Areal der VI. Bereitschaftspolizeiabteilung Dachau*, 31).

69   Dachau Mayor Reitmeier displaying the city tourist brochure after the Dachau survivors' association allowed him to distribute free copies in the memorial site museum, Sept. 1985. Reitmeier saw this event as one of the highpoints of his campaign to promote the "other Dachau" (photo Nils Jørgensen).

70   Mayor Reitmeier shaking hands with East German President Erich Honecker, 11 September 1987. Members of the Amperthaler club in traditional dress behind Reitmeier wait to present a boxed three-volume set of Reitmeier's published collection of Dachau paintings to Honecker. The concentration camp entrance gatehouse is visible in the background (photo Nils Jørgensen).

71   Commemorative torchlight march by the German trade union youth on the anniversary of the 10 November 1938 pogroms, 7 November 1992. Since 1953 the trade union youth have sponsored this annual ceremony. In the early 1960s attendance peaked at 7,000. At the 1992 event Social Democratic Party chief and member of parliament Hans-Jochen Vogel, who had been mayor of Munich and Federal Minister of Justice, delivered the keynote address (photo Nils Jørgensen).

Comparison of Visitor Counts
and Catalog Sales

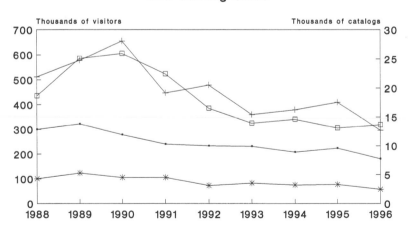

72   Graph showing the number of German (✳) and non-German (□) language museum catalogs sold at the memorial site, 1988–96. Comparison with changes in the rough counts of German (•) and foreign (+) visitors confirms that the number of visitors to the site fell off in the 1990s (author).

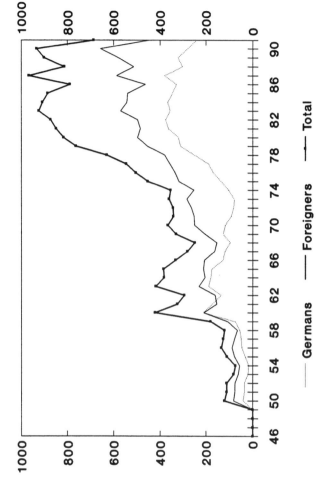

Number of Visitors to Dachau
(thousands)

——— Germans ——— Foreigners ——— Total

73   Graph of the number of foreign and German visitors to the Dachau memorial
      site, 1950–91 (author).

Number of Visitors
to major tourist attractions

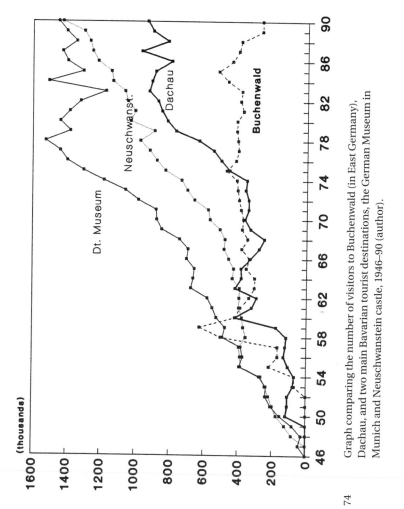

Graph comparing the number of visitors to Buchenwald (in East Germany), Dachau, and two main Bavarian tourist destinations, the German Museum in Munich and Neuschwanstein castle, 1946–90 (author).

75 *(above)* Demolition of the World War I munitions factory buildings near the former entrance to the SS camp, August 1985. In order to make the Bavarian state police barracks in the former SS camp more private, in the 1980s a number of historical buildings were torn down and high earthen mounds were thrown up (author).

76
Portion of the railroad track leading into the camp that was preserved as a memorial in 1987, May 1991. The sign reads "Railroad track to the former SS camp where between 1933 and 1945 tens of thousands of prisoners were transported into the concentration camp." The rest of the track was torn up in 1985 when young Germans suggested using the right of way to make a bicycle path from the town to the memorial site. The memorial's location is marked in ill. 1 (author).

77   Directional sign on a highway near the memorial site, July 1980. Since the
      1950s local authorities have resisted installing adequate signage directing
      visitors to the Dachau memorial site. Only in the 1980s did the situation
      begin to improve (photo Ursula Höhne).

78   Main directional sign seen by visitors arriving in Dachau by train, 1995.
      Poorly lit in the pedestrian tunnel under the tracks, the memorial site bus
      lines are given in small type (author).

79   Street signs at Resistance Square in downtown Dachau, 1995. The signs read:
"Resistance Square," "Reference to the resistance by Dachau citizens against
the NS regime (1945)," "Delivery vehicles permitted." The square was named
in November 1945, but during the following decades the name was lost. In
1981 a journalist found a reference to it in an old newspaper, and a new sign
was quickly installed. See ill. 1 for location (author).

80   Main entrance to the memorial site on a typical Monday, after the Monday
closing was instituted in January 1983. The closing was instituted instead of
increasing the maintenance staff so that the grounds could be adequately
maintained. Although thousands of people are turned away on Mondays
each year, until 1999 the Bavarian government refused even to consider
measures to reopen the site on Mondays (photo Nils Jørgensen).

81   Group of Roma (gypsies) seeking asylum from their forced repatriation to war-torn Yugoslavia in the Protestant Church of Reconciliation, 18 May 1993. The cross on the wall depicts the main entrance of Auschwitz-Birkenau. In the late 1970s persecuted groups in West Germany began to use concentration camp memorial sites to highlight their plight (Leonhardt Frank, dpa).

82   Group of German homosexuals carrying a memorial plaque from the Protestant church to the official commemorative room in the museum, 18 June 1995. The inscription on the pink granite plaque reads "BEATEN TO DEATH / KILLED AGAIN BY SILENCE / To the homosexual victims of National Socialism / The homosexual initiatives of Munich, 1985" (photo Zehnder).

83   One of the signboards with large historical photographs erected in 1985 in an attempt to convey more vividly the history of the site, which is now barren except for a second generation of poplar trees, August 2000. About a half-dozen such signs were erected in the mid-1980s. From 1999 to 2001 about thirty smaller, more text-based tablets are being added (author.

84   Group of German students weeding the reconstructed ditch, ca. 1996. Since the early 1980s many youth groups have come to Dachau for week-long seminars about the concentration camp. Until 1998, when the Dachau youth guest house opened, most of them came in the summer and stayed in a tent camp. Note the scaffolding in the background: when the roof was repaired, dormer windows were added to make the caretaker's attic apartments more comfortable (photo courtesy of *Dachauer Nachrichten*).

85

The first visit by a Bavarian minister president to the Dachau concentration camp memorial site took place in March 1993. Here Minister President Max Streibl (right) is accompanied by Simon Snopkowski, the president of the Israelite Cultural Community. Streibl also visited the crematorium and bowed before the ovens. In the 1980s visits by foreign dignitaries became common (see ill. 70), but Bavarian government leaders avoided the site until the 1990s (Augstein, dpa).

86

Russian General Lebed visited the Dachau memorial site in January 1997. Here memorial site director Barbara Distel is showing Lebed and his wife a model of the camp in the museum. Note the inscription on the roof of the model of the service building (photo Nils Jørgensen).

87   The concentration-camp-era inscription "smoking prohibited" discovered on a wall in the west wing of the former service building during renovation work in 1998, August 2000. When at first only the word "prohibited" was visible, experts were enthusiastic about preserving and displaying this original relic. When the entire inscription was uncovered, revealing a banal prohibition at odds with common conceptions of life in concentration camps, the enthusiasm for its preservation and display waned (author).

88   Also discovered in the west wing, on a wall added after 1945, were three murals depicting snow-covered mountains, a Hawaiian sunset, and a view of Manhattan (pictured here), August 2000. These murals document how the US army attempted to take symbolic possession of the site after 1945. They would provide a powerful backdrop for an exhibition on the postwar uses of the former concentration camp. However, some experts want to tear down the wall because it is not original (Nazi-era) (author).

13

The 1970s: redefining the three myths and ending ignorance

In 1970, although the Nazi era had ended twenty-five years earlier, the myth of victimization was alive and well. Victimization by the Nazis since 1933 and by the Allies at the end of the war was no longer primary, however. Conservative members of the generation of the 1920s felt themselves to be victims of, to use Armin Mohler's phrase, "professional masterers of the past," who, in this view, indiscriminately assumed that all Germans past and present were responsible for the Nazi crimes. On the other hand, for reasons of age, the myth of ignorance was rapidly losing importance as an element of self-exoneration. The 1948er cohort of Mayor Reitmeier and Chancellor Kohl replaced it with a "myth of tender age." Finally, the myth of resistance had increased in importance. It had originally been undercut because resistance was predicated on knowledge of the crimes, and thus it conflicted with the myth of resistance. As the issue of knowledge became less important, the aspect of resistance could grow in magnitude, as it did. Originally, purported ignorance had been coupled with examples of victimization to establish innocence, with claims of resistance playing a secondary, supporting role to that same end. By 1970 innocence was presumed, and claims of continuing victimization were coupled with calls for resistance to establish an explicit "right" to pursue whatever goals the claimant wished to attain. This phenomenon applied as much to leftist 1968ers as to conservative 1943ers and 48ers such as Reitmeier, Kohl, and CSU politician Franz Josef Strauss, who claimed in 1969 that West Germany's economic achievements gave it a "right not to want to hear about Auschwitz."[1]

We can trace the rise and fall of this second generation of myths in a series of debates on the editorial pages of the local Dachau newspapers. Seven times from 1971 to 1981 the Dachau populace used its newspapers as a forum to debate the city's relationship to the Nazi past, as embodied by the concentration camp memorial site.

From victims of Nazism to victims of tourism and the media

On 23 May 1971 West German national TV Channel One broadcast a film entitled "DAH – Dachau's Mark of Cain" (DAH are the letters on the license plates of cars registered in Dachau county). The main thrust of the program was twofold. First it contrasted daily life in the city of Dachau, as epitomized by the annual *Volksfest* (similar to Munich's famous *Oktoberfest*), with the horrors of the concentration camp. Then it showed how the residents of the town "suffer" from the consequences of most foreigners' equation of the town and the KZ. The title of the program was derived from stories dating back to the early 1950s, in which cars with Dachau plates were allegedly vandalized in foreign countries.[2] A TV journalist interviewed several Dachau groups and businesses, for example the Boys' Choir and the Dachau Paper Works, which had experienced negative reactions due to the town/camp's negative image abroad. Following the broadcast the local newspapers and the mayor received what they called a "flood" of letters from all over Germany.[3]

The mayor released to the press a selection of the letters he had received regarding the TV report. All of those published emphasized two main themes: (1) that the town of Dachau bore and bears no guilt or responsibility for the events in the concentration camp above and beyond that borne by any other German town, and (2) that the "other" or "actual" Dachau, namely the residence of a seventeenth-century Electoral Prince and the artists' retreat, received too little coverage in the program. The published letters thus support the newer version of the myth of victimization: Dachau township was now being unjustly vilified by foreigners and the national media.

One of the letters invoked a correspondingly updated version of the myth of resistance in order to highlight the injustice of the victimization. The local Social Democratic Party (SPD) organization no longer claimed the townspeople had aided the camp prisoners during the Nazi era. Rather, spokesperson Wolfgang Spreitler highlighted postwar local support for the survivors' effort to create a memorial site. This, he claimed, was evidence that the townsfolk were not trying to cover up the unpleasant past. In this view, the TV report neglected to show the "countless instances of assistance for *former* KZ prisoners and *especially* within the framework of the dissolution of the refugee camp [1962–4], how by its establishment of the East Dachau settlement [new housing for the barracks residents], the town of Dachau proved its will to practice genuine mastery of the past" (emphasis added).[4]

The "bad tourist"

In March 1972 the next outpouring of popular sentiment was also triggered by Dachau's perceived postwar victimization, but this time the emphasis was shifted to the perpetrator of that victimization. The letters were prompted by the *Munich Merkur*'s request that readers respond to its report about letters Morton Frank, a US doctor who had visited the camp, had written to the German Consulate in Washington and the Dachau Tourist Office. In those letters Frank complained about the town's lack of sensitivity towards the Nazi past.[5] Frank noted that the city bus line that went by the memorial site ran only once per hour, that it was painted red and covered with advertising slogans, and that the main street leading to the site is named Sudetenlandstrasse, after the area of Czechoslovakia which Chamberlain had conceded to Hitler in an attempt to stave off war in 1938. It was also a region of postwar victimization of Germans, because they were expelled from Czechoslovakia after the end of the war.[6]

Published opinion in Dachau had hitherto portrayed the city as the victim of insensitive national news media and foreign tourists flocking to the site. This time the local letter-writers went on the offensive, led by the *Merkur*'s report, which did its best to trivialize Frank's suggestions. The letter-writers were outraged, for instance, at the suggestion that the memorial site bus be devoid of advertising. However, there is nothing inherently absurd about specially marking the bus as a sign of respect for the dead of the concentration camp. After all, voices in Dachau, including some contributors to this debate, continue to point out the "disrespectful" attire of tourists who visit the site.

Morton Frank was branded as a representative of a country which had not only "exterminated the native Indian population," threatened to "reduce [the town of] Dachau to ashes and rubble," and eradicated Hiroshima, but also recently napalm-bombed Vietnam and perpetrated the massacre at My Lai, as no fewer than six of eighteen letter-writers pointed out. Several writers noted that foreign, especially US, visitors were as impious as Frank alleged the Dachauers were, wearing "tasteless shorts" to the memorial site, and talking loudly there.

These portrayals of Dachau township's detractors as "perpetrators" were not new. As we have seen, the perception that camp survivors were criminals was already common in the 1950s. The most interesting feature of these 1972 letters was not so much their content, but their massive number: the readers explicitly understood the newspaper's call for responses as a call to resist the defamation of their city. Andreas Liegsalz wrote: "People who think and make demands similar to those of Dr. Morton Frank should be decisively opposed." And E. Schmalz enjoined his fellow citizens: "We should finally muster the courage to face foreign troublemakers . . . I think that it is finally time to emancipate ourselves from this collective guilt." At this time, however, the suggested solutions to the victimization perpetrated by visitors such as Frank were still self-defensive, ranging from renaming the town "Thoma City" (after the town's famous-son author), to expanding the memorial site to include all the mass killings of history, so that foreign visitors would see that their countries were no more or less guilty than Dachau or Germany.

Eradication as resistance

A much more radical means of resisting Dachau's continuing victimization was proposed in a public exchange in January 1975. It began when a letter to the editor calling for the elimination of the Dachau memorial site was printed in the format of a news report with a by-line and photographs under the headline "End the Shameful Spectacle." This article triggered the longest and most varied public debate about the uses and abuses of the memorial site since the war.[7]

While the initial responses employed the standard arsenal of mythical arguments to make their point, their phraseology was a step more explicit than in the responses to Morton Frank in 1972. The perpetrators of Dachau's victimization were more imaginatively portrayed. In an appeal for "mercy" from the "sons and daughters of Israel," the first author complained that the "brats of civilization" with their "flaccidly bored faces" were coming to Dachau "voracious for adventure," to see a "chamber of horrors." When they were finished, Dieter Hentzschel noted, they would eat "hot dogs with lots of ketchup." However, his primary concern was to resist such impiety, to put an end to the victimization of Dachau's reputation. With reference to his young age, this first author explicitly abandoned the myth of ignorance, replacing it with the myth of tender age. As a "squirt" standing at the side of the road, Hentzschel wrote, he saw both the cattle cars entering the camp with "clawlike hands" and "white faces" in the ventilation slits, and the oxcarts full of corpses leaving it for the Leiten gravesite.[8] It was "indebtedness to these dead," he claimed, that obligated him to advocate the closure of the memorial site.

The elimination of remains as a form of resistance remained a major theme of the exchange, accompanied by the familiar stigmatization of critics as perpetrators. A Dachau reader who responded critically to the initial letter-article was in turn reprimanded by a third reader who pointed out that, in his opinion, 90 percent of the visitors were indeed rubbernecks looking for gruesome thrills, and, in light of Vietnam and 66 million victims of Soviet concentration camps since 1918, those foreign visitors (or their countries) were no better than the Germans. If the memorial site should continue to exist, he concluded, then it should be given a primarily religious character with chapels and convents, in which literature about all crimes against human rights the world over would be available. Somewhat anachronistically relying on the "good Nazi" stereotype of the 1950s, a fourth reader claimed to be intimately familiar with the camp because he had been interned there after the war, and then employed by the US army.[9] He described Dachau as a "reception and transit camp for other KZs and not an extermination camp." He claimed to be "for the memorial site in Dachau," but only if everything shown there reflected his "true" version of its innocuous history. A fifth reader suggested that Dachau be turned into a "memorial park" with "quiet playgrounds for small children, flowers, bushes, trees." The former central KZ building and the museum in it were to "disappear," since the documents and pictures could be "summarized in a book." The German Dachau survivors' association put an end to this wishful speculation by requesting an official statement from the Dachau city council. Since the memorial site was guaranteed by an international treaty and under the care of the Bavarian government, the council would have been foolish to support the readers' demands. In a judiciously worded statement – published as a letter to the editor – Mayor Reitmeier announced the council's standpoint. After conceding that the suggestions were "purely theoretical," the council stated that it was "united" with the survivors in condemning the KZ crimes. Nonetheless, the statement continued, it also "valued the fundamental right of free expression of opinion" of all Dachau citizens, "even with respect to the memorial site."[10] Still, Dachau's elected council concluded, in the interest of the "decent Dachau," it would be better not to damage Dachau township's reputation in the worldwide media by publicly demanding the removal of the site.

Reitmeier's 1975 letter put a temporary end to local public demands for eradicating the memorial site, but it did not end quieter efforts to eradicate historical remains of the concentration camp.[11] In fact, his statement implied that when eradication might not damage the city's reputation, it could be practiced. And indeed it was, well into the 1990s. In March 1983, for example, the West German association of Dachau survivors requested that the city council preserve a section of the railroad track leading into the concentration camp.[12] At that time, the council took no action. Two years later, when an association of pro-memorial-site interest groups began to lobby for the creation of a bicycle path from the town to the memorial site along that track, it was quickly torn up.[13] After another two years the survivors scored a minor victory. In 1987 the West German camp survivors requested that another section of concentration camp track leading along the perimeter of the former SS complex be preserved as a memorial.[14] Their request was granted, and the memorial stands today – in an alley well hidden from public view (ills. 1, 76).

That small victory did not mean that the town fathers were willing to preserve remains if they did not have to. In fact, it was probably a concession for the unannounced demolition, earlier that year, of the villa constructed for the camp commandant in 1938. Shortly after it was suggested as a site for an international youth hostel and education center, the town elders had it torn down (compare ill. 75).[15] In order to ensure that the nearby World War I-era quadriplexes for the armaments factory officials could not be used for the youth center either, they were also quietly demolished.[16] In both cases, the historic buildings could have been renovated to alleviate Dachau township's serious shortage of housing, as local groups had already suggested in 1980.[17]

In the 1990s, the destruction of buildings associated with the concentration camp continued. Early in the decade a number of barracks were torn down so that the housing project "Roman Grove" could be built abutting the south wall of the memorial site, overlooking the museum. Similarly, numerous buildings just outside the *Jourhaus* were torn down to clear the back entrance to the riot police compound. (Some of these are visible in ill. 3.) In 1998 the city of Dachau was still unwilling to preserve the remaining greenhouses from the camp plantation, even as the Bavarian Office of Historic Preservation was planning to add the plantation buildings to the list of historically protected objects.[18]

Cultural heritage as resistance

An alternative way of resisting Dachau's victimization than closing the memorial site and destroying historic remains was to emphasize the positive features of the town's history. When in 1977 a local newspaper reader criticized the tourist information available in the Dachau train station for ignoring the memorial site, the "right" of the townsfolk to improve Dachau's image became the explicit theme of the champions of Dachau's honor.[19]

City council member Bernd Sondermann of the center-left party SPD
pointed out that his party had spearheaded an initiative to put up new signs
at the main bus stops directing visitors to the memorial site (compare ills.
77, 78), but he also conceded that Dachau had a "legitimate right . . . to call
to mind not only the horrible events of the Nazi years."[20] A local businessman claimed that he had been able to "straighten out . . . the crooked image
of Dachau that obviously exists abroad" in personal conversations with his
business partners. He noted, however, that his private successes were
dwarfed by the prejudicial picture tens of thousands of visitors received at
the memorial site. He argued rhetorically:

> Why can't the other side be clearly shown, namely how the populace helped
> the prisoners and what the consequences for them were? The nonpartici-
> pants, primarily youthful visitors, develop emotions and aggressions against
> the populace because they identify it with the KZ. Only with comprehensive
> information could the site serve to help prevent new injustice.

Finally, Mayor Reitmeier himself felt obliged to present his position on the
issue. He emphasized his own "resistance": "As first mayor I have worked
intensively to restore the good name of the city of Dachau since I took
office in 1966, and at every opportunity I emphasized the 'other Dachau.'
I hardly need to name further details." He went on, however, to name quite
a number of details about measures he had taken to reestablish Dachau's
good reputation: posting welcome signs on the city limits and a special
sign "near the KZ" (sic) referring to the "other Dachau," touting Dachau's
artistic past in public presentations, and attempting to convince the camp
survivors to permit the distribution of the town's "elegant brochure" in the
memorial site museum, in which the "true relationship between the town
and the horrors of the camp are explained" (compare ill. 69).

   Those negotiations were, he pointed out, especially difficult because of
the attitude of those he was bargaining with, whom he named the
"International KZ Committee" – probably so that he could avoid using the
name "Dachau" in its proper title ("International Dachau Committee").
Reitmeier's formulation inadvertently recalls Nazi propaganda stereotypes
of victims as perpetrators, such as "international Jewry" and "international
Bolshevism." At the end of his letter the mayor justified his inaction on
the issue with the myth of (present) victimization: no other changes in the
memorial site could be made because, according to his assessment of the
situation, the "KZ-Committee . . . would unfortunately not permit us to
undertake them." Thus, he concluded, "we must reconcile ourselves to the
realities."

The end of ignorance: re-realizing the Nazi past

Already in the late 1960s the Mitscherlichs had argued that what they called a "derealization" of the Nazi past was responsible for some of the deficits in the political culture of West Germany. In the 1970s West German pedagogues and historians alike accepted this analysis and began to take steps to remedy the situation. At the university level, from 1970 to 1978, the twenty-two largest West German universities offered a total of 650 courses on the period, an average of just under two per university per term.[21] Although the vast majority of them were probably taught with the traditional abstract approach (only two explicitly examined the murder of the Jews!), a cohort of young teachers was being trained to teach about the period.

During those same years, the broader West German public began to reexamine the person of Adolf Hitler. What became known as the "Hitler wave" began in 1973, with the publication of journalist Joachim Fest's popular biography *Hitler*, and a well-publicized study revealing school-children's ignorance about Hitler.[22] Fest's (b. 1926) portrayal emphasized how Hitler had "seduced" the German people – quite in line with the exonerating myth of victimization. When a film version of Fest's biography was released in 1977, it was a box office hit, reaching a true mass audience.[23] The highpoint of this Hitler wave, and perhaps the best evidence of the depth of popular German misconceptions about Hitler, was reached in the spring of 1983, when the West German illustrated magazine *Stern* announced that it had sixty-two volumes (!) of Hitler's hitherto unknown personal diaries in its possession.[24] Public interest – and *Stern*'s sales – skyrocketed, in spite of the implausibly benevolent image of Hitler presented by the forgeries. Although the diaries were soon unmasked as fakes, the initial widespread acceptance of the improbable "Adolf the Amiable" image presented by the texts reveals the general lack of knowledge about fundamental aspects of Hitler's character and his criminal state.

During this time of great popular interest in distorted portrayals of Hitler, further studies of schoolchildren's knowledge about him revealed no improvement in their dismal misconceptions about Nazism's revered Führer.[25] These studies cast a negative light on the educational establishment, prompting it to take at least face-saving action. In April 1978 the Standing Conference of all West German State Ministers of Education passed a resolution "On the Treatment of National Socialism in Teaching."[26] The resolution was very short; it merely ordered the Ministers of Education to direct their schools to implement the guidelines set forth in the wake of the antisemitic incidents in 1960.[27] This action reveals how empty the commitment to improve education about Nazism had been up to that time. In fact, much of the innovative curricular material on Nazism available in the 1970s was developed by individual teachers without state support.[28]

At the same time, the "history of everyday life" (*Alltagsgeschichte*) movement – similar to the history workshop movement sweeping through the Anglo-Saxon world – began to take hold in West Germany.[29] The mammoth project "Bavaria in the NS Period," begun by Martin Broszat at the Munich Institute for Contemporary History in 1973, was a major breakthrough for focusing this movement on the National Socialist period.[30] It included the first, and as of this writing, still the only detailed history of the Dachau camp by a West German historian.[31]

By the end of the 1970s there is evidence that the myth of ignorance and its corollary image of the "clean camp" were being replaced by a wealth of historical detail in local historical consciousness in Dachau. In March 1978 the Dachau edition of the *Süddeutsche Zeitung* published a 16-year-old schoolboy's report about his visit to the memorial site. In response a retired minister claimed that "Dachau was a prison camp," as the headline over the letter put it, and that no one had ever been gassed there.[32] The detailed responses to that claim not only helped to establish a standard of public knowledge about the crimes committed in the camp, but also clearly revalued learning about those crimes as more important than continuing to profess past ignorance about them.[33]

The definitive end to the public expression of the myth of ignorance in Dachau, however, did not come until 1981. It was predicated on one longer-term and one short-term development. The longer-term development was the emergence of a new cohort, the 1979ers (born 1954–66), who were comparatively free from mythic legacies; the short-term one was the 1979 broadcast of a TV miniseries that made the Holocaust so concrete that the 1933ers admitted some knowledge in order to participate in a discussion with their 1979er grandchildren.

The TV miniseries *Holocaust*: learning the victims' point of view

In the context of the rising interest in the history of everyday life in the United States during the 1970s, ABC-TV's film version of Alex Haley's epic biographical novel about black slavery in the United States, *Roots*, was a phenomenal success. Seeking a similarly spectacular media event, ABC's competitor NBC commissioned Gerald Green, author of several books about Nazi Germany, to write a family-based miniseries about the Nazi attempt to exterminate all Jews.[34] Green's miniseries was a great success when it was broadcast in the US in April 1978, even though it did not attract quite as many viewers as *Roots*. Peter Märthesheimer, a producer for the West German TV station WDR, immediately began to negotiate bringing the miniseries to Germany. It was broadcast by the BBC in England, then in Belgium, and in September 1978 in Israel.[35] Although there were many reservations about broadcasting a fictionalized Hollywood version of the German attempt to exterminate the Jews, the telecasts in other countries made the German resistance to showing the film look awkward. In October 1978 a German telecast date in January 1979 was announced, and a flurry of preparatory activity ensued.

Educational organizations commissioned teaching aids and TV guides, magazines published special issues, and national surveys were conducted.[36] On 9 November 1978, the fortieth anniversary of *Kristallnacht*, the persecution of the Jews was discussed as never before on the pages of newspapers from the largest cities to the smallest towns.[37] That heightened the anticipation of the film. In mid-January German Channel One broadcast two historical documentaries, *Antisemitism*, and *Final Solution*.[38] During all of this public pre-film activity, German critics from across the political spectrum were almost unanimously negative in their anticipatory assessments of the film.[39] However, after a two-day WDR press seminar led by Margarete Mitscherlich on 11–12 January 1979, the media assessment began to turn.[40] Both the fear of breaking the taboo of silence and the fear of trivialization were replaced by an acceptance of the didactic benefits of broadcasting the film.

The four-night broadcast beginning on 28 January sparked an unexpected and completely unprecedented audience response. Over the course of the four nights the ratings rose from 31 to 40 percent of the entire TV viewing audience, and ultimately 48 percent of the entire West German population over 14 years of age saw at least one segment of the series.[41] The call-in shows after each installment attracted from 11 to 18 percent of the viewing audience with a total of over 33,000 calls, four times the number received by NBC during the US broadcast. Contemporary observers noted that the public discussion prompted by the film rivaled that of *The Diary of Anne Frank* in the late 1950s and of Rolf Hochhuth's drama *The Deputy* in 1962.[42] While some indicators, such as public opinion polls, suggest that within a few months of the broadcast public opinion about issues such as racism and antisemitism had returned to pre-broadcast levels, other evidence shows that the West German broadcast of *Holocaust* catalyzed a preexisting trend toward a less mythically tabooized discussion of the Nazi past.[43] Historian Jeffrey Herf assessed its impact succinctly:[44]

> *Holocaust* did fracture continuity in consciousness in West Germany. It put the Right on the defensive. It was . . . a prod to the Left to give up some of its "defensive gestures" . . . that precluded a more fruitful discussion within the Left of National Socialism and the Holocaust.

A closer examination of the topics discussed both by the mainstream mass audience and among the German left reveals challenges to and transformations of the three founding myths.[45] (The criticism from the right merely reflects the continuing adherence of that group to the three myths.) Herf outlines four predominant themes in the left-wing reception of the series. First, left critics claimed that the show and its broadcast reflected capitalist and Zionist interests. This identification of Americans and Jews as perpetrators was a direct reflection of the myth of victimization, as was the fourth theme Herf names, the comparison of the Holocaust to the war in Vietnam. The second left-wing criticism focused on the possible reading of the film as implying that National Socialism had ended in 1945, instead of pointing out the putatively fascist structures that persisted in present-day Germany. This criticism was both a reaction to the decades of silence engendered by the myth of ignorance, and a consequence of the 1968ers' legacy of the myth of resistance: the determination to snuff out possible fascist tendencies. The third theme Herf observes shows that the resurgence of the myth of resistance in the 1970s did not go unnoticed: some left-wing critics worried that the film might foster a "mythology of [German] resistance where none in fact took place."[46] As we will see, this fabrication of resistance is precisely what was happening in Dachau.

These four left-wing topics, however, were not the primary concerns of the mainstream West German populace, represented by the callers and letter-writers after the broadcast. By far the most heatedly discussed issue was what contemporaries had known about the systematic murder of the Jews.[47] Public confessions by the editors of the illustrated magazines *Spiegel* and *Stern* opened the doors to a national reckoning with the myth of ignorance. In the first issue of his magazine after the broadcast, *Stern* editor Henri Nannen (b. 1913), a 1933er, wrote: "I, at any rate, I knew that in Germany's name defenseless people were being exterminated in the way vermin are extinguished. And unashamed, I wore the uniform of an officer in the German air force. Yes, I knew about it and was too cowardly to resist."[48] This public outpouring reflects at the national level another phenomenon we have already observed in Dachau: the rejection of the myth of ignorance by the postwar cohorts, forcing its abandonment, at least in public pronouncements, by their elders.

Most German critics and foreign commentators such as Herf put aside their doubts about *Holocaust*'s educational, historical, and aesthetic merits when confronted by the massive public reaction triggered by the film.[49] Clearly a taboo had been broken, making a change in West Germany's recollection of the Nazi past possible. The victims became living, breathing people, instead of statistics and piles of emaciated corpses. As the evidence of change at the local level indicates, a transformation was in the offing. Peter Märthesheimer, the producer who initiated the West German broadcast, expressed this when he noted after the broadcast that "the shock of *Holocaust* was not caused primarily by any special quality of the series itself, but rather by the particular situation of our country, in our particular history, in our consciousness – and in our subconscious."[50] Indeed, following the extremist "resistance" that culminated in the terrorist "hot autumn" of 1977 (see chapter 12), a more rational examination of continuities between past and present set in.

The impact of the TV broadcast of *Holocaust* was so unexpected and so powerful that it is often portrayed as an isolated event, rather than as the result of changes that had been building for some time. We have already seen how the number of young visitors to Dachau mushroomed from the early 1970s, and how the history of everyday life movement had already begun to focus on the National Socialist period. A cluster of books published in the late 1970s, in which 1943er and 1948er children of 1918er and 1933er parents active in the Nazi period publicly "searched for the missing time" in their fathers' lives, is further evidence that the time was ripe for the victims of brown-collar crimes to be "re-realized" empathetically in the mass media.[51] These children's public search for their parents' Nazi past coincided with the rising interest of an even younger generation, the 1979er grandchildren of the 1933ers, in the lived history of National Socialism. This emerging interest provided an opportunity for the survivors of Nazi persecution and genocide to finally counter their mythical stigmatization as perpetrators. "Angry old men," as a 1979 publication called them, who had opposed Nazism found a receptive audience especially among these 1979er "grandchildren."[52]

Let us examine one member of this group, to see how this interest developed prior to the TV broadcast.

A 1979er discovers Nazism

In 1974 Jürgen Z. was among a group of 16-year-old tenth graders from a high school in Bavaria that visited the Dachau memorial site with their history teacher.[53] The trip was part of a history unit about the Nazi period. In the early 1970s only a modest proportion of all Bavarian high school classes visited a concentration camp memorial site (or even studied the Nazi period), although by the early 1980s a majority did both. In 1974 Jürgen Z.'s class was one of just over 1,000 groups of young people to tour the memorial site. Z., one of the brighter and more motivated students in that group, had prepared a special assignment researching the persecution of the Jews. Z.'s teacher, like Detlef Hoffmann, had been influenced by the ideas of the student movement in the late 1960s, and he devoted substantial classroom time to the study of Nazism. On the field trip to Dachau, Z. walked by himself at times because the unserious behavior of some classmates bothered him. The "subterranean shock" (as he later described it) of the visit, however, did not immediately prompt him to concern himself more deeply with the National Socialist past in Germany, although it did make him more sensitive to the plight of political prisoners.

A few years later, in 1977, as a member of Amnesty International, Jürgen Z. began to work in support of political persecutees in the Soviet Union. Human rights in socialist systems were his particular concern. Z. thought little about concentration camps until the early 1980s, when he moved to the town because his wife had taken a position in a Dachau textile factory. Z. began a journalism apprenticeship at the local newspaper. While writing a story about a local group working to improve the memorial site, he was caught up in the, as he put it, "magnetism" of the topic and its actors. Although he had not been able to watch the TV miniseries *Holocaust* when it was broadcast in January 1979, he noted that he was indeed affected by the impulses that were triggered by the film. Many close contacts with Dachau survivors deepened his knowledge and strengthened his commitment to keep the memory of the camp alive. He became one of the activists in the local politics of memory.

In the decade after Jürgen Z.'s first visit to the memorial site an abundance of opportunities opened up for students to follow up on such a visit in their home communities. Most of those opportunities arose from the "history of everyday life" movement, in which Z. also became active. This new "dig where you stand" approach to history was both localized and personal, focusing on individual people in their own home town. In 1988 Z., for example, began working in a Dachau group which investigated the fate of Dachau's Jews on *Kristallnacht* in 1938. Work such as this led Jürgen Z. to become an outspoken advocate of a center for youth encounters in Dachau, where young people could stay to deepen their experience of the history of the concentration camp (see chapter 15).

14

The 1980s: relinquishing victimization

By the end of the 1970s the myth of ignorance and its legacy of vague knowledge of life under Nazism had lost their hegemony in the West German public sphere. A younger cohort of Germans who came of age during that decade, their curiosity piqued by the TV miniseries *Holocaust* in 1979, began to investigate the history of everyday life (*Alltagsgeschichte*) during the Nazi era. The 1980s' West German history workshop movement, in contrast to its counterparts in the US and other Western European countries, thus focused specifically on the Nazi period. These local groups unearthed a wealth of detailed information about the Nazi-era populace's knowledge of the systematic persecution of "non-Aryan" victims. The West German history workshop movement soon revolutionized the teaching about Nazi history in the secondary schools and universities.

As public interest in the intentional victims of Nazism increased, a number of prominent 1943ers and 1948ers responded by pressing their own claims of German victimization, both under Hitler and after World War II, more stridently. This countereffect was most vividly represented by a 1948er filmmaker's wildly popular German answer to *Holocaust*, the TV miniseries *Heimat*, telecast in 1984. Its explicit intent was to portray everyday life under Nazism from the perspective of "ordinary" Germans. At the same time, a series of high-profile fortieth and fiftieth anniversary commemorations of Nazi-era events provided additional opportunites for the 48ers to impress the myth of victimization on younger cohorts, but they met with little success. By the end of the decade, West German politicians' pronouncements of past victimization fell upon overwhelmingly deaf ears. When the Berlin Wall, the paramount symbol of German victimization after World War II, was torn down during the unification of East and West Germany in 1989–90, the myth of victimization's fate was sealed. Its last proponents, members of organizations of ethnic Germans expelled from Eastern Europe in the 1940s, were gradually relegated to the margins of public discourse.

The effects of *Holocaust* on the educational establishment

One of the most concrete and immediate political effects of the 1979 TV broadcast was to focus public attention on the fourth parliamentary debate about the removal of the statute of limitations on mass murder, which, as discussed in chapter 7, had been extended for ten years in 1969.[1] In the discussions following the broadcast and in the debate itself in March, the question of the brown-collar crimes was brought up time and again. The film's empathetic personalization of the crimes created substantial public pressure to continue prosecution. A poll prior to the broadcast yielded 15 percent who thought that prosecution of brown-collar crimes should remain possible indefinitely; afterwards 39 percent of those who had seen the film and even 25 percent of those who had not seen it advocated removal of the limitation.[2] Even opponents of further prosecution cited the film as evidence that all of the trials to date had done little to educate the broader public, so that their educational effect could not be used to justify them. This time, parliament voted to extend the statute of limitations for murder in perpetuity.

The astonishing public reaction to the film also finally prompted the West German educational establishment to do more than pay lip service to improving instruction about the National Socialist period. In addition to lower profile measures such as further improvement of history textbooks and increased distribution of relevant publications by the Centers for Political Education, one of the furthest reaching changes was the selection of National Socialism as the topic of the annual national school competition for the "President's Prize."[3] Prior to 1980 typical topics had been "The 1848 Revolution" (1974), or, after the history of everyday life had taken hold, "The Working World" (1977), "Housing" (1978), and "Leisure Time" (1979). Because of *Holocaust*, however, in 1980 the directors doubled the length of time to complete projects and chose the themes "Everyday Life under National Socialism" prior to 1939 (1980–1), and during the war (1982–3), and then "Life in the Postwar Period" (1983–4).

The effects of the film on the competition were dramatic. Whereas between 3,000 and 5,000 pupils had participated in the earlier competitions, the number roughly tripled to almost 13,000 participants, a record that still has not been superseded.[4] The number of projects tripled as well, to over 2,100. Beneath these figures lies an even more important effect: a new generation of "1979er" German historians emerged from these competitions to play an important role in public education about the brown-collar crimes. On the local and national levels, their work has done a great deal to fill vacuous conceptions of life under Nazism with concrete detail, as the following examples illustrate.[5]

Anna Rosmus (b. 1960), a participant in the 1980–1 competition, became the most notorious member of this cohort of amateur historians when her story was made into a feature film, *The Nasty Girl*, in 1989.[6] While researching the history of anti-Nazi resistance in Passau, she encountered the myth of resistance, namely that church officials and many of the town's leading citizens had not been the anti-Nazis they claimed to have been.[7] Rosmus was denied access to documents, defamed, sued and denounced. After an arson attack and a threat to kidnap her daughter, Rosmus' case caught the attention of the national and international media. Finally, her study was published in 1984 with a preface by one of the justices of the West German Supreme Court. That same year she received the prestigious "Scholl Siblings Prize" in memory of the Munich student resisters, and in 1987 Kurt Tucholsky's widow bequeathed a death mask of the famous author to her in recognition of her steadfastness.

Rosmus went on to write several other historical books about Passau's Nazi past before leaving for Boston University to write a dissertation on the history of the Jews in Passau with Elie Wiesel.[8] She raised a great deal of local ire by unearthing the unsavory past activities of her fellow townsfolk. One doctor successfully sued her in a local court to remove information about him from her 1993 book about the treatment of pregnant slave laborers in the town – even though he could not disprove her allegations.[9]

Michael Brenner (b. 1964), whose case study of Jewish life in the town of Weiden during the Nazi period won a first prize in the 1982–3 competition, went on to become an acclaimed historian.[10] Brenner lectured at Brandeis University, and, when he accepted the University of Munich's brand new chair in Jewish History and Culture in 1997, became one of the youngest full professors in the country.[11] His institute at the University of Munich has rapidly become a center for research and education about German–Jewish history.[12] Brenner's success is just one example of the mushrooming German interest in learning about its eradicated Jewish culture. Whereas in the two decades prior to 1984 about 270 German studies of Jewish communities had been published, by 1990 about 1,700 more had appeared – an eighteenfold increase in average annual output![13]

In Dachau, the impact of the film was reflected numerically in the visitors' statistics. The number of German school classes and youth groups visiting the site shot up 55 percent from the 1978 level (which, by the way, had already seen a huge increase of 45 percent from the year before) (see ill. 73).[14] The rise in the total number of German visitors was large at 61,500, although it was essentially equal to the increase the previous year.[15] That the 1979 increase was a phenomenon especially among young Germans is indicated by the number of foreign visitors to the memorial site, which increased "only" 19 percent in 1979, with the number of foreign school and youth groups increasing 18 percent.[16] These were still substantial increases, since the figures for foreigners vary in general much less than those for Germans.

This quantitative jump was accompanied by qualitative changes, although they were somewhat slower in coming. One of the awards in the first President's history competition about the National Socialist period was won by Dirk Rumberg, with a study about "Everyday Life in Dachau in 1933."[17] While Rumberg was from the neighboring village of Haimhausen, there was also a marked increase in the research done by natives of Dachau, both for the history prize and on their own.[18] The most significant long-range development was the establishment, in 1981, of a local history workshop devoted to studying the Nazi period. The orientation and goals of this group and its leader, Hans-Günter Richardi, have shaped and continue to exert a strong influence on the local politics of the Nazi past in Dachau.[19] It is worth looking at the origins of this influential history club and its founder in greater detail.

Richardi, an older member of the 1968er cohort, went from Berlin to Munich in the early 1960s to begin a journalistic apprenticeship at the illustrated magazine *Quick*. Since he had found housing in nearby Dachau, the editor for whom he was working showed him an article he had recently written about the Dachau memorial site.[20] In 1975 Richardi met several Dachau survivors at the annual commemorative ceremony, and as a hobby he began to conduct research on the history of the town and the concentration camp. The first volume of that research, covering the years 1933 and 1934, was eventually published in 1983.[21] (In 1999 Richardi was still looking for a publisher for the second volume.) Meanwhile, in 1979, Richardi had made a name for himself by publishing the first tourist guide in German that included both the town and the concentration camp.[22]

With interest in the history of the camp soaring in the wake of *Holocaust*, Richardi organized local historians into an association he originally named "Why Only Dachau?" (*Warum gerade Dachau?*).[23] Its goal was to show that Dachau had been no different (at least not more pro-Nazi) than other German cities during the Nazi period. Based on that presumption, its members hoped to make the local populace amenable to learning more about the Dachau camp.

The Dachau branch of the conservative CSU invited Richardi to present his research findings after a convocation in October 1981. In classic formulations of the three myths Richardi argued three theses: (1) it was absolutely false that anyone in Dachau had any financial advantages because of the existence of the concentration camp – on the contrary, the SS had taken advantage of Dachau's "dire situation" and high unemployment; (2) prior to 1942 the Dachau citizens could not have known what happened behind the KZ walls, and (3) especially in Dachau there were a multiplicity of activities demonstrating solidarity and the will to help the prisoners.[24] After Richardi's presentation, the cultural coordinator in the city administration, Heinrich Rauffer, a member of the CSU, contradicted the first two of Richardi's theses by relating his personal experience. Rauffer, who had been a child at the time, told how his own parents' store near the camp had profited from the camp's business, and how customers in the store had talked, albeit mutedly ("*hinter vorgehaltener Hand*"), about what went on in the camp.

Thus contradicted by an essentially unassailable source, over the following two years Richardi and his history workshop jettisoned the myth of ignorance and concentrated on buttressing the myth of resistance. They collected anecdotes about instances where townspeople had helped camp inmates, and published them early in 1983 as a series of articles in the major Munich newspaper *Süddeutsche Zeitung*, where Richardi was an editor, then as a booklet, and finally, with the support of his history workshop (which had soon been renamed "For Example Dachau"), as an exhibition in the lobby of city hall.[25] Richardi's collection reveals the inherent contradiction between the myths of ignorance and resistance, since each anecdote illustrates how public the horrific conditions in the concentration camp were. It would have been absurd to attempt to uphold the myth of ignorance in light of that material.

Rediscovering "forgotten persecutees"

Another development catalyzed by the broadcast of *Holocaust* in 1979 was the public recognition of groups which came to be known as "forgotten persecutees" (*vergessene Verfolgte*), such as gypsies, homosexuals, prostitutes, Jehovah's Witnesses, slave laborers, soldiers who deserted from the army, and the victims of forced sterilization, to name the largest groups. We will look at two groups in greater detail.[26]

The gypsies, more correctly known by the tribal names Sinti and Roma, were the first of these groups to take advantage of the popular empathy for victims of brown-collar crimes after the broadcast of the TV miniseries. In November 1979 they staged a hunger strike in the memorial site at Bergen-Belsen to press their demands for a lump sum *Wiedergutmachung* payment similar to what the Jewish Claims Conference had received after 1953.[27] They also drew attention to the fact that Sinti survivors had received a compensation payment of only DM5 per day in a concentration camp, as compared to the DM10 per day Jewish survivors had received. After the hunger strike the Sinti were officially recognized with an inscription on the Belsen monument. In 1979 the first books discussing their persecution under the Nazis, and continuing persecution in West Germany, were published – given the time lag in the publication process, an indication that interest had been growing for some time before the broadcast of *Holocaust*.[28]

The Sinti used hunger strikes and occupations at the concentration camp memorial sites in Dachau and Neuengamme to good effect in pressing their political goals throughout the 1980s and 1990s. Over Easter 1980 in Dachau, for instance, they conducted a hunger strike to draw attention to discriminatory West German laws.[29] Publicity in the local, regional, and national media was predominantly positive. After the strike, however, when local groups suggested that a cultural center for the Sinti be established in Dachau, an outcry from local conservatives, quite in line with outspoken resistance spawned by the myth of resistance, ensued.[30] None the less, a compromise was reached and in November 1980 the city of Dachau hosted a "Day of Sinti Culture."[31] By 1993, when forty Macedonian Roma threatened by extradition to war-torn former Yugoslavia sought asylum in the Dachau memorial site, a broad coalition of local groups supported them for over two months (ill. 81).[32] During the economic recession of the early 1990s, however, the subject of constructing a cultural center in Dachau dropped from view.

In the 1970s homosexuals also began to draw on the history of their victimization under National Socialism to press for political recognition in the present. During a meeting of homosexuals in Munich in the summer of 1976, a man streaked naked across the Dachau memorial site to the international memorial, where he demanded financial compensation for homosexuals who had survived imprisonment in the Nazi concentration camps.[33] Then in 1977 the "National Working Group Repression against Gays" sent several letters to the international Dachau survivors' committee CID asking why no pink triangle, the color homosexuals were forced to wear in the camps, was included on the chain sculpture in the international memorial in Dachau (see ill. 61).[34] Although internal correspondence reveals that the German Dachau survivors attributed the omission to the prevailing anti-gay climate of the early 1960s, in its response the CID merely noted that the pink triangle could be found on a chart in the museum, and it ceased to answer the group's letters.

Six years later another organization of homosexuals made a second attempt at official recognition in the memorial site. The second initiative began in December 1984, when the Protestant "Action Sign of Atonement," which had been actively sponsoring full-time volunteers in the Dachau memorial site since 1979, hosted an exhibition on "Homosexuality and Politics since 1900."[35] In February 1985, with reference to that exhibition, the Munich branch of "Homosexuals and the Church" wrote to the CID. This time they were first put off because a change to the memorial would require a meeting of the full organization. Then four local organizations of homosexuals joined the initiative. They mustered letters of support from a Belgian organization of homosexuals, from Otto Schily, a member of the West German parliament, and from Helmut Gollwitzer, a prominent member of the West German Protestant Church. In October 1985, they commissioned a triangular pink granite plaque with the text "Beaten to death / Killed [again] by silence / To the homosexual victims of National Socialism / The homosexual initiatives of Munich, 1985" (ill. 82).

The four local groups petitioned the CID to allow them to display this plaque in a room of the museum reserved for ribbons and other private signs of remembrance. Again, the committee refused, and the plaque was put on display in the reading room of the Protestant Church of Reconciliation at the rear of the memorial site. Finally, in 1994, after the aging leadership of the CID had changed again, the plaque was allowed to be displayed in the museum.

Thus the willingness to recognize victimized groups increased over the course of the 1980s. In this case members of the group were able to use their social recognition to press the survivors of political repression to change their exclusionary stance. The political survivors' reluctance to broaden the category of victims of Nazism is not surprising, since they had faced decades of competing claims of victimization from Germans who had overwhelmingly supported the Nazi regime.

The boomerang effect: 1948ers revive German victimization

As we have seen, by informing a mass audience in an emotionally moving and plausible way about the brown-collar crimes, the American film

Holocaust catalyzed the end of the myth of ignorance. By providing the populace with empathetic images of Jews and a concrete story of their victimization, it challenged the myth that Germans had been victims of Nazism. As additional groups of victims of brown-collar crimes began to publicly press their claims in Germany, members of the 1943er and 1948er cohorts responded by reviving the claim that Germans had also been victims of Nazism. We will examine this phenomenon in film, national memorials, and commemorative anniversaries.

Filmmaker Edgar Reitz (b. 1932) responded to the re-realization of nonmainstream German victims of Nazism by creating an epic portrayal of German victimization: a 15½ hour film entitled *Heimat*, roughly translatable as "Homeland." Immediately after the telecast of *Holocaust*, Reitz set to work on his German "answer" to the American film.[36] *Heimat*, which was aired as a nine-part series on national television in 1984, portrays life in the director's own village from the turn of the century, when the main character Maria is born, until her death in 1982.

Reitz's film was the second-largest film event in West German TV history, with approximately 9 million viewers tuning into each segment (*Holocaust* had the largest audience, with 10–13.4 million watching each episode). Reitz consciously excluded every reference to the annihilation of the Jews from his melodrama (he told an interviewer that that would have given the film "a different direction"), and he included only the slightest hint that the populace had known about the concentration camps. Instead, his portrayal of idyllic village life buffeted by the events of larger history presents powerful images of "decent, normal citizens" who are victimized from time to time, as *New York Times* German correspondent James Markham noted.[37] Historian–journalist Timothy Garton Ash was more explicit:[38]

> When you show the 1930s as a golden age of prosperity and excitement ... when you are shown the Germans as victims of the war, then you inevitably find yourself asking: But what about the other side? What about Auschwitz? ... To which the color filters insistently reply: "...this is a film about what Germans remember. Some things they remember in full color. Some in sepia. Others they prefer to forget."

National politics, anniversaries, and diplomacy

The 1943ers' and the 1948ers' revival of the myth of German victimization in response to *Holocaust* was not limited to film; it was propagated at the highest levels of scholarship and government as well. Major commemorative anniversaries provided the opportunities for that.

In the emerging historical interest in the Nazi period in the early 1960s, "round year" anniversary commemorations of Nazi-era events focused on signal events of German victimization, namely the Nazi assumption of power (thirtieth anniversary in 1963); ignorance, namely the "unexpected" outbreak of World War II (twenty-fifth anniversary in 1964); and resistance, namely the 20 July resistance movement (twentieth anniversary in 1964).[39] The victims of brown-collar crimes were so marginal in public consciousness at that time that, for instance, the twenty-fifth anniversary of *Kristallnacht* in 1963 barely figured in contemporary national discourse. By the 1980s this situation had changed dramatically.

An increase in the visibility of public commemorations of the victims of Nazism's brown-collar crimes began at the end of the 1970s. Especially noteworthy was the fortieth anniversary of *Kristallnacht* in 1978, when 1943ers Chancellor Helmut Schmidt (b. 1918) and President Walter Scheel (b. 1919) delivered nationally reported speeches in the Cologne synagogue.[40] On the one hand, Schmidt beat around the bush on the question of mythic ignorance:

> The truth is also that many Germans disapproved of the crimes and the misdemeanors; also, that very many others at the time knew nothing or almost nothing. The truth is that, nevertheless, all this took place before the eyes of a large number of German fellow citizens.

On the other hand, he admitted some deficits in German political culture deriving from the continued propagation of the three myths. Support for democracy and respect for the dignity and freedom of the individual "had been inadequate for generations," he said, adding that although most Germans alive in 1978 were "individually free from blame," they too could become guilty, "if they fail to recognize the responsibility for what happens today and tomorrow deriving from what happened then."[41] Schmidt called for support of independent thinking; respect for others; rejection of scapegoating, extremism, and violence; and acceptance of responsibility for one's actions.

At the same time, a major political shift was underway in West Germany. The SPD–FDP left–center coalition, begun under Willy Brandt in 1969, had ruled by a slim majority since the 1976 elections, when CDU opposition candidate Helmut Kohl received 48.6 percent of the vote. When 1943er President Scheel (FDP) was replaced by CSU candidate 1933er Karl Carstens (b. 1914) in 1979, it became evident that a political shift toward the right was underway. In 1982, with 1.8 million people unemployed – the highest number since the early 1950s – the conflict between the worker-friendly SPD and the employer-friendly FDP came to a head.[42] When the FDP Minister of Economics leaked a sensitive government memorandum to the press in August 1982, Chancellor Schmidt threatened to fire all four FDP ministers from the cabinet. He called for a vote of confidence in the parliament, which failed, the parliament instead selecting Helmut Kohl.

In the 6 March 1983 national elections (coincidentally the day after the fiftieth anniversary of the national election that confirmed Adolf Hitler as chancellor with 44 percent of the national vote in 1933), Kohl's CDU received 49 percent of the vote and the FDP 7 percent, while the SPD dropped to 38 percent, the lowest it had received since the founding of West Germany in 1949. While this was a significant blow to the major center-left party, for the first time since 1957 a fourth party managed to surpass the 5 percent threshold: the left-wing environmental Green Party, which was a collecting point for leftists from the 1968er cohort. Their "long march through the institutions," begun in 1969–70, had finally arrived in parliament. They had matured politically but had not lost the contrary spunk that had characterized their politics more than a decade earlier, and they constantly challenged the exoneratory, victim-based politics of the past spearheaded by Kohl during the 1980s.

The fiftieth anniversary of Hitler's January 1933 nomination as chancellor marks the beginning of a series of spectacles of commemoration that shows no sign of abating even after the turn of the millennium. In January 1983 an international conference of prominent historians was convened in the Reichstag in Berlin to discuss the latest research on how Hitler moved from chancellorship to dictatorship in such a short period in 1933–4.[43] The most controversial presentation at the conference was the closing address by neoconservative philosopher Hermann Lübbe (b. 1926), a 1948er who claimed that the period of mythical inversions through the mid-1950s had been "a social-psychologically and politically necessary means of transforming our . . . population into the citizenry of the Federal Republic." Thus, for instance, the reintegration of the former Nazis into the government had facilitated the emergence of a consensus for democratic governance. While that was undoubtedly true, Lübbe went on to deny the negative consequences that the ignoring and ignorance of the Nazi past had had for West German political culture, as the Mitscherlichs, for example, had pointed out. Instead, he accused the 1968ers of antidemocratic behavior because they had fostered rancor by breaking the healing taboo of silence.

Chancellor Kohl, who had a history Ph.D., was very much in agreement with Lübbe's point of view, and immediately after taking office he initiated the creation of historical museums that would portray a consensual vision of Germany's past. In two of his early official executive announcements, he proposed the construction of a "House of the History of the Federal Republic" in Bonn (Oct. 1982), and of a "German Historical Museum" in Berlin (May 1983).[44] On 8 May 1983 the private but officially recognized People's Association for the Care of German War Graves (Volksbund deutsche Kriegsgräberfürsorge) proposed the construction of a "national memorial for the war-dead of our people" in Bonn.[45] This project, which included only German victims, was also quickly endorsed by Kohl.

Although such projects were popular among Kohl's constituency, they roused the ire of the left, especially of the leftist 1968ers organized in the Greens, who soon published documentation with arguments against the projects.[46] Kohl was undeterred, however. As mentioned above, during his January 1984 visit to Israel he proclaimed his innocence due to the "grace of late birth." Kohl's press secretary Peter Boenisch's preventive resistance to the anticipated victimization of Germans was even more glaring. Boenisch, clad in a full-length black leather coat reminiscent of those worn by the SS, warned right upon arrival in Israel that "the Jews should not always lay Auschwitz on Germany's doorstep."[47] The West German press soon dubbed the Israel trip a "visit of embarrassments."[48]

Although Kohl's professions of German innocence in Israel had been embarrassing, the visit was short, made few waves, and – except for Kohl's memorable declaration of the "grace of late birth" – soon forgotten. That was not the case with Kohl's next commemorative debacle: his visit to the German military cemetery at Bitburg with US President Reagan on 5 May 1985.

Dachau vs. Bitburg, 1985

Shortly after the Israel trip a new opportunity arose for Kohl to receive international validation that his country had finally emerged from its term of imposed historical penitence. In the spring of 1984 leaders of the postwar Western military alliance NATO were planning to convene in Normandy to commemorate the fortieth anniversary of the June 1944 D-Day landing. It was to be attended by US President Ronald Reagan, British Queen Elizabeth, and French President Mitterrand, as well as heads of state from Belgium, Canada, Luxembourg, the Netherlands, and Norway.

Although West Germany now belonged to the alliance, Kohl recognized that it would have been embarrassing for a representative of the country that had caused the loss of so many lives to participate in the military commemoration. Instead, he accepted the French premier's offer to find a more appropriate opportunity to demonstrate France's recognition that the new Germany had nothing to do with the old.[49] The leaders of the Western alliance were especially indebted to Kohl because of the high political costs he had incurred by allowing NATO to station Cruise missiles and Pershing II rockets on West German soil in the fall of 1983. The vigorous West German peace movement had mobilized against Kohl for making Germany a staging ground and primary target for the next World War.

Mitterrand repaid his symbolic debt to Kohl in September 1984 with a ceremony on the World War I battlefield at Verdun. In a solemn gesture the two heads of state stood silently holding hands in front of two huge wreaths symbolizing German–French reconciliation. Reagan was next in line to repay the favor to his German partner. The May 1985 world economic summit in Bonn presented an ideal opportunity, since it was to take place a few days before the fortieth anniversary of the end of World War II. Kohl broached the subject when he visited the White House in November 1984.

As it prepared the Kohl–Reagan meeting, the West German Foreign Office worried that Reagan might visit only a former concentration camp during his stay in Germany, which the press would portray as his most significant stopping point.[50] Their solution was for the German chancellor to suggest that the US president visit both Dachau and a World War II battlefield.[51] Before he left the US, Kohl, seeking to underscore West Germany's contrite worthiness of being let out of the historical doghouse, announced that he himself would give a speech in a former concentration camp in May 1985.[52]

Although nothing had been officially announced about Reagan's itinerary, on 16 January 1985 the German Chancellor's Office announced that Kohl might accompany him to Dachau to commemorate the anniversary of the end of the war.[53] On 21 January *Der Spiegel* reported that the German government had not been able to convince Reagan not to visit a camp, so that Chancellor Kohl would accompany him to Dachau, along with President Weizsäcker and Bavarian Minister President Strauss.[54] It added that the German government had also requested that Reagan visit a site of especially heavy World War II combat and shake hands with Kohl as a "gesture of reconciliation" between the former enemies that would "compensate for

... the unpleasant KZ visit." The Foreign Office immediately denied every-thing reported by *Spiegel* (and *Welt am Sonntag*), stating that the only sure thing was that Reagan would be in Bonn for the summit from 2 to 4 May.[55] In fact, although the left-wing West German press repeatedly reported rumors that Kohl was trying to dissuade Reagan from visiting a former camp, there is no hard evidence to support that contention.[56] Rather, it appears that Kohl remained silent on the matter of visiting a camp from when he initially proposed it in November until mid-April, when he reiter-ated the suggestion.

In spite of the uncertainty about Dachau, the January report that Reagan would visit Dachau galvanized local politicians, who worried that such a visit "would only reinforce and rejuvenate the negative image" of the town, as deputy mayor Georg Englhard said.[57] The Munich edition of the mass circulation *Bild* reported in a front-page headline on 22 January: "Dachauers don't want Reagan / 'KZ visit hurts us.'"[58] More seasoned local politicians transcended this passive feeling of victimization and proposed at the local level what Kohl had done at the national: Reagan should visit both the former camp and the city, and thus become acquainted with the "other Dachau."[59] Mayor Reitmeier and the county governor wrote a letter to Minister President Strauss, asking that he "do everything in his power to see that President Reagan . . . also comes to the city."

This local effort to resist what was perceived as the city's ongoing victim-ization was premature, however, since on 24 January White House press secretary Speakes announced that the US president would not visit Dachau.[60] The president, he said, felt that "today's Germans did not have anything more to do with the genocide of the Jews," and that a visit in Dachau might be misunderstood. Instead, Reagan wanted to com-memorate 8 May with ceremonies that would "demonstrate reconciliation and friendship" and emphasize West Germany's "return to democracy."[61] Reagan clearly sympathized with Kohl's agenda of ignoring the past, and wanted to avoid anything that might hurt "the souls or the hearts" of his West German allies, as Mitterrand had phrased it.[62]

In spite of the January denial that Reagan was planning to visit Dachau, in early February and again in late March presidential aide Michael Deaver visited Dachau and other Holocaust sites to see if they would be suitable for a visit by the president. He found the memorial site "worthy for the president to visit."[63] Deaver also found the German military cemetery in Bitburg suitable for the "balancing" gesture so coveted by Kohl. On 21 March and again on 1 April Reagan reiterated that he would not visit a con-centration camp memorial site during his time in Germany, because "the bulk of German citizens had not gone through the experience of World War II."[64] This unleashed a storm of protest in the US, especially among those who could very well remember having gone through the experience of the war – especially war veterans and Jews. The press pointed out that Auschwitz doctor Mengele was the same age as Reagan, while Gestapo chief Klaus Barbie was three years younger. At that time an intensive manhunt was on for Mengele, whose body was found on 7 June in Brazil, while Barbie had been extradited to France in February 1983 and was awaiting his 1987 trial.[65]

On 11 April Reagan added insult to the injury of ignoring the Holocaust by announcing that he would indeed visit a German military cemetery. Kohl's team began damage control with a 15 April cable to the White House reminding Reagan that the chancellor had suggested a visit to Dachau "because we knew it would be a political necessity."[66]

At that point Mayor Reitmeier returned to his effort to champion his victimized town, this time writing directly to President Reagan, with copies to Kohl and Strauss: "When you come to Dachau to pay homage to the victims of the KZ, you should also visit the other Dachau, the honorable Dachau, the ancient city with its 1,200 year history."[67] This time, instead of being criticized by mythically inclined conservatives, Reitmeier was chastised by the other side: the 1968ers and 1979ers who did not wish to exclude the brown-collar crimes from Dachau's past. The chairman of the local trade union association wrote an open letter to the mayor criticizing his invitation because it implied that the camp/memorial site was part of a "dishonorable" Dachau. The mayor replied immediately with another open letter in which he clarified that the memorial site "certainly" belonged to the "honorable" Dachau.[68]

It is crucial to note that *from the beginning* both Mayor Reitmeier and Chancellor Kohl accepted that their foreign guest would visit a former concentration camp, and they were willing to accompany him there.[69] Thus by the mid-1980s many 1948ers were ready to recognize publicly that there had been "dirty" camps. Although they no longer publicly supported the myth of Nazi-era victimization, they were determined to resist Germany's (Dachau's) present victimization by forcing the recognition of the "other," non-Nazi Germany that had unwittingly been sullied by the brown-collar crimes. That this recognition of the "good Germany" was the single most important element of Kohl's agenda became clear in the further course of the scandal. In spite of enormous political costs, Kohl remained adamant in his refusal to release Reagan from his pledge to visit a battlefield or military cemetery as a site of the "good Germany's" victimization.

362

The Dachau mayor's balancing act between proponents and opponents of the mythically reenvisaged past was minuscule compared to the criticism the US president faced at home because of his desire to ignore the brown-collar crimes during his visit. On 15 April news reports revealed that there were graves of some four dozen SS soldiers at the Bitburg cemetery, prompting fifty-three US senators to sign a 17 April letter strongly urging Reagan to drop that site from his itinerary. The next day Reagan committed the greatest gaffe of the whole affair during a meeting with the press. He defended the planned Bitburg visit with one of the most pointed expressions of the myth of victimization ever spoken publicly:[70]

> There's nothing wrong with visiting that cemetery where those young men are victims of Nazism also . . . They were victims, just as surely as the victims in the concentration camps.

Not only was this the epitome of mythic victimization, it was predicated on complete ignorance of what had happened in Nazi Germany. The pressure on Reagan peaked on 18 April, at Washington's official Holocaust Remembrance Day ceremony. After Reagan awarded the Congressional Gold Medal of Honor to the 56-year-old Holocaust survivor Elie Wiesel, the Nobel prizewinner implored the president not to visit Bitburg – in a speech televised live throughout the United States. Reagan immediately announced that he would visit a former concentration camp in addition to Bitburg. This time, Belsen was chosen instead of Dachau. A Reagan administration official told the press: "The President was not hot to go to a camp. You know, he is a cheerful politician. He does not like to grovel in a grisly scene like Dachau."[71] Belsen, which had been burned to the ground after the war, was now, as Wiesel put it, "prettier" than Dachau because all traces of the "dirty" camp had been eradicated in 1945.[72] Kohl himself went to Bergen-Belsen for a commemorative ceremony on 21 April to emphasize that he had no intention of denying "Germany's historical responsibility for the crimes of Nazi tyranny."[73]

As pressure in the US and abroad mounted for Reagan to abandon his visit to Bitburg, it was clear that he was waiting for permission from Kohl.[74] Still, the West German chancellor remained steadfast in his desire to celebrate the "good Germany," refusing to release Reagan from his commitment to visit Bitburg, as 257 members of the US House of Representatives had requested in an open letter to him on 25 April.[75] Interestingly, Kohl was overwhelmingly supported by the West German political mainstream: the German parliament cast 398 votes in support of Kohl's agenda, against the 24 Greens, who introduced the US House's request as a motion on the West

German House floor. The dismal failure by the 1968er cohort to thwart the 1948ers' resistance to their perceived ongoing victimization revealed how strong and pervasive those mythic legacies still were.

As things turned out, Reagan did visit both Bergen-Belsen and Bitburg, on 5 May, the day after the world economic summit. At the Bitburg cemetery, the symbolic handclasp was performed by 90-year-old American General Matthew Ridgway, who had participated in the final assault on Germany in the winter of 1944–5, and former Luftwaffe General Johannes Steinhoff (1913–94) The two heads of state remained grimly silent as their military commanders tried to symbolically close the book on Germany's aggressively militarist past. After driving back past scores of jeering demonstrators,[76] in his speech at the Bitburg military base Reagan narrated a sentimental anecdote about good Nazi-era Germans.[77] He told how, on Christmas eve 1944, first four US GIs, then three Wehrmacht soldiers, came knocking at a local farmhouse door. After sharing a meal, the German medic tended the frostbitten and wounded Americans. The next morning the men shook hands before the Germans showed the Americans the way back to their own lines. Reagan then alluded to John Kennedy's famous 1963 "Ich bin ein Berliner" speech, and expressed his solidarity with all victims in the world:

> Well, today freedom-loving people around the world must say, I am a Berliner, I am a Jew in a world still threatened by anti-Semitism, I am an Afghan, and I am a prisoner of the Gulag, I am a refugee in a crowded boat foundering off of the coast of Vietnam, I am a Laotian, a Cambodian, a Cuban, and a Miskito Indian in Nicaragua. I, too, am a potential victim of totalitarianism.

Kohl could not have wished for a more eloquent recognition of West Germany's postwar victimhood, given first place even before the Jews. However, the international and domestic reactions before and after the speech ensured that Bitburg would not go down in history as a symbol of the end of Germany's post-Nazi probation, but as a reminder of the deficiencies in Germany's process of coming to terms with its Nazi heritage.[78]

The Weizsäcker speech and the "Historians' Controversy"

Several other events in 1985–6 indicate that this attempted revival of the myth of victimization was not going unchallenged.[79] Three days after the symbolic handclasp at Bitburg, West German President von Weizsäcker addressed the parliament on the fiftieth anniversary of the end of the war.[80] In sharp contrast to the blurring of victimization practiced by Kohl and Reagan, Weizsäcker's speech was explicitly anti-mythical. At the outset, he specifically recognized and enumerated the groups of victims of Nazism, whom he "commemorated" in the name of all Germans: the murdered Jews, the nations that suffered in the war, the Sinti and Roma, the homosexuals and mentally ill, the hostages and the resistance movement. In the same paragraph he did also mention the German "compatriots who perished as soldiers, during air raids at home, in captivity or during expulsion," but he subordinated them by only recognizing "mourning" for them, and by briefly returning only to the expellees once later in the speech. Then Weizsäcker unequivocally repudiated the myth of ignorance:

> Who could remain unsuspecting after the burning of the synagogues, the plundering, the stigmatization with the star of David, the deprivation of rights, the ceaseless violation of human dignity? Whoever opened his eyes and ears and sought information could not fail to notice that Jews were being deported. The nature and scope of the destruction may have exceeded human imagination, but in reality there was . . . the attempt . . . not to take note of what was happening. There were many ways of not burdening one's conscience, of shunning responsibility, looking away, keeping mum. When the unspeakable truth of the Holocaust then became known at the end of the war, all too many of us claimed that we had not known anything about it or even suspected anything.

He continued with a clear distinction between Germans as perpetrators and Germans as victims, stating clearly that the former had created the latter: "The initiative for the war . . . came from Germany," and "without Hitler, [the division of Germany] would not have happened at all."

Weizsäcker's clear recognition of German responsibility for the Nazi crimes was widely acclaimed, both in Germany and abroad. Kohl's history museum and national victims' memorial projects ground to a halt after Bitburg and remained on ice until after unification in 1990. Another public battle, this time among historians, remained to be fought before the myth of victimization lost its public legitimacy. A year after Weizsäcker's standard-setting speech, a left-wing social philosopher mounted a public attack on a number of conservative historians who were still brazenly pushing the "Germans as victims" line.

In June 1986 Jürgen Habermas triggered what came to be known as the "Historians' Controversy" by publishing an exposé of this blossoming historiography of victimization in *Die Zeit*.[81] Habermas focused on three recently published texts that spun the myth of victimization to new heights. The first was a political essay by historian Michael Stürmer (b. 1938), a neoconservative 1968er who occasionally wrote speeches for Helmut Kohl. Stürmer's gloss, published in different versions as "History in a Land without History" in the *Frankfurter Allgemeine* and then as "Search for Lost Memory," in the Bonn governmental weekly *Das Parlament*, sought to justify Kohl's attempts to foster a positive conception of German national history.[82] Habermas took this rather unremarkable piece of programmatic conservative fare and examined how recent works by two 1943er historians fulfilled its agenda.

The first was an essay that historian Ernst Nolte (b. 1923) had written for a conference about "the past that will not go away," which Nolte ultimately did not attend.[83] Nolte suggested that Hitler and the National Socialists had perpetrated an "Asiatic deed," namely the Holocaust, because they feared they might become the victims of another "Asiatic deed," namely the Soviet gulags, which Nolte saw as "more primary than Auschwitz." He equated German with Jewish victimization by comparing "the [1980s'] talk about 'the guilt of the Germans'" to the National Socialist "talk about 'the guilt of the Jews.'"

Habermas's second target was a 1986 book by Andreas Hillgruber (b. 1925), *Two Different Sorts of Demise: The Shattering of the German Reich and the End of European Jewry*, which combined two of Hillgruber's recent lectures.[84] In the first essay Hillgruber sought to justify the German army's fight to the bitter end by describing in moving detail with numerous examples the horrors the civilian population suffered under the Soviet advance. He claimed that a German historian could only view this history from that perspective of resisting victimization, not through the eyes of the Jews or the resistance movement against Hitler. In contrast, Hillgruber's essay on the Jews was a rather dry academic piece examining "the historical position of the annihilation of the Jews." The combination of the two essays in one volume cast the self-pitying victimization of the first piece in an especially crass light.

Throughout the summer and fall of 1986, historians from the 1948er cohort battled on the pages of West Germany's major daily and weekly newspapers over whether Germans had been perpetrators or victims.[85] Within a year the newspaper articles were collected and published as a monograph, and nearly all major scholarly journals of European history published interpretative essays.[86] Soon a number of monographic assessments appeared as well.[87] When the dust settled, it was fairly clear that the dominant block of West German historians – most of them 1948ers – decisively rejected the myth of victimization, as did essentially all of the non-Germans who wrote about the debate. Of course, a residual fringe of German historians, mostly 1968ers and 1979ers, are still pushing the apologetic agenda.[88]

Thus in the wake of the Historians' Controversy the myth of victimization was no longer acceptable in public discourse. In 1988 the continuing popular interest in the history of everyday Nazism and its victims at the local level provided the basis to make the fiftieth anniversary of *Kristallnacht* the largest commemoration of the organized anti-Jewish pogrom ever.[89] Local initiatives across West Germany organized an impressive array of exhibitions, memorials, and commemorative ceremonies.[90] In Dachau a working group researched what had been done to Dachau's fifteen Jews, and exhibited its results in the lobby of city hall.[91] A more permanent reminder of *Kristallnacht* was established on the outside of the building, where Mayor Reitmeier dedicated a plaque commemorating the six Jewish families driven from Dachau.

In Bonn, parliamentary president Philipp Jenninger (b. 1932), a 1948er who had cultivated a much closer relationship to German Jews than Kohl, asked to give the commemorative address to parliament.[92] Soon after beginning his speech, which he delivered in a detached monotone, Jenninger tried to explain how the Germans had been seduced and thus victimized by Hitler. When he began asking rhetorical questions such as "Didn't Jews have too much power?" and described antisemitic stereotypes at length, left-wing members of parliament walked out of the assembly in protest. As the following passage from the beginning of the speech indicates, Jenninger's formulations implicitly recapitulated the mythic inversion that made Jews into perpetrators and non-Jewish Germans into victims:[93]

> And as for the Jews: Hadn't they in the past presumed a role – as was said back then – that they weren't entitled to? Shouldn't they have finally had to accept restrictions? Didn't they perhaps even deserve to be put in their place? And especially: Didn't the propaganda – aside from a few wild exaggerations that couldn't be taken seriously – correspond in the main points with their own suspicions and convictions?

Jenninger's speech was completely inappropriate for the occasion – it contained too much Nazi vocabulary and diction, and it did not express the shame and loss that many Germans felt about the events of November 1938. As SPD minority leader Hans-Jochen Vogel wrote to Jenninger the next day:[94]

> you used phrases and terms from the NS regime of violence . . . in a way that
> reveals an alarming lack of sensitivity and a complete misjudgment of the
> thoughtfulness and linguistic empathy and care required of someone
> speaking for the whole parliament on such an occasion.

Leaders of Jewish organizations in Germany, used to a lack of empathy from non-Jewish Germans and aware that Jenninger was their ally, reserved judgment, but many Germans of the 1968er cohort angrily demanded his resignation. After two days of trying to justify his intention, Jenninger resigned. For mythically inclined Germans, that was further evidence that they were again being victimized by the Jews. Nonetheless, published opinion, by then under the sway of the postwar cohorts, overwhelmingly accepted the resignation.

Jenninger's resignation can be seen as a harbinger of the end of the myth of victimization, with regard both to perceived victimization during the Nazi period, and to victimization by those "masterers of the past" who felt that the brown-collar crimes should be remembered. Mythic victimization's demise was accelerated when the most visible consequence of what Germany suffered as a result of its blind loyalty to Hitler, namely the postwar division of the Nazi Reich, ended. With the opening of the Berlin Wall in November 1989 and the unification of West and East Germany in October 1990, West Germans had reason to feel "whole" again. Still, some of the legacies of mythic victimization continue to influence German politics. Higher rates of violence against foreigners and anti-immigrant sentiment, noticeable from the grass roots to the halls of parliament during the economic recession of the 1990s (especially in the "five new states" of former East Germany), are some of the more visible manifestations.[95]

Looking back over the 1980s, we can see that by the end of the decade the myth of ignorance had disappeared completely from the mainstream political discourse. Official commemorative speeches now generally conceded that the Germans had known much about the brown-collar crimes. Even Jenninger had said at the outset, "Everyone saw what happened, but almost everyone looked away and remained silent."[96] Mythic ignorance's legacy of unempathetic, abstract knowledge of the crimes had been overcome by a groundswell of local historians of everyday life (see table 2). Their efforts to make the victims of Nazi Germany come alive to younger generations were supported by history teachers armed with excellent curricular materials, as well as by the mass media. In Dachau, a rotating team of full-time teachers was employed to give tours and develop new curricular materials.

By the end of the 1980s, the myth of victimization, too, had become publicly unacceptable. Increased historical knowledge about the victims helped to dispel the myth itself, and the unification of Germany in 1989 helped to relegate its legacy of underdog mentality to political irrelevance. Before we turn to the 1990s, the story of another postwar Dachau mayor shows in an individual example how the fading of the myths of ignorance and victimization prior to that decade prepared the way for a powerful challenge to the myth of ignorance in the 1990s.

Kurt Piller (b. 1959), mayor of Dachau 1996–

Kurt Piller was born in Dachau in 1959.[97] His father, like many of the 1948ers, had been drafted into the army in 1945 at age 17. (This last-gasp recruitment of all German males from 16 to 60 was known as the *Volkssturm*, or "People's Army.") Although his father had often expressed his disapproval that boys so young should be sent to war, Kurt Piller never thought about that very much. Around 1972, when he was 12 or 13, Piller's class visited the Dachau memorial site. No aspects of this visit left special traces in Piller's memory. A few years later he wrote a term paper about the concentration camp and visited the memorial site on his own as well. Soon he began to read books about the National Socialist period on his own, too. For instance, a trip to Amsterdam in the late 1970s prompted him to reread *The Diary of Anne Frank*. He also read excerpts from Hitler's *Mein Kampf* and the publication of Hitler's informal *Table Talk*, as well as a popular recent biography of Hitler by Joachim Fest.

In 1978, when he completed secondary school, Kurt Piller decided to visit Israel. He had heard of the 1967 and 1973 Israeli–Arab wars, and was interested in the "pioneering spirit" in the young country. Jerusalem, the cultic center of three world religions, also fascinated him. When he was in the Holy City, Piller also visited Yad Vashem, Israel's central Holocaust memorial and museum in the hills above Jerusalem. In Israel, Piller met Jews who had emigrated from Germany, whom he recalls as nostalgic, not hateful. He also remembered sitting in a circle on the ground and discussing historical legacies with young Israelis. Although people in Israel "were of course taken aback at first" when they heard he was from Dachau, they were always impressed by his honesty and openness. Such reactions were not limited to Israel, either. Piller loves to travel, and has been to India, Australia, and the United States, as well as to many European countries. Essentially all of his encounters with foreigners ("99.9 percent," as he put it) ended on a positive note. Clearly Piller has a very open, uncomplicated relationship with his own origins. His 1948er father's young age (b. 1928)

369

and clear innocence during the Nazi period provided an objective basis for this forthrightness, while the desire to give his own young child an honest conception of the past motivated him to work publicly toward that goal.

When Piller began university studies in political science and history, his personal interest in the Nazi period increased. As a student he saw Gerald Green's TV miniseries *Holocaust* when it was broadcast in West Germany in 1979 or rebroadcast in 1981. In 1997 he recalled that the series had made a "deep impression" on him, as had a film about the concentration camp survivor and Nazi hunter Simon Wiesenthal, of whom he had also read a biography. After changing majors to law and legal history Piller came across documents from the Nazi period. Files from the notorious "people's court" stand out in his memory. In spite of all of these encounters with the Nazi past, Piller did not realize its political implications for the present until May 1985, when, in the wake of US President Ronald Reagan and West German Chancellor Helmut Kohl's visit to the World War II military cemetery in Bitburg, West German President Richard von Weizsäcker presented his exceptionally candid speech about Germany's relationship to the brown-collar crimes. That speech also made a "deep impression" on Kurt Piller. He suddenly understood the implications of Dachau Mayor Reitmeier's continual emphasis that Dachau was first and foremost an artists' colony, and that the concentration camp had really been more on Prittlbach's territory than Dachau's.

Weizsäcker's speech gave Piller what he calls his "first insight" about Dachau and its past: "The history of the city and the concentration camp are not divisible." A second insight, which was prepared by his experiences in Israel and other foreign countries, came to him during a six-month legal internship in Australia in 1988–9. Piller's Australian supervisor, upon learning that he was from Dachau, introduced him to the chief justice of the Australian Supreme Court, who had been a Spitfire pilot over Germany in World War II. The legal intern from Dachau and the highest Australian judge had a very cordial talk. Piller, impressed by the Australian's unpretentiousness, concluded that "openness is the best policy," or, as he rephrased it, "I realized that people respond with openness when one approaches them with openness." This insight has become a guiding principle of Piller's politics since he was elected mayor of Dachau in 1996.

Even before he officially assumed office in May of that year, Kurt Piller represented the city at the annual "day of encounters," an informal catered event after the official commemorative ceremony, sponsored by local groups for concentration camp survivors and local residents. In contrast to his predecessor Reitmeier, Piller sees the Dachau camp's central role in

370

the Nazi period as an opportunity for the city, not as a burden. He has replaced the semi-private chamber of commerce with an official "Office for Culture, Tourism and Contemporary History," a combination unique to Dachau. As its first head he hired Silke Schuster, another 1979er, who was interested in the position primarily because it offered an opportunity to shape Germany's presentation of the Nazi past.[98]

Mayor Piller introduced several other initiatives to this end. He regularly takes time to meet with groups of survivors. He completely revamped the dismal bus service from the town to the memorial site, adding a special new line with larger buses and drivers trained to deal professionally and sensitively with visitors' concerns. Piller is visiting cities in Israel, Poland, and the Netherlands in a serious attempt to find "partner cities" for Dachau, which would provide additional opportunities for Dachau residents to interact with foreigners. He has begun raising funds to endow a historical–cultural foundation in the city that would include a library, sponsor cultural events, host visiting scholars, and perhaps even support an endowed contemporary history professorship at the University of Munich. Piller has already gained the endorsement of Weizsäcker's successor as German president, Roman Herzog, who built his retirement home in Dachau (where Herzog's son lives). Piller also played a key role in rerouting the street access from the city to the former camp more along the historical route through the former SS camp that had belonged to the Bavarian state police since 1971 (ill. 1).[99]

Mayor Piller's initiatives with regard to the Dachau memorial site since his election in 1996 are indicative of a broad-based transition in united Germany's public recollection of the Nazi past. As the generations of perpetrators and survivors are dying out and the 1979ers accede to positions of political and cultural power, the public debates about the Nazi crimes are characterized less by personal recriminations, whether perceived or actual, and more by a search for meaning and implications. In other words, they are less oriented towards the past, and more towards the present and future.

15

The 1990s: resistance vs. education

The re-realization of the Nazi past in the 1980s created a critical mass of Germans in positions of public influence who accepted that their national collective had been perpetrators, not victims. For that sector of the recollective community, the myth of resistance was rapidly becoming untenable. Commemorations of "Dachau" and other brown-collar crimes in the 1990s can be understood as conflicts over the validity of mythic resistance. As we will see, these 1990s' conflicts also carry the hallmarks of mythic resistance's legacy of hypersensitivity.

This final chapter is devoted to the myth of resistance and the educational efforts currently underway to counteract that myth's exoneration of Nazi-era German society. The myth of resistance has been by far the most difficult of the three myths to dislodge: it has the deepest roots in public consciousness, and it had penetrated the 1968 cohort more deeply than the other myths. Additionally, most 1990s' events that contribute to anti-mythic post-ignorance and post-victimization scenarios do not debunk the myth of resistance, but rather bolster it. In contrast to the other myths, mythic resistance has been uncritically accepted since German rearmament in the 1950s. It has an entrenched institutional infrastructure of historical monographs and textbooks, professorial chairs, museums, memorial sites, and commemorative holidays.[1] Finally, as the last of the myths upholding the older generation's innocence, it is being defended with special desperation. There is reason for optimism, however. Even if the myth itself is tenacious, one of its postwar products, the determination to expose self-serving untruths, is alive and well. Sooner or later, I predict, it will go the way of the other myths.

Let us return to the 1970s to see why mythic resistance was ascendant when the other myths were under fire. Because the mythic image of the "good Nazi" was so improbable, it was a focus of scrutiny when the re-realization of the Nazi past began in the 1970s. As the collaborationist nature of traditional military resistance groups became clear, curiosity about grassroots groups increased. In the 1980s the previously positive assessment of the collaborationist elites who backed the 20 July 1944 assassination attempt was reversed, and resistance by women and the "White Rose" students in Munich was rediscovered.[2] This research soon made clear that resistance of any kind had been the exception, not the rule. In a face-saving attempt to rescue the notion of the "good (everyday) Nazi," Martin Broszat introduced the term *Resistenz* ("impedance") to distinguish between active resistance to Nazi dictates (*Widerstand*), and behavior that indicated nonacceptance of Nazi policies, even if it did little or nothing to alter those policies.[3]

As the 1980s' and 1990s' Germans learned more about the plight of the true victims of Nazism, they realized that the token noncompliance of *Resistenz* had been overshadowed by thick layers of apathy and collaboration. They also recognized how complex the issue of true resistance was. Resistance involved more than planting a bomb under Hitler's desk, for although Hitler held together all strands of power, his system had soon developed its own genocidal momentum, which needed to be brought to a halt. And resistance meant more than leaving a cooked potato on the sidewalk for passing inmates, or harboring a fugitive prisoner, for although that may have softened the crushing onslaught of the genocidal juggernaut, it did nothing to stop it.

The city of Dachau offers an almost allegorical illustration of the early 1980s' rediscovery of active anti-Nazi resistance after decades of focus on the ineffectual "resistance" of mythic "good Nazis." As we have seen, while under the scrutiny of the Allies immediately after the end of war, German civil authorities made an effort to publicly propagate examples of genuine German resistance. In March 1946 Mayor Schwalber gave a commemorative speech at the graves of the victims of the pre-liberation Dachau uprising, and in May 1947 he spoke again when the VVN dedicated a plaque opposite city hall where the bodies of the executed insurgents had lain (ill. 13). In preparation for 9 November 1946, the first anniversary of his revealing speech discussed in part II, Schwalber introduced a motion in the town council to name six city streets after resistance fighters from Dachau, "in order to express the bonds between the residents of Dachau and the prisoners, and especially to keep the memory of the joint fight for freedom alive."[4] The council also decided to name a square in the heart of the old city "Resistance Square" (see ill. 79). At some later date – some residents suspect during the 1950s or 1960s, but no one knows for sure – the latter street sign was removed. Its disappearance was not noticed until 1981, when a local journalist found a reference to the renaming in an old article.[5] This discovery sparked a local scandal and the rededication of the square.

Only once in the decades from the 1940s to the 1980s (in February–March 1960, when Mayor Zauner was in trouble for calling the camp inmates "criminals and homosexuals") did the city of Dachau even consider establishing a memorial in the town for the victims of the camp, but it decided against the project.[6]

Another interesting change took place over the course of the 1980s. As we saw at the end of chapter 13 (p. 346), in 1979 there was an outpouring of literary works in which members of the 1968er cohort accused and challenged the silence of their 1933er parents. In the course of the 1980s this generational conflict shifted from a reflexive condemnation of the parents' past to a reflective examination of the consequences of being raised by Nazi-tainted parents during the mythically imbued 1950s and 1960s. In 1987 Ralph Giordano coined a term for the burden incurred by the postwar cohorts: "the second guilt" of not being able to connect emotionally with the Nazi past.[7] The first publications to examine the effects of this second guilt were Peter Sichrovsky's *Born Guilty: Children of Nazi Families* and Dörte von Westernhagen's *The Children of the Perpetrators*, both printed in 1987 and widely discussed in the media.[8] Additional reflective personal accounts followed in 1989, such as Sabine Reichel's *What Did You Do in the War, Daddy?*, and Gabriele von Arnim's diary of her year-long quest to break through mythic ignorance, *The Great Silence*.[9] At the same time, more scholarly and comprehensive collections than Sichrovsky's initial book began to appear, most importantly Dan Bar-On's *Legacy of Silence* (1989), and Gerald Posener's *Hitler's Children: Sons and Daughters of Leaders of the Third Reich* (1991).[10]

We have seen how the cohort of 1968ers, born between 1937 and 1953, debunked the myth of ignorance in the 1970s, and we have seen how the barefoot historians of the second postwar cohort of 1979ers, born 1954–66, challenged the myth of victimization in the 1980s. In this chapter we will see how the third postwar cohort, born after 1966 and embracing a more reflective attitude towards the Nazi past, has attempted to come to terms with the legacies of mythic resistance in the 1990s. This story begins with an overview of the national events arising from and impinging upon the process of coming to terms with mythic resistance. It then moves to the local arena in Dachau, where the attempt to establish an international center for youth encounters in the town illustrates how determined 1979ers overcame the mythically rooted resistance of the preceding cohorts. In conclusion we will examine the plans for the projected renovation of the site in 2000–2001, especially the extent to which those plans reflect mythic legacies, and the ways they might be modified to better overcome those legacies in the education of the cohorts of Germans born after the mid-1970s.

The dialectic of mythic resistance

The revival and realization in 1993 of Helmut Kohl's pet project of a national memorial for all German victims offers a first illustration of how attitudes towards mythic resistance began to change in the 1990s.[11] Kohl had ceased actively to pursue his national victims' memorial project after a rancorous debate about the project in the Bundestag in April 1986. That debate was immediately followed by the Historians' Controversy of 1986–7. Before Kohl could restart his initiative, momentous things began to happen in German history: in the fall of 1989 the East German government began to totter, leading to the opening of the Berlin Wall in November and the incorporation of East Germany into the West in October 1990. On 20 June 1991 the West German parliament, swelling with nationalist pride after the happy ending of the Cold War, decided in a close 338:320 vote, against all economic rationality, to restore the former Reich capital Berlin as the new national capital. To complete the symbolic trappings of the former and future capital, Kohl immediately revived his national victims' memorial project. He proposed to reutilize a classicist revival guardhouse built after the Napoleonic Wars in 1815, which the democratic Prussian SPD government had rededicated as a "memorial site for the fallen of the Great War" in 1931.[12] Since 1962 it had served as East Germany's national memorial to the "victims of militarism and fascism" (which, in the perverse logic of East German mythic resistance, included the Nazi-era German army, the Wehrmacht).

Kohl's proposal stipulated that a small meditative sculpture by the socialist artist Käthe Kollwitz would be enlarged as the central motif in the interior. It depicted a mourning mother hugging her dead, uniformed son on her drawn-up knees. When this proposal was debated in parliament in May 1993, the three main political parties CDU, SPD, and FDP were unanimous in their support.[13] The memorial was readied in record time for its third rededication on *Volkstrauertag*, the religious German national day of mourning on 14 November. Members of the 1968er and 1979er cohorts, organized in the Greens and "Coalition 1990," protested vigorously against the plan. Kohl mobilized support from some of the 1980s' opponents, including the head of the Central Council of Jews in Germany, by adding a text derived from President Weizsäcker's May 1985 address as a more detailed dedication on a plaque next to the memorial's entrance.[14] Stubborn resistance was mustered by the Berlin Jewish community, the political survivors' organization VVN, some members of the SPD, the Coalition 90/Greens, the East German socialist PDS party, and cultural figures with roots in the 1968 movement. They categorically rejected the idea of commemorating the victims of Hitler's genocidal programs along with "victims" who helped him to implement those programs in one memorial. However, they were unable to prevent the realization of the project. Since its dedication, this "national memorial to the victims of war and tyranny" has, in spite of its location in the heart of Berlin, faded from the limelight of the politics of the past. It is more a relic of a bygone period of mythic victimization than a future-oriented symbol of German recollection.

The national victims' memorial has been overshadowed by a much larger and far more controversial memorial project for Berlin: a national memorial "for the murdered Jews of Europe." This other memorial has yet to be realized, although millions of marks have already been spent on design competitions and convocations of experts.[15] Its roots go back to 1988, when TV talk show hostess Lea Rosh (b. 1937), after narrating a documentary TV series entitled *Death is a Master from Germany*, started a private initiative to establish such a memorial.[16] Rosh, who changed her name from Edith Rohs to express the Jewish identity she felt (one of her grandparents had been Jewish), is a typical example of the anti-Nazi, pro-victim attitude of the mythically resisting 1968ers.[17] Helmut Kohl offered her organization a prime piece of real estate in Berlin as part of his effort to gain support for his own German victims' memorial project in 1993. Because of this gift and some prodding by Rosh and her supporters, the murdered Jews project became a matter of Kohl's prestige. Underwritten by the national and Berlin city governments, a design competition in 1994 brought in 528 entries, none of which was ultimately found to be acceptable. A series of colloquia was held in early 1997 to discuss fundamental questions of why Germany needed such a memorial, where it could be located, and how it might look. A second, limited competition yielded nineteen proposals in November 1997, several of which were deemed acceptable. However, the realization of the project stalled once again prior to the September 1998 national elections. Even though Chancellor Kohl lost the election to SPD candidate Gerhard Schröder, the project had already progressed so far that it could not be abandoned.[18] At that time three agencies had to come to an agreement before the project could be realized: the national government (the chancellor with his cabinet), Rosh's private foundation, and the government of the city-state of Berlin (the mayor and the cabinet). The project remained stalled for months after the election because the three parties could not agree to close the competition. Finally, they decided that the federal parliament should decide between two competing designs (a monolithic text "Do not murder," and a symbolic graveyard with 2,700 huge concrete stelae and an "informational space"), or no memorial at all.

This projected national memorial for the murdered Jews of Europe is informed both by the myth of resistance and the challenge against that myth. It is mythic in that the enormous expenditure of funds on it compensates for the lack of sincere governmental efforts to confront the Nazi past at the hundreds of existing memorial sites, most notably sites of national significance such as the Berlin Gestapo headquarters or the Sachsenhausen concentration camp on the outskirts of Berlin. While the national government was investing so many financial and public relations resources into Rosh's project, it explicitly rejected the creation of a permanent national foundation to support the existing concentration camp memorial sites. Initially, DM15 million were budgeted for the Berlin "murdered Jews" memorial – the lion's share from government funds. When the suggestion of integrating a library and research institution into the "murdered Jews" memorial was suggested, federal Minister of Culture Michael Naumann thought a hyperbolic DM150 million and then even 180 million might be an appropriate amount.[19] In contrast, the national parliament doled out only token amounts for the concentration camp memorial sites, for instance a paltry DM500,000 for the overhaul of Dachau in 1997.[20] For the entire Dachau project, an issue of international importance, the Bavarian authorities refused to budget more than DM8.5 million – about 75 percent of the DM14 million deemed necessary by experts.[21]

The issue of national financial support for concentration camp memorial sites was particularly acute in the early 1990s because the memorial sites in eastern Germany were facing a dire financial crisis. In contrast to the West, where local and regional support groups had evolved since the 1960s to lobby for the memorials, in the East government endorsement from the beginning obviated the need for local and regional networks of support. After unification in 1990 the West German model of "cultural autonomy of the states" (*Kulturhoheit der Länder*), which includes financial responsibility, took effect in the East. Instead of recognizing the grave need also to renovate and expand the western sites, on 29 June 1994 parliament decided to create a temporary (ten-year) program to support only the sites in former East Germany. By the time the ten-year period expires in 2004, it is likely that the mythic inhibitions will have subsided enough to allow the creation of a national foundation to support the memorial sites. Some progress has already been made in this direction: in September 1998 DM5.5 million was budgeted for the preservation and restoration of Sachsenhausen and Ravensbrück.[22]

The planned national memorial for the murdered Jews of Europe, however, is also a symbol of weakening mythic resistance. Stated simply, it is a public recognition that Germans did indeed perpetrate the Holocaust, and a sign that at least the political elites are willing to accept, symbolically if not morally, their national community's responsibility for perpetrating it. (True moral acceptance would entail a clear recognition of restitution and compensation obligations, without regard to financial consequences.) The importance of that sign would clearly be heightened if there were a show of broad popular support for the memorial, such as an outpouring of donations for its realization. However, to date the German populace has remained reticent, skeptically eyeing this initiative "from above."

Numerous other events of the 1990s illustrate the dialectic of debunking mythic resistance: events that weaken it often serve to propagate it as well.[23] Steven Spielberg's blockbuster Holocaust film *Schindler's List* is probably the clearest example of this phenomenon.[24] As with the film *Holocaust* in 1979, the German release of *Schindler's List* in March 1994 was a major media event. Again, prior to the German premiere many essayists were reserved about the film's educational potential, but, after the effusive popular reception became clear, educators scrambled to make the film available to schools and to produce teachers' guides.[25] Many young Germans – the audience with which the film was most popular – claimed, in spite of all previous exposure to the topic in the mass media and at school, that this film was the first time they had learned about the Holocaust.[26] (Most of them probably meant that this was the first time that they had felt an emotional connection to the events.) Although the film was thus anti-ignorance and anti-victimization, Schindler's story as portrayed by Spielberg undergirded the myth of resistance. It featured a German hero whose brown-collar exploitation of Jewish labor paled in comparison to his dramatic rescue of several hundred Jews. The counter-mythic implication that if Schindler saved Jews, many other Germans could have done so but did not, was only brushed upon in the public discussion.

Personalizing the perpetrators: "Crimes of the German Army" and the Goldhagen debates

The year 1995 marks a turning point in the struggle against mythic resistance.[27] A controversial international commemoration of the fiftieth anniversary of the liberation of Auschwitz in January was the first in a series of events that revealed a dramatic transformation in united Germany's public attitude toward the Nazi past. These events included the June 1995 parliamentary decision to create a national day of Holocaust remembrance, a vigorous public debate about a 1995 exhibition documenting the German army's participation in systematic mass murder, and the stormy public discussions in summer and fall 1996 of political scientist Daniel Goldhagen's controversial bestselling book indicting most pre-1945 Germans as "Hitler's willing executioners."

The 26 January 1995 ceremony in Auschwitz was attended by representatives from around the world, including Nobel prizewinner Elie Wiesel, German President Herzog, and Polish President Walesa. The German delegation included two of four vice presidents of the German parliament as well.[28] In a statement read for him, Chancellor Kohl told the audience that "the darkest and most horrible chapter of German history was written in Auschwitz," and that "one of our priority tasks is to pass on this knowledge to future generations so that the horrible experiences of the past will never be repeated." This unequivocal statement of acceptance of Germany's brown-collar past was a far cry from Kohl's homage to German victimhood at Bitburg a decade earlier, although he did return to more vacuous statements on German victimhood in an 8 May 1995 commemorative speech.[29]

As the 8 May 1995 anniversary of the end of the war approached, it became clear that this would be a commemoration of superlatives – the last of the "round number" anniversaries which could be attended by substantial numbers of living witnesses. In fact, it is likely that overall attendance was higher at the 1995 ceremonies than at any other time since the end of the war, and it is certain that the media coverage surpassed even the 1945 media blitz.[30] In Dachau a Bavarian Minister President attended a commemorative ceremony in the former camp for the second time ever (the first time was on 20 March 1993), speaking to an audience of 5,000, including about 2,000 survivors (ill. 85).[31] In Berlin, President Herzog gave the keynote address, which devoted substantial space to the brown-collar crimes. At that same ceremony in the soon-to-be-wrapped Reichstag building, Ignaz Bubis, the head of the Central Council of Jews in Germany, suggested that Germany create a national day of remembrance for the victims of National Socialist persecution and genocide. Three weeks later the parliament approved a bill naming 27 January, the day Auschwitz was liberated, the Day of Commemoration for Victims of National Socialism, beginning in 1996.

While German elected officials were symbolically affirming their country's moral debt to the victims of brown-collar crimes, an exhibition about ordinary German soldiers' participation in genocidal undertakings began touring Germany and Austria. As part of the Hamburg Institute for Social Research's research program on violence and destruction in the twentieth century, two scholars used hundreds of photographs and unsent letters collected by Soviet investigators from captured Germans during World War II to create a traveling exhibition. In picture after picture, letter after letter, and report after report, the exhibition detailed the daily participation of all ranks of the German army in executions and hangings of unarmed civilians, and the deportation and mass murder of Jews across the eastern front. These graphic documents made clear beyond doubt that large numbers of Germans from all walks of life had heard and seen firsthand testimony about brown-collar crimes.

Although these personal documents had been known to scholars for some time, they had not been widely known among the broader public. Hannes Heer and Klaus Naumann of the Hamburg Institute completed the exhibition of personal photographs and letters in early 1995.[32] It drew substantial but not spectacular audiences in various German and Austrian cities until March 1997, when it was shown in Munich.[33] By that time, it had been seen by 130,000 visitors in sixteen cities. After conservative Bavarian officials denounced it and a demonstration of 5,000 neo-Nazis drew even more attention to it, 88,400 visitors – more than four times the projected 20,000 – saw the show during its six-week sojourn in the Bavarian capital.[34] The Munich controversy prompted the national parliament to debate whether the exhibition should receive an official endorsement. The March and April 1997 parliamentary discussions were characterized by moving personal statements from 1948ers.[35] Another controversy ensued when the exhibition opened in April 1997 in St. Paul's Church in Frankfurt, where the first democratic German parliament had convened in 1848. By early 1999 the exhibition had been shown to 860,000 visitors in thirty-two German and Austrian cities, with bookings for fifty more locations and requests from thirty more.[36] The organizers had amassed an archive of over 30,000 press clippings about the exhibition. Venues for English, French, and Dutch translations were already scheduled.[37] As with the *Holocaust* TV series, the Historians' Controversy, and

Schindler's List, following the intense media reporting, numerous interpretative and documentary collections were published, making in-depth
examinations and discussions in schools and universities possible.[38]

A third 1990s' highpoint of the German interest in brown-collar perpe-
trators was reached in 1996 with the frenzied reception of Daniel
Goldhagen's book *Hitler's Willing Executioners*.[39] As soon as the English
edition was published in March 1996, a flood of German reviews ensued.[40]
The weekly *Die Zeit* published an eight-part series of opinions on the book
prior to its German publication in August.[41] When the author arrived in
Germany for a book tour in September, he became the darling of the
German public. TV talk shows could not book him often enough, and
panel discussions sold out without exception.[42] As a book of letters
Goldhagen received from his German audiences indicates, the televised
discussion of his theses reached a far greater audience than is usual for a
scholarly work.[43]

The book's central thesis struck at the heart of all three myths.
Goldhagen argues that most Germans not only knew about and did not
resist the Holocaust, but that they openly embraced and perpetrated it
when offered the opportunity. This claim, given the almost universal
scholarly rejection in Germany and abroad, might be called the "myth of
eager perpetration." Interestingly, in spite of all of the cogent scholarly ref-
utations, the German public enthusiastically embraced the book and
cheered the author at numerous public appearances in 1996.[44]

Jürgen Habermas, the philosopher who had initiated the Historians'
Controversy in 1986, gave the book one of its strongest endorsements in a
March 1997 speech when Goldhagen received a privately sponsored
"German Democracy Prize."[45] For Habermas, the book's scholarly merits
or failings were unimportant. Rather, he considered it praiseworthy
because of its contribution to the "ethical-political process of public self-
understanding" in Germany – in other words, its role in fostering awareness of the three myths and their legacies. Although Habermas admitted
that some of Goldhagen's claims were insupportable, he still found the
"agitated reactions" of some German historians incomprehensible.[46] A
categorization of the reactions according to the cohorts of the historians,
however, reveals that 1948ers such as Hans Mommsen were clearly more
"agitated" about Goldhagen's book than their 1979er colleagues such as
Norbert Frei (b. 1955) and Thomas Sandkühler (b. 1962).

The older scholars of the 1948er and 1968er cohorts, driven by anti-
mythic zeal – itself a legacy of the myth of resistance – were guarding
against arguments they felt were falling back to older, monocausal

models. They did not realize that their own more complex explanatory models were often too abstract, too far removed from the gruesome behaviors so richly portrayed by Goldhagen, to be plausible to younger audiences. As we have already seen with the popular reactions to *Schindler's List* and the exhibition about the crimes of the German army, it was the graphic portrayal of the mental world of the perpetrators that resonated with a public tired of the half-truths at the core of the myth of resistance.

One reviewer suggested that Goldhagen's book's rave popularity stemmed from the emotionally empathetic portrayal of the victims, as had been the case with the films *Holocaust* and *Schindler's List*.[47] However, the gruesome descriptions in Goldhagen's book do not make the victims come to life, even metaphorically (nor, for that matter, was the empathetic portrayal of victims the distinguishing feature of *Schindler's List*). Rather, both paint a rich picture of the personalities, thoughts, and motivations of the brown-collar murderers.

As these events of the late 1990s show, younger Germans are less tolerant of public portrayals of Germans as victims.[48] Instead, there has been a clear increase in willingness to learn about Germans as perpetrators, about how quite ordinary citizens from the "middle of society" could become brown-collar criminals. The visibility of the 1933ers' and 1943ers' professions of ignorance and the 1948ers' presumption of innocence is receding as these generations leave the public stage. These older cohorts' strident insistence on a right to ignorance is giving way to the willingness in the younger, post-1968er cohorts to confront the question of legacies and responsibility head on.[49] By the end of the 1990s institutions such as the German Protestant Church, and organizations such as the German Society of Pediatrics, were vying to profess their Nazi-era participation in the Holocaust.[50] This willingness also manifests itself in recent efforts to institutionalize education about the brown-collar crimes, especially at sites such as Dachau.

Mythic resistance in Dachau: the creation of a youth center, 1983–1998

Education, especially emotionally moving education, was the primary means by which the three founding myths have been challenged and overcome. The initial Allied reeducation program in 1945–6 failed to make Germans reflect on the brown-collar crimes because it failed to strike an empathetic chord. Anne Frank's story in the 1950s, and the TV miniseries *Holocaust* in 1979, as well as *Schindler's List*, the *Wehrmacht* exhibition and Goldhagen events of the 1990s were so spectacular in their success precisely because they were so emotionally resonant. This insight has important consequences for the design of concentration camp memorial sites, which draw most of their educational power from visitors' knowledge that they are at the very sites where the brown-collar crimes were committed.

Since 1945 advocates of anti-Nazi educational efforts had recognized that a strong emotional aura surrounded the sites of the brown-collar crimes. For that reason the Allies chose the Nazi judicial center Nuremberg and the concentration camps at Dachau and Belsen as the locations for the trials of brown-collar perpetrators. In spite of German efforts in the late 1940s to ignore, and in the early 1950s to efface, the traces of the Nazi atrocities, interest in those authentic sites remained. The most brazen attempt at effacement, Dachau County Governor Junker's July 1955 parliamentary motion to close the crematorium to visitors, prompted the first documented suggestion to create a permanent educational facility instead. In response to Junker's demolition proposal, Professor Baruch Graubard, the vice president of the Israelite Cultural Communities in Bavaria, suggested that an "international youth or student center" with a library of documents about the Hitler period, or perhaps even an "institute for Jewish studies" or an "international memorial site" could be erected by the town. Then, instead of insisting that they had been victimized by the Nazis, the townsfolk could point out their present commitment to humanitarian values.[51]

Over the following decade an international memorial site was indeed created, albeit more against than with the will of the town, which resisted supporting the memory of the concentration camp until the late 1980s. In 1960, when Mayor Zauner made his insulting remarks about concentration camp inmates having been criminals, a proposal that the town erect a simple monument for the victims of the camp was considered, but quickly rejected once the international attention had waned. In 1970, a year in which the twenty-fifth anniversary of liberation provoked a heightened interest in the commemoration of the Dachau KZ, CSU city councillor Alfred Kindermann initiated a resolution suggesting the establishment of a "Peace Research Institute." This time the idea was approved by the city council and sent on to the Bavarian Minister of Culture. However, once the anniversary year had passed no further action was taken, and the city did not follow up its own suggestion.[52]

As the number of young visitors continued to climb in the 1970s – from about 1,100 youth groups in 1972 to over 3,600 in 1978 – the issue of opening a youth hostel in Dachau was raised again. An inquiry in 1978 revealed that 50 percent of the guests at the two Munich youth hostels visited the Dachau memorial site.[53] Nonetheless, the city of Dachau still resisted the idea of offering young people a place to stay locally. Yet another attempt to link the city and the memorial site, this time through the establishment of a cultural center for Sinti and Roma in Dachau in 1980, was also quickly shelved, even though Mayor Reitmeier noted the city's empathy with the discriminated group. In a classic expression of the legacy of the myth of victimization, he said:[54]

> Dachau's citizens share the deplorable fate of most gypsies, in that they have to live with a bad reputation through no fault of their own. Especially we Dachauers know the hardships of minorities, because we, too, belong to a quite small, persecuted minority.

Yet another attempt at reviving the peace research institute project, in 1982, this time by a Berlin salesman who had moved to Dachau in 1980, gained the support of the local Social Democratic Party. However, when Mayor Reitmeier stated publicly that the city council had already discussed such proposals "enough to make one vomit [zum Erbrechen]," that project once again faded into bureaucratic oblivion.[55]

By that time, however, the anti-mythic movement of the late 1970s was gaining momentum. In 1981, the Polish town of Oświęcim (in German: Auschwitz) began construction of an international youth hostel with financial support from the West German government. In the fall of that year a group of interested people in Dachau met to discuss the establishment of a similar center in Dachau.[56] Survivors of the camp joined with volunteers working at the memorial site, other interested local citizens, and the newly founded history workshop "For Example Dachau" to work towards their goal.[57] This time the city government was informed from the beginning, even if it declined to participate. The support association enlisted international advocates for their effort. Local religious and human-rights groups (such as the Dachau and Bavarian Youth Rings, and the local chapter of Amnesty International), the international Dachau survivors' committee, and prominent public figures such as authors Heinrich Böll and Ralph Giordano, vice president of the national parliament Heinz Westphal, national SPD chairman Hans-Jochen Vogel, and former Austrian chancellor Bruno Kreisky were among the members of a special "advocacy group" supporting the youth center project. In August 1984, as part of the preparations for the coming "International Year of Youth," the city of Munich committed DM300,000 to the project.

The support association for the youth hostel did not wait for the construction of a building to begin its work. From the summer of 1983 until 1998, when the center was finally opened, each summer an "international youth encounter tent camp" was organized.[58] The number of participants rose steadily from 117 in 1983 to 404 in 1988. The coalition of support groups gained practical experience in working with individuals and groups for periods averaging from four days to over a week. In 1985 the support association accelerated its public relations work. In May 1985, two months after the Dachau CSU rejected the project out of hand, the association obtained the endorsement of President Weizsäcker, who had just delivered his memorable post-Bitburg speech.[59] Public relations successes followed thick and fast: in 1986 the association was awarded the Theodor Heuss medal, and at a conference sponsored by the Bavarian Youth Ring in March 1987 to discuss its own draft proposal for the project, national parliamentary representatives from the SPD, CDU, and CSU expressed their support for the project.[60]

The Dachau CSU did not yield to this mounting pressure. At an election rally during the Dachau *Volksfest* in 1986 (the same occasion Minister Baumgartner had used in 1955 to call for the "disappearance" of the crematorium), Dachau CSU chairperson Georg Englhard (b. 1929) suddenly called out to the 1,500-person audience during his welcoming speech: "We want to know if we need such an institution [youth encounters center] – who is for it?"[61] When only a few people raised their hands, he declared, "We know who the supporters are." Such veiled threats, however, did not deter the proponents. Their continuing progress infuriated the local "resisters" even more.

At a climactic city council committee meeting in March 1987 Manfred Probst (a member of the 1968er cohort), the head of the CSU fraction in the town council, declared that he would "fight to the last drop of blood" against the construction of the center.[62] Drawing on the image of the "food donor," the most frequently mentioned form of mythically overblown local "resistance," Probst's colleague Englhard claimed that Dachau natives derived a "moral right to resist the center . . . from the right to resist of their parents who helped KZ prisoners."[63] The local CSU did not leave it at verbal gaffes. In September the hostile *Dachauer Nachrichten* printed a "survey" in its free weekly edition, asking readers to answer yes or no to two questions and send in the clipping. The questions were a one-two punch of mythic victimization and resistance:[64]

yes___ no___ I support the *Dachau News*'s suggestion to include a
multilingual documentation in the memorial site . . . that
establishes [sic!] that the KZ was forced upon the city of
Dachau by the NS powerholders, that many Dachau citizens
were imprisoned in the KZ, that no Dachau citizen was ever a
member of the guard detachments, and that many citizens
helped the prisoners.

yes___ no___ I support the suggestion to emphasize in an appropriate way
inside the KZ memorial site the Dachau citizens who selflessly
helped the prisoners.

The response to this consoling attempt to rewrite history by acclamation
was overwhelming: a month later the *News* had received 1,711 answers, all
of them (according to the report) marked "yes."[65] For the local CSU leadership this was a clear mandate for their efforts to ensure that the city of
Dachau would not "be thrown into one pot with the horrors."

With international attention focused on such antics, the behavior of
the Dachau CSU was becoming an embarrassment for the Bavarian
parent party. The controversy had already begun to shift out of Dachau's
purview into the Bavarian parliament. In April 1987, after Probst's "last
drop of blood" speech, the Bavarian Minister of Culture asked the city
and county of Dachau to respond officially to the Bavarian Youth Ring's
draft proposal. In October, splitting clearly along party lines, both the
city and county councils rejected it.[66] Responding to media reports of
these rejections, three members of the US Congress wrote to Bavarian
Minister President Strauss, urging him to "use his good offices" to ensure
the realization of the project. The Bavarian government then attempted
to find a compromise solution, first by renaming the project, from
"center for youth encounters" to "youth guest house," to emphasize that
the visitors would be guests of the town as well as of the memorial site.
Second, the Bavarian politicians tried to exclude the advocacy group
from the activities of the planned center and place local officials in
charge.

After a public hearing in January 1988, at which the only objections were
raised by Mayor Reitmeier and Dachau's county governor, the Culture
Ministry released a proposal giving Dachau officials 50 percent control of
the youth center. In its November 1988 plan for "improving the pedagogical support of young visitors and for a youth guest house in the city of
Dachau," the Bavarian government planned an oversight board composed solely of representatives of the Ministries of Culture and Finance
(long in the hold of the CSU), and the mayor and county governor of
Dachau. This lopsided plan excluded all experts and experienced groups

386

that had been working towards the realization of the project. Criticism of such local politicking drew national attention once again.[67]

During another four years of wrangling the support group succeeded in broadening the oversight committee slightly to include the Bavarian Youth Ring. Finally in April 1992, Dachau city council accepted the project, with only the three delegates of the extreme-right Republikaner Party dissenting. Even in the face of overwhelming odds, however, local officials did not give up their resistance – the myth of resistance had done an excellent job preparing the local political elites to resist another "victimization" after the one they had been quick to embrace in 1933. Delay tactics were now the preferred method. First a series of public hearings about potential locations were held, in which neighbors voiced their fears that the "revelry of the masterers of the past" would disturb their sleep.[68] Eventually, however, a favored site emerged: at the edge of the former SS camp, about midway between the town and the camp (ill. 1). Now officials suggested that toxic residues might be buried underground, necessitating a round of expensive tests, which yielded no results except further delays.

However, in accordance with the 1995 "turn" of public opinion mentioned above, Dachauers voted a new mayor into office who truly welcomed the youth center as an opportunity to bring fresh impulses into the local political culture. Ground was finally broken in March 1997, but not without a remnant of mythic resistance.[69] Not only were neighbors still complaining about the "racket" that would be made by young people who had been "incited by the concentration camp," but the support group that had sustained the initiative for more than a decade, and without which the project would never have progressed that far, was neither mentioned in the speeches nor allowed to make public statements.

The youth guest house was officially opened on 8 May 1998.[70] Looking back over more than two decades of dogged resistance, it appears that 1948er Dachauers had learned one lesson from their 1933er parents' willingness to tolerate and support Nazism even where they had sensed it was immoral. The progeny resisted verbally and symbolically until the bitter end. Their ability to stand up and fight for their belief that the memorial site was "wrong" for the town is, from this perspective, quite laudable. It was only overcome by the equally dogged engagement of 1968ers and 1979ers for the memorial site and youth center.

The difference between the opponents and proponents lay not in their conviction, but in the moral basis for that conviction. While the 1948ers tended to focus on their own narrowly conceived self-interest, later cohorts usually took a more universalistic outlook. As the following examination of plans to redesign the Dachau memorial site suggests, fostering more humane and universal value orientations is emerging as the primary goal of "education after Auschwitz" in the new millennium. However, in spite of the rough consensus around that goal, different cohorts of educators have widely varying views as to the most effective means to achieve it.

Intellect vs. emotion: Dachau as a "site of learning"

As the Nazi period has receded in time, the increased use of the Dachau memorial site for educational purposes has propelled the augmentation of the didactic infrastructure. In 1969 a twenty-minute documentary film summarizing the history of the camp was completed. In 1978 a catalog documenting the exhibition was published in German and English, with French and Italian versions following slightly later.[71] In September 1980 the Bavarian government recognized the skyrocketing number of school classes visiting the memorial by assigning four school teachers to work with groups at the site each year.[72] The number of these transient official guides climbed to nine by the end of the decade. Within a short time additional aids were developed for teachers who were unable to visit the site themselves before bringing their classes, and the first substantive studies of the experiences of school classes at the site were conducted.[73] In 1985 the memorial site began publication of an annual scholarly journal, the *Dachauer Hefte*, that makes historical documents and cutting-edge research on the camp available to an interested readership. The series was so successful that in 1992 it won the prestigious Geschwister Scholl Prize (named for a brother-and-sister pair who belonged to the White Rose resistance group in Munich) and was reprinted in a popular paperback edition.[74] At the turn of the millennium it was still the only scholarly journal in German devoted exclusively to Germany's brown-collar past.

In spite of these additions, the Bavarian government continued to resist making other important changes at the site. Instead of increasing maintenance and museum staff to meet the demands of the heavy traffic, in January 1984 a Monday closing was introduced. Each year this leaves literally tens of thousands of visitors from all over Europe and abroad standing in front of closed doors (ill. 80).[75] Although a relatively modest increase in personnel would enable the site to open every day, Bavarian officials showed no interest in remedying that situation.[76]

In September 1988 the Bavarian Ministry of Culture, which had just taken over responsibility for the site from the Ministry of Finance, released a plan for improving the site. However, it took no action for another five years.[77] In 1989 the Bavarian parliament passed a resolution to turn the "memorial site" into a "place of learning" (*Lernort*), a plan endorsed by the international survivors' organization, CID. In the 1990s the pressure to augment or redesign the memorial site to better serve the needs of young visitors increased further. The number of young people visiting the memorial site in organized groups (the only reasonably reliable statistic for this period) increased by about 17 percent from over 160,000 (6,000+ groups) in the late 1980s, to more than 190,000 (7,000+ groups) in the 1990s.[78]

Still the Bavarian government's foot-dragging continued. In response to a July 1992 inquiry, a Ministry of Culture representative admitted that "we still haven't gotten to the substantive issues." In the face of this official lethargy, in 1993 a coalition of local groups formed to lobby for improvements in the pedagogical facilities. This coalition's first initiative illustrates how the 1968er cohort's emphasis on cognitive learning, a product of its own emotionally rarefied conception of the Nazi period, came to be recognized through a learning process among the 1979ers.

At the May 1993 liberation ceremony some of the new coalition's members petitioned the CID for permission to sell "For Example Dachau" founder Hans-Günter Richardi's book about the early years of the concentration camp in the memorial site.[79] (According to the 1966 contract between the Bavarian government and the CID, the latter determines which books can be sold at the memorial site. The survivors have been very conservative in this regard, limiting the list to CID publications, primarily the museum catalog and the various issues of the new annual journal *Dachauer Hefte*. The CID also receives the proceeds from those sales, which comprise a substantial portion of its income.)

The petitioners were mainly local residents who had been voluntarily offering tours of the concentration camp memorial site. Their leading figure was Helmut Rez from neighboring Hebertshausen, at that time a doctoral student in political science at the University of Munich. Many of its members were also members of "For Example Dachau." CID president André Delpeche, perhaps annoyed by Richardi's past attempts to heroize resistance by Dachau citizens in order to win their approval of the memorial site, gruffly refused to consider the request. When the group petitioned him again two months later, Delpeche said that he would present their concern to the CID executive committee at its next meeting, but that they should not expect any changes.[80] The petitioners then constituted themselves more formally as the "Working Group 'Future of the Memorial Site.'" Instead of waiting to find a *rapprochement* with the CID, the Working

Group went on the offensive. In August 1993 it produced a comprehensive "Memorandum for a Better Memorial Site," which it sent to the chairwoman of the cultural policy committee in the Bavarian parliament with a letter asking whom it should approach to implement such changes.[81]

As we have seen, strident self-righteousness was one of the legacies of the myth of resistance. It was often accompanied by a haughty stance *vis-à-vis* the camp survivors, itself reminiscent of the attitude underlying the "'bad' survivor" trope of the 1950s. One of the Rez group's members gave this position a particularly pointed expression in a letter to the editor in early October 1993:[82]

> Under the present state of affairs improvements may only be made with the consent of the CID, which, however, has been adamantly blocking any changes whatsoever in a manner we cannot [sic!] accept. Such an important (learning) place as the memorial site cannot, in my opinion, be the "private property" of a small Comité.

Richardi, in spite of his personal stake in the book-selling question, also showed the same insensitivity, calling the CID's "obstinate position" an "annoyance."

The Rez group's demand was not unjustified, since other memorial sites in Germany, such as Buchenwald and even the much smaller Neuengamme, offer dozens of relevant publications for sale. However, for Delpeche and many other survivors of the concentration camps, a former concentration camp is primarily a site to memorialize and commemorate, honor, and ritually mourn. Only secondarily is it an educational institution. In this view, Germans need first to connect emotionally with the victims and begin the labor of mourning before they can start a truly transformative educational process. This phenomenon has been recognized by people who have worked intensively with young people in memorial sites such as Dachau. For instance Jürgen Zarusky, who had worked closely with survivors for more than a decade, pointed out:[83]

> The memorial site is first of all a site of commemoration and not a book store. The vast majority of visitors don't buy any publications at all, with the possible exception of the catalog [actually purchased by at most 8 percent of visitors; see ill. 72[84]]. It would indeed be a small enhancement of the memorial site if a broader offering of literature were available to interested visitors. However, its quality as a site of learning certainly does not depend on whether one can purchase the newest book by Richardi.

Norbert Reck, another local resident with substantial experience working with survivors and youth groups, made the same point years earlier in a paper summarizing his half-decade of experience working with teachers and their classes visiting the memorial site:[85]

> A memorial site is indeed a site of learning also, but not *only*. Whoever brings a group to the memorial site solely so that the group will learn something, and whoever does not also want to commemorate there from the depths of their heart, misuses the memorial site – and, if I may say it – insults the honor of the dead. Whoever uses a memorial site only as a means to an end should not be surprised when young people ignore this "means" as they ignore other media, and don't display the proper respectful attitude at the site.

The message is clear: the use of the memorial site exclusively for cognitive learning, without attention to the emotional aspects of a visit, is not apt to promote the kind of learning that these teachers want to take place at a memorial site.

During the 1990s, the insight that memorial sites should give priority to the emotional side of the learning experience gained wide acceptance among people working in education about brown-collar crimes. In 1997, for example, David Altschuler, the director of a Holocaust museum in New York City, observed:[86]

> A museum is only one medium of education. It is outstanding at achieving certain goals and irrelevant to others. For learning factual information, books and courses in school can be more effective. But some kinds of information – some kinds of feelings, emotions – can be unlocked with a billboard, with an advertisement, with a museum, that no college course will ever unlock.

What applies to Holocaust museums in the United States applies even more to memorial sites for the victims of brown-collar crimes in Germany: they should draw especially on their unique strength, namely the emotional appeal of a genuine historical site with authentic remains, and leave most of the intellectual learning for other, more suitable situations.

Film scholar Alison Landsberg has written one of the most detailed arguments in favor of this position. In her 1997 essay "Toward a Radical Politics of Empathy," she conceives of Holocaust museums (and by extension, concentration camp memorial sites) as "transferential spaces" where people enter into experiential relationships with events they did not experience, thereby gaining access to "sensually immersed knowledges, knowledges which would be difficult to acquire by purely cognitive means."[87] She suggests further that:

> It might be the case that for the event to become meaningful enough to retain as part of one's intellectual and emotional archive, upon which one's

actions in the future might be based, it needs to be significant not just on a cognitive level, but palpable in an individual, affective way.

This should not imply that concentration camp memorial sites should be devoid of factual information, nor that they should aim to make the greatest possible emotional impact. It merely underscores the need to strike a balance between the two. Numerous scholars have pointed out the danger of neglecting the cognitive.[88] Ludwig Eiber, the former director of the Neuengamme concentration camp memorial site and initially in charge of the Dachau exhibition redesign, noted that:[89]

> The location determines the exhibition . . . but the location is not self-
> explanatory. Visitors need help in recognizing the meaning of a camp,
> digesting the impressions they receive, and sorting out the information they
> learn.

Since most visitors know relatively little about the specifics of the Nazi concentration camps before they arrive, comprehensive onsite information is indispensable. Additionally, it is a didactic truism that too much emotion clouds the intellectual penetration of a given subject.[90] An affective connection to the material may be necessary to motivate a potential learner to engage with the subject matter, but after a certain point it is not conducive to achieving an understanding that encompasses multiple perspectives of that topic. Thus memorial site designers must guard against emotionally overwhelming visitors to those sites. Cognitive information in the form of written documents, charts, and narratives should be employed both to heighten emotional impact and to limit it.

Let us examine how the redesign of the Dachau memorial site at the turn of the millennium negotiates between the scylla of intellectual abstraction and the charybdis of emotional obfuscation.

Myths and enlightenment: the 1996 Dachau renovation guidelines

The establishment of a panel of experts called for in the Bavarian Ministry of Culture's 1988 plan did not take place until March 1995, when an "advisory council" to draw up guidelines for the planned renovation of the site was finally constituted. Under the leadership of Professor Wolfgang Benz of the Technical University of Berlin, one of the co-editors of the annual journal *Dachauer Hefte*, the advisory council was composed of four Dachau survivors and seven historians. In June 1995 it solicited input from a broad range of groups, including Helmut Rez's Working Group, Richardi's "For Example Dachau," and the Support Association for the Youth Center, as well as the Bavarian Youth Ring, the Documentation and Cultural Center for German Sinti and Roma,[91] and a few other groups.

A year later, in May 1996, the advisory council released its draft recommendations, which it summarized in six guidelines:[92]

1) Visitors will enter the memorial site through the original entry gate on the west side, instead of through the provisional gate in the southeast corner.

2) Several hitherto unused buildings will be incorporated into the tour and contain exhibitions: the entrance gate, the camp prison ("bunker"), the west wing of the service building, and the second (reconstructed) barrack.

3) The entrance to the museum will be moved from the east wing to the west wing of the service building (near the new entrance), which will contain the movie theater and rooms for discussions, multimedia offerings, and special exhibitions.[93]

4) The main exhibition will be modernized, and complemented by special exhibitions in other buildings corresponding to their functions (entry gate, bunker, barracks, crematorium).

5) The redesign of the outside spaces will be governed by the following principles:
   (a) no reconstructions or stagings will be implemented;
   (b) the watchtowers will not be accessible (avoidance of the perspective of the perpetrators);
   (c) outside of the main exhibition the history only of KZ Dachau will be addressed (no references to the situation in other KZs); only texts and pictures of KZ Dachau will be exhibited.

6) The memorial site will have four distinct functional areas:
   • authentic sites throughout the terrain, with their own exhibitions;
   • the main exhibition;
   • a "communication and media" area with a movie theater and special exhibition space, and seminar and lecture rooms with a separate entrance;
   • an enlarged "library and archive" area for scholarly, public relations, and pedagogical uses.

Most of these points are eminently reasonable. They take advantage of the Dachau site's ability to promote experiential learning. Having visitors enter the memorial site as prisoners once entered the camp, and having them traverse the exhibition as newly entering prisoners were once administratively and physically "processed" in the service building (gathering of personal data, confiscation of clothing, shaving of all hair, showering, etc.) certainly makes for a more intuitive understanding of how the camp functioned. Similarly, the use of authentic buildings for in-depth presentations of specific aspects unburdens the main exhibition and allows visitors to focus on those themes in buildings with emotionally resonant auras.

However, especially the guidelines in item 5 deserve closer consideration. They indicate that mythic legacies may also be at work, to the detriment of Dachau's effectiveness as a memorial site. First, principle 5(a) states categorically that nothing will be reconstructed or "staged." This limits the aspects of the site that can be used to promote experiential learning to the few remains that were coincidentally preserved or previously reconstructed. Since most original remnants of the camp were drastically modified in the late 1940s and early 1950s, and finally bulldozed in 1964–5, this prohibition amounts to allowing apologetic past visions of the "clean camp" to determine the future appearance and impact of the memorial site.

Consideration of the contingent nature of what was preserved reveals how illogical this categorical statement is. If County Governor Junker had succeeded in having the crematorium torn down in 1955, or if Curate Roth had not stopped the demolition of the watchtowers in 1956, would these buildings not be worthy of reconstruction? The crematorium–gas chamber building, because of the extreme atrocity it documents, would probably not be reconstructed. In that case, because the installation's authenticity has repeatedly been challenged, only the original would be so far beyond doubt that it could represent itself. Since the immediate postwar period, when SS internees circulated the rumor that the crematorium had been built by German prisoners working for the Americans after the war, deniers have used Dachau and Auschwitz to bolster their claims. The gas chamber in Auschwitz I, which was reconstructed from various remains of the demolished gassing facilities in Auschwitz II in 1947, is still a favorite "proof" offered by proponents of the "Holocaust as hoax" myth.[94]

The watchtowers, in contrast, as comparatively innocuous trappings of the camp, would probably be, and indeed were, reconstructed. The prisoners' barracks are on a level with the watchtowers. The camp survivors, aware of the difficulty of preserving all of the barracks, suggested in their 1962 plan that selected ones should be preserved, and the end walls of the rest left standing. The Bavarian government at that time, anxious to demolish as many remains of the camp as possible, did not accept even that compromise. In this case two new barracks were built to represent the originals. However, they were built to a much higher standard, with concrete slab floors and reinforced concrete supports (see ill. 30). Instead of recreating the end walls, the other thirty-two barracks were marked by low cement curbs, which many visitors mistakenly assume are genuine foundations. These thirty-two monotonous cement rectangles convey no impression of the daily life borne by some prisoners for a full twelve years. The hierarchies among the prisoners, and their segregation in different barracks according to nationality, severity of punishment, condition of health, or religion are neutralized. Nothing conjures up the subtle advantages of living in a barrack closer to the kitchen, which, for example, not only shortened by up to 500 meters the distance the huge kettles of broth had to be carried, but lengthened the time one had to eat it as well. How would kitchens, showers, a library, canteen, brothel, and greenhouse fit into our picture of a concentration camp?

The advisory council's categorical prohibition thus perpetuates the sanitizing efforts of the Bavarian government more than thirty years ago, instead of at least retroactively honoring the wishes of the survivors. The real question is not *whether* there should be reconstructions, but *which* reconstructions there should be.

In considering this question, it is useful to distinguish between genuine and authentic: while genuine means the original itself, one meaning of authentic (which also means genuine) is that something is "marked by close conformity to an original, accurately and satisfyingly reproducing essential features" of it.[95] Not only are the concrete reinforced barracks inauthentic, so are the watchtowers. The originals had different window coverings and no doors entering into the camp. The roof of the service building, without its clean-camp inscription about the "milestones to freedom," and with the addition of dormer windows on the east wing in the 1997 renovation, is not authentic in a narrow sense, either (see ill. 84).

Clearly there are gradations in the degree of authenticity. What was a "satisfying reproduction" at one time may not be sufficient at another time. Most camp survivors and many adults today would find that machine guns and search lights overstep the bounds of appropriate reconstruction. Max Mannheimer, one of the Dachau survivors on the advisory council, stated this position concisely when he told a reporter in 1996 that the memorial site "should not become a horror story," as one might find "re-created at Disneyland."[96]

This is a valid concern, but it should not obscure the fact that a great deal could be reconstructed before there is any danger of the Dachau memorial site becoming a historical theme park or "chamber of horrors," as critics have worried in the local press since the early 1950s. The crucial point is not that all reconstructions should be avoided, but that some reconstructions may be inappropriate or misleading. Memorial site designers must thus not only decide which reconstructions are appropriate, but also how explicitly they can and should be recognizable as reconstructions.

To take the example of the watchtowers: for young people with little foreknowledge of the history, such graphic elements as machine guns might be effective in creating an experiential sense of what the original camp was like. In the United States Holocaust Memorial Museum in Washington, D.C., visitors pass through an original deportation boxcar and walk through an arrangement of original shoes; in the Simon Wiesenthal Center's Beit Hashoah–Museum of Tolerance in Los Angeles, the tour ends with visitors passing through a replica concentration camp gate into a simulated gas chamber. Many younger visitors report that these are powerful experiences; some older visitors are overwhelmed by them. In these cases, however, the museum context makes clear that these are only simulated experiences. At an actual concentration camp site, that distinction is not as clear, and it becomes much more important explicitly to distinguish reconstructions from original remains.

An examination of the camp features that have already been reconstructed illustrates the broad range of possibilities for marking reconstructions. The most salient feature of the barracks area is also a recent reconstruction: the two rows of poplar trees along the central camp street. The original trees were planted during the expansion of the camp in 1938. They were felled in the early 1960s when the barracks were torn down, and then replanted in the 1980s (see ills. 4, 29). Especially when they are in full foliage, these "second generation" trees dominate the barrackless camp and make a strong impression on visitors. Why, of all of the original elements of the barracks area, are they alone worthy of reconstruction? Without distraction by other reconstructions, they lend the memorial site an eerie, almost parklike quality. The atmosphere of the memorial site would be quite different if, say, the barbed wire fencing that once stood between some barracks, isolating some groups of prisoners from others, were reconstructed. The interior fences would reinforce visitors' impression of the harshness of life in the camp, instead of giving today's barren site a serene, gardenlike quality.

Another problematic area of reconstruction is the security system enclosing the camp. From the gate inscription "Arbeit macht frei" to the one and one-half new watchtowers on the east side, essentially all of the existing barrier system around the camp was reconstructed after 1960.

Only two segments of the ditch and barbed wire barrier were rebuilt: near the 1965–2001 entrance in the southeast corner, and near the (postwar) gate to the crematorium in the northwest corner (see ill. 2). The concrete wall, which may or may not mimic the original, was erected after 1965 (ill. 80).[97] A well-tended strip of grass replaces the ditch and barrier around most of the rest of the camp. This haphazard reconstruction gives a highly distorted impression of the security of the original installation, but it is sufficient to illustrate the original security system.

One of the didactically most problematic changes in the presentation of the original security system is the broad path connecting the prisoners' compound and the crematorium area. It misrepresents the complete inaccessibility of the murder and corpse disposal installation for prisoners in the camp. During the KZ period this installation was behind the barrier, ditch, and wall, and strictly off limits to all but the few prisoners who were required to work there. Today a broad bridge crosses the ditch and penetrates the wall to connect the two. There are practical reasons for this artificial connection. In addition to shortening the distance visitors have to walk from the barracks area to the crematoria, this bridge physically represents the close functional connection between persecution and genocide that evolved in the concentration camps in 1941–2. However, other ways of achieving those ends might distort the original situation in the camp less. For instance, a clearly modern ramp or catwalk *over* the barbed wire barrier, moat, and wall would allow visitors physically to experience their privilege of being able to transcend the prisoners' compound and examine the crematoria. A separate, ground-level bridge further down along the wall could provide access for disabled visitors and maintenance personnel.

Last but not least is the question of barrack reconstructions. As mentioned above, two new barracks were reconstructed adjacent to the roll-call square in 1965, after all of the originals had been demolished. Although a prisoner infirmary and a canteen barrack (where more privileged prisoners could buy additional food and other items) originally stood at that site, these barracks were reconstructed as dormitory barracks.

The advisory council's 1996 recommendations barely address the issue of the inauthenticity of these preexisting, "staged" barracks. The more detailed plan released in 1998 suggests a more detailed dormitory reconstruction, with the formerly empty rooms at the east end of the former infirmary barrack devoted to an exhibition about its original function.[98] In the second barrack, where the canteen was, the 1996 plan and 1998 specifications foresee exhibitions about the various groups of prisoners, such as political prisoners of various affiliations and nationalities, Jews,

Jehovah's Witnesses, and homosexuals, with "special emphasis on resistance and solidarity in the camp." A biographical approach is intended to balance the structural emphasis of the main exhibition, which is based primarily on perpetrator records. However, the fact that in that very barrack certain prisoners could purchase a limited number of foodstuffs and personal items, thus reinforcing the divisive hierarchy among the prisoners, is not mentioned in the recommendations, nor is the existence of a prisoner library and classrooms in the adjacent barrack.

Since these superficially benign camp-era facilities do not lend themselves to a simple "dirty camp" narrative, re-creating them would raise more questions than it would answer. The advisory council may have omitted such reconstructions from its list in order to keep the message of the memorial site straightforward, thus avoiding potentially confusing or even "wrong" impressions.[99] If that is the case, the council's calculation may be counterproductive. As argued above, memorial sites with generally limited time for visits are best suited to evoking emotional reactions that can function as a starting point for longer-term, cognitive interactions with the historical record. Creating dissonant impressions and raising difficult issues is a more promising way of fostering the development of an emotional connection than an attempt to administer the most direct anti-Nazi message possible. Additionally, the exclusive "dirty camp" narrative is not only inauthentic, it is the least accessible to empathetic understanding.

On the question of the prisoner barracks, the advisory council implicitly recognized the insupportability of its categorical prohibition of reconstructions and stagings. The recommendations suggest namely that "frames constructed out of black metal poles in the outlines of individual barracks or parts of barracks" might be used to point out the special functions of some of the demolished buildings.[100] Documentary photographs and texts could be attached to the black poles to illustrate the special barracks functions. This kind of abstract staging elegantly solves the problem of distinguishing the authentic but nongenuine from the original by making no pretense of verisimilitude.

However, in that it did not recommend which specific barracks should be marked by framing poles, the council avoided the difficult issue of selecting aspects to emphasize. Before its recommendations can be realized, someone must decide which images of "Dachau" the memorial site should represent. The "dirty," inhuman camp would be symbolized by marking the punishment, quarantine, and even the infirmary barracks (since experiments on human subjects were also performed there); the "clean," "reeducation" aspects of the camp might be highlighted by marking the library, the canteen, and the chapel for religious services. The infirmary, library, and chapel could also be used to underscore the solidarity and resistance of the inmates, since they were used for clandestine and highly dangerous subversive activities. These issues will be decided by symposia of specialists as the renovation work progresses.[101]

Striking a balance between the various aspects of the original camp to be emphasized in the memorial site will not be easy. Given the traditional emphasis on icons of the "dirty camp" in memorial sites, and the continuing desire on the part of visitors to take away a positive "lesson" from the site, it is likely that genocidal aspects and inmate resistance will be highlighted. Both also respond to myths prevalent in the 1960s: underscoring the genocidal nature of the concentration camps reverses the "goodness" of the elder Nazi-era cohorts, while the emphasis on the inmates' resistance helps to clear the survivors' "bad" reputation.

Equally important for the development of intuitive understanding among future post-mythic cohorts, however, will be the documentation of the ideological construct of the "clean camp." As we have seen, evidence suggests that post-1968er cohorts find these streamlined iconic "dirty" camps unconvincing. The example of 1979er Stefanie discussed on p. 313 is a case in point.[102] Stefanie's 1968er history teacher had lectured the class on "victims, nothing but victims," and then exploded with frustration when a student asked him to explain the causes of the genocide in a way that made the behavior of the perpetrators comprehensible: "Tell us, where was the madness? Why did all those people shout hurrah and Heil? ... There must have been something to it." This desire to understand the perpetrators was at the core of the major discussion-provoking events during the 1990s: *Schindler's List*, the exhibition "Crimes of the German Army," and Daniel Goldhagen's book *Hitler's Willing Executioners*, to name only the three most salient.

This brings us to a second questionable statement in guideline 5: the stipulation that the "perspective of the perpetrators" be avoided.[103] Explaining the recommendation that the watchtowers remain inaccessible, a member of the advisory council told the author in 1997 that young Germans "already had enough experience with the perspective of the perpetrators" and should "for once experience the perspective of the victims when they come to a [concentration camp] memorial site." It is likely that another mythic legacy is at work here: the 1968ers' powerful identification with the victims. Attempting to control the visitor experience in this way is tantamount to railroading a particular view, a particularly unempathetic view, of the Nazi period into the minds of Dachau's visitors. It is likely to be as ineffectual with post-1979ers as it was with Stefanie and skeptics among her cohort.

Finally, the 1996 guidelines indicate that another mythic legacy, this time from the myth of ignorance, may also be at work: the privileging of cognitive over experiential learning. In a special section entitled "pedagogy of the memorial site," there is an explicit call to subordinate the emotional appeal of the site to a completely "rational" approach. Although it is not amplified in the suggestions that follow, the programmatic introductory sentence states: "The memorial site is not only a site of commemoration and warning, but especially a site of cognitive learning. For that reason the importance of cognitive learning shall be explicitly emphasized."[104] In a 1998 interview, advisory council member Hans Günter Hockerts, a professor of contemporary history in Munich, underscored this point, linking it to the "perspective" question: "There will be no theatrical stagings. Visitors will not be allowed to go into a watchtower, because then they might slip into the role of a perpetrator. No one will be allowed to play a virtual SS man – there is enough of that in those awful video games."[105] This statement ignores the didactic insight outlined above: that memorial sites are especially suited to fostering a personal, emotional connection to historical events.

Since the guidelines were completed in 1996, the realization plans have been modified several times. The Ministry of Culture first commissioned the Bavarian State Center for Political Education to oversee the project, while the task of redesigning the main exhibition was delegated to the House of Bavarian History, the official state historical museum.[106] Given the difficult task of designing an exhibition for 50,000 square feet on a limited budget of DM1 million, the House of Bavarian History convened a colloquium of experts in June 1998.[107] In December 1998 concrete plans and a timetable were finally released to the public.[108]

As additional problems emerged, the council modified its suggestions. For instance, when survivors recounted the importance of the rooms in the west wing of the service building, the advisory board decided that the movie theater should not be moved into that wing. It would have prevented the documentation of the original functions of those rooms.[109] However, some board members' desire to make the museum as "original" as possible has led to several counterproductive results. When part of an original inscription " . . . verboten" was discovered behind a cabinet, they decided to strip the wall down to the first coat of paint and leave that as the setting for the historical exhibition (ill. 87). Thus visitors must view the documents in a distinctively dirty and unpleasant setting, resembling a construction site more than any situation that was ever present in the concentration camp. Critics call this a "brick fetishism" that overcompensates for the massive destruction of other historical relics, while giving the historical exhibition a cheap, unfinished and unserious character.

In contrast to this fetishism for original Nazi-era substance, some of the same experts advocate the destruction of murals painted in the west wing by the US army after 1945. The murals depict pleasant scenes in the soldiers' homeland: snow-covered mountains, a Hawaiian sunset, and the Manhattan skyline (ill. 88). These paintings document how the US army attempted to take symbolic possession of the site after 1945. Although the murals would provide a powerful backdrop for the planned exhibit on the postwar uses of the camp, the wall carrying them is slated for demolition, ostensibly because it was added after 1945.[110] The demolition advocates may think that the destruction of these original relics will heighten the impression of the former concentration camp they want to convey. Since the wall would only marginally impair the experience of the Nazi-era admitting room's original function, however, its demolition is not necessary. Rather, the demolition may be motivated by countermythic overcompensation and lack of attention of future generations' need to understand their own mediated relationship to the Nazi era. In spite of strong opposition from some advisory board members, and contrary to decisions to preserve and exhibit postwar remains at sites such as Sachsenhausen and Buchenwald, in Dachau anti-mythic purists may yet have their way.[111]

The use of the original concentration camp entrance also became a particularly charged issue.[112] Although Bavarian officials repeatedly confirmed that a portion of the former SS camp would be taken from the present Bavarian state police compound for this purpose, Dachau residents (in marked contrast to their 1930s counterparts) have been lobbying hard to prevent any changes to the area, thus leaving the awkward and artificial 1965 entrance situation intact. In December 1999 the Bavarian Ministries of the Interior (responsible for the state police) and Culture tried to renege on the promised restoration of the original entrance. They were vigorously opposed by memorial site director Barbara Distel, Dachau mayor Kurt Piller, and the German Dachau survivors association, with backing from Federal Minister of Culture Michael Naumann. Naumann went so far as to imply that the Bavarian state police might have to leave entirely some day, since it is "not reasonable to expect young policemen and memorial site visitors to tolerate the accommodation of state police in former SS barracks directly adjacent to the memorial site."

Ultimately the needs and assumptions of future visitors to the memorial site should determine what balance between emotion and cognition should be maintained. The advisory council notes in its preface that in the year 2000 the memorial site will be visited primarily by young people who have "no life-historical relationship to the events" because even their parents and teachers "only learned about National Socialist crimes . . . in school or college." This assumption is both misleading and untrue.[113] The parents of the post-2000 visitors, namely 1979ers, may have learned more information at school, but they also heard the mythically colored portrayals of their 1948er parents and 1933er grandparents. Most of the 1979ers interested in the Nazi past heard or even worked with camp survivors, and they often developed strong personal feelings about the brown-collar crimes and their relevance for the present. It is precisely because of their own strong feelings that the 1968er designers of the new memorial site, whose 1989er children will be the teachers of those post-2000 visitors, are so concerned with controlling the experience of visitors to the memorial site.[114]

After the year 2000 youth groups visiting concentration camp memorial sites will increasingly be guided by members of the 1989er cohort, whose *parents* were 1968ers. Those guides will probably have first learned about the brown-collar crimes in their teen years, that is, during the 1980s. In conclusion we will examine the stories of a few 1989er teachers who came to have a stronger than average connection to the events of Germany's National Socialist past. The process by which 1989ers forged stronger connections to the Nazi period is probably the best indication we have about how that process might take place in future generations. It also offers anecdotal evidence about the role memorial sites can play in that learning process.

The 1989ers: from reflex to reflection

By the late 1980s the largest group of the first-time visitors to concentration camp memorial sites were the 1989er children of 1968er parents. The parents' politically formative years had been the 1950s, the heyday of West Germany's "economic miracle," not the period of occupation, migration, and shortage that followed the devastation of Hitler's reign in Germany. Since the Nazi period had already been a mediated experience for these 1968er parents, their 1989er children found other sources of information about it. Their 1943er grandparents told personal stories about the Nazi period, but these biographical anecdotes were so distorted by the three myths that they lacked credibility, and the 1989er grandchildren did not relate empathetically to them. Thus the 1989er Germans, born after the mid-1960s, learned more about the Nazi period from films and books, and in school, than from family members. Nazism only took on personal significance for them if some special individual or experience transmitted it to them. We can already see the phenomenon of "Nazism as history" in the stories of Kurt Piller and Jürgen Z., although familial connections still played some role in the relationship those 1979ers developed to that history. The following stories are based on interviews with 1989ers.[115] They were conducted during a 1997 bus trip through Poland to Auschwitz and Cracow with a group of German students studying to be secondary school teachers.

Both Klaudia K. and Tanja K. were born in smaller German cities in 1970.[116] Klaudia's father and mother were born in 1932 and 1942, Tanja's parents in 1942 and 1951. The oldest parent, Klaudia's father, was evacuated from Pforzheim, which was more than 75 percent destroyed in Allied bombing attacks, as a 13-year-old. He often talked, "naively," as his daughter put it, about what he had experienced during the Nazi period. One of his favorite anecdotes was how he, as a small boy, had seen Pforzheim's Jews being taken away (in 1938 or 1941). He had recognized the local pharmacist at a collection point, and he ran after the departing train (truck?), shouting in confusion, "but Herr Grossmann, but Herr Grossmann ..." His emphasis in telling this and other anecdotes was to show that he had not understood what had been happening to the Jews.

Both girls were introduced to the topic of the persecution of the Jews when they were about 10 years old, by their parents. Tanja's parents had watched the TV miniseries *Holocaust* with her in 1979, sending her out of the room during the most gruesome scenes. Her family also stopped at the Flossenbürg concentration camp memorial site in northern Bavaria at the beginning of a vacation trip in 1980, primarily because Tanja's 1968er father wanted to see it. There she "learned a lot," as she put it. This statement is especially interesting in light of the fact that at that time Flossenbürg had only the most meager of documentary exhibitions, with perhaps one or two dozen shabby panels in a drafty, half-demolished cement barrack. The only other remains in the luxuriant parklike terrain were the small crematorium and a large pyramidal grave of ashes. What Tanja probably meant was that this was the first time she felt a strong personal connection to the historical events.

Klaudia's first encounter with the Nazi persecution of the Jews came in 1979, when her Catholic religion instructor (b. 1942) showed her class a film about the Polish priest Maximilian Kolbe, who had assisted Jews, and had the students read a book about a Roma child's experience of Nazi persecution, *When Hitler Stole the Pink Rabbit*. She had also been taken to the memorial site in Bergen-Belsen, which was near her grandparents' home, because her devoutly Catholic mother, a child of German refugees who fled from eastern Poland in 1945, had wanted to pray for the dead buried there. In 1980 her mother selected *The Diary of Anne Frank* to read as one of the traditional family activities on the four advent Sundays before Christmas.

The two girls' interest in the topic grew slowly over the next two years. In both cases adults younger than their parents played an important role. Looking back after almost fifteen years, Tanja emphasized the importance of a young (1968er) teacher who had intensively researched the history of Jews in their town. Tanja still felt the woman's enthusiasm for the topic and remembered the documents the teacher had shown the class, as well as answers the class had received to letters they had written to former Jewish residents who had fled to the United States. Klaudia had heard many stories about the war from her conservative grandfather, who was a member of an organization of German refugees from Eastern Europe, which by nature had a revanchist, nationalist orientation. In her case it was a 1968er aunt, born in the early 1950s, about ten years after Claudia's mother, who shaped her political attitudes and supported her interest in filling in the gaps in her grandfather's stories. Klaudia also read a number of novels about victims of Nazism on her own. She said she had wanted to balance out the distortions presented by her high school German teacher, who avoided the Holocaust even though it was a mandatory part of the curriculum.

Tanja did not pursue the topic further for many years, although she did participate in demonstrations against neo-Nazis at her school (her home town is notorious as a hotbed of neo-Nazism). Additionally, as a frequent traveler in Europe, she occasionally heard remarks about her last name, which sounds like that of a famous Nazi general. She clearly remembers her self-consciousness about being German when she was an exchange student in France at age 17, but since then she has decided that it is better not to hide her origin. That decision gave her, as she said, an opportunity "to show that you can't lump my generation together with the past." Undoubtedly not only her age, but the confidence she derived from her concrete knowledge of the Nazi past, helped her to understand such encounters as opportunities, not victimizing burdens. When Tanja traveled to Amsterdam with Klaudia during a college vacation, it was quite natural for the two twenty-year-olds to visit the Anne Frank house. She planned to take a bicycle trip in Israel in 1997, something only young Germans fairly secure in their relationship to their country's past would want to do.

Klaudia's experience was slightly different, in that she continued reading books about the Nazi period through her teen years, and then decided to study history in college. (Tanja studied economics and

English.) Klaudia took a number of college and graduate courses about the Nazi period, taught the film *Schindler's List* when she was a teaching intern at a high school, and took a job transcribing interview tapes for a professor conducting oral history research with concentration camp survivors. She, too, is very open when talking about the Nazi past. Even though she had already finished her required coursework, in 1997 she decided to participate in a course that culminated in a bus trip to Poland to visit Auschwitz (among other places) with a group of Polish students. It was she who invited Tanja along on that trip, since a few spaces were available to students who had not participated in the seminar.

Tanja and Klaudia's college classmate Mathias F. was also born in 1970, of 1948er/1968er cohort parents born in 1935 and 1939.[117] His experience, and that of several other young men of his generation, raises the question whether there are typically gender-specific processes whereby young teens develop a more personal interest in the human costs and consequences of Nazism. While by no means all of the young German men whose stories I heard followed this path, most of them share common features with it. On the other hand, several of the aspects of Mathias's and other men's stories were not present in the interviews with women.[118]

Both of Mathias's parents had come to Germany in 1945 as the children of German refugees from Poland. At gatherings of his extended family there was often talk about how things had been in the old homeland, and he was interested in finding out more about what life had been like for Germans in "the east." He was keenly interested in the history of the Nazi period in school, including the persecution of the Jews. But he was interested not so much in the human consequences of that persecution (the biographies of local Jews or Anne Frank, for instance), as in the mental world of the elites of the Nazi empire: Himmler, Hess, Hitler, Göring, Heydrich, Frank, Goebbels, von Schirach, Ribbentrop, and Schacht were the names he mentioned. Mathias struggled to make sense of the policies these men put into practice, for example their "waste" of human resources – not only the personnel employed to murder Jews, but the Jews themselves, many of whom, he thought, would have been glad to fight for the German army instead of going to the gas chambers. He also wondered why so many soldiers had been "wasted" in the battle of Stalingrad, when they could have been flown or marched out in time. Mathias was also curious about his next-door neighbor, a former colonel in Hitler's army. The man said "Heil" instead of "hello" when they met on the street – until 1987, when Rudolf Hess, the last member of Hitler's inner circle, died.

Mathias's interest in the war and the mental world of the top Nazis changed suddenly when he was about 20. He told how he had bought a big book about World War II at a used-book store, but when he sat down to read it he found he was no longer interested in the war. At about the same time his girlfriend, who had noticed his interest in the Nazi period, gave him *The Diary of Anne Frank* to read. Mathias did not visit a concentration camp memorial site until well after he began college, and his memory of the pertinent books he had read in school was hazy. Although by the time of the Auschwitz trip his interest had shifted more towards the human side of Nazi persecution, it was still motivated more by the desire to find out the causes of his own family's suffering than by empathy with Hitler's intentional victims. At the time of the interview it was unclear whether he had developed that extra measure of engagement characteristic of teachers who move their students beyond rote learning. It would be interesting to know what role the absence of an empathy-triggering experience played in Mathias's rather convoluted path of inquiry into the history and legacies of Nazism.

Little is known about questions such as the gender specificity of interest in different aspects of the history of National Socialism, or the role that a visit to a concentration camp memorial site might play in the direction or strength of those interests. In all of the many interviews and conversations I have conducted on these subjects, one fact clearly emerges: any visit to a concentration camp memorial site has to be seen in the context of the previous life experiences of the visitor – who their parents were, what happened to them as individuals, and what significant political events shaped their lives. As these preconditions evolve on a collective scale, they will affect both what is done and what should be done at a memorial site. This book is an account of the often painful and disturbing tension between the two.

Throughout this book we have heard the stories of people who visited the Dachau concentration camp after the war. From the very start they were surprised by what they found, but they generally recognized that the present state of things might be more appropriate to the contemporary social and political situation than their own preconceived expectations. The Dachau memorial site must change to keep pace with the changing prerequisites of present and future visitors. We, the custodians of such sites, must endeavor to cut ourselves loose from our own mythic moorings to shape the site according to the needs of those it will serve. We must strike a balance between the antiquarian preservation of confusing details, monumental portrayals of resistance to emulate or atrocities to reject, and critical deconstructions of mythic histories.

Notes

Dachau: past, present, future

1 See Hans-Günter Richardi, *Schule der Gewalt: Das Konzentrationslager Dachau, 1933–1934* (Munich: Beck, 1983; republished Munich: Piper, 1995), 247.

2 Directions to the site can also be found on the world wide web at sites sponsored by the history workshop Zum Beispiel Dachau, the memorial site, and the city tourist office: http://members.aol.com/zbdachau/index_e.htm, http://www.infospace. de/ gedenkstaette/english/index.html, and http://www.infospace.de/vv-dachau/html/ igedenk.htm.

3 A bus schedule from 1973 is published in Jochen Gerz and Francis Lévy, *Exit: Das Dachau-Projekt* (Frankfurt: Roter Stern, 1978), unnumbered plate.

4 See ibid.

5 Historians are not quite sure why the gas chamber was never used. Perhaps by the time it was completed disease and maltreatment already generated enough corpses.

6 Marcus Smith, *The Harrowing of Hell: Dachau* (Albuquerque: University of New Mexico, 1972), 95. It is also described in Nerin Gun, *The Day of the Americans* (New York: Fleet, 1966).

7 For a broad overview of recent literature, see John Gillis (ed.), *Commemorations: The Politics of Identity* (Princeton: Princeton University Press, 1994), 1–24. For more recent discussions, see Susan Crane and Alon Confino's contributions to the AHR Forum "History and Memory," *American Historical Review*, 102:5 (Dec. 1997), 1372–1403; also Noa Gedi and Yigal Elam, "Collective Memory – What Is It?" *History and Memory*, 8:1 (spring 1996), 30–51. For a sophisticated discussion of the interrelationships between history and memory with detailed case studies, see John Bodnar, *Remaking America: Public Memory, Commemoration, and Patriotism in the Twentieth Century* (Princeton: Princeton University Press, 1990).

Part I Dachau 1890–1945: a town, a camp, a symbol of genocide

1 Introduction to the glossy color pamphlet *Dachau* which has been available near the exit of the concentration camp memorial from 1985 to 1999 (see Rainer Rutz, "In der KZ-Gedenkstätte: Für das 'andere Dachau' darf jetzt geworben werden. OB Reitmeier spricht von 'entscheidendem Durchbruch,'" *SZ/DN*, 12 Sept. 1985). Reitmeier was mayor from 1966 to 1996. This translation is taken from the English edition of the brochure.

All translations in this book, unless otherwise noted, are by the author.

1 Dachau: a town and a camp

1 For an overview of Dachau's history prior to 1914, see Hans-Günter Richardi, *Dachau: Führer durch die Altstadt, die Künstlerkolonie und die KZ-Gedenkstätte* (Passau: Passavia, 1979), 19f, 29f, 38ff, 50–9. The quotation at the end of the paragraph is taken from p. 7. See also p. 58.

2 Richardi, *Dachau: Führer*, 53; the following quotations are from pp. 54 and 57f.

3 See Allan Mitchell, *Revolution in Bavaria, 1918–1919: The Eisner Regime and the Soviet Republic* (Princeton, Princeton University Press, 1965). This book contains much factual material, even if its central thesis has proven to be untenable. Sebastian Haffner, *Failure of a Revolution* (Chicago: Banner, 1986), chapter 13, contains an overview of the Bavarian revolution and its demise. For the events in Dachau see Heinrich Hillmayr, "Rätezeit und Rote Armee in Dachau," *Amperland* (1960), no. 3, 74–80, no. 4, 90–5.

4 The following history of Dachau is based on the excellent history of this period by Sybille Steinbacher, *Dachau – die Stadt und das Konzentrationslager in der NS-Zeit: Die Untersuchung einer Nachbarschaft* (Frankfurt: Peter Lang, 1993), 35–48.

5 Ibid., 42. The brochure cited on p. 15 claims that ca. 20 percent (1,400 of 7,100) of Dachau residents received welfare payments in 1928; Steinbacher (45 n. 157) cites a similar figure for spring 1932.

6 Ibid., 77–84.

7 The following quotations are taken from the excellent study by Johannes Tuchel, *Konzentrationslager: Organisationsgeschichte und Funktion der "Inspektion der Konzentrationslager," 1934–1938* (Boppard: H. Boldt, 1991), 35ff. On Hitler's knowledge of turn-of-the-century British and Spanish camps, see also Andrzej Kaminski, *Konzentrationslager 1896 bis heute: Eine Analyse* (Stuttgart: Kohlhammer, 1982), 34–8. The evidence suggesting that Hitler may have been inspired by late-1920s camps in the Soviet Union is inconclusive at best. See ibid., 38, 46ff (whereby the pre-Soviet Czarists drew on Prussian models), and Hans-Ulrich Wehler, *Entsorgung der deutschen Vergangenheit? Ein polemischer Essay zum "Historikerstreit"* (Munich: Beck, 1988), 46, 150ff. On Kaminski's comparison of Nazi concentration camps and Soviet gulags, see Tuchel, *Konzentrationslager*, 23f.

8 Tuchel, *Konzentrationslager*, 36, quoting Eberhard Jäckel and Axel Kuhn (eds.), *Hitler: Sämtliche Aufzeichnungen 1905–1924* (Stuttgart: DVA, 1980), 233.

9 Tuchel, *Konzentrationslager*, 36, quoting Kurt Gossweiler, *Kapital, Reichswehr und NSDAP, 1919–1924* (Cologne: Pahl-Rügenstein, 1982), 503.

10 Tuchel, *Konzentrationslager*, 37, quoting *Völkischer Beobachter*, 11 Aug. 1932.

11 Tuchel, *Konzentrationslager*, 37, quoting Cuno Horkenbach, *Das Deutsche Reich von 1918 bis heute: Ausgabe 1933* (Berlin: Verlag für Presse, Wirtschaft und Politik, 1935), 106.

12 Steinbacher, *Dachau – Die Stadt*, 81ff.

13 Ibid., 87.

14 The following portrayal is based on a chronicle of the camp drawn up by the SS in March 1938. It was found by Tuchel in the Federal Archive in Koblenz (BaKo), in the files of the Reich Finance Ministry (BaKo, R2/28350). See Tuchel, *Konzentrationslager*, 124 n. 13.

15 *Münchner Neueste Nachrichten*, 26 Mar. 1933; see also Richardi, *Schule der Gewalt*, 47.

16 "Les Deux visages de l'Hitlérisme," *Vu* (Paris), no. 268 (3 May 1933), 671ff; reprinted in Fédération Nationale des Déportés et Internés Résistants et Patriotes, *Le choc 1945: la presse révèle l'enfer des camps nazis* (Paris: FNDIRP, 1985).

17 *Trial of the Major War Criminals before the International Military Tribunal, Nuremberg, 14 November 1945–1 October 1946* [hereafter *IMT*], vol. 26, doc. 778-PS, 294 (see also Tuchel, *Konzentrationslager*, 146f). The full text of the regulations is reprinted in Barbara Distel and Ruth Jakusch, *Konzentrationslager Dachau, 1933–1945* (Munich: n.p., 1978), 68f.

18 The early history of the Dachau camp is portrayed in detail by Richardi, *Schule der Gewalt*, passim, and Tuchel, *Konzentrationslager*, 121–58. Martin Broszat, "The Concentration Camps, 1933–1945," in Broszat and Helmut Krausnik, *Anatomy of the SS State*, trans. by Dorothy Long and Marian Jackson (Frogmore/St. Albans: Paladin, 1970; reprinted 1973), 173–83, gives the best summary of the creation of the rules. Wäckerle's code is reprinted in *IMT*, vol. 26, doc. 922.

19 Richardi, *Schule der Gewalt*, 100f.

20 *Münchner Neueste Nachrichten*, 6 Aug. 1933, quoted in Richardi, *Schule der Gewalt*, 179f.

21 Letter by Eicke to Himmler, 10 Aug. 1936, in Eicke's personnel file; quoted in Tuchel, *Konzentrationslager*, 151.

22 Rudolf Höss, *Death Dealer: The Memoirs of the SS Kommandant at Auschwitz*, ed. by Steven Paskuly, trans. by Andrew Pollinger (Buffalo: Prometheus, 1992), 83, 93f. I have modified the translation slightly to bring it closer to the original. See the German edition by Martin Broszat (Munich: dtv, 10th edn, 1985), 58, 66f.

23 Steinbacher, *Dachau – Die Stadt*, 112.

24 Ibid., 101–16.

25 *Dachauer Zeitung*, 22 Mar. 1933, quoted in Steinbacher, *Dachau – Die Stadt*, 94.

26 Report by Mayor Lambert Friedrichs, 15 May 1935, DaA; quoted in Steinbacher, *Dachau – Die Stadt*, 98.

27 Tuchel, *Konzentrationslager*, 152f. On the inscription see Höss, *Kommandant*, 65, with note by Broszat.

28 For a concise but detailed portrayal of the Röhm Affair in English, see Norbert Frei, *National Socialist Rule in Germany: The Führer State 1933–1945* (Cambridge, Mass.: Blackwell, 1993), 3–27; see also Tuchel, *Konzentrationslager*, 175–81.

29 *Völkischer Beobachter*, 14 July 1934, quoted in Tuchel, *Konzentrationslager*, 177.

30 On the control of information in general, see Willi Boelcke (ed.), *Kriegspropaganda 1939–1941: Geheime Ministerkonferenzen im Reichspropagandaministerium* (Stuttgart: DVA, 1966), introduction.

31 For examples of restrictions on information about the concentration camps, see Gordon Horwitz, *In the Shadow of Death: Living Outside the Gates of Mauthausen* (New York: Free Press, 1990), 37, 49, 62, 70, 76, 89, 94f. On the general limitation of information about the camps after 1934, see Marlis Steinert, *Hitler's War and the Germans*, trans. Thomas de Witt (Athens: Ohio University Press, 1977), 55 (after Walter Hagemann, *Publizistik im Dritten Reich* [Hamburg: Heitmann, 1946], 168); also Hermann Kaienburg, "'sie nächtelang nicht ruhig schlafen liess': Das KZ Neuengamme und seine Nachbarn," *Dachauer Hefte*, 12 (1996), 34–57, 34.

32 In addition to the evidence below, see Klaus Drobisch, "Zeitgenössische Berichte

über Nazikonzentrationslager 1933–1939," *Jahrbuch für Geschichte* (East Berlin), 26 (1982), 103–33; Muriel Favre, "'Wir können vielleicht die Schlafräume besichtigen': Originalton einer Reportage aus dem KZ Oranienburg (1933)," *Rundfunk und Geschichte*, 24:2/3 (Apr./July 1998), 164–9. In 1997 Ute Wrocklage of the University of Oldenbourg received a dissertation fellowship from the German Historical Institute to conduct research on "Fotografien der Konzentrationslager, 1933–1945." Robert Gellately is also working on a similar project.

For a contemporary document, see Himmler's Jan. 1937 presentation to army trainees about the "nature and tasks of the SS and police," Nuremberg doc. 1992, 70, cited in Heinz Huber and Arthur Müller (eds.), *Das Dritte Reich: Seine Geschichte in Texten, Bildern und Dokumenten* (Munich: Desch, 1964), 483–6. Himmler claimed that the camp statutes were based on the Prussian penitentiary statutes of 1914–18, and that cruelty and sadism were not practiced there.

33 "Die Wahrheit über Dachau," *Münchner Illustrierte Zeitung*, 16 July 1933.

34 Louis Lochner (trans.), Rolf Memming (ed.), "A Dissident Nazi: Hans-Jörg Maurer's Würzburg Diary," *Wisconsin Magazine of History*, 50:4 (summer 1967), 347–91, 355 (entry 20 Nov. 1935).

35 Friedrich Franz Bauer, "Konzentrationslager Dachau," *Illustrierter Beobachter*, 3 Dec. 1936, 2014–17, 2028.

36 In addition to the evidence cited below, see Lee Kersten, "W. Macmahon Balls Bericht über das KZ Sachsenhausen: Eine Reportage im Herbst 1938 im australischen Rundfunk," *Dachauer Hefte*, 11 (1995), 124–32; also an official two-page illustrated newspaper report about the camps in 1939 which shows exclusively pictures of prisoners at work in order to disprove the "hair-raising things" being said about the camps abroad: *Münchner Illustrierte Presse*, 3 Aug. 1939.

37 Werner Schäfer, *Konzentrationslager Oranienburg: Das Anti-Braunbuch über das erste deutsche Konzentrationslager* (Berlin: n.p., 1934). Schäfer's book contrasts news reports, letters, pictures, and even tables listing the gain in weight of prisoners, with German rumors and foreign published reports about barbaric conditions in the camp. The following quotations are from p. 23.

This book was written in response to World Committee for the Victims of German Fascism, *The Brown Book of the Hitler Terror and the Burning of the Reichstag* (London: Gollancz, [Sept.] 1933). The German edition, entitled *Braunbuch über Hitler-Terror und Reichstagsbrand* (Basel: Universum, [Aug.] 1933), was reprinted in 1973 by Röderberg in Frankfurt.

The early documentary reports about life in the camps also set the tone for the memoir literature that was to come after 1945. See Claude Conter, "KZ-Literatur der 30er Jahre oder die Genese der KZ-Darstellung," in Conter (ed.), *Literatur und Holocaust* (Bamberg: Universität Bamberg, 1996), 24–30.

38 The letter was published in the *Glonntal-Bote*, 1 Apr. 1934, reprinted in Distel and Jakusch, *Konzentrationslager Dachau*, 80.

39 Tuchel, *Konzentrationslager*, 308f. Quotations from similar letters were published in Schäfer, *Konzentrationslager Oranienburg*, as well.

40 Hitler apologists such as the British historian David Irving have capitalized on this sort of evidence in their attempt to exonerate Hitler from certain crimes. See Martin Broszat, "Hitler und die Genesis der 'Endlösung': Aus Anlass der Thesen von David Irving," *VfZ*, 25 (1977), 739–75; reprinted in Martin Broszat, *Nach Hitler: Der schwie-*

rige Umgang mit unserer Geschichte (Munich: Oldenbourg, 1987), 187–229. Broszat cites the relevant reviews of Irving's work.

41 On the (re-)discovery of this evidence since the late 1970s, see chapter 13, below. For one example, see the letter Bavarian Justice Minister Gürtner wrote to Reich Interior Minister Frick on 14 May 1935, in which Gürtner describes the mistreatment of prisoners. In: *IMT*, vol. 33, doc. 3751-PS, 56–60.

42 See testimony of Dachau survivor Dr. F. Blaha in *IMT*, vol. 3, 201ff, 208f, 213ff (11 Jan. 1946). See also General von Eberstein's description of his "many visits": *IMT*, vol. 20, 330, 342f (3 and 5 Aug. 1946). For a visit in 1935, see General Milch's testimony in vol. 9, 84ff, 110f. The description of an 8 May 1936 tour for top Nazi officials in the 9 May 1936 *Münchner Neueste Nachrichten* is summarized in Hans-Günter Richardi, Eleonore Philipp, and Monika Lücking (eds.), *Dachauer Zeitgeschichtsführer* (Dachau: Stadt Dachau, 1998), 110f. See also the contemporary German photographic report about Dachau reprinted in the US: "Life Inside a Nazi Concentration Camp," *New York Times Magazine* (14 Feb. 1937), 16.

43 On Gudrun Himmler's visits, see Diane Westergaard, "Gudrun Himmler visits Dachau," *Prairie Schooner*, 59:1 (spring 1985), 14, and Gun, *Day of the Americans*, 306 (1959 interview). Gudrun Himmler-Burwitz rediscovered her childhood diary after her mother died in the late 1970s. See Ingrid Kolb, "Töchter und Väter," *Stern*, 6 Jan. 1983, 60–5. On Himmler-Burwitz's continued work assisting SS "veterans," see Siegfried Helm, "Himmlers Tochter hilft den alten Gefährten," *Berliner Morgenpost*, 19 Apr. 1998 (after a report in the London *Times* on 18 Apr. 1998).

44 Felix Kersten, *The Kersten Memoirs, 1940–1945* trans. Constantine Fitzgibbon and James Oliver (New York: Macmillan, 1957), 287. I have changed the translation of *Erziehungslager* (1952 German edition, 376) to reeducation camp (instead of "training camp") in accordance with the summary of Masur's description of the meeting in Yehuda Bauer, *Jews for Sale? Nazi-Jewish Negotiations, 1933–1945* (New Haven: Yale University Press, 1994), 247, 289 n. 20. Masur's description was published in Swedish in 1945: Norbert Masur, *En Jude Talar med Himmler* (Stockholm: Albert Bonniers Förlag, 1945). Kersten did not include this exchange with Masur in the 1947 English version of his "diary" (see 284f of that first edition), although he did mention Himmler telling him a similar story in the summer of 1942 (113–16). Kersten may have created this first-person quotation for the 1952 German edition based on Masur's memoir. A rudimentary version of the incident (not in the first person) can be found in Kersten's slightly embellished 1948 Dutch edition, *Klerk en Beul: Himmler van Nabij* (Amsterdam: Meulenhoff, 1948), 186. On the reliability of Kersten's diaries as a source, see Bauer, *Jews for Sale?*, 102f.

45 For a general overview of this period, see Klaus Drobisch and Guenter Wieland, *Das System der NS-Konzentrationslager, 1933–1939* (Berlin: Akademie, 1993).

46 Tuchel, *Konzentrationslager*, 299, 303, 308f.

47 Ibid., 325.

48 Ibid., 335–8.

49 Tuchel, *Konzentrationslager*, 339ff, after Karl Doerner, memorandum, 8/9 Apr. 1938, BaKo, R22/1333.

50 The testimony at Nuremberg of F. Blaha, a Czech doctor imprisoned in Dachau, describes the elaborate preparation for and the program of such official visits, which took place quite frequently. *IMT*, vol. 3, 201–3, 208f, 213–15.

51 Even if concentration camp tours were not obligatory for Justice Department officials, it seems that whole classes of government trainees from other ministries were regularly taken on tours. At a denazification trial in 1946, a Finance Ministry trainee recalled that when his freshmen class of the Finance Academy in Berlin-Tegel was taken to Sachsenhausen in March 1938, "the majority of prisoners were homosexuals and Jehovah's Witnesses. The prisoners were separated and marked by group. They looked very good. The sanitary facilities were perfect." While a bureaucrat on trial in 1946 had good reason to lie about the conditions, there was little advantage for him in inventing the context of a regular tour, which he probably assumed was common knowledge. See Tuchel, *Konzentrationslager*, 340f, after Heinrich Appelkamp, sworn statement in the Darmstadt Internment Camp, 9 June 1946, Staatsarchiv Nürnberg, KV-Anklage, Verteidigung, III 154.

52 According to Eberstein, the Americans visited the Dachau camp before 1939. See *IMT*, vol. 20, 342ff and the AP report in *New York Times* (*NYT*), 4 Aug. 1946, 4. It would be interesting to find contemporary reports about these visits.

53 The following information is after Steinbacher, *Dachau – Die Stadt*, 118–23. For a portrayal of similar negotiations in Weimar about Buchenwald, see Jens Schley, "Weimar und Buchenwald: Beziehungen zwischen der Stadt und dem Lager," *Dachauer Hefte*, 12 (1996), 196–214, 210f.

54 Charles W. Sydnor, Jr., *Soldiers of Destruction: The SS Death's Head Division, 1933–1945* (Princeton: Princeton University Press, 1977; rev. edn, 1990), 323.

55 Distel and Jakusch, *Dachau*, 204; Günther Kimmel, "Das Konzentrationslager Dachau: Eine Studie zu den nationalsozialistischen Gewaltverbrechen," in Martin Broszat and Elke Fröhlich (eds.), *Bayern in der NS-Zeit*, vol. II (Munich: Oldenbourg, 1979), 349–413, 370f.

56 Details about the pogrom in the town and the camp can be found in Hans Holzhaider, *Vor Sonnenaufgang . . . Das Schicksal der jüdischen Bürger Dachaus* (Munich: Süddeutsche Zeitung, 1984), and Arbeitskreis "Reichskristallnacht" (ed.), *Dachau ist somit judenfrei* (Dachau: n.p., 1988).

57 It is characteristic of the undeveloped state of research in this area that no one has yet investigated the possibility that these preparations may have been in anticipation of a large influx of prisoners for other reasons, for instance if Neville Chamberlain had not conceded the Sudetenland at the infamous Sept. 1938 Munich conference.

58 Steinbacher, *Dachau – Die Stadt*, 126–36. For the number of deaths see ibid., 156, and Kimmel, "Das Konzentrationslager Dachau," 372.

59 Steinert, *Hitler's War and the Germans*, 157f, 166–9.

60 Fritz Spiesser, *Das Konzentrationslager* (Munich: Eher, 1940; 5th edn, 1943).

61 The use of the Boer War in Nazi anti-British propaganda merits a study in its own right. On the 1941 film *Ohm Krüger* about the Boer War, see Erwin Leiser, *Nazi Cinema* (New York: Macmillan, 1974 [Hamburg: Rowohlt, 1968]), 99–103. The topic concerned British officials for decades after the demise of the Nazi regime. In his book *Return of the Swastika?* (London: Robert Hale, 1968) about neo-Nazi activities in West Germany, Lord Russell of Liverpool included an appendix about "German Anti-British Propaganda" (188–92), in which he attempted to disprove the veracity of the Nazi claims. For a recent summary, see Anette Wieviorka, "L'Expression 'camp de concentration' au 20e siècle," *Vingtième Siècle*, 54 (1997), 4–12, esp. 4f and 8.

62 Enno Georg, *Die wirtschaftlichen Unternehmungen der SS* (Stuttgart: DVA, 1963), 59f.

63 Ibid., 25ff, 38ff; see also Wolfgang Sofsky, *Die Ordnung des Terrors* (Frankfurt: Fischer, 1993; Engl. edn, 1997), 51.

64 See excellent summaries in Ian Kershaw, *The Nazi Dictatorship: Problems and Perspectives of Interpretation* (London: Edward Arnold, third edn, 1993), 60–8; Michael Marrus, *The Holocaust in History* (Hanover: University Press of New England, 1987), 30–46.

65 Christopher Browning, "Beyond 'Intentionalism' and 'Functionalism': A Reassessment of Nazi Jewish Policy from 1939 to 1941," in Thomas Childers and Jane Kaplan (eds.), *Reevaluating the Third Reich* (New York: Holmes and Meier, 1993), 211–33.

66 Karl Schleunes, *The Twisted Road to Auschwitz: Nazi Policy toward German Jews, 1933–1939* (Urbana: University of Illinois Press, 1970). See also Uwe-Dietrich Adam, *Judenpolitik im Dritten Reich* (Düsseldorf: Droste, 1972).

67 See Hermann Graml, *Antisemitism in the Third Reich*, trans. Tim Kirk (Oxford: Blackwell, 1992), 146–51.

68 According to Hans Filbinger, *Die geschmähte Generation* (Munich: Universitas, 1987), 64, in only a few months at the end of the war, 2.5 million people were evacuated from Norway. Given the order of magnitude of that undertaking, the proposed Jewish deportation was not impossible, even though the sea route to Madagascar was much longer.

69 Browning, "Beyond," 219, after Jürgen Förster, *Das Deutsche Reich und der Zweite Weltkrieg*, vol. IV (Stuttgart: DVA, 1983), 414, 416, 427.

70 Heinz Höhne, *The Order of the Death's Head: The Story of Hitler's SS*, trans. Richard Barry (New York: Coward-McCann, 1970), 358f. This statement was taken from p. 28 of Ohlendorf's plea in mitigation during his sentencing review in July 1950, which Höhne found in the possession of Ohlendorf's wife. (Compare Höhne, 607 n. 77 and 609 n. 57.) See also Omer Bartov, *The Eastern Front, 1941–1945: German Troops and the Barbarization of Warfare* (New York: St. Martins, 1986).

71 Mathias Beer, "Die Entwicklung der Gaswagen beim Mord an den Juden," *VfZ*, 35 (1987), 403–17.

72 For this and the following, see the excellent portrayal by Henry Friedlander, *The Origins of Nazi Genocide: From Euthanasia to the Final Solution* (Chapel Hill: University of North Carolina Press, 1995), esp. 284ff, 296ff.

73 Adalbert Rückerl, *NS-Vernichtungslager im Spiegel deutscher Strafprozesse* (Munich: dtv, 1977), 87–242; see also Eugen Kogon, Hermann Langbein, and Adalbert Rückerl (eds.), *Nazi Mass Murder: A Documentary History of the Use of Poison Gas* (New Haven: Yale University Press, 1994), chapter 5.

74 See Yitzhak Arad, *Belzec, Sobibor, Treblinka: The Operation Reinhard Death Camps* (Bloomington: Indiana University Press, 1987), 119–24, 437.

75 According to Arad, ibid., 364, about 130–40 Jews from Sobibor and Treblinka survived until the end of the war. It is impossible to make reliable estimates of the number of escapees from the other camps, since most of them did not survive until the end of the war. On the survivors of Sobibor, see Richard Rashke, *Escape from Sobibor* (Urbana: University of Illinois Press, 1982; 2nd edn, 1995). A 1987 film based on this book is available on videotape.

76 See Kogon, Langbein, and Rückerl, *Nazi Mass Murder* (German edn, Frankfurt: Fischer, 1983), 204f, and Deborah Dwork and Robert-Jan van Pelt, *Auschwitz, 1200 to the Present* (New York: Norton, 1996), 292f.

77 For a revealing example of this extrapolation from Dachau to all camps, see John Cobden, *Dachau: Reality and Myth* (Newport Beach, Calif.: Institute for Historical Review, 1994). See also Erich Kern, *Meineid gegen Deutschland* (Oldendorf: K. W. Schütz, 1968; 2nd edn, 1971).

78 See Arad, *Belzec*, 170; also Ino Arndt and Wolfgang Scheffler, "Organisierter Massenmord an Juden in nationalsozialistischen Vernichtungslagern," in Hans-Dietrich Bracher et al. (eds.), *Nationalsozialistische Diktatur, 1933–1945: Eine Bilanz* (Bonn: Bundeszentrale, 1986), 539–71, 553 n. 28, 566 n. 58, and Rückerl, *NS-Prozesse*, 77ff.

79 For further references on the so-called Aktion 1005, see Raul Hilberg, *The Destruction of the European Jews* (New York/London: Holmes and Meier, rev. edn, 1985), vol. III, 977–9; Kogon, Langbein, and Rückerl, *Nazi Mass Murder*, German edn, 187–90; and Jon Bridgman, *The End of the Holocaust: The Liberation of the Camps* (Portland: Areopagitica, 1990), 14–22. These books document and describe the staggering clean-up work done by prisoners under SS supervision since March 1943 at Belzec, Sobibor, and Treblinka.

80 Falk Pingel, *Häftlinge unter SS-Herrschaft: Widerstand, Selbstbehauptung und Vernichtung im Konzentrationslager* (Hamburg: Hoffman und Campe, 1978), 125–8; see also Dwork and van Pelt, *Auschwitz*, 334, and Sofsky, *Ordnung des Terrors*, 51f.

81 Sofsky, *Ordnung des Terrors*, 55, after compilation by Gudrun Schwarz, *Die nationalsozialistischen Lager* (Frankfurt/New York: Campus, 1990). By way of comparison, by the mid-1990s there were approximately as many McDonald's franchises in Germany.

82 Steinbacher, *Dachau – Die Stadt*, 145–9.

83 Robert Sigel, "Heilkräuterkulturen im KZ: Die Plantage in Dachau," *Dachauer Hefte*, 4 (1988), 166–8, 171.

84 Imma Maria Mack, *Why I Love Azaleas: Remembrances of my Trips to the Plantation of the Concentration Camp in Dachau, May 1944–April 1945* (St. Ottilien: EOS, 1989). Shortly after its first German publication in 1988, this book became a local and even regional bestseller, going through several editions within a year. At public presentations and in private discussions and interviews in the early 1990s, many people from Dachau referred me to Mack's book as an example of "what it was really like" in the town. The reasons for this are discussed as the "myth of resistance" later in this book.

85 For the data on the priests see Kimmel, "Konzentrationslager Dachau," 375f. Kimmel's main sources are a manuscript by former camp record-keeper Domagala, and Eugen Weiler, *Die Geistlichen in Dachau sowie in anderen Konzentrationslagern und in Gefängnissen*, vol. I (Mödling: Missionsdruckerei St. Gabriel, 1971).

86 See Leonhard Roth, "1500 Geistliche in drei Stuben zusammengepfercht," *MM/DN*, 10 Sept. 1955.

87 Kimmel, "Konzentrationslager Dachau," 376f.

88 After Louis Köckert, *Dachau . . . Und das Gras wächst . . .: Ein Report für die Nachgeborenen* (Munich: Freies Volk, 1980), 41.

89 Reproduced in Distel and Jakusch, *Konzentrationslager Dachau*, 168.
90 See Jean-Claude Pressac and Robert-Jan van Pelt, "The Machinery of Mass Murder at Auschwitz," in Yisrael Gutman and Michael Berenbaum (eds.), *Anatomy of the Auschwitz Death Camp* (Bloomington: Indiana University Press, 1994), 183–245, 186.
91 On the Dachau gas chamber/crematorium building, see the article by Falk Pingel, "'Barrack X' in Dachau: A Special Case," in Kogon et al. (eds.), *Nazi Mass Murder*. See also the reproductions of the plans in Distel and Jakusch, *Konzentrationslager Dachau*, 161–7.

2 Dachau: a symbol of genocide

1 See Arad, *Belzec*, 170–8.
2 See Yehuda Bauer, "The Death-Marches, January–May 1945," *Modern Judaism*, 3:1 (1983), 1–23, and Daniel Goldhagen, *Hitler's Willing Executioners: Ordinary Germans and the Holocaust* (New York: Knopf, 1996), 327–54. For a detailed description of the evacuation marches from Dachau, see Klaus-Dietmar Henke, *Die amerikanische Besetzung Deutschlands* (Munich: Oldenbourg, 1995), 895–913. Henke's long section on "Die Befreiung des Konzentrationslagers Dachau" (862–931) covers some of the same topics as I do in this chapter. His portrayal is the first German scholarly work on the final phase of the Dachau camp. It includes US military reports and testimony of survivors of the evacuation marches that have not previously been examined.
3 Quoted after Raymond Phillips (ed.), *Trial of Joseph Kramer and 49 Others: The Belsen Trial* (London: W. Hodge, 1949), 163–6.
4 Henke, *Die amerikanische Besetzung*, 882–95, offers a detailed analysis of Himmler's negotiation attempts and evacuation policies. He draws on the published memoirs of participants such as Masur and Schellenberg.
5 See Bauer, *Jews for Sale?*, 249.
6 For a discussion of the command and its effects in Dachau see Stanislav Zàmecnik, "'Kein Häftling darf lebend in die Hände des Feindes fallen': Zur Existenz des Himmler-Befehls vom 14./18. April 1945," *Dachauer Hefte*, 1 (1985), 219–31. For a discussion of the command in the context of Himmler's personal politics, see Herbert Obenaus, "Die Räumung der hannoverschen Konzentrationslager im April 1945," in Rainer Fröbe et al., *Konzentrationslager in Hannover: KZ-Arbeit und Rüstungsindustrie in der Spätphase des Zweiten Weltkriegs*, vol. II (Hildesheim: August Lax, 1985), 493–544, 493ff. Folke Bernadotte, *The Curtain Falls: The Last Days of the Third Reich* (New York: Knopf, 1945), offers an eyewitness's perspective. For further references see Henke, *Die amerikanische Besetzung*, 895 n. 566.
7 On Gardelegen, see Seymour Freidin, "Sickened Nazis Made to Dig Up Burned Bodies / Americans Keep Civilians at Reinterment Task at Gardelegen Death House," *NYHT*, 22 Apr. 1945, 1, and Herbert Obenaus, "Das Ende der Kranken aus dem Lager Stöcken im Massaker von Gardelegen," in *Konzentrationslager in Hannover*, vol. II, 536–44 with illustrations 110–28. *Christian Science Monitor*, 23 July 1945; Allan H. Mick (ed.), *With the 102d Infantry Division Through Germany* (Washington: Infantry Journal Press, 1947), 211–16. On Leipzig-Mochau see

Margaret Bourke-White, *Dear Fatherland, Rest Quietly: A Report on the Collapse of Hitler's "Thousand Years"* (New York: Simon and Schuster, 1946).

8 The plans to liquidate Dachau were well known among the inmates and occupy a central position in almost all descriptions of the days prior to liberation. To name just two examples: Arthur Haulot, "Lagertagebuch Januar 1943 – Juni 1945," *Dachauer Hefte*, 1 (1985), 129–203, 190ff; and Nico Rost, *Goethe in Dachau* (Frankfurt: Fischer, 1983), 233–40. For an analysis of the conflicting orders and plans of the responsible Nazi authorities, see Paul Berben, *Dachau: The Official History* (London: Norfolk, 1975), 180–4. See also the account by British secret service agent Peter Churchill, *The Spirit in the Cage* (London: Hodder and Stoughton, 1954).

9 For an overview of the behavior of the local populace during this final phase, with references to important secondary sources, see Steinbacher, *Dachau*, 181–5. Horwitz, *In the Shadow of Death*, 144–63, also treats this aspect in detail.

10 The mortality figures can be found in Günther Kimmel, "Das Konzentrationslager Dachau: Eine Studie zu den Nationalsozialistischen Gewaltverbrechen," in Broszat and Fröhlich (eds.), *Bayern in der NS-Zeit*, vol. I, 349–413, 385.

11 For a concise summary of the liberation of Dachau see Barbara Distel, "The Liberation of the Concentration Camp at Dachau," *Dachau Review*, 1 (1985), 3–11. Henke, *Die amerikanische Besetzung*, 913–19, gives a more detailed account of Dachau's liberation.

12 The first and to date only attempt to document this *putsch* attempt is Hans Holzhaider, *Die Sechs vom Rathausplatz* (Munich: Süddeutscher, 1982; 2nd edn, 1995); see also Hans-Günter Richardi et al., *Die Stadt und das Lager: Nationalsozialismus und Widerstand in Dachau* (Munich: Süddeutscher, 1983), 25.

13 This is mentioned in various accounts of liberation, such as Gun, *Day of the Americans*.

14 The most reliable portrayal of Dachau's liberation to date is Jürgen Zarusky, "'That is not the American Way of Fighting': Die Erschiessungen gefangener SS-Leute bei der Befreiung des KZ Dachau," *Dachauer Hefte*, 13 (1997), 27–55. Zarusky corrects several errors in Henke, *Die amerikanische Besetzung*. For detailed English-language accounts of the liberation of Dachau and its context, see Robert Abzug, *Inside the Vicious Heart: Americans and the Liberation of Nazi Concentration Camps* (New York: Oxford University Press, 1985); Bridgman, *End of the Holocaust*, 103–9; and Douglas Botting, *From the Ruins of the Reich: Germany 1945–1949* (Harmondsworth: Penguin, 1985), 36–49.

15 Howard Buechner, *Dachau: The Hour of the Avenger* (Metairie, La.: Thunderbird, rev. edn, 1987), 54f, 122. See also Flint Whitlock, *The Rock of Anzio: From Sicily to Dachau: A History of the 45th Infantry Division* (Boulder: Westview, 1998), 351–90. Good selections of documents on German military resistance at the end of the war can be found in Gerhard Förster and Richard Lakowski (eds.), *1945: Das Jahr der endgültigen Niederlage der faschistischen Wehrmacht, Dokumente* (East Berlin: Militärverlag der DDR, 1975), and Generallandesarchiv Karlsruhe (ed.), *Der deutsche Südwesten zur Stunde Null* (Karlsruhe: Generallandesarchiv, 1975).

16 Andrew Mollo, "The Webling Incident," *After the Battle*, 27 (1980), 30–3.

17 In addition to the precise analysis by Zarusky, the following story draws on Bill Walsh, "Een Amerikaanse Bevrijder Vertelt," in Til Gardeniers-Berendson (ed.),

Dachau 1945–1985 (Amsterdam: n.p., 1985), 42–4; Buechner, *Dachau: The Hour,* passim; Whitlock, *Rock of Anzio,* 359–82; Abzug, *Inside the Vicious Heart,* 90–4. Information has also been drawn from my correspondence with Howard Buechner about Walsh (in particular a letter of 14 July 1990) and several other accounts of the liberation of Dachau. Henke, *Die amerikanische Besetzung,* 919–26, offers the most detailed scholarly portrayal. Henke, who relies uncritically on Buechner and calls the shooting of the SS guards "the worst, but not the only war crime American soldiers committed on German soil," appears to be working on a study of such events (see 926 n. 767).

18 P[rivate] F[irst] C[lass] John Degro, quoted in Buechner, *Dachau: The Hour,* xxii. As noted above, "Dachau" was not only a concentration camp, but included a garrison with barracks for two SS divisions, a major SS hospital, clothing factories and stores for the entire SS, as well as the personnel and pay offices for the SS's death's head divisions. See Sydnor, *Soldiers of Destruction,* 323. This garrison was four to five times as large as the prisoners' compound (*Schutzhaftlager*); the soldiers approaching from the west entered the SS garrison first.

19 On Weiss see Karl Roder, *Nachtwache: 10 Jahre KZ Dachau und Flossenburg* (Vienna: Bohlau, 1985), 270–3. According to Zarusky, "'That is not,'" Weiss was arrested on 2 May 1945 in Muehldorf.

20 For the original report, see Internationales Komitee vom Roten Kreuz, Geneva, *Die Tätigkeit des IKRK zugunsten der in den deutschen Konzentrationslagern inhaftierten Zivilpersonen (1939 – 1945),* trans. Internationaler Suchdienst, Arolsen (3rd edn, April 1947), 149ff: "Bericht über das Lager Dachau, 27.4.-2.5." See also Smith, *The Harrowing of Hell,* 256. Wicker and Maurer agreed on three conditions for the surrender: guards were to remain in the towers in order to keep the prisoners in check, other camp guards were to remain unarmed in a courtyard, and the entire garrison of troops stationed there was to be allowed to retreat to German lines. This was similar to the surrender negotiated for Belsen, where guards were indeed allowed to retreat to German lines, although not all of them chose to do so. See Derrick Sington, *Belsen Uncovered* (London: Duckworth, 1946), 90f.

According to the notes taken by a reliable prisoner in Dachau, Carel Steensma, a white flag was hung from the entry building (*Jourhaus*) at 7 a.m. See Michael Selzer, *Deliverance Day: The Last Hours of Dachau* (Philadelphia: Lippincott, 1978), 83. Selzer's rendition is fictionalized and contains some dramatic embellishment, but is the only published account based on Steensma's notes. (Steensma figures in the narrative under the pseudonym "Piet Maas.")

21 Color film footage of some of the beaten and slain SS is included in George Stevens, Jr., *From D-Day to Berlin* (New Liberty Productions, 1995).

François Goldschmitt, *Elsässer und Lothringer in Dachau: Die letzten Tage von Dachau,* vol.V (Metz: Pierron, 1947), 40, describes how a shot went off as a prisoner attacked a surrendering guard; US soldiers immediately shot the entire group of SS men.

For the account of Hans Linberger, a German survivor of one of the shootings, see Erich Kern, *Meineid gegen Deutschland* (Oldendorf: K.W. Schütz, 2nd edn, 1971 [1st edn, 1968]), 244–7, and 314f.

22 See Barbie Zelizer, *Remembering to Forget: Holocaust Memory through the Camera's Eye* (Chicago: University of Chicago, 1998); Abzug, *Inside the Vicious Heart,* 21–44;

and Norbert Frei, "'Wir waren blind, ungläubig und langsam': Buchenwald, Dachau und die amerikanischen Medien im Frühjahr 1945," *VfZ* 35 (1987), 385–401, 388f. I thank Astrid Eckart, who is writing her dissertation on this topic, for her comments on this section.

23 On the liberation of Buchenwald see Abzug, *Inside the Vicious Heart*, 45–59; and on the surrender of Belsen: Sington, *Belsen Uncovered*, 9–25. See also Bridgman, *End of the Holocaust*, 49ff, 80ff.

24 Obenaus, "Das Ende der Kranken," 544 on Gardelegen; Abzug, *Inside the Vicious Heart*, 80f on Penig and 74ff on Thekla. *Life* photographer Margaret Bourke-White describes the discovery of Leipzig-Mochau (Thekla) in *Dear Fatherland*. On the liberation of death-march prisoners and of the Flossenbürg main camp on 23 April, see Peter Heigl, *Konzentrationslager Flossenbürg in Geschichte und Gegenwart* (Regensburg: Mittelbayerische Druckerei, 1989), 37, 57ff.

25 See Ronald Brownstein, "The *New York Times* on Nazism (1933–39)," *Midstream*, 26:4 (Apr. 1980), 14–19, and especially the exceedingly rich study by Andrew Sharf, *The British Press and Jews under Nazi Rule* (Oxford: Oxford University Press, 1964), esp. 70–100: "Belief and Atrocities." For a collection of documents see Robert Abzug, *America Views the Holocaust, 1933–1945: A Brief History in Documents* (New York: St. Martin's, 1999).

Nazi reprisals on inmates may explain some of the media's reticence in portraying conditions in the German camps. For example, after *Manchester Guardian* exposures of conditions in the Nazi camps in 1937, Jews in Dachau were subjected to two months' solitary confinement in darkened barracks. In 1938 the New York weekly *New Republic* reported that the *Manchester Guardian* "has specialized in accurate information about conditions in Germany," and it summarized a recent *Guardian* report about Buchenwald (7 Sept. 1938, 96).

26 Curt Daniel, "'The Freest Theatre in the Reich': In the German Concentration Camps," *Theatre Arts*, 25 (Nov. 1941), 801–7.

27 "Our Three Concentration Camps," *American Magazine*, 133 (8 Jan. 1942), 46–8.

28 Especially the *Christian Science Monitor*, the *New Republic*, and *Nineteenth Century* printed reports of the German camps. Numerous listings for the Nazi era can be found in the *Reader's Guide to Periodical Literature* under the heading "Prisons, Germany." I have deposited a collection of copies of all of these articles at the archive of the Dachau memorial site (DaA).

Additionally, most pre-liberation books about the camps presume that readers knew that conditions there were very bad, and seek to document that they were even worse. See, for instance, G. R. Kay, *Dachau, the Nazi Hell* (London: F. Aldor, 1939); Peter Wallner, *By Order to the Gestapo* (London: J. Murray, 1941); *Dachau* (London: W. Gardner, Darton and Co., 1942); Georg Karst, *Beasts of the Earth* (New York: Unger, 1942).

29 See David Wyman, *The Abandonment of the Jews: America and the Holocaust, 1941–1945* (New York: Pantheon, 1984), 190.

30 Abzug, *Inside the Vicious Heart*, 27–30, gives a vivid description of the generals' visit to Ohrdruf based on the testimony of several eyewitnesses. See also Frei, "'Wir waren blind,'" 385; Bridgman, *End of the Holocaust*, 82; Brewster Chamberlin and Marcia Feldman (eds.), *The Liberation of the Nazi Concentration Camps 1945: Eyewitness Accounts of the Liberators* (Washington, D.C.: US Holocaust Memorial

Council, 1987), 75ff (Lewis Weinstein). I do not believe that Eisenhower visited Buchenwald itself, as David Hackett writes in *The Buchenwald Report* (Boulder: Westview, 1995), 10, 382 n. 6.

31 Abzug, *Inside the Vicious Heart*, 30. This reaction was echoed by the headline of a mimeographed newsletter put out by the 45th Infantry Division after the liberation of Dachau: Bill Barrett, "We Have Seen Dachau: Now We Know What We Are Fighting For." (Quoted after Gun, *The Day of the Americans*, 36.) Excerpts of this newsletter are printed in Buechner, *Dachau: The Hour*, xxviiif.

32 The text of the telegram is quoted after the final report of the congressional delegation, "Atrocities and Other Conditions in Concentration Camps in Germany," 79th Congress, 1st session, Senate document no. 47 (Washington: Government Printing Office, [15 May] 1945); reprinted in *IMT Documents in Evidence* (blue series), vol. 37 (Nuremberg, 1949), 606. A slightly different version of the telegram can be found in Alfred Chandler (ed.), *The Papers of Dwight D. Eisenhower: The War Years* (Baltimore/London: Johns Hopkins University Press, 1970), vol. IV, 2623. That version, also quoted by Frei ("'Wir waren blind'", 386), may have been a draft, since Eisenhower was less definite about inviting a British delegation.

33 The British delegation's report was published as "Buchenwald Camp: The Report of a Parliamentary Delegation," Command Paper 6626 (London: His Majesty's Stationery Office, April 1945). That report was also printed by the London *Times* on 28 Apr. 1945, and published in translation by the French Ministry of Information. See Fédération Nationale des Déportés et Internés Résistants et Patriotes, *Le choc 1945*, 60–2. The report notes that among the ten volunteers selected to go to Buchenwald there was one woman, two MDs, and one Jewish lawyer. See also David Hackett (trans. and ed.), *The Buchenwald Report* (Boulder: Westview, 1995), 9–15; Jürgen Zieher, "Amerikanische Reaktionen auf die Befreiung der deutschen Konzentrationslager (April bis November 1945)" (MA thesis, University of Mannheim, August 1996), 24–38.

On Eisenhower's telegram see Chandler, *The Papers*, 2623 n. 1. Chandler erroneously gives the date of the British visit as 20 April. He reports that Churchill immediately requested permission to send a second delegation; Eisenhower acceded. See also *NYHT*, 22 Apr. 1945 (ap report), and *NYHT*, 23 Apr. 1945. The first British delegation returned to London on 23 April.

34 See *NYHT*, 22 April 1945. The US congressional representatives were Clare Luce (Conn.), John Kunkel (Penn.), and Leonard Hall (N.Y.).

35 The following information is taken from the delegation's report, cited above (note 33). Very little has been published about the tour. Hermann Weiss, "Dachau and International Public Opinion: Reactions to the Liberation of the Camp," *Dachau Review*, 1 (1987), 12–31, 16 n. 11 gives a list of important newspaper reports on the visit; Abzug, *Inside the Vicious Heart*, 130–3 also contains a brief description. The congressional report has been reprinted in the Emory University "Witness to the Holocaust" publication series (no. 3, 1980).

36 *Buchenwälder Nachrichten*, 26 April 1945 (reprint edited by Bodo Ritscher, Weimar, 1983, 18).

37 On the replacement of the corpses for the later visits, see Volkhard Knigge, "Die Gedenkstätte Buchenwald: Vom provisorischen Grabdenkmal zum National-denkmal," in *Antifaschismus: Geschichte und Neubewertung* (Berlin: Aufbau

Taschenbuch, 1996), 309–31, 310; also Volkhard Knigge, "Buchenwald," in Detlef Hoffmann (ed.), *Das Gedächtnis der Dinge: KZ-Relikte und KZ-Denkmäler, 1945–1995* (Frankfurt: Campus, 1998), 92–173, 96f.

38 Frei, "'Wir waren blind,'" 389. The delegation included representatives of the newspapers *New York Times, Washington Star, St. Louis Post-Dispatch, Minneapolis Star-Journal, Chicago Sun, Detroit Free Press, Los Angeles Times, Houston Chronicle, Kansas City Star, Fort Worth Star-Telegram* and *New Orleans Times-Picayune*, as well as of the newspaper chains Hearst and Scripps-Howard. The magazines *Saturday Evening Post, Collier's, This Week Magazine, American Magazine*, and *Reader's Digest* also sent reporters. Frei offers an excellent portrayal and analysis of their tour and subsequent efforts to publicize the German atrocities in the US. Unless otherwise noted, all information on this delegation is from Frei's essay. Frei draws most of his information from the collection of the delegations' reports, articles, diaries, and speeches in box 98 of the Joseph Pulitzer II papers held by the Library of Congress. It is not known why the full delegation did not visit Dachau; perhaps the other members had seen enough at Buchenwald and Ohrdruf. The four members who visited Dachau were: Izak, Mott, Saltonstall, and Short.

39 See "America to see Nazi Atrocities in Army Film," *NYHT*, 27 Apr. 1945, about a preview showing of an eleven-minute version of the film. See also Jeffrey Shandler, *While America Watches: Televising the Holocaust* (New York: Oxford University Press, 1999), 8–22.

40 "Atrocities: Capture of the German Concentration Camps Piles up Evidence," *Life*, 18 (7 May 1945), 32–7. *Newsweek* also ran a series of illustrated articles. In vol. 25 (1945) see the issues of 30 Apr. (56f), 7 May (58), 28 May (34f), and 11 June (10). *Time*'s main report, entitled "Dachau," ran on 7 May 1945, 32f.

41 Ben Hibbs, editor-in-chief of the *Saturday Evening Post*, in that magazine, 9 June 1945, 21, quoted after Frei "'Wir waren blind,'" 390. Eisenhower's own retrospective assessment of his publicity efforts shows how seriously he took this task. In a telegram to Marshall on 4 May 1945 he wrote: "We have just uncovered another camp in the south. My own belief is that if America is not now convinced, in view of the disinterested witnesses we have already brought over, it would be almost hopeless to attempt to convince them through bringing anyone else." Quoted after Chandler (ed.), *The Papers*, vol. IV, 2679.

42 Harold Hurwitz, *Die Stunde Null der deutschen Presse: Die amerikanische Pressepolitik in Deutschland 1945–1949* (Cologne: Wissenschaft und Politik, 1972), 94.

43 This was the text of a proclamation issued on 16 April by the mayor of Weimar; see Walter Bartel (ed.), *Buchenwald: Mahnung und Verpflichtung* (East Berlin: Deutscher Verlag der Wissenschaften, 4th edn, 1983), 559. The translation is after Bridgman, *End of the Holocaust*, 82.

   A number of army cameramen were on hand to record the event in Weimar, and footage of the visit is contained in the early Western Allied films on the atrocities, such as *The Nazi Concentration Camps*, and *Death Mills*. See Brewster Chamberlin, "Todesmühlen: Ein früher Versuch zur Massen-'Umerziehung' im besetzten Deutschland," *VfZ*, 29 (1981), 420–36, 424, 432, and David Culbert, "American Film Policy in the Re-education of Germany after 1945," in Nicholas Pronay and Keith Wilson (eds.), *The Political Re-education of Germany and her Allies after World War II* (London: Croom Helm, 1985), 173–202, 199.

There were earlier tours, but less is known about them. Already in July 1944 the Soviets had taken German prisoners on a tour of Maidanek; see "Nazi Mass Killing Laid Bare in Camp," *NYT*, 30 Aug. 1944. The results of the Maidanek investigation were published in Central Commission for the Investigation of German War Crimes in Poland, *German Crimes in Poland* (New York: Fertig, 1982).

There were also other forced tours in early April. Shortly after 6 April, Lt. Col. James Van Wagenen, a Military Government officer, ordered that the mayor of Ohrdruf be led through the camp near that town. The mayor agreed to summon twenty-five prominent men and women for a subsequent tour. The mayor and his wife subsequently committed suicide. See Earl Ziemke, *The US Army in the Occupation of Germany, 1944–1946* (Washington: Government Printing Office, 1975), 231f, and Charles McDonald, *The Mighty Endeavor* (New York: Oxford University Press, 1969), 476ff. Contemporary news reports about the tour in Ohrdruf differ slightly from this official version. See the ap report of 11 April (in *NYHT*, 12 April 1945): "Even Germans Are Shocked by Ohrdruf Camp / Townsfolk, Taken for Tour of Horror Prison, Profess Disgust and Disbelief," which names Col. Hayden Seale as the initiator and counts forty citizens on the tour.

44 In fact, as noted above (note 37), some of the piles of corpses had already been cleared away, and were brought back before the citizens' tour.

45 *NYHT*, 21 Apr. 1945, reports by Howard Barnes and Marguerite Higgins. For a contextualized narrative of the experience of the 24-year-old Higgins at Buchenwald, see Antoinette May, *Witness to War: A Biography of Marguerite Higgins* (New York/Toronto: Beaufort, 1983), 82–5. In that same issue of the *NYHT*, headlines on other articles read "SS Men Bury Torture Dead at Belsen," and "Nazis Roasted Captives Alive in Leipzig Camp." All four articles were illustrated with large photos, and it was reported that after the Buchenwald tour the mayor of Weimar and his wife committed suicide.

46 Shirer's column appeared, for example, in *NYHT*, 22 April 1945. For a brief summary of Shirer's attitude towards Germany and his influence in the United States, see Martin Broszat, "William Shirer und die Geschichte des Dritten Reiches," *Historische Zeitschrift*, 196 (1963), 112–23, 112f.

47 According to Ziemke, *The US Army*, 245, there were standing instructions from Eisenhower to "make the Germans bury atrocity victims in the most prominent and suitable spot in the nearest town." I have not been able to document any official order to this effect. On 21 April, an ap photo of three civilian men kneeling amidst charred human remains in Gardelegen carried the caption: "Following a policy of forcing German citizens to view the horrors of prison camps operated by the Nazis, these burgomasters from towns in the vicinity of Gardelegen were brought in by 9th Army units." See *NYHT*, 22 April 1945 (ap/signal photo).

48 Very little has been published about these incidents, but brief mentions of many examples can be found in a widely dispersed literature. I have been able to document twenty-four cases. See Abzug, *Inside the Vicious Heart*, 33–9 (Nordhausen), 78 (Thekla), 82 (Namering), and 83 (Flossenbürg); "Buchenwald Camp: The Report of a Parliamentary Delegation," 4, 6 (Buchenwald); Sam Bloch (ed.), *Holocaust and Rebirth: Bergen-Belsen 1945–65* (n.p.p.: n.p., 1965), 57, and Sington, *Belsen Uncovered*, illustrations (Celle); Bourke-White, *Dear Fatherland*, 102f (Duisburg and Ruhr cities); Florian Freund, *Arbeitslager Zement: Das Konzentrationslager*

Ebensee (Vienna: Verlag für Gesellschaftskritik, 1989), 435 (Ebensee); Heigl, *Konzentrationslager Flossenbürg*, 19 (Tittling near Passau), 91f (Flossenbürg), 129ff (Schwarzenfeld), 135–140 (Neuenburg v. W.), 147 (Wetterfeld); Obenaus, "Das Ende der Kranken," 544 (Gardelegen); Edith Raim, "'Unternehmen Ringeltaube': Dachaus Außenlagerkomplex Kaufering," *Dachauer Hefte*, 5 (1989), 193–213, 212 (Kaufering 4); Rainer Schulze (ed.), *Unruhige Zeiten: Erlebnisberichte aus dem Landkreis Celle 1945–1949* (Munich: Oldenbourg, 1990), 77, 83 (Belsen); *Stars and Stripes*, 30 April 1945 (Landsberg); US Army, 71st Division, *The Seventy-First Came*, 22, 26 (Gunskirchen); Ziemke, *The US Army*, 245 (Leipzig/Thekla). A selection of pictures of these forced visits/burials can be found in the brochure "KZ," see below. In the films *The Nazi Concentration Camps*, and *Death Mills*, similar scenes in Arnstadt, Fehrballin, Hadamar, Naumbach, Offenburg, and Remsdorf are shown.

Some of these incidents were also reported in the German-language newspapers published by Military Government. See, for example, *Hamburger Nachrichten-Blatt*, 14 May and 2 June 1945 (Ebensee).

A German master's thesis offers an excellent overview of the US media reporting about the concentration camps, including many hitherto unpublished documents collected by the United States Holocaust Memorial Museum in Washington, D.C. See Zieher, "Amerikanische Reaktionen auf die Befreiung der deutschen Konzentrationslager".

49 See Abzug, *Inside the Vicious Heart*, 68ff.
50 For an excellent and reliable account of this work at Dachau by the physician in charge, see Smith, *Harrowing of Hell*, 79–119. Sington, *Belsen Uncovered*, 26–69, describes the measures taken in Belsen.
51 For example Heigl, *Konzentrationslager Flossenbürg*, 130, 131, 137; Abzug, *Inside the Vicious Heart*, 34f, 71, 82, 83. Dagmar Barnouw, *Germany 1945: Views of War and Violence* (Bloomington: Indiana University Press, 1996), although often rather speculative in its interpretation of individual images, also discusses these incidents at length and reproduces many of the photographs. See esp. 6–34, 39–41, 51–9, 65–71, and 77–83.
52 Marguerite Higgins, "Army Forces Weimar Citizens to View Buchenwald's Horrors. Americans March 1,000 Germans, Weeping and Protesting, Past Heaps of Dead, Victims of Gestapo, and Through Torture Chambers," *NYHT*, 18 April 1945, 1.

For another contemporary example, see the statement by Fred Bohm about the villagers of Nordhausen, quoted in Abzug, *Inside the Vicious Heart*, 33. (Abzug's figure of 2,000 conscripted civilians in Nordhausen is probably exaggerated. See Ziemke, *The US Army*, 234, where only "several hundred German civilians" are mentioned.)
53 Tony Barta, "Antifaschismus und demokratischer Neubeginn: Die Stadt Dachau im ersten Jahr nach dem Nationalsozialismus," *Dachauer Hefte*, 1 (1985), 62–87, 71. (English translation: "After Nazism: Antifascism and Democracy in Dachau, 1945," in Michael Dobkowski and Isidor Wallimann (eds.), *Radical Perspectives on the Rise of Fascism in Germany, 1919–1945* [New York: Monthly Review, 1989], 289–318.) The criteria according to which the committee selected these particular men from their lists of Nazi Party members is not known.
54 See Smith, *Harrowing of Hell*, 138–41. For the date, see Frantizek Kadlec, prisoner no. 20,601, "Tagebuch der Gruppe tschechischer Belegschaft des Blocks Nr. 8 und

Nr. 14 des Konzentrationslager Dachau," 16, DaA. The Polish newspaper article cited by Weiss, "Dachau and International Public Opinion," 29f is also of interest. If each procession carried 400 corpses, there were probably two processions per day, not one, as the report states. According to a newspaper article several years later, the transports lasted from 5 to 10 May 1945, and each of the twelve carts carried approximately thirty corpses (*Dachauer Nachrichten*, 16 Dec. 1949).

55 Michael Groiss, letter to the editor, *SZ/DN*, 6 May 1985. See also Dietrich Hentschel, letter to the editor, *SZ/DN*, 11 Jan. 1975, and the statement by Georg Englhard (local CSU leader), quoted in *SZ/DN*, 6 Apr. 1985, 9.

56 The tour took place on 8 May 1945. It is described in *Der Aufbau* (New York), 18 May 1945, quoted by Hermann Weiss, "Dachau und die internationale Öffentlichkeit," *Dachauer Hefte*, 1 (1985), 12–38, 34. The translation of Weiss's article in *Dachau Review*, 1 (1985), 28 is somewhat misleading in this case. For the date of the tour see *Der Antifaschist: Stimme der Deutschen aus Dachau*, 9 May 1945 (mimeographed newsletter, DaA). Footage of this tour is included in the film shown daily at the Dachau memorial site.

Patricia Lochridge, "Are Germans Human?," *Women's Home Companion* (Springfield, Ohio), 72 (July 1945), 4, 96, also describes the tour. Lochridge, who used pseudonyms in the article, wrote that the tour group was selected by the "newly liberated" and "newly appointed" mayor of Dachau. The person who most closely fits the bill is Georg Scherer, a participant in the 28 April uprising. Scherer, however, was released well before liberation, and was not "imprisoned for helping a French boy escape slave labor," as Lochridge wrote.

57 Josef Schwalber, "Dachau in der Stunde Null," *Amperland*, 4 (1968), 83–7, 87.

58 Richard Titze in *Mitteilungsblatt der Lagergemeinschaft Dachau* (Dec. 1984); Interview William Ronson, 5 May 1990.

59 Schulze (ed.), *Unruhige Zeiten*, contains several reports that daughters or wives were compelled to go to Belsen to care for the sick. The film *The Nazi Concentration Camps* shows German female nurses from one of the towns (Nordhausen?) who were being forced to care for the liberated prisoners. As the examples of Ludwigslust and Weimar show, women were equally required to participate in the tours. Photographs show that they were also, if not always, compelled to perform burial work. See Heigl, *Konzentrationslager Flossenbürg*, 129, 135–40, and Barnouw, *Germany*, 15, 22–5, 32–4.

60 See International Prisoners' Committee minutes, 9 May 1945 (DaA); *Der Antifaschist*, 11 May 1945 (DaA); Smith, *Harrowing of Hell*, 158; interview given by Col. Paul Roy to Voice of America on 22 July 1945 (Archive of the *Neue Zeitung*, microfilm in the Presse- und Informationsamt der Bundesregierung, Bonn), excerpts printed in *Washington Evening Star*, 3 Aug. 1945.

61 See Lochridge, "Are Germans Human?" For information on the "mayor" Edmund Suse interviewed by Lochridge, see 7th US Army (William Quinn), *Dachau* (n.p.: n.p.p., [1945], reprinted in Witness to the Holocaust Publication Series [Atlanta: Emory University Center for Research in Social Change, 1979; 2nd edn, 1983]), 62. It should be noted that Lochridge had an "interpreter sergeant" with her who "had looked in vain for three members of his family known to have been imprisoned in Dachau." Judging by some of the reactions Lochridge recorded, however, most of her interlocutors were not inhibited by his presence. Additionally, the statements

she records prefigure so precisely the protective subterfuges documented for later months and years that it is unlikely that she made them up.

62 Franz Neumann, "Re-educating the Germans: The Dilemma of Reconstruction," *Commentary*, 6 (June 1947), 517–25, 517.

63 See Nicholas Pronay, "'To Stamp Out the Whole Tradition,'" in Pronay and Wilson (eds.), *The Political Re-education of Germany and her Allies*, 1–36, 18f.

64 Keith Wilson, "Great War Prologue," in Pronay and Wilson (eds.), *Political Re-education*, 37–58.

65 See Lothar Kettenacker, "The Planning of 'Re-education' During the Second World War," in Pronay and Wilson (eds.), *Political Re-education*, 59–81, 62f.

66 Edward Carr, *Conditions of Peace* (New York: Macmillan, 1942), 233. This passage is also quoted by Kettenacker, "Planning of 'Re-education,'" 63. Carr (1892–1982) was originally a diplomat who had worked with Vansittart in the British "News Department" (the name originally proposed was "Propaganda Department") before becoming a historian after World War I. He is best known for his seven-volume *History of Soviet Russia* (1950–64).

67 Vansittart's (1881–1957) major work in this respect is *Roots of Trouble: The Black Record of Germany Past, Present and Future* (Toronto/London: Hamish Hamilton, 1941). See also his *Lessons of My Life* (New York: Knopf, 1943), and *Bones of Contention* (New York: Knopf, 1945). Lutz Niethammer, *Entnazifizierung in Bayern: Säuberung und Rehabilitierung unter amerikanischer Besatzung* (Frankfurt: Fischer, 1972), 32–52 contains an excellent discussion of the spectrum of opinions on denazification/reeducation in US policy. In the United States, Secretary of Finance Henry Morgenthau's (1891–1967) name is more commonly associated with this position. However, he did not develop a full-fledged doctrine, as Vansittart did. See Henry Morgenthau, *Germany is Our Problem* (New York: Harper, 1945).

68 Kettenacker, "Planning of 'Re-education,'" 68f.

69 Klaus Bergmann and Gerhard Schneider (eds.), *1945: Ein Lesebuch* (Hannover: Fackelträger, 1985), 41–61 offers an excellent collection of documents and reports about futile but determined resistance efforts in the last days of the war. For a general discussion, see Marlis Steinert, *Hitler's War and the Germans: Public Mood and Attitude during the Second World War* (Athens: Ohio University Press, 1977), 547ff. On the organization of resistance, see Charles Whiting, *Hitler's Werewolves: The Story of the Nazi Resistance Movement, 1944–1945* (New York: Stein and Day, 1972). For a scholarly history of the development of the werewolf program, see Helmuth Auerbach, "Die Organisation des 'Werwolf'", in *Gutachten des Instituts für Zeitgeschichte*, vol. I (Munich: Selbstverlag IfZ, 1958), 353–5, and Arno Rose, *Werwolf 1944–1945* (Stuttgart: Motorbuch, 1980). Karl-Heinz Füssl has found archival materials on the group: NARA RG 319/XE 049888: Werewolf Activities. Heiner Wember, *Umerziehung im Lager: Internierungslager in der Britischen Zone* (Düsseldorf: Klartext, 1991), 14, discusses an underground radio station run by werewolves which fueled Allied fears of a guerrilla movement.

70 Based on the archival documentation of reeducation by the agencies that developed it, Karl-Heinz Füssl argues that the reeducation program was a well-conceived means of achieving rational goals. However, his evidence does not suggest that the program *as implemented* actually achieved these goals. His footnotes offer an excellent survey of the latest literature on the topic. See Karl-Heinz

Füssl, "Zwischen NS-Traumatisierung und Demokratie: Die Erziehungspolitik der USA in der deutschen Nachkriegsgeschichte (1945–1952)," *Paedagogica Historica*, 33:1 (1997), 221–46.

71 Chamberlin, "Todesmühlen," 421 (citing NARA RG 208, Office of War Information, entry 404, box 803, folder 2).

72 Ibid. (citing NARA RG 260, OMGUS, 17–3/10, folder 13, excerpts of the OWI German committee meeting minutes, 23 Feb. 1945; retranslation H. Marcuse).

73 Chamberlin, "Todesmühlen," 421, 424f.

74 For a general overview of atrocity reporting in occupation newspapers, see Elisabeth Matz, *Die Zeitungen der US-Armee für die deutsche Bevölkerung, 1944–1946* (Münster: Fahle, 1969), 53f. For an example of a didactic series, see *Hamburger Nachrichten-Blatt*, issues from 14 to 24 May 1945. Each issue contained reports of atrocities committed in concentration camps; every second day there appeared a large, illustrated front-page article about a concentration camp. The first article about KZ Ebensee on 14 May presumed that the readers were already familiar with Dachau and Buchenwald. See also Bourke-White, *Dear Fatherland*, 135ff, and Kitty Fischer, "'Ich bin Kriegswaise," *Dachauer Hefte*, 6 (1990), 94–103, 100, for two examples of the experiences of contemporaries with the newspaper campaign. See also Zelizer, *Remembering to Forget*, passim; Cornelia Brink, *Ikonen der Vernichtung: Öffentlicher Gebrauch von Fotografien aus nationalsozialistischen Konzentrationslagern nach 1945* (Berlin: Akademie, 1998), 47–58.

75 See Cornelia Brink, "'Ungläubig stehen oft Leute vor den Bildern von Leichenhaufen abgemagerter Skelette. . .' Konzentrationslager-Fotografien auf Plakaten – Deutschland 1945," in Fritz-Bauer-Institut (ed.), *Auschwitz: Geschichte, Rezeption und Wirkung* (Frankfurt: Campus, 1996), 189–222; and Barbro Eberan, *Luther? Friedrich 'der Grosse'? Wagner? Nietzsche?: Wer war an Hitler schuld?: Die Debatte um die Schuldfrage 1945–1949* (Munich: Minerva, 1983), 22. Some of the other captions were: "Diese Schandtaten: Eure Schuld?" (These shameful acts: your guilt?), "Wessen Schuld?" (Whose guilt?), "Das ist eure Schuld" (This is your guilt). "Schuld" translates directly as "guilt"; although in these phrases it would more appropriately be rendered as "fault," for which there is no German equivalent, or "responsibility," which is more accurate, albeit not as pithy.

An article in *Die Gegenwart* (Freiburg, 1 [1946], 10ff) entitled "Kollektivschuld," begins with the sentence: "When the first German soldiers released from Allied POW camps returned home they found on walls, billboards and advertising pillars those identical posters that they had already seen over and over again on the way . . . pictures of the horrors in the concentration camps." See also Morris Janowitz, "Atrocities: A Study of German Reactions," *American Journal of Sociology* (Sept. 1946), 143. On the posters in Military Government offices, which were visited by Germans for many reasons, see Jon Gheorghe, *Automatic Arrest* (Leoni: Drüffel, 1956), 180. Gheorghe quotes the two titles he could remember among posters of emaciated corpses in the Oberursel interrogation room as: "Keine Verbrüderung" and "Ausrottung des deutschen Militarismus ist humanitäre Pflicht" (the originals were presumably in English: "No Fraternization," and "Extermination of German Militarism is a Humanitarian Duty"). In an article on fraternization in *Stars and Stripes*, 7 July 1945, there are sketches of three posters directed at US soldiers: one shows a crematory oven with a doorway full of corpses next to it (caption: "Lest We

Forget"); a second depicts a blonde woman in traditional German dress standing smiling in the middle of a field of corpses with a gallows and a smoking chimney in the background. See also Brink, *Ikonen*, 70–8.

76 See Schulze (ed.), *Unruhige Zeiten*, 261 (Hermannsburg); Barnouw, *Germany*, 10 (Beckum/Westphalia); and Horwitz, *In the Shadow*, illustration opposite p. 115 (Linz); also Zelizer, *Remembering to Forget*, 136f.

77 Especially noteworthy in this respect is *KZ: Bildbericht aus fünf Konzentrations-lagern*, a 54-page illustrated brochure produced by the US Office of War Information in late April 1945 for distribution in Germany. Its printing, however, was delayed until early July. For details on the distribution, see Chamberlin, "Todesmühlen," 420 n. 1. The introduction of the brochure reads: "Thousands of Germans who live near these places were led through the camps to see with their own eyes which crimes were committed in their name. But it is not possible for most Germans to view a KZ. This pictorial report is intended for them."

A number of other brochures were printed in English, presumably for distribution among Allied soldiers: 7th US Army, *Dachau* (see above), of which 10,000 copies were printed (Chamberlin and Feldman [eds.], *The Liberation*, 33), and US army, 71st Division (Willard Wyman), *The Seventy-First Came to Gunskirchen Lager* (n.p.p.: n.p. [1945]). All three aforementioned brochures were reprinted in the Emory University "Witness to the Holocaust" series in 1979–83. See also: US army, 667th Infantry, Missouri, *Dachau: Something to Remember* (n.p.p.: n.p., ca. July 1945).

78 According to Janowitz, "German Reactions," 143, Radio Luxembourg and the BBC were the main sources of information on the camps in Germany in May 1945. Radio London repeatedly broadcast reports about German concentration camps in mid-May (*Hamburger Nachrichten-Blatt*, 16 May 1945). See also Ursula von Kardorff, *Berliner Aufzeichnungen aus den Jahren 1942 bis 1945* (Munich: Nymphenburger, 1976), 250 (20 April 1945): "Die Entdeckung des KZ Oranienburg ruft bei den Alliierten unvorstellbares Entsetzen hervor. *Ich hörte es im englischen Rundfunk.* Was jetzt zutage tritt, muss über alle Massen grauenhaft sein. Selbst wir, die in Berlin viel erfuhren und noch mehr ahnten, sind fassungslos" (emphasis added).

79 Culbert, "American Film Policy," 177–9. See also the announcement in the *Hamburger Nachrichten-Blatt*, 26 May 1945, that "one of the first documentary films about the concentration camps" would soon be shown. Some films may have been shown locally at earlier dates. See Barnouw, *Germany*, 224 n. 18.

80 For some examples of public talks held by former Dachau inmates after returning home, see Walter Feuerbach, *55 Monate Dachau – Ein Tatsachenbericht* (Lucerne: Rex, 1945); Max Lackmann, *Schuld und Gnade: Eine Heimkehr aus Dachau: Aus einem Vortrag Juli 1945*, (Aalen: n.p., 1945); and Fritz Wandel (city councillor in Reutlingen), "Ein Weg durch die Hölle: Dachau wie es wirklich war" (ms. 1945), Dokumentationsarchiv des deutschen Widerstands, Frankfurt (DDW), (excerpts published in *Mitteilungen der Militärregierung in Reutlingen* and *Schwäbisches Tagblatt* as well as other newspapers); Ernst Wilm, *Dachau – Bericht auf der Gemeindeversammlung, Sonntag den 28.10.1945 in der evangelischen Kirche zu Mennighüffen* (Dortmund: Evangelischer Vortragsdienst, 1948); "Aus der Hölle von Dachau," *Neue Westfälische Zeitung* (Oelde), 14 Aug. 1945, reprinted in Bergmann and Schneider (eds.), *1945: Ein Lesebuch*, 102. Joel Sack, *Dawn after Dachau* (New

York: Shengold, 1990), 84f describes a reading by two Buchenwald survivors in an emergency shelter in Nuremberg in July 1945.

On the autobiographical accounts published immediately after the war, see Helmut Peitsch, *Deutschlands Gedächtnis an seine dunkelste Zeit: zur Funktion der Autobiographik in den Westzonen Deutschlands und den Westsektoren von Berlin 1945 bis 1949* (Berlin: Sigma, 1990); Helmut Peitsch, "Autobiographical Writing and *Vergangenheitsbewältigung* (Mastering the Past)," *German History*, 7 (1989), 47–70.

There is also evidence that liberated survivors invited villagers into the camp to have a look for themselves, as the story of Lorenz Reitmeier in the introduction shows. Some survivors also offered to go to schools to tell their stories. See August Hochrein to A. Fischer, Ministry of the Interior, 25 Aug. 1945, Bavarian Main State Archive (BayHsta), State Chancellory files (Stk) 113 624.

81 Janowitz, "German Reactions," 143.

82 Chamberlin, "Todesmühlen," 428 n. 41 (NARA RG 260, OMGUS 17–3/10, folder 4: PWD Monthly Report for July 1945). See also Heide Fehrenbach, *Cinema in Democratizing Germany: Reconstructing National Identity after Hitler* (Chapel Hill: University of North Carolina Press, 1995), 56f.

83 The study was undertaken in June 1945 by Morris Janowitz, who later became an eminent sociologist at the University of Chicago. See note 75. The original report dated 21 June 1945 is preserved in NARA, RG 260, 5/261–2, folder 14 (see Chamberlin, "Todesmühlen," 420 n. 1). About 100 Germans in seven cities and several villages were questioned; seventy were interviewed in depth.

For biographical information on Janowitz, see James Burk, "Introduction," in Morris Janowitz, *On Social Organization and Social Control* (Chicago/London: University of Chicago, 1991), 1–56.

84 Janowitz, "German Reactions," 144. The following quote was also taken from this source.

85 Chamberlin, "Todesmühlen," 422f (NARA RG 260, OMGUS, 17–3/10, folder 4, Material Needed for Proposed Motion Picture on German Atrocities, 5 May 1945).

86 The film script is printed in Culbert, "American Film Policy," 199f. This was a typical Vansittartist stance; see Kettenacker, "Planning of 'Re-education,'" 60: "whatever their virtues may be, the German people have a very definite vice of choosing vicious leaders and of following them both willingly and blindly" (quote after the Vansittartist Orme Sargent, ca. 1939).

87 Frank Trommler, "'Deutschlands Sieg oder Untergang': Perspektiven aus dem Dritten Reich auf die Nachkriegsentwicklung," in Thomas Koebner, Gert Sautermeister, and Sigrid Schneider (eds.), *Deutschland nach Hitler: Zukunftspläne im Exil und aus der Besatzungszeit 1939–1949* (Opladen: Westdeutscher, 1987), 214–28, convincingly develops an alternative explanation for the powerful obedience to the dictates of National Socialist leaders right up to the bitter end: that the identification with the Nazi regime actually dissipated in the early 1940s and was replaced by an "existentialism of work" which continued to supply meaning after the Nazi vision of the future had suppressed all other possible futures and then lost credibility itself.

88 See Hermann Graml, "Die Kapitulation und ihre Folgen," in Martin Broszat and Norbert Frei (eds.), *Das Dritte Reich im Überblick: Chronik-Ereignisse-Zusammenhänge* (Munich: Piper, 1989), 161–74. Also interesting in this respect is a

report quoted by Ziemke, *The US Army*, 246, which describes how quickly Nazi par-
tisans switched from underground resistance to collaboration with Allied authorities (SHAEF G-5, historical section, "Germany – April 1945," 5 May 1945). See also
the references in note 69, above.

89 Bourke-White, *Dear Fatherland*, 4f. See also Arnold Sywottek, "Tabuisierung und
Anpassung in Ost und West: Bemerkungen zur deutschen Geschichte nach 1945,"
in Koebner, Sautermeister, and Schneider (eds.), *Deutschland nach Hitler*, 229–60,
231.

90 In contrast, some of the more morally conscious Allies included themselves in the
circle of guilty. See, for example, the conclusion of American reporter Martha
Gellhorn in "Dachau: Experimental Murder," *Collier's* (23 June 1945), 16, 28, 30: "We
are not entirely guiltless, we the Allies, because it took us twelve years to open the
gates of Dachau. We were blind and unbelieving and slow." Frei ("'Wir waren
blind,'" 401) selected this quotation as the title of his essay about the media blitz.
Even though Frei is no apologist, it is interesting to note that this German historian
selected an Allied "mea culpa" as the title of his superb essay. See also the quote
after E. H. Carr in Kettenacker, "Planning of 'Re-education,'" 63; Dorothy
Thompson, "The Lesson of Dachau," *Ladies Home Journal*, 62 (6 Sept. 1945), with
Peter Kurth, *American Cassandra: The Life of Dorothy Thompson* (Boston: Little,
Brown, 1990), 378; also Hannah Arendt's Jan. 1945 essay "Organized Guilt," in
Arendt, *The Jew as Pariah* (New York: Grove, 1978). For background on the female
journalists, see Nancy Caldwell Sorel, *The Women Who Wrote the War* (New York:
Arcade, 1999).

91 Gert Sautermeister, "Messianisches Hoffen, tapfere Skepsis, Lebensbegehren:
Jugend in den Nachkriegsjahren; Mit einer Nachrede wider die Trauer-Rhetorik," in
Koebner, Sautermeister, and Schneider (eds.), *Deutschland nach Hitler*, 261–300.

92 See Chamberlin, "Todesmühlen," 429, and Hanus Burger, *Der Frühling war es wert:
Erinnerungen* (Munich: Bertelsmann, 1977; reprinted Frankfurt: Ullstein, 1981)
232–66 (esp. 236–40). Burger describes how hard he worked to overcome the opposition to the production of the film and admits that the film did not achieve the
effect he had wanted.

93 Burger, *Der Frühling*, 258.

94 Chamberlin, "Todesmühlen," 430. The final version of the film script is printed in
Culbert, "American Film Policy," 197ff.

95 Helmut Regel, "Der Film als Instrument alliierter Besatzungpolitik in
Westdeutschland," in Klaus Jaeger and H. Regel (eds.), *Deutschland in Trümmern:
Filmdokumente der Jahre 1945–1949* (Oberhausen: K. M. Laufen, 1976), 39–50, 43;
cited after Fehrenbach, *Cinema*, 275 n. 19.

96 See notice in *VVN-Nachrichten*, 1 April 1948.

97 For statistics, see Quinn, *Dachau*; Kimmel, "Das Konzentrationslager Dachau," 374;
Weiss, "Dachau und die internationale Öffentlichkeit," 34.

98 This phase of the camp is described in detail in Wolfgang Benz, "Between Liberation
and the Return Home: The Dachau International Prisoners' Committee and the
Administration of the Camp in May and June 1945," *Dachau Review*, 1 (1987), 32–54.

99 Sack, *Dawn after Dachau*, 47ff.

100 The reliable report by the US military doctor in charge: Smith, *The Harrowing of
Hell*, is an invaluable source for the measures taken after liberation.

101 For a general summary, see M. J. Proudfoot, Report on the conditions in Dachau concentration camp on 2 July 1945, 9 July 1945; NARA RG 331, box 50, entry 47, reprinted in USHMM, *The Year of Liberation: 1945* (Washington: USHMM, 1995), 172–5.

7th US Army, *Dachau*, 65 lists 31,432 liberated inmates by nationality; an additional ca. 30,000 were in Dachau's subsidiary camps at that time. Between liberation and the end of May, 2,226 survivors of the main camp died. See Berben, *Dachau: The Official History*, 219, 223. On the remaining inmates, see also Gun, *Day of the Americans*, 26; *Gli Italiani in Dachau*, no. 37, 29 June 1945 (DaA); Sack, *Dawn after Dachau*, 60ff, 96.

Some of the Russians were members of the so-called Vlasov army, an organization of Russian POWs who fought for the Germans under Russian leadership. Many Jews and those who had enlisted in Soviet satellites such as Lithuania or the Baltic states did not wish to return to their native countries.

102 Oskar Müller to mayor of Dachau, 30 May 1945; Müller to "Lagerältesten, Blockältesten, sämtliche Nationalkomitees, Dienststellen, Arbeitskommandos, Kameraden," 31 May 1945, DDW, OM.

103 Eugène Ost, "Nach 30 Jahren," *Rappel*, special edn (Luxembourg, 1975), 219–25, 222, DaA; interview, Richard Titze, May 1990.

104 Hans Schwarz, Komitee ehemaliger politischer Gefangener, Hamburg, Situationsbericht über die Betreuung ehemaliger politischer Gefangener in den deutschen Städten, 13 July 1945, StAHH, BfEuL Ab IV 8d.

105 The history of these early centers has barely been explored. Various letters in file 21 of the Anton Pfeiffer papers, BayHsta, show that the Munich *KZ-Betreuungsstelle*, established prior to July 1945, was affiliated with the Dachau center. The Munich center was located at Goethestr. 64. Other institutions concerned with former prisoners, such as the Bavarian Red Cross's "Department of Political Persecutees," were also located there. For more information, see StMü, BuR 2526. According to Schattenhofer, *Chronik*, 74, 92, a report about the Munich center was presented at the fifth meeting of the Munich city council on 6 Sept. 1945, and a meeting of KZ care representatives from all over Bavaria was held in Munich on 20 Oct. The "Landesausschuss der politisch Verfolgten" was also stationed at Goethestr. 64; see *Landesausschuss* to Military Government, 5 Feb. 1947, BayHsta, OMGBY 13/141–1/1.

106 Interview Titze, May 1990; information Barbara Distel, 1990, who was in intermittent contact with Cieslik. In April 1949 Paul Hussarek was president of the IIO, see invitation to "Tag der Befreiung in Dachau," 29 Apr. 1946, BayHsta, Stk 113 624. In May 1947 the German Ernst Beer was apparently in charge. See L. Roth to Ernst Beer, 10 May 1947, BayHsta, JS102. Roth resigned from his position there because the VVN did not allow for a Christian service during the commemorative ceremonies on 17 and 18 May 1947. This indicates that the VVN was closely connected with the *KZ-Betreuungsstelle*.

107 For a short biography of Titze (1912–1990) see Jürgen Müller-Hohagen, "Richard Titze," in Hans-Günter Richardi et al. (eds.), *Lebensläufe: Schicksale von Menschen, die im KZ Dachau waren* (Dachau: Verein Zum Beispiel Dachau, 1990), 47–9.

108 Ost, "Nach 30 Jahren," 222. The museum is not mentioned in other contemporary reports, such as those by Arthur Haulot and Otto Färber. When interviewed by me

in 1990, Haulot said that he could not remember whether he had seen an exhibition in the crematorium building in Nov. 1945. Views of the museum can be found
on a Dec. 1945 film held by NARA, Motion Pictures Branch, #111 ADC 5610.

109 USHMM, *The Year of Liberation*, 172f.

110 C. E. Straight, "Report of the Deputy Advocate for War Crimes to the Judge Advocate,
European Command," 29 August 1948, Archive of the Institut für Zeitgeschichte
(IfZ), Munich, sets the date at ca. 8 July. A former concentration camp inmate sup-
plying the camp with vegetables wrote on 7 July of the "recently reoccupied" camp
(Hanns Hornung to Josef Schwalber, 7 July 1945, BayHsta, JS). The capacity is given
in *SZ*, 9 Oct. 1945.

111 See Arthur Haulot, "Lagertagebuch," *Dachauer Hefte*, 1 (1985), 129–203, esp. 196f,
202f.

112 Elmer Plischke, "Denazifying the Reich," *Review of Politics*, 9 (1947), 159f.

113 Bradley F. Smith, *The Road to Nuremberg* (New York: Basic, 1981), 34, 45ff, 63f, 190f.
It is a common misperception that Stalin was the staunchest advocate of summary
executions. Smith found that Churchill promoted the plan more tenaciously than
either Roosevelt or Stalin. See also the well-documented summary by Michael
Marrus, *The Nuremberg War Crimes Trial, 1945–46: A Documentary History* (Boston:
Bedford, 1997), 22ff.

114 See Smith, *Road to Nuremberg*, 218ff for the final policy change of the British.
Niethammer, *Entnazifizierung*, 35–68, also contains an excellent portrayal of this
development. Frank Buscher, *The US War Crimes Trial Program: 1946–1955* (New
York/Westport: Greenwood, 1989), 14–20 offers a narrow but concise summary in
English.

115 United States Department of State, *Foreign Relations of the United States: The
Conference of Quebec 1944* (Washington: Government Printing Office, 1972), 123ff;
see Smith, *Road to Nuremberg*, 54–7; Buscher, *US War Crimes Trial Program*, 16.

116 Smith, *Road to Nuremberg*, 33, 54 (Maidanek), 114–18 (Malmédy), 201–6. See also
James Weingartner, *Crossroads of Death: The Story of the Malmédy Massacre and
Trial* (Berkeley: University of California Press, 1979).

117 Niethammer, *Entnazifizierung*, 150–6, and United States Department of State,
Foreign Relations of the United States: 1945, vol. III, 434ff. This compromise resolution was intended to apply only during an interim period after the end of the war
in Europe, but since its harsh but vaguely worded regulations shielded shifts in
policy from public criticism, it was not reformulated and remained officially in
effect until March 1947. See Niethammer, *Entnazifizierung*, 66–8; also John Gimbel,
The American Occupation of Germany: Politics and the Military, 1945–1949
(Stanford: Stanford University Press, 1968), 28–33, 166f.

118 "OMGUS Denazification Policy Board Report," 15 January 1946, NARA RG 260,
OMGUS 124–3/15, reported 117,512 persons interned in the US zone on 6
December 1945. See also Niethammer, *Entnazifizierung*, 255; Plischke,
"Denazifying the Reich," 157.

119 An acrimonious debate about possible intentional neglect of German POWs, which
may have claimed millions of casualties, was sparked by Canadian journalist James
Bacque's book, *Other Losses: An Investigation into the Mass Deaths of German
Prisoners at the Hands of the French and Americans after World War II* (Toronto:
Stoddart, 1989; Rockland, Calif.: Prima, 1991). Historians have since found that

although there was a high death rate among German POWs, it was not nearly as high as Bacque claimed. See Günter Bischof and Stephen Ambrose (eds.), *Eisenhower and the German POWs: Facts against Falsehood* (Baton Rouge: Louisiana State University Press, 1992).

120 See Roland Foerster, Christian Greiner, Georg Meyer, Hans-Jürgen Rautenberg, and Norbert Wiggershaus, *Anfänge westdeutscher Sicherheitspolitik 1945–1956: Von der Kapitulation bis zum Pleven-Plan* (Munich: Oldenbourg, 1982), vol. I, 604.

121 See Hanno Müller (ed.), *Recht oder Rache? Buchenwald 1945–1950: Betroffene erinnern sich* (Frankfurt: dipa, 1991), 9; Nationale Mahn- und Gedenkstätte Sachsenhausen (ed.), *Speziallager Nr. 7: Sachsenhausen, 1945–1950* (Berlin: Brandenburgisches Verlagshaus, 1990), passim. For a comprehensive bibliography of relevant literature, see Bodo Ritscher et al. (eds.), *Die sowjetischen Speziallager in Deutschland 1945–1950: Eine Bibliographie mit einem Anhang: Literatur zum historisch-sozialen Umfeld der Speziallager* (Göttingen: Wallstein, [May] 1996), which lists over 300 entries.

122 Harold Marcuse, "Gefängnis als Gedenkstätte? Die Geschichte des ehemaligen Konzentrationslagers Neuengamme, 1945–1960," unpublished seminar paper, 4 October 1984, copy in NA 6f (quoted in Fritz Bringmann and Hartmut Roder, *Neuengamme: Verdrängt – Vergessen – Bewältigt?* [Hamburg: VSA, 1987], 34). See also Wember, *Umerziehung im Lager*, 70–3.

123 Wember, *Umerziehung im Lager*, 28f, 81–3. The centralization of former concentration camp guards captured in the British zone at Esterwegen, one of the better-known early KZs (Carl von Ossietzky was still imprisoned there when he received the Nobel Peace Prize in 1935), is further evidence of the symbolic nature of the reuse of the German KZs.

124 KZ Flossenbürg in northeastern Bavaria was used as a POW camp from July 1945 to April 1946. See Heigl, *Konzentrationslager Flossenbürg*, 79.

125 "Im Internierungslager Langwasser," *Telegraf*, 2 Dec. 1947, typescript copy in BayHsta, MSo 2061.

126 Recent studies of the internment camps, such as Wember, *Umerziehung im Lager*, and Christa Schick, "Die Internierungslager," in Martin Broszat, Klaus-Dietmar Henke, and Hans Woller (eds.), *Von Stalingrad zur Währungsreform: Zur Sozialgeschichte des Umbruchs in Deutschland* (Munich: Oldenbourg, 1988), 301–25, reconstruct the administrative history of the internment camps, but they rely on sparse information gleaned from memos from authorities only tangentially concerned with the camps, reports by investigative commissions, and chance testimony from former internees for their portrayal of life (and death – an especially touchy subject) in the internment camps. See also Niethammer, *Entnazifizierung*, 255.

127 Gheorghe, *Automatic Arrest*, 197f.

128 My interview with the Hamburg historian Fritz Fischer, 14 Nov. 1983. Because of crimes committed by persons with the same name (an SS doctor in Buchenwald and a German administrator in southern France), Professor Fischer was interned in the Dachau War Crimes Enclosure from January 1946 until February 1947, when his true identity was established.

129 Interview D. J. (amateur historian and retired lecturer for the Bavarian state police stationed in the former Dachau SS camp), 27 July 1990. D. J. had interviewed several men who had served time in the Dachau War Crimes Enclosure.

130 Gheorghe, *Automatic Arrest*, 197f.

131 See Robert Sigel, *Im Interesse der Gerechtigkeit: die Dachauer Kriegsverbrecher-prozesse 1945–1948* (Frankfurt: Campus, 1992), 40–75; and Buscher, *US War Crimes Trial Program*. The Belsen trial began in September and ended in early November with eleven death sentences. The trials of the murderers of the pilots took place in Ludwigsburg and Dachau.

132 Photograph in possession of the Keystone Picture Service, Hamburg, copy in DaA. The picture was printed in *Schwäbische Landeszeitung*, 13 Nov. 1945, 3. The same scene shortly after liberation, after the corpses had been removed, is depicted in Selzer, *Deliverance Day*, 201.

133 Quinn, *Dachau*, 66.

134 Ibid. See also 33f, where the gassing procedure is described. It was also believed that the five clothing disinfection chambers were used to gas prisoners.

135 After Distel and Jakusch, *Konzentrationslager Dachau*, 204f. The figure 206,206 is based on a calculation by Jan Domagala, a prisoner who as camp secretary was responsible for the master index. Kimmel ("Konzentrationslager Dachau," 377f) found discrepancies in that calculation and says that the best estimate would be "more than 200,000 prisoners" in total. The number of deaths was compiled by the Tracing Service of the International Red Cross, which attempts to document as many deaths in the camps as possible.

136 The higher figure was cited again and again by individuals such as Philipp Auerbach and Martin Niemöller, as well as in a number of hastily researched articles and reports about Dachau. See, for example, the caption of the picture of the newly dedicated statue in front of the Dachau crematorium, *MM*, 1 May 1950. Auerbach is cited as the source of the number in *SZ*, 2 May 1950, 1.

137 "Die Wahrheit über das KZ Dachau / Wurden in Dachau 238 756 Menschen ermordet oder gab es im ganzen Altreich keine Gaskammern?" *DNZSZ*, 3 Mar. 1961. On the *DNZSZ* in general, see Karsten Reinecke, "Die 'Deutsche National-Zeitung und Soldaten-Zeitung': Ein Organ der 'Heimatlosen Rechten' in der Bundesrepublik" (Ph.D. dissertation, Erlangen-Nuremberg, 1970), esp. 194–219. Reinecke does not explicitly mention the "gas chamber lie." In June 1960, shortly before its merger with the *Deutsche National-Zeitung*, the *Deutsche Soldaten-Zeitung* printed a relatively balanced article based on a recent press announcement by Bishop Neuhäusler, "Weihbischof Neuhäuslers offene Worte: Im KZ Dachau gab es keine Gaskammern," *DSZ*, 1 June 1960.

138 Bringmann and Roder, *Neuengamme*, 91.

139 Sigel, *Im Interesse der Gerechtigkeit*, 60, 65, 75.

140 For a detailed description of the event, see Irving Dilliard, "28 Dachau Killers are Hanged at Landsberg," *Stars and Stripes*, 30 May 1946.

141 Eugen Kogon, *Der SS-Staat: Das System der deutschen Konzentrationslager* (Munich: Heyne, 1974; 13th printing, 1983), 410, 409. Kogon's book was written in 1945 and published in 1946. On the origins of this book, see Hackett, *The Buchenwald Report*, introduction. The English translation of Kogon, Heinz Norden (trans.), *The Theory and Practice of Hell: The German Concentration Camps and the System Behind Them* (New York: Farrar, Straus and Co., 1950) does not contain this concluding chapter, which was originally published as "Gericht und Gewissen" in *Frankfurter Hefte*, 1:1 (Apr. 1946), 25–37.

Anyone interested in the intellectual climate of that time would be well advised to compare Kogon's essay with the German philosopher Karl Jaspers' widely read and discussed exposition of "The Question of German Guilt," which was based on a series of lectures held at Heidelberg University in January and February 1946. See Karl Jaspers, *Die Schuldfrage* (Heidelberg: Lambert Schneider, 1946); *The Question of German Guilt*, trans. Ernst Basch (New York: Dial, 1948). For a contemporary's assessment of Jaspers as "basically [a] conformist," see Neumann, "Re-educating," 524, with references. For recent discussions of Jaspers and postwar guilt, see Anson Rabinbach, "The German as Pariah: Karl Jaspers' The Question of German Guilt," in Rabinbach, *In the Shadow of Catastrophe: German Intellectuals between Apocalypse and Enlightenment* (Berkeley: University of California Press, 1997), esp. 141–52, and Dan Diner, "On Guilt Discourse and Other Narratives: Epistemological Observations Regarding the Holocaust," in Gulie Ne'eman Arad (ed.), *Passing into History: Nazism and the Holocaust beyond Memory: In Honor of Saul Friedlander on his Sixty-fifth Birthday* (Bloomington: Indiana University Press, 1997) (*History and Memory*, 9:1/2 [fall 1997], 301–20).

Part II Dachau 1945–1955: three myths and three inversions

1 Josef Schwalber, manuscript of speech for 9 Nov. 1945, BayHsta, js101, and draft of speech for 9 Nov. 1945, JS25. Also printed in *Augsburger Zeitung*, 15 Nov. 1945, 1.

2 On the creation of the 9 November commemorative date, see John Bornemann, "Reconstructions of History: From Jewish Memory to Nationalized Commemoration of Kristallnacht in Germany," in Michael Bodemann (ed.), *Jews, Germans, Memory: Reconstructions of Jewish Life in Germany* (Ann Arbor: University of Michigan Press, 1996), 179–223.

3 *Augsburger Zeitung*, 15 Nov. 1945, 1. There is also a handwritten note to this effect on the final manuscript. I did not find reports that the speech was actually broadcast in the US. It was, after all, in German.

4 For a good survey of the literature on politically relevant myths, see Andreas Doerner, *Politischer Mythos und symbolische Politik* (Opladen: Westdeutscher, 1995). See also Herfried Münkler, "Politische Mythen und nationale Identität: Vorüberlegungen zu einer Theorie politischer Mythen," in Wolfgang Frindte and Harold Pätzolt (eds.), *Mythen der Deutschen: Deutsche Befindlichkeiten zwischen Geschichten und Geschichte* (Opladen: Westdeutscher, 1994), 21–27; Herfried Münkler, Interview, in *Blätter für deutsche und internationale Politik*, 40:10 (1995), 1179–90.

For uses of the term similar to mine, see Antonia Grünenberg, *Antifaschismus, ein deutscher Mythos* (Reinbek: Rowohlt, 1993), and Hans-Peter Rouette, "Die Widerstandslegende: Produktion und Funktion der Legende vom Widerstand im Kontext der gesellschaftlichen Auseinandersetzungen in Deutschland nach dem Zweiten Weltkrieg" (Ph.D. dissertation, Free University of Berlin, 1983).

5 Josef Schwalber, manuscript "Einweihung Gedenkstein Waldfriedhof," 28 Apr. 1946; BayHsta, JS XVIII/101. I am indebted to Jürgen Hepe for the transcription of this stenographic text.

6 Most recently, this position was publicly suggested by Martin Walser in his accep-

tance speech for the Peace Prize of the German Publishers in Frankfurt on 11 Oct. 1998. On that speech and the reactions by Ignaz Bubis and others, see Frank Schirrmacher (ed.), *Die Walser-Bubis Debatte: Eine Dokumentation* (Frankfurt: Suhrkamp, 1999), and Gerd Wiegel and Johannes Klotz (eds.), *Geistige Brandstiftung: Die Walser-Bubis-Debatte* (Cologne: Papyrossa, 1999).

3 "Good" Nazis

1 Hans Zauner, *Erinnerungen* (Dachau: private publication, n.d. [ca. 1961]). This book is available in the Bayerische Staatsbibliothek in Munich, and from Zauner's daughter-in-law in the Zauner stationery store in downtown Dachau. Some biographical information was obtained from Zauner's Nazi Party file at the Berlin Document Center, and "Hans Zauner ist 85 Jahre alt," *MM/DN*, 28 Dec. 1970.
2 Berlin Document Center, file Hans Zauner, born 28 December 1885 in Bad Tölz, index card and evaluation by the Kreisleitung on 4 February 1938. For an additional evaluation of Zauner's behavior as *Kreismeister für Handwerk*, see also "Dachau's Political Review," 27 Jan. 1947, in NARA RG 260, 7/55/30/5, box 48.
3 It is not clear just what the threat was. The usual version is the threat of shelling by the Allies. However, that is a rather implausible albeit firmly entrenched element of local memory. That particular myth was debunked in 1975, but persisted in some circles into the 1990s. See Steinbacher, *Dachau – Die Stadt*, 216–20; also *Mitteilungen LGD* (winter 1985–6).
4 Zauner, *Erinnerungen*, "Die Nachkriegszeit."
5 See Llew Gardner, "So Stark the Memories – But They Say 'Let's Forget'," *Sunday Express* (London), 10 Jan. 1960; reprinted as "How Can Germany Forget?" *Washington Daily News*, 18 Jan. 1960, 14; translated in *MM/DN*, 24 Feb. 1960. Zauner gave a number of additional explanatory interviews, e.g., "Schwamm über die Hölle von Dachau-Ost?," *Elan* (Mar. 1960), and "Dachau: After 15 Years a Memorial in the German Terror Camp," *Daily Mail*, 30 Apr. 1960, 11.
6 See Gert Naumann, *Besiegt und "befreit:" Ein Tagebuch hinter Stacheldraht in Deutschland, 1945–1947* (Leoni: Drüffel, 1984), esp. 139–201. The page references in parentheses in the main text refer to this diary.
    For similar narratives see Karl Vogel, *M-AA-509: Elf Monate Kommandant eines Internierungslagers* (Memmingen: Selbstverlag, 1951), and Ernst von Salomon, *Der Fragebogen* (Hamburg: Rowohlt, 1951). For a woman's experience, see Melita Maschmann, *Fazit: Mein Weg in die Hitler-Jugend* (Munich: dtv, 1979 [orig. edn, 1963; English edn, 1964]), 195–207.
7 "PW – die wahre Geschichte der Kriegsgefangenschaft," *Quick*, no. 44, 1959; after Schornstheimer, *Bombenstimmung und Katzenjammer: Vergangenheitsbewältigung: Quick und Stern in den 50er Jahren* (Cologne: Pahl-Rugenstein, 1989), 42f. In this case the film screening was in Camp McCain in Mississippi, and the German POW who shouted out explicitly referred to German victimization in rejecting the film's message: "Think of Dresden, Hamburg and Cologne."
    On German POWs' reactions to a screening in Utah in the summer of 1945, see Allan Kent Powell, *Splinters of a Nation: German Prisoners of War in Utah* (Salt Lake City: University of Utah Press, 1989), 144f.

See also Werner Kleinhardt, *Jedem das Seine* (Frankfurt: Suhrkamp, 1982), 99ff. Also relevant in this regard was my interview with history professor Fritz Fischer (born 1908), 14 Nov. 1983. Fischer was in Dachau for a short time because other men with the same name had committed atrocities.

8 Based on my interview with Ludwig H. (1911–91), 27 Jan. 1990, and on H.'s personnel file in the Berlin Document Center.

9 Dr. Karl Schnell, *Kriegstagebuch*, vol. VII: *756 Tage hinter Stacheldraht: Kriegsgefangenschaft und Internierung, 1945–1947*. Schnell was in Dachau with Naumann and the General Staff officers (8 Oct. 1945 to 19 Feb. 1946, 3 June to 11 Nov. 1946): see vol. VII, 101–40, 183–224. In a 15 Aug. 1993 telephone conversation Schnell told me that he had read Naumann's book and recommended it to me.

10 See John Gimbel, *The American Occupation of Germany: Politics and the Military, 1945–1949* (Stanford: Stanford University Press, 1968), 2f, 85–90. Gimbel documents how the OMGUS Information Control Division heralded the speech as a watershed of US policy formulation. The speech itself was published as US Department of State, "Restatement of US Policy on Germany," *Department of State Bulletin* (Washington: Office of Public Service, Bureau of Public Affairs), vol. 13, 960–4. See also Günter Moltmann, "Zur Formulierung der amerikanischen Besatzungspolitik in Deutschland am Ende des Zweiten Weltkrieges," *VfZ*, 15 (June 1967), 299–322.

11 Gimbel, *American Occupation*, 131–40.

12 Ibid., 150f, 162–9.

13 *NYHT*, 28 Apr. 1945. The term "denazification" was coined by a member of Eisenhower's political advisory board in April 1945 as a section heading for a number of occupation statutes. Hitherto terms such as "Eradication of Nazism" or "Control, Disarmament, and Disbandment of Para-Military and Police Organizations" had been used. See Elmer Plischke, "Denazifying the Reich," *Review of Politics*, 9 (1947), 153–72, 155 n. 3.

14 Jörg Friedrich, *Die kalte Amnestie: NS-Täter in der Bundesrepublik* (Frankfurt: Fischer, 1984), 36, after Gimbel.

15 John Herz, "The Fiasco of Denazification in Germany," *Political Science Quarterly*, 63 (Dec. 1948), 569–94, 577.

16 For an etymological discussion, see Peter Novick, *The Holocaust in American Life* (Boston: Houghton Mifflin, 1999), 133f; also Omer Bartov, *Murder in our Midst* (New York: Oxford University Press, 1996), 56–60.

17 Friedrich, *Kalte Amnestie*, 74, after *Trials of War Criminals before the Nuremberg Military Tribunal* (The Justice Case), vol. III (Washington, 1951). For Jahrreis' statement see also Wilbourn Benton and Georg Grimm (eds.), *Nuremberg: German Views of the War Trials* (Dallas: Southern Methodist University Press, 1955), 31–75. Hannah Arendt made the same point in a 17 Aug. 1946 letter to Karl Jaspers. See Lotte Kohler and Hans Saner (eds.), *Correspondence of Hannah Arendt and Karl Jaspers, 1926–1969* (New York: Harcourt Brace Jovanovich, 1992), 54.

18 See Adalbert Rückerl, *NS-Verbrechen vor Gericht: Versuch einer Vergangenheitsbewältigung* (Heidelberg: C. F. Müller, 1982). In my opinion, the best discussion of these crimes, both in their specific nature and legal problematics, is Herbert Jäger, *Verbrechen unter totalitärer Herrschaft: Studien zur nationalsozialistischen Gewaltkriminalität* (Frankfurt: Suhrkamp, [1967], 1982).

19 In a 1965 interview, Karl Jaspers offered the following illogical explanation: "War crimes are crimes against humaneness. Crimes against humaneness – unfortunately the difference is only this clear in the German language, which distinguishes between humaneness and humanity – crimes against humaneness are all of the horrors which are called war crimes, committed against enemies. A crime against humanity is the claim to decide which groups of people and peoples are allowed to live on earth, and the implementation of that decision by extermination. Today it is called genocide." (See Karl Jaspers, "Für Völkermord gibt es keine Verjährung: Gespräch mit Rudolf Augstein," *Der Spiegel*, 10 March 1965, 49ff; reprinted in Jaspers, *Die Schuldfrage: Für Völkermord gibt es keine Verjährung* (Munich: Piper, 1979), 97–123, 104.

At Nuremberg, "crimes against humanity" was a category created to include state-sanctioned murder of Germans by Germans. The genocide against non-German Jews was a war crime. See also Peter Steinbach, *Nationalsozialistische Gewaltverbrechen: Die Diskussion in der deutschen Öffentlichkeit nach 1945* (Berlin: Colloquium, 1981), 23f, 43f; Ulrich Brochhagen, *Nach Nürnberg: Vergangenheitsbewältigung und Westintegration in der Ära Adenauer* (Hamburg: Junius, 1994), 256, 428 n. 69; Gerhard Griem, "Der Tatbestand des Verbrechens gegen die Menschlichkeit in der Rechtssprechung der Nürnberger Gerichtshöfe unter Hinweis auf die hiervon abweichende Rechtssprechung deutscher Gerichte" (Jur. Diss., Munich, 1951).

20 See, to cite only two of many examples, Robert M. W. Kempner, *SS im Kreuzverhör: Die Elite, die Europa in Scherben schlug* (expanded new edn, Nördlingen: Delphi Politik, 187; original edn, 1964), 18f; Friedrich, *Kalte Amnestie*, 147, 213. Nuremberg prosecutor Telford Taylor wrote about this translation problem in Telford Taylor, *Die Nürnberger Prozesse* (Zürich: Europa, 1951). To my knowledge, the only exception is Jäger, *Verbrechen unter totalitärer Herrschaft*, e.g. 329f, who uses the term "Menschheitsverbrechen."

21 For general assessments of contemporary German perceptions of denazification, see Herz, "Fiasco of Denazification," 573–81; Niethammer, *Entnazifizierung*, 663–6; Kurt Tauber, *Beyond Eagle and Swastika: German Nationalism since 1945*, vol. I (Middletown: Wesleyan University Press, 1967), 36f.

22 *Simpl*, no. 6 (1946), reprinted in Dieter Galinski and Wolf Schmidt (eds.), *Jugendliche erforschen die Nachkriegszeit: Materialien zum Schülerwettbewerb deutsche Geschichte 1984–1985* (Hamburg: Körber, 1984), and Clemens Vollnhals (ed.), *Entnazifizierung: Politische Säuberung und Rehabilitierung in den vier Besatzungszonen, 1945–1949* (Munich: dtv, 1991), 331.

23 See Niethammer, *Entnazifizierung*, 13, for a general discussion of "wash" associations. For several especially crass cases of *manus manum lavat*, see files relating to post-trial activities: NARA RG 338, 29/42/2, box 3 (e.g. Hans Schmidt). Sigel, *Im Interesse*, 69f, lists the references former Dachau capo Peter Betz obtained for his clemency petition.

24 Niethammer, *Entnazifizierung*, 613f.

25 George Orwell, "Revenge is Sour," *Tribune*, 9 Nov. 1945, reprinted in Sonja Orwell (ed.), *The Collected Essays, Journalism and Letters of George Orwell*, vol. IV, *1945–1950* (New York: Harcourt, Brace and World, 1968), 3–6.

26 Ralph Giordano, *Die zweite Schuld, oder von der Last Deutscher zu sein* (Hamburg: Rasch und Röhring, 1987), 88f.

27 See Niethammer, *Entnazifizierung*, chapter IV.5: "Endkrise: Westintegration und beschleunigte Rehabilitation", 483–537. For the 8 May deadline, see 513. See also Angelika Schafflik, "Im Schatten der Nürnberger Urteile: Die Dachauer Prozesse unter besonderer Berücksichtigung des Weiss-Prozesses" (Zulassungsarbeit Staatsexamen, Munich, 1986), 19f.

28 Internees to Bezold, 6 July 1948, BayHsta, MSo 2062.

29 Typescript copy of letter from local CSU chair Teufelhardt to Schwalber, 10 June 1948; copy of letter from Special Ministry to Teufelhardt, 12 July 1948, both in BayHsta, JS02.

30 Copy of letter from Justice Minister Müller to Special Minister Hagenauer, 19 July 1948; letter from Junker to Schwalber, 27 Apr. 1949, both in BayHsta, JS02.

31 See Lagerleiter Vogel to Sonderministerium Abteilung VI, 16 Apr. 1948, BayHsta, MSo 2015; Herz, "The Fiasco of Denazification in Germany," 569–94, 576.

32 List of persons in Dachau, 1 June 1948 with penciled update 20 July, BayHsta, MSo 2091. At this time the Bavarian authorities were just starting to refurbish the denazification chambers with stoves for the winter, new tables, curtains, etc., when they were suddenly informed by the US military that they should cancel all contracts immediately and prepare to take over the camp themselves.

33 Already on 20 July 1945 Munich Cardinal Faulhaber and Protestant Bishop Meiser raised their objections to the "mass persecution and wholesale condemnation of all SS men" by Military Government. See Michael Ratz et al., *Die Justiz und die Nazis: Zur Strafverfolgung von Nazismus und Neonazismus seit 1945* (Frankfurt: Röderberg, 1979), 56. (Ratz quotes Johannes Neuhäusler, "Entnazifizierung und katholische Kirche," *Der Überblick: Nachrichtendienst aus der christlichen Welt*, 17 Mar. 1948, 4–8.)

34 See the characterization of Minister Alfred Loritz's policy by FDP deputy Linert, which Denazification Minister Loritz applauded, *Verhandlungen des Bayerischen Landtags*, 30 Jan. 1947. Loritz was a very controversial figure. Because of his rhetorical skill, *Aufbau* gave him the epithet "budding Hitler." See Auerbach to Ehard, 29 Mar. 1947, BayHsta, Stk 114 262.

35 Friedrich, *Kalte Amnestie*, 145.

36 As reported by the journal *Quick* (17:43 [25 Oct. 1964]), lawyer Heinecke argued that Hitler's motives were not base and the murders were not cruel: "A national leader who decides to exterminate people in order to save his country does not act from base motives . . . Hitler and his inner circle had no interest in letting the Jews suffer during or prior to the killing, or in having them tortured . . . His only motive was to exterminate the Jews, whom he considered pests." Quoted after Helmut Hammerschmidt (ed.), *Zwanzig Jahre danach: Eine deutsche Bilanz, 1945–1965* (Munich: Desch, 1965), 314.

37 In other cases, the reasoning was applied in the other direction. Otto Ohlendorf's lawyer defended him by placing the blame on Hitler. See Norbert Frei, *Vergangenheitspolitik: Die Anfänge der Bundesrepublik und die NS-Vergangenheit* (Munich: Beck, 1996), 229 n. 139, after *Spiegel*, 31 Jan. 1951, 9. For further examples see Ingo Müller, *Furchtbare Juristen: Die unbewältigte Vergangenheit unserer Justiz* (Munich: Kindler, 1987), 250f.

38 Steinbacher, *Dachau – Die Stadt*, 65. Steinbacher gleaned some of her information from Nazi-era newspapers; she also had access to Wülfert and Huber's denazification files. See also pp. 67, 93, 140, 145–7.

39 They were officially not allowed to be more than 60 percent of normal wages. According to Rüdiger Hachtmann, *Industriearbeit im "Dritten Reich": Untersuchungen zu den Lohn- und Arbeitsbedingungen in Deutschland 1933–1945* (Göttingen: Vandenhoeck und Ruprecht, 1989), 51, 104–7, 111, 127, from 1941 to 1944 untrained German male workers earned about RM40/week, or RM6.60/day. Skilled workers cost on average about RM8/day or ca. 33 percent more than KZ slaves. In an unskilled, labor-intensive industry such as canning, the 40 percent differential would have bolstered profits substantially.

For more general discussions of the topic, see Gerhard Hoch and Rolf Schwarz (eds.), *Verschleppt zur Sklavenarbeit: Kriegsgefangene und Zwangsarbeiter in Schleswig Holstein* (Bremen: W. Geffken, 1985), 127; Hermann Kaienburg, *"Vernichtung durch Arbeit": Der Fall Neuengamme* (Bonn: Dietz, 1990), 199, 406; Ulrich Herbert, *Hitler's Foreign Workers: Enforced Foreign Labor in Germany under the Third Reich* (New York: Cambridge University Press, 1997[Berlin/Bonn: Dietz, 1985]).

40 Lawyer Max Rau to Headquarters Judge Advocate EUCOM, 28 Mar. 1948, DaA, Rau papers.

41 *MM/DN*, 26 Nov. 1948.

42 Ibid., 10 Dec. 1948.

43 *VVN-Nachrichten*, 18 May 1949.

44 This was noted in the interpellation about the Leiten Affair in the French National Assembly (see p. 146f). See *Annales de l'Assemblée nationale*, 13 Dec. 1949, 6805.

45 See *MM/DN*, 27 Sept. 1972 and 28 Sept. 1973.

46 For an excellent overview of the first trial and its background, see Michael Marrus, *The Nuremberg War Crimes Trial 1945–46: A Documentary History* (Boston: Bedford, 1997). Very little work has been done on the twelve successor trials. See the documentation: *Trials of War Criminals before the Nuremberg Military Tribunals under Control Council Law No. 10*, 15 vols. (Washington: Government Printing Office, 1951–2). Extensive microfilm records of these trials are available from the Washington National Archives. Of the 184 accused in the successor trials, 142 were found guilty; twenty-four were sentenced to death and twelve death sentences were carried out, the rest received varying prison terms.

47 See Frei, *Vergangenheitspolitik*, 21 n. 28, 22, 28, 155, 158, 234. The German terms were *Kriegsverurteilte, Militärverurteilte, kriegsgefangene Deutsche*, and *verurteilte Soldaten*. The quotation marks were first added by Neuhäusler in an Oct. 1948 telegram to US President Truman. Even Frei uncritically uses the term "war criminal" to substitute for the more precise German term "NS crimes." This vagueness stands in sharp contrast to Frei's recognition of the euphemistic use of the term, and to his reasoning for coining the term "politics of the past" (see ibid., 13f).

48 Sigel, *Im Interesse*, 37, 159. See also Frei, *Vergangenheitspolitik*, 143 n. 29.

49 Another statistical overview can be found in Rolf Vogel (ed.), *Ein Weg aus der Vergangenheit: Eine Dokumentation zur Verjährungsfrage und zu den NS-Prozessen* (Frankfurt/Berlin: Ullstein, 1969), 10.

50 Memo from Col. Harbaugh to Col. Fleischer, 26 Aug. 1948, NARA RG 338 29/42/2, box 5. See also the rosters of inmates at Landsberg contained in the same box. The roster of 30 Sept. 1948 contains a statistical summary. For the data for 1955 and 1957, see Sigel, *Im Interesse*, 192f.

51 Most of the information that follows is from Sigel, *Im Interesse*, 65f. See also Friedrich, *Kalte Amnestie*, 217, and Werner Scherf, "Strafverfolgung von Ärzteverbrechen im KZ Buchenwald," *Wissenschaftliche Zeitschrift der Humboldt Universität zu Berlin, Reihe Gesellschaftswissenschaften*, 37:5 (1988), 503–6. The reasoning for the 1948 recommendation can be found in Judge Advocate Division, War Crimes Branch, General Administrative Records, Press release of 30 Dec. 1948, NARA RG 338 29/40/6, box 3.

52 See the account by Werner Bergmann, *Antisemitismus in öffentlichen Konflikten: Kollektives Lernen in der politischen Kultur der Bundesrepublik 1949–1989* (Frankfurt: Campus, 1997), 200–4. Bergmann draws primarily on contemporary newspaper reports, esp. "Der unglaubliche Fall Eisele," *SZ*, 9 July 1958.

53 Friedrich, *Kalte Amnestie*, 95f (after *IMT*, vol. 4, case 9) (my retranslation).

54 Ibid., 121f, after an Oct. 1980 Berlin radio broadcast of excerpts of the trial by Rainer Ott entitled "Ausblick in die Vergangenheit" (see ibid., 418).

55 Rudolf Höss, *Death Dealer: The Memoirs of the SS Kommandant at Auschwitz*, ed., by Steven Paskuly, trans. by Andrew Dollinger (Buffalo: Prometheus, 1992), 162, 164.

56 Dachau Internees to Ehard, 29 June 1948; Dachau Internees to Entnazifizierungsausschuss, 6 July 1948, BayHsta, Stk 113 953; Internees to Bezold, 6 July 1948, BayHsta, MSo 2062. Unless otherwise noted, the following quotes are taken from these petitions, which differ only slightly from one another.

57 In June 1948 ten denazification courts were working in the Dachau internment camp, trying an average total of 20–30 cases per week, so that the last of the 300 internees could anticipate release in about ten weeks, or by mid-September.

58 Internierten des Internierungs- und Arbeitslagers Dachau to Ministerpräsident Ehard, 17. Feb. 1948, BayHsta, MSo 2061. The letter concludes with thirty-four pages containing 1,935 signatures. This petition prompted a report broadcast by Radio Munich on 3 Apr. 1948. See *Stimmen aus Dachau*, May 1948, which reprints the report. See also letter from Lagerältester des Interniertenlagers Dachau to Ministerpräsident Ehard, 12 Apr. 1948, BayHsta, Stk 113 953. At that time, 2,551 were still in the camp. Schick, "Internierungslager," 325, reports similar statistical findings for the camp Nuremberg-Langwasser.

59 Report from Kulturabteilung der I.- und A.lagers Dachau über den Besuch des Dichters Carl Zuckmayer und Herren der Tagespresse, 29.2.48, BayHsta, MSo 2061.

60 A number of examples of the use of survivor, prison camp, and barbed wire imagery in the early 1950s can be found in Robert Moeller, "War Stories: The Search for a Usable Past in the Federal Republic of Germany," *AHR*, 101:4 (Oct. 1996), 1008–48, 1010, 1013, 1027f.

61 Letter "Die Internierten des Internierungs-u. Arbeitslagers Dachau an das Bayerische Staatsmin. für Sonderaufgaben," 29 June 1948, Stk 113 953. The phrase is also used in a letter of 3 May 1948, Stk 113 953.

62 See, for example, Karl Vogel, *M-AA-509: Elf Monate Kommandant eines Internierungslagers* (Memmingen: Selbstverlag, 1951), passim. The articles from newspapers Vogel quotes are also a valuable source. See 70 (*Tiger Cub*, n.d., explicit comparison of Garmisch with KZ Dachau), 87 (*The Thundering Herd*, 13 Oct. 1945 about Garmisch), and 133 (*Stars and Stripes*, 11 Dec. 1945 about Moosburg). See also the published diary quoted at length on pp. 81–5: Naumann, *Besiegt und "befreit."*

63 Niethammer, *Entnazifizierung*, 178f. See also Wember, *Umerziehung im Lager*, 91–104, esp. 94ff.

64 Anonymous, "Kazet – Internierungslager?," *Der Lagerspiegel* (Regensburg), 11 Sept. 1947; copy in BayHsta, MSo 1986.

65 Gustave Gilbert, *Nürnberger Tagebuch* (Frankfurt: Fischer, 1962 [New York: Farrar, Straus 1947, 1961; Da Capo, 1995]), 1947 edn., p. 256.

66 After Friedrich, *Kalte Amnestie*, 102f, after *Trials of War Criminals*, vols. VII–VIII (case 6, I. G. Farben) (Washington, 1952).

67 For a much more exacting examination of civilian employees' knowledge about Auschwitz, see also Silvester Lechner, "Ernst D. oder Entsetzen über Auschwitz," *Dachauer Hefte*, 12 (1996), 123–38.

68 Retranslation after Giordano, *Zweite Schuld*, 112f.

69 Ibid., 113. The German text uses the awkward verb form "konnte gerettet werden" which allows the court to say that the defendant saved them without emphasizing his agency.

70 Friedrich, *Kalte Amnestie*, 203.

71 For a good portrayal of these lobbying efforts, see Buscher, *US War Crimes Trial*, 91–113. For a general overview, see Brochhagen, *Nach Nürnberg*, 33–53. The most detail is offered by Frei, *Vergangenheitspolitik*, 133–306.

72 File folders bursting with these materials can be found in NARA RG 338 29/40/6, box 6, and 29/42/2, box 3.

73 Bishops Meiser, Niemöller, Wurm, and Wüstermann to Clay, 20 May 1948, NARA RG 338, box 462, Bishop Wurm file, cited after Buscher, *US War Crimes Trial*, 98.

74 Neuhäusler to Clay, 11 Nov. 1948, BayHsta, OMGBY 13/123–1/5. Buscher, *US War Crimes Trial*, found copies of these documents in NARA RG 338 and 466 (McCloy papers); Frei, *Vergangenheitspolitik*, found copies in the IfZ archive.

75 Neuhäusler to Clay, 20 Jan. 1951, copy in BayHsta, Stk 113 891.

76 McCloy to Neuhäusler, 16 Jan. 1951, copy in ibid.

77 Brochhagen, *Nach Nürnberg*, 32, describes this dual demonstration as well.

78 Michel to Ehard, 10 Jan. 1951, BayHsta, Stk 113 891.

79 The following is based on documents published in Beate Klarsfeld, *Die Geschichte des PG 2,633,930 Kiesinger: Dokumentation mit einem Vorwort von Heinrich Böll* (Darmstadt: J. Melzer, 1969), esp. 11f, 15f, 23, 34, 64–7. See also Beate Klarsfeld, *Wherever They May Be!* (New York: Vanguard, 1975), 28–34. Klarsfeld's campaign to expose Kiesinger is discussed below in chapter 12, p. 304.

80 The following is after Friedrich, *Kalte Amnestie*, 294–8. Friedrich's information is from the documentation by Reinhard Strecker, *Dr. Hans Globke* (Hamburg: Rütten und Loening, 1961). See also Giordano, *Zweite Schuld*, 106–11.

81 For the most famous example of successful protest by the "Aryan" spouses of Jews, see the excellent monograph by Nathan Stoltzfus, *Resistance of the Heart: Intermarriage and the Rosenstrasse Protest in Nazi Germany* (New York: Norton, 1996). Stoltzfus offers a wide-ranging account of German–Jewish intermarriages throughout the 1930s.

82 Helmut Hammerschmidt and Michael Mansfeld, *Der Kurs ist Falsch* (Munich: K. Desch, 1956), 24–40, 68ff. The man responsible for hiring personnel at the Foreign Office, a former I. G. Farben official, later published artificially low percentages. See Wilhelm Haas, *Beitrag zur Geschichte der Entstehung des Auswärtigen Dienstes der*

Bundesrepublik Deutschland (Bonn: H. Köllen, 1969), 58. For the assessment, see Brochhagen, *Nach Nürnberg*, 414 n. 5 and n. 1. In the text Brochhagen cites figures from the French High Commissioner in line with the statistics I cite (191f). See also Friedrich, *Kalte Amnestie*, 202f.

Further statistics can be found in Curt Garner, "Public Service Personnel in West Germany in the 1950s: Controversial Decisions and their Effects on Social Composition, Gender Structure, and the Role of Former Nazis," *Journal of Social History*, 29:1 (fall 1995), 25–81, 40–4, reprinted in Robert Moeller (ed.), *West Germany under Construction: Politics, Society and Culture in the Adenauer Era* (Ann Arbor: University of Michigan, 1997), 135–95. For a broader perspective, see Friedrich, *Kalte Amnestie*, and Brochhagen, *Nach Nürnberg*, 173–258. See also the statistics for Bavaria cited on p. 151.

83 Lewis Edinger, "Post-Totalitarian Leadership: Political Elites in the German Federal Republic," *American Political Science Review*, 54 (1960), 58–82.

84 Ferdinand Hermens, "Denazification or Renazification?" in Julia Johnson (ed.), *The Dilemma of Postwar Germany* (New York: Wilson, 1948), 174–80, cited after Brochhagen, 176 and 410 n. 10. By 1951 the term was in common use. See *American Jewish Yearbook*, 53 (1952), 438, and 54 (1953), 307, which called "civil service renazification" a "mass phenomenon in 1951–52."

85 See Frei, *Vergangenheitspolitik*, 29–53, and Friedrich, *Kalte Amnestie*, 213f. The crimes mentioned below are "Freiheitsberaubung" and "Körperverletzung (mit Todesfolge)."

86 Friedrich, *Kalte Amnestie*, 214f describes two cases where this actually happened.

87 For a careful analysis of the realization of Article 131 see Frei, *Vergangenheitspolitik*, 69–100. In English, see James Diehl, *The Thanks of the Fatherland: German Veterans after the Second World War* (Chapel Hill: University of North Carolina Press, 1993), 141–62. See also Friedrich, *Kalte Amnestie*, 272–81, 422, and Michael Ratz et al., *Die Justiz und die Nazis: Zur Strafverfolgung von Nazismus und Neonazismus seit 1945* (Frankfurt: Röderberg, 1979), which includes the text of the law (63ff). The legal aspects are discussed by Michael Kirn, *Verfassungsumsturz oder Rechtskontinuität? Die Stellung der Jurisprudenz nach 1945 zum Dritten Reich, insbesondere die Konflikte um die Kontinuität der Beamtenrechte und Art. 131 Grundgesetz* (Berlin: Duncker und Humblot, 1972).

88 For examples of high-ranking Nazis who had been sentenced to death *in absentia* in France but were working in West Germany, see Ratz et al., *Die Justiz*, 70–4. Further examples can be found in David C. Large, "Reckoning without the Past: The HIAG of the Waffen-SS and the Politics of Rehabilitation in the Bonn Republic, 1950–1961," *Journal of Modern History*, 59 (March 1987), 79–113.

89 On the quota system, see Frei, *Vergangenheitspolitik*, 69–100, and Garner, "Public Service Personnel," 50f.

90 On the Foreign Office see Garner, "Public Service Personnel in West Germany in the 1950s."

91 Friedrich, *Kalte Amnestie*, 143.

92 For his positive assessment of the long-term consequences of denazification (as opposed to its short-term results), see ibid., 201f. A similar position is held by Steinbach, *Nationalsozialistische Gewaltverbrechen*, 42f, and Frei, *Vergangenheitspolitik*, 404ff.

93 An explicit argument for this positive assessment of denazification can be found in Hermann Graml, "Die verdrängte Auseinandersetzung mit dem Nationalsozialismus," in Martin Broszat (ed.), *Zäsuren nach 1945: Essays zur Periodisierung der deutschen Nachkriegsgeschichte* (Munich: Oldenbourg, 1990), 169–83.

94 Mary Fulbrook, *The Divided Nation: A History of Germany, 1918–1990* (Oxford: Oxford University Press, 1991), 279f.

95 The following portrayal of the "Gauleiter conspiracy" follows Frei, *Vergangenheitspolitik*, 361–96, and Friedrich, *Kalte Amnestie*, 305f. The quotation from the newsletter was published by Naumann's lawyer Friedrich Grimm, *Unrecht im Rechtsstaat: Tatsachen und Dokumente zur politischen Justiz, dargestellt am Fall Naumann* (Tübingen: Verlag der Deutschen Hochschullehrer-Zeitung, 1957), 241. For the longer-term consequences of the affair, see also Marion Gräfin Dönhoff, "Vertanes Erbe," *Die Zeit*, 1 Dec. 1955, and letters to the editor, *Die Zeit*, 15 Dec. 1955.

96 See also Manfred Jenke, *Verschwörung von Rechts: Ein Bericht über den Rechtsradikalismus in Deutschland nach 1945* (Berlin: Colloquium, 1961), 155–79, and 427–39 (documents). In fact, Werner Naumann was not interested in a revival of unreconstructed National Socialism. He worked to curtail "negative" influences from the older members of the movement (e.g. disregard of legal rights, persecution of Jews). See Jenke, *Verschwörung von Rechts*, 168f.

97 On the rearmament of West Germany, see David Clay Large, *Germans to the Front: West German Rearmament in the Adenauer Era* (Chapel Hill: University of North Carolina Press, 1996).

98 Adenauer said: "After all that I have read and heard about him, he was always on the side of the more decent group – I don't say the decent group, just the more decent group." Konrad Adenauer, *Teegespräche 1959–1961*, ed. by Hanns Jürgen Küsters (Berlin: Siedler, 1988), 199ff (12 Feb. 1960).

99 On the Landsberg incident, see Brochhagen, *Nach Nürnberg*, 108f and 392 n. 79. There is a large literature about Oberländer. On the pro side, see Kurt Ziesel, *Der rote Rufmord* (Tübingen: Schlichtenmayer, 1961); Hermann Raschhofer, *Der Fall Oberländer: eine vergleichende Rechtsanalyse der Verfahren in Pankow und Bonn* (Tübingen: Schlichtenmayer, 1962); Hermann Raschhofer, *Political Assassination: The Legal Background of the Oberländer and Stashinsky Cases* (Tübingen: Schlichtenmayer, 1964), and most recently Siegfried Schutt, *Theodor Oberländer: Eine dokumentarische Untersuchung* (Munich: Langen Muller, 1995) with a preface by Oberländer himself. On the contra side, see Ausschuss für deutsche Einheit, *Die Wahrheit über Oberländer: Braunbuch über die verbrecherische Vergangenheit des Bonner Ministers* (East Berlin: n.p., 2nd edn, 1960).

Oberländer's past had already been debated in the Bavarian parliament when he became Bavarian Minister of Refugee Affairs in the early 1950s. See Brochhagen, *Nach Nürnberg*, 436 n. 15 for a US consular report about a discussion in 1950, and *Verhandlungen des Bayrischen Landtags* (7 Oct. and 28 Oct. 1952), vol. 4, 126, 288. The latter date contains Oberländer's reply.

After Oberländer entered Adenauer's cabinet, the federal parliament debated his past as well, with foreign observers watching closely. See *Verhandlungen des Deutschen Bundestags* (9 Apr. 1954), 1016; also an article mentioning him clipped by US officials: "Nazi Death Camp Records Going Back to the Germans," *New*

York Post, 12 Apr. 1954 (in: NARA RG 338, 29/40/6, box 3), and *Der Spiegel*, 21 Apr. 1954.

100 It is interesting to note that Josef Müller, the Bavarian CSU minister who supported the communist former Dachau prisoners in the Leiten Affair, 1949–50, was proud of having been the "foster-father" of Strauss in the CSU, even though their political behavior was very different.

101 On the Spiegel Affair, see David Schoenbaum, *The Spiegel Affair* (New York: Doubleday, 1968), and Jürgen Seifert (ed.), *Die Spiegel-Affäre*, vol. I: "Die Staatsmacht und ihre Kontrolle," vol. II: "Die Reaktionen der Öffentlichkeit" (Freiburg: Walter, 1966).

102 This string of affairs is documented in Bernt Engelmann, *Das neue Schwarzbuch: Franz Josef Strauss* (Cologne: Kiepenhauer und Witsch, 1980). Strauss never contested Engelmann's portrayal. See also Joachim Schoeps, *Die Spiegelaffäre des Franz Josef Strauss* (Hamburg: Rowohlt, 1983), 27–42.

103 The following is after Engelmann, *Das neue Schwarzbuch*, 11–43 and 106–12. The corresponding documents are reproduced on 204–20.

104 For a detailed account of the early history of the CSU, see Wolfgang Benz, "Parteigründungen und erste Wahlen. Der Wiederbeginn des politischen Lebens," in Benz (ed.), *Neuanfang in Bayern, 1945 bis 1949: Politik und Gesellschaft in der Nachkriegszeit* (Munich: Beck, 1988), 9–35, 25ff.

105 Police report about the "Diskussionskreis ehemaliger Angehöriger der Allgemeinen- und Waffen-SS," 23 Jan. 1953, StMü, BuR 2469. The meeting ultimately did not take place, since it was prohibited by Bavarian Minister of the Interior Hoegner (SPD).

106 See Günter Wallraff, *Ganz Unten* (Cologne: Kiepenhauer und Witsch, 1985), 26f (also 14).

107 Giordano, *Zweite Schuld*, 242–50, 252f, 358f.

108 Engelmann, *Das neue Schwarzbuch*, 176. *Die Zeit*, 43:41 (7 Oct. 1988), 2 dates the quotation in 1969. The original German reads: "Ein Volk, das diese wirtschaftlichen Leistungen vollbracht hat, hat ein Recht darauf, von Auschwitz nichts mehr hören zu wollen!"

109 Martin Walser's 11 Oct. 1998 acceptance speech for the Peace Prize of German Book Dealers in St. Paul's Church in Frankfurt is an example of the tenacity of such mythic legacies. See the essays in *Universitas*, 12 (1998) and p. 433 n. 6, above.

110 Niethammer, *Entnazifizierung*, 509–15.

111 For an excellent portrayal of how these new victim groups emerged, see Moeller, "War Stories," passim.

112 *Amtliches Handbuch des Bayerischen Landtags* (Munich, 1948). Stang was interned in KZ Dachau from 31 Aug. to 14 Oct. 1944 in "Operation Thundercloud," the code name for the blanket arrests of former SPD members after the 20 July 1944 assassination attempt against Hitler. See the bound typescript list of prisoners held by the DaA, 5825.

113 *Verhandlungen des Bayerischen Landtags* (24 Apr. 1951), vol. 1, 479.

114 Hans Ehard, "Gedenken der KZ-Opfer im Landtag," 24 Apr. 1951, BayHsta, Stk 112 548; also printed in the proceedings of parliament. Ehard should not be confused with Ludwig Erhard, who was the West German Minister of Economics from 1949 to 1963, and Federal Chancellor from 1963 to 1966.

115 Weitmann, police report on the meeting of the VVN in the Collosseum on 21 April, 24 Apr. 1951, StMü, BuR 2467.
116 Langer, [police] report on the Tag der Opfer des Krieges und des Nazismus, 11 Sept. 1951, StMü, BuR 2467.
117 See Heinemann to the Ministers of Interior of the States, 13 June 1950 (minutes of the meeting of Ministers of the Interior), StAHH, Senatskanzlei II, 020.62–2/3, "Gedenkfeiern f. d. Opfer des Nationalsozialismus, 1945–1953." In 1950, the State Ministers of the Interior discussed whether that day was to be made a national holiday. Meinhold Lurz has written on the history of *Volkstrauertag* and *Heldengedenktag*: Meinhold Lurz, *Kriegerdenkmäler in Deutschland* (Heidelberg: Esprint, 1987), vol. V, 383f, vol. VI, 509f.
118 Federal Minister of Expellee Affairs to Ehard, 5 Oct. 1950, BayHsta, MArb 114 829. See also Moeller, "War Stories," 1021 with n. 36.
119 Ministry of Labor to State Chancellory, 20 Oct. 1950, BayHsta, MArb 114 829. On the nature of the private interest group that the government had decided to support on that day, see *Verhandlungen des Bayerischen Landtags* (19 Oct. 1950), vol. 6, 1167.
120 In addition to the correspondence relating to preparations each year in the file BayHsta, MArb 114 829, see the State Chancellory's file of speeches with Ehard's speeches of 24 Nov. 1951 (*Tag der Opfer des Krieges*), 16 Nov. 1952 (*Volkstrauertag*), 25 Oct. 1953 (*Kriegsgefangenengedenkwoche*), 23 May 1954 (Rally of War Victims in Bamberg); see also *Verhandlungen des Bayerischen Landtags* (22 Oct. 1952), vol. 4, 275 (speech by Hundhammer). On the former Hero's Day (13 March) in 1954, Federal Parliamentary President Ehlers spoke at a rally of the "Union of German Soldiers" (VdS) in Bonn, see NARA RG 338, 29/40/6, box 3 (with ap and dpa news reports).
121 For a summary of the Moscow trip, see Dennis Bark and David Gress, *History of West Germany* (Cambridge, Mass.: Blackwell, 1989), I, 358–65. More depth is offered by Josef Foschepoth, "Adenauer's Moskaureise 1955," *Aus Politik und Zeitgeschichte*, 22 (1986), 30–46, and Brochhagen, *Nach Nürnberg*, 240–8.
122 See Large, *Germans to the Front*, 62–4.
123 See Friedrichs, *Kalte Amnestie*, 244–7.
124 Ibid., 246 after Tauber, chapter 8, 254ff (see citation on p. 484 n. 31, below).
125 "Zweierlei Erinnerungen," *Neue Zeitung*, 12 Nov. 1951. The *Neue Zeitung* was by-lined the "American newspaper in Germany." It was produced by returned German émigrés in the US High Commissioner's Information Service Division. The headline translates as: "Two Different Memories."
126 Another example of US support of brown-collar anticommunist groups was the "Shock-Troop against Bolshevist Subversion" ("Stosstrupp gegen bolschewistische Zersetzung"), which was led by former SS men but received financial support from the US army. Modifying a German figure of speech, Bavarian Minister President Hoegner warned that "the lessons of the past should prevent us from allowing brown billy-goats to be our gardeners." See *Verhandlungen des Bayerischen Landtags* (29 Oct. 1952), vol. 4, 308, 313.
     On 23 Oct. 1952, US support of paramilitary organizations was debated in the federal parliament as well. In the interest of anticommunism the Federal Minister for All-German Affairs requested that the Bavarian Ministry of Justice refrain from prosecuting such groups, even though they had drawn up lists of SPD members who were to be shot if the Soviet Union should invade West Germany.

127 See Large, *Germans to the Front*, 69, 74–81.
128 See Frei, *Vergangenheitspolitik*, 194–234.
129 See Bark and Gress, *History of West Germany*, vol. I, 297–302.
130 See Bergmann, *Antisemitismus in öffentlichen Konflikten*, 200.

4 "Bad" inmates

1 For a recent example of the prevalence of this term, even among people who see the survivors favorably, see Detlev Garbe, *Die vergessenen KZs?* (Bornheim-Merten: Lamuv, 1983), 43, 50, 57, 76, 85, 105, 187, 210ff. Of course, the term "survivor" is also used by these authors (see 50, 58, 187f). At that time the term *Zeitzeuge* ("historical witness") was just making its appearance (117).

The captions in the film shown to visitors of the Buchenwald memorial site since 1996 offer a particularly egregious 1990s' example of the persistence of the use of the term "KZ prisoner" (at times without the modifier "former"). See Ursula Junk, *KZ Buchenwald. Aushalten. Wir eilen euch zu Hilfe* (WDR, 1995).

2 For examples of the use of the term before 1945 by Hitler's opponents, see Constantin Goschler, *Wiedergutmachung: Westdeutschland und die Verfolgten des Nationalsozialismus, 1945–1954* (Munich: Oldenbourg, 1992), 25–30. This book offers the best overall historical treatment of the subject.

3 The most detailed collection of evidence on looting are the interviews conducted in the Bergen-Belsen area in 1946 by Hanna Fuess. See Rainer Schulze (ed.), *Unruhige Zeiten: Erlebnisberichte aus dem Landkreis Celle 1945–1949* (Munich: Oldenbourg, 1990), passim. Specific examples are cited below.

4 There are many allusions to fear of rape in the Fuess interviews, although no specific cases are mentioned. In Buchenwald, another of the first camps to be liberated, it was reported that the mayor of Weimar's daughter was raped.

5 Lutz Niethammer discusses the process by which expectations and isolated incidents are combined in memory to produce exaggerated results in Niethammer (ed.), *"Hinterher merkt man, daß es richtig war, daß es schiefgegangen ist": Nachkriegserfahrungen im Ruhrgebiet* (Bonn: Dietz, 1983), 17–38. For a discussion of the postwar silence about mass rape in the case of the Red army, see Norman Naimark, *The Russians in Germany: A History of the Soviet Zone of Occupation, 1945–1949* (Cambridge, Mass.: Harvard University Press, 1995), 69–76.

6 Caspar Schrenck-Notzing, *Charakterwäsche* (Stuttgart: Seewald, 2nd edn, 1965), cited by Friedrich, *Kalte Amnestie*, 191. In 1996 there was a debate in Germany surrounding the planned publication of a book that documented a postwar camp in Poland where a Jewish survivor brutalized German inmates: John Sack, *An Eye for an Eye: The Untold Story of Jewish Revenge against Germans in 1945* (New York: Basic, 1993).

7 For instance, on 22 April 1945 the entire German population of the village of Bergen was evacuated in order to house liberated concentration camp survivors, POWs, and slave laborers. See Schulze (ed.), *Unruhige Zeiten*, 293. Although some Germans were able to return after 2–4 weeks, others had to wait up to six months.

8 Zauner, *Lebenserinnerungen*, section "Die Nachkriegszeit."

9 "Kleine Wiedergutmachungen," *Hamburger Nachrichten-Blatt*, 25 May 1945.

10 "Mitteilungen für die Zivilbevölkerung: Ablieferung von Kleidung," *Hamburger Nachrichten-Blatt*, 28 May 1945.

Notes to pages 130–2

11 Cited after Friedrich, *Kalte Amnestie*, 123.

12 Eugen Kogon, "Der politische Untergang des europäischen Widerstands," *Frankfurter Hefte*, 5 (1949), ca. 405.

13 Schulze, *Unruhige Zeiten*, 81 (looting by "KZ-Leute"), 85 (plunder after release of prisoners), 109 (armed Italian and Russian slaves, "KZ-Leute" loot), 112–16 (plunder and revenge by "KZ-Polen"), 120f (looting by "KZ-Juden"), 123 (Russian plunderers, slaughter of livestock), 133 ("KZ-Leute" prevented from looting), 139 (slaughter of livestock by Poles and Russians), 169 (feeding "hordes of KZ-Leute"), 181ff (voluntary care of "KZ-Leute," then looting by "KZ-Haufen"), 187 (suffering under "KZ-Bettler"), etc. The two reports 326–39 are especially interesting in this regard.

14 For a general overview, see Michael Marrus, *The Unwanted: European Refugees in the Twentieth Century* (New York: Oxford University Press, 1985); for a more recent, more detailed portrayal, see Angelika Königseder and Juliane Wetzel, *Lebensmut im Wartesaal: Die jüdischen DPs (Displaced Persons) im Nachkriegsdeutschland* (Frankfurt: Fischer, 1994). For the following figures, see 7, 18.

15 Hans Schwarz, "Situationsbericht über die Betreuung ehemaliger politischer Gefangener in den deutschen Städten," 13 July 1945, StAHH, BfEuL Ab IV 8d.

16 See Walter Schwarz, "Die Wiedergutmachung nationalsozialistischen Unrechts durch die Bundesrepublik Deutschland: Ein Überblick," in Ludolf Herbst and Constantin Goschler (eds.), *Wiedergutmachung in der Bundesrepublik Deutschland* (Munich: Oldenbourg, 1989), 33–54, esp. 34–9.

17 For example, the books by Walter Schwarz and Constantin Goschler. An informal survey on the internet discussion list H-German conducted by me in October 1996 confirmed the prevalence of this notion. See the 29 Oct. 1996 query at http://h-net2.msu.edu/; responses in my possession.

18 See, for example, Deutsche Liga für Völkerbund (ed.), *Die Friedensforderungen der Entente: Vollständige revidierte deutsche Übersetzung der Versailler Bedingungen, Volksausgabe* (Berlin: Engelmann, 3rd edn, 1919), 99ff. This text was the official German version based on a translation made under Allied auspices in Versailles in May 1918, and on a provisional translation independently compiled in Berlin. Although this euphemistic term was accepted in Germany at first, by the early 1920s it was replaced in common parlance by the more direct translation *Reparationen*. See, for example, the draft of an official protest against the treaty discussed by the Reich cabinet on 28 June 1919, which considers the *Wiedergutmachung* for the destruction caused by German troops *recht und billig*, in contrast to other demands, which it terms *Wiedervergeltung*. Anton Golecki (ed.), *Das Kabinett Bauer, 21. Juni 1919 bis 27. März 1920* (Boppard: Harold Boldt, 1980), 31. After 1921 *Wiedergutmachung* was rarely used in the published official documents. I thank Gerald Feldman for this reference.

19 A detailed overview of the earliest measures in Bavaria is given by Goschler, *Wiedergutmachung*, 76–81. See also Marita Krauss, "Verfolgtenbetreuung und Wiedergutmachung am Beispiel von München und Oberbayern, 1945–1952," unpubl. ms. (Munich, 1988) (copy held by the Munich Landesentschädigungsamt).

20 See Hans-Dieter Kreikamp, "Zur Entstehung des Entschädigungsgesetzes der amerikanischen Besatzungszone," in Herbst and Goschler (eds.), *Wiedergutmachung,*

446

61–76. First the prospect of a currency reform, which finally took place in June 1948, and then considerations of equity and liquidity between the various German states were primarily responsible for the delay. Very rich in material, but as a government-sponsored project rather one-sidedly positive in its interpretations is the five-volume series: Bundesminister der Finanzen and Walter Schwarz (eds.), *Die Wiedergutmachung nationalsozialistischen Unrechts durch die Bundesrepublik Deutschland*, 5 vols. (Munich: Beck, 1974–85). See esp. Walter Schwarz, "Rückerstattung nach den Gesetzen der Alliierten Mächte," in vol. I, 28ff; Schwarz, "Wie kam die Rückerstattung zustande? Neue Erkenntnisse aus den amerikanischen und britischen Archiven," in vol. II, 801–14; Ernst Féaux de la Croix, "Vom Unrecht zur Entschädigung: Der Weg des Entschädigungsrechts," in vol. III, 14–37.

21 See Rudolf Huhn, "Die Wiedergutmachungsverhandlungen in Wassenaar," in Herbst and Goschler (eds.), *Wiedergutmachung*, 139–61, 143f.

22 *Gesetzesverordnungsblatt* (Bavaria), 1946, 258: law of 5 March [/1 August] 1946 concerning confiscation of assets.

23 BayHsta, Stk 114 242, folder entitled: "Wiedergutmachung: Gesetz Nr. 35 über die Bildung eines Sonderfonds zum Zwecke der Wiedergutmachung, 1946–1950." The "Stiftung zur Wiedergutmachung nationalsozialistischen Unrechts" received RM68 million from the inventory of the Dachau concentration camp prior to Nov. 1948; see Krauss, "Verfolgtenbetreuung," 48 with n. 271.

24 Wilhelm Hoegner, *Der schwierige Aussenseiter: Erinnerungen eines Abgeordneten, Emigranten und Ministerpräsidenten* (Munich: Isar, 1959), 271ff. Otto Aster was chosen to head the agency for political persecutees, Hermann Aumer the one for Jews.

25 Unless otherwise indicated, the source of the following information is "Auf der Sonnenseite des Lebens," *Hochland-Bote, Zeitung für Landkreise Garmisch-Partenkirchen . . .*, 5 Feb. 1946.

26 Aumer to Hoegner, 14 Feb. 1946; Gottfried Branz to Minister of the Interior Seifried, 23 Feb. 1946, BayHsta, Stk 113 624.

27 File re ordinance "über die Aufhebung des Staatskommissariats für die Betreuung der Juden in Bayern und des Staatskommissariats für die politisch Verfolgten," BayHsta, Stk 114 263.

28 Memo 16 Oct. 1946 re Hermann Aumer, BayHsta, Stk 114 262. The charges against Aumer were dropped on 16 October.

29 Auerbach (1906–52) was the son of a wholesale exporter in Hamburg. He managed a chemical factory in Antwerp until 1940, when he was interned as a German by the Belgians. He was extradited to Vichy France and then deported to Germany in 1942 because he had supported international brigades in the Spanish Civil War; late in 1943 he was sent to Auschwitz, where he was put in charge of pest control (*Ungezieferbekämpfung*). In January 1945 he was evacuated to Buchenwald, where he was liberated by the US army. See Constantin Goschler, "Der Fall Philipp Auerbach: Wiedergutmachung in Bayern," in Herbst and Goschler, *Wiedergutmachung*, 77–98, 78, and Krauss, "Verfolgtenbetreuung und Wiedergutmachung," 25. There are a number of puzzling aspects in this biography which I have not been able to resolve. Auerbach's dissertation: "Wesen und Formen des Widerstands im 3. Reich," (Erlangen, 22 Aug. 1949) (ms. in DaA), does not contain a curriculum vitae. See also H.-A. Müller-Türmitz, *Steuerzahler Dr. Auerbach: Wiedergutmachung* (Munich: Treuga, 1951) (copy in DDW).

30 Hoegner, *Der schwierige Aussenseiter*, 272. Auerbach officially took office on 10 Oct. 1946, *Verhandlungen des Bayerischen Landtags* (9 Mar. 1954), vol. 6, 894ff (concluding report of the investigation of the Landesentschädigungsamt). On 16 Nov. 1948 Auerbach's position was renamed "Generalanwalt für die Wiedergutmachung"; on 22 Nov. 1949 he became acting president of the Landesentschädigungsamt. For a detailed summary of Auerbach's postwar career in Bavaria, see Goschler, "Der Fall Philipp Auerbach," 77–98, esp. 91f on the reorganization of his office. On Auerbach's initial appointment, see also Annual Historical Report of the US Army, July 1946 to June 1947, IfZ. On 16 Dec. 1948 the Staatskommissariat für rassisch, religiös und politisch Verfolgte was renamed Landesamt für Wiedergutmachung, see *Verhandlungen* (16 Dec. 1948), vol. 3, 406ff. Draft law to become effective on 15 Sept. 1946, BayHsta, Stk 114 263.

31 Regional Board of Political Persecutees (Landesausschuss der politisch Verfolgten), communication to Military Government, 5 Feb. 1947, BayHsta, Office of Military Government for Bavaria (OMGBy) 13/141–1/1. The following delegates were present: Ernst Holzer and Heinrich Pflüger (CSU); Oskar Zelger, Anton Aschauer (SPD); Maximilian Fuchs, Gerhard Hirsch (FDP); Adolf Maislinger, Anton Hermannsdorfer (KPD); Hans Otto (Süddeutsche Ärzte- und Sanitätshilfe); and Bernhard Levi (Bayerisches Hilfswerk für die durch die Nürnberger Gesetze Betroffenen).

32 Resolutions of the Tegernsee meeting of interzone (US, GB, F) conference on questions of racial, religious and political persecutees, 7, 8, 9 Dec. 1946, BayHsta, OMGBy 13/141–1/1.

33 See *Mitteilungsblatt des Landesausschusses der politisch Verfolgten in Bayern*, no. 4, 1947, IfZ. For a general history of the VVN, see Max Oppenheimer, *Der Weg der VVN: Vom Häftlingskomitee zum Bund der Antifaschisten* (Frankfurt: Röderberg, 1972), 5–83, esp. 10ff. The need to establish a national organization of former persecutees had already been discussed at an interzonal meeting of delegates in Berlin in July 1946, where it was decided that it would be expedient to establish official regional groups first. See also Albin Stobwasser, *Die den roten Winkel trugen* (Hamburg: VVN, 1983), 28.

34 Hoegner, *Der schwierige Aussenseiter*, 272. Hoegner was the introductory speaker at the congress of liberated Jews.

35 See Philipp Auerbach and Ludwig Schmitt, *Was wir wollen: Referate auf der Gründungsversammlung der VVN in München, 26 Januar 1947* (Munich: n.p., 1947), copy in DaA. Auerbach's speech was entitled "Der Stand der Wiedergutmachung in Bayern."

36 See, e.g., Helga and Hermann Fischer-Hübner (eds.), *Die Kehrseite der "Wiedergutmachung": Das Leiden von NS-Verfolgten in den Entschädigungsverfahren* (Gerlingen: Bleicher, 1990); Jörg Friedrich, "Verbrechen, die sich auszahlen: Aus der Geschichte der Bundesrepublik: Nazi-Opfer und Nazi-Täter vor dem Entschädigungsamt," *Die Zeit*, 23 June 1989, 41–3; "Eklat wegen Wiedergutmachung," *Die Tageszeitung*, 2 June 1990. The entitlement of enslaved Poles to restitution was one of the major points of contention when soon-to-be-reunified Germany was negotiating an international treaty with Poland. See "Die Verbitterung über Kohl wächst – Es geht um Wiedergutmachungsleistungen für Zwangsarbeiter," *Die Tageszeitung*, 5 Mar. 1990, 3.

37 Earl Harrison's report is reprinted in Leonard Dinnerstein, *America and the Survivors of the Holocaust* (New York: Columbia University Press, 1982), 291ff. On the background of the delegation, see 34ff, and Yehudah Bauer, *Flight and Rescue: Brichah* (New York: Random House, 1970), 76–80. See also Königseder and Wetzel, *Lebensmut im Wartesaal*, 35–46.

38 On US army stereotypes see Königseder and Wetzel, *Lebensmut*, 26–30; on German stereotypes see ibid., 135–8, and Wolfgang Jacobmeyer, *Vom Zwangsarbeiter zum Heimatlosen Ausländer: Die Displaced Persons in Westdeutschland, 1945–1951* (Göttingen, 1985), 209–15. For a survivor's view, see Gun, *Day of the Americans*, 200f.

39 In addition to the statistics given by Jacobmeyer, see Abraham Peck, "Liberated but Not Free: Jewish Displaced Persons in Germany after 1945," in Walter Pehle (ed.), *November 1938: From "Reichskristallnacht" to Genocide* (New York/Oxford: Berg, 1991), 222–36, and Juliane Wetzel, "'Mir szeinen doh": München und Umgebung als Zuflucht von Überlebenden des Holocaust 1945–1948," in Broszat, Henke, and Woller (eds.), *Von Stalingrad zur Währungsreform*, 327–64, 342f. For one of the many contemporary accounts, see Leo Schwarz, *The Redeemers: A Saga of the Years 1945–1952* (New York: Farrar, Straus, and Young, 1953), 37f.

40 See Robert Sigel, "Heilkräuterkulturen im KZ: Die Plantage in Dachau," *Dachauer Hefte*, 4 (1988), 164–73.

41 The State Holding Authority was set up prior to 25 June 1946 at the behest of the OMGUS Berlin. Hoegner to Ehard, 22 June 1946, BayHsta, Stk 112 253. It should be noted that Auerbach was also a member of the administrative council of the State Holding Authority, so that he was privy to inside information. Meyer-König to Schwalber, 17 Nov. 1947, BayHsta, JS02.

42 Schmitt to Pfeiffer, 14 Feb. 1948, BayHsta, OMGBy 10/88–2/11. See also Schmitt to Hoegner, 5 Feb. 1948, BayHsta, Stk 113 645. Schmitt claims that in 1947 General Clay said that the persecutees could have the complex, but I found no record of such a promise.

43 See Minister of Education Hundhammer to Minister President, letter re "Deutsche Versuchsanstalt für Ernährung und Verpflegung GmbH Dachau," 1 Aug. 1947, BayHsta, Stk 113 645.

    Titze's biography is summarized by Jürgen Müller-Hohagen in Richardi et al., *Lebensläufe*, 47–9. Anton Gill, *The Journey Back from Hell: An Oral History: Conversations with Concentration Camp Survivors* (New York: Morrow, 1989), 244f contains an interview with Titze. In an interview with me in 1990, Titze was unable to recall details of his work in the corporation. Two taped interviews with Titze from ca. 1975 and ca. 1980 are in the possession of Hans-Günter Richardi; I was not able to listen to those tapes.

44 State Chancellory to State Holding Authority, 7 July 1947; State Holding Authority Branch Dachau to Deutsche Versuchsanstalt, 24 July 1947 (copy of copy), BayHsta, Stk 113 645. The latter letter contains the translation of an undated letter from OMGBy Finance Division. "Deutsche Versuchsanstalt für Ernährung und Verpflegung, GmbH" (German Experimental Facility for Nutrition and Foodstuffs, Inc.) was the official title of the SS corporation that had run the plantation complex; the name was retained after the war. See Sigel, "Heilkräuterkulturen," 166.

45 Resolution of the *Betreuungsstelle* Ansbach, 29 July 1947; *Betreuungsstelle* Arnsberg and vicinity to Ehard, 30 July 1947; *VVN-Bezirksstelle* Feuchtwangen to Ehard,

1 Aug. 1947; *Betreuungsstelle* Kulmbach to Staatsregierung, 2 Aug. 1947; Auerbach to Ehard, 7 Aug. 1947, BayHsta, Stk 113 645.

46 The co-signatories of the letter are largely identical to the representatives of the Regional Board of Political Persecutees named in note 31.

47 See Hundhammer to Minister President, 1 Aug. 1947, BayHsta, Stk 113 645. Hundhammer also mobilized a number of organizations to write letters in support of his proposal. See: Landesverband für Heilpflanzenbeschaffung to Minister President, 13 Aug. 1947; Alfred Köhler to Minister President, 20 Aug. 1947; Hundhammer to State Holding Authority and Minister President, 15 Oct. 1947. A later letter (Auerbach to Ehard, 7 Jan. 1948) refers to a letter Hundhammer wrote to Regierungspräsident (county manager) Oesterle on 23 Dec. 1947 alleging five violations by trustee Huber. All in BayHsta, Stk 113 645.

48 See Alois Hundhammer, *Mein Beitrag zur bayerischen Politik, 1945–1965* (Munich: Neuer Presseklub, 1965), 5. At the end of the 1950s Hundhammer became one of the leading figures in the *Kuratorium* that lobbied for the creation of the present memorial site.

49 Interview Titze, May 1990.

50 After the plantation went bankrupt in April 1949, that same specialist, Dr. Boas, carried out experiments in "biological-dynamic" agriculture there. See "Der Dachauer Kräutergarten besteht noch," *Mitteilungsblatt des Bayerischen Hilfswerks*, no. 20 (July 1949).

51 Hundhammer to State Holding Authority and Minister President, 15 Oct. 1947; also cabinet minutes of 11 Feb. 1948, BayHsta, Stk 113 645.

52 Auerbach summed up the results of the visit in a letter to Hundhammer on 7 Jan. 1948; he gave additional details in a letter to the Minister President on 19 Jan. 1948 (both in BayHsta, Stk 113 645).

53 According to his personnel file in the Berlin Document Center, Hörhammer had indeed been an industrious Nazi. Born in 1907 in Freising near Munich, he joined the SA in 1933. He became a member of the NS Students' League and joined the NSDAP on 1 May 1937. In June 1941 he became the party *Blockleiter* on his street. Before he was given a professorship on 20 July 1944 he was evaluated by the Nazi league of university teachers: "Nor are there any objections with respect to Hörhammer's politics . . . He is one of the most enthusiastic members of the National Socialist League of University Instructors." His *Ortsgruppe* in Nymphenburg wrote: "This is one thoroughly reliable National Socialist from whom one can always expect positive participation."

54 Marginal notes on Auerbach to Ehard, 19 Jan. 1948, BayHsta, Stk 113 645. There was also a cabinet meeting on 19 Jan. 1948 during which the plantation was discussed, but the minutes were not accessible for research. Ministerialrat Leusser sent drafts of the minutes of the meetings of 17 Jan. and 19 Jan. to the Ministry of Education for approval; Leusser to Ministry of Culture, 27 Jan. 1948, BayHsta, Stk 113 645.

55 Sigel, "Heilkräuterkulturen," 166–8, 171.

56 Schmitt to Ehard, 5 Feb. 1948 and 19 Feb. 1948; Huber to Wirtschaftsminister Anton Pfeiffer, 20 Feb. 1948; Auerbach to Ehard, 26 Feb. 1948; all in BayHsta, Stk 113 645.

57 Ministry of Trade and Commerce to the State Chancellory about claims by the VVN, 4 Aug. 1948, BayHsta, Stk 113 645. In this letter, the ministry admitted that the Staatliche Erfassungsgesellschaft (State Registering Agency; STEG) had sold

machines from the plantation to a company which had been dismantled by Military Government (*demontagegeschädigt*) because of its Nazi affiliations. This sheds light on the leanings of the State Holding Authority.

58 Draft contract (10pp.), 1 Mar. 1948; Müller to Rheinfelder/Kultus, 21 Apr. 1948; Hundhammer to State Chancellory with final version of contract, 5 May 1948; Ehard to Hundhammer, 31 May 1948; unsigned memorandum, 5 July 1948. All in BayHsta, Stk 113 645.

59 Unsigned stenographic minutes of meeting in the plantation, 28 July 1948; Ringelmann [Ministry of Finance], summary of results of meeting, 28 July 1948; [Josef Mayer, Ministry of Education], memorandum, 2 Aug. 1948; excerpt from minutes of cabinet meeting, 2 Aug. 1948; all in BayHsta, Stk 113 645. Since the cabinet members were not informed about the details of the meeting until after 2 August, it is probable that Auerbach was able either to move Military Government to intervene, or to show that the proposed contract contravened one of the laws of the occupiers.

60 About twenty representatives were there: Ringelmann and Kiefer from the Ministry of Finance; Auerbach and Aster from the State Commissionership; three members of the State Holding Authority; Junker for Dachau county; Geheimrat (privy councillor) Hepp for the Botanical Society; Winkler for the farm in Rothschwaige; trustee Ullmann and members of the current plantation administration; and Professor Boas from the Technical University. Representatives of the VVN and its subsidiary, the Bayerisches Aufbauwerk, and Mayer and Koenigsdorfer from the Ministry of Education were brought in some time after the meeting had begun.

61 At a press conference in early December 1947, Auerbach explained that he wanted to attempt to realize Himmler's plan to make Germany self-sufficient in the production of some spices and medicinal herbs. After the currency reform, it was clear that that would not be economically feasible. See Karl-Heinz Moser, "Himmlers Kräutergarten," *NZ*, 8 Dec. 1947, and "Himmlers Kräutergarten," *Welt am Abend* (Vienna), 19 Dec. 1947 (the latter is in BayHsta, JS02).

62 The proceeds from the 1948 harvest were not sufficient to both pay the workers and buy seed and fertilizer for the next year.

63 See "Der Dachauer Kräutergarten besteht noch" (p. 450 n. 50), which is based on an article by Walter Neff in *Heilpflanzen-Rundschau*, no. 17 (1 June 1949). See also *SZ*, 16 Apr. 1949 and *NZ*, 21 May 1949. The latter contains a substantial number of factual errors and distortions.

64 For a more detailed summary of these developments, see Fulbrook, *Divided Nation*, 157–66.

65 For a recent interpretation of Schumacher's time in Dachau, with references to the relevant literature, see Ulla Plener, "Kurt Schumacher und Kommunisten in den Konzentrationslagern (1933–1943)," *Utopie Kreativ*, 65 (1996), 31–40.

66 Quoted after Schwarz, *Redeemers*, 302.

67 W. E. Süskind, "Judenfrage als Prüfstein," *SZ*, 2 Aug. 1949. As an example of the continuing difficulties Germans have with antisemitic prejudices, in 1988 Wetzel, who has done a considerable amount of work on Jews in postwar Germany, referred to this editorial as a "refreshing exception" to the widespread antisemitism in Germany after the war (Wetzel, "'Mir szeinen doh,'" 357).

68 Adolf Bleibtreu [pseudonym meaning "stay loyal"], letter to the editor, *SZ*, 9 Aug. 1949. As a sample of the viciousness: "I am employed by Americans, and several of them have already said that they forgive us everything except one thing: that we did not gas all of the Jews, for now many are enjoying life in America . . . Rest assured that I am doing everything possible to enlighten many Americans. I assure you that I am not a Nazi, but a hundred percent German. I belong to the so-called 'Silent People' who carry on a whispering propaganda campaign that has far more effect than a hundred newspapers . . . We are a small circle as yet. We know all the ropes" (translation by Schwarz, *Redeemers*, 302).

69 Schwarz, *Redeemers*, 302ff. Schwarz was an eyewitness; this printed account is based on his diary. See also his assessment of other published accounts (376f, esp. of Norbert Muhlen's article in *Commentary*, Oct. 1949, 355–60).

70 *SZ*, 11 Aug. 1949. See also the open letter from Bavarian Commissioner van Waggoner to "Bleibtreu," *SZ*, 13 Aug. 1949.

71 See, for instance, *Time*, 22 Aug. 1949, and *Palestine Post*, undated article in BayHsta, OMGBy 13/144–2/7. Almost exactly one year prior to this incident, the Bavarian parliament discussed a rash of desecrations of Jewish cemeteries in Bavaria. See *Verhandlungen des Bayerischen Landtags* (22 and 28 July 1948), vol. 2, 1650 and 1748. At that time, however, the negative publicity subsided very quickly.

72 See file on antisemitic incidents, BayHsta, Stk 113 610; correspondence re antise-mitic letter to *SZ*, BayHsta, OMGBy 13/144–2/7; letters re protests by Jewish DPs in Munich, BaKo, OMGUS/CAD 15/118–1/43.

Frank Stern offers a brief summary of this event and interprets it, in my estima-tion incorrectly, as relatively unimportant in the context of the major political issues of the day. See Frank Stern, *The Whitewashing of the Yellow Badge: Antisemitism and Philosemitism in Postwar Germany* (New York: Pergamon, 1992), 337–41, esp. 339. The flurry of public relations activity reveals the importance accorded the incident by German and occupation authorities. Stern cites the OMGUS materials in NARA, RG 260.

73 O. Holewa, "Die Gräber von Dachau: Ihre Pflege ist Pflicht der Lebenden," *VVN-Nachrichten*, 28 Sept. 1949, 7.

74 VVN Dachau to Landratsamt Dachau, 9 Aug. 1949; VVN Dachau to VVN Munich, 12 Aug. and 19 Aug. 1949, Institut für die Geschichte der Arbeiterbewegung – Zentrales Parteiarchiv, Berlin, now Stiftung Archiv der Parteien und Massenorganisationen der DDR im Bundesarchiv (SAPMo), V 278/2/159. For the name of the finder, see Titze interview, May 1990.

75 Landratsamt Dachau/Lutz to VVN Dachau, 23 Aug. 1949, SAPMo, V 278/2/159.

76 VVN Dachau to VVN Landesleitung, and VVN Dachau to Landratsamt Dachau/Lutz, 19 Aug. 1949, SAPMo, V 278/2/159.

77 On 10 September 1949 the Bavarian government said that Military Government could expect an answer to the inquiry of 22 August in "8 to 10 days." "KZ-Gräber wurden vernachlässigt," *NZ*, 10 Sept. 1949.

78 "Um die neuerlichen knochenfunde in Efzenhausen," *MM/DN*, 12 Sept. 1949.

79 VVN Dachau to Hans Schwarz/Rat der VVN, 4 Sept. 1948, SAPMo, V 278/2/159.

80 Wolff/VVN Munich to Hans Schwarz, 8 Sept. 1949, BayHsta, Stk 113 628. The Munich VVN was deeply divided on the question of whether international public-ity would help or hurt the reputation of German former camp inmates.

81 "Germans Unearth Dachau Graves for Commercial Use," *New York Times*, 7 Sept. 1949; "Neues KZ-Massengrab entdeckt," *NZ*, 9 Sept. 1949. A Military Government press release distributed by UP was printed in *Stars and Stripes*, 10 Sept. 1949 ("MG to Investigate Alleged Desecration of Dachau Graves," 1). Later reports are somewhat confusing; they falsely attribute the front-page *Times* article to the *New York Herald-Tribune* (which printed only a three-paragraph UP report on page 10), and claim that it was reprinted in *Stars and Stripes* on 11 Sept. See the French National Assembly debate, note 104 below, and *SZ*, 15 Dec. 1949.

82 *NZ*, 9 Sept. 1949. The star of David may have been made out of a yellow wood swastika that the SS had erected on the hill (Titze interview, May 1990).

83 "Gedenkfeiern für die Opfer des Faschismus / Generalanwalt Dr. Auerbach über den Gräberfund bei Dachau," *SZ*, 13 Sept. 1949.

84 "Der Leitenberg ist ein Leichenberg," *MM*, 24 Sept. 1949.

85 "20,500 Opfer auf dem Leitenberg," *MM*, 28 Sept. 1949. The calculation that resulted in this estimate can be found in Paul Hussarek, "Der Berg der Toten," *Dachauer Stimmen*, 2 Nov. 1949 (DaA, Leiten notebook).

86 "Lageplan der Massengräber gefunden," *SZ*, 28 Sept. 1949. This was a chance discovery, as Landrat Junker related in an interview decades later. See ibid., 22 Nov. 1981.

87 The only newsworthy event was the discovery on 13 October of the corpse of the French General Delestraint who had been executed in April 1945; see *SZ*, 14 Oct. 1949.

88 See *Franc Tireur*, 29 Sept. 1949.

89 Memorandum about telephone call from the Federal Chancellory Office (*Bundeskanzlei*), 7 Nov. 1949, BayHsta, Stk 113 625.

90 Bolds to McCloy, 22 Nov. 1949, BayHsta, OMGBy 13/110–2/7.

91 Bolds to Ehard, 21 Nov. 1949 (English with German translation), BayHsta, Stk 113 628.

92 "Dachauer Massengräber unter Staatsobhut," *NZ*, 23 Nov. 1949.

93 "Französische Widerstandskämpfer besuchen Dachau," *NZ*, 26 Nov. 1949.

94 "Rapport de la commission d'enquête de la F.N.D.I.R.P. sur le scandale de Dachau," 29 Nov. 1949, DaA, Leiten file. Two German translations by Harry Kuhn can be found in SAPMo, V 278/2/161. The members of the commission were: Charles Serre, Marcel Rosenblatte, Armand Mottet, Noé Vilner, Abbé Ploton, and Raymond Prunières. The group also met with Minister President Ehard.

95 "*Ein Verbrechen ... an der ganzen europäischen Kulturwelt.*" See *Verhandlungen des Bayerischen Landtags* (30 Nov. 1949), vol. 5, 212; *NZ*, 1 Dec. 1949.

96 The original reads: "Le Dr Auerbach ... a permis l'exploitation industrielle concédée par les Chemins de fer à l'entreprise Gotler." The plot of land in question was part of a railway right of way and was leased to the Munich firm Göttler. Carola Karg of the Munich VVN later pointed out the misunderstanding; see "Übersetzungsfehler im Leitenberg-Communique?," *SZ*, 10 Dec. 1949. At the time of the delegation's visit, steam shovels were still working only 10 m from the site of the original discovery.

97 "Bewusste Störung der Verständigung," *Frankfurter Allgemeine Zeitung*, 1 Dec. 1949; "Französische Vorwürfe abgelehnt," *SZ*, 2 Dec. 1949; "Übelste politische Brunnenvergiftung," *Frankfurter Neue Presse*, 1 Dec. 1949; report about press conference by Bolds, Radio Frankfurt, 3 Dec. 1949, DaA, clippings file. See also

"Scandaleuse profanation," *Franc Tireur*, 1 Dec. 1949; "A Dachau, une commission d'enquête a constaté la profanation des charniers du camp," *Le Figaro*, 2 Dec. 1949. The French government maintained a file of clippings about the incident, Archives nationales, Paris, 72 AJ 1892: "Coupures de presse relatives à la profanation des tombes de Dachau."

98 "Ein kleiner untersetzter Mann mit . . . listigen Augen." See "KP-Intrige gegen deutsch-französische Verständigung," *MM*, 1 Dec. 1949, 1.

99 "Staatsregierung auf dem Leitenberg," *SZ*, 2 Dec. 1949.

100 Since the first French delegation in mid-November had been kept out of the media by Bolds, the press refers to this third French delegation as the second one. See "Politischer Streit um den Leitenberg," *SZ*, 7 Dec. 1949. The other members of the delegation were Pertaut, Bellier, and Maurer; see unsigned memo, 7 Dec. 1949, BayHsta, Stk 113 625.

101 Gumppenberg, memorandum re visit of the executive committee of the union of former French prisoners of Dachau, 7 Dec. 1949, BayHsta, Anton Pfeiffer papers, 73. See also transcript of radio report, 6 Dec. 1949, BayHsta, Stk 112 998; "Das Streiflicht," *SZ*, 8 Dec. 1949.

102 "Bayerische Behörden ohne Schuld," *MM*, 8 Dec. 1949; Dr. Baumgartner, memorandum, 8 Dec. 1949, BayHsta, Stk 113 625.

103 "Schuld und Versäumnis," *MM*, 8 Dec. 1949.

104 Annales de l'Assemblée nationale, séance du 13 décembre 1949, 6797–6811. A German translation of the text by Helmut Stein is in DaA, Leiten notebook, and DDW, AN2837.

105 Since a high proportion of Frenchmen were killed when ships loaded with evacuees from Neuengamme were mistakenly bombed by the Royal Air Force, this discovery also provoked a strong French reaction. See *Le Monde*, 9 Dec. 1949, and "Massengräber ertrunkener KZ-Häftlinge wurden an der Neustädter Bucht gefunden," *NZ*, 8 Dec. 1949.

106 See *Bundesgesetzblatt*, part II, 1955, 215ff; Eberhard Jäckel, *Die deutsche Frage 1952–1956: Notenwechsel und Konferenzdokumente der vier Mächte* (Frankfurt/ Berlin: Alfred Metzner, 1957).

107 Press release, 14 Dec. 1949, BayHsta, Stk 113 625. See also "Ehard nimmt Stellung," *NZ*, 15 Dec. 1949; "Ehard: Kommunistische Urheberschaft festgestellt," *SZ*, 15 Dec. 1949. In addition to the transcript of the interpellation, see "La profanation de l'ossuaire de Dachau: 'Négligence de la part des autorités allemandes' déclare M. R. Schuman," *Libération*, 14 Dec. 1949; "L'Assemblée, unanime, s'élève contre la profanation des tombes de Dachau," *L'Aube*, 14 Dec. 1949; "Protestation unanime contre la profanation des tombes des déportés à Dachau," *Le Monde*, 15 Dec. 1949.

108 Sattler, memorandum, 9 Dec. 1949, BayHsta, Stk 113 626. At this time, the ceremony was planned for Sunday, 18 December, but was soon changed to the preceding Friday.

109 Landesamt für Wiedergutmachung/Preuss, lists of invited guests, ca. 12 Dec. 1949, BayHsta, Stk 113 625.

110 Proposal by Kurz (CSU), *Verhandlungen des Bayerischen Landtags* (13 Dec. 1949), vol. 5, 315; see also 292f.

111 "Mahnung einer furchtbaren Vergangenheit: Feierliche Einweihung des KZ-Friedhofes Leitenberg," *SZ*, 17 Dec. 1949. The first visitors' book preserved in the

DaA begins with three pages of signatures of the VIPs present at the ceremony.
112 The investigation was begun in September and restarted on 20 December. See *SZ*, 24 and 29 Sept. 1949; Auerbach to Ankermüller, 26 Sept. 1949, BayHsta, Stk 113 625; Bolds to Ehard, 21 Nov. 1949, BayHsta, Stk 113 628; and *NZ*, 21 Dec. 1949.
113 "'Landrat und Bürgermeister haben keine Schuld!'" *Dachauer Nachrichten*, 16 Dec. 1949, 1.
114 According to the VVN, Wittmann had been a supporting member of the SS. He owned part of the Leitenberg, for which he received DM60,000 from the Bavarian government in December 1949. Verlautbarung der VVN zum amtlichen Untersuchungsergebnis Leitenberg, 20 Jan. 1949, DaA, Leiten notebook.
115 In its reply, the VVN duly noted this indication of a guilty conscience on the part of the city council, see "VVN zur Kreistagssitzung," *Dachauer Nachrichten*, 21 Dec. 1949.
116 The term "final solution" was also used in another newspaper article containing references to the Leiten Affair: see "Mr. McCloy in München," *SZ*, 10 Jan. 1950.
117 A copy of the twelve-page report can be found in BayHsta, JS25.
118 "Auerbach schuldlos," *Abendzeitung*, 17 Jan. 1949; "Zusammentreffen widriger Umstände," *SZ*, 19 Jan. 1949; "Walter: Kein Verschulden am Leitenberg," *MM*, 19 Jan. 1949; "Das Untersuchungsergebnis über den Leitenberg," *Dachauer Nachrichten*, 7 Feb. 1950.
119 Auerbach to Ehard, 23 Jan. 1950; Sattler to Ehard, 27 Jan. 1950, BayHsta, Stk 113 628.
120 See "Bau eines Ehrenmals als Staatsaufgabe," *Dachauer Nachrichten*, 7 Feb. 1950.
121 See Auerbach to Ehard, 30 Jan. 1950, Landratsamt Hersbruck to Auerbach, 2 Feb. 1950, and correspondence through March 1950, all in BayHsta, Stk 113 627; *Südbayerische Volkszeitung*, 2 Feb. 1950; *SZ* and *MM*, 3 Feb. 1950; *Verhandlungen des Bayerischen Landtags* (7 Feb. 1950), vol. 5, 627. On the discovery of a mass grave of ashes near the Dachau crematory on 22 March, see *SZ*, 30 Mar. 1950; *Dachauer Nachrichten*, 1/2 Apr. 1950. For a summary about recently uncovered mass graves throughout Germany, see "Eine Mauer des Schweigens," *Allgemeine*, 14 Apr. 1950.

   In Hubmersberg, a village in the vicinity of Flossenbürg, another gravesite was found in June. See Elmer Luchterhand, "Knowing or Not Knowing: Involvement in Nazi Genocide," in Paul Thompson (ed.), *Our Common History: The Transformation of Europe* (Atlantic Highlands: Humanities Press, 1982), 251–72.
122 Communiqué Ehard to Bolds, 1 Feb. 1950, BayHsta, Stk 113 625; *SZ*, 2 Feb. 1950; with correction, 3 Feb. 1950.
123 "Leitenberg bleibt KZ-Gedenkstätte," *SZ*, 13 Mar. 1950. For the results of the US report, see Press Release of the Office of the Land Commissioner for Bavaria, 9 Mar. 1950, BayHsta, Stk 113 625; also *SZ*, 10 Mar. 1950.
124 *NZ*, 11 Mar. 1950.
125 Bolds to Ehard (English and German translation), 27 Apr. 1950, BayHsta, Stk 113 625; "Bolds kritisiert Zustand der KZ-Gräber," *SZ*, 28 Apr. 1950.
126 Preuss to Auerbach, 10 Apr. 1950, BayHsta, Stk 113 625. The radio program was written by Walter von Cube and broadcast by Reimund Schnabel, a former Dachau inmate who became a professional writer. See Reimund Schnabel, *Macht ohne Moral: Eine Dokumentation über die SS* (Frankfurt: Röderberg, 1957), and *Die Frommen in der Hölle: Geistliche in Dachau* (Frankfurt: Röderberg, 1965).
127 Memorandum re *Grundsteinlegung*, 27 Mar. 1950, BayHsta, Stk 113 625. The

Minister President offered to pay travel expenses for ten former Dachau inmates. This file contains a large number of personal invitations and negative replies.

128 "Bundeskanzler Figl kommt zum Befreiungstag," *SZ*, 26 Apr. 1950.

129 See "Die Befreiungsfeier in Dachau," *SZ*, 2 May 1950; "Der Staatsakt in Dachau," *Südost-Kurier*, 3 May 1950.

130 Minutes of the third Leitenberg jury meeting, 19 May 1950, BayHsta, Stk 113 627. At that time DM400,000 had already been spent. The total amount was later increased to DM650,000; see memorandum about the landscaping of the Leitenberg, 10 Oct. 1950, BayHsta, JS25. For the contemporary public reaction to the magnitude of the sum, see minutes of the meeting of 20 Feb. 1950 in the settlement Dachau-Ost, BayHsta, MArb 755, 6.

131 Auerbach to Ehard, 19 June 1950, BayHsta, Stk 113 627. Auerbach had inspected 450 of 493 sites since January; only sixty of them had been in an acceptable condition. See also the earlier list of cemeteries, individual graves, and KZ memorial sites, undated [ca. Jan. 1950], BayHsta, Stk 113 626. At that time, only 23 sites of 249 (11 percent) were slated for improvements.

132 One of the more public of these rededications was the burial of 4,111 urns with human ash found in Dachau at liberation in the Perlach Forst cemetery in Munich on 12 September 1950. See Wimmer to VVN, 7 Sept. 1950, StMü, BuR 2560; Stadtrat Munich to Regierung Oberbayern, 27 Dec. 1949, BayHsta, Stk 113 626.

133 See "Never again! Nie wieder! Jamais plus!," *Mitteilungsblatt des Landesentschädigungsamts*, no. 9 (Sept. 1950), 5; also *SZ*, 5 Sept. and 7 Sept. 1950; *NZ*, 5 Sept. 1950. The museum displays are discussed on pp. 170ff, 174, below.

134 Memo, 23 Nov. 1953, LEA, file "Prüfungsmitteilungen des Bayerischen Obersten Rechnungshofes über Verwendung der Spendengelder aus der 'Denkmalspende Dachau' / . . . / Erich Preuss."

135 Preuss, memo, 15 Feb. 1951; concluding report, 3 Feb. 1951, BayHsta, Stk 113 626. The street was completed in June 1951: see *SZ*, 28 June 1951. It went along the western perimeter of the former camp, where the Carmelite convent now stands (see ill. 46).

136 Troberg to Anton Karl, 7 Sept. 1954, LEA, file "Prüfungsmitteilungen."

137 Auerbach to Ehard, 19 Jan. 1949, BayHsta, Stk 113 645.

138 Hitler had a personal grudge against Hoegner, who had initiated the Bavarian parliamentary subcommittee that investigated Hitler's abortive *putsch* attempt in 1923. See *Bayerischer Staatsanzeiger*, 12 Apr. 1991, 31 (after *Amtliches Handbuch des Bayerischen Landtags*, 1948).

139 *Verhandlungen des Bayerischen Landtags* (16 Dec. 1948), vol. 3, 406.

140 Ibid. (motions of 20 and 21 July 1949), vol. 4, 476 and 530.

141 Ibid., vol. 4, 507.

142 Unsigned memorandum about a demonstration of the VVN in parliament, 17 Mar. 1950, BayHsta, Stk 113 626. The statistic was presumably compiled by the organization of former persecutees, VVN, but it mirrors both the findings of US social scientists and West German investigators at the national level. See Arnold Brecht, "Personnel Management," in Edward Litchfield (ed.), *Governing Postwar Germany* (Ithaca: Cornell University Press, 1953), vol. I, 262–93, 269ff. See also David Childs, *Germany in the Twentieth Century* (New York: HarperCollins, 1991), 154ff. See also the Land Commissioner for Bavaria's 1949 report to US High Commissioner

McCloy, "Some Aspects of Renazification," in which he reports that 81 percent of the 924 Bavarian judges and prosecutors were former Nazis. NARA RG 56, 321ff, cited in Müller, *Furchtbare Juristen*, 205.

143 The resolution is commonly known as the *Unvereinbarkeitsbeschluss.* See Susanne Miller, "Die Behandlung des Widerstands gegen den Nationalsozialismus in der SPD nach 1945," in Ursula Büttner (ed.), *Das Unrechtsregime* (Hamburg: Christians, 1986), vol. II, 407–20; Stobwasser, *Die den roten Winkel trugen*, 41.

144 For an example of such tacit solidarity at the grass roots in Hamburg in Sept. 1948, see Harold Marcuse, "Das Gedenken an die Verfolgten des Nationalsozialismus in Hamburg" (unpubl. MA thesis, University of Hamburg, 1985), 20–2. Social Democrat former KZ inmates negotiated with the city government about official patronage of a commemorative ceremony as if they were the sole organizers; in actuality they left most of the organization to the Communist former prisoners.

145 See note 150, below. Schattenhofer, *Chronik der Stadt München*, 373, falsely claims that on 11 June 1948 Auerbach resigned from the VVN in order to preserve his SPD membership. On 422 (7 Oct. 1948), Schattenhofer correctly reports that Auerbach chose to remain in the Munich VVN which, in contrast to other VVN organizations in West Germany, refrained from participating in party politics.

146 Stobwasser, *Die den roten Winkel trugen*, 44.

147 For example, the VVN was outlawed in Hamburg on 1 Aug. 1951 and in Frankfurt on 2 Aug.; see Stobwasser, *Die den roten Winkel trugen*, 45. Oppenheimer, *Vom Häftlingskomitee zum Bund der Antifaschisten*, 18, reports that the central offices of the VVN in Frankfurt were sealed by the police on 23 Feb. 1953. In contrast, courts in Lower Saxony threw the case against the VVN out of court on 2 Apr. 1954, and the administrative court in Regensburg determined on 25 May 1955 that the VVN in Bavaria was neither anticonstitutional nor outlawed. See ibid.

148 For the ordinance from September 1949 against "extreme political parties, organizations and persons" who might disrupt the public order, see StMü BuR 2468 (1952), passim. The original *Entschliessung* of the Bavarian Ministry of the Interior of 16 Sept. 1949 carried the file number KB 3–3055a11; a revised resolution passed on 12 Dec. 1951 went into effect on 7 Jan. 1952.

149 For the documentation of the trial, see Gerd Pfeiffer and Hans-Georg Strickert (eds.), *KPD-Prozess: Dokumentarwerk zu dem Verfahren über den Antrag der Bundesregierung auf Feststellung der Verfassungswidrigkeit der Kommunistischen Partei Deutschlands vor dem Ersten Senat des Bundesverfassungsgerichts*, 3 vols. (Karlsruhe: C. F. Müller, 1955). Volume I contains the minutes of the proceedings concerning activities prior to the beginning of the trial; see 63 for the January confiscation date. Volume II (28th to 44th days) deals with the hearings on the goals of the KPD; volume III (to 51st day) contains the closing arguments and the text of the verdict.

150 "Dr. Auerbach nicht mehr SPD-Mitglied," DENA report in *Münchner Abendzeitung*, 22 Dec. 1948. Waldemar von Knoeringen gave the notice to Auerbach.

151 *SZ*, 14 Apr. 1950.

152 See AG Dachau to Ministry of Culture, 29 Mar. 1950 and answer, 5 Apr. 1950, BayHsta, Stk 113 625. The VVN event with ca. 1,000 participants is described in a police report in Stk 113 627, and in *SZ*, 17 Apr. 1950. On the official state ceremony, see *SZ*, 26 Apr. and 2 May 1950.

153 The *Hamburger Abendblatt*, 9/10 Sept. 1950, reported the use of police violence to disperse ceremonies in Frankfurt and Hanover when speakers criticized the development of atomic weapons. For a similar situation in Hanover a year earlier, see Herbert Obenaus, "Zur Nachkriegsgeschichte der hannoverschen Konzentrationslager", in Rainer Fröbe et al. (eds.), *Konzentrationslager in Hannover. KZ-Arbeit und Rüstungsindustrie in der Spätphase des Zweiten Weltkriegs* (Hildesheim: August Lax, 1985), vol. II, 545–85, 566f.

154 The damage to Bavaria's reputation persisted much longer than the negative media attention. See *Dagbladet* (Oslo), 2 July 1951. The Norwegian graves authority responded to charges by the German Volksbund Deutsche Kriegsgräberfürsorge that a German cemetery in Oslo had been neglected by pointing out that the Germans had used soil from a Dachau KZ cemetery for commercial purposes. The report was discussed in the Bavarian parliament, see *Verhandlungen* (25 Sept. 1951), vol. 2, 221.

In April 1952 French former KZ inmates, their families, and surviving family members of dead inmates visited Dachau. The representative of the French Graves' Commission for Germany and Austria said in his speech that the Leiten Affair was known in France as "Le scandale de Dachau." See "Französische Pilger gedenken der KZ-Toten," *MM/DN*, 1 Apr. 1952.

155 Weitmann, Munich Police Presidium, report of 12 March 1951, StMü, BuR 2467. In the Federal Republic, the use of public space for assemblies is subject to prior approval by the police, who may prohibit meetings if they perceive any danger to public safety. Police decisions are in turn subject to appeal in court.

156 Ibid., see also *SZ*, 12 Mar. 1951.

157 Weitmann/Marr, report on the Christmas celebration, 28 Dec. 1950, StMü, BuR 2468. A protest meeting called by the AG Dachau on 27 September 1952 was similarly dispersed. See Heigl/Kagerbauer, report on protest meeting of the Arbeitsgemeinschaft Dachau, 3 Oct. 1952, StMü, BuR 2468.

158 When the Bavarian cabinet discussed the cornerstone-laying of the memorial hall on the Leiten on 23 Mar. 1950, Müller tried to coordinate the state ceremony with that of the VVN. See memorandum re discussion in the cabinet on 23 Mar., 27 Mar., 1950, BayHsta, Stk 113 626. Although the cabinet decided not to participate officially in the VVN ceremony, Müller gave the keynote speech. See *SZ*, 14 Apr. 1950; also the police report about the events of 16 Apr. 1950 in Dachau, 18 Apr. 1950, BayHsta, Stk 113 627. Müller was severely criticized by Peter Lütsches, formerly a leading member of the VVN who then headed the CDU/CSU persecutee group, BVN. See Lütsches to Ehard, 24 Apr. 1950, BayHsta, Stk 114 623.

159 See Josef Müller, *Bis zur letzten Konsequenz: Ein Leben für Frieden und Freiheit* (Munich: Süddeutscher, 1975), 325–35, 357–60. Müller, the patron of Franz Josef Strauss, also publicly supported former Nazis. For general background see Wolfgang Benz, "Parteigründungen und erste Wahlen: Der Wiederbeginn des politischen Lebens", in Benz (ed.), *Neuanfang in Bayern, 1945 bis 1949: Politik und Gesellschaft in der Nachkriegszeit* (Munich: Beck, 1988), 9–35, 25ff.

160 Just two weeks earlier, Schwarz had invited the international Amicale Dachau, which had planned to visit Dachau and Flossenbürg on 29 April, to come a few days earlier in order to participate in the German ceremony. See Schwarz to Walraeve, 27 Feb. 1951, FstHH, HS, notebook 13–4–4–3.

161 Weitmann, report of 17 April 1951, StMü, BuR 2467.

162 "Gedenkfeier der 'Arbeitsgemeinschaft Dachau,'" *SZ*, 16 Apr. 1951.

163 See Vormerkung betreff: Gedächtnisstätte auf dem Leitenberg, 4 May 1951, BayHsta, Stk 113 628, 5 for the state's reasons for sponsoring an evening of theater instead of holding an official commemorative event, namely the "occurrences in the Restitution Office" (a reference to Auerbach's arrest) and the "differences among the political persecutees."

164 *SZ*, 10 Apr. 1951.

165 Report by the state police, 16 Apr. 1950, BayHsta, Stk 113 627. The figure "700–800" is the police estimate. A newspaper reporter estimated 1,000 marchers. See "VVN begeht Dachauer Befreiungstag," *SZ*, 17 Apr. 1950.

166 *SZ*, 2 May 1950, 1.

167 Auerbach to Ehard, 19 June 1950, BayHsta, Stk 113 627. The letter contains a detailed description of eight dedication ceremonies and five additional cemeteries that Auerbach visited.

168 "Gedenktag für die Opfer des Nationalsozialismus," *Mitteilungsblatt des Landesausschusses der politisch Verfolgten in Bayern*, no. 47 (1 Oct. 1950), 2f. This article contains reports about four ceremonies: Perlach Forst cemetery in Munich, Leiten in Dachau, Waldfriedhof Dachau, and crematory Dachau, and mentions several other smaller events in Munich.

   Although events that day were widely announced, they were hardly reported in the press at all. See "Zum Tag der Opfer des Nationalsozialismus," *Dachauer Anzeiger*, 7 Sept. 1950, in which an editorial proclaimed "High participation by the populace ought to be one of the human obligations that we have today."

169 Eisinger to city finance authority, 12 Sept. 1950, VVN to city council member "comrade" Lettenbauer, 6 Oct. 1950, Wimmer to finance authority, 24 Oct. 1950, StMü, BuR 2560.

170 Various police reports, StMü, BuR 2468.

171 Aumüller/Weitmann, police report on the gathering of the Arbeitsgemeinschaft Dachau on 4 May, 7 May 1952, StMü, BuR 2468.

172 See Goschler, "Der Fall Philipp Auerbach," 95–8.

173 "Erstmals keine Befreiungsfeier," *SZ*, 1 May 1953.

174 The report noted that the two persecutee groups, the Landesrat für Freiheit und Recht and the Union of Former Polish KZ Inmates, were "disgruntled" by the lack of participation of official representatives. Similarly, on 6 Oct. 1953 the "IG der Opfer des Nazismus," which met in the Salvatorkeller and marched to the graves of victims of the Nazis in the Perlach Forest, complained that no official representatives responded to its invitation. StMü, BuR 2469.

175 *Verhandlungen* (23 June 1953), vol. 5, 1561. For further examples, see Moeller, "War Stories," 1014, 1018, 1021.

5 "Clean" camps

1 After Cornelia Berning, *Vom "Abstammungsnachweis" zum "Zuchtwart": Vokabular des Nationalsozialismus* (Berlin: de Gruyter, 1964), 112. See *Meyers Lexikon*, 7th edn, vol. VI, col. 1725, and 8th edn, vol. VI, col. 1416. The 1939 definition reads: "Besser Verwahrungs- und Erziehungslager. Sie haben seit 1933 den Zweck a)

Gewohnheitsverbrecher . . . aufzunehmen, b) Kommunisten und andere Feinde des nationalsozialistischen Staates . . . vorübergehend unschädlich zu machen und zu brauchbaren Volksgenossen zu erziehen."

2 Ausschuss für Sozialpolitik, proposal by Hans Hagn and Comrades re "Freimachung von Lagern zur Benützung als Arbeitslager für asoziale Elemente," 21 Nov. 1947; BLA, bound volumes of committee minutes.

3 *Verhandlungen* (1947/48), vol. 2, 587 and 589 with supplement no. 871.

4 For instance, an illustrated magazine article about Dachau concentration camp reported in July 1933 that "Volksgenossen, die artfremden Verführern zum Opfer fielen . . . werden durch die heilende Wirkung produktiver Arbeit und straffer Disziplin zu brauchbaren Mitgliedern des nationalsozialistischen Staates erzogen." *Münchner Illustrierten Presse,* July 1933. A legible photograph of the title page of the article is printed in Hans-Günter Richardi and Verein zum Beispiel Dachau (eds.), *Die Stadt und das Lager* (Munich: Süddeutscher, 1983), 16. It should be noted that at the time of publication at least twelve people had already been brutally murdered in Dachau. See Richardi, *Schule der Gewalt,* 88–107.

5 Another example of conversion of a Nazi penal institution into a prison in the postwar period is the Plötzensee facility in Berlin, which is used as a juvenile correctional institution. See Friedrich Zipfel et al., *Gedenkstätte Plötzensee* (Berlin: Landeszentrale für politische Bildungsarbeit, 1972), 2.

6 Prison authority to the Senate, 21 October 1947, NA; quoted by Marcuse, "Gefängnis als Gedenkstätte," 9; in turn quoted by Fritz Bringmann and Hartmut Roder, *Neuengamme. Verdrängt – vergessen – bewältigt? Die zweite Geschichte des Konzentrationslagers Neuengamme* (Hamburg: VSA, 1987), 38f.

7 Herbert Blank, "Hinter dem Gitter . . . schmeckt der Honig bitter," *Nordwestdeutsche Hefte* (Hamburg), 1 (Dec. 1946), 17–22, 20.

8 Gefängnisbehörde to Senate, 21 Oct. 1947, NA. The author was Oberlandgerichtsrat Walter Buhl, a legal official who had served the Nazi state from 1933 to 1945. See Bringmann and Roder, *Neuengamme,* 39.

9 Prior to 1933 Koch had created a novel liberal juvenile correctional institution on an island in the Elbe river near Hamburg (Hahnöfersand). Interview Konrad Hoffmann, Sept. 1984.

10 *Niederdeutsche Zeitung,* 21 Aug. 1948.

11 *Die Welt,* 27 Jan. 1949 (report about a press conference and prison tour in Glasmoor).

12 See, for instance, *Hamburger Abendblatt,* 13 Nov. 1954: "Gefangene mit Verantwortung: Ein Blick in die Anstalt Neuengamme – Lebensertüchtigung für Häftlinge"; *Welt,* 4 Apr. 1959: "Alle wollen gerne nach Neuengamme: Gefängnis oder Sanatorium? Hamburg ist nett zu seinen Dieben." Both articles are quoted in Marcuse, "Gefängnis als Gedenkstätte," 14.

13 Plans for a second major expansion of the prison on the grounds of the former KZ brought the conflict to a head in 1989. The net result was that the expanded facility was relocated to a nearby site, and the existing institution gradually phased out. See *Die Tageszeitung,* Hamburg edition, 18 July 1989. As of 1999 some former concentration camp buildings have been integrated into the memorial site, but no replacement prison facility is under construction. See also chapter 15, below.

14 Bavarian Minister President Hoegner (SPD), who was commissioned by the parliament to negotiate with US Military Government, was later a staunch supporter of

the memorial site. I was not able to locate any sources which would clarify this question, however.

15 See United States Department of State, *Germany 1947–1949: The Story in Documents* (Washington: Government Printing Office, 1950), 54.

16 Volker Berghahn, *Modern Germany: Society, Economy and Politics in the Twentieth Century* (Cambridge: Cambridge University Press, 1982), 255.

17 Ibid. The difference between expellees and refugees is in many cases academic. Still unsurpassed as a concise summary is Leo Schwarz, *Refugees in Germany Today* (New York: Twayne, 1957); see esp. 15–31, 53–60. For a general summary and contextualization see Michael Marrus, *The Unwanted: European Refugees in the Twentieth Century* (New York/Oxford: Oxford University Press, 1985), 296–351.

18 *Statistisches Jahrbuch für Bayern*, 1947, 26.

19 Data and charts from the Statistisches Landesamt, Nov. 1947, BayHsta, OMGUS 10/43–2/4.

20 *Verhandlungen* (1947/48), vol. 2, 1346, amendment proposed by Frau Dr. Probst from the Committee for Refugee Questions. The original text contains euphemistic expressions and syntax common in Nazi German: "bei der Neueinweisung in die frei gewordenen Unterkünfte [wird] weitestgehend dem zweckmässigen Arbeitseinsatz und dem Grundsatz einer familiengerechten Unterbringung Rechnung getragen."

21 Christa Schick, "Die bayerischen Internierungslager", in Broszat et al. (eds.), *Von Stalingrad*, 301–25, 312 (Headquarters USFET to Commanding Generals, 13 July 1946, in NARA RG 260, 3/174–2/8 and 17/55–2/13).

22 List of construction measures carried out since the transfer of the camp in Oct. 1947, 8 May 1948, in BayHsta, MSo 2062.

23 See letter from camp leader Vogel/Dachau to Sonderministerium Dept. VI, 16 Apr. 1948, in BayHsta, MSo 2015. For a general discussion of the releases, see Schick, *Internierungslager*, 324. See also *NZ*, 12 Apr. 1948 and *SZ*, 25 May 1948. BayHsta, Stk 113 953 contains correspondence between the Minister of Special Affairs and the Dachau internees which allows a fairly accurate reconstruction of the rate at which prisoners were discharged. See also Headquarters, European Command, to OMGUS, 14 Apr. 1948, in BaKo, OMGUS/CAD 3/158–1/4.

24 Sachs to Abteilung 1/Hertle, 13 Aug. 1948, BayHsta, MSo 358.

25 Verwaltungsdirektor Hertsch to Leiter des I.- und A.lagers Dachau betr. Lagerauflösung, 6 July 1948, in BayHsta, MSo 2062.

26 "Programm des Internationalen Ferienkurses der Bayerischen Hochschulen," 24 July – 13 Aug. 1948, OMGBY 13/150–2/6; memo by Schuster, 22 Sept. 1948, BayHsta, MArb 645, 2.

27 Memorandum by Arnulf Enders, Deutsche Studentenschaft, 6 Aug. 1948; Deutsche Studentenschaft (Nicolai) to Staatssekretär für das Flüchtlingswesen Jaenicke, 12 Aug. 1948, BayHsta, MArb 79/645, 2. Professor Bondy (USA) accompanied the students.

28 Nicolai to Jaenicke, 12 Aug. 1948, BayHsta, MArb 645. Jaenicke (1881–1968) was the son of a mayor of Breslau; he became Regierungspräsident of Breslau in 1919 and of Potsdam in 1930. He was also a member of the Reichstag in the Deutsche Staatspartei until 1932. He later became the first West German ambassador to Pakistan (1952–4) and then emissary to the Vatican (1954–7). See Krauss,

"Verfolgtenbetreuung," 24, n. 106, n. 125 (after Franz Josef Bauer, *Flüchtlinge und Flüchtlingspolitik in Bayern 1945–1950* [Stuttgart: Klett–Cotta, 1982], 61f, n. 147). Jaenicke was appointed Secretary for Refugee Affairs on 31 Jan. 1947; *Verhandlungen* (1947), vol 1, 108.

29 Sierig, minutes of the protest meeting of 18 Aug. 1948, BayHsta, MArb 1057; report George Jacobsen CAD/Dachau to OMGBy ID and CAD, 6 Sept. 1948, BayHsta, OMGBy (13/310). See also Lagerleiter Reg. Dulag Dachau Karl Wagner to Jaenicke, 24 Aug. 1948, BayHsta, MArb 79/1057.

30 Herrmann was born in 1899 in Brno. An inheritance made it possible for him to study psychology and attend lectures by Sigmund Freud. As a writer he came to Germany at the end of the 1920s, but reemigrated to Czechoslovakia when the Nazis came to power in 1933. He was drafted into the German army in 1942, but released because of a heart condition in 1945. He was expelled from Prague in May 1948. See "Egon Herrmann Angeklagter und Ankläger," *Schwäbische Landeszeitung*, 25 Feb. 1949.

31 Rothschwaige was built in 1942 to quarter deported foreign workers before they were distributed to area farmers. After the war, the Rothschwaige camp was in the possession of the State Labor Authority (Landesarbeitsamt), which made it available to the refugee authority on 10 Dec. 1945 (memo Dr. Strassmann, 10 Oct. 1948, BayHsta, MArb 645). The camp had been a Reg. Dulag at least since May 1947. See Wagner to Jaenicke, 24 Aug. 1948, BayHsta, MArb 79/1057 (Wagner had been in charge of the Dachau camp since 15 May 1947). Dachau-Rothschwaige and Allach II were run by the same *Lagerleiter.*

32 Report by Piehler (SPD) about a visit to Dulag Dachau, *Verhandlungen* (23 Sept. 1948), vol. 3, 91.

33 Gernbeck to Jaenicke, 28. Aug. 1948, BayHsta, MArb 645, 1. Gernbeck was the Government Commissioner for Refugee Affairs in Upper Bavaria (Regierungs-beauftragter für das Flüchtlingswesen in Oberbayern).

34 Ibid.

35 Press release from Ministerialdirigent Adam, 2 Sept. 1948; telegram Kontroll-auschuss Reg. Dulag Dachau to Prime Minister Ehard, 5 Sept. 1948, BayHsta, MArb 79/645.

36 Telegram Augsburg I, II, III to Staatssekretariat Flüchtlingswesen, 4 Sept. 1948, BayHsta, MArb 1057; telegrams Neu Ulm and Rosenheim-Holzhof, 8 Sept. 1948, BayHsta, MArb 645; Report George Jacobsen CAD/Dachau to OMGBy ID and CAD, 6 Sept. 1948, BayHsta, OMGBy (10/108–3/20).

37 Report about the meeting of delegates in camp Dachau on 2 Oct. 1948, BayHsta, MArb 1057; "Kommunistische Umtriebe in Flüchtlingslagern?" *Echo der Woche*, 8 Oct. 1948.

38 Memorandum by Janauschek about meeting of 8 Sept. 1948, BayHsta, MArb 645. A twelve-minute report was also broadcast in New York on 11 September, BayHsta, OMGBy 10/108–3/20.

39 Transcript of DENA radio announcement, 9 Sept. 1948, 8:45, BayHsta, MArb 645.

40 Unsigned memo, communication from Janauschek, 9 Sept. 1948; [Jaenicke,] written confirmation of oral promises, 10 Sept. 1948, BayHsta, MArb 645.

41 In addition to the two quotes cited above, see, *inter alia*, memo Landesamt für Vermögensverwaltung und Wiedergutmachung Dachau, 7 Oct. 1948: meeting in

"ehem. I.-u.A.Lager Dachau"; Rau to Jaenicke, received 6 Nov. 1948: "Flüchtlings-wohnlager Dachau (ehem. Interniertenlager)," BayHsta, MArb 1057; Deichel to Jaenicke (excerpt from minutes of Dachau City Council), 11 April 1949: "ehem. Interniertenlager Dachau," BayHsta, MArb 645.

The term "internee" was never used to refer to former concentration camp inmates, but only to Germans being held as suspects by the Allies.

42 Since Jaenicke later denied having made several of those promises it is important to note that an observer for Military Government reported about the meeting of 9 Sept. that: "A so-called 'Wohnlager' will be established in part of the Internment camp, that will be given to the refugees by AUERBACH." Unsigned memo re meeting of Jaenicke, Auerbach, and refugees on 9 Sept., BayHsta, OMGBy 10/108–3/20. The memo also confirms that Jaenicke agreed that the refugees could elect their own camp leader.

43 Neubauer to Jaenicke, Neubauer to Ehard, Neubauer to Plonner, 29 Sept. 1948, BayHsta, MArb 645, 7. The *Entlassungslager* was immediately to the south of the KZ prisoners' compound (Titze interview, May 1990). With the construction of condominiums in 1989 Neubauer's proposal found belated realization; today the "Siedlung am Römerhain" overlooks the former KZ walls (see ill. 1).

44 Gumppenberg to Jaenicke, 5 Oct. 1948, BayHsta, MArb 645.

45 F. Fischer/Oberste Baubehörde to Jaenicke, 18 Oct. 1948, ibid.

46 Jaenicke to Gumppenberg, 26 Oct. 1948; Jaenicke to Haussleiter, and Jaenicke to Neubauer, 27 Oct. 1948, ibid., 7.

47 *Verhandlungen* (22 Sept. 1948), vol. 3, 87.

48 Ibid. (2 Dec. 1948), vol. 3, 359.

49 Report by Bauleiter Wrba [ca. Dec. 1949], BayHsta, MArb 645.

50 Rau to Jaenicke, 6 Nov. 1948, BayHsta, MArb 1057.

51 Fischer's figure may have included ca. DM1,000,000 development costs, which were supposedly saved by using existing water, sewage, and electrical facilities in the former KZ. However, Fischer referred explicitly only to "building costs." See Report by Bauleiter Wrba [ca. Dec. 1949], 20, BayHsta, MArb 645.

52 Minutes of meeting in Dachau-Ost, 20 Feb. 1950, BayHsta, MArb 755. The figure was for units actually built in Wolfratshausen ten months after Fischer's estimate.

53 Memo by Schuster about the situation in Allach II and Dachau, 22 Sept. 1948, BayHsta, MArb 645.

54 Communication from Janauschek about meeting of 8 Sept. 1948; transcript of DENA radio announcement, 9 Sept. 1948, 8:45, ibid. Even the student advocates of the refugees found Herrmann too extreme: see Nicolai to Jaenicke, 7 Oct. 1945, ibid. On 29 October the new camp supervisor Hangkofer reported that most refugee camps did not want Herrmann as their spokesperson: see report about meeting in Dulag Dachau, 30 Oct. 1948, ibid., 1.

55 Nicolai to Van Wagoner/OMGBy, 6 Sept. 1948, ibid., 2.

56 The Dachau Non-Profit Building Cooperative was able to build sixty units ready for occupancy from 1 May to 1 Nov. 1949: see Gemeinnützige Baugenossenschaft Dachau to Ministry of the Interior, 15 Mar. 1950, ibid.

57 Report by Bauleiter Wrba [ca. Dec. 1949], ibid.

58 Detailed correspondence regarding these measures can be found in the archived files of the Bavarian Ministry for Work, BayHsta, MArb.

59 "Friedland zwischen unfriedlichem Land," *Fränkische Landeszeitung*, 24 June 1950.

60 For an example of the older term, see the quotation from Jaenicke's 10 Sept. 1948 confirmation notice, cited on page 163 (note 40), above.

61 Memo from Agent Heinrich Kaltenegger (SPD) to CID commanding officer, 25 Aug. 1948, BayHsta, OMGBy.

62 It is important to note that in the early years there was a strong grass roots sentiment in support of the union. Kurt Schumacher (SPD leader in the West) was one of its staunchest opponents. See Hermann Weber, *SED: Chronik einer Partei* (Cologne: Wissenschaft und Politik, 1976); Werner Müller, "Sozialdemokratische Politik unter sowjetischer Militärverwaltung: Chancen und Grenzen der SPD in der sowjetischen Besatzungszone zwischen Kriegsende und SED-Gründung," *Internationale wissenschaftliche Korrespondenz zur Geschichte der deutschen Arbeiterbewegung*, 23 (1987), 170–206.

63 Nicolai to van Wagoner, 6 Sept. 1948, BayHsta, MArb 645.

64 In a personal letter to Secretary Jaenicke the next day, the students emphasized that the hunger strike was *not* a subversive activity planned by communists, but a natural reaction of immiserated people. Nicolai to Jaenicke, 7 Sept. 1948, BayHsta, MArb 645.

65 Stenographic notes, Intelligence Coordinating Meeting, 9 Sept. 1948, BayHsta, OMGBy 10/92–2/2, fiche 3.

66 Quotes after Dr. Seiffert (1) and Egon Herrmann (7), in Report about the meeting of delegates in camp Dachau on 2 Oct. 1948, BayHsta, MArb 1057. See also the article "Kommunistische Umtriebe in Flüchtlingslagern," *Echo der Woche*, 8 Oct. 1948, 1.

67 Report about the meeting of delegates in camp Dachau on 2 Oct. 1948, 1, BayHsta, MArb 1057. This quote also shows the low standing of the Nuremberg trials in public opinion ("*not even* in Nuremberg").

68 Ibid. The phonetic orthography of proper names and faultless use of the verb forms of indirect speech indicate that this nineteen-page document was prepared by a professional stenographer. The document contains marginal comments and underlining by Jaenicke. The next meeting of refugees passed a resolution that no one would be allowed to take stenographic notes, see report by Lagerleiter Hangkofer re meeting of 3 Nov. 1948, 4 Nov. 1948, BayHsta, MArb 645.

69 Memo by Schuster re visit by Reiter, 11 Oct. 1948, BayHsta, MArb 1057; secret report by Jacobsen/FOD to CAD Refugee Branch, BayHsta, OMGBy 15/102–2/7.

70 *MM*, 12 Nov. 1948, 3. See memo by government commissioner Petreck, 16 Nov. 1948, BayHsta, MArb 1057; memo by Dr. Ahnelt, 1 Apr. 1952, BayHsta, MArb 645, 4.

71 English translation of report by Lagerleiter Hangkofer re meeting of 14 Nov. 1948, 15 Nov. 1948, BayHsta, MArb 1057. I have corrected slight errors of orthography. See also *Kölner Volksstimme*, 15 Nov. 1948.

72 German version of report by Lagerleiter Hangkofer re meeting of 14 Nov. 1948, 15 Nov. 1948, BayHsta, MArb 1057. This quote was underlined heavily several times by Secretary Jaenicke.

73 Memo by Kristof about deposition of Planck, 29 Nov. 1948, BayHsta, MArb 645, 1. See also Letter to OMGBy, Welfare Section, accompanying translation of report Hangkofer to Schuster of 23 Oct. 1948, 25 Oct. 1948, ibid. Over the short term, Jaenicke unsuccessfully tried to ban Herrmann from public speaking. See "Redeverbot," *DENA*, 28 Oct. 1948, Presse- und Informationsamt der Bundesregierung, Egon Herrmann file.

74 Translation of van Wagoner to Ehard, 19 Nov. 1948, BayHsta, MArb 1057.

75 Report about meeting on 28 Nov. 1948, 1500 hrs, BayHsta, OMGBy 10/108–3/20. Herrmann's trial (24 Feb. to 15 March 1949) resulted in a suspended sentence of one year imprisonment for slander and disturbing the peace. See *NZ*, 18 March 1949.

76 *Fränkische Landeszeitung*, 24 June 1950.

77 On the founding of the cooperative, see "Protokoll über Sitzung am 20.2.50 in Siedlung Dachau-Ost," BayHsta, MArb Abgabe 1979, file 755; and "Egon Herrmann schaltet um: 250 neue Wohnungen auf ehemaligem SS-Grund geplant," *Dachauer Anzeiger*, 28 Feb. 1950.

78 References to population figures can be found throughout the MArb files. See, e.g., Konrad to Jaenicke re Gemeinschaftsverpflegung, 8 Aug. 1950, BayHsta, MArb 1979, 755 ("over 2,000 residents").

79 "Der Grundstein zur Friedlandsiedlung ist gelegt: Pater Roth vollzog die Weihe / Förderer von 'Friedland' zu Ehrenmitgliedern ernannt," *MM/DN*, 6 June 1950.

80 See Gemeinnützige Wohnungsbaugenossenschaft Dachau GmbH to Office of Refugee Affairs, 15 Mar. 1950; Adam/Refugee Affairs to Regierung Obb., 2 Sept. 1950; both in BayHsta, MArb Abgabe 1979, 645. Because the Bavarian government still did not support it, Herrmann's cooperative applied to US authorities for support. See Ernst Klement/Soziale Baugenossenschaft to High Commissioner McCloy, 27 Apr. 1951, BayHsta, Stk 115 048.

81 "Zum zweiten Male: Dachau," *Die neue Demokratie im Bild* (Baden-Baden), 4 (29 Jan. 1949), 6f.

82 "Dachau: Heute ein Gefängnis der Armut," *Neuer Tag*, 25 May 1950.

83 "Besteht noch das KZ in Dachau? Wie es in dem Umsiedler-Lager Dachau-Ost aussieht – Ein aktuelles Denkmal der 'abendländischen Kultur'," *Südbayerische Volkszeitung* (KPD), 31 Mar. 1951. See also "A Dachau: Hier camp de concentration nazi, aujourd'hui centre d'hébergement," clipping from an illustrated magazine, ca. 1955, DaA.

At the beginning of the 1950s such critical remarks were limited to left-leaning publications, but by the second half of the decade, especially after the publication of Nico Rost's *Ich war wieder in Dachau* in 1956, similar criticism of the camp can be found in literally dozens of newspapers, including many in the mainstream.

84 See, e.g., "Dachau-Ost bleibt staatliches Lager," *MM*, 15 Feb. 1951; *Verhandlungen* (27 Feb. 1951), vol. 1, 234 (inquiry prompted by local unrest); Titze/Wohnsiedlung to Regierung Obb. re "Beschwerde der Stadtgemeinde Dachau an den Bayerischen Landtag," 4 June 1951, BayHsta, MArb 1979, 755.

85 See p. 248, below.

86 See *Mitteilungen LGD*, Dec. 1959.

87 My interview with Frau Itzek, who grew up in the camp from 1948 to 1962, 17 July 1987; also Inge Weigert and Josef Schneider, "'Eine Art kleines Getto': Wohnen im ehemaligen Konzentrationslager und erste neue Heimat in Dachau-Ost," *SZ/DN*, 28 Feb. 1989.

88 Ost, "Nach 30 Jahren," 222. The museum is not mentioned in other contemporary reports, such as those by Arthur Haulot and Otto Färber. When interviewed by me in 1990, Haulot said that he could not remember whether he had seen an exhibition in Nov. 1945.

89 The twenty-three-page pamphlet is entitled *Dachau! Ein Tatsachenbericht in*

Bildern (n.p.p., n.d.), DaA. This is the only copy of the brochure I was able to locate. The title page is missing, so that no definitive information about its publication is available. The caption under the final picture refers to the judgments already passed on Dachau SS guards. The pictures can also be found in *Gedenkboek*, an album of pictures on red paper produced by Belgian Dachau survivors. Copies of this red album are held by DaA and DDW. Several undated photographs of at least two different arrangements of the mannequins are held by the DaA.

90 Some of the pictures of the train duplicate those published in the US army booklet by Quinn published in May 1945. The crematory sequence is reprinted in Ludo Vaneck, *Le Livre des Camps* (Leuven: Kritak, 1979), 63. The series also exists as a set of postcards preserved in the photograph collection of the DaA; they were donated to the collection by the IfZ, which probably received them from a private donor.

91 It would be interesting to examine similar exhibitions created during these years. The following references provide a starting point for such an investigation.

In January 1946 in Munich "Opfer und Widerstand" was shown. The opening was announced on a program for the "Day of Victims of Fascism," 27 Jan. 1946, StMü, BuR. 2526. The title was probably derived from a radio series prepared by the former Dachau inmate Reimund Schnabel which was aired in Munich in Dec. 1945 and the first months of 1946. That title is quoted in the introduction to Arthur Haulot, "Das waren Kameraden," *SZ*, 21 Dec. 1945. See also Reimund Schnabel to Hans Schwarz, 4 Mar. 1970, FStHH, HS 13-4-4-3. According to that letter, the twenty-four-part series of thirty-minute weekly broadcasts under the title "Opfer, Widerstand, Ansporn" began on 16 Dec. 1945.

In Sept. 1946 an "antifascist" exhibition was opened by Viktor Matejka (who later directed the Mauthausen memorial site) of the Amt für Kultur und Volksbildung in Vienna. See the publication *Niemals Vergessen: Katalog zur Antifaschistischen Ausstellung* (Innsbruck: Handelsakademie, August 1947), copy in DaA. In 100 days, 250,000 people saw that exhibition. See also Brink, *Ikonen*, 185.

In September 1947 in Hamburg "Kampf und Opfer" was shown. See Albin Stobwasser, *Die den roten Winkel trugen: Zur Geschichte der VVN-Bund der Antifaschisten, Hamburg* (Hamburg: n.p., 1983), 23f, 29f.

On 13 Sept. 1947 an exhibition entitled "Die dagegen waren: Widerstand im Dritten Reich" opened on the Schlossplatz in Stuttgart. See Hans Gasparitsch, *Aus meinem Schubladen gekramt: 1918–1988* (privately published, March 1988), 27 (copy in DaA).

92 Several copies in DaA, which lists the IIO as editor. A bibliography published in 1948 also names the IIO as editor and 1946 as the date of publication; the title is listed as *Album Dachau*. See Franz Ahrens, *Widerstandsliteratur: Ein Querschnitt durch die Literatur über die Verfolgungen und den Widerstand im Dritten Reich* (Hamburg: VVN, 1948), 36, 24.

Since the Statue of Liberty motif described below bears the date "29.IV.1945," I assume that the brochure was published before the first anniversary poster (with the date "29.IV.1946") was printed (ill. 12).

93 An original postcard with the New York Statue of Liberty is held by the DDW; it differs from the illustration in the brochure in that it bears the anniversary date "29.IV/1946".

94 For a detailed analysis of this figure, see Harold Marcuse, "Dachau: The Political Aesthetics of Holocaust Memorials," in Peter Hayes (ed.), *Lessons and Legacies III* (Evanston: Northwestern University Press, 1999), 138–68, 147f; also Detlef Hoffmann (ed.), *Das Gedächtnis der Dinge: KZ-Relikte und KZ-Denkmäler 1945–1995* (Frankfurt: Campus, 1998), 57–61.

95 See Harold Marcuse, *Nazi Crimes and Identity: Collective Memories of the Former Dachau Concentration Camp, 1945–1990* (Ann Arbor: University Microfilms, 1992), 275–80.

96 It is possible that the exhibition from 1945 did not exist continuously until it was reopened in 1950. A resolution by the International Prisoners' Committee in 1957 contains the sentence: "Even the museum which existed from 1946 to 1948 has disappeared." ("Resolution des Int. Dachau-Komitees" in Vienna, 29 June 1957, DaA, OK.) However, those dates might have been based on conjecture and even confusion with the 1950–3 exhibition. Not only would it have been unusual to refer only to the earliest exhibition and not also to the one that most members had seen (very few members of the CID [e.g. Otto Kohlhofer and Arthur Haulot, whom I asked] had been in the camp from 1946 to 1948), but even a witness who had lived continuously in Dachau (Richard Titze) equated the two exhibitions because they were both run by Preuss. This, however, does not rule out a gap from 1946 to 1948.

97 Only hybrid versions of this 59pp. publication (Munich: Philipp Rauscher, n.d.) are preserved by the memorial site. On page 4 of a brochure bound in a cover with the title *Never Again*, reference is made to a "former publication 'Never Again,'" which was extended as the present booklet, entitled "Remember That" (it does *not* bear that title). Thus the cover of the original *Never Again*, bound around a revised text which was supposed to bear a new title, is the only indication that this version ever existed. The subsequent trilingual version discussed below does bear the title *Remember That*, but it is in 8″× 6″ format, not 6″× 6″, so that it belongs to a still later edition; it also refers to the "former publication 'Never Again.'"

98 As mentioned in the previous note, I could not locate any copies with a properly titled cover. The following quotation is from p. 4.

99 Erich Preuss, *Nie Wieder / Never Again / Jamais Plus: Ein Kurzbericht in Wort und Bild über Leben und Leid im KZ-Dachau 1933–45* (Munich, 1950), ed. by KZ-Gräber Fürsorge Dachau with drawings by Jan Komski, 64pp. The only copy of this edition I could locate is in DDW and bears a handwritten dedication from Preuss (presumably to Auerbach):

> On 10 September 1950 / my book was published punctually
> made in the shortest amount of time / truly – enough work
> but there were two of us / Each one in his place
> As a river emanates from its source / Thus with your help this book went into circulation
> And now "[unreadable]" I only wish for the one for whom it was written –
> "Good Sales!"

The odd formulation "for whom it was written" might refer to the fact that Auerbach's reputation had been damaged by the previous exhibition.

100 Erich Preuss, *Remember That / Denket Daran! / Pensez-Y* (Munich: Rauscher, n.d.). Two copies are held by DaA.

101 Preuss, Gedächtnisprotokoll, 27 July 1950, BayHsta, Stk 113 626.

102 The primary source for this narrative is Alfred Werner, "Return to Dachau," *Commentary* (Dec. 1951), 542–5. For Werner's biography, see Alfred Werner, "Christmas at Dachau, 1938," *Commonweal*, 33 (20 Dec. 1940), 227–9; Werner, "Infamous Dachau," *The American Hebrew* (New York), 115:6(1945), 6–11; Werner, "Inward Man at Dachau," *The Jewish Forum*, 31:8 (1948), 284–6. See also p. 511 n. 2 for other instances of visitors in the 1950s who had similar reactions.

103 From 1949 until his death in 1979 Werner published popular monographs on such artists as Ernst Barlach, Marc Chagall, Lovis Corinth, Raoul Dufy, Amadeo Modigliani, Chaim Soutine, Maurice Utrillo, and many others.

104 Joachim Steinmayr, "Wenn das Grauen zur Sehenswürdigkeit wird . . . Sieben Jahre nach der Befreiung ist das KZ Dachau ein düsterer Anziehungspunkt für Fremdenverkehr," *SZ*, 12 Jan. 1952.

105 "Das Streiflicht," ibid.

106 Joachim Steinmayr, "Was der Jude 27660 erlebte: Auch unser Berichterstatter besuchte die Verbrennungsöfen in Dachau," *Ruhr Nachrichten*, 25 Jan. 1952.

107 It was published with the source attribution "NP" (Nordpress), for instance as J. St., "An der Stätte des Grauens: KZ Dachau lockt die Fremden an / 'Hängetanne' als Andenkenfoto," *Grenz Echo*, 22 Feb. 1952.

108 Max Löhrich (photos), "Damit wir es nicht vergessen . . .," *Zeit und Bild*, 19 Apr. 1952.

109 "Konzentrationslager Dachau heute: Gedächtnisstätte oder Touristenattraktion? – Sonderstempel aus dem Krematorium," *Nordpress-Standard, München*, no. 375, 15 July 1952.

110 In March the Minister of the Interior suggested that the Minister President unambiguously clarify the question of responsibility (Ankermüller/Interior to Ehard, 3 Mar. 1950, BayHsta, Stk 113 627). The Minister President circulated a memorandum to the various ministries on 5 May 1950; the replies were summarized in a memorandum circulated by the Interior Ministry on 6 June, in which the Interior Ministry temporarily took charge (all memos ibid.).

111 An official decision to place the sites under the care of the Restitution Office was probably made in early August 1950, because when Auerbach inquired about landscaping in Flossenbürg in July, he was told to wait because the cabinet would "shortly" resolve the general issue of care for the former concentration camps; when the Leiten cemetery was discussed in October, Auerbach's authority was already in charge. See Brand to Auerbach/Landesentschädigungsamt, 24 July 1950, BayHsta, Stk 113 624, and excerpt from cabinet minutes, 9 Oct. 1950, Stk 113 627. A brief summary can be found in Schwend/Staatskanzlei to Brenner/Kultus, 22 May 1951, BayHsta, Stk 113 628.

112 Memos of 12 Oct. 1950, and 25 Jan. 1951 (regarding cabinet meeting of 22 Jan.), BayHsta, Stk 113 627.

113 Schwalber/Culture to Zietsch/Finance regarding cabinet meeting of 19 Feb. 1952, 5 Mar. 1952, BayHsta, JS25.

114 Goschler, "Der Fall Philipp Auerbach," 95–8.

115 The Press and Information Office of the federal government has a large file of newspaper clippings on the Auerbach case.

116 I was not able to document the exact date of the transfer because the Castle

Administration repeatedly denied me access to their records. In Oct. 1952 that authority was already in charge, as indicated by its request for round-the-clock access to the crematory. See Schlösserverwaltung/Kiefer to Ministry of Finance, 22 Oct. 1952, BayHsta, Stk 113 628.

117 The date of the cabinet meeting is given in Ministère des anciens combattants et victimes de guerre to Ambassadeur de France, 3 Apr. 1954, DaA (hanging file "Lager Dachau nach 1945, Bereich Krematorium").

118 Typescript copy of Bayerische Verwaltung to Erich Preuss, 12 May 1953, and carbon copy of Preuss to Finance Minister Zietsch, 13 May 1953, BayHsta, Stk 113 628.

119 "KZ-Gedächtnisausstellung geräumt," *SZ,* 28 May 1953; "Dachau kämpft gegen die Schatten der Vergangenheit: Unkontrollierbare Propaganda auf dem ehemaligen KZ-Gelände trieb mit dem Entsetzen Missbrauch," *MM,* 30 May 1953; "Bayern schliesst Dachauer KZ-Museum: Privater Aussteller untergräbt die Versöhnungspolitik des Landes," *Rhein-Neckar-Zeitung* (Heidelberg), 6 June 1953. This exhibition is described on p. 172f, above.

120 Arbeitsgemeinschaft Dachau, "Aufruf zur Teilnahme an einem internationalen Pilgertreffen," BayHsta, JS. The invitation was signed by, among others, Georg Scherer and Alfred Klein, Dachau; Walter Vielhauer, Heilbronn; Kurt Kellner, Würzburg; Artur Ketterer, Stuttgart; Willi Müller, Bremen; also Victor Matejka, Vienna; Bob Claessens and J. Jeegers, Belgium; and representatives from Holland and France.

121 The first such pilgrimage I was able to document took place on 16 June 1947. See "Wallfahrt nach Dachau," *Heute* (Berlin/Vienna), 1 July 1947, 6–7 (in SAPMo, V 278/2/161). Annual French pilgrimages are documented beginning in 1951. The DaA may soon receive copies of the early editions of the French prisoners' newsletter, which would provide more detail on this issue.

122 See Clarac/Observateur Français en Bavière to Ambassadeur de France, 28 July 1953, DaA. I was not able to locate the articles by Michelet, whose papers are held by a French provincial archive.

123 Brand/State Chancellory to Ministry of Finance, 10 Aug. 1953, and Ministry of Finance to French General Consulate (re inquiry of 23 July), 7 Sept. 1953, BayHsta, Stk 113 628; French translation of the latter letter, DaA.

124 When Auerbach was blamed for the neglect of the Leiten graves in the fall of 1949, he offered to resign if the Minister President did not have full confidence in him. See Auerbach to Ehard, 22 Nov. 1949, BayHsta, Stk 113 625. Although I did not find an answer to this letter, the correspondence between Auerbach and Ehard in the subsequent months makes it very clear that Auerbach was strongly backed by Ehard.

125 I did not find any articles besides Steinmayr's criticizing the exhibition in the various Bavarian and national clippings collections I examined.

126 In addition to the French protests and the articles by Michelet, see Ernest Landau, "Über den Boden von Dachau darf kein Gras wachsen," *MM,* 6 June 1953, which was also published in an expanded version "Das Gras darf nicht wachsen: Ein Wort zur Demontage der Gedächtnisausstellung im Konzentrationslager Dachau," *AWJD,* 19 June 1953.

127 "Dachau kämpft," *MM,* 30 May 1953.

128 Preuss was probably one of the creators of the exhibition set up in 1945 under US

authority. But even at that time, as an employee of the Dachau Information Office, he was paid by the Dachau County Governor's Office. Preuss had worked for the Bavarian Restitution Office since January 1948. See press release by Auerbach (naming Preuss as head of public relations), 24 Jan. 1948, BayHsta, Stk 114 263.

129 "Bayern schliesst," *Rhein-Neckar-Zeitung*, 6 June 1953. This article also mentions that Preuss's brother Hugo (1860–1925) was a well-known German Democratic Party (DDP) politician who was, as Reich Minister of the Interior from Nov. 1918 to June 1919, one of the primary drafters of the democratic Weimar constitution.

130 See file "Prüfungsmitteilungen des Bayerischen Obersten Rechnungshofes über Verwendung der Spendengelder aus der Denkmalspende Dachau / . . . / Erich Preuss," LEA. See esp. the overview sent by the Oberster Rechnungshof to the Ministry of Finance on 25 September 1953.

131 Clarac to Ambassador, 28 July 1953, DaA. I could not ascertain the reason for Preuss's imprisonment, but he could not have worked at the International Information Office after liberation if he had been a common criminal.

132 Armand Gérard/Bad Godesberg to Madame de Lipkowski/Association Nationale, 31 Mar. 1954, DaA. Lipkowski's letter placed the removal of the exhibition in the same context as the accidental profanation of the Leiten cemetery in 1949. See Délégation Générale/Ministère des anciens combattants et victimes de guerre to Ambassadeur de France/Bad Godesberg, 3 Apr. 1954, DaA.

133 Notes by Preuss and protocol of interrogation of Wladyslaw Dluzak, 27 July 1950, BayHsta, Stk 113 626.

134 Memorandum by Staatssekretär Brenner/Kultus (7pp.), 4 May 1950, BayHsta, Stk 113 627. In January 1951, with the approval of State Secretary Sattler (Culture), Auerbach commissioned Preuss to take charge of the exhibition. See Schwend to Brenner, 22 May 1951, BayHsta, Stk 113 628.

In the late fall of 1951 a guide at Flossenbürg was indeed fired because he had been selling human ash. See Bericht des Landesentschädigungsamts über Abgabe von Asche aus dem Krematorium in Flossenbürg, 30 Nov. 1951, BayHsta, Stk 113 624. This incident reveals that there were indeed people interested in purchasing human ashes.

135 Landrat Junker to Ministry of Finance, 30 Sept. 1953, archive of Dachau County Governor's Office (LRA), files 063–064.

136 Based on daily estimates published in newspaper reports, I have calculated that in the early 1950s there were approximately 100,000 visitors to the Dachau memorial sites each year, of which the vast majority (ca. 80 percent) were foreigners. Official tallies were not made until December 1953. See ill. 73.

137 Ministry of Finance/Trassl to Landratsamt Dachau, 30 Oct. 1953, LRA, 063–4. See also memorandum from town council to Junker, 7 Nov. 1953, ibid. It should be noted that in the 1965 contract between the Bavarian state and the Comité International de Dachau governing responsibility for the museum and grounds, the Bavarian government explicitly reserved the right to prohibit the sale of publications in the museum. Thus today the scholarly journal *Dachauer Hefte* is subject to censure by the state government.

138 Junker to Ministry of Finance, 30 Sept. 1953, ibid.

139 The "concentration camp" files of the Presse-Archiv des Deutschen Bundestags and of the Presse- und Informationsamt der Bundesregierung begin with Steinmayr's

1952 article criticizing the Dachau exhibition. The Leiten Affair occurred prior to the creation of those offices, so it did not prompt collecting activity, but one would expect that Federal President Heuss's speech on 30 November 1952 in Bergen-Belsen would have generated a larger amount of material than the isolated articles preserved in those two archives. (I was not able to examine the clippings collection in the Bundespräsidialamt, but Heuss's papers in the BaKo contain numerous articles on his Nov. 1952 speech in Bergen-Belsen.)

140 Gaston Coblentz, "Dachau Crematorium is Kept as Memorial," *NYHT*, 8 March 1954, 1 (copy in *SZ* archive).

141 Terence Prittie, "Dachau Revisited," *Manchester Guardian Weekly*, 16 Dec. 1954.

142 Junker to Presse- und Informationsamt der Bundesregierung, 22 Apr. 1954, LRA, 063-4 (response to inquiry of 13 Apr. 1954).

143 *Mitteilungsblatt des Beirats für Wiedergutmachung*, no. 77 (June 1953).

144 On Junker's *mehrmonatige Parteianwartschaft*, see Landrat Junker to Staatssekretär Schwalber, 27 April 1949, BayHsta, JS02. In this letter, Junker describes his problems with the head of the Dachau denazification court, Zola Philipp (who coincidentally found the bones that triggered the Leiten scandal in Sept. 1949). Philipp classified Junker as "exonerated" on 19 Dec. 1946, but after Junker used his influence with the Denazification Minister to clear a friend, Philipp reopened Junker's case. Junker now wanted his CSU colleague Schwalber to use his influence with the CSU Denazification Minister Hagenauer "in the interest of the party's reputation" to have the new charges struck down. Since he never became a member of the Nazi Party, there is no file on Junker at the Berlin Document Center.

145 Junker to State Commissionership, 19 July 1948; Auerbach to Junker, 2 July 1948; Junker to Ministry of the Interior, 21 Aug. 1948; Auerbach/Ministry of the Interior to Junker, 27 Aug. 1948, BayStaA, LRA 128 069.

146 Junker to VVN Bezirksstelle Dachau, 29 April 1949, BayStaA. Junker claimed that he had not ordered the confiscation out of personal animosity, but because of a "legal obligation."

147 See "Wir schwören, uns zu widersetzen," *Die Tat*, 4 June 1955 (col. 4).

148 I was unable to locate the text of the original motion. This information was pieced together from the various reports about and protests against the resolution cited below. Both the County Governor's Office and the archive of the Bavarian parliament told me that they could find no record of the motion, and since it was never actually debated on the House floor, it is not contained in the published proceedings.

149 See *SZ*, 20 July, 21 July 1955; *Abendzeitung*, 21 July 1955; *Bayerischer Landtagsdienst*, 27 July 1955; *FR*, 29 July 1955.

150 The articles in the *SZ* containing the original announcement also reported that the Landesrat für Freiheit und Recht, the Arbeitsgemeinschaft verfolgter Sozialdemokraten and Staatssekretär Panholzer protested against the bill. In a press conference on 21 July Minister President Hoegner expressed his disapproval, and on 22 July Kurat Roth, a former prisoner working in the refugee settlement, wrote a letter of protest (see Kellner/State Chancellory to Kurat Roth, 28 July 1955, BayHsta, Stk 113 628). See also VVN Bayern to Minister President and Landtag deputies, 21 July 1955, and Polish Union of Former Political Prisoners, Munich to Hoegner, 25 July 1955, both BayHsta, Stk 113 628. For the media reaction, see *SZ*, 22

July (editorial) and 26 July 1955 (Jewish US soldiers stationed in Dachau); *FR*, 29 July 1955; *Die Tat*, 30 July 1955.

151 Quoted after: "Landrat schlecht beraten," *Abendzeitung*, 21 July 1955. Zietsch also told reporters: "I think it is right that we not forget what happened so quickly." See "Cernàk-Attentat bleibt im Dunkel," *SZ*, 23 July 1955.

152 See *Combat* (Paris), 13 Aug. and 17 Aug. 1955; *SZ*, 13 Aug. 1955 (Polish former prisoners in London); Georg Kahn-Ackermann (SPD member of the federal parliament from Dachau), "Unternehmen Wasserkopf," *Abendzeitung*, 5 Sept. 1955; "SPD gegen Krematoriumsschliessung," *Fürstenfeldbrucker Tagblatt*, 5 Sept. 1955; and summarizing those two reports, "'In Bruck rührt sich was', sagt man im Landtag," *MM*, 6 Sept. 1955.

153 I have discovered a sole example of supralocal support for Junker's motion. See Karl Stankiewitz, "Touristen besuchen die Gaskammern: Das Grauen als Sehenswürdigkeit / Das Konzentrationslager Dachau soll gesperrt werden," *Westdeutsche Allgemeine* (Essen), 3 Aug. 1955. An accompanying photograph shows cars parked directly at the crematory wall.

154 "Dr. Baumgartner: 'Krematorium muss verschwinden!'," *MM/DN*, 11 Aug. 1955; *SZ*, 11 Aug. and 12 Aug. 1955. A report was also distributed by the Associated Press (see, e.g., "Streit um Dachauer Krematorium geht weiter," *FR*, 12 Aug. 1955; "Nouvelle tentative de fermer au public le camp de Dachau," *Le Monde*, 12 Aug. 1955). On Baumgartner see Klaus-Dietmar Henke and Hans Woller (eds.), *Lehrjahre der CSU: Eine Nachkriegspartei im Spiegel vertraulicher Berichte* (Stuttgart: DVA, 1984), 27, 92, 122f.

155 "Schliessung des Dachauer Krematoriums verstiesse gegen Vertrag mit Frankreich," *SZ*, 8 Sept. 1955; "Dachau Crematorium to Stay Open / Proposal to Close Memorial Resisted," *The Times* (London), 22 Sept. 1955.

156 "Wieder Kreuz und Davidstern auf dem Leitenberg," *Bayerischer Landtagsdienst*, 20 Sept. and 5 Oct. 1955; "Dachauer Gedächtnisstätte soll bleiben," *SZ*, 21 Sept. 1955. The establishment of abstract and physically distant memorials may originally have been a strategy to defuse the opposition by showing that the "crematorium-closers" were not against *all* reminders of the camp. Baumgartner said in his 10 Aug. speech: "In order to honor the people who died in the camps and not to forget their sacrificial deaths, a genuine memorial site in the form of a dignified monument would be enough" (*MM*, 11 Aug. 1955).

157 Adolf Bauer, "Irreführung in Dachau," *SZ*, 22 Oct. 1955. A US army photograph of one of the doors is printed, *inter alia*, in Gun, *Day of the Americans*, 129; Andrew Mollo, "Dachau," *After the Battle*, 27 (1980), 1–29, 17; Selzer, *Deliverance Day*, 247.

158 "Junker tarnt KZ-Verbrechen," *Bayerisches Volksecho*, 10 Oct. 1955. A solitary sign reading "Access to the Cemetery on the Leiten" was erected in such a way that visitors coming on the main road from Dachau could not read it.

Part III Dachau 1955–1970: groups and their memories

1 This phenomenon is described and illustrated with many examples in Harold Marcuse, Jochen Spielmann, and Frank Schimmelfenning, *Steine des Anstosses: Nationalsozialismus und Zweiter Weltkrieg in Denkmalen, 1945–1985* (Hamburg: Museum für Hamburgische Geschichte, 1985).

2 See Volkhard Knigge, "Vom Reden und Schweigen der Steine: Zu Denkmalen auf dem Gelände ehemaliger nationalsozialistischer Konzentrations- und Vernichtungslager," in Sigrid Weigel and Birgit Erdle (eds.), *Fünfzig Jahre danach: Zur Nachgeschichte des Nationalsozialismus* (Zurich: Hochschulverlag, 1996), 193–235, 207. Knigge attributes his insight to a conversation with historian Jörn Rüsen.

6 The first representations of Dachau, 1945–1952

1 "Germans Honor Victims / Forced to Build Memorials to 3,500 Dachau Dead," *NYT*, 15 June 1945, 4. I have corrected some typesetting errors. See also Marcus Smith, *The Harrowing of Hell: Dachau* (Albuquerque, University of New Mexico, 1972), 139. A Military Government communication from Jan. 1946 says that the monument was originally ordered by the Area Commander of the 7th US Army, Colonel Adams of the 45th Division. See JTM to Capt. Rae, 8 Jan. 1946, BayHsta, Stk 113 623. The memo erroneously places the monument in the Dachau city cemetery, where the ca. 2,000 inmates who died after liberation were buried.
2 *Mitteilungen des Antifaschistischen Aktions-Ausschusses in Dachau*, no. 1 (14 June 1945), BayHsta, JS01. This was probably the only number of the *Mitteilungen* that was published. For a more detailed description based on a 1974 interview with Max Gorbach, one of the committee members, see Tony Barta, "Antifaschismus und demokratischer Neubeginn: Die Stadt Dachau im ersten Jahr nach dem Nationalsozialismus," *Dachauer Hefte*, 1 (1985), 62–87, 69f.
3 Walther, "Report about the result of the investigation of the delay in the decoration of the gravesites on the Leiten near Dachau," 12 Jan. 1950, 4, BayHsta, Stk 113 628. Walther claims that Buechner's design was published in the *Dachauer Amtsblatt*, but I was not able to find any reference to it in that publication.
4 See JTM to Capt. Rae, 8 Jan. 1946, BayHsta, Stk 113 623; and speech by former County Governor Kneuer, in "Am Grabmal des unbekannten KZlers: Richtfest der Gedächtnishalle auf der Leiten," *MM/DN*, 19 Sept. 1951. The project had also been endorsed by Munich Cardinal Faulhaber: see *MZ*, 14 July 1945, quoted by Schattenhofer, *Chronik der Stadt München*, 63. The rejection is documented in the *Stadtratsprotokoll*, 27 July 1945, BayHsta, JS01. This was the first meeting designated as "city council meeting." The protocols of the meetings of the Dachau county governor and the US regional commandant, which began in May and continued through Sept., and from which excerpts were published by Barta (see "Antifaschismus," 73 n. 16, 74–7), do not contain references to the project. A complete set of the protocols can be found in BayHsta, JS VIII/106. The set used by Barta in the Munich *Staatsarchiv* has been transferred to the neighboring *Hauptstaatsarchiv*.
5 From 1945 to 1948 the military exchange rate was RM10 = $1 (see R. L. Bidwell, *Currency Conversion Tables: A Hundred Years of Change* [London: Rex Collings, 1970], p. 23); the inflation factor from 1945 to the late 1990s, based on the consumer price index, is about 9 (see NASA's inflation calculator at http://www.jsc.nasa.gov/bu2/inflateCPI.html). Thus RM500,000 would be about $450,000 today. This gives only a partial indication of the costs, since prices for monuments have soared in the meantime. In Dec. 1949 the new Leiten memorial was to cost DM1–2 million ($3–600,000, or $2.1–4.2 million in 1999). The international memorial dedicated in

Apr. 1967 in Auschwitz-Birkenau cost DM3.5 million ($900,000 in 1967 dollars, $4.5 million in 1999); the Vietnam Veterans' Memorial in Washington, D.C. cost $8,000,000 in 1980–2 ($13.5 million today); the planned Berlin National Holocaust Memorial was budgeted for DM15 million in 1998 ($10 million), with the possible addition of a research library costing up to DM150 million ($70 million).

6 The cross can be seen in contemporary photographs and drawings, for instance in an ink sketch published in the Christmas 1947 issue of *Der Ausblick*, a magazine created by the Germans interned in the postwar Dachau camp.

7 Survivor Richard Titze told me that the yellow-painted star of David was fashioned from a swastika that the SS had erected on the site. A photograph of this temporary memorial was published in "Neues KZ-Massengrab entdeckt," *NZ*, 9 Sept. 1949.

8 Harold Marcuse, *Nazi Crimes and Identity: Collective Memories of the Former Dachau Concentration Camp, 1945–1990* (Ann Arbor: University Microfilms, 1992), 318.

9 A sketch of this design can be found in Wiedemann, blueprint of memorial site, 16 Nov. 1960, DaA, OK. See also Stefan Schwarz, memo re meeting in Finance Ministry, 9 Mar. 1962, LEA. The sketch is published in Detlef Hoffmann, *Das Gedächtnis der Dinge: KZ-Relikte und KZ-Denkmäler, 1945–1995* (Frankfurt: Campus, 1998), 78.

10 Knappe's best-known work is probably the reliefs in the "tomb of the unknown soldier" in front of the Army Museum in Munich; see "Offener Brief an den Bürgermeister von Dachau," *SZ*, 13 Nov. 1945. Knappe, a professor at the Munich Academy of the Arts, later designed a communion bench and a pulpit for the "Atomic Church" in Hiroshima, and stained glass windows for the Munich Dom. See the exhibition catalog *Skulptur und Macht: Figurative Plastik im Deutschland der 30er und 40er Jahre* (Berlin: Akademie der Künste, 1983), 163.

A contemporary evaluation of Knappe (JTM to Capt. Rae, 8 Jan. 1946, BayHsta, Stk 113 623) found that "his [denazification] questionnaire is fine," that he was locally considered "left," and that he was probably selected by the Communist second mayor of Dachau, Georg Scherer. In a 1960 letter to Josef Schwalber, who had been Scherer's assistant in 1945, Knappe wrote: "the idea developed with your support." See Knappe to Schwalber, July 1960, BayHsta, JS89; also *MM/DN*, 30 July 1960. The 12 Jan. 1950 report about the Leiten investigation states that Knappe was chosen by "a Dachau artist."

An article in the first postwar edition of a major German architectural journal claimed that Knappe had been a "decorator for the big Hitler celebrations." See er, "Das Dachauer Gedächtnis- und Befreiungsmal", *Der Baumeister*, 1:1 (Jan. 1946), 24.

11 "Das Befreiungsmal von Dachau," *SZ*, 26 Oct. 1945 (report datelined Dachau, 22 Oct.). The Bavarian State Chancellory saved this clipping, see BayHsta, Stk 113 623. A model of the monument was displayed in Dachau castle during the 9 Nov. 1945 international memorial ceremony.

Photographs (6″×8″) of the model can be found in the Dachau County Governor's Office, LRA, 064. One photograph was published in *MM/DN*, 30 July 1960. Knappe gave the model to Schwalber, who in turn gave it to the city of Dachau (memo by Schwalber, 22 Sept. 1960, BayHsta, JS89). In 1991 it could no longer be found; city archivist Gerhard Hancke presumed that it had been discarded by Mayor Böck in the early 1960s (letter to me, 10 May 1991).

12 *Befreiungsmal* is the term used to denote the project in most sources prior to 1946, except in a Bavarian State Chancellory memo of 8 Nov. 1945, which refers to it as *Sühnemal* ("monument of atonement"). See Pfister, memo, 8 Nov. 1945, BayHsta, Stk 113 623. After the public criticism of the design in Nov. 1945, *Sühnemal* and *Gedächtnismal* ("commemorative marker") became prevalent.

13 Knappe to Schwalber, July 1960, BayHsta, JS89, published in *MM/DN*, 30 July 1960.

14 The published drawing bears close resemblance to the "Reichsehrenmal für die im Osten gefallenen Soldaten" of the First World War, constructed in St. Annaberg (Silesia) in 1938 by the Volksbund deutsche Kriegsgräberfürsorge. That monument is pictured in Harold Marcuse, Frank Schimmelfenning, and Jochen Spielmann, *Steine des Anstosses: Nationalsozialismus und Zweiter Weltkrieg in Denkmalen, 1945–1985* (Hamburg: Museum für Hamburgische Geschichte, 1985), 6. Kathrin Hoffmann-Curtius adds a religious dimension to my interpretation; see her essay "Denkmäler für das KZ Dachau," in Claudia Keller (ed.), *Antifaschismus: Geschichte und Neubewertung* (Berlin: Aufbau, 1996), 280–309, 288f.

15 Hans Eckstein/Lochham to Minister President Hoegner, 29 Oct. 1945, BayHsta, Stk 113 623. The Nazi monument was allegedly in Riederau am Ammersee. Eckstein also claimed that Knappe had been denied permission to teach in Munich because of "cultural Bolshevism." On 14 Nov. 1945 Hoegner forwarded a copy of the letter to the Monuments and Fine Arts Section of Military Government in Munich, which was apparently unable to confirm the allegation.

16 Union of Munich Architects (Ungelehrt, Döllgast, Haeusser), "'Das Befreiungsmal von Dachau': Offener Brief an den Bürgermeister von Dachau," *SZ*, 13 Nov. 1945; "Das Dachauer Gedächtnis- und Befreiungsmal," *Der Baumeister*, 1 (1946), 24.

The comparison in the latter article to the Castel del Monte (an eight-sided twelfth-century fortress in Italy) was probably based solely on the sketch published in the *SZ* on 26 Oct. In fact, as the photographs of the model show, the building had a semicircular base and was quite dissimilar to the Castel del Monte. The *Baumeister's* remark that such monumentality would be more fitting "in the Libyan desert" than on the Leiten was prescient: in 1953 a German soldiers' monument replicating the Castel del Monte was built by the Volksbund deutsche Kriegsgräberfürsorge at El Alamein in the Egyptian desert. I was not able to ascertain whether Knappe was involved in the design of that building.

17 On 15 Nov. the wire service DANA sent out a report with the title "Denkmal oder Krankenhaus?," and on 27 Dec. 1945 the *Tagesspiegel* in Berlin printed an editorial in support of the criticism. Copies of both can be found in SAPMo, V 278/2/161.

18 Minutes of city council, 28 Dec. 1945, BayHsta, JS01.

19 JTM to Capt. Rae, 8 Jan. 1946, BayHsta, Stk 113 623.

20 Hoegner to General Walter J. Muller, director of the Office of Military Government for Bavaria, 23 Mar. 1946, BayHsta, Stk 113 623. An overview of the developments in 1946 based on Ministry of Culture documents not available to the author can be found in Walther, "Report about the results of the investigation of the delay in the decoration of the gravesites on the Leiten near Dachau," 12 Jan. 1950, 5f, BayHsta, Stk 113 628.

The "Ausschuss für das Dachauer Gedächtnismal" included Ministerialrat Jacob (Kultus), E. Hanfstaengl (Direktor der Gemäldesammlungen), G. Lill (Direktor des Denkmalamts), the mayor of Dachau (Schwalber), Captain Steener of Military

Government's Fine Arts Section, the artists Prof. A. Schinnerer and Dieter Sattler, and Referent Kurt Pfister. Sattler was chairman of the professional association of architects and construction engineers; see Sattler to Ehard, 27 Jan. 1950, BayHsta, JS25. In Jan. 1947 he began working for the Ministry of Culture.

21 The English translation is taken in part from Pfister to Steener/Fine Arts, 15 Apr. 1946, BayHsta, Stk 113 623.

22 See "Ausschreibungsunterlagen zum Wettbewerb auf der Leiten," 5 June 1946, BayHsta, Stk 113 623. The materials included two mimeographed pages and plans scaled 1:25,000, 1:5,000, and 1:500. Photographs could be ordered from Paul Sessner, Augsburgerstr. 27 in Dachau.

It was incorrect that the crematory had been "inoperative" from Nov. 1944 to May 1945; it had not been able to keep pace with the daily mortality rate.

23 See "Dachau bei München: Denkmal im Konzentrationslager," *Baumeister-Rundschau*, no. 5 (1946), 62; "Denkmal im Konzentrationslager Dachau," *Neue Bauwelt*, no. 17 (1946), 12. Actually, a design by Hans Friedrich was deemed the best, but he was disqualified when his denazification questionnaire revealed that he had been a member of the SA.

The minutes of the meetings of the prize commission on 10 Sept. and 4 Oct. 1946 are in Stk 113 623. The commission's members were: Minister President Hoegner and his Referent Kurt Pfister, Alfred Jacob from the Ministry of Culture, Mayor Schwalber, Ministerialrat Berndt, Prof. Lill (Denkmalpfleger), Prof. Hanfstaengl/Sammlungen, Prof. Karl Sattler, Prof. Schinnerer, and Prof. Henselmann.

24 The four purchased designs were from the sculptor Augustin Lohr, the architect Richard Steidle, the architect Wolfgang Vogel and his partner Lindl, and the engineer Hellmuth von Werz. The new artists were Döllgast, Sepp Ruff, Gustav Gsänger, Leitensdorfer, Hocheder, Hunselmann, and Otto Roth.

25 A number of memos are to be found in BayHsta, Stk 113 623. The original four prize-winning artists finally received their payment in the spring of 1947. See Jacob to Landeshauptkasse, 10 May 1947, BayHsta, MFin 67404. On the destruction by fire see Sattler, memo, 7 Dec. 1949, 3, BayHsta, Stk 113 625.

26 In *Dachauer Stimmen*, no. 1, 2 Nov. 1949 (DaA, Leiten notebook) Paul Hussarek wrote that former prisoners had negotiated with the Bavarian government in the spring of 1949 to have a memorial grove planted on the Leiten. I have not been able to find any confirmation of that plan. Since at precisely that time former Buchenwald inmates successfully lobbied for the creation of a memorial grove at Buchenwald's mass graves by the government of Thuringia, it is possible that Hussarek confused the two plans. According to Heinz Koch, *Nationale Mahn- und Gedenkstätte Buchenwald: Geschichte ihrer Entstehung* (Weimar–Buchenwald: NMG Buchenwald, 1988), 17, on 13 June 1949 the state parliament of Thuringia appropriated [East German] M160,000 for the grove, which was dedicated on 11 Sept., the Day of Victims of Fascism. See Gitta Günther, *Buchenwald* (Weimar: Weimarer Schriften, no. 9, 1983), 88f.

27 See Max Oppenheimer, *Der Weg der VVN: Vom Häftlingskomitee zum Bund der Antifaschisten* (Frankfurt: Röderberg, 1972), 7–10.

28 Ibid., 11–13; Max Oppenheimer (ed.), *Antifaschismus – Position, Politik, Perspektive: Geschichte und Ziele der VVN-Bund der Antifaschisten* (Frankfurt: Röderberg, 1978), 11f. Oppenheimer cites a facsimile reprint of the papers and resolutions of that

meeting: *30 Jahre VVN – Referate und Entschliessungen der Gründungskonferenz 1947* (Frankfurt: Röderberg, 1977). See also "1. Dachau-Gedächtnis-Kundgebung," *VVNN*, 28 May 1947.

29 See Franz Ahrens, *Widerstandsliteratur: Ein Querschnitt durch die Literatur über die Verfolgungen und den Widerstand im Dritten Reich* (Hamburg: VVN, 1948), 43. According to Ahrens, Karl Schirdewan's speech was published in a special issue of *Unser Appell* (VVN Berlin) in February 1948.

30 See Koch, *Nationale Mahn- und Gedenkstätte*, 14. Three thousand participants came to Weimar, 1,300 from the Soviet zone, 800 from the western zones, 500 from Berlin, and 400 from foreign countries. According to "Befreiungsfeier – Weimar 1948," *VVNN*, no. 3, Apr. 1948, working groups for Buchenwald, Sachsenhausen, Dachau, Ravensbrück, Neuengamme, and Auschwitz were formed on the first day. See also Karl Wagner/VVN-Württemberg-Baden to Josef Lorenz, Arnstadt/ Thüringen, 30 Apr. 1948, DaA notebook "Mitteilungen der Lagergemeinschaft Dachau, I."

A mimeographed "Liste der Verantwortlichen der Arbeitsgemeinschaft [Dachau] in den einzelnen Ländern," Apr. 1948, FstHH, HS 13–4–4–3 reads like a "Who's Who" of central figures in the organization of German Dachau inmates for the next two decades, including Hans Kaltenbacher, Karl Wagner, Gustl Gattinger, Georg Koch, Hans Schwarz, Willi Müller, Walter Vielhauer, Robert Gehrke, and Walter Reede (Dresden). Some letters in Schwarz's private correspondence also refer to the meeting in Weimar. See, e.g., Walter Reede to Schwarz, 26 Aug. 1948.

See also Walter Vielhauer to Karl Wagner, VVN-Stuttgart, 26 Apr. 1948, DDW, Walter Vielhauer papers, file 44, which contains a mimeograph mentioning a *Prüfungskommission* for the history of KZ Dachau, and a six-page list of former Dachau inmates living in Germany.

31 A circular entitled "Arbeitsgemeinschaftstagungen am 13. September 1948" lists a talk by Hans Schwarz with thirty-nine listeners and twelve participants in the discussion. In "Generalsekretariat Hochschulgruppen," SAPMo, V 278/2/22.

32 Mimeographed circular from Hans Schwarz/Rat der VVN to the "Ländervorsitzenden, Mitglieder des Präsidiums der Dachauer Arbeitsgemeinschaft," 9 July 1949, FstHH, HS 13–4–4–3. The planned meeting in late Aug. 1949 was to consider the following four points: (1) reports from the working groups in each federal state; (2) information about underground work and resistance in KZ Dachau; (3) report about a book about KZ Dachau, and (4) "international cooperation and our German obligations."

On the effect of the discovery of graves on the Leiten, see Dachauer Arbeitsgemeinschaft beim Sekretariat des Rates der VVN, Maria-Louisen-Str. (Hamburg) (ed.), *Dachauer Stimmen*, no. 1, 2 Nov. 1949, DaA, Leiten notebook. This report mentions "representatives from seventeen German federal states," in mid-August, with 150 Austrians and forty Germans expected to attend. See VVN-Dachau to Regierungsrat Lutz/Landratsamt, 19 Aug. 1949, SAPMo, V 278/2/159.

33 Documents in the Jean Stock papers at the Archive of Social Democracy in Bonn contain information about these resignations. See report about the *Landesvorstandssitzung* on 12 May 1949 in file 82, and reply by the VVN Aschaffenburg to Stock's resignation from the VVN, 28 Feb. 1949, file 83. At the Munich meeting, Auerbach, Franz X. Fackler, Heinrich Pflüger, W. Seutter v. Lützen, and Alois

Ullmann (Planegg) resigned. The latter had been the trustee of the entire former KZ Dachau since 5 Mar. 1948 (file 83).

34 See pp. 145–50, above, and VVN-Bezirksstelle Dachau to Rat der VVN/Schwarz, 4 Sept. 1949, SAPMo, V 278/2/159, in which the dangers for the reputation of the VVN are mentioned. Werner Gross/Nürtingen to Rat der VVN Hamburg, re "Dachauer Arbeitsgemeinschaft," 15 Dec. 1949, FstHH, HS, offers an example of a former Dachau inmate (no. 84) who thought the VVN was culpable.

35 In May 1948 the international association of former political prisoners, the Fédération Internationale des Anciens Prisonniers Politiques (FIAPP; in the early 1950s reorganized as the Fédération Internationale des Résistants, FIR), voted to accept the German VVN as a member organization. See Oppenheimer, *Der Weg der VVN*, 14 (Warsaw meeting on 29 May 1948), and 18; Oppenheimer (ed.), *Antifaschismus*, 12f.

On the cooperation of the FIAPP and the VVN in the Leiten Affair, see VVN-Bezirksstelle Dachau to Rat der VVN/Schwarz, 4 Sept. 1949, SAPMo, V 278/2/159, and "Rapport de la commission d'enquête de la F.N.D.I.R.P. sur le scandale de Dachau," 29 Nov. 1949, DaA, Leiten notebook. The FNDIRP was the French association in the FIAPP. See also the correspondence between FIAPP and the VVN in SAPMo, V 278/2/161 (e.g., letters of 14 Dec. and 16 Dec. 1949). For an assessment of the importance of this international work, see "Verlautbarung" of the VVN Munich about the official Leiten investigation, 20 Jan. 1950, DaA, Leiten notebook. The help from the FIAPP was also lauded at the founding meeting of the Dachauer Arbeitsgemeinschaft discussed below.

36 A picture of the sculpture was printed on an invitation to a September 1949 commemorative ceremony and appeal for donations distributed by Auerbach's office. See Auerbach to Mayor Wimmer, 30 Aug. 1949, StMü, BuR 2277, and Auerbach, printed Call for Donations, 1 Sept. 1949, BayHsta, MSo 134.

37 On Koelle, see Germanisches Nationalmuseum Nürnberg (ed.), *Dokumente zu Leben und Werk des Bildhauers Fritz Koelle (1895–1953)*, 4. Sonderausstellung des Archivs für Bildende Kunst (exhibition catalog, n.p.p., n.d.). The 1.44 meter high Dachau sculpture from 1946 is depicted on p. E29. For biographical information, see Hans Vollmer, *Allgemeines Lexikon der Bildenden Künstler* (Leipzig: E. A. Seemann, 1956), vol III, 79.

38 For a comparison of this sculpture to similar groups see Harold Marcuse, "Dachau and the Political Aesthetics of Holocaust Memorials," in *Lessons and Legacies II* (Evanston, Ill.: Northwestern University Press, 1999), 138–68. The other groups include a World War I memorial in the monastery garden of Rot an der Rot; the 1946 Dachau International Information Office poster discussed above; and Nathan Rapoport's bronze sculpture *Liberator* (1985) in New Jersey. The latter is depicted and discussed in detail in James E. Young, *The Texture of Memory: Holocaust Memorials and Meaning* (New Haven: Yale University Press, 1993), 155–84. Artist Willi Lammert's 1957 sculpture of two female inmates at Ravensbrück makes an interesting comparison as well.

39 Dachau survivor Hans Schwarz wrote to French survivors that the sculpture was "universally condemned" because it "immortalized the horrors." Letter from Schwarz to Noe Vilner and others, 2 Dec. 1949, SAPMo V 278/2/161.

40 See "Wettbewerbsausschreibung einer Gedächtnishalle," *Bayerischer Staatsan-*

zeiger, 11 Feb. 1950, and *SZ*, 11 Feb. 1950. On the 30 Apr. 1950 commemorative ceremony, marked by the participation of a large number of prominent persons, see pp. 149f.

41 Ehard to Land Commissioner Bolds, 1 Feb. 1950, BayHsta, Stk 113 625.

42 "Staatsregierung und Landtag auf dem Leitenberg: Landrat Junker mit der Ausgestaltung betraut," *MM/DN*, 3/4 Dec. 1949. For the cost estimate see Sattler, memo, 7 Dec. 1949, 5, BayHsta, Stk 113 625.

43 Wolfgang Petzet, "Das Ergebnis des Leitenberg-Wettbewerbs," *MM/DN*, 4 May 1950. The latter references are to the Bavarian Valhalla near Regensburg and the Ruhmeshalle at Kelheim.

44 Sattler, minutes of the first meeting of the jury for the Leiten competition, 25 Apr. 1950, BayHsta, Stk 113 627. The document lists the artists and describes the nine best entries, which were displayed for two weeks in the Hochschule für bildende Künste in Munich. The fifteen-person jury included Ungelehrt (one of the authors of the Nov. 1945 open letter), von Werz (architect of one of the winning entries in 1946), and six professors, but no representatives of the Dachau survivors.

See also "Familie Lang siegt im Leitenberg-Wettbewerb," *Abendzeitung*, 29 Apr. 1950; J.v.H., "Denkmals-Wettbewerb für den Leitenberg," *SZ*, 3 May 1950.

The two best entries were from the sculptor and passion-play director Georg Johann Lang, his son architect Ernst Maria Lang, and from the Munich architect Wunibald Puchner in collaboration with the sculptor Hans Vogel.

45 "Urkunde zur Grundsteinlegung auf der Leiten bei Dachau," 29 Apr. 1950, BayHsta, Stk 113 628. A photocopy of the document, which was published in the *Abendzeitung* of 2 May 1950, is held by the Dachau memorial site.

46 Dieter Sattler, report about the third meeting of the jury on 19 May 1950, 20 May 1950, and memo by Gummpenberg, 14 June 1950, BayHsta, Stk 113 627. On Roth and Hiller's design, see H. Fischer, "Gedächtnishalle auf dem Leitenberg bei Dachau," *Die Bauzeitung* (Stuttgart), Jan. 1951, 17–23, in which plans and sketches of the other two winning entries are also published.

47 See "Gedächtnishalle auf dem Leitenberg," *MM*, 28 Aug. 1950. At that time, construction was to begin "in the fall," with completion slated for April 1951. The fourth jury meeting was on 22 June and the fifth on 8 Aug. (minutes in BayHsta, Stk 113 626). See also "Besprechung über die Gestaltung des Leitenbergs," 10 Oct. 1950, BayHsta, JS25.

48 See Erich Preuss, report about the construction project on the Leiten, 3 Feb. 1951, BayHsta, Stk 113 627, and Preuss/Landesentschädigungsamt, memo regarding the repositioning of the cornerstone, 15 Feb. 1951, Stk 113 626. At that time the projected costs were ca. DM630,000.

The verse cited below (p. 197 and note 52) intimates that bad weather, incomplete blueprints, and technical difficulties exacerbated the bureaucrats' lethargy.

49 For descriptions of the event, see "Am Grabmal des unbekannten KZlers: Richtfest der Gedächtnishalle auf der Leiten / Dr. Zdralek und Dr. Kneuer sprachen," *MM/DN*, 19 Sept. 1950; "Richtfest für das Mahnmal," *Dachauer Volksbote*, 19/20 Sept. 1950; Kneuer to Ehard, 26 Sept. 1951, BayHsta, Stk 113 628.

A report and a photograph were sent out by Associated Press. See *NZ*, 18 Sept. 1951. At that time, final completion was scheduled for Apr. 1951, see "Richtfest am Leitenberg," *SZ*, 18 Sept. 1951. This article repeated the erroneous figure of 20,000 dead buried in the cemetery.

50 They are the traditional authors of such ditties. The other possibility is that Preuss wrote the poem, but since it contains a jest about him it is not likely that he was the author. After describing how money for construction ran out in the winter, the poem continues: "Doch sagt man A, sagt man auch O / und der Preuss, als Verwalter war froh, / konnte er doch weiter nach Art der Preissen / umherdisponieren und sachgemäss weisen." On the other hand, Preuss dedicated a copy of the new exhibition brochure in Sept. 1950 to Auerbach with verse not dissimilar to this. See the copy of the brochure held by the DDW, Frankfurt quoted on p. 467 n. 99, above.

51 *SZ*, 2 Feb. 1950 with correction 3 Feb. 1950. See also p. 149, above.

52 "Richtspruch zur Hebweinfeier der Gedächtnishalle Leitenberg," 17 Sept. 1951, BayHsta, Stk 113 628. The original reads: "So schwankten die Entwürfe zumal / vom Typ Kalkofen bis Völkerschlachtsdenkmal. Die richtige Mischung ergab nach Roth'scher Norm, / dieses Modell, à la Wasserturm. // Doch nun frug Jeder, wer zahlt? wer gibt Geld? / So färbten sich Akten und Bäume gelb, bis endlich im Herbst 1950 dann / zum Winter hinein der Bau begann."

53 A Deutsche Presse-Agentur wire service announcement dated 24 Sept. 1950 summarized the article in *Combat*. Copy in the archive of the *SZ*. See also Kneuer to Ehard, 26 Sept. 1951, BayHsta, Stk 113 628. Preuss was responsible for the cake and the organization of the ceremony.

54 Plans and photographs of the building were published in G. H., "Landschaft – Bauwerk – Symbol: Gedächtnisstätte auf dem Leitenberg bei Dachau," *Deutsche Bauzeitung*, no. 12 (1956), 507–9. Two of the same photographs were published in *Der Baumeister*, no. 12 (1954), 796.

55 See Marcuse, *Nazi Crimes*, 263–7, also Meinhold Lurz, "Die Heldenhaine und Totenburgen des Volksbundes deutsche Kriegsgräberfürsorge," *Arch+*, 71 (Oct. 1983), 66–70. Tannenberg was erected 1924–7 near Allenstein in what is now Poland; see *Festschrift zur Einweihung des Tannenberg-Denkmals am 18. September 1927* (Königsberg: n.p., 1927). The Annaberg (in Poland, near Gliwice) monument was built to commemorate the counterrevolutionary Freikorps forces of 1919. In the 1940s Wilhelm Kreis, who had won a competition for a model Bismarck tower at the turn of the century, designed even larger but formally similar structures for Warsaw and Stalingrad as well.

56 Zietsch/Finance Ministry to State Chancellory, 29 Sept. 1952, BayHsta, Stk 113 628. In November the Bavarian Castle and Garden Administration, which had just taken over responsibility from the Restitution Office (which had been occupied by the police since March 1952), checked the correctness of the thirty-three heraldic shields which had already been mounted in the memorial hall. See Kiefer/Bayerische Verwaltung der staatlichen Schlösser, Gärten und Seen to Staatskanzlei, 10 Nov. 1952; State Chancellory to Auswärtiges Amt, 1 Dec. 1952; Auswärtiges Amt to State Chancellory, 27 Apr. 1953; all in BayHsta, Stk 113 628.

57 See "Auf dem Leitenberg werden KZ-Opfer exhumiert: 1,200 Familien wünschen Überführung ihrer Toten nach Frankreich," *MM*, 2 Nov. 1955; "Ein neues Grab für die Opfer von Dachau: Auf dem Leitenberg werden ehemalige französische Häftlinge umgebettet," *SZ*, 12 Nov. 1955. The French project included an innovative procedure for identifying skeletal remains based on medical records. For further information, see the French dissertation by Georges Fully, copy in DaA.

58 In *Verhandlungen* (23 May 1956), vol. 3, 2066f, a parliamentary decision to erect a

"tall cross and a Jewish gravestone" is mentioned. The realization of the two monuments was delayed for a number of years: see *Bayerischer Landtagsdienst*, 10 Aug. 1956, SZA. I did not find any further mention of these two objects, which still stand today.

7 Rising public interest, 1955–1965

1 I use the term *Kristallnacht* instead of the term "Pogrom Night," which became fashionable after 1988, not because of its euphemistic connotations, but because it originally had a subversive, anti-Nazi meaning. See Alf Lüdtke, "'Coming to Terms with the Past': Illusions of Remembering, Ways of Forgetting Nazism in West Germany," *Journal of Modern History*, 65:3 (1993), 542–73; also Y. Michael Bodemann, "Reconstructions of History: From Jewish Memory to Nationalized Commemoration of Kristallnacht in Germany," in Bodemann (ed.), *Jews, Germans, Memory: Reconstructions of Jewish Life in Germany* (Ann Arbor: Michigan University Press, 1996), 179–223.

2 Peter Steinbach, *Nationalsozialistische Gewaltverbrechen: Die Diskussion in der deutschen Öffentlichkeit nach 1945* (Berlin: Colloquium, 1981), 46. To support his claim Steinbach refers to Helmut Schelsky's sociological study of West German youth from 1945 to 1955: *Die skeptische Generation: Eine Soziologie der deutschen Jugend* (Dusseldorf/Cologne: Diederichs, 1957). For Schelsky's characterization of the postwar generation, see esp. 84–95.

3 For the *SZ* archive the figures are (1950–55): 49, 7, 5, 2, 3, 23, whereby two of the 1954 articles were in English newspapers, and forty of the 1950 articles fell in the Jan.-June period. Although I did not keep an exact count, this striking tendency was confirmed by a systematic reading of the four-page daily *MM/DN* from 1949 to 1954, where the former concentration camp is hardly mentioned between 1951 and 1954, in marked contrast to the preceding years.

4 I suspect that the German archives' figures for 1955 are somewhat low because German collectors had become unused to clipping articles on the camps. Whereas the collections often duplicate each other (if they contained any articles at all) during 1950–4, in 1955 each collection contained a number of unique articles. However, I did not systematically note the presence of duplicate articles, so I cannot tabulate exact numbers for each archive.

5 *New York Times Index*, 1949–56. The most important headings were "Minorities – Nazi Policies," and "Germany – War Crimes and Criminals." I have only considered articles that refer explicitly to the history of the camps themselves. In 1954, for instance, there are sixteen articles listed, but all of them have to do with pardoning convicted Nazi criminals.

6 See Alvin Rosenfeld, "Popularization and Memory: The Case of Anne Frank," in Peter Hayes (ed.), *Lessons and Legacies* (Evanston, Ill.: Northwestern University Press, 1991), 243–278. Anna Steenmeijer (ed.), *A Tribute to Anne Frank* (New York: Doubleday, 1971) includes a description of the German reception and reprints a number of personal letters to Otto Frank. For a personal memoir, see Hans Speier, *From the Ashes of Disgrace: A Journal from Germany, 1945–1955* (Amherst: University of Massachusetts Press, 1981), 72f (6 Oct. 1955).

7 On the importance of this new edition, see Hermann Langbein, *Im Namen des*

deutschen Volkes: Zwischenbilanz der Prozesse wegen nationalsozialistischer Verbrechen (Vienna: Europa Verlag, 1963), 35.

8 The memorandum is reprinted in Walter Stahl (ed.), *Education for Democracy in West Germany: Achievements, Shortcomings, Prospects* (New York: Praeger, 1961), 265f. It was also published in *Die Welt* and the *Börsenblatt des deutschen Buchhandels*. It is also cited by Ulrich Brochhagen, *Nach Nürnberg: Vergangenheitsbewältigung und Westintegration in der Ära Adenauer* (Hamburg: Junius, 1994), 434 n. 70.

9 On the play, see Rosenfeld, "Popularization and Memory," 259 and 251–4. The statistics are after Brochhagen, cited above. The sharp rise in popularity was not limited to West Germany; the Dutch edition went through twenty printings from 1955 to 1958 (ibid., 258). The German paperback edition (Frankfurt: Fischer) had reached 2,355,000 copies in sixty-seven printings by August 1989 (262). Rosenfeld does not include the concurrent East German edition (E. Berlin: Union, 1955) in his statistics. The texts of contemporary US reviews and articles about the play are available at the *New York Times* web site: http://www.nytimes.com/books/97/10/26/reviews/971026.26leitert.html#1.

10 See H. G. van Dam, "Monument der Unmenschlichkeit: Wächst Gras darüber?," *Allgemeine Wochenzeitung der Juden in Deutschland*, 8 June 1956.

11 Erich Lüth, *Ein Hamburger schwimmt gegen den Strom* (Hamburg: C. Kayser, 1981), 109. See also Alex Sagan, "Examining Optimism: Anne Frank's Place in Postwar Culture," in Alex Grobman and Joel Fishman (eds.), *Anne Frank in Historical Perspective: A Teaching Guide for Secondary Schools* (Los Angeles: Martyrs Memorial and Museum, 1995), 55–66, 61.

An interesting sidenote on the impact of the play is how it prompted Nazi-hunter Simon Wiesenthal to discover the Gestapo man who had arrested the Franks. See Joseph Wechsberg (ed.), *The Murderers Among Us: The Simon Wiesenthal Memoirs* (New York: McGraw-Hill, 1967), 171–83.

12 See, e.g., Georg Zimmermann, "Die Einsamkeit brechen: Kinder fahren nach Bergen-Belsen / Wer hilft?," *Hamburger Abendblatt*, 20 Feb. 1957. See also "Wieder Pilgerfahrt der Jugend zu den Massengräbern von Bergen-Belsen," *Freie Presse Bielefeld*, 13 Jan. 1958. Rosenfeld, "Popularization and Memory," 262f, mentions the renaming of schools and the 1959 creation of an Anne Frank refugee haven in Wuppertal.

13 "Gedenkfeier in Bergen-Belsen," *Hannoveranische Allgemeine Zeitung*, 15 Apr. 1957.

14 "Demonstration für Menschenrechte: Fünfhundert junge Gewerkschafter fuhren nach Bergen-Belsen und gedachten der Opfer des Nazi-Terrors," *Freie Presse Bielefeld*, 3 June 1957.

15 "'Der Ungeist ist noch nicht vertilgt!' Die Gedenkstunde an den Gräbern von Bergen-Belsen," *WJD*, 18 Apr. 1958; see also *Stuttgarter Zeitung*, 14 Apr., *SZ*, and *Hannover Presse*, 20 Apr. 1958.

16 Seff Schmidt, "10.000 Jugendliche kamen nach Bergen-Belsen," *Westdeutsche Allgemeine* (Essen), 25 May 1959.

17 "Jugend in Belsen," *Frankfurter Allgemeine Zeitung*, 22 June 1959 (translation of a report from the *Manchester Guardian*).

18 See Rosenfeld, "Popularization and Memory," 266–9.

19 For this assessment, see Anette Insdorf, *Indelible Shadows: Film and the Holocaust* (Cambridge: Cambridge University Press, 2nd edn, 1986), 6f, 15; Ilan Avisar, *Screening the Holocaust: Cinema's Images of the Unimaginable* (Bloomington: Indiana University Press, 1988), 116–22. See also Rosenfeld, "Popularization and Memory," 252–4, and Sagan, "Examining Optimism."

20 Ernst Schnabel, *Anne Frank: Spur eines Kindes* (Frankfurt: Fischer, 1958; 1988: 165,000th copy printed); Ernst Schnabel, *Anne Frank: A Portrait in Courage*, trans. R. and C. Winston (New York: Harcourt, Brace and World, 1958). At the time of its publication Schnabel's book was serialized as a radio play (interview D. Hoffmann, 28 Apr. 1991).

21 Karl Korn, "Nacht und Nebel," *Frankfurter Allgemeine Zeitung*, 13 April 1956. For a general discussion of *Night and Fog*, see Walter Euchner, "Unterdrückte Vergangenheitsbewältigung: Motive der Filmpolitik in der Ära Adenauer," in Rainer Eisfeld and Ingo Müller (eds.), *Gegen Barbarei: Essays Robert Kempner zu Ehren* (Frankfurt: Athenäum, 1989), 346–59, 347f.

22 *Die Europäische Zeitung* (Bonn), 20 Nov. 1956.

23 *Die Zeit*, 7 March 1957.

24 Verband deutscher Studentenschaften (ed.), *Erziehungswesen und Judentum* (Munich: Ner Tamid, 1960), 134–9, cited after Stahl (ed.), *Education for Democracy*, 236.

25 Günter Moltmann, *Der Dokumentarfilm Nacht und Nebel* (Hamburg: Kuratorium für staatspolitische Bildung, 1957; Düsseldorf, 1960).

26 Helmut Hofer, "Einführung und geschichtlicher Rückblick," in Bayerischer Jugendring (ed.), *Lernort Dachau: Protokoll einer Fachtagung im Institut für Jugendarbeit des Bayerischen Jugendrings* (Munich: BJR, 1988), 66–9, 67.
    The cemetery was located on the Ungererstrasse. It is possible that a DP camp was located there. Prior to January 1948 the US army had a "stockade" in that street (Rinke, memorandum, 13 Jan. 1948, re Dienstfahrt nach I.- und A.-Lager Dachau, BayHsta, MSo 2061). In Sept. 1948 one of seventeen Dachau barracks given back to the Bavarian government by the US army was relocated to the Ungererstrasse (Wrba, report about the expansion of the settlement Dachau-Ost, ca. Dec. 1949, BayHsta, MArb, Abgabe 1979, 645). On 30 Apr. 1950 the Israelite Community in Munich held a commemorative ceremony there (unsigned memo to Preuss, BayHsta, Stk 113 625).

27 [Helmut Hofer], "Aktivitäten der DGB-Jugend Bayern zur Reichspogromnacht von 1952 bis 1988," 3pp. typescript, 1988, 2 (copy in DGB-Landesbezirk Bayern, Abt. Jugend). Hofer, "Einführung," 67, sets the ceremony in November 1953, but the later typescript explicitly corrects the anniversary date.

28 No reports were contained in any of the clippings collections, and a search of November issues of the *SZ* and the *MM/DN* prior to 1956 yielded no results. I found brief reports on most of these events in the December issues of the Bavarian Youth Ring's monthly magazine *Jugendnachrichten*.

29 "Wiederaufleben nationalistischer und militaristischer Jugendorganisationen," *Jugendnachrichten*, Oct. 1954. See also the responses in ibid., Dec. 1954, 1–4.

30 See *Verhandlungen* (25 Apr. 1956), vol. 3, 1969–75. In the detailed discussion, a number of media reports on neo-Nazi youth activities were mentioned (e.g. "Im alten Geist ungebrochen weiter," *Vorwärts*, 13 Apr. 1956).

31 The definitive work on post-World War II German nationalism notes no sharp breaks in youth activity during the 1950s, although there may have been a phase of consolidation ca. 1955. See Kurt Tauber, *Beyond Eagle and Swastika: German Nationalism since 1945* (Middletown, Conn.: Wesleyan University Press, 1967), vol. I, esp. charts preceding 393; also 412–28, 826–42. Incidents such as the government's support of a meeting of long-standing right-wing youth organizations in Oct. 1956 (421f) indicate that the "boom" suggested by contemporary reports was merely a change in the public perception of the groups.

32 "Gewerkschaftsjugend ehrt Widerstandskämpfer," *SZ* (Landkreisausgabe), 6 Nov. 1956. Ludwig Linsert from the executive committee of the DGB was the keynote speaker. I was not able to locate any additional information about this ceremony in Linsert's papers, which have not yet been cataloged (Archiv der sozialen Demokratie, Bonn).

33 "Jugend gedenkt der KZ-Opfer," *SZ* (main edition), 11 Nov. 1957; "Gewerkschaftsjugend gedachte der NS-Opfer: An der eindrucksvollen nächtlichen Feierstunde im Konzentrationslager Dachau nahmen viele prominente Politiker teil," *Stimmen der Arbeit aus Bayern*, 15 Nov. 1957 (DaA, H. Stöhr notebook). A photograph of the ceremony can be found in *Die Tat*, special edition, Jan./Feb. 1958.

34 "Erinnerung an die Kristallnacht," *Jugendnachrichten*, Nov. 1958; "Stark besuchte Gedenkfeiern in Dachau und Flossenbürg," ibid., Dec. 1958; "Jugend ehrt die Opfer," *Die Tat*, 22 Nov. 1958 (see also photographs in ibid., 15 Nov. 1958); "Gedenkfeier im Konzentrationslager," *SZ* (Landkreisausgabe), 11 Nov. 1958.

35 In addition to the reports in the preceding note, see the announcements in *Münchner Stadtanzeiger*, 7 Nov. 1958, and *SZ* (main edn), 8 Nov. 1958. The low attendance of 500 in Dachau does not necessarily reflect a decrease in interest among Bavarian teenagers, since 2,000 northern Bavarians went to Flossenbürg, where Heinrich Stöhr spoke. There were also competing events in Munich (e.g. for the White Rose resistance group). Trade union leader Ludwig Koch and Dachau survivor Nico Rost gave keynote speeches in Dachau.

36 Hans-Dieter Roos, "Dachau: Denkmal deutschen Vergessens," *Colloquium*, Sept. 1956, 6f, with editorial, 3.

37 *Colloquium*, Süddeutsche Redaktion, to CID, 14 Sept. 1956, DaA, OK.

38 "Bekenntnisfeier im ehemaligen KZ," *SZ* (Landkreisausgabe), 18 June 1957.

39 See Anne Bauer to Otto Kohlhofer, 7 June 1959, DaA, OK. The broadcast of 27 May 1959 was entitled "Wächst Gras darüber? Die deutsche Vergangenheit im Urteil junger Menschen."

40 See "Dachau: After 15 Years a Memorial in the German Terror Camp," *Daily Mail*, 30 Apr. 1960, 11.

41 See Ausschuss für kulturpolitische Fragen, "Antrag von Hoegner, Essl und Frakt. betr. Besichtigung der Denkstätten der KZ-Lager in Bayern," (Beilage 849), 11pp., BLA, and "Schülerfahrten zu KZ-Gedenkstätten," *SZ*, 13 May 1960.

42 *Verhandlungen* (31 May 1960), vol. 4/2, 1882 with Beilage 849.

43 See inquiry re Bavarian radio broadcast, "Zeitgeschichte in den bayerischen Volksschulen," *Verhandlungen* (29 June 1960), vol. 4/2, 2050.

44 "400 Lehrkräfte besichtigen das KZ / Weihbischof Neuhäusler zeigt Katholische Erziehergemeinschaft die Gedenkstätten," *MM/DN*, 8 Nov. 1960.

45 See "Sühne für die Untaten im KZ: Zu Fuß von München nach Dachau," *Abendzeitung*, 5 Aug. 1960; Ursula von Kardorff, "Sühne-Wallfahrt nach Dachau: Tausende von jungen Katholiken aus aller Welt bei der Einweihung der Todesangst-Christi-Kapelle," *SZ*, 6 Aug. 1960.

46 See "Feierstunde auf dem Leitenberg," *SZ*, 14 Nov. 1960.

47 Nicola Reichel, "Gedenkstunde zur Kristallnacht: Kundgebungen in Dachau und Flossenbürg / Fackeln und Kränze," *SZ*, 12 Nov. 1962, 16; Ursula Peters, "Gedenken an die Ermordung der Juden: Feiern im ehemaligen Konzentrationslager Dachau zum 25. Jahrestag der 'Kristallnacht,'" *SZ*, 11 Nov. 1963. According to "'Das Grauen darf nicht vergessen werden': Gedenken an den 9. November des Jahres 1938," *MM/DN*, 11 Nov. 1963, only 3,000 not 5,000 were in attendance. See also the mimeographed script of the skit by Meyer-Amery held by DaA.

48 The *Geschäftsbericht* of the DGB Landesausschuss, 1963, reported 6,000 at Dachau; the *Jugendnachrichten* of the BJR, no. 12 (1964), estimated 7,000. None of the many newspaper reports gave an attendance estimate for Dachau.

49 The planning for this event is well documented in two notebooks of documents organized by Hermann Kumpfmüller and held by the office of the BJR in Munich.

50 In November 1959 Minister Hundhammer gave the keynote speech, with Minister of Culture Schwalber, former Minister President Hoegner and former Minister of Justice Müller attending (*SZ*, 9 Nov. 1959), and in 1960 Pater Roth and Nico Rost spoke (*SZ*, 14 Nov. 1960). Then in November 1961 Xaver Senfft and Artur Bader of the Youth Ring spoke (*Mitteilungen der Lagergemeinschaft Dachau*, Dec. 1961); in 1962 Bader and CID president Guérisse, a Gaullist (*SZ*, 12 Nov. 1962); in 1963 a state pastor from Nuremberg, Karl-Heinz Neukamm, with a dramatic reading of a text by Meyer-Amery (*SZ*, 11 Nov. 1963); in 1964 trade unionist Ludwig Rosenberg and Munich Mayor Hans-Jochen Vogel (*SZ*, 9 Nov. 1964); in 1965 Youth Ring president Kumpfmüller and author Gerhard Schoenberner (*SZ*, 8 Nov. 1965).

51 See Ernst Nolte, *Die Deutschen und ihre Vergangenheiten* (Frankfurt: Propyläen, 1995), 104. Nolte's chapter on "Vergangenheitsbewältigung nach 1945" is fairly accurate. Nolte writes that the group published in the Stuttgart journal *Die Kultur*, 1 (Oct. 1952)–10 (Apr. 1962), that it was on friendly terms with the Frankfurt school, and that a number of pedagogues were "quite active" in the group. I found no other references to its activities.

52 Reinhard Henkys, *Die nationalsozialistischen Gewaltverbrechen: Geschichte und Gericht* (Stuttgart: Kreuz, 1964), 196f. The following summary is also after Henkys, who does not name his sources.

53 Ibid., 197; Langbein, *Im Namen des deutschen Volkes*, 36; Peter Steinbach, *Nationalsozialistische Gewaltverbrechen: Die Diskussion in der deutschen Öffentlichkeit nach 1945* (West Berlin: Colloquium, 1981), 46ff; Martin Broszat, "Siegerjustiz oder strafrechtliche 'Selbstreinigung': Aspekte der Vergangenheitsbewältigung der deutschen Justiz während der Besatzungszeit 1945–1949," *VfZ*, 29 (1981), 477–544, 541. See also Gert Kalow's essay "Aug in Auge mit unserer Geschichte," *FAZ*, 3 Dec. 1958, reprinted in Gert Kalow, *Hitler – das deutsche Trauma: Zur Kritik des politischen Bewusstseins* (Munich: Piper, 1967; 2nd edn, 1974), 7–29.

54 For a fine-grained description and excellent analysis of the activities of such task forces and their development over time, see Christopher Browning, *Ordinary Men:*

Reserve Police Battalion 101 and the Final Solution in Poland (New York: HarperCollins, 1992, rev. edn 1998).

55 The standard work on the task forces is Helmut Krausnick and Hans-Heinrich Wilhelm's *Truppe des Weltanschauungskrieges: die Einsatzgruppen der Sicherheitspolizei und des SD, 1938–1942* (Stuttgart: DVA, 1981). An *Einsatzkommando* such as Fischer-Schweder's was only one unit in an *Einsatzgruppe.*

56 In West Germany, judicial authorities are responsible only for investigating and prosecuting all crimes committed within their area of jurisdiction.

57 For practical reasons, the Zentrale Stelle der Landesjustizverwaltungen zur Aufklärung [Verfolgung] nationalsozialistischer Gewaltverbrechen was set up at Ludwigsburg near Stuttgart. The formation of the office had been decided upon at a meeting of the State Ministers of Justice and Judicial Senators in Bad Harzburg in October 1958. See Henkys, *Die nationalsozialistischen Gewaltverbrechen,* 197, 353.

58 The trial of Gustav Sorge and Wilhelm Schubert lasted from 13 Oct. 1958 to 6 Feb. 1959. See ibid., 55–8. The entire trial proceedings are published in Hendrik George Van Dam and Ralph Giordano (eds.), *KZ-Verbrechen vor deutschen Gerichten: Dokumente aus den Prozessen,* 2 vols. (Frankfurt: EVA, 1962, 1966), vol. I, 151–510.

59 Ralph Giordano, *Hier fliegen keine Schmetterlinge: Zwei Dokumentarfilme* (Hamburg: Kuratorium für Staatspolitische Bildung, 1961).

60 See Henkys, *Die nationalsozialistischen Gewaltverbrechen,* 197. A list of the exact dates and judgments of these trials can be found in Langbein, *Im Namen des deutschen Volkes,* 150–97.

61 See chapter 3, above. The 1974 docudrama *The Odessa File* provides a good illustration of how old-Nazi networks hindered the prosecution of brown-collar criminals in the early 1960s. Beate Klarsfeld documents the workings of an old-Nazi network in her *Wherever They May Be!* (New York: Vanguard, 1972), 36ff; and Frankfurt prosecutor Fritz Bauer tipped the Israeli secret service off about the whereabouts of Adolf Eichmann because he feared his own office would leak the information. See Gerhard Werle and Thomas Wandres, *Auschwitz vor Gericht: Völkermord und bundesdeutsche Strafjustiz: Eine Dokumentation des Auschwitz-Urteils* (Munich: Beck, 1995), 47f. Simon Wiesenthal devoted much of his life to tracing such networks: see his autobiography *The Murderers Among Us,* esp. 78–95 on Odessa, and 96–128 on Eichmann.

62 Henkys, *Die nationalsozialistischen Gewaltverbrechen,* 210–12, gives seven examples and mentions that "the list could be extended" not only by adding other main perpetrators, but by including a "great number" of police officer-witnesses who gave testimony at the various trials as well. See also Nationale Front des demokratischen Deutschlands (ed.), *Braunbuch: Kriegs- und Naziverbrechen in der Bundesrepublik: Staat, Wirtschaft, Armee, Justiz, Verwaltung, Wissenschaft* (E. Berlin: Staatsverlag der DDR, 2nd edn, 1965; 3rd edn, 1968).

63 See Ingo Müller, *Furchtbare Juristen: Die unbewältigte Vergangenheit unserer Justiz* (Munich: Kindler, 1987), 240–61; *Hitler's Justice: The Courts of the Third Reich* (Cambridge, Mass.: Harvard University Press, 1991); Barbara Just-Dahlmann and Herbert Dahlmann, *Die Gehilfen: NS-Verbrechen und die Justiz nach 1945* (Frankfurt: Athenäum, 1988); Bundesministerium der Justiz (ed.), *Im Namen des deutschen Volkes: Justiz und Nationalsozialismus, Katalog zur Ausstellung des Bundesministers der Justiz* (Cologne: Wissenschaft und Politik, 1989). Barbara

Dahlmann was a state prosecutor who translated Polish affidavits for the Ludwigsburg Central Office. She gave a number of public presentations on this subject in the early 1960s.

64 Henkys, *Die nationalsozialistischen Gewaltverbrechen*, 230f.

65 On the exhibition, see especially Michael Kohlstruck, "Das zweite Ende der Nachkriegszeit: Zur Veränderung der politischen Kultur um 1960," in Gary Schaal and Andreas Wöll (eds.), *Vergangenheitsbewältigung: Modelle der politischen und sozialen Integration in der bundesdeutschen Nachkriegsgeschichte* (Baden-Baden: Nomos, 1997), 113–27. In addition to this article based on the main organizer's private archive, see *Der Spiegel*, 13 Jan. and 17 Feb. 1960. The exhibition is also discussed by Klaus Bästlein, "'Nazi-Blutrichter als Stützen des Adenauer-Regimes': Die DDR-Kampagne gegen NS-Richter," in Helga Grabitz et al. (eds.), *Die Normalität des Verbrechens* (Berlin: Hentrich, 1994), 408–43, 415. See also the exhibition brochure: Wolfgang Koppel (ed.), *Ungesühnte Nazijustiz: Hundert Urteile klagen ihre Richter an* (Karlsruhe: Selbstverlag, 1960). See also Werner Bergmann, *Antisemitismus in öffentlichen Konflikten: Kollektives Lernen in der politischen Kultur der Bundesrepublik, 1949–1989* (Frankfurt: Campus, 1997), 259f.

66 My discussion follows the excellent summary by Steinbach, *Nationalsozialistische Gewaltverbrechen*, 54–68. The most important documentary works on these debates are Rolf Vogel (ed.), *Ein Weg aus der Vergangenheit: Eine Dokumentation zur Verjährungsfrage und zu den NS-Prozessen* (Frankfurt: Ullstein, 1969), and Germany (West) Bundestag (ed.), *Zur Verjährung nationalsozialistischer Verbrechen: Dokumentation der parlamentarischen Bewältigung des Problems 1960–1979*, 3 vols. (Bonn: Presse- und Informationszentrum, 1980).

67 In the following years the relevance of "following orders" was a hotly debated topic. See Henkys, *Die nationalsozialistischen Gewaltverbrechen*, 221–3, 265 n. 364; also H. Jäger, "Betrachtungen zum Eichmann-Prozeß," *Monatsschrift für Kriminologie und Strafrechtsreform*, no. 3/4 (1962), 7; Erwin Schüle, "Die Justiz der Bundesrepublik und die Sühne nationalsozialistischen Unrechts," *VfZ*, 9 (1961), 440–3; Erwin Schüle, "Die Zentrale der Landesjustizverwaltungen zur Aufklärung nationalsozialistischer Gewaltverbrechen in Ludwigsburg," *Juristenzeitung* (1962), 241–4; Erwin Schüle, "Die strafrechtliche Aufarbeitung des Verhaltens in totalitären Systemen – Der Eichmann-Prozess aus deutscher Sicht," in Karl Forster (ed.), *Möglichkeiten und Grenzen für die Bewältigung historischer und politischer Schuld in Strafprozessen* (Würzburg: Studien und Berichte der Katholischen Akademie in Bayern, Heft 19, 1962), 83ff.

68 FDP representative Bucher, cited after Steinbach, *Nationalsozialistische Gewaltverbrechen*, 55.

69 Bergmann, *Antisemitismus in öffentlichen Konflikten*, 282.

70 The publication of Ernst Nolte's comparative study, *Three Faces of Fascism: Action Française, Italian Fascism, National Socialism*, in 1963 marks the beginning of that discussion, which was continued by the New Left in several special issues of the Berlin journal *Das Argument* beginning in 1965. The original title of Nolte's book was *Der Faschismus in seiner Epoche* (Munich: Piper, 1963); the English translation was published in 1965. For an assessment of its significance, see Geoff Eley, "What Produces Fascism," in Eley, *From Unification to Nazism* (Boston: Allen and Unwin, 1986), 254–82, 255. On the significance of the fascism discussion in *Das Argument*,

see Ronald Fraser et al., *1968: A Student Generation in Revolt* (London: Chatto and Windus, 1988), 50.

For examples of an emerging functionalist school, see Martin Broszat, *Der Staat Hitlers* (Munich: dtv, 1969), and Karl Schleunes, *The Twisted Road to Auschwitz: Nazi Policy toward German Jews* (Urbana: University of Illinois Press, 1970).

71 Excellent discussions can be found in Bergmann, *Antisemitismus in öffentlichen Konflikten*, 235–50, and Brochhagen, *Nach Nürnberg*, 276–305.

The West German government published a "white book" on the incidents: Germany, Federal Government (ed.), *The Antisemitic and Nazi Incidents from 25 December 1959 until 28 January 1960* (Bonn, 1960); for another contemporary portrayal of the events, see Peter Schönbach, *Reaktionen auf die Antisemitische Welle im Winter 1959/1960* (Frankfurt: EVA, 1961) (Frankfurter Beiträge zur Soziologie, special issue 3).

72 On the role of East German agitators, see Bergmann, *Antisemitismus in öffentlichen Konflikten*, 245f, n. 151. Michael Wolffsohn, *Die Deutschland-Akte: Juden und Deutsche in Ost und West, Tatsachen und Legenden* (Munich: Ferenczy bei Bruckmann, 1995), 18–27, presumes stronger East German involvement but offers no proof.

73 Karl Borcherding, *Wege und Ziele politischer Bildung in Deutschland: Eine Materialsammlung zur Entwicklung der politischen Bildung in den Schulen 1871–1965* (Munich: Olzog, 1965), 85–9, reprints the 30 Jan. 1960 statement and the 11 Feb. resolution. Adenauer's speech can be found in the "white book": Federal Government (ed.), *The Antisemitic and Nazi Incidents*.

74 An extremely valuable resource for the study of this rising interest is the anthology Walter Stahl (ed.), *Education for Democracy in West Germany: Achievements – Shortcomings – Prospects* (New York: Praeger, 1961). This collection of translated articles was compiled by the Atlantik Brücke in Hamburg, a private organization promoting German–American understanding. It contains many references to contemporary events and newspaper articles, as well as translations of articles from the journal *Gesellschaft Staat, Erziehung (GSE)*, which was founded in 1956 and functioned as an important forum of debate on such issues. The anthology includes a translation of Adorno's celebrated essay "Was bedentet: Aufarbeitung der Vergangenheit?," for example, which was published in *GSE* (see n. 81, below).

For an excellent summary including the most recent research, see Bergmann, *Antisemitismus in öffentlichen Konflikten*, 261–6; also Peter Dudek, *"Der Rückblick auf die Vergangenheit wird sich nicht vermeiden lassen": Zur pädagogischen Verarbeitung des Nationalsozialismus in Deutschland, 1945–1990* (Opladen: Westdeutscher Verlag, 1995).

75 For a discussion of the effect of the antisemitic incidents on the West German educational establishment, see Klaus Köhle, "Die Vergangenheitsbewältigung – Geschichte eines Problems," in Raimund Baumgärtner, Helmut Beilner, and Klaus Köhle, *Das Dritte Reich* (Munich: Bosco, 1972), 9–30, 19f.

76 Borcherding, *Wege und Ziele*, 85–9, reprints the 30 Jan. 1960 statement. For an official report, see Karl Mielcke, *1917–1945 in den Geschichtsbüchern der Bundesrepublik* (Hannover: Niedersächsische Landeszentrale für politische Bildung, 1961), 58–68.

For one of the unofficial examinations, see Vereinigung der Verfolgten des Naziregimes (ed.), *Unbewältigte Vergangenheit und die Vordringlichkeit der*

Vermittlung eines objektiven Geschichtsbildes (Frankfurt: VVN, 1961), which collects numerous examples from the press, schoolbooks, and politicians' public pronouncements that illustrate the prior neglect of the topic.

On 29 June 1960 Bavarian State Radio broadcast a report critical of the treatment of the Nazi period in school textbooks. See inquiry re Bavarian radio broadcast "Zeitgeschichte in den bayerischen Volksschulen," *Verhandlungen des Bayerischen Landtags*, fourth period vol. 2, 2050.

77 Hannah Vogt, *Schuld oder Verhängnis: 12 Fragen an Deutschlands jüngste Vergangenheit* (Frankfurt: Diesterweg, 1961); an English translation by Herbert Strauss was published by Oxford University Press in 1964. Vogt was one of the editors of *GSE*.

Also in 1961, Christian Geissler produced an excellent anthology on the Nazi period: Christian Geissler (ed.), *Das Dritte Reich mit seiner Vorgeschichte, 1918–1945* (Ebenhausen: Langewiesche-Brandt, 1961).

Two guides for history teachers published that same year should also be mentioned here: Gerhart Binder, *Lebendige Zeitgeschichte, 1890–1945: Handbuch und Methodik* (Munich: Kaiser, 1961), and Hans-Joachim Winkler, *Legenden um Hitler* (W. Berlin: Colloquium, 1961) (in the series "Zur Politik und Zeitgeschichte," ed. by Landeszentrale für politische Bildung and Otto-Suhr-Institut der FU Berlin, no. 7).

78 Some textbooks of the immediate postwar period that were in use until ca. 1950 had included detailed treatments of the concentration camps. See Peter Meyers, "Vom 'Antifaschismus' zur 'Tendenzwende': Ein Überblick über die Behandlung des Nationalsozialismus in der historisch-politischen Bildung seit 1945," in Bundeszentrale für politische Bildung (ed.), *Der Nationalsozialismus als didaktisches Problem* (Bonn: Bundeszentrale, 1980), 43–63, 51f.

79 In the 1964 introduction to the English edition of Vogt's textbook, Gordon Craig noted that the antisemitic incidents of 1959–60 were the direct inspiration for the book, which sold 400,000 copies in the first two years. See Vogt, *Burden of Guilt*, xv.

80 The importance of this term, which can also mean "coming to terms with the past," has been discussed at length since the 1980s. For a contemporary assessment, see Hans Wenke, "'Bewältigung der Vergangenheit' und 'Aufarbeitung der Geschichte': Zwei Schlagwörter, kritisch beleuchtet," *Geschichte in Wissenschaft und Unterricht*, 11 (1960), 65–70. I have found early references that the term was coined by Federal President Theodor Heuss, or at a 1953 conference at the Evangelische Akademie in the Haus am Kleinen Wannsee in Berlin, but I have not been able to confirm either one.

81 Theodor Adorno, "Was bedeutet: Aufarbeitung der Vergangenheit," *Gesellschaft, Staat Erziehung*, 5:1 (1960), 3ff; more accessible in Theodor Adorno, *Eingriffe: Neun kritische Modelle* (Frankfurt: Suhrkamp, 1963), 125–46; or Theodor Adorno, *Gesammelte Schriften* (Frankfurt: Suhrkamp, 1970), vol. X, pt. 2, 555–72, with a new postscript, 816f. It has been translated into English as "What does 'Digesting the Past' Mean?" in Stahl (ed.), *Education for Democracy*, 87–101, and as "What Does Coming to Terms with the Past Mean?" in Geoffrey Hartmann (ed.), *Bitburg in Moral and Political Perspective* (Bloomington: Indiana University Press, 1986), 114–29. I prefer the translation "working through" because it is closer to the original German and reflects Adorno's emphasis on an open-ended process.

82 On *Bewältigung* and mastery, see Peter Hofstätter, "Bewältigte Vergangenheit?" *Die Zeit*, no. 24 (14 June 1963), 9. See also Gerhard Schoenberner, "Was heisst Bewältigung der Vergangenheit?" *Die Zeit*, no. 28 (9 Aug. 1963).

83 See Horst Schallenberger, "Zur Darstellung der Schoah im deutschen Schulbuch der Gegenwart," *Tribüne*, 17:67 (1978), 32–58, 36f. A 1959 study revealed that "books" and "parents" were named by young people as sources of knowledge of contemporary history more often than "school." See Kurt Fackiner, "Jugend, Schule, Nationalsozialismus," *Frankfurter Hefte*, 14 (1959), 549–60, 552f and table VI. (See also his *GSE* essay reprinted in Stahl (ed.), *Education for Democracy*, 64–9.) Since the early 1960s, television has also played a major role: see Georg Feil, *Zeitgeschichte im Deutschen Fernsehen: Analyse von Fernsehsendungen mit historischen Themen, 1957–1967* (Osnabrück: Fromm, 1974). This fascinating study includes tables listing all historical television broadcasts from 1958 to 1967 grouped by topic (162–76), and the percentage of viewers for the shows about National Socialist topics (47ff).

84 Rolf Schörken, "National Socialism in the Eyes of 15 and 16 Year-Old High School Pupils," in Stahl (ed.), *Education for Democracy*, 60 (translated from *GSE*, 1959). Schörken listed illustrated magazines and parents as the boys' primary sources of information (57ff).

85 See Heinrich Bodensiek, "Zeitgeschichte in Bilddokumenten," *Neue Politische Literatur*, 12 (1967), 483–93. This is a review of the book publication that resulted from the TV series discussed below.

On two other important films shown on television, Radio Free Berlin's *The Best Years of our Lives*, and Erwin Leiser's *Mein Kampf* (1960), see Grace Richards Conant, "German Textbooks and the Nazi Past," *Saturday Review*, 46 (20 July 1963), 52f.

86 Heinz Huber and Arthur Mueller (eds.), *Das Dritte Reich: Seine Geschichte in Texten, Bildern und Dokumenten*, 2 vols. (Munich: K. Desch, 1964). The following quotation is taken from 11f.

87 See Sabine Reichel, *What Did You Do in the War, Daddy? Growing up German* (New York: Hill and Wang, 1989), 33–43.

88 Michael Schornstheimer, *Bombenstimmung und Katzenjammer: Vergangenheitsbewältigung: Quick und Stern in den 50er Jahren* (Cologne: Pahl-Rugenstein, 1989), 20f. See also his completely revised *Die leuchtenden Augen der Frontsoldaten: Nationalsozialismus und Krieg in den Illustriertenromanen der fünfziger Jahre* (Berlin: Metropol, 1995).

89 I would like to note that another detailed examination of illustrated magazines, Ullrich Kröger, "Die Ahndung von NS-Verbrechen vor westdeutschen Gerichten und ihre Rezeption in der deutschen Öffentlichkeit 1958 bis 1965 unter besonderer Berücksichtigung von 'Spiegel,' 'Stern,' 'Zeit,'" (Ph.D. thesis, Hamburg, 1973), has a good empirical base but is very apologetic in its interpretations. (This contradicts the assessment by Steinbach, *Nationalsozialistische Gewaltverbrechen*.)

90 Ludwig Friedeburg and Peter Hübner, *Das Geschichtsbild der Jugend* (Munich: Juventa, 1964), 51. This study is an important source on the topic for Peter Meyers, "Vom 'Antifaschismus' zur 'Tendenzwende'" (1980), 59, and Sybille Hübner-Funk, "Hitler's Grandchildren in the Shadow of the Past: The Burden of a Difficult Heritage," *Tel Aviver Jahrbuch für deutsche Geschichte*, 19 (1990), 103–15, 107. See

also Peter Hübner's "Zur Bedeutung zeitgeschichtlichen Wissens für das politische Verhalten von Jugendlichen," *GSE*, 10:3 (1965), 254–63.

91 Walter Jaide, "Die Jugend und der Nationalsozialismus," *Die neue Gesellschaft*, 12:3 (1965), 723–31, 730.

92 For instance, when the 1964 study was republished in 1970, its authors wrote: "Although the younger generation's political sensibilities and readiness to become politically involved have remarkably expanded, its ahistorical relationship to the past has not changed." See Friedeburg and Hübner, *Geschichtsbild der Jugend* (Munich: Juventa, 2nd edn, 1970), 5.

93 For an overview of the trial and its effects, see Steinbach, *Nationalsozialistische Gewaltverbrechen*, 51–3, and Tom Segev, *The Seventh Million: The Israelis and the Holocaust* (New York: Hill and Wang, 1993), 323–66. For a contemporary summary, see Hans Holthusen, "Hannah Arendt, Eichmann und die Kritiker," *VfZ*, 13:2 (Apr. 1965), 178–90.

94 Steinbach, *Nationalsozialistische Gewaltverbrechen*, 53.

95 For a comprehensive bibliography organized by country, see Randolph Braham, *The Eichmann Case: A Source Book* (New York: World Federation of Hungarian Jews, 1969). To name just a few of the German publications: *Eichmann und die Eichmänner: Dokumentarische Hinweise auf den Personenkreis der Helfer und Helfershelfer bei der "Endlösung"* (Ludwigsburg: Schromm, 1961); Siegfried Einstein, *Eichmann: Chefbuchhalter des Todes* (Frankfurt: Röderberg, 1961); Robert Kempner, *Eichmann und Komplizen* (Stuttgart/Zurich: EVA, 1961); Robert Pendorf, *Mörder und Ermordete: Eichmann und die Judenpolitik des Dritten Reiches* (Hamburg: Rütten und Loening, 1961); Albert Wucher, *Eichmanns gab es viele: Ein Dokumentarbericht über die Endlösung der Judenfrage* (Munich: Knaur, 1961).

96 "Eichmann-Ausstellung in München," *Tat*, 18 Feb. 1961. At the same time, the exhibition "Unrepentant Nazi Justice" was shown in the Munich gallery where the White Rose student resistance group had met.

97 Hans Lamm (ed.), *Der Eichmann-Prozess in der deutschen öffentlichen Meinung: Eine Dokumentensammlung* (Frankfurt: Ner-Tamid, 1961); Regine Schmidt and Egon Becker, *Reaktionen auf politische Vorgänge: Drei Meinungsstudien* (Frankfurt: EVA, 1967), 113ff; Council for Jews from Germany (ed.), *Nach dem Eichmann Prozess: Zu einer Kontroverse über die Haltung der Juden* (Jerusalem/New York: Council for Jews from Germany, 1963). See also Henkys, *Die nationalsozialistischen Gewaltverbrechen*, 370 (#123, 125), and Gerhard Schoenberner, "Der Prozess Eichmann und die Folgen," *Frankfurter Hefte*, 16 (July 1961), 433ff.

98 Akiva Deutsch, *The Eichmann Trial in the Eyes of Israeli Youngsters: Opinions, Attitudes and Impact* (Ramat-Gan: Bar-Ilan University Press, 1974).

99 American Jewish Committee (ed.), *The Eichmann Case in the American Press* (New York: Institute for Human Relations Press, 1962); Pierre Papadatos, *The Eichmann Trial* (New York: Praeger, 1964). For a more personal example of the US reception, see Kay Boyle, *Breaking the Silence: Why a Mother Tells Her Son about the Nazi Era* (New York: Institute of Human Relations Press, 1962).

100 Günther Anders, *Wir Eichmannsöhne: Offener Brief an Klaus Eichmann* (Munich: Beck, 1964). See also Heinar Kipphardt, *Bruder Eichmann* (Reinbek: Rowohlt, 1983).

101 Rolf Hochhuth, *Der Stellvertreter* (Hamburg: Rowohlt, [February] 1963). The publication information is calculated from the March 1979 edition, which brought the

total to 496,000 copies. The play was translated into English by Robert Macdonald, *The Representative* (London: Methuen, 1963), and Richard and Clara Winston, *The Deputy* (New York: Grove, 1964).

102 On the public discussion of Hochhuth's play, see Fritz Raddatz (ed.), *Summa iniuria oder Durfte der Papst Schweigen? Hochhuths "Stellvertreter" in der öffentlichen Kritik* (Hamburg: Rowohlt, [September] 1963), and Eric Bentley, *The Storm over the Deputy* (New York: Grove, 1964).

103 To name just some: Walter Adolph, *Verfälschte Geschichte: Antwort an Rolf Hochhuth* (Berlin: Morus, 1963); Desmond Fisher, *Pope Pius XII and the Jews, an Answer to Hochhuth's Play, Der Stellvertreter (The Deputy)* (Glen Rock, N.J.: Paulist, 1963); Joachim Günther, *Der Steit um Hochhuths "Stellvertreter"* (Basel: Basilius Presse, 1963); Hans Rudolf Tschopp-Brunner, *Kritische Bemerkungen zum "Stellvertreter": Theater und Verantwortung* (Basel: H. R. Tschopp-Brunner, 1963); Josef-Matthias Gorgen, *Pius XII, Katholische Kirche, und Hochhuths "Stellvertreter"* (Buxheim: Martin Verlag, 1964); and Dolores and Earl Schmidt, *The Deputy Reader: Studies in Moral Responsibility* (Chicago: Scott Foresman, 1965).

104 See Henkys, *Nationalsozialistische Gewaltverbrechen*, 197. A list of the exact dates and rulings of these trials can be found in Langbein, *Im Namen des deutschen Volkes*, 150–97.

105 On the importance of the Auschwitz trial, see Ulrich Schneider (ed.), *Auschwitz, ein Prozess: Geschichte, Fragen, Wirkungen* (Cologne: Papyrossa, 1994), 112 (Reinhard Kühnl) and 151 (Peter Gingold). The trial itself is documented in Hermann Langbein (ed.), *Der Auschwitz-Prozess: Eine Dokumentation in zwei Bänden* (Frankfurt: EVA, 1965). The Frankfurt Fritz Bauer Institute has begun a large research project on the trials and their reception. For a report about a first scholarly conference, see *Newsletter: Informationen des Fritz Bauer Instituts*, 8:17 (fall 1999), 8–18.

106 See Werle and Wandres, *Auschwitz vor Gericht*, 46–54; also Fritz Bauer, "Im Namen des Volkes: Die strafrechtliche Bewältigung der Vergangenheit," in Helmut Hammerschmidt (ed.), *Zwanzig Jahre danach: Eine deutsche Bilanz, 1945–1965* (Munich: Desch, 1965), 301–14, 305.

107 On Bauer's biography, see Heinz Düx, "Singuläre Erscheinung von historischem Rang: Fritz Bauer," in Schneider (ed.), *Auschwitz, ein Prozess*, 74–81.

108 Bauer, "Im Namen," 302. For a detailed personal description of the popular response to the trials, see Horst Krüger, *Das zerbrochene Haus: Eine Jugend in Deutschland* (Munich: Rütten and Loening, 1966), 237–84.

109 See Eugen Kogon, "'Auschwitz und eine menschliche Zukunft,' Eröffnungsrede zur Ausstellung von Dokumenten von und über Auschwitz in der Frankfurter Paulskirche, Busstag [November] 1964," *Frankfurter Hefte*, 19 (1964), 830–8.

110 Karl Jaspers, *Wohin treibt die Bundesrepublik? Tatsachen – Chancen – Gefahren* (Munich: Piper, 1966), 47–123; in English: *The Future of Germany* (Chicago: University of Chicago Press, 1967).

111 Ulrich Sonnemann, *Das Land der unbegrenzten Zumutbarkeiten: Deutsche Reflexionen* (Hamburg: Rowohlt, 1963), esp. 44ff.

112 Kurt Sontheimer, "Der Antihistorismus des gegenwärtigen Zeitalters," *Neue Rundschau* (1964), 611–31.

113 Martin Walser, "Unser Auschwitz," *Kursbuch*, 1 (1965), 189–200, and *Stuttgarter Zeitung*, 20 March 1965.

114 Peter Weiss, *Die Ermittlung* (Frankfurt: Suhrkamp, 1965; Reinbek: Rowohlt, 1969), *The Inquiry* (New York: Random House, 1966). On this oratorium see Andreas Huyssen, "The Politics of Identification: 'Holocaust' and West German Drama," *New German Critique*, no. 19 (winter 1980), 117–36, 131f.

115 Bernd Naumann, *Auschwitz: Bericht über die Strafsache gegen Mulka u.a. vor dem Schwurgericht Frankfurt am Main* (Frankfurt: Athenäum, 1965; reprinted 1995); also in English with a preface by Hannah Arendt (New York: Praeger, 1966).

116 The following portrayal follows Steinbach, *Nationalsozialistische Gewaltverbrechen*, 56–68. See also the documentary collections: Presse- und Informationszentrum des Bundestags (ed.), *Zur Verjährung nationalsozialistischer Verbrechen: Dokumentation der parlamentarischen Bewältigung des Problems 1960–1979* (Bonn: Presseamt, 1980), and Rolf Vogel (ed.), *Ein Weg aus der Vergangenheit: Eine Dokumentation zur Verjährungsfrage* (Frankfurt/Berlin: Ullstein, 1969). For another English-language discussion, see Jeffrey Herf, *Divided Memory: The Nazi Past* (Cambridge, Mass.: Harvard University Press, 1997), 337–42.

117 Karl Jaspers, "Für Völkermord gibt es keine Verjährung," first published in *Der Spiegel* in 1965, then in Jaspers, *Wohin treibt?*, 17–45, and Jaspers, *Die Schuldfrage* (Munich: Piper, 1979), 97–123.

118 Simon Wiesenthal (ed.), *Verjährung? 200 Persönlichkeiten des öffentlichen Lebens sagen nein: Eine Dokumentation* (Frankfurt: EVA, 1965).

119 Behind-the-scenes manipulations reveal that this consequence was well known, albeit not publicly. See the discussion in Ulrich Herbert, *Best: Biographische Studien über Radikalismus, Weltanschauung und Vernunft, 1903–1989* (Bonn: Dietz, 1996).

120 Steinbach, *Nationalsozialistische Gewaltverbrechen*, 67.

121 See, for instance, Leon Jick, "The Holocaust: Its Uses and Abuses," *Brandeis Review* (spring 1986), 25–31, 27f: "The situation began to change in the early 1960s, slowly at first but with increasing intensity." See also Michael Marrus, *The Holocaust in History* (Hanover, N.H./London: University Press of New England, 1987), 2: "Since the beginning of the 1960s, we have seen extensive historical investigation of the Holocaust."

122 For a listing of the relevant titles see the catalog of German dissertations: Alfred Milatz (ed.), *Hochschulschriften zur neueren deutschen Geschichte: Eine Bibliographie* (Bonn: Kommission für Geschichte, 1956). An example would be: Gerhard Griem, "Der Tatbestand des Verbrechens gegen die Menschlichkeit in der Rechtssprechung der Nürnberger Gerichtshöfe unter Hinweis auf die hiervon abweichende Rechtssprechung deutscher Gerichte," (Diss. Jur., Munich, 1951).

123 An overview of the publications from the immediate postwar years can be found in Franz Ahrens, *Widerstandsliteratur: Ein Querschnitt durch die Literatur über die Verfolgungen und den Widerstand im Dritten Reich* (Hamburg: VVN, 1948).

The best bibliographic guides to the literature available in the 1950s are: Günther Weisenborn (ed.), *Der lautlose Aufstand: Bericht über die Widerstandsbewegung des deutschen Volkes 1933–1945* (Hamburg: Rowohlt, 1953); Heinz Brüdigam, *Wahrheit und Fälschung: Das Dritte Reich und seine Gegner in der Literatur seit 1945: Versuch eines kritischen Überblicks* (Frankfurt: Röderberg, 1959), esp. 30–5; and Henkys, *Die nationalsozialistischen Gewaltverbrechen*, 355–71. For more recent bibliographic discussions, see Falk Pingel, *Die nationalsozialistischen Konzentrationslager* (Hamburg: Hoffmann und Campe, 1978), 318–28; Gudrun Schwarz, *Die nationalsozialistischen Lager* (Frankfurt/New York: Campus, 1990), 8–11; Johannes Tuchel,

Konzentrationslager: Organisationsgeschichte und Funktion der "Inspektion der Konzentrationslager," 1934–1938 (Boppard: Harold Boldt, 1991), 15–27; Ulrich Herbert, "Der Holocaust in der Geschichtsschreibung der Bundesrepublik Deutschland," in Ulrich Herbert and Olaf Groehler, *Zweierlei Bewältigung* (Hamburg: Ergebnisse, 1992), 67–86. One of the most comprehensive bibliographic listings to date was published by the Central Commission for the Investigation of German Crimes in Poland, *Biuletyn Głównej Komisji Badania Zbrodni Hitlerowskich w Polsce,* vol. XXX (Cracow: Wydawn Ministerstwa Sprawiedliwosci, 1981), which contains ca. 3,500 titles.

124 See Helmut Peitsch, *Deutschlands Gedächtnis an seine dunkelste Zeit: Zur Funktion der Autobiographik in den Westzonen Deutschlands und den Westsektoren von Berlin, 1945 bis 1949* (Berlin: Sigma, 1990); for an English summary see Peitsch, "Autobiographical Writing and Vergangenheitsbewältigung (Mastering the Past)," *German History,* 7 (1989), 47–70.

125 Eugen Kogon, *Der SS-Staat: Das System der deutschen Konzentrationslager* (Frankfurt: EVA, 1958; Munich: Heyne, 1974; 13th edn, 1983); *The Theory and Practice of Hell: The German Concentration Camps and the System Behind Them* (New York: Farrar, Straus and Co., 1950; new editions 1960, 1973, 1998).

126 Günther Weisenborn (ed.), *Der lautlose Aufstand: Bericht uber die Widerstandsbewegung des deutschen Volkes 1933–1945* (Hamburg: Rowohlt, 1953; Frankfurt: Röderberg, 1981).

127 Hans-Günther Adler, *Theresienstadt 1941 bis 1945: Das Antlitz einer Zwangsgemeinschaft: Geschichte, Soziologie, Psychologie* (Tübingen: Mohr, 1955; rev. edn, 1960).

128 Léon Poliakov and Josef Wulf, *Das Dritte Reich und die Juden: Dokumente und Aufsätze* (Berlin: Arani, 1955). This book was based on Poliakov's *Bréviaire de Haine: La IIIe Reich et les Juifs* (Paris: Calman-Levy, 1951); it was published in English as *Harvest of Hate* (Syracuse, N.Y.: Syracuse University Press, 1954; Westport, Conn.: Greenwood, 1971; New York: Holocaust Library, 1979). German-Jewish commentator Henryk Broder recalled that Wulf's books had a small readership in the 1950s; see his *Erbarmen mit den Deutschen* (Hamburg: Hoffmann und Campe, 1993), 75. Broder (with Frans van der Meulen) also made a film about Wulf.

129 Edward, Lord Russell of Liverpool, *Geissel der Menschheit: Kurze Geschichte der Nazikriegsverbrechen* (Frankfurt: Röderberg; E. Berlin: Volk und Welt, 1956); *The Scourge of the Swastika: A Short History of Nazi War Crimes* (London; New York: Philosophical Library, 1954). This book was also published in Yiddish in 1956 (Tel Aviv: Gluyot), and a companion volume about Japan was published soon afterwards: *The Knights of Bushido: The Shocking History of Japanese War Atrocities* (New York: Dutton, 1958).

130 Gerald Reitlinger, *Die Endlösung: Hitlers Versuch der Ausrottung der Juden Europas, 1939–1945* (West Berlin: Colloquium, 1956; 4th edn, 1961; 5th edn, 1979). The original English edition was published in 1953 under the title: *The Final Solution: The Attempt to Exterminate the Jews of Europe, 1939–1945* (New York: Beechhurst/London: Vallentine, 1953; New York: Yoseloff, 1968). See also Gerald Reitlinger's *Die SS: Tragödie einer deutschen Epoche* (Munich: Desch, 1957); *The SS: Alibi of a Nation, 1922–1945* (New York: Viking, 1957; New York: Da Capo, 1989).

131 Léon Poliakov and Josef Wulf, *Das Dritte Reich und seine Diener: Dokumente* (Berlin: Arani, 1956). The same authors published *Das Dritte Reich und seine*

Denker in 1959, and Wulf wrote *Das Dritte Reich und seine Vollstrecker: Die Liquidation von 500,000 Juden im Ghetto Warschau* in 1961 (all Berlin: Arani). A shorter version of Wulf's book on the Warsaw Ghetto was published by the Bundeszentrale für Heimatdienst in 1958.

132 Walther Hofer, *Der Nationalsozialismus: Dokumente 1933–1945* (Frankfurt: Fischer, 1957; 40th edn, 1990).

133 There are some early documentary and historical works written by Germans within the academic system, but the authors were either closely connected with former persecutees, or themselves Jews. The most salient examples include Fred Mielke and Alexander Mitscherlich, *Das Diktat der Menschenverachtung* (Heidelberg: Lambert Schneider, 1947), and the only dissertation completed in the 1950s dealing with brown-collar crimes, Hans Lamm, "Über die Entwicklung des deutschen Judentums im Dritten Reich," (Ph.D. thesis, Erlangen, 1951). Lamm, later the editor of the *Allgemeine Wochenzeitung der Juden in Deutschland* (Düsseldorf), was also a friend of West German President Theodor Heuss. See Hans Lamm (ed.), *Theodor Heuss an und über Juden: Aus Schriften und Reden 1906–1963* (Düsseldorf: Econ, 1964).

134 Hermann Mau and Helmut Krausnick, *Deutsche Geschichte der jüngsten Vergangenheit, 1933–1945* (Tübingen: Wunderlich / Stuttgart: Metzler, 1956). This overview was originally published in Peter Rassow (ed.), *Deutsche Geschichte im Überblick* (Stuttgart: Metzler, 1953). Mau was killed in an automobile accident before finishing the manuscript; the concluding sections on *Verfolgung, Widerstand,* and *Zusammenbruch* were written by Krausnick (see postscript to the 1956 ed., 201–3). An English translation by E. and A. Wilson was published several years later: *German History 1933–1945: An Assessment by German Historians* (London: Wolff, 1959).

Another work by a professional German historian dealing with the National Socialist persecution of the Jews, Hermann Graml's *Der 9. November 1938: Reichskristallnacht* (Bonn: Bundeszentrale für Heimatdienst, 1953), was published somewhat earlier, but it is not a work of academic historiography, and was intended to fulfill a more concretely political purpose: to win popular support for the West Germany–Israel Restitution Treaty, which was concluded in that year. See also Graml's *Reichskristallnacht: Antisemitismus und Judenverfolgung im Dritten Reich* (Munich: dtv, 1988).

135 Compare Mau and Krausnick, *Deutsche Geschichte*, 50–69 (Röhm *putsch*), 160–71 ("Verfolgung"), and 172–88 (20 July 1944).

136 Research since the 1980s has documented the extensive participation of the German army in the brown-collar crimes. See p. 555 n. 32, below.

137 Quoted from the trial brief of the Ulm Task Force trial, 671, in Van Dam and Giordano (eds.), *KZ-Verbrechen*, vol. II, 62.

138 Wolfgang Scheffler, *Judenverfolgung im Dritten Reich, 1933–1945* (Berlin: Colloquium, 1960, 1964).

139 Martin Broszat, *Der Nationalsozialismus: Weltanschauung, Programm und Wirklichkeit* (Stuttgart: DVA, 1960). Broszat published *Nationalsozialistische Polenpolitik, 1939–1945* (Stuttgart: DVA, 1961) a year later.

140 Karl Dietrich Bracher, Wolfgang Sauer, and Gerhard Schulz, *Die nationalsozialistische Machtergreifung; Studien zur Errichtung des totalitären Herrschaftssystems in Deutschland 1933/34* (Cologne: Westdeutscher, 1960, 1962).

141 For Broszat's own assessment, see Martin Broszat, "'Holocaust' und die Geschichtswissenschaft,"*VfZ*, 27 (1979), 285–93; reprinted in *Nach Hitler: Der schwierige Umgang mit unserer Geschichte* (Munich: Oldenbourg, 1987), 271–86, esp. 282ff.

142 For a general discussion, see Hans-Peter Rouette, "Die Widerstandslegende: Produktion und Funktion der Legende vom Widerstand im Kontext der gesell-schaftlichen Auseinandersetzungen in Deutschland nach dem Zweiten Weltkrieg" (Ph.D. dissertation, Free University of Berlin, 1983), esp. chapter 3. For a good over-view of the literature at that time, see Helmut Esters (ed.), *Stand und Problematik der Erforschung des Widerstandes gegen den Nationalsozialismus* (Bad Godesberg: Friedrich-Ebert-Stiftung, 1965).

143 Eberhard Kolb, *Bergen-Belsen: Geschichte des "Aufenthaltslagers" 1943–1945* (Hanover:Verlag für Literatur und Zeitgeschehen, 1962; reprinted Göttingen, 1986).

144 *Studien zur Geschichte der Konzentrationslager* (Stuttgart: DVA, 1970) (Schriftenreihe der *VfZ*, 21), with essays about Hamburg-Fuhlsbüttel (Henning Timpke), Neuen-gamme (Werner Johe), Mauthausen (Gisela Rabitsch), Ravensbrück (Ino Arndt), Bergen-Belsen (Eberhard Kolb), and Dora-Mittelbau (Manfred Bornemann and Martin Broszat). The manuscript upon which Heinrich Smikalla's presentation about Dachau was based was too long to be included in the volume (see 8); it has, in fact, never been published. The essay about Mauthausen was based on that author's unpublished dissertation (University of Vienna); Broszat was able to use a number of East German publications about Dora for the essay on that camp.

145 Hans Rothfels, "Augenzeugenbericht zu den Massenvergasungen (Quellenkritische Edition des Gerstein-Berichts)," *VfZ*, 1 (1953), 188–94, and "Denkschrift Himmlers 'über die Behandlung der Fremdvölkischen im Osten' vom Mai 1940," *VfZ*, 5 (1957), 194–8. The Gerstein report with an essay by Helmut Krausnick, "Zur Zahl der jüdi-schen Opfer des Nationalsozialismus," was reprinted in 1956 as the ninth publica-tion of the Bundeszentrale für Heimatdienst (Bonn); it was first published as a document in the Nuremberg trials. Martin Broszat's annotated edition of Auschwitz commander Rudolf Höss's autobiographical writings (Stuttgart: DVA, 1958; paper-back Munich: dtv, 1963; 10th edn, 1985; London: Weidenfeld and Nicolson, 1959) should also be mentioned in this context, as should a 1960 essay by Hans-Günther Adler about "Selbstverwaltung und Widerstand in den Konzentrationslagern der SS," *VfZ*, 8 (1960), 221–36.

146 The Institute for Contemporary History was founded in 1947 for reasons of politi-cal expedience; one of its main purposes was to legitimate historiographically the separation between German conservative elites and supporters of the Nazi regime. See John Gimbel, "The Origins of the 'Institut für Zeitgeschichte': Scholarship, Politics and the American Occupation, 1945–1949", *American Historical Review*, 70 (Oct. 1964), 714–31. Members of the institute did not agree with this judgment; see Helmut Krausnick, "Zur Arbeit des Instituts für Zeitgeschichte," *Geschichte in Wissenschaft und Unterricht*, 19 (1968), 90–6, and Hellmuth Auerbach, "Die Gründung des Instituts für Zeitgeschichte," *VfZ*, 18 (1970), 529–57.

For a contemporary assessment of the institute's establishment, see Paul Kluke, "Das Institut für Zeitgeschichte in München," *Schweizerische Beiträge für allge-meine Geschichte*, 12 (1954), 238–44. The institute was originally called "Deutsches Institut für die Geschichte der nationalsozialistischen Zeit."

147 *Gutachten des Instituts für Zeitgeschichte* (Munich: Selbstverlag, 1958); a second volume was published in 1966 (Stuttgart: DVA).

148 Hans Buchheim, "Die SS – das Herrschaftsinstrument," Martin Broszat, "Konzentrationslager," Hans-Adolf Jacobsen, "Kommissarbefehl," Helmut Krausnick, "Judenverfolgung," in *Anatomie des SS-Staates*, 2 vols. (Olten: Walter, 1965; Munich: dtv, 1967; London: Collins, 1968).

149 The fact that these books were reprinted so often indicates that they were not superseded by new research for about twenty years. The paperback edition of the two volumes was published for the sixth time in 1994 (50,000 total copies); the fourth edition of vol. I was published in 1984 (39,000 copies), and vol. II for the third time in 1982 (33,000 total copies).

8 Catholics celebrate at Dachau

1 For the data on the priests see Günther Kimmel, "Das Konzentrationslager Dachau: Eine Studie zu den nationalsozialistischen Gewaltverbrechen," in *Bayern in der NS-Zeit* (Munich: Oldenbourg, 1979), 375f. Kimmel's main sources are a manuscript by former camp record-keeper Domagala, and Eugen Weiler, *Die Geistlichen in Dachau sowie in anderen Konzentrationslagern und in Gefängnissen*, vol. I (Mödling: Missionsdruckerei St. Gabriel, 1971).

2 Emmerich Hornich, untitled report, *Stimmen aus Dachau*, spring 1970, 16. Hornich says that he was present at several meetings between Pies, Pfanzelt, and Patton. In the first discussion between Pies and Pfanzelt, Pies suggested a monastery to be called "Eternal Worship"; Pfanzelt wanted to construct a monastery at the entrance to the SS camp from the city, where "Kennedy Square" is today.

3 This was point no. 7 in excerpt from the minutes of Dachau city council, 27 July 1945, BayHsta, JS01. At that time the official military exchange rate was RM10 = \$1.

4 "Wallfahrtsort Dachau?," *Münchner Zeitung*, 28 July 1945. The news was reported by the rector of a Jesuit collegium in Maastricht, Dachau survivor Pater von Gestel. Faulhaber's negotiations are also mentioned in *Stimmen aus Dachau*, Aug. 1963, in a report about the laying of the cornerstone of a convent in Dachau on 28 Apr. 1963.

5 Carl Hupfer, "Die Weihe des Dachauer Sühneklosters," *SZ*, 23 Nov. 1964. The quotation was attributed to Cardinal Faulhaber by his successor Cardinal Döpfner in a speech at the dedication of the convent mentioned in the preceding note. Döpfner may have had access to notes preserved in Faulhaber's papers. Sigmund Benker, the archivist of the archbishopric of Munich and Freising, told me that he was not able to locate any such records concerning the monastery project (letter of 28 Feb. 1989). The original reads: "aus der Stätte gottloser menschlicher Verirrung eine Stätte des Gebets und der Sühne zu machen zur Erbauung und Aneiferung aller Lagerbesucher und zum Frieden der Welt."

6 According to Hornich, untitled report.

7 See *Reallexikon zur deutschen Kunstgeschichte*, vol. IV, article "Doppelkapelle"; H. Buschow, "Studien über die Entwicklung der Krypta im deutschen Sprachgebiet" (Ph.D. dissertation, Würzburg, 1934). On the Catholic cult use of relics in general, see Josef Braun, *Die Reliquiare des christlichen Kultes und ihre Entwicklung* (Freiburg: Herder, 1940); M. Förster, *Zur Geschichte des Reliquienkultes in*

Altengland (Sitzungsberichte der Bayrischen Akademie der Wissenschaften, Philosophisch-Historische Abteilung, no. 8, 1943).

8 See Otto Färber, "Erlösung von Dachau," *Schwäbische Landeszeitung*, 13 Nov. 1945, with a picture of the structure. Färber also mentions and illustrates a crucifixion scene painted on one of the barracks by a Belgian former inmate.

An article, "Une visite à Dachau: Théâtre des crimes Nazis," in *Le Patriote Illustré*, published after the judgments of the first Nuremburg trial were passed in Oct. 1946, also depicts the catafalque structure. The accompanying caption claims that the scaffolding stems from the "former camp gallows." As far as I know, no formal gallows was used in KZ Dachau; prisoners were usually hanged in a courtyard adjacent to the tract of individual cells or from the crematory rafters. The article contains a number of factual errors and distortions tending towards a more sensational portrayal, so the information about the scaffolding is not reliable. Copy in DaA, map drawer.

9 The church was dedicated on 28 Dec. 1945. See *Amtsblatt für Stadt und Landkreis Dachau*, 30 Jan. 1946, and Detlef Hoffmann, *Das Gedächtnis der Dinge: KZ-Relikte und KZ-Denkmäler, 1945–1995* (Frankfurt: Campus, 1998), 43.

10 Färber, "Erlösung von Dachau," mentions that the church was under construction in Nov. 1945. A watercolor by the architect is held by the DaA.

The benediction by Faulhaber is mentioned by Leonhard Roth, "Wie steht es jetzt mit unserem KZ Dachau?," *Stimmen aus Dachau*, Oct. 1959, and Michael Höck: "'Richtigstellung und Ergänzung,'" *MM/DN*, 13 Feb. 1975.

11 On the reuse of a barrack see Färber, "Erlösung von Dachau." A detailed description of the church can be found in "The Way Back," *Time*, 21 Apr. 1947.

12 Memo "Übergabe des Interniertenlagers Dachau von den Amerikanern," 15 Oct. 1947, BayHsta, MSo 2060.

13 Report by the "Kulturabteilung der I.- und A.lagers Dachau über den Besuch des Dichters Carl Zuckmayer und Herren der Tagespresse," 29 Feb. 1948, BayHsta, MSo 2061.

14 Memo from Office of MG Supervisor, Ernest E. Jones, OMGBy Camp Supervisor re gate 5, 3 Mar. 1948, BayHsta, MSo 2061.

15 See monthly report for Aug. 1948, 30 Aug. 1948, BayHsta, MSo 2063.

16 Presentation by Kurt Petreck (Angestellter beim Regierungsbeauftragten für das Flüchtlingswesen, Obb.) at a press conference in the "Wohnsiedlung Dachau-Ost," 31 Jan. 1950, BayHsta, MArb 79/71. That annex also included the west wing of the service building, the tract of cells behind the service building, and the gatehouse.

17 The barracks of the refugee settlement had a different numbering system than the "blocks" of the KZ. Thus barrack 32 was actually former block 27 of the KZ punishment detail. See Foit, "Lageplan Wohnlager Dachau-Augustenfeld," 22 Oct. 1948, BayHsta, MArb; reprinted in Hoffmann, *Gedächtnis der Dinge*, 43. Roth set up the new church in barrack 32 in Nov. 1949. See "40 Jahre Gemeinde Hl. Kreuz – 25 Jahre Pfarrkirche Hl. Kreuz," *MM/DN* special edition, 8 Apr. 1989.

18 Pfarrkuratie Heilig Kreuz, Dachau (ed.), *Heilig Kreuz, Dachau: Zur Weihe der Kirche, 12. April 1964* (revised edn, n.d.), 6ff. See also "40 Jahre Gemeinde Hl. Kreuz – 25 Jahre Pfarrkirche Hl. Kreuz," *MM/DN*, special edition, 8 Apr. 1989.

19 When the roll-call square was cleared in the early 1960s the church was moved to Dachauer Str. in Ludwigsfeld, where it still stands today.

20 See Roth to Minister President Hoegner, 9 Apr. 1956, BayHsta, Stk 113 629; Kurat

Roth, letter to the editor, *Abendzeitung*, 11 Apr. 1956; Kohlhofer to CID, 12 Apr. 1956, DaA; Oskar Müller to Roth, 13 Apr. 1956, DDW, OM; Ursula von Kardorff, "Lager Dachau – Elf Jahre danach," *SZ*, 13 Apr. 1956.

21 At a meeting with the Finance Ministry in Apr. 1958 the CID suggested that the two churches (a Protestant counterpart had been erected in 1951, see below) be left standing with explanatory signs. See "Lager Dachau wird Mahnmal: Internationales Komitee verhandelt mit dem bayerischen Finanzministerium," *SZ*, 23 Apr. 1958.

22 A blueprint by Vander Auvera dated 7 Aug. 1958 (DaA, OK) designates the church as "à détruire."

23 *CID Informationen*, no. 10, 17 Dec. 1959, copy in FStHH, HS 13-4-4-2.

24 Manzenreiter, "Niederschrift über das Ergebnis der Besprechung am 9.3.62 im Bayer. Staatsministerium der Finanzen betr. die Gestaltung der Gedenkstätte in Dachau," 9 Mar. 1962, FstHH, HS 13–4–4–2. Neuhäusler presided over the session, which was attended by the architect of the new Catholic chapel, representatives of the German Protestant Church, the Israelite Community, the CID, the Ministry of Culture, and the Ministry of Finance. See also the report about the meeting in *Stimmen aus Dachau*, July 1962.

25 The church still stood in April 1964: see Oberbaurat Schelling/Schlösserver-waltung, blueprint of the memorial site, 20 Apr. 1964, DaA, OK. In Dec. 1964 Hans Schwarz reported that the roll-call square was being bulldozed at that time. See circular to Dachauer Kameraden, Dec. 1964, FstHH, HS 13–4–4–3.

26 *Stimmen*, March 1959.

27 *CID Informationen*, no. 10, 17 Dec. 1959, copy in FstHH, HS 13-4-4-2.

28 Even Roth was acutely aware of the difference in importance between the KZ chapel and the postwar churches. When Austrian survivors requested that Neuhäusler read a pontifical mass for them in the camp during a pilgrimage in June 1958, Roth told Neuhäusler that the SS church would be more adequate in size, but that it was not a "place of the KZ," so that his church in the former punishment barrack 27 might be more suitable. See A. Hyross to Neuhäusler, 21 May 1958, and Roth to Neuhäusler, 2 June 1958, AEMF, Johannes Neuhäusler papers.

29 "Mit der Königin des Friedens in eine gemeinsame Zukunft: Gedächtniskapelle ita-lienischer Freiheitskämpfer auf dem Leitenberg wurde eingeweiht," *Münchner Katholische Kirchenzeitung*, 11 Aug. 1963.
   The organizer of the dedication ceremony in 1963 mentioned that the "initiator" of the chapel was the president of the Italian Petroleum Company, Dr. Mattei, who had since died in an accident. See A. Voltolini to Schwalber, 10 July 1963, BayHsta, JS25.

30 KNA report, "Papst Pius stiftet Kelch für Dachauer," *SZ*, 14 Feb. 1957. The chalice was presented to the president of the Dachau committee by the archbishop of Verona.

31 This rhetorical question was rather absurd, since the baroque style had originated in Rome, where Bavarian masters had gone to study it. "'Campo Santo'-Stil im Dachauer Land: Italienische Votivkirche soll gebaut werden – sie passt nicht in die Gegend," *MM/DN*, 25 June 1958. The editorial includes a picture of the model.

32 Ibid.

33 See "Italiener gedenken ihrer KZ-Toten: Feier an der Kapelle auf dem Leitenberg – Urkunde eingemauert," *MM/DN*, 9 Aug. 1960.

34 I have not been able to confirm this relatively high figure. Liliana Picciotto Fargion, "Italien," in Wolfgang Benz (ed.), *Dimensionen des Völkermords* (Munich: Oldenbourg, 1991), 199–229, 216, estimates that 7,500 Italian Jews were murdered in Germany.

35 "Mit der Königin des Friedens in eine gemeinsame Zukunft: Gedächtniskapelle italienischer Freiheitskämpfer auf dem Leitenberg wurde eingeweiht," *Münchner Katholische Kirchenzeitung,* 11 Aug. 1963.

36 Wilhelm Maschner, "So geschehen in Dachau: Eine Weihestunde auf dem Totenhügel, der es am Rande an Würde mangelte," *Die Welt,* 2 Aug. 1963.

37 Nikola Reichel, "Worte der Versöhnung in Dachau: Italiens Staatspräsident Segni und Bundespräsident Lübke bei der Feier auf dem Leitenberg," *SZ,* 1 Aug. 1963, 17.

38 "Vierzehn Stationen bis zur Kapelle: Der Kreuzweg zum Leitenberg steht kurz vor der Vollendung," *MM/DN,* 3 Sept. 1962. These stations were an integral part of the votive chapel project, whose planned dedication was postponed from 9 Sept. (the former Day of the Victims of Fascism, and the day the KZ priests met in 1950 and 1955) to 29 Sept. 1962 because the way of the cross was not yet complete.

39 See the reprint of a newspaper article about Neuhäusler's eightieth birthday in *Stimmen von Dachau: Mitteilungen der KZ-Priestergemeinschaft,* winter 1967–8.

40 On Neuhäusler's relationship to and opinion of Pacelli, see Johannes Neuhäusler, "Karmel Heilig Blut Dachau," *Zeitschrift für Politik,* 10 (Oct. 1963), 257–62. On Pacelli himself, see Gitta Sereny, *Into that Darkness: An Examination of Conscience* (New York: Vintage, 1983 [1974]), 277–84.

41 Johannes Neuhäusler, *Kreuz und Hakenkreuz: Der Kampf des Nationalsozialismus gegen die katholische Kirche und der kirchliche Widerstand* (Munich: Katholische Kirche Bayerns, 2nd edn, 1946). Later he wrote *Saat des Bosen: Kirchenkampf im Dritten Reich* (Munich: Manz, 1964).

42 See Office of Military Government, War Crimes Branch, records relating to post-trial activities, 1945–57, file Neuhäusler, NARA, RG 338, 29/42/2, box 11.

43 Quoted by Hans-Ulrich Engel, "Dachau, eine Stadt lebt mit einem Vorurteil," *Westdeutscher Rundfunk,* 1 Nov. 1968, DaA.

44 The original brochure was entitled *So war es in Dachau;* under the title *Wie war das im KZ Dachau? Ein Versuch, der Wahrheit näherzukommen* the brochure has been printed in numerous editions in four languages (over 150,000 total copies by 1964).

45 See *Stimmen,* March 1959. The article notes that the project of creating a religious memorial site was not pursued because "we had the impression that locally serious barriers were raised."

For documentation of the 1950 and 1955 congresses, see Pe., "Gedenkfeier im Lager Dachau," *SZ,* 5 Dec. 1950; "Ehemalige Häftlingsgeistliche ehren tote KZ-Kameraden," *NZ,* 5 Sept. 1950; "Von Anfang an Gegner von Unfreiheit und Gewalt: KZ-Priester sehen sich nach zehn Jahren wieder – Kardinal Wendel erstmals in Dachau," *MM/DN,* 12 Sept. 1955; "Gegen die Schwätzer und Schwärmer von der 'Menschlichkeit,'" *Dachauer Anzeiger,* 13 Sept. 1955; *Stimmen,* Dec. 1955 (this was the first issue of *Stimmen* since Dec. 1948). The only other large meeting of the over 500 members of the KZ-Priestergemeinschaft during that period that I could document was in June 1952, on the fortieth anniversary of *Blockvater* Canon Reinhold Friedrichs' ordination. See "KZ-Priester trafen sich," *Welt,* 6 June 1952.

46 Curate Roth, "Kapelle ehrt Italiener als Nation," *MM/DN,* 23 Dec. 1958.

47 Roth to Oskar Müller, 3 March 1960, DDW, OM.

48 See *Stimmen*, Apr. 1960; Wilhelm Maschner, "Im KZ Dachau wohnen auch heute noch Menschen / Weihbischof Neuhäusler will 225000 Mark für den Bau einer Erinnerungsstätte sammeln," *Die Welt*, 24 May 1960, 1. Cheshire, who by that time had established twenty-eight "Cheshire Foundations," and his group spent a night praying in one of the Dachau barracks. Before they left Munich, they expressed their disappointment at the condition of the camp to Neuhäusler. On the visit, see "Priesterbaracke wird freigemacht: Grössere Wallfahrtsgruppen aus England und Frankreich angemeldet," *MM*, 27 Aug. 1959; "Abwurf der Atombombe über Hiroshima beobachtet: Wallfahrten in das ehemalige KZ Dachau sollen eine ständige Einrichtung werden," *MM*, 4 Sept. 1959. The German sources often refer to Cheshire as "Ryder Cheshire," mistaking his wife's name, Sue Ryder, for his surname.

49 "Komitee pflegt KZ-Gedenkstätten: Feierstunde mit Minister Hundhammer in Dachau," *SZ*, 9 Nov. 1959. About 1,000 young people attended the ceremony; they expressed their desire to be responsible for the care of the sixty-five Bavarian KZ gravesites.

50 See Ursula Peters, "Ein Mahnmal gegen den Terror / Weihbischof Johannes Neuhäusler besichtigt Dachauer Baustelle / Steine aus der Isar," *SZ*, 25 May 1960, 12; "Gaskammer ist nie fertig geworden / Weihbischof Neuhäusler über das KZ Dachau – Sühnekapelle entsteht," *MM*, 24 May 1960. Neuhäusler was referring to an article in the *Melbourne Herald*, 31 Mar. 1960. See Johannes Neuhäusler, *What was it like in the Concentration Camp at Dachau?* (Munich: Manz, 1960), 10th edn, 68. (The date "March 3" referring to the Melbourne article is a printing error.)

51 See Kurt Schade, "Ein Konzentrationslager mahnt: Dachau ist noch nicht vergessen," *Mann in der Zeit*, 8 July 1960.

52 "Spendenaufruf," AEMF, Neuhäusler papers. The text of this call was published, *inter alia*, in "Schwer enttäuscht vom Zustand des KZ Dachau: Weihbischof Dr. Johannes Neuhäusler zur Errichtung eines Sühnemals," *MM/DN*, 14 May 1960.

   In a similar vein a committee of leading Dachau citizens that had been formed to support the fund drive announced: "Germany and the world will watch attentively to see to what extent Dachau itself will make its contribution to this . . . memorial site." See ibid. and "Kapelle als Sühnedenkmal," *SZ* (Landkreisausgabe), 16 May 1960.

53 In spite of its hagiographic tendencies, the best general overview of Roth's life is Hans-Günter Richardi, "Leonhard Roth," in Richardi et al. (eds.), *Lebensläufe: Schicksale von Menschen, die im KZ Dachau waren* (Dachau: Verein Zum Beispiel Dachau, 1990; Dachauer Dokumente, vol. II), 39–46. Additional information was obtained from the clippings files on Roth in the DaA and the Press and Information Office of the German Federal Government, from interview Otto Kohlhofer, 15 July 1987, and from the papers of Oskar Müller (DDW) and Josef Schwalber (BayHsta). Of special importance is a collection of documents prepared by Friedrich Haugg in the Müller papers. See also the five-part series in *SZ/DN*, 16–28 Oct. 1992.

54 Roth's homosexuality is, in my opinion, the more probable reason. The circumstances of Roth's arrest and the fact of his extradition, his masochistic self-denial, the Church's postwar refusal to give him a post outside the camp, and later confirmation of his homosexual orientation all strongly indicate that Roth may

have been doing self-imposed penance for a self-recognized sin. In Dec. 1946 Roth told a newspaper reporter that he was arrested because he refused to serve in the German army (*SZ*, 28 Dec. 1946); in 1947 he told *Time* magazine that he was arrested as an anti-Nazi (*Time*, 21 Apr. 1947).

55 See "The Way Back," *Time*, 21 Apr. 1947 (interview with Roth), and Karl Kirsch, unpublished memoirs, description of Roth's efforts during the Dachau trials, DaA.

56 "Ehemalige KZ/Häftlinge antworten Zauner: Heftige Angriffe Pater Roths – Versammlung im überfüllten Birgmannsaal endete mit Tumult," *MM/DN*, 21 Mar. 1960; "Empörung über Pater Roth: 'Er hat das Andenken an Prälat Pfanzelt verunglimpft,'" and "Zauner reagiert nicht auf anonyme Einladungen: Eine Antwort an die ehemaligen Dachauer KZ-Häftlinge," *MM/DN*, 22 Mar. 1960.

57 Roth to Müller, 21 Mar. and 23 Mar. 1960, DDW, OM; see also Roth to Alfred [Haag], 26 Mar. 1960, DaA, Roth notebook. On Roth's dismissal, see N. Reichel, "Kurat Roth von Dachau abberufen: Der Seelsorger des Barackenlagers in Urlaub / Generalvikar Fuchs stellt richtig," *SZ*, 16 Apr. 1960.

58 Immediately after Roth's discharge a large local following including several prominent Dachauers protested at the Vicar's office. See Karl Stankiewitz, "Der 'Engel von Dachau' soll gehen: Pater Roth in Zwangsurlaub – Barackeninsassen des ehemaligen Konzentrationslagers fordern Rückkehr," *Der Tag* (CDU), 28 Apr. 1960. Egon Herrmann, refugee settlement leader Willi Tietz, and Capt. Jones of the US army post were among those who protested Roth's dismissal.

59 Johannes Neuhäusler, "Rundbrief (streng vertraulich) an Schriftleitungen der Katholischen Kirchenzeitungen, betr. Kurat Roth, Dachau," DaA, Roth notebook.

60 Nikola Reichel, "Häftlingspater Roth tödlich verunglückt," *SZ*, 18 Aug. 1960.

61 On Roth's later reputation see "Pater Roth an Prälat Pfanzelt: Zwei Briefe aus dem Jahr 1955," *MM/DN*, 24 Mar. 1960; Paul Brandt, "Zum 15. Todestag von Pater Roth . . . Der Kurat von Hl. Kreuz in Dachau noch nicht vergessen," *MM/DN*, 23 Aug. 1975; Ferdl Miedaner, "Selbstmord auf dem Zwölferkopf: Über die späte Ehrung des Dachauhäftlings Pater Roth," *Österreichische Zeitung*, 31 Dec. 1986. The latter report was prompted by a city council decision to name a street after Roth. See also Richardi, "Leonhard Roth," passim.

62 See "Dachaus Silbermöwe ist ein KZ-Priester: Katholiken der Stadt sammeln für Erzbischof Adam Kozlowiecki," *MM/DN*, 22 Mar. 1960. The program was called "Action Silver Gull" because the first missionary who was thus financed was a Native American with that name.

63 See "Schwer enttäuscht vom Zustand des KZ Dachau: Weihbischof Dr. Johannes Neuhäusler zur Errichtung eines Sühnemals," *MM/DN*, 14 May 1960.

64 See "Einige Betriebe fehlen noch / Nicht alle fühlten sich vom Aufruf des Landrats angesprochen," *MM/DN*, 4 June 1960.

65 See photograph of Zauner, the reporter, and the interpreter in front of the Agony of Christ construction site, *MM/DN*, 28 Apr. 1960. The article itself was: "Dachau / After 15 Years a Memorial in the German Terror Camp," *Daily Mail*, 30 Apr. 1960, 11.

66 Rudolf Rentsch, "Die Kräfte des Lichts," *MM/DN*, 11 June 1960.

67 "Gedächtniskapelle für KZ-Opfer: Bundeswehr übernimmt Transport von Steinen aus der Isar," *SZ*, 12 Apr. 1960.

The original design had called for the natural stone *Nagelfluh* as a construction material, but to reduce the cost of the chapel from the original projection of

DM700,000, the free river stones were selected instead. See *Stimmen aus Dachau,* no. 12 (spring 1970), 12f.

68 "Zuschuss für Dachauer Sühnemal," *SZ,* 19 May 1960.

69 *SZ,* 28 May 1960; "KZ-Ehrenmal Dachau," *Kirche und Leben: Aus dem Bistum Münster,* 19 July 1960. A Westphalian nursery added a truckload of decorative bushes to the shipment.

70 "Erfolgreiche Sammlung," *SZ* (Fernausgabe), 23 July 1960.

71 "Ein KZ-Denkmal aus dem Jahre 1945: Oberste Baubehörde entzog der Stadt die Zuständigkeit – Jetzt vergessen," *MM/DN,* 30 July 1960.

72 The *Stimmen aus Dachau* of the KZ priests estimated 30–40,000 (Nov. 1960); the *MM* 50,000; the *Tölzer Kurier* 50,000; the *SZ* 60,000.

73 The texts of the speeches were published in *Statio Orbis* (Munich: Kösel, 1961, 1962), vol. II, 164–69; a description of the celebration in vol. I, pp. 55f. Excerpts from Friedrichs' introduction and Hengsbach's sermon can be found in Neuhäusler, *Wie war das im KZ Dachau?,* 72f. The speeches were also distributed as mimeographed press releases, some of which are contained in LEA, file d.kz-g. Neuhäusler's papers in AEMF contain a large selection of newspaper reports about the celebration. There are also several Bavarian government files on the event in BayHsta, Stk 114 080 (Kultusministerium): "Eucharistischer Weltkongress München 1960," Bd. 1, Az. 4713.

74 "Noch 10000 Wagen hätten Platz gehabt / KZ-Gedächtnisfeier vorzüglich organisiert – 'Dachauer freundliche Leute'," *MM/DN,* 8 Aug. 1960. See also "'Vorzügliche Organisation'," *SZ* (Landkreis), 9 Aug. 1960.

The initial local newspaper reports on the Saturday after the Friday event focused on the number of participants and the names of the prominent visitors. See "Sühnekapelle am 'Tag des Kreuzes' geweiht / Über 50000 Gläubige aus aller Welt im ehemaligen KZ – Häftlinge berichten," *MM/DN,* 6 Aug. 1960.

75 See, for example, "Zuschuss für Dachauer Sühnemal," *SZ,* 19 May 1960.

76 There is a substantial literature by and about Schacht. See his *Abrechnung mit Hitler* (Hamburg: Rowohlt, 1948), and *1933: Wie eine Demokratie stirbt* (Düsseldorf: Econ, 1968). For an example of the critical contemporary reception of *Abrechnung* see Wolfgang Harich in *Die Weltbühne,* 3 (1948), 1253–8. About his dismissal see "Dr. Schacht Dismissed," and "The Schacht Affair," *Times* (London), 21 Jan. and 23 Jan. 1939. Schacht's file in the Berlin Document Center contains critical assessments of him by high Nazi personalities.

77 See "Schacht gegen Besuche im Konzentrationslager," *Stuttgarter Zeitung,* 14 May 1960. The article was reprinted in the CID *Bulletin Information,* no. 12 (June 1960).

The story came to the attention of the press after the incident was discussed in a meeting of the Commission for Cultural Politics of the Bavarian parliament on 12 May. The minutes of that meeting, at which the official endorsement of school visits to Dachau was discussed, are printed in *Ausschuss für kulturpolitische Fragen,* BLA, Beilage 849: "Antrag von Hoegner, Essl und Fraktion betr. Besichtigung der Denkstätten der KZ-Lager in Bayern," 12 May 1960.

78 See, e.g., "Gedächtniskapelle für 30000 KZ-Opfer in Dachau / Weihe durch Bischof Dr. Johannes Neuhäusler in Gegenwart von 70000 Menschen – Sühnewallfahrt der Jugend," [*MM?*], 6 Aug. 1960 (AEMF, Neuhäusler papers); "Kapelle im ehemaligen KZ Dachau," *Neue Zeit,* 6 Aug. 1960.

79 See Herbert Liebmann, "Gedächtnisfeier in Dachau," *SZ*, 13 Aug. 1960, who suggested that it would have been better if Schacht had participated as a private person, and Dr. Hjalmar Schacht, Reichsbankpräsident a.D., Düsseldorf, letter to the editor, *SZ*, 19 Aug. 1960.

80 "Nachträgliche Kritik," *SZ*, 19 Aug. 1960; "Personalien," *Der Spiegel*, 24 Aug. 1960, 62. See also Valentin Schwan, "Die Konzentrationslager waren staatlich," *SZ*, 10 Sept. 1960, for a rebuttal of Schacht's apologetics. Both the KZ priests and the West German camp association were also critical of Schacht's attendance, as was the Bavarian Youth Ring. See *Stimmen*, Nov. 1960; *Mitteilungen LGD*, Sept. 1960; "Feierstunde auf dem Leitenberg," *SZ*, 14 Nov. 1960.

81 "Das sind die Weisen, die durch Irrtum zur Wahrheit reisen / die bei dem Irrtum verharren, das sind die Narren." *Spiegel*, 7 Sept. 1960, 79.

82 See *SZ*, 23 May 1960.

83 Schwarz, memo re memorial sites in Dachau, 18 Jan. 1962, LEA. Schwarz reports that at a meeting in the camp, architect Wiedemann showed an overall plan with a model, whereby Neuhäusler suggested that "the barracks area be landscaped as a grove and the [Protestant and Jewish] chapels be erected in the barracks area." Otto Kohlhofer protested vigorously against Neuhäusler's plan.

84 Nikola Reichel, "Sühnekloster in Dachau: Ehemaliges Konzentrationslager soll zur Stätte des Gebets von Karmelitinnen werden," *SZ*, 21 Mar. 1963; *Stimmen*, Aug. 1963.

85 S*timmen*, Aug. 1963.

86 The quotations from Neuhäusler's brochure are cited by Reichel, "Sühnekloster in Dachau", and Nikola Reichel, "Stätte des Grauens – dem Gebet geweiht: Am Sonntag wird der Grundstein des Sühneklosters Heilig Blut in Dachau gelegt," *SZ*, 27 Apr. 1963.

87 The sermon is printed as Johannes Neuhäusler, "Karmel Heilig Blut Dachau," *Zeitschrift für Politik*, 10 (Oct. 1963), 257–62.

88 This and the following quotes are taken from Nikola Reichel, "Sühne am Berg der deutschen Schuld / Der Wortlaut der Urkunde," *SZ*, 29 Apr. 1963.

89 See "Erster Spatenstich für Sühnekloster," *SZ*, 27 Aug. 1963, and Gerhard Wolfrum, "Ein Kloster zur Sühne: Karmel im ehemaligen Konzentrationslager Dachau ist im Rohbau fertig," *SZ*, 3 July 1964.

90 Carl Hupfer, "Die Weihe des Dachauer Sühneklosters: Kardinal Döpfner hält eine Messe / Bauarbeiten dauerten 15 Monate / Museum im Wachtturm," *SZ*, 23 Nov. 1964.

91 See Carol Rittner and John Roth (eds.), *Memory Offended: The Auschwitz Convent Controversy* (New York: Praeger, 1991). For contemporary reports, see Iwona Irwin-Zarecka, *Neutralizing Memory: The Jew in Contemporary Poland* (New Brunswick: Transaction, 1989), 154–6; Wladzslaw Bartoszewski, *The Convent at Auschwitz* (New York: G. Braziller, 1991), 7; "Das Kloster in Auschwitz bleibt umstritten," *FR*, 3 June 1989; Barbara Just-Dahlmann, "Der wirkliche Hintergrund der jüdischen Proteste," *FR*, 26 June 1989, 15.

92 The Pope's call, during his 7 June 1979 visit, for a beacon of piety amid the evil of Auschwitz-Birkenau is also cited as a reason for the Carmelites' project. See Debórah Dwork and Robert Jan van Pelt, *Auschwitz, 1270 to the Present* (New York: Norton, 1996), 369.

93 See ibid., 370.

94 Kohlhofer to CID, 8 July 1964, DaA, OK.

95 See *Stimmen,* Easter 1966, and Söhngen to Striffler, 8 Feb. 1966, EZB.

9 The survivors negotiate a memorial site

1 Protocol of the founding meeting of the Dachau Arbeitsgemeinschaft on 28 Jan. 1950, 3 Feb. 1950, DDW, OM. On meetings of the group since May 1947, see VVN to Hans Schwarz, 12 Mar. 1951, FStHH, HS 13–4–4–3.

   For a more detailed treatment of the Dachau survivors' early organizational efforts, see Harold Marcuse, *Nazi Crimes and Identity: Collective Memories of the Former Dachau Concentration Camp, 1945–1990* (Ann Arbor: University Microfilms, 1992), 287ff.

2 See Alfred Klein/Arbeitsgemeinschaft Dachau (Goethestr. 64) to Kultusminister Dr. Schwalber, 29 May 1953, BayHsta, JS, with a printed call to attend the ceremony. A poster calling attention to the event is held in the poster collection, DaA. See also mimeographed circular Hans Schwarz to comrades, 30 May 1953, HS 13–4–4–3. The international announcement of the "pilgrimage" was made in the first issue of the German journal of the FIR. See the moving article by Walter Vielhauer, "Internationales Pilgertreffen in Dachau," *Der Widerstandskämpfer,* 1/1 (Apr.–May 1953), 22, 24.

3 See Alain Joubert, "Dachau: Bericht vom Internationalen Treffen der ehemaligen Häftlinge des Lagers," *Der Widerstandskämpfer,* 1/2 (June–July 1953), 26f. A twenty-page protocol of the meeting in Dachau castle was printed as a special issue of the *Dachauer Stimmen* that month. An original is in DDW, notebook newsletter of the Dachau Association; a copy has been deposited at the DaA.

4 For instance, there was a meeting in Antwerp on 27 Sept. 1953. See *L'Union Belge,* no. 29 (Oct./Nov./Dec. 1953); copy in DDW, Walter Vielhauer papers 19, and *Der Widerstandskämpfer,* 1/3 (Aug.–Sept. 1953), 32.

5 See interview Kohlhofer, 15 July 1987, and "Einig wie in Dachau! Bericht über die Zusammenkunft der 'Dachauer,'" *Die Tat,* 1 Jan. 1955. In Kohlhofer's papers one notebook begins with a typed copy of that resolution, and contains letters pertaining to the practical organization of the congress. See, e.g., Kohlhofer to Comité International de Dachau, 28 Feb. 1955, DaA. The following information is taken from various documents in this notebook.

6 See Heinz Koch, *Nationale Mahn- und Gedenkstätte Buchenwald: Geschichte ihrer Entstehung* (Weimar-Buchenwald: NMG Buchenwald, 1988), 42, and Gitta Günther, *Buchenwald* (Weimar: Weimarer Schriften, no. 9, 1983), 88f; also my interview with Otto Kohlhofer, 15 July 1987.

7 See protocol of a meeting of the Internationale Lagergemeinschaft Dachau, 17 Feb. 1955, DaA. Information about the preparations for the Landesrat's celebration can be found in BayHsta, Stk 112 120. See also the undated printed letter from Kohlhofer and Maislinger to comrades with program of 8 May 1955, DDW, OM.

8 The text of Hoegner's speech on 24 Apr. 1955 is in BayHsta, Stk 112 557 (copy deposited in DaA); "Dachau – Erinnerung und Mahnung: Häftlinge aus sieben Nationen gedenken des 10. Jahrestages ihrer Befreiung," *SZ,* 25 Apr. 1955. The speeches were also published in a brochure: *Gedenkfeier zum 10. Jahrestag der Befreiung des*

Konzentrationslagers Dachau am 23./24. April 1955 (n.p., n.d.), IfZ, Dn 200. Franz Böhm also spoke at the occasion. (The printed brochure implies that Böhm spoke at the camp in Dachau, not in the Munich palace.)

9 "Eindrucksvolle Manifestation des europäischen Widerstands / Walter, Landesrat für Recht und Freiheit [sic]: Einheit aller Verfolgten ist unerlässlich," *Die Tat*, 14 May 1955. See also "Internationales Treffen in Dachau – 3000 beim Marsch zum Leitenberg," *Die Tat*, 14 May 1955, 4.

10 For the example of Baden-Württemberg, see "Die 'Dachauer' trafen sich in Stuttgart," *Die Tat*, 26 Mar. 1955, and circular from Walter Leitner to comrades and survivors, 19 Mar. 1955, DaA, Lagergemeinschaft notebook. Leitner reported difficulties with the Stuttgart police, who prohibited the public collection of donations to support the ceremony, a further indication of the marginalization of camp survivors in West Germany in the 1950s.

11 Philipp Greiff et al. to comrades, 20 Mar. 1955; Niemöller to Greiff, 29 Mar. 1955; Greiff et al. to Niemöller, 6 Apr. 1955, Zentralarchiv der Evangelischen Kirche in Hessen und Nassau, Darmstadt, 62/2450. For a discussion of the 1947 expulsion, see the chapter on Protestant memory, pp. 277f below. Niemöller expressed his support for the CID after reading Nico Rost's *Ich war wieder in Dachau* in 1957. He began publicly supporting the CID with a telegram of greetings delivered at a June 1958 pilgrimage. See Niemöller to Rost, 7 Dec. 1957, DaA, OK, and: "Das Warnen nicht vergessen," *Tat*, 5 July 1958.

12 See *NYT*, 9 Mar. 1955 (8:1), and 12 Apr. 1955 (12:3); *Die Tat*, 14 May 1955 (1). A pilgrimage of 300 French and Belgian survivors went to Dachau on 29 May as well. That trip was sponsored by seven French groups (FNDIR, FNDIRP, UNADIF, ADIR, ADJF, ANFFMRF, ANFROMF) and thirteen camp associations. See "Pfingsten 1955: Grosses internationales Treffen im ehemaligen KZ Dachau," *Die Tat*, 28 May 1955, 1.

13 See "Wichtige Tagung in Brüssel: Internationales Dachau-Komitee gegründet," *Tat*, 17 Dec. 1955, 8; also Kohlhofer to Leitner, 18 Oct. 1955, DaA, Lagergemeinschaft notebook.

14 "Wichtige Tagung in Brüssel," *Tat*, 17 Dec. 1955.

15 See R. T. [Richard Titze], "KZ-Archive in die Verwaltung der europäischen Widerstandsorganisationen übergeben," *Tat*, 2 July 1955.

16 "Nico Rost bittet um Mitarbeit," *Tat*, 24 Nov. 1956. According to Rost, who was responsible for gathering the material, the decision was reached at a CID meeting on 8 Sept. 1956.

17 The following narrative is based primarily on Nico Rost, *Ich war wieder in Dachau* (Frankfurt: Röderberg, 1956). Biographical information can be found in the published version of the diary Rost kept in Dachau: *Goethe in Dachau* (Hamburg: Konkret, 1981; Frankfurt: Fischer, 1983 [original Dutch edition 1948]). See also Simon Andrä, "Nico Rost," in Hans-Günter Richardi et al., *Lebensläufe: Schicksale von Menschen, die im KZ Dachau waren* (Dachau: n.p., 1990), 84–90.

18 On Kohlhofer's ability to bridge wide divisions between various groups and people see Barbara Distel, "Otto Kohlhofer in memoriam," *Dachauer Hefte*, 5 (1989), 277–83, 281.

19 Kohlhofer to Hoegner, 12 Feb. 1955, DaA, OK. The German term is *Geist der Lagerstrasse*. It may have originated with Edmond Michelet. It was also an explicit theme of the May 1967 speeches by Senator Jean Mandel and Minister of

Agriculture Hundhammer at the dedication of the Jewish memorial building. See the chapter on Jewish memory, p. 271, below.

20 In the 1990s this issue was debated at length. See Lutz Niethammer (ed.), *Der "gesäuberte" Antifaschismus: Die SED und die roten Kapos von Buchenwald* (Berlin: Akademie, 1994), and Niethammer, "Die SED und die roten Kapos von Buchenwald," in Claudia Keller (ed.), *Antifaschismus: Geschichte und Neubewertung* (Berlin: Aufbau, 1996), 333–50, 350 n. 8.

21 Roth held memorial sermons on 29 Apr. 1946 ("Jahrestag der Befreiung," *SZ*, 26 Apr. 1946; program of "Tag der Befreiung in Dachau," 28 Apr. 1946, BayHsta, Stk 113 624); 28 Apr. 1947 (program of second anniversary of liberation, 28 Apr. 1947, BayHsta, AP22), and again on All Souls' Day 1951, (*NZ*, 1 Nov. 1951).

22 See Leonhard Roth, "1500 Geistliche in drei Stuben zusammengepfercht: Heute beginnt in Dachau der KZ-Priester-Kongress," *MM/DN*, 10 Sept. 1955.

23 Interview Kohlhofer, 15 July 1987.

24 See "Wünsche ehemaliger Häftlinge," *SZ*, 9 Apr. 1956; "KZ Dachau ohne Kirchen," *Abendzeitung*, 9 Apr. 1956; Leonhard Roth, letter to the editor, *MM*, 10 Apr. 1956 and *Abendzeitung*, 11 Apr. 1956. Roth also sent the letter to the Minister President; see Roth to Hoegner, 9 Apr. 1956, BayHsta, Stk 113 629. The letter was forwarded to Hoegner by General Vicar Johann Fuchs on 16 Apr., and answered by Panholzer of the Finance Ministry on 3 May.

25 Ursula von Kardorff, "Lager Dachau – Elf Jahre danach: Das ehemalige Konzentrationslager sollte endlich zu einer würdigen Gedenkstätte werden," *SZ*, 13 Apr. 1956, 3. This half-page illustrated article is held by the clippings collections of the *SZ*, Bavarian Radio, North German Radio, the Press Office of the Federal Government, and the federal parliament.

26 "KZ-Türme sollen abgebrochen werden," *SZ*, 25 July 1957; "Um den Abbruch des Wachturmes," *SZ*, 26 July 1957; "Abbruch der Dachauer KZ-Wachtürme gestoppt," *Tat*, 3 Aug. 1957.

27 A picture of the banner on the watchtower was printed in the *AWJD*, 12 July 1957. See also "Transparente über den KZ-Baracken," *MM*, 8 June 1957; "Resolution der Bewohner der Baracken von Dachau-Ost," *Tat*, 8 June 1957; L. Roth, "Dachau muss Gedenkstätte werden," *Tat*, 27 July 1957.
   The refugees had already attended a CID meeting after the 1956 liberation ceremony: see *Tat*, 12 May 1956.

28 Panholzer/Finanzministerium to Fuchs, 3 May 1956, BayHsta, Stk 113 629; Dr. el., "Wohnlager Dachau-Ost bedarf endgültiger Lösung: Neue Forderungen ehemaliger Häftlinge," *MM/DN*, 10 Apr. 1956. I was unable to locate any more precise information about this meeting. It is likely that the minutes are preserved by the Ministry of Finance and/or the Castle and Garden Administration.

29 See vice president of the federal parliament Richard Jäger (Dachau) to Hoegner, 17 July 1956 and 22 July 1957, and MdB Kahn-Ackermann to Hoegner, 10 Sept. 1956, all in BayHsta, Stk 114 892.

30 Protocol of a meeting of Walraeve and Kohlhofer on 29 July 1956 in Frankfurt, DaA, OK.

31 The speech was reprinted in *SZ/DN*, 20 Apr. 1989. A copy of Roth's morning sermon, "Kampf für Ordnung und Menschenrecht," is preserved in DDW, OM, file "Dachau-Geschichte" (copy deposited in DaA).

32 Latin was chosen so as not to favor any individual nation. The original text reads: "Primus lapis monumenti in victimarum nazismii memoriam errigendi quae in carceribus dachauae intra annos 1933–1945 mortem subier positus est A.D. IV id Sept 1956."

33 "Die alten Münchner reden über Dachau," *Tat*, 19 May 1956.

34 See "Transparente über den KZ-Baracken," *MM*, 8 June 1957; L. Roth, "Dachau muss Gedenkstätte werden," *Tat*, 27 July 1957.

35 Some documents on the federal support for the Dachau evacuation project are kept by the Bundesarchiv in Koblenz, but they were unavailable for this research due to the thirty-year rule. (The files cover the period extending to 1963.)

36 After completion of 121 apartments in 1962, 500 residents still lived in former KZ Dachau. In April of that year the Finance Committee of the Bavarian parliament appropriated money for a special construction program. See *SZ*, 30 Apr. 1962. In Nov. 1962, final evacuation was slated for Dec. 1963: see memo of 12 Nov. 1962, LEA. In Dec. 1963, when eleven barracks had already been demolished, final clearance was slated for spring 1964 (*SZ*, 6 Dec. 1963), but in the summer of that year it was clear that year's end was the earliest possible date (*SZ*, 12 Aug. 1964). In April 1965 the last so-called "asocials" were forcibly removed (*FAZ*, 21 Apr. 1965).

37 Roth first suggested this in a memorandum to Minister President Hoegner on 9 Apr. 1956; original in BayHsta, Stk 113 629. On the CID position, see Kohlhofer to CID, 12 Apr. 1956, DaA, OK; Oskar Müller to Roth, 13 Apr. 1956, DDW, OM; Lagergemeinschaft Dachau, "Erklärung," 29 Apr. 1956, DDW, OM. The first indication that the CID itself accepted this position is: "Internationales Komitee verhandelt mit Finanzministerium," *SZ*, 23 Apr. 1958.

38 At a meeting between Kohlhofer and the Ministry of Finance a specialist from the building department said that the twenty-one year old barracks had been built in 1937 with a life expectancy of ten years, and that they were built on wooden posts, not foundations. See Kohlhofer to CID, 22 Mar. 1958, DaA, OK.

39 Nerin Gun, *The Day of the Americans* (New York: Fleet, 1966), 32, reconstructed the saying below the pig mural in the crematorium from memory. Descriptions of the murals can also be found in contemporary reports. See, for example, Marcus Smith, *The Harrowing of Hell: Dachau* (Albuquerque: University of New Mexico, 1972), 95. The inscription "Eine Laus – der Tod" can still be seen on some of the barrack rafters in Auschwitz-Birkenau today.

40 Oskar Müller to Roth, 1 Dec. 1959, DDW, OM.

41 "Eine so pittoreske kleine Stadt," *Blätter für deutsche und internationale Politik* (Feb. 1966), 157.

42 Christopher Warman, "Cleaned-up Dachau Disappoints Survivors," *Times* (London), 9 Sept. 1968.

43 See Roth to Minister President Hoegner, 9 Apr. 1956, BayHsta, Stk 113 629; Kurat Roth, letter to the editor, *Abendzeitung*, 11 Apr. 1956; Dr. el., "Wohnlager Dachau-Ost bedarf endgültiger Lösung. Neue Forderungen ehemaliger Häftlinge – Staat muss sich entschließen," *MM/DN*, 10 Apr. 1956.

44 See Koch, *Nationale Mahn- und Gedenkstätte*, 45, 47f. According to Walter Bartels, the museum had a twofold purpose: "Visitors are to take two impressions of the museum with them when they leave: a) abhorrence of fascist barbarism, and b) respect for the victims of fascism and the heroes of the antifascist resistance. Both

impressions are to help convince them deeply of the necessity of the fight against fascism and militarism."

45 German translation of the statutes of the CID, 4 June 1958, DaA, OK. The goals were also published as a translation from the Belgian state gazette of 20 Dec. 1958 in *CID Informationen*, no. 5 (23 Jan. 1959), FstHH, HS 13–4–4–2.

46 Vander Auvera, blueprint of two barracks, 7 Aug. 1958 with modifications Mar. 1960, DaA, OK. This blueprint has since been integrated into the regular collection of the memorial site.

A blueprint by Vander Auvera of the entire south end of the prisoners' camp (1:500; 27 Oct. 1958) shows these two barracks as the two *behind* the first infirmary and canteen barracks. The plan to preserve four barracks instead of just two was dropped some time prior to 1960.

47 See "Service Technique du Mémorial," *Informationen*, no. 4 (19 Dec. 1958), and *CID Informationen*, no. 5 (23 Jan. 1959), both in FstHH, HS 13–4–4–2.

48 See Ministry of Finance to CID/Brussels, 9 July 1960, Archive of the Bavarian Youth Ring (BJR), notebook "Jugend und Widerstand," sect. I. The letter carries the ministry's reference code: "AZ: O 1481/E – 53 273 D 450." See also "Ausstellung von KZ-Dokumenten," *SZ*, 23 July 1960, "Dachauer Dokumente," *SZ*, 28 July 1960, and "Mahnung für die kommenden Generationen: Eröffnung des Dachauer KZ-Museums / Eine internationale Gemeinschaftsarbeit," *SZ* (Landkreis), 1 Aug. 1960. An invitation to the inauguration on 30 July is preserved in DaA, OK.

The CID decision to set up a provisional museum in the crematory (instead of a partial museum in a barrack) for the World Congress may have been prompted by the German discussion of an article in the English newspaper *Daily Mail* criticizing the lack of historical information available at the site. See rtsch., "Keine Auskunft im KZ," *MM*, 29 June 1960. However, at a CID meeting in Nov. 1959 it was decided that the barrack museum should become a higher priority so that "it would at least be partially complete" before the Catholic congress. See Otto Kohlhofer, memo re CID meeting in Brussels on 7–8 Nov. 1959, 21 Nov. 1959, pt. 5c, DaA, notebook "Bayerisches Staatsministerium – CID, 1958–1964."

49 On the commissioning of the model see CID Service Technique du Memorial, *Informationen*, no. 4 (19 Dec. 1957), FstHH, HS 13–4–4–2.

50 N[ikola] R[eichel], "Mahnung für die kommenden Generationen: Eröffnung des Dachauer KZ-Museums / Eine internationale Gemeinschaftsarbeit," *SZ* (Landkreis), 1 Aug. 1960.

51 I owe this insight to Barbara Distel. In a conversation of 19 May 1991 she reported how, at a 1990 conference on the Eichmann trial at the London Goethe Institute, she learned how shocked and impressed the German Dachau survivors had been by the trial, after which they decided to give the extermination of the Jews an important place in the exhibition. Most of the photographs in the 1965–2001 Dachau exhibition were taken from Gerhard Schoenberner's book *Der gelbe Stern* (Gutersloh: Bertelsmann, 1960). Schoenberner was a member of the advisory committee for the 1965 Dachau exhibition.

52 The photographs and texts are reproduced in Barbara Distel and Ruth Jakusch (eds.), *Konzentrationslager Dachau, 1933–1945* (Munich: n.p., 1978), 157ff (Hartheim) and 168f (Hebertshausen).

53 Nico Rost, "Quelques remarques suite à ma visite au musée en Novembre 1962,"

FstHH, HS 13–4–3. A strikingly similar critique, although directed against (the Communist) Alfred Haag "and his friends," to whom Rost probably belonged, was registered by an unknown survivor: see unsigned carbon copy, "Der Aufbau unseres Museums und die Urkunde von Luxemburg" (n.d., ca. Aug. 1963), FstHH, HS 13–4–3.

54 Distel and Jakusch (eds.), *Konzentrationslager Dachau*, 5. See also Gisela Lehrke, *Gedenkstätten für Opfer des Nationalsozialismus: Historisch-politische Bildung an Orten des Widerstands und der Verfolgung* (Frankfurt: Campus, 1988), 99–104.

55 The 1965 exhibition is documented in the catalog: Distel and Jakusch (eds.), *Konzentrationslager Dachau*.

56 Cornelia Brink, "Visualisierte Geschichte: Zu Ausstellungen an Orten nationalsozialistischer Konzentrationslager" (unpubl. Master's thesis, Freiburg, 1990, copy in NA), 72; see also Lehrke, *Gedenkstätten*, 99.

57 N[ikola] R[eichel], "Mahnung für die kommenden Generationen."

58 Estimates of their number vary widely; the most often cited number is 6,000 (for instance in a 4pp. guide distributed at the entrance to the Dachau museum). In 1947 the priest Otto Pies cited a figure of 4–5,000: see "Block 26," *Klerus-Blatt*, 31 May 1947. The most specific figures are given in a letter to the *SZ* from a Russian former Dachau inmate: 600 in one train late in 1941, 2,009 in another of several trains in 1942, for a total of "over 7,000." See Illarion Panow, "Das Los der Häftlinge in Dachau," *SZ*, 29 Apr. 1966, 8. In January 1950 Hans Kaltenbacher, who had reason to amplify the number, spoke of 12,000: see protocol of founding meeting of the Arbeitsgemeinschaft Dachau, 3 Feb. 1950, DDW, OM. See also Reinhard Otto, *Wehrmacht, Gestapo und sowjetische Kriegsgefangene im deutschen Reichsgebiet 1941/42* (Munich: Oldenbourg, 1998).

59 A visit to the Hebertshausen site was planned for the June 1961 meeting "Youth and Resistance": see "Informations-Bulletin über das Treffen der Jugend und Widerstandskämpfer aus Europa . . . in Dachau und München," May 1961, FstHH, HS 13–4–4–2. See also "Europäische Pilgerfahrt 1961," *Mitteilungen LGD*, Dec. 1961.

60 "Einweihung des Gedenksteines am ehem. SS-Schiessplatz Hebertshausen," *Mitteilungen LGD*, Dec. 1964. For a positive, non-West German opinion of the monument, see also unsigned carbon copy, "Der Aufbau unseres Museums und die Urkunde von Luxemburg" (n.d., ca. Aug. 1963), FstHH, HS 13–4–3.

61 The meeting took place in the collaborationist capital of Vichy, of all places. See "Hier, à Vichy, le général de Gaulle a présidé le banquet de clôture des anciens de Dachau," *La Tribune*, 7 May 1956. Otto Kohlhofer attended that meeting.

62 Detlef Hoffmann, "Menschen im Stacheldraht: Das Denkmal auf dem Gelände des Schutzhaftlagers Dachau," *Wiener Jahrbuch für jüdische Geschichte, Kultur und Museumswesen*, 3 (1997–8), 96–126, 107.

63 *CID Informationen*, no. 8 (17 Aug. 1959), FstHH, HS 13–4–4–2. Twelve entries were from Germany, eleven from England, eight from Yugoslavia, seven from France, three each from the Netherlands, Belgium, and Denmark, the remaining sixteen from other countries.

64 *CID Informationen*, no. 10 (17 Dec. 1959), FstHH, HS 13–4–4–2. The 4 November ceremony was organized by Arthur Haulot. Detlef Hoffmann cites different dates and figures for this competition, based on a compilation in "Historique du Monument," *CID Bulletin*, no. 125 (1989), 10–14. According to that document,

beginning on 5 Sept. [Nov?] 1959, six projects were exhibited in Brussels. The prize committee met from 2 to 4 Nov. 1959. See Hoffmann, "Menschen im Stacheldraht," 107.

65 *CID Informationen*, no. 10 (17 Dec. 1959), FstHH, HS 13–4–4–2. In his article "Menschen im Stacheldraht" Hoffmann describes the six prize-winning designs based on photographs of the Brussels exhibition.

66 Hoffmann, "Menschen im Stacheldraht," 113–15.

67 Interview Kohlhofer, 18 July 1987. The artist's first name is Nandor, last name Glid.

68 See Hansdietmar Klug, "Dachau – Appell an den Menschen: Entwürfe für ein Monument im ehemaligen KZ Dachau," *Die Kunst und das Schöne Heim*, 25 (Nov. 1966), 49–52; "Dachau," *Bauwelt Zeitung*, 47 (22 Nov. 1965), 1339–40; *SZ*, 28 Nov. 1967.

69 On the 1923 Weimar memorial, see Dietrich Schubert, "Das Denkmal der Märzgefallenen in Weimar," *Jahrbuch der Hamburger Kunstsammlungen*, 21 (1976), 199ff.

70 Ds., "Ein Mahnmal für Dachau," *SZ*, 17 Aug. 1965.

71 Kuratorium, mimeographed memo, 22 Dec. 1966, LEA; "Bonner Spende für Dachau," *SZ*, 7 June 1967.

72 Neuhäusler's architect Josef Wiedemann told Detlef Hoffmann in an Aug. 1996 interview that Neuhäusler originally thought that his chapel would be used by Jews and Protestants as well. See Hoffmann, "Menschen im Stacheldraht," 126 n. 47f.

10 Jews represent the Holocaust at Dachau

1 For an example of a Dachau narrative by an Austrian Catholic clergyman similar to those from this group, see Georg M. Karst, *The Beasts of the Earth*, trans. Emil Lengyel (New York: A. Unger, 1942).

2 Bruno Bettelheim, "Returning to Dachau: The Living and the Dead," *Commentary*, 21 (1956), 144–51. Bettelheim, a *Kristallnacht* survivor and a regular contributor to *Commentary* (see his article in the Sept. 1951 issue), probably read Alfred Werner's article; in any case his experience was very similar to Werner's. Other instances of non-Jewish foreign visitors to Dachau in the 1950s who reacted similarly are: Morris Philipson, "Pilgrimage to Dachau," *Commonweal*, 65 (March 1957), 657–9, and Nerin Gun, *Day of the Americans*, 296–309 (visit in 1959). For another example of a Jewish émigré visiting another former concentration camp in Germany, see Lower Saxony Ministry of the Interior to Office of Federal President, 27 Feb. 1959 re letter from Fred Strauss, Berlin/New York, 17 Nov. 1958, BaKo B122, 2081. Werner Cahnman[n], introduced below, is an exception to this rule.

3 For examples of memoirs from this group, see Joel Sack, *Dawn after Dachau* (New York: Shengold, 1990), and Art Spiegelman, *Maus: A Survivor's Tale*, vol. II: *And Here My Troubles Began* (New York: Pantheon, 1991), esp. 88, 91–7, 104–13. The second volume's title refers to Spiegelman's father's arrival in Dachau, which at that time in 1945 was comparatively worse than Auschwitz.

Shortly after liberation Sack compiled a two-volume list of the liberated Jewish Dachau survivors (including those from the branch camps in Freimann, Landsberg, Schleissheim, Pensing, St. Ottelia, Neustift, Feldafing, Pasing, Buchberg, Mittenwald, Garmisch, and Buchenwald): Abraham Klausner and Yoel Zak, *Sharit*

Ha-Platah [Book of the Living], 2 vols. (Dachau, 1945). It would be a valuable research project to trace this group of survivors and systematically examine their memoirs.

4 For a perceptive criticism of the limited sociological scope of analyses of life in the camps, see Falk Pingel, "The Destruction of Human Identity in Concentration Camps: The Contribution of the Social Sciences to an Analysis of Behavior under Extreme Conditions," *Holocaust and Genocide Studies*, 6:2 (1991), 167–84. See 178f for a discussion of Jewish culture in the camps. Notably, even Wolfgang Sofsky's standard-setting 1993 sociology of the concentration camps, *The Order of Terror* (Princeton: Princeton University Press, 1997; Frankfurt: Fischer, 1993), does not include any discussion of prisoners' cultural pursuits in the camps.

A noteworthy exception to the unidimensional perspective criticized by Pingel is Paul Neurath, *Social Life in the German Concentration Camps of Dachau and Buchenwald* (Ann Arbor: University Dissertations, 1951). This study is, however, based primarily on the author's personal experience, not a systematic collection of evidence.

5 See Michael Selzer, *Deliverance Day: The Last Hours of Dachau* (Philadelphia: Lippincott, 1978), 192f, and Gun, *Day of the Americans*, 23f. For a short account of Loy's experience of liberation, see Howard Buechner, *Dachau: The Hour of the Avenger* (Metairie, La.: Thunderbird, rev. edn, 1987), 73–6.

6 Sack, *Dawn after Dachau*, 19f. Sack also describes the second Jewish service by Eichhorn, 46f.

7 David Max Eichhorn, "Sabbath Service in Dachau Concentration Camp," *Dachau Review*, 1 (1985), 96–105.

8 Ibid., 101.

9 Alex Grobman, "American Jewish Chaplains and the *Shearit Hapletah*: April–June 1945," *Simon Wiesenthal Center Annual*, 1 (1984), 89–111, 92, 94.

10 On the Jewish settlement in Belsen see Sam Bloch (ed.), *Holocaust and Rebirth: Bergen–Belsen 1945–1965* (New York and Tel Aviv: Bergen-Belsen Memorial Press of the World Federation of Bergen-Belsen Associations, 1965), and Derrick Sington, *Belsen Uncovered* (London: Duckworth, 1946), 177ff. See also the interview with Wilhelm Niebuhr, a German teacher who worked in the construction group that built the monument, in Rainer Schulze (ed.), *Unruhige Zeiten: Erlebnisberichte aus dem Landkreis Celle 1945–1949* (Munich: Oldenbourg, 1990), 285. A photograph of the monument can be found in Sybil Milton and Ira Nowinski, *In Fitting Memory: The Art and Politics of Holocaust Memorials* (Detroit: Wayne State, 1991), 175.

11 Hans Ehard, speech at the dedication of the Munich synagogue, 20 May 1947, BayHsta, Stk 112 539.

12 There probably were other specifically Jewish commemorations during this time, but documentation is sparse. In Dachau on 28 Apr. 1946, for example, the Jews had a separate ceremony, as did the Catholics, Protestants, and Poles. See the program published in *SZ*, 26 Apr. 1946; original in BayHsta Stk 113 624.

13 See [Hans Carl,] "Wiedersehen in Dachau: 1. Dachau-Gedächtniskundgebung in München am 17. und 18. Mai 1947," *Stimmen*, 1 June 1947.

14 "Full Jews" (*Volljuden*) were, according to Nazi racial doctrine, Jews with no history of intermarriage. For the quote see *Stimmen*, 15 June 1947.

15 The basic background literature on West German antisemitism in the late 1940s

includes: Frank Stern, *Whitewashing the Yellow Badge: Antisemitism and Philosemitism in Postwar Germany*, trans. William Templer (New York: Pergamon, 1992); Abraham Peck, "Liberated but Not Free: Jewish Displaced Persons in Germany after 1945," in Walter Pehle (ed.), *November 1938: From "Reichskristallnacht" to Genocide* (New York/Oxford: Berg, 1991), 222–36; Juliane Wetzel, "'Mir szeinen doh': München und Umgebung als Zuflucht von Überlebenden des Holocaust 1945–1948," in Martin Broszat, Klaus-Dietmar Henke, and Hans Woller (eds.), *Von Stalingrad zur Währungsreform: Zur Socialgeschichte des Umbruchs in Deutschland* (Munich: Oldenbourg, 1998), 327–64; Leo Schwarz, *The Redeemers: A Saga of the Years 1945–1952* (New York: Farrar, Straus, and Young, 1953), Marita Krauss, "Verfolgtenbetreuung und Wiedergutmachung am Beispiel von München und Oberbayern (1945–1952)," unpubl. ms., Munich 1988, LEA.

16 See *Verhandlungen* (22 and 28 July 1948), vol. 2, 1650, 1748–50. The Bavarian Minister of the Interior reported two cases in Sept. 1947, and twenty-one since Mar. 1948.

17 Copy of Landpolizei to Präsident, 18 Apr. 1950, BayHsta, Stk 113 627.

18 For the background in Auerbach's trial for embezzlement and perjury (Ohrenstein was a co-defendant) and his subsequent suicide, see p. 177 above, and Werner Bergmann, *Antisemitismus in öffentlichen Konflikten: Kollectives Lernen in der politischen Kultur der Bundesrepublik 1949–1989* (Frankfurt: Campus, 1997), 145–74.

19 Stefan Schwarz, memo re meeting in Finance Ministry, 9 Mar. 1962, LEA. Schwarz notes that Heinz Meier, the president of the Landesverband der israelitischen Kultusgemeinden in Bayern, suggested that a synagogue be erected in Dachau at a meeting of the Landesverband in 1960, after Wiedemann, the architect of the Catholic chapel, had reported Rabbi Blumenthal's opinion. The suggestion of columns with cross and star of David flanking the Catholic chapel is documented by Wiedemann, blueprint of memorial site, 16 Nov. 1960, DaA, Kohlhofer papers.

20 See Raul Hilberg, *The Destruction of the European Jews* (New York/London: Holmes and Meier, rev. edn, 1985), preface, and Leon Jick, "The Holocaust: Its Uses and Abuses," *Brandeis Review* (spring 1986), passim. For a historical etymology of the term, see also Geoff Eley, "Holocaust History," *London Review of Books* (3 March 1982), 6–9, 6.

21 See Bergmann, *Antisemitismus in öffentlichen Konflikten*, 251.

22 Dipl. Ing. Schwarz, memo re "Errichtung einer Gedenk-Synagoge im ehem. KZ-Lager Dachau," Jan. 1961, LEA. Schwarz planned and discussed his visit with Otto Kohlhofer. See also Schwarz, memo, 11 Dec. 1960, LEA.

23 See Amos Elon, *The Israelis: Founders and Sons* (New York: Penguin, 1984), 197–209, and Segev, *The Seventh Million*, 427–36.

24 Schwarz to LEA president Heinz Meier, 9 Mar. 1961, LEA.

25 Schwarz, memo, 6 June 1960, LEA.

26 Memo about a meeting in the Finance Ministry, 11 July 1962, FstHH, HS 13-4-4-2; *Mitteilungen LGD*, Dec. 1962. The visitors were from the Bamberg County Governor's Office. See "Europäische Pilgerfahrt 1961," *Mitteilungen LGD*, Dec. 1961.

The following anecdote illustrates how some Dachau citizens have tried to modify the potent collective memory of this restaurant: in a conversation in 1985 Hans-Günter Richardi, one of the leading sanitizers of local history, told me that this restaurant had been located at a crossroads a substantial distance from the camp. That is completely untrue and was probably well known to Richardi.

27 See summary of the results of a meeting in the Finance Ministry on 9 Mar. 1962, LEA and HS 13–4–4–2, and *Stimmen*, July 1962. See also Nikola Reichel, "Barackenlager Dachau wird geräumt," *SZ*, 5 Apr. 1962; *Mitteilungen*, June 1962.

28 "In Dachau entsteht eine Sühne-Christi-Kirche . . . Übersicht zur gegenwärtigen Planung," *FAZ*, 11 Nov. 1963.

29 On the brothel see Christa Paul, *Zwangsprostitution: Staatlich errichtete Bordelle im Nationalsozialismus* (Berlin: Edition Hentrich, 1994), 64. I found no documentation on the demolition, only a reference that the building housed a kindergarten in the early 1950s.

30 "Gedenkfeier jüdischer KZ-Häftlinge," and "Probst Grüber bei Dachauer Gedenkfeier," *SZ*, 4 May and 8 May 1963; Walter Leitner, "Dachau-Befreiungsfeier 1963," *Mitteilungen LGD*, Aug. 1963. Siegfried Neuland, the president of the Munich Jewish Community, spoke for the Verband der jüdischen KZ-Invaliden.

31 This claim is based on the newspaper reports of those events collected by me. The speakers were Heinrich Stöhr (1957), Nico Rost (1958, 1960), Alois Hundhammer (1959), Albert Guérisse (1962), Karl-Heinz Neukamm (1963), and Ludwig Rosenberg (1964), head of the DGB (the German national trade union association), who may have been Jewish.

32 Cahnman[n] (1902–80) was imprisoned in KZ Dachau for two months before he emigrated to London in June 1939 and from there to the United States in 1940. See Werner Cahnman[n], "In the Dachau Concentration Camp," *Chicago Jewish Forum*, 23:1 (fall 1964), 18–23. See also the long interview with Cahnman[n]: Nikola Reichel, "Dachau-Komitee kritisiert Behörden: Verzögerungen beim Bau der Gedenkstätte / Vorwürfe gegen Amerikaner," *SZ*, 24 July 1963, and the corrections by Werner Cahnman[n], "Mahnmal in Dachau" (letter to the editor), *SZ*, 31 July 1963.

33 On Cahnman[n]'s US career, see Joseph Maier and Chaim Waxman, "Werner Cahnman: An Introduction to his Life and Work," in Maier and Waxman (eds.), *Ethnicity, Identity, and History: Essays in Memory of Werner J. Cahnman* (New Brunswick/London: Transaction, 1983), 1–12.

34 "Mahnmal für KZ-Opfer," *Abendzeitung*, 29 Apr. 1964; Gerhard Wolfrum, "Gedenken an den Todesmarsch nach Dachau: Jüdische Verfolgte errichten ein Mahnmal / Morgen Feier der Lagergemeinschaft in Hebertshausen," *SZ*, 2 May 1964; "Zum Gedenken der jüdischen Opfer von Dachau," *Mitteilungen LGD*, Dec. 1964. A photograph of the monument was published in the *Abendzeitung* on 2 May.

35 This monument was desecrated in Dec. 1966. See Landesverband der jüdischen Verfolgten e.V., memo, Apr. 1967, LEA. The Jewish monument on the Leiten was also desecrated in May 1967, shortly before the dedication of the Jewish memorial in the camp. See "Jüdischer Gedenkstein beschmiert," *SZ*, 3 May 1967.

36 On Belsen, see below, p. 280; on the convent in Auschwitz, pp. 240 and 504 n. 91f, above.

37 Gerhard Wolfrum, "Gedenken an den Todesmarsch nach Dachau," *SZ*, 2 May 1964. One may recall that when Auerbach was commissioned with the renovation of the ca. 450 KZ gravesites in Bavaria in 1950, he avoided consolidating the graves.

38 For examples of these early monuments, see American Jewish Congress, *In*

Everlasting Remembrance: Guide to Memorials and Monuments (New York: AJC, 1969); also James Young, "Holocaust-Gedenkstätten in den USA: Ein Überblick," *Dachauer Hefte*, 6 (1990), 230–9; Milton and Nowinski, *In Fitting Memory*, 202, 248–68.

39 Schwarz to Präsidium des Landesverbands, 24 Sept. 1964, LEA. When Munich city council pledged DM50,000 for the Catholic chapel in 1960, it also reserved DM30,000 each for the planned Protestant and Jewish monuments. See also Hans Meier to Mayor Vogel, 8 July 1960, LEA.

40 "Das Konzentrationslager Dachau: Ein Schandfleck deutscher Geschichte," *MM/DN*, 8 May 1965.

41 Guttmann to Schwarz, 15 May 1965, LEA.

42 The original German is: "Stelle, oh Ewiger, ihnen eine Warnung hin! Erfahren sollen die Völker, dass sie Sterbliche sind." See Schwarz to Landesrabbiner of Hesse, Lichtigfeld, 25 May 1967. The inscription had been approved by Lichtigfeld in Apr. 1963. This letter was written to discuss Cahnman[n]'s criticism that Psalm 9 was a "Rachepsalm."

43 Schwarz to Lichtigfeld, 25 May 1967. See also Schwarz's opinion in Rudolf Hohlweg, "Jüdische Gedenkfeier in Dachau," *SZ*, 2 May 1966: "KZ Dachau shall become a place to commemorate the dead that shows as if in a mirror what people can do to other people 'simply because they are Jews.'"

44 Schwarz to Guttmann, 18 Aug. 1966, LEA.

45 For a description of the building and its intended symbolism see Stefan Schwarz, *Die jüdische Gedenkstätte in Dachau* (Munich: Landesverband, 1972), esp. 33–7. See also the plans in Hoffmann, *Gedächtnis der Dinge*, 80.

46 "Um das Dachauer Krematorium," *SZ* (Landkreis), 6 Sept. 1955. For a short biography of Graubard, whose 22-year-old daughter Alina, a survivor of Auschwitz, committed suicide in June 1955, see Baruch Graubard, "In den Fängen des Todes," *Dachauer Hefte*, 6 (1990), 118–20.

47 The only earlier plan for the historical education of young people at the site was a June 1950 bill introduced by the Munich SPD into the city council to support visits by school classes to the Leiten cemetery (*SZ*, 14 June 1950). However, that suggestion did not include the creation of any didactic facilities.

48 See Martin Urban, "Vermächtnis der Toten erfüllt: Jüdische Gedenkstätte auf dem ehemaligen KZ-Gelände in Dachau eingeweiht," *SZ*, 8 May 1967; *Stimmen*, spring/summer 1967; and Hermann Lewy, "Aufruf an das Gewissen: Zur Einweihung der jüdischen Gedenkstätte in Dachau," *AWJD*, 12 May 1967, 1. The prepared text of Mandel's speech is printed in Schwarz, *Die jüdische Gedenkstätte*, 13f.

49 See Harold Marcuse, "The Revival of Holocaust Awareness in West Germany, Israel, and the United States," in Carole Fink, Philipp Gassert, and Detlef Junker (eds.), *1968: The World Transformed* (Cambridge: Cambridge University Press, 1998), 421–38.

50 A special exhibition on athletes persecuted under National Socialism was displayed in the second reconstructed barrack during the Olympics.

51 For a detailed but somewhat euphemistic report, see Rolf Vogel, "Das Leid ruft die Jugend der Welt zum Engagement: Vorolympische Gedenkstunde in Dachau," *AWJD*, 1 Sept. 1972; more objective is Rudolf Grosskopff, "Nur wenige Sportler fuhren zum Lager Dachau," *FR*, 26 Aug. 1972.

On the 1 Sept. ceremony, see "Israels Olympia-Team in Dachau: Gedenken im ehemaligen KZ – 'Deutschland ein anderer Staat geworden,'" *MM*, 4 Sept. 1972; Karl-Heinz Krumm, "Nationalsozialistische Vergangenheit streifte das olympische Dorf," *FR*, 5 Sept. 1972.

52 Hans-Jochen Vogel (b. 1926) was Lord Mayor of Munich from 1960 to 1962, chairman of the Bavarian SPD from 1972 to 1977, member of parliament 1972–82 and 1983– , Cabinet Minister for Housing and Urban Development 1972–4, and Minister of Justice 1974–81. In 1987 he became chairman of the national SPD. In the 1980s he initiated a law criminalizing the denial of the Holocaust, and in the 1990s he co-founded the organization "Against Forgetting." He is an excellent example of what I will call the cohort of 1948ers, who devoted substantial energy to the attempt to come to terms with the legacies of Nazism.

53 See Midge Decter, in "Germany 1967: Nine American Writers and Editors, back from a Tour to Berlin and Major West German Cities, Give their Personal Impressions of Germans Today," *Atlantic*, 219:5 (May 1967), 50–3.

54 See Irving Halperin, *Here I Am: A Jew in Today's Germany* (Philadelphia: Westminster, 1971), chapter "Dachau: 1964," 106–13. See also Edward Wakin, "Visit to a Munich Suburb: The Railroad Now Used Daily by Commuters Once Carried Human Cargo to Dachau," *America*, 111 (5 Sept. 1964), 235f. Halperin is a professor who specialized in literature by Holocaust survivors; Wakin is a progressive academic. Both have extensive lists of publications.

55 Silvia Tennenbaum, "Return to Germany," *Midstream*, 22 (Dec. 1976), 39–45. The quotations are from pp. 43, 45, 44. Tennenbaum was about 6 years old when her secular Jewish family emigrated from Germany in 1936.

56 Carolyn Bronstein, "A Bridge out of Darkness," *Seventeen*, 47 (Sept. 1988), 166–8. I also conducted a telephone interview with Bronstein on 10 Sept. 1998; notes in my possession.

57 Interview with Belinda Davis (b. 1959), 2 Mar. 1992, Ann Arbor, Michigan; notes in my possession. Compare interviews with Irene Marcuse-Silver (b. 1953), visit in Sept. 1981, interview 1 Mar. 1992; Diana Saso, (b. 1971), visit in 1991, interview 10 May 1993; and Kevin Wong, (b. 1967), visit in 1985, interview 12 Mar. 1993.

11 Protestants make amends at Dachau

1 Following standard practice, I use Protestant as the translation of *evangelisch*, which includes the Lutheran, Reformed, and United Churches. In Germany the two Christian denominations Catholic and Protestant vastly outnumber all others.

2 For recent exceptions see the excellent studies by Doris Bergen, *Twisted Cross: The German Christian Movement in the Third Reich* (Chapel Hill: University of North Carolina Press, 1996), and Günter Brakelmann (ed.), *Kirche im Krieg: Der deutsche Protestantismus am Beginn des Zweiten Weltkriegs* (Munich: Kaiser, 1979). However, even the two-volume standard work on German churches during the Nazi period ends in 1934: Klaus Scholder, *The Churches and the Third Reich*, trans. John Bowden (Philadelphia: Fortress, 1987–8; Berlin: Ullstein and Siedler, 1977 and 1985). See also Ursula Büttner, "'Die Judenfrage wird zur Christenfrage': Die deutsche evangelische Kirche und die Judenverfolgung im Dritten Reich," *Zeitschrift für Geschichtswissenschaft*, 45:7 (1997), 581–96.

3 See Bergen, *Twisted Cross*, 1–14.

4 Niemöller was a highly decorated submarine officer in World War I. In the 1920s he became a theologian, in 1931 an ordained minister. Niemöller retrospectively described his own political position in 1934 as "stocknational." See Hans-Joachim Oeffler (ed.), *Martin Niemöller: Reden, Predigten, Denkanstösse 1964–1976* (Cologne: Pahl-Rugenstein, 1977), 258.

5 See Martin Greschat (ed.), *Die Schuld der Kirche: Dokumente und Reflexionen zur Stuttgarter Schulderklärung vom 18./19. Oktober 1945* (Munich: Kaiser, 1982), 91ff, 110ff. Although Dibelius's vague text was chosen as the basis, Niemöller argued successfully that the stronger statements in Asmussen's draft be included in the final version. They are indeed the most cited passages of the text. For historical contextualization see Clemens Vollnhals, "Die Evangelische Kirche zwischen Traditionswahrung und Neuorientierung," in Broszat, Henke, and Woller (eds.), *Von Stalingrad zur Währungsreform*, 113–69, 132–6; also Clemens Vollnhals, *Evangelische Kirche und Entnazifierung, 1945–1949: Die Last der nationalsozialistischen Vergangenheit* (Munich: Oldenbourg, 1989).

6 The visit took place on 8 Nov. 1945 and was recorded in Niemöller's diary. See Wilhelm Niemöller, *Neuanfang 1945: Zur Biographie Martin Niemöllers nach seinen Tagebuchaufzeichnungen aus dem Jahre 1945* (Frankfurt: Stimme, 1967), 64. For the following description of the visit see also the various versions of a speech Niemöller originally gave on 3 July 1946 in Stuttgart: Martin Niemöller, *Der Weg ins Freie* (Stuttgart: Franz Mittelbach, 1946); Martin Niemöller, "Ich – Du – Wir alle", *Nordwestdeutsche Hefte* (Hamburg), 1/8 (Nov. 1946), 58–9. Niemöller also gave the speech on 25 Jan. 1947 in New York. See "Pastor Niemöller: Amerikanische Predigt," *VVNN*, 21 June 1947 (complete text), and 16 Aug. 1947 (excerpts).

7 Niemöller quotes a German text: "Hier wurden / in den Jahren 1933 bis 1945 / 238756 Menschen verbrannt." Contemporary photographs show a sign with the English text: "This area is being retained as a shrine to the 238,000 individuals who were cremated here. Please don't destroy."

8 Actually, although in the often repeated speech Niemöller attributed the revelation to his visit in Dachau, he must have "discovered" his personal responsibility before that time. That insight was a prerequisite for the October 1945 "Stuttgart Declaration of Guilt."

9 After Greschat (ed.), *Schuld der Kirche*, 110f.

10 See Christoph Klessmann, "Kontinuitäten und Veränderungen im protestantischen Milieu," in Axel Schildt and Arnold Sywottek (eds.), *Modernisierung im Wiederaufbau: Die westdeutsche Gesellschaft der 50er Jahre* (Bonn: Dietz, 1993), 403–18.

11 See *SZ*, 14 Aug. 1959.

12 Niemöller had a short statement read for him in Dachau on 19 June 1958 (see *Der Widerstandskämpfer*, June/July 1958); he spoke personally on 12 Nov. 1960 in Flossenbürg (see Niemöller papers, Zentralarchiv der Evangelischen Kirche in Hessen und Nassau, Darmstadt), and on 3 May 1964 in Dachau (*Mitteilungen LGD*, Dec. 1964). He also gave a sermon at the church dedication on 30 Apr. 1967 (*Stimme der Gemeinde*, clipping in DDW, OM), and spoke again on 4 May 1980.

13 See minutes of meeting of Rat der EKD, 3 Nov. 1960, EZB, file 6172/5 (hereafter EZB5).

14 Minutes of meeting of Rat der EKD, 12 May 1961, ibid.

15 At a 1992 conference in Brussels Annegret Ehmann, one of the planners of the new memorial site "Haus der Wannseekonferenz" in Berlin, told how she had found evidence that Protestant Church officials developed, on their own initiative, an index card system for tracing Jewish ancestry based on church registers. The irony is that a crucifix is a depiction of Christ, who was of course a Jew.

16 The pastor was Krop from Groningen. Given the timing of the request, it would be interesting to find out if Neuhäusler or the CID prompted him to make the request in order to push the EKD to take action. In light of the January 1963 meeting discussed below, this is a probable scenario.

17 Wilm to Scharf, 14 Aug. 1961, EZB5.

18 Wilm to Lilje, 20 Sept. 1962, ibid.

19 This is false. Approximately 50,000 people died in KZ Belsen, while Dachau's official death toll is ca. 32,000 (+ ca. 6,000 Soviet POWs). Even if one takes the term "buried" literally (most corpses in both camps were cremated), Belsen had about 20,000 in mass graves, Dachau 5–6,000. Wilm erred because he was using the figure of 75,000 victims of KZ Dachau that had been calculated by VVN and Lagergemeinschaft researchers. See the report about Wilm's speech of 9 Nov. 1963: *SZ*, 11 Nov. 1963.

20 In November 1952 Federal President Heuss spoke there, and in 1960 Chancellor Adenauer.

21 Wilm to Kunst and von Harling about reaction in Berlin, 10 Dec. 1962, EZB5.

22 Wilm to Bavarian Bishop Dietzfilbinger, 9 Feb. 1963, ibid.

23 Niedersächsisches Innenministerium to Kirchenkanzlei in Hannover, 26 Feb. 1963, ibid.

24 Wilm to Kunst and von Harling, 14 Aug. 1963, and Wilm to Scharf, 16 Sept. 1963, ibid.

25 The early discussion is summarized in Wilm to Scharf, 19 Apr. 1963, ibid.

26 See draft of minutes of the meeting of the working committee of the EKD, 20 Jan. 1964, EZB9; excerpt from the minutes of the Ratssitzung in Berlin, 20 March 1964. The name "Jesus-Christus-Kirche" was also considered.

27 For the exact text of the call see Kurt Scharf, "Spendenaufruf für den Bau einer Evangelischen Kirche in Dachau," in Kirchenamt Hannover to all parishes, 20 May 1964, EZB8a.

28 Wagenmann, Circular G10/64 re construction of a Protestant memorial church in Dachau, 20 May 1964, EZB8a.

29 See minutes of working committee, 20 Jan. 1964, EZB5. The architects were A. Zamstra (Amsterdam), Friedhelm Amslinger (Munich), Egon Eiermann (Karlsruhe), Johann Ludwig (Munich), Dieter Oesterlen (Hannover), Helmut Striffler (Mannheim), and Hans Christoph Müller (Berlin).

30 Ibid.

31 Niederschrift über die Sitzung des Preiskomitees, 10pp., 24 July 1964, ibid.

32 See D. Scharf, Dr. Luskey, and A.L. Bouman, "Versöhnungskirche im Lager Dachau," 4pp. brochure (Berlin, 1965); and Helmut Striffler, "The Building," in Christian Reger, *Protestant Church of Reconciliation in the Former Concentration Camp at Dachau* (n.p.p.: n.p., n.d.[ca. 1968])(brochure available at the Protestant Church in the KZ Dachau memorial site).

33 Additional pictures are available on the Church of Reconciliation's web site: http://www.epv.de/versoehnungskirche.

34 The German reads: "Zuflucht ist unter dem Schatten Deiner Flügel." This inscrip-

tion from Psalm 36:8 was approved at a meeting of the building committee on 4 Aug. 1964. See O. Söhngen, minutes of meeting of 3./4.8.64, 8pp., EZB5.

35 Reger, *Protestant Church of Reconciliation.*

36 Minutes of the meeting of the prize committee, 10pp., 24 July 1964, EZB5.

37 Oskar Söhngen, Ergebnisprotokoll von Sitzungen des Bauausschusses, 3 and 4 Aug. 1964, 8pp., ibid.

38 Horn, memo re discussion between CID and state church council in Munich on 16 Feb. 1965, 17 Feb. 1965, ibid. At the end Guérisse reiterated that he had been "shocked" by the dimensions of all six Protestant designs but did not say so because he had not been a voting member of the prize committee, and that his concerns were "solely aesthetic."

39 Copy of Castle Administration to Kohlhofer, 4 Mar. 1965, LEA.

40 On the size reduction of the Jewish memorial, see Oberkirchenrat Horn to Söhngen, 27 Dec. 1966, EZB, Söhngen files. On the relocation of the Jewish memorial (originally 25 m closer was suggested), see the minutes of the 3–4 Aug. 1964 meetings, EZB5.

41 Schwarz, memo re memorial sites in Dachau, 18 Jan. 1962, LEA. At the meeting reported in this memo Neuhäusler suggested that "the barracks area be landscaped as a grove and the [Protestant and Jewish] chapels be erected in the barracks area." Otto Kohlhofer protested vigorously against the greening of the memorial site. The original blueprint of the grove plan from the Dachau Parks Office is discussed and reprinted in Hoffmann, *Gedächtnis der Dinge,* 78f, redrawn here as ill. 46.

There are other formulations of this conciliatory "green" conception of remembrance. See, e.g., Emmerich Hornich, letter to "Liebe Freunde [Comité International de Dachau]," 11 Aug. 1961, BayHsta, JS88.

42 Copy of Castle Administration to Kohlhofer, 4 Mar. 1965, LEA. The quotation after Wiedemann is taken from Schelling to Striffler, 14 Dec. 1966, EZB6.

43 There is a long and detailed correspondence about this in the personal files of Oskar Söhngen. See especially Neuhäusler's final letter to Horn, 22 Feb. 1967. The quotation after Horn is from Horn to Söhngen, 27 Dec. 1966, EZB, Söhngen files.

44 For the final cost of the entire project, see estimate by Striffler, 27 Feb. 1965, and Kirchenkanzlei to Wilm and Collmer, 15 Apr. 1965, both EZB5. The original estimate was DM850,000. See minutes of meeting in Munich, 31 Oct. 1964, ibid.

45 On the decision to finance the building by donations, see Wilm to Scharf, report about discussion in Munich and Dachau, 4pp., 19 Apr. 1963, ibid.

46 State Church Council of Lippe, circular with call for donations on Pentecost Sunday, 3pp., 14 Apr. 1964, EZB8a.

47 Minutes of a meeting of the construction committee, 4 Mar. 1965, EZB5. A total of DM328,000 had been raised. For the proportional table, see Wilm to Collmer, 15 Apr. 1965, ibid.

48 Overview of the donations account with key and percent fulfillment, 23 Sept. 1965, EZB8a; minutes of meeting of the construction committee, 31 March 1966, EZB9.

49 Circular to Landeskirchen, 17 March 1967, EZB6.

50 This account of the origin of AS was told by a volunteer in Israel in 1964 to an American visitor. The official who made the suggestion was judge Lothar Kreyssig. See Halperin, *Here I Am,* 131f.

51 Peter Pragal, "Bausteine zur Völkerversöhnung: Jugendliche helfen bei der Errichtung einer Kirche im ehemaligen Dachauer Lager," *SZ,* 26 Nov. 1965.

52 Wilm to Lilje, 20 Sept. 1962, EZB5. The participation of AS volunteers was discussed again in Oct. 1964: see minutes of the working committee, 31 Oct. 1964, ibid.

53 Peter Pragal, "Bausteine zur Völkerversöhnung: Jugendliche helfen bei der Errichtung einer Kirche im ehemaligen Dachauer Lager," *SZ*, 26 Nov. 1965.

54 See Wilm to Lilje, 20 Sept. 1962, and mimeographed diary of the Dachau group, 2 Sept. 1965 – 30 Jan. 1966. I thank Angelika Berghofer-Sierra for a copy of the latter document. For the general history of AS, see Karl-Klaus Rabe, *Umkehr in die Zukunft: Die Arbeit der Aktion Sühnezeichen/Friedensdienste* (Bornheim-Merten: Lamuv, 1983). The 1965–6 Dachau group is only briefly mentioned, see 67. AS volunteers also assisted in the construction of the "Document House" in Bergen-Belsen in 1966.

55 Evangelischer Pressedienst (epd), "Dachau: Museums-Baracke als Unterkunft ungeeignet / Bayerisches Finanzministerium zu Vorwürfen der 'Aktion Sühne-zeichen,'" 4 Jan. 1966, EZB.

56 Pragal, "Bausteine," *SZ*, 26 Nov. 1965.

57 See diary entry for 25 Jan. 1966. The Munich visit took place on 28 Jan. See also Max-Hermann Bloch, "Dachaus unbewältigte Vergangenheit," *Augsburger Allgemeine*, 9 Feb. 1966, reprinted in *Stimmen*, Easter 1966. See also typescript copy of Köberlin, Pfarramt Dachau-Friedenskirche to Landeskirchenamt Munich, 19 Feb. 1966, EZB6. Köberlin says that Bloch's article also appeared in the *Nürnberger Nachrichten*, 11 Feb. 1966.

58 Klaus Heienbrok, Concluding report of group Dachau I/Israel VII, 7pp., undated, EZB6. The quotation is from p. 3.

59 See Gerhard Wolfrum, "KZ-Häftlinge feiern den Tag der Befreiung: Delegationen aus 14 europäischen Ländern in Dachau / Grundstein für evangelische Versöh-nungskirche gelegt," *SZ*, 10 May 1965.

60 Martin Urban, "Stätte des Friedens im ehemaligen KZ: Evangelische Versöhnungs-kirche in Dachau eingeweiht / Niemöller gegen neuen Nationalismus," *SZ*, 2 May 1967; re., "Evangelische Versöhnungskirche in Dachau eingeweiht: Millionen-Spende aus allen Teilen Europas – Sowjetzonen-Delegation erhält keine Ausreise-genehmigung," *MM*, 2 May 1967; "Versöhnungskirche in Dachau eingeweiht," *FAZ*, 2 May 1967.

61 The text of the prepared speech is contained as an enclosure to "Einweihung der Evangelischen Versöhnungskirche / Informationen für Hörfunk und Fernsehen," 24 Apr. 1967, EZB, Oskar Söhngen files.

62 See Striffler to Söhngen, ca. 5 May 1967 (letter accompanying article "Versöhnungs-kirche in Dachau eingeweiht," *FAZ*, 2 May 1967), and attached copy of Söhngen to Striffler, EZB, Söhngen files. Striffler found Niemöller's comments "inappropriate, thin," while Söhngen found them "a scandal."

63 The text of Niemöller's speech was published in *Stimme der Gemeinde*, no. 11 (1 June 1967)(copy in DDW, OM), and *Evangelische Welt* (1 June 1967)(in EZB, Söhngen files).

12 The 1968 generation: new legacies of old myths

1 Karl Mannheim is the seminal theorist on this issue. See esp. his 1927 essay, "The Sociological Problem of Generations," in Paul Kecskemeti (ed.), *Karl Mannheim: Essays on the Sociology of Knowledge* (London: Routledge, 1952, 1972), 276–320.

Please note that I do not follow Mannheim's distinction between "generation" and "cohort." I prefer the term "cohort" to "generation" because it emphasizes the importance of pivotal historical events in individual biographies, whereas "generation" implies biological linkages between cohorts. Although "generation" might thus be more appropriate to describe the "children" cohorts that become relevant after the mid-1960s, I find the switch in terminology confusing.

For a discussion of Mannheim's thoughts on the two terms, see Peter Loewenberg, "The Psychohistorical Origins of the Nazi Youth Cohort," *American Historical Review*, 76:5 (Dec. 1971), 1457–1502, 1465. For an excellent discussion of the literature in general, see Helmut Fogt, *Politische Generationen: Empirische Bedeutung und theoretisches Modell* (Opladen: Westdeutscher, 1982), 6–25.

2 For other discussions of age cohorts shaped by pivotal experiences, see Hans Jaeger, "Generationen in der Geschichte: Überlegungen zu einer umstrittenen Konzeption," *Geschichte und Gesellschaft*, 3 (1977), 429ff; Heinz Bude, *Bilanz der Nachfolge: Die Bundesrepublik und der Nationalsozialismus* (Frankfurt: Suhrkamp, 1992), chapter 6, and "Die Erinnerung der Generationen," in Helmut König, Michael Kohlstruck, and Andreas Wöll (eds.), *Vergangenheitsbewältigung am Ende des zwanzigsten Jahrhunderts* (Opladen: Westdeutscher, 1998), 69–85; Norbert Frei, "Farewell to the Era of Contemporaries: National Socialism and its Historical Examination en route into History," in Gulie Ne'eman Arad (ed.), *Passing into History: Nazism and the Holocaust beyond Memory: In Honor of Saul Friedlander on his Sixty-fifth Birthday* (Bloomington: Indiana University Press, 1997) (*History and Memory*, 9:1/2 [fall 1997]), 59–79; Kristin Platt and Mihran Dabag, *Generation und Gedächtnis: Erinnerungen und kollektive Identitäten* (Opladen: Leske and Buderich, 1995). I am indebted to A. D. Moses for his incisive and insightful comments on the question of cohorts, especially with regard to the group that I call the 48ers.

3 In 1934 Columbia University sociology professor Theodore Abel conducted an essay competition for "the best personal life history of an adherent of the Hitler movement." Close to 70 percent of the 683 Nazis who responded were born between 1895 and 1916. For an excellent analysis of this material, see Peter Merkl, *Political Violence under the Swastika: 581 Early Nazis* (Princeton: Princeton University Press, 1975).

4 For a sophisticated five-country examination of the 1918er cohort, see Robert Wohl, *The Generation of 1914* (Cambridge, Mass.: Harvard University Press, 1979). See 239f for numerous references to the literature of generation and cohort theory.

5 For a detailed discussion of seminal experiences of the cohort born between 1900 and 1915, see Loewenberg, "The Psychohistorical Origins of the Nazi Youth Cohort," passim. The experiences are diagrammatically illustrated on p. 1462. See also Ulrich Herbert's discussion of this cohort, including an examination of contemporary 1930s' literature that discerned the phenomenon, in his *Arbeit, Volkstum, Weltanschauung: Über Fremde und Deutsche im 20. Jahrhundert* (Frankfurt: Fischer, 1995), 31–58, with bibliographic notes on p. 234. For the most detailed intellectual biography of a member of this cohort, see Ulrich Herbert's *Best: Biographische Studien über Radikalismus, Weltanschauung und Vernunft, 1903–1989* (Bonn: Dietz, 1996). Johannes Steinhoff, Peter Bechel, and Dennis Showalter (eds.), *Voices from the Third Reich: An Oral History* (New York: Da Capo,

1994 [1989]) offers a collection of 157 interviews, the vast majority taken from people with birth years between 1909 and 1925.

6 See Gesine Schwan, *Politik und Schuld: Die zerstörerische Macht des Schweigens* (Frankfurt: Fischer, 1997), 133, 147. Schwan uses the cutoff date of 1925. As an example of the common use of the term, see Jürgen Habermas, "Der Zeigefinger: Die Deutschen und ihr Denkmal," *Zeit*, 31 Mar. 1999. The term *Tätergeneration*, while accurate, contains a collective reproach that belies its coining by 1968ers. I prefer the term "careerist Nazis" because it characterizes the activity of this cohort more neutrally without branding everyone as criminally guilty.

7 For concise biographical interviews with numerous 1943ers, see Henry Ries, *Abschied meiner Generation* (Berlin: Argon, 1992) (thirty-seven interviews range from birth years 1899 to 1924, with most between 1917 and 1924); also Karl Heinz Jahnke, *Hitlers letztes Aufgebot: Deutsche Jugend im sechsten Kriegsjahr 1944/45* (Essen: Klartext, 1993); Ludwig Marcuse (ed.), *War ich ein Nazi? Politik – Anfechtung des Gewissens* (Munich: Rütten und Loening, 1968) (nine authors whose birth years range from 1903 to 1922). On women, see Trude Unruh, *Trümmerfrauen: Biografien einer betrogenen Generation* (Essen: Klartext, 1987). For typical "victims'" perspectives: Siegfried Knappe (b. 1916) and Ted Brusaw, *Soldat: Reflections of a German Soldier, 1936–1949* (New York, Orion, 1992); Heinz Edler, *Die missbrauchte Generation: Erlebnisse, Erfahrungen, Erkenntnisse eines Unbekannten aus sechs Jahrzehnten* (Frankfurt: R. G. Fischer, 1989); G. R. Karl Rammelt, *Die Gescholtenen: Die Generation zwischen 1918 und 1933* (Leoni: Druffel, 1991); Anton Braunstätter, *Die verratene Generation* (Vienna: Lagerkreis REWDA, 1996).

8 This is especially evident in the examples collected in Steinhoff, Bechel, and Showalter, *Voices.*

9 Strauss is discussed on pp. 118f, above. On Noelle-Neumann's Nazi-era career, see Christopher Shea, "Nazi Apologist or Distinguished Scholar?" *Chronicle of Higher Education*, 8 Aug. 1997.

10 See, for example, Hans Filbinger, *Die geschmähte Generation* (Munich: Universitas, 1987), esp. 167, for remarks on this cohort.

11 See also the biography of the concentration camp guard Anna Fest (b. 1920) in Alison Owings, *Frauen: German Women Recall the Third Reich* (New Brunswick: Rutgers University Press, 1993), 313–41. See also the case of Melita Maschmann (b. 1918), discussed on pp. 298f, below.

12 For examples and discussions of this cohort, see Alfons Heck (b. 1928), *The Burden of Hitler's Legacy* (Frederick, Colo.: Renaissance House, 1988); Rolf Schörken, *Jugend 1945: Politisches Denken und Lebensgeschichte* (Opladen: Leske and Budrich, 1990; Frankfurt: Fischer, 1994); Gabriele Rosenthal and Claudia Gather, *Die Hitlerjugend-Generation: Biographische Thematisierung als Vergangenheitsbewältigung* (Essen: Blaue Eule, 1986); Heinz Bude, *Deutsche Karrieren: Lebenskonstruktionen sozialer Aufsteiger aus der Flakhelfer-Generation* (Frankfurt: Suhrkamp, 1987); Friedhelm Boll, "Hitler-Jugend und 'skeptische Generation': Sozialdemokratie und Jugend nach 1945," in Dieter Dowe (ed.), *Partei und soziale Bewegung: Kritische Beiträge zur Entwicklung der SPD seit 1945* (Bonn: Dietz, 1993), 33–58.

13 An excellent example of this ambivalence can be found in the 1997–8 revelation that 1933er historians Werner Conze (b. 1910) and Theodor Schieder (b. 1904) were

heavily complicit in producing historical justification for Nazi policies. Their 1948er students during the 1950s, for example Hans-Ulrich Wehler (b. 1931), were chastised by even younger German historians for defending the 1933ers. A superb documentation of this discussion can be found at http://hsozkult.geschichte. hu-berlin.de/beitrag/diskusio/nszeit.htm. This includes the text of Michael Fahlbusch's presentation at the Sept. 1998 Frankfurt Historikertag, and Fahlbusch's review of Peter Schoettler (ed.), *Geschichtsschreibung als Legitimationswissenschaft 1918–1945* (Frankfurt: Suhrkamp, 1997). See also Jürgen Kocka's commentary and Hans-Ulrich Wehler's interview in the Berlin *Tagesspiegel*, 8 Dec. 1998. For a fascinating series of interviews with German historians born in the 1930s, see: http://hsozkult.geschichte.hu-berlin.de/beitrag/intervie/index.htm.

14 Oral history projects such as Lutz Niethammer (ed.), *Lebensgeschichte und Sozialkultur im Ruhrgebiet 1930 bis 1960*, 3 vols. (Bonn: Dietz, 1983, 1985; 2nd edn, 1986), and scholarly works such as Broszat, Henkel, and Woller, *Von Stalingrad zur Währungsreform*, also found that 1948 was a more important subjective turning point than 1945. Memoirs such as those by Alfons Heck and Melita Maschmann emphasize the gradual reorientation after 1945.

The term forty-fiver is used by A. D. Moses, "The Forty-Fivers: A Generation between Fascism and Democracy," *German Politics and Society*, 17:1 (spring 1999), 94–126. Moses takes the term from Joachim Kaiser (b. 1928), "Phasenverschiebungen und Einschnitte in der kulturellen Entwicklung," in Martin Broszat (ed.), *Zäsuren nach 1945: Essays zur Periodisierung der deutschen Nachkriegsgeschichte* (Munich: Oldenbourg, 1990), 69–74. Using the designation 1945ers would be equivalent to calling my 1918ers 1914ers (emphasizing the start of World War I, not its end), or my 1933ers 1929ers (using the dissolution of Weimar as the defining moment, not the start of Nazism). I am not completely consistent in that I bow to common usage and ease of pronunciation in calling the youngest cohort 1989ers instead of 1990ers.

15 The phrase may have first been used by Günter Gaus. See p. 536 n. 10, below.

16 For a number of reflections on their schooling by members of the 48er and 43er cohorts who became leading public figures in the 1960s and 1970s, see Geert Platner and Students of the Gerhart-Hauptmann-Schule in Kassel (eds.), *Schule im Dritten Reich: Erziehung zum Tod* (Cologne: Pahl-Rügenstein, 4th augmented edn, 1988), 79–126. The contributors include Karl Carstens (b. 1914), Alfred Dregger, Helmut Kohl, Manfred Rommel (the general's son), Franz Josef Strauss (1915–88), and Richard von Weizsäcker (b. 1920). Their generally neutral and distanced recollections stand in sharp contrast to the documentary evidence in the same collection.

17 Typically, however, the 1948er cohort of historians did not confront their mentors directly. This is superbly documented in the 1999 interview project conducted by researchers at the Berlin Humboldt University: "Fragen, die nicht gestellt wurden! Oder gab es ein Schweigegelübde der zweiten Generation?" ("Second generation" refers to the 1948ers.) The interviews are archived at: http://hsozkult.geschichte.hu-berlin.de/beitrag/intervie/inteview.htm. See also Winfried Schulze and Otto Gerhard Oexle (eds.), *Deutsche Historiker im Nationalsozialismus* (Frankfurt: Fischer, 1999).

18 Further examples of authors from this generation who were concerned with legacies of Nazism are: Hans Magnus Enzensberger (b. 1930), Rolf Hochhuth (b. 1931),

Walter Kempowski (b. 1929), and Jakov Lind (b. 1927). Walter Jens (b. 1923), although slightly older, might be counted among this group.

19 For examples from this cohort, see Heinz Bude, *Das Altern einer Generation: Die Jahrgänge 1938–1948* (Frankfurt: Suhrkamp, 1995).

20 Günther Anders, *Wir Eichmannsohne: Offener Brief an Klaus Eichmann* (Munich: Beck, 1964). The terms "children of the perpetrators" and the more metaphorical "children of Hitler" came into common use in the late 1980s (see chapter 15, p. 374 with p. 553 note 10). See also Helmut Dubiel, *Niemand is frei von der Geschichte: Die nationalsozialistische Herrschaft in den Debatten des Deutschen Bundestages* (Munich: Hanser, 1999), chapter 3: "Die 70er Jahre: Kinder Hitlers oder Kinder der Demokratie."

21 A group of such books published in 1979–80 is discussed on p. 346 with n. 51. For a collection of biographical interviews, see Peter Sichrovsky, *Born Guilty: Children of Nazi Families* (New York: Basic, 1988), *Schuldig geboren: Kinder aus Nazifamilien* (Cologne: Kiepenhauer und Witsch, 1987). For an individual account, see Niklas Frank (b. 1939), *Der Vater: Eine Abrechnung* (Munich: Bertelsmann, 1987), *In the Shadow of the Reich* (New York: Knopf, 1991).

22 Sabine Reichel, *What Did You Do in the War, Daddy? Growing up German* (New York: Hill and Wang, 1989); *Zwischen Trümmern und Träumen: Aufgewachsen im Schatten der Schuld* (Hamburg: Hoffmann und Campe, 1991); Ursula Duba, *Tales from a Child of the Enemy* (New York: Penguin, 1997 [Twin Soul, 1995]); Ursula Hegi, *Tearing the Silence: On Being German in America* (New York: Simon and Schuster, 1997).

23 Based on interview with Detlef Hoffmann, 28 Apr. 1991, Hamburg, Germany; notes in my possession. Hoffmann detailed his views on remembrance of the Nazi period in a presentation at the international conference of heads of memorial sites in Auschwitz in Nov. 1987. See also D. H., "Erinnerungsarbeit der 'zweiten und dritten' Generation und 'Spurensuche' in der zeitgenössischen Kunst," *Kritische Berichte*, 16:2 (1988), 31–46. For other examples, see Reichel and Hegi, cited above, and Claudia Koonz, "Between Memory and Oblivion: Concentration Camps in German Memory," in John Gillis (ed.), *Commemorations: The Politics of Identity* (Princeton: Princeton University Press, 1994), 258–80, 265.

24 Ernst Schnabel, *Anne Frank: Spur eines Kindes* (Frankfurt: Fischer, 1958); trans. as *Anne Frank: A Portrait in Courage* (New York: Harcourt Brace, 1958). Schnabel was an editor at Northwest German Radio in Hamburg.

25 Alexander Mitscherlich and Fred Mielke, *Das Diktat der Menschenverachtung* (Heidelberg: Lambert Schneider, 1947); *Medizin ohne Menschlichkeit* (Frankfurt: Fischer, 1949); *Doctors of Infamy: The Story of the Nazi Medical Crimes*, trans. Heinz Norden (New York: Schuman, 1949; Ann Arbor: University Microfilms, 1983).

26 See also his articles: "Fotografierte Lager: Überlegungen zu einer Fotogeschichte deutscher Konzentrationslager," *Fotogeschichte*, 54 (1994), 3–20; "Menschen hinter Stacheldraht," in Yasmin Doosry (ed.), *Representations of Auschwitz: 50 Years of Photographs, Paintings, and Graphics* (Oświęcim: Auschwitz State Museum, 1995), 87–94, and D. Hoffmann (ed.), *Das Gedächtnis der Dinge: KZ-Relikte und KZ-Denkmäler, 1945–1995* (Frankfurt: Campus, 1998).

27 In the words of Hermann Eich, (*Die unheimlichen Deutschen* [Düsseldorf: Econ, 1963]; *The [Unloved] Germans*, trans. Michael Glenny [New York: Stein and Day,

1965], 216): "1960 saw the emergence in West Germany of a highly subjective literature of condemnation and personal exculpation."

28 Christian Geissler, *Anfrage* (Hamburg: Claassen, 1960); translated as *Sins of the Fathers* (New York: Random House, 1962). Geissler published other books relevant in this context, including a TV drama, *Schlachtvieh: Ein Fernsehspiel* (Hamburg: Classen, 1963); *Ende der Anfrage* (Munich: Rütten und Loening, 1967), about a 1965 trip to the "euthanasia" institute Hartheim; *Das Dritte Reich mit seiner Vorgeschichte* (Munich: Langewiesche, 1961), and books on the terrorist movement of the 1970s.

Gudrun Tempel, *Deutschland? Aber wo liegt es?* (Hamburg: Rowohlt, 1962); *Germany: An Indictment of My People*, trans. Sophie Wilkins (New York: Random House, 1963). Chapter 8 of the translation contains letters from readers and discusses the book's reception in Germany. The title of the British edition was *Speaking Frankly about the Germans: A Personal History and a Challenge* (London: Secker and Warburg, 1963). In Richard Matthias Müller's father–son dialogs, *Über Deutschland* (Olten: Walter, 1965), the father is informed, while the postwar son denies the brown-collar crimes.

29 The German publication was William Shirer, *Aufstieg und Fall des Dritten Reiches* (Cologne: Kiepenheuer und Witsch, 1961). For a discussion of the reception in Germany, see Gavriel Rosenfeld, "The Reception of William L. Shirer's *The Rise and Fall of the Third Reich* in the United States and West Germany, 1960–62," *Journal of Contemporary History*, 29 (1994), 95–128, 115. In a 9 May 1996 posting on H-German Rosenfeld noted the similarity between Shirer's popularity in the early 1960s and Daniel Goldhagen's in the mid-1990s. The posting can be retrieved from the discussion logs at: http://www.h-net.msu.edu/~german/.

30 Eich, *The [Unloved] Germans*. The adjective "unloved" does not appear on the title page of the edition I examined, but it is on the header of every left page, and it is used in some library listings of the title. Thus the English publisher seems to have been uncertain as to how much sympathy for the Germans the title should invoke. The following quotation is on p. 129 of the English edition.

31 For a discussion of the crass lack of empathy toward Jewish victims in 1950, see Hannah Arendt, "The Aftermath of Nazi Rule: Report from Germany," *Commentary*, 10:10 (Oct. 1950), 342–53, 342f.

32 Melita Maschmann, *Fazit: Kein Rechtfertigungsversuch* (Stuttgart: DVA, 1963; Munich: dtv, 1979); trans. as *Account Rendered: A Dossier on My Former Self*, by Geoffrey Strachan, with a foreword by Lord Russell of Liverpool (New York: Abelard-Schuman, 1964).

33 See Ludwig Marcuse (ed.), *War ich ein Nazi?*

34 For scholarly analyses of this cohort, see Rolf Schörken, *Luftwaffenhelfer und Drittes Reich: Die Entstehung eines politischen Bewusstseins* (Stuttgart: Klett-Cotta, 1984); Schörken, "Singen und Marschieren: Erinnerung an vier Jahre Jungvolk 1939 bis 1943," *Geschichte in Wissenschaft und Unterricht*, 7 (July/Aug. 1998), 447–61; Christian Schneider, Cordelia Stillke, and Bernd Leineweber, *Das Erbe der Napola: Versuch einer Generationengeschichte des Nationalsozialismus* (Hamburg: Hamburger Edition, 1996).

35 A. D. Moses, "The Forty-Fivers: A Generation between Fascism and Democracy," *GPS*, 17:1 (spring 1999), 94–126, 119.

36 According to Christoph Klessmann, *Zwei Staaten, eine Nation: Deutsche Geschichte*

1955–1970 (Göttingen: Vandenhoeck und Ruprecht, 1988), 181, the 1950s' silence with regard to the Nazi past contributed to the "rigidity and intolerance" of the student movement. Klessmann later notes that this movement was by no means limited to students but was a generational phenomenon, with most activists born between 1943 and 1949 (272). See also p. 276, where Klessmann notes the "ignorance" of young leftists about the importance of civil society's achievements.

37 "Ein Volk, das diese wirtschaftlichen Leistungen erbracht hat, hat ein Recht darauf, von Auschwitz nichts mehr hören zu wollen." Cited as a quotation from 1969 in *Die Zeit*, 43:41 (7 Oct. 1988), 2.

38 Jillian Becker, *Hitler's Children: A Story of the Baader–Meinhof Terrorist Gang* (Philadelphia: Lippincott, 1977), 58. Becker claims that this statement was used to repudiate guilt; I disagree. The 1968ers did not feel personal guilt, but were trying to justify their activism against political injustice. A. D. Moses points out that it was not guilt, but the "psychological consequences of guilt" that were passed from the 1933er and 1943er cohorts to the 1968ers.

39 Seven examples are cited by Martin Kloke, *Israel und die deutsche Linke: Zur Geschichte eines schwierigen Verhältnisses* (Frankfurt: Haag und Herchen, 2nd expanded edn, 1994), 171 n. 67.

40 Ibid., 164. On the resurfacing of this stigmatization of Israeli Jews as "Nazis" during the Gulf War in 1991, see 308–26, and Buruma, *Wages of Guilt*, 14–31, esp. 16, 19.

41 For East German accusations see Ausschuss für deutsche Einheit (ed.), *Die Wahrheit über Oberländer: Braunbuch über die verbrecherische faschistische Vergangenheit des Bonner Ministers* (E. Berlin: Ausschuss, 1960); and Nationale Front des demokratischen Deutschlands (ed.), *Braunbuch: Kriegs- und Naziverbrechen in der Bundesrepublik: Staat, Wirtschaft, Armee, Justiz, Verwaltung, Wissenschaft* (E. Berlin: Staatsverlag der DDR, 1960, 1965, 1968).

For the West German Zind, Eisele, and Nieland cases, see Bergmann, *Antisemitismus in öffentlichen Konflikten*, 192–221.

42 For example, the high proportion of former Nazis in the Foreign Office reported in a popular Munich radio series in 1955 did not prompt any official response. See Helmut Hammerschmidt and Michael Mansfeld, *Der Kurs ist Falsch* (Munich: K. Desch, 1956), 24–40, 68ff. For a broader historical perspective, see Brochhagen, *Nach Nürnberg*, 173–258.

The so-called Gauleiter Conspiracy of 1952–3 only sparked short-term public interest and had no important political repercussions. See the discussion in chapter 3, pp. 115f, above.

43 For a survey of the reactions to important incidents, see T. H. Tetens, *The New Germany and the Old Nazis* (New York: Random House, 1961). See also the documentation, Vereinigung der Verfolgten des Naziregimes (ed.), *Die unbewältigte Gegenwart: Eine Dokumentation über Rolle und Einfluss ehemals führender Nationalsozialisten in der Bundesrepublik Deutschland* (Frankfurt: VVN, 1962), and Bergmann, *Antisemitismus*, 192–221. See also Lewis Edinger, "Continuity and Change in the Background of German Decision-Makers," *Western Political Quarterly*, 14 (Mar. 1961), 17–36.

44 For a good summary of the affair, see David Schoenbaum, *The Spiegel Affair* (New York: Doubleday, 1968). See also Joachim Schoeps, *Die Spiegel-Affäre des F.-J. Strauss* (Hamburg: Rowohlt, 1983), and Ronald Bunn, *German Politics and the*

Spiegel Affair: A Case Study of the Bonn System (Baton Rouge: Louisiana State University Press, 1968).

45 For an example of Adenauer's concern about comparisons with the Gestapo, see Schoenbaum, *Spiegel Affair*, 113; for media examples, see 157.

46 For a good overview of these early 1960s' political developments, see Mary Fulbrook, *The Divided Nation: A History of Germany, 1918–1990* (Oxford: Oxford University Press, 1991), 198f.

47 For a discussion of the rise of right-wing parties, see Klessmann, *Zwei Staaten, eine Nation*, 209–14. On the economic basis of the NPD's success, see Lutz Niethammer, *Angepasster Faschismus: Politische Praxis der NPD* (Frankfurt: Fischer, 1969), 27–31.

48 Niethammer, *Angepasster Faschismus*, 98–229, offers a state-by-state examination of the election results.

49 For a detailed history of the emergency laws, see Michael Schneider, *Demokratie in Gefahr? Der Konflikt um die Notstandsgesetze: Sozialdemokratie, Gewerkschaften und intellektueller Protest (1958–1968)* (Bonn: Neue Gesellschaft, 1986). The protests against the laws are discussed on 182–8, 230f, 239f. As a sidenote, similar laws (Art. 48 of the Weimar constitution) had been invoked dozens of times during crises in the 1920s.

50 On the history of the APO, see Gerd Langguth, *Protestbewegung: Entwicklung, Niedergang, Renaissance: Die Neue Linke seit 1968* (Cologne: Wissenschaft und Politik, 1983); Klessmann, *Zwei Staaten*, 256–98.

51 See Beate Klarsfeld, *Wherever They May Be!* (New York: Vanguard, 1972), 50–63, and Dennis Bark and David Gress, *A History of West Germany* (Cambridge, Mass.: Basil Blackwell, 1989), vol. II, 127. Bark and Gress claim that Böll, who sent a bouquet of roses to thank Klarsfeld after the event, as well as Grass and Jaspers, were claiming a "grace of late birth" for themselves. In fact they did just the opposite by not exempting themselves from their own public calls that Germany must take responsibility for its Nazi past. On Kiesinger's Nazi past, see p. 109f, above.

52 See Beate Klarsfeld, *Die Geschichte des PG 2633930 Kiesinger: Dokumentation mit einem Vorwort von Heinrich Böll* (Darmstadt: Melzer, 1969), 75.

53 See *Der Spiegel*, 24:51 (14 Dec. 1970), 27, 29–31; 24:52 (21 Dec. 1970), 7; 24:53 (28 Dec. 1970), 7; also Willy Brandt, *Begegnungen und Einsichten: Die Jahre 1960–1975* (Hamburg: Hoffmann und Campe, 1976), 524f, 533 (English edn, 399f).

54 Hermann Giesecke, "Ist die Geschichte des Dritten Reiches noch ein politisches Thema für die Jugendbildung?" in *Deutsche Jugend*, 11 (1963), 274, translation quoted after Hübner-Funk, "Hitler's Grandchildren," 106 (see also 112).

55 Fritz Vilmar, "Der Nationalsozialismus als didaktisches Problem," *Frankfurter Hefte*, 21:10 (Oct. 1968), 683–90, 683.

56 Ludwig Friedeburg and Peter Hübner, *Das Geschichtsbild der Jugend* (Munich: Juventa, 1964, 2nd edn, 1970), 5. Friedeburg, who had been director of the Frankfurt Institut für Sozialforschung since 1966, became the Hessian Minister of Culture in 1969. Thus he can be seen as a trail blazer on the "long march through the institutions."

57 For older members of the 1968er cohort, the educational experiences may have been comparatively worse. See, for example, Ursula Duba, *Tales from a Child of the Enemy*, 14–19, 44–6.

58 Günther van Norden, *Das Dritte Reich im Unterricht* (Frankfurt: Hirschgraben,

1970), 82. Otherwise, however, this book develops a sophisticated pedagogy against "derealization," based on the Mitscherlichs' analysis. For example, it suggests that teachers encourage pupils to talk to their parents and grandparents about the Nazi past, and it recommends convening a meeting with parents before starting the curricular unit, because "it might avoid a direct contradiction between parent and teacher."

59 Reichel, *What Did You Do in the War?*, 104–10. See also Bergmann, *Antisemitismus*, 230, and the nuanced discussion in Hübner-Funk, "Hitler's Grandchildren," 106f. For an example of a better-intended but equally questionable pedagogy in the late 1950s, see Dorothee Sölle (b. ca. 1928), "God Was Very Small in those Times," in Carol Rittner (ed.), *Anne Frank in the World* (Armonk, N.Y.: M. E. Sharpe, 1998), 42f.

60 On the need for portraying feeling as well as fact, see also Kay Boyle, *Breaking the Silence: Why a Mother Tells Her Son about the Nazi Era* (New York: Institute of Human Relations, 1962), 24; Ido Abram and Matthias Heyl, *Thema Holocaust: Ein Buch für die Schule* (Hamburg: Rowohlt, 1996), 128ff.

61 On the 1960s' treatments of National Socialism in schoolbooks, see Gerhard Matzker, "Die Zeit des Nationalsozialismus im Unterricht," *Neue Deutsche Schule*, 19:21 (1967), 413–16; Edgar Wieck (ed.), *Deutscher Widerstand 1933–1945: Aspekte der Forschung und der Darstellung im Schulbuch* (Heidelberg: Lambert Schneider, 1967); Jürgen Redhardt, *NS-Zeit im Spiegel des Schulbuchs: Konzeptionen und Fehlkonzeptionen für westdeutsche Schüler, dargestellt am hessischen Beispiel* (Frankfurt: Röderberg, 1970).

62 Gerhard Schoenberner, *Der gelbe Stern: Die Judenverfolgung in Europa, 1933 bis 1945* (Munich: Bertelsmann, 1960, 1962, 1968), *The Yellow Star* (London: Corgi, 1969, 1978; New York: Bantam, 1973, 1979); see also his collection of text documents, *Wir haben es gesehen: Augenzeugenberichte über Terror und Judenverfolgung im Dritten Reich* (Hamburg: Rütten und Loening, 1962).

For examples of literature recommendations for schools, see Heinz Huber and Arthur Muller (eds.), *Das Dritte Reich: Seine Geschichte in Texten, Bildern und Dokumenten* (Munich: K. Desch, 1964), vol. II, 541; Scheffler, *Judenverfolgung*, 92ff; Wolfgang Kleinknecht, Herbert Krieger, and Wolfgang Lohan, *Handbuch des Geschichtsunterrichts* (Frankfurt: Diesterweg, 1963), vol. V, 375f.

63 Other relevant titles would be: Robert Antelme, *Das Menschengeschlecht* (Berlin: Aufbau, 1949, 1956), Tadeusz Borowski, *Die steinerne Welt* (Munich: Piper, 1959, 1963), Elie Wiesel, *Die Nacht zu begraben Elischa* (Munich: Bechtle, 1959, 1961), and Jorge Semprún, *Die grosse Reise* (Hamburg: Rowohlt, 1964). I thank Barbara Distel for her help compiling this list.

64 Bruno Apitz, *Nackt unter Wölfen* (Halle: Mitteldeutscher, 1958; Zurich: Aurora, 1963; Frankfurt: Röderberg, 1979); *Naked among Wolves*, trans. Edith Anderson (Berlin: Seven Seas, 1960). The book went through at least fifty-eight German editions by 1968, and was translated into many languages. On the book's reception, see Ingrid Hähnel and Elisabeth Lemke, "Millionen lesen einen Roman: Bruno Apitz' 'Nackt unter Wölfen'" in Inge Münz-Koenen (ed.), *Werke und Wirkungen* (Leipzig: Reklam, 1987), 21–59.

65 On this point see Antje Efkes, "Tatsachenbericht oder Lehrbuch des Kommunismus? Zu Bruno Apitz' *Nackt unter Wölfen*" in Claude Conter (ed.), *Literatur und Holocaust* (Bamberg: Universität Bamberg, 1996), 43–55.

66 Primo Levi, *Se questo e un uomo* (Turin: Einaudi, 1947; 2nd edn, 1957); *If This Is a Man*, trans. Stuart Woolf (New York: Orion, 1959); *Survival in Auschwitz* (New York: Collier, 1961); *Ist das ein Mensch*, trans. Heinz Riedt (Frankfurt: Fischer, 1961, 1979; Munich: Hanser, 1988, 1991; dtv, 1992, 8th edn 1999). On the reception, see also Myriam Anissimov, *Primo Levi: Tragedy of an Optimist* (Woodstock: Overlook, 1999), 280–93.

67 See Primo Levi, *The Drowned and the Saved* (New York: Vintage, 1988), 175–97 (chapter 8: "Letters from Germans").

68 Some references regarding the discussion in the 1960s can be found in Richard Matthias Müller, *Normal-Null und die Zukunft der deutschen Vergangenheits-bewältigung* (Schernfeld: Süddeutsche Hochschulverlagsgemeinschaft, 1994), 28.

69 Peter Hofstätter, "Bewältigte Vergangenheit?" *Die Zeit*, 24 (14 June 1963), 9; "Was verspricht man sich vom Schulfach Zeitgeschichte?" *Die Zeit*, 25 (21 June 1963); "Wir Deutschen – wer sind 'wir'?" *Die Zeit*, 29 (23 Aug. 1963). For a summary of the debate and its reception, see Bergmann, *Antisemitismus*, 283–90. Hofstätter had begun his academic career toeing the Nazi line at an Austrian university.

70 On the contemporary nonelite reception of the Auschwitz trials, see Horst Krüger, *Das zerbrochene Haus: Eine Jugend in Deutschland* (Munich: Rütten und Loening, 1966), 238–76.

71 Karl Jaspers, *The Future of Germany* (Chicago: University of Chicago Press, 1967); *Wohin treibt die Bundesrepublik? Tatsachen, Gefahren, Chancen* (Munich: Piper, 1966, with nine editions through 1968). See also his *Antwort zur Kritik meiner Schrift "Wohin treibt die Bundesrepublik?"* (Munich: Piper, 1967).

72 Gert Kalow, *The Shadow of Hitler: A Critique of Political Consciousness*, trans. Betsy Ross (London: Rapp and Whiting, 1968); German edn: *Hitler: Das gesamtdeutsche Trauma* (Munich: Piper, 1967). For the genesis of the book, see the preface to the English edition, vii. On Kalow's relationship to Jaspers, see xi. The quotations below are taken from 8 and 116.

73 The biographical information is taken from Armin Mohler, *Vergangenheits-bewältigung, oder wie man den Krieg nochmals verliert* (Krefeld: Sinus, 1980, 1981), 119–22.

74 Armin Mohler, *Vergangenheitsbewältigung: Von der Läuterung zur Manipulation* (Stuttgart: Seewald, 1968); republished as *Vergangenheitsbewältigung, oder wie man den Krieg nochmals verliert*. This book should be viewed in the context of Mohler's *Was die Deutschen fürchten: Angst vor der Politik/Angst vor der Geschichte/Angst vor der Macht* (Stuttgart: Seewald, 1965; Berlin: Ullstein, 1967), and his *Der Nasenring: Die Vergangenheitsbewältigung vor und nach dem Fall der Mauer* (Munich: Langen Müller, 1991). A comparison shows how his opinions took shape and hardened into dogmatic polemics.

75 Mohler, *Vergangenheitsbewältigung*, 1980 edn, 55.

76 For some of the few more serious authors supporting Mohler's position, Müller, *Normal-Null und die Zukunft der deutschen Vergangenheitsbewältigung* (1994) and the works of Michael Wolffsohn, especially his *Ewige Schuld?: 40 Jahre deutsch-jüdisch-israelische Beziehungen* (Munich: Piper, 1988); English edn: *Eternal Guilt? Forty Years of German-Jewish-Israeli Relations*, trans. Douglas Bokovoy (New York: Columbia University Press, 1993). Herf, *Divided Memory* (1997), also supports this position.

77 Antonia Grünenberg made this remark at a conference in Berkeley in 1995. The book is Alexander and Margarete Mitscherlich, *Die Unfähigkeit zu trauern: Grundlagen kollektiven Verhaltens* (Munich: Piper, 1967; new edn, 1977; 15th printing 1983); in English: *The Inability to Mourn: Principles of Collective Behavior* (New York: Grove, 1975).

78 For background on the book, see Alexander Mitscherlich's title-giving keynote speech in Helmut Becker (ed.), *Hemmen Tabus die Demokratisierung der deutschen Gesellschaft? – Bergedorfer Protokolle* (Hamburg: R. v. Decker, 1965); also Hans-Martin Lohmann, *Alexander Mitscherlich: Mit Selbstzeugnissen und Bilddokumenten* (Reinbek: Rowohlt, 1987).

79 For some examples of the English-language reception, see Andreas Huyssen, "The Politics of Identification," (1980), 120; Eric Santner, *Stranded Objects: Mourning, Memory, and Film in Postwar Germany* (Ithaca: Cornell University Press, 1990); Fulbrook, *Divided Germany*, 284 (applied to the wrong generation); Moeller, "War Stories," (1996), 1011; Moses, "The Forty-Fivers," 99ff.

80 See esp. Mitscherlichs, *Inability*, 27f.

81 The diary of Max von Westernhagen (1863–1943) offers an excellent example of this identification with the *supermensch*. See the discussion in Dörte von Westernhagen (b. 1943), *Die Kinder der Täter: Das Dritte Reich und die Generation danach* (Munich: Kösel, 1987), 11–40.

82 The quotations are taken from Tilman Moser, "Gibt es die 'Unfähigkeit zu trauern'? Zur psychischen Verarbeitung des Holocaust in der BRD," in Bernhard Moltmann (ed.), *Erinnerung: Zur Gegenwart des Holocaust in Deutschland-West und Deutschland-Ost* (Frankfurt: Haag und Herchen, 1993), 149–61, and "Die Unfähigkeit zu trauern: Hält die These einer Überprüfung stand?" *Psyche*, 46 (May 1992). See also Mitscherlichs, *Die Unfähigkeit* (1977 edn), pt. I, section 10, and pt. III, theses 28, 29; Margarete Mitscherlich, *Erinnerungsarbeit: Zur Psychoanalyse der Unfähigkeit zu trauern* (Frankfurt: Fischer, 1987), passim.

83 Mitscherlich, *Erinnerungsarbeit*, 11, 61.

84 Hans Buchheim, "Die Bundesrepublik und das Dritte Reich," in Buchheim, *Aktuelle Krisenpunkte des deutschen Nationalbewusstseins* (Mainz: Von Hase, 1967), 33–66.

85 For a more detailed discussion of the role of Nazism in the 1968 conjuncture, see Harold Marcuse, "The Revival of Holocaust Awareness in West Germany, Israel, and the United States," in Carole Fink, Philipp Gassert, and Detlef Junker (eds.), *1968: The World Transformed* (New York: Cambridge University Press, 1998), 421–38.

86 For an early example, see Klessmann, *Zwei Staaten*, 265, which mentions a February 1959 petition at the Berlin Free University which called for the ousting of professors with Nazi records. Michael Naumann, Federal Cultural Commissioner for Chancellor Schröder since 1998 and one of the most engaged proponents of the National Holocaust Memorial in Berlin, participated in this movement in 1964. See Michael Jürgs, "Ein 68er am Weg zur Hölle: Michael Naumann, Kulturbeauftragter des Kanzlers: Früher schrieb er gegen das Vergessen – heute finanziert er das Erinnern," *SZ*, 16 Oct. 1999.

87 See Rolf Seeliger, *Braune Universität*, nos. 1–6 (Munich: Seeliger, 1963–6). Seeliger (b. 1925) was somewhat older than most students because he had not been able to study during the Nazi period. A student in the late 1950s, he became a freelance journalist and took an active role in publicizing the Eichmann trial in 1961 (my tele-

phone conversation with Seeliger, Munich, August 1994). On the Eichmann exhibition, see "Massenmord im Zeichen des Hakenkreuzes," *Tat*, 25 Feb. 1961. See also Seeliger's articles on Dachau Curate Roth, for example "Prediger in der Wüste: Der Dachauer Häftlingspater," *Freie Presse* (Bielefeld), 16 Sept. 1960 (other articles are collected in the Roth file at DDW). Seeliger later published a documentary on the APO: *Die ausserparlamentarische Opposition* (Munich: Seeliger, 1968).

88 The lectures were published in Andreas Flitner (ed.), *Deutsches Geistesleben und Nationalsozialismus: Eine Vortragsreihe der Universität Tübingen* (Tübingen: Wunderlich, 1965). The series was initiated by the student editors of a university newspaper. See Becker (ed.), *Hemmen Tabus*, 99.

89 See the review of the publications resulting from these three lecture series: Ernst Nolte, "Die deutsche Universität und der Nationalsozialismus," *Neue Politische Literatur*, 12 (1967), 236–9. The other series were published as: Freie Universität Berlin (ed.), *Nationalsozialismus und die deutsche Universität: Universitätstage 1966* (Berlin: FU Berlin, 1966), and Universität München (ed.), *Universität im Dritten Reich: Eine Vortragsreihe der Universität München* (Munich: n.p., 1966).

90 Most of the critical analyses were by 1948ers such as Dahrendorf in the Tübingen series, Hans Maier in the Munich series, and Abendroth, Bracher, Lieber, Helge Pross, and Sontheimer in the Berlin series. I thank A. D. Moses for his comments about these lectures.

91 Wolfgang Fritz Haug, *Der hilflose Antifaschismus: Zur Kritik der Vorlesungsreihen über Wissenschaft und Nationalsozialismus an deutschen Universitäten* (Frankfurt: Suhrkamp, 1967, 1968, 1970; 4th edn, with a new preface, Cologne: Pahl-Rügenstein, 1977). The essay with all prefaces was reprinted as the first part of Wolfgang Fritz Haug, *Vom hilflosen Antifaschismus zur Gnade der späten Geburt* (Hamburg: Argument, 1987).

92 Mitscherlich, *Erinnerungsarbeit*, 8.

93 Statement by Stefanie, in Sichrovsky, *Born Guilty*, 30f. The publication of this statement prompted much reflection in the literature. See ibid., 160–4; Neue Gesellschaft für bildende Kunst (ed.), *Inszenierung der Macht* (Berlin: Nishen, 1987), 11; Buruma, *Wages of Guilt*, 140f. It should be noted that Stefanie was a grandchild of a perpetrator, not a child, as were the other interviewees in Sichrovsky's study. For similar experiences by Anna Rosmus, see Hans-Dieter Schütt, *Anna Rosmus: Die Hexe von Passau* (Berlin: Dietz, 1994), 39, 41f.

94 Lea Fleischmann, *Dies ist nicht mein Land: Eine Jüdin verlässt die Bundesrepublik* (Hamburg: Hoffmann und Campe, 1980), 104–15.

95 See the text of a 3 Feb. 1966 poster reprinted in Karl A. Otto, *APO: Ausserparlamentarische Opposition in Quellen und Dokumenten (1960–1970)* (Cologne: Pahl-Rügenstein, 1989), 209f.

96 "Anti-U.S. Posters at Dachau," UPI report of 7 Nov. 1966, *NYT*, 8 Nov. 1966, 18.

97 See Stefan Aust, *The Baader-Meinhof Group: The Inside Story of a Phenomenon* (London: Bodley Head, 1987), 40–6. Fulbrook, *Divided Nation*, 282, notes that Springer controlled 80 percent of the popular daily newspapers at that time.

98 Becker, *Hitler's Children*, 40.

99 "Demonstrieren – Ja! Randalieren – Nein!" *Bild*, 3 June 1967; quoted after Otto, *APO*, 236.

100 See Wilhelm Backhaus, *Sind die Deutschen verrückt? Ein Psychogramm der Nation*

und ihrer Katastrophen (Bergisch Gladbach: Gustav Lübbe, 1968), 253f. The original German was: "Bei meinen Kollegen und Verwandten liegen ab sofort Hundepeitschen und Weichmacher bereit," and "Ungeziefer muss man mit Benzin begiessen und anzünden. Tod der roten Studentenpest!" For another example, in Hamburg in 1967, see Becker, *Hitler's Children*, 156.

101 Becker, *Hitler's Children*, 41 and 72. Later, in prison, Ensslin wrote, "The difference between the dead section and isolation is the difference between Auschwitz and Buchenwald." See Aust, *Baader-Meinhof Group*, 543.

102 In 1967 analogies to World War II were actually even more prevalent in Israel than in West Germany. See Marcuse, "The Revival of Holocaust Awareness in West Germany, Israel, and the United States," 421–38, esp. 432f. By the 1980s, however, the mainstream West German media were full of comparisons between Israel and Nazi Germany. See Kloke, *Israel*, 224–32.

103 Rolf Vogel (ed.), *The German Path to Israel: A Documentation* (London: Wolff, 1969), 304–15.

104 Ulrike Meinhof, "Drei Freunde Israels," in *Konkret*, no. 7 (1967), 2f. Cited after Kloke, *Israel*, 113. Meinhof had long battled remnants of Nazism in West German society. In 1961 she published a lead article in *Konkret* entitled "Hitler in You," which railed against Armaments Minister Franz Josef Strauss. The article ended with the words, "As we ask our parents about Hitler, someday our children will ask us about Herr Strauss." When Strauss sued Meinhof for slander, she was successfully defended by Gustav Heinemann, who became president of West Germany in 1969. Her parents were 1933ers, born in 1901 and 1909. See Becker, *Hitler's Children*, 109ff, 139f.

105 Prefatory remark of the SDS Bundesvorstand to the publication of its Near East statement on 5 June 1967, SDS papers, cited after Kloke, *Israel*, 113f. This can be compared to Himmler's 1943 speech, in *IMT*, vol. 29, doc. 1919–PS.

106 On the actions against Springer, see Heinz Grossmann and Oskar Negt (eds.), *Die Auferstehung der Gewalt: Springerblockade und politische Reaktion in der Bundesrepublik* (Frankfurt: EVA, 1968). The comparison between Dutschke and Hitler was not limited to the Springer press; see the letters to the editor received by *Der Spiegel*, 22:18 (29 Apr. 1968), 8–10.

107 *Stern*, 3 March 1968.

108 After Becker, *Hitler's Children*, 49.

109 *Der Spiegel*, 22:17 (22 Apr. 1968), 69, 25.

110 See Klessmann, *Zwei Staaten*, 249. See also 269–72.

111 There were also moderates among the first postwar cohort. The Jusos, the official youth organization of the Social Democratic Party, were uncomfortable supporting their party's stance in favor of the emergency laws, but they also rejected the APO's use of violence. In May 1968 the national congress of delegates explicitly distanced itself from violence as a form of protest. See "Entschliessung des Bundeskongresses der Jungsozialisten zur Ausserparlamentarischen Opposition, 11./12. Mai 1968," *Sozialistische Hefte*, no. 5 (1968), 309f, reprinted in Otto, *APO*, 275.

112 See Jürgen Habermas et al., *Student und Politik: Eine soziologische Untersuchung zum politischen Bewusstsein Frankfurter Studenten* (Neuwied: Luchterhand, 1961).

113 See Jürgen Habermas, "Kongress 'Hochschule und Demokratie,'" in Habermas, *Protestbewegung und Hochschulreform* (Frankfurt: Suhrkamp, 1969), 137–52.

Excerpts from the other contributions to the Hannover discussion can be found in Otto, *APO*, 239–48.

114 For Habermas's retraction, see *Protestbewegung*, 146–52, and Jürgen Habermas, "Scheinrevolution unter Handlungszwang," *Der Spiegel*, 22:24 (10 June 1968), 57f. For reactions from the left and right, see Wolfgang Abendroth et al., *Die Linke antwortet Jürgen Habermas* (Frankfurt: EVA, 1968), and Karl-Dietrich Bracher, *Zeitgeschichtliche Kontroversen um Faschismus, Totalitarismus, Demokratie* (Munich: Piper, 1976). See also Haug, *Vom hilflosen Antifaschismus zur Gnade*, 145–52.

115 Richard Löwenthal, *Romantischer Rückfall* (Stuttgart: Kohlhammer, 1970), 13.

116 For an excellent short summary of these developments with references to recent literature, see A. D. Moses, "The State and the Student Movement, 1967–1977," in Gerald De Groot (ed.), *Student Protest: The Sixties and After* (London: Longman, 1998), 139–50.

117 For the details of the arson attack, see Becker, *Hitler's Children*, 65, 79f, 82f. Any examination of this incident should include the 22 May 1967 Brussels department store fire and the Berlin fliers calling for similar actions in Germany. See ibid., 54f.

118 Ibid., 297–303 contains short biographies of most of the terrorists. The hard core leadership (except for Meinhof) was born between 1938 and 1944; the bulk of the "membership" from 1944 to 1951. None of the known activists were born after 1954. Thus the 1968er cohort yielded the first generation of Red Army Faction (RAF) terrorists.

119 Ibid., 88.

120 It would be necessary to differentiate between different terrorist groups. The "Movement June 2" split off from the RAF because its members professed greater closeness to the working class. See Jeremy Varon, "Shadowboxing the Apocalypse: New Left Violence in the United States and West Germany" (Ph.D. thesis, Cornell University, 1998).

121 See Becker, *Hitler's Children*, 92, 96, 101, 104f.

122 See Gerd Langguth, *Die Protestbewegung in der Bundesrepublik, 1968–1976* (Cologne: Wirtschaft und Politik, 1976), 46–8.

123 P. J. Winters, "Ulrike Meinhof lässt sich nur Stichworte geben," *FAZ*, 15 Dec. 1972, 6, cited after Kloke, *Israel*, 167. See also Aust, *Der Baader Meinhof Komplex* (Hamburg: Hoffmann und Campe, 1985), 260–3.

124 See Kloke, *Israel*, 168, 172f.

125 Hans-Joachim Klein, *Rückkehr in die Menschlichkeit: Appell eines ausgestiegenen Terroristen* (Hamburg: Rowohlt, 1979). See esp. 80f, 89, 185, 200. See also Klein's remarks for a French TV series by Daniel Cohn-Bendit, *Wir haben sie so geliebt, die Revolution* (Frankfurt: Philo, 1987), 160ff.

126 Aust, *The Baader-Meinhof Group*, 543.

127 The left-wing Berlin daily *taz* offers the most detail in its reports on the RAF.

128 See Kohlhofer to CID, 18 June 1968, DaA, CID box 12. The correspondence relating to this issue has not yet been cataloged by the DaA. I found it among twenty-four boxes of material sent to the memorial site in 1993 by the Brussels office. The memorial site has a copy of my provisional listing of the contents of those boxes, which I will cite hereafter as "cid##."

129 Kumpfmüller to CID, 2 July 1968, DaA, cid12. This was an official confirmation of

the conditions that Kohlhofer had already passed on to the CID. See the mimeo-graphed CID letter to its member organizations, Guérisse and Walraeve to Chers Camarades, 24 June 1968, with responses 27 June (Theis and Ost, Luxembourg), and 1 July (Blaha, Czechoslovakia).

130 Carbon copy of minutes of working meeting in Munich, 18 July 1968, DaA, cid12. See also Walraeve to Pat [Guérisse], 18 July 1968.

131 "NATO-Militär in Dachau auf dem Appellplatz: Die Vorbereitungen für die Feiern in dem ehemaligen Konzentrationslager," *Tat*, 17 Aug. 1968.

132 Franzel (b. 1901) was a conservative historian whose magnum opus is *Geschichte des deutschen Volkes* (Munich: Adam Kraft, 1974). On the conservative Deutschland Stiftung, founded in 1966, see Deutschland-Stiftung, e.V. (ed.), *Die Deutschland Stiftung, ein Vermächtnis Konrad Adenauers: Eine Dokumentation* (Würzburg: Holzner, 1967). One of the foundation's first deeds was to award a prize to Armin Mohler, the former Nazi sympathizer who called for a "closing of the book" on the Nazi past.

133 Detailed documentation of this ceremony can be found in the DaA in a notebook marked "Mahnmal 1968." A number of foreign and domestic press clippings can be found in cid12 as well.

134 See Becker, *Hitler's Children*, 43, 50.

135 It is not clear whether both of these last two chants were called out, or whether the "Ho Chi Minh" reported by the press was actually a mis-hearing of "tessera," as a representative of the Greek resistance movement explained in a letter to the editor. See *SZ*, 24 Sept. 1968.

136 See Louis Köckert, *Dachau . . . und das Gras wächst . . .: Ein Report für die Nach-geborenen* (Munich: Freies Volk, 1980), 108.

137 See Cahnman[n] to Walraeve, 7 Oct. 1968; Blaha (CSSR) to Guérisse/Walraeve, 16 Oct. 1968; Thalheim/Bruschke (DDR) to CID, 28 Dec. 1968, all DaA, cid12.

138 See Präsidium der Lagergemeinschaft Dachau [Kohlhofer and Eisinger], "Zur Einweihung des Mahnmals," 11 Sept. 1968, DaA, OK. On the distribution of the text see Guérisse/Walraeve to Kohlhofer and Eisinger, 27 Sept. 1968, DaA, OK.

139 Kumpfmüller/BJR to CID, 16 Sept. 1968, DaA, cid12.

140 Later examples of this politically more creative use of the memorial site would be when Beate Klarsfeld let herself be arrested there (see Ursula Peters, "Beate Klarsfeld lässt sich verhaften: Demonstrativer Auftritt im ehemaligen Konzen-trationslager Dachau," *SZ*, 18 Apr. 1974); when Bertolt Brecht's daughter Hanna Hiob led an "anachronistic parade" to the site (see "'Da gibt es keine Ausnahmen': Initiatoren des 'Anachronistischen Zuges' durften nicht auf das Gelände der Bereitschaftspolizei," *SZ/DN*, 18 Sept. 1980); also when "Remstal Rebel" Palmer protested against the highly placed former brown-collar judges Filbinger and Blass on 19 Jan. 1981.

141 Peter Knorr, "Warum nicht gleich KZs? Auf Wiedersehen in Dachau," *Pardon*, 8:2 (Feb. 1969), 36–9.

142 See "Gedenken durch Diskussion: Veranstaltung des Bayerischen Jugendrings im ehemaligen KZ Dachau," *SZ*, 30 Oct. 1969; A. Z., "Dachau – nicht nur zum Gedenken: Bayerische Jugend im ehemaligen KZ Dachau," *Tat*, 15 Nov. 1969; regis-tration postcard for event on 8 Nov. 1969, in DaA, notebook "Besondere Veranstaltungen." The *Tat* report counted ca. 500 participants.

143 See Marcuse, *Nazi Crimes and Identity in West Germany*, 399. These statistics are available at the Dachau memorial site. The number of visiting groups is very reliable, in sharp contrast to the estimates of individual visitors.

144 Heinemann's words were: "Auch nach allem materiellen Wiederaufbau und über allem fortschreitenden Generationenwechsel hinweg bleibt die Aufhellung unserer eigenen Geschichte um unserer Zukunft willen geboten." Gustav Heinemann, *Allen Bürgern verpflichtet: Reden des Bundespräsidenten 1969–1974* (Frankfurt: Suhrkamp, 1975), 15. Also in *Verhandlungen des Deutschen Bundestags*, 70 (1969), 13,664ff.

145 "Jungsozialisten zum Thema KZ," *Dachauer Volksbote*, 18 Mar. 1970.

146 See Kurt Göttler, "Jusos kurbeln das Gespräch an: Dachau und das KZ im Kreuzverhör / Diskussionsabend der Jungsozialisten bringt zahlreiche Vorschläge," *MM/DN*, 24 Apr. 1970.

Part IV Dachau 1970–2000: new age cohorts challenge mythic legacies

1 I have not been able to find much material on this (my own) cohort. Reinhard Mohr, *Zaungäste: Die Generation, die nach der Revolte kam* (Frankfurt: Fischer, 1992), uses the term "78ers." Since there was no single crucial political experience that left its stamp on this cohort, it might more properly be called the "1970s cohort." However, for the sake of brevity and consistency, I have chosen to call it after the year of the first German broadcast of the TV miniseries *Holocaust*.

2 Reitmeier's recollections have been taken primarily from Lorenz Reitmeier, "Dachau, 29. April 1945," *SZ/DN*, 27 Apr. 1985; see also "Ansprache des 1. Bürgermeisters der Stadt Dachau Dr. Lorenz Reitmeier anlässlich des 25. Jahrestages der Befreiung des Konzentrationslagers Dachau (gehalten in der Sondersitzung des Stadtrates vom 29.4.1970)," DaA; Hans Holzhaider, "Reitmeier zur KZ-Gedenkstätte: Hier geschieht Grosses / Sondersitzung des Stadtrats zum 40. Jahrestag der Befreiung," *SZ/DN*, 27 Apr. 1985.

3 For the 1966 ceremony see "Feierstunde vor Krematorium," *MM/DN*, 9 May 1966. Reitmeier was also at the ceremonies in the memorial site in 1983, 1984, 1985, and 1988, among others.

4 *MM/DN*, 6 May 1969; *Mitteilungen LGD*, Dec. 1969.

5 Mayor Reitmeier, "Mehr als Aufklärungsschrift nicht möglich," *MM/DN*, 24 June 1977; see also Hans-Ulrich Engel, "Dachau, eine Stadt lebt mit einem Vorurteil," broadcast of the Westdeutscher Rundfunk, 30 Nov. 1968, manuscript DaA; and "22. März – Dachau und das KZ," *MM/DN*, 22 Mar. 1983, 19.

6 "Ansprache des 1. Bürgermeisters der Stadt Dachau Dr. Lorenz Reitmeier anlässlich des 25. Jahrestages der Befreiung des Konzentrationslagers Dachau," DaA. (During Reitmeier's tenure this text was available upon request at the Dachau city hall.) Excerpts are reprinted in Hans-Günter Richardi, *Von der Roten Armee zum Schwarzen Corps: Dachaus Weg ins Dritten Reich* (Munich: Süddeutscher, 1983), 61.

7 See, for example, Craig Whitney, "Life goes on in Dachau, but Always with a Memory," *NYT*, 27 Jan. 1976.

8 This claim is a long-standing element of the myth of victimization; for some examples of its use, see Kaltenbacher to Walraeve, 20 Aug. 1953, in box 3, folder XII of CID materials sent to DaA in 1993; Ursula Peters, "Wo Dreissigtausend sterben

535

mussten," *SZ*, 16 Nov. 1963; Hans-Ulrich Engel, "Dachau, Eine Stadt lebt mit einem Vorurteil," broadcast of the Westdeutscher Rundfunk, 30 Nov. 1968, manuscript DaA; "Dachau mit den Augen eines Amerikaners gesehen: Immer wieder berichten grosse ausländische Zeitungen über die Amperstadt und ihre Vergangenheit," *MM/DN*, 14 Jan. 1974; Richardi and Verein Zum Beispiel Dachau (eds.), *Die Stadt und das Lager*, 11; and Wolfgang Schäl, "Gedenkfeier zum 50. Jahrestag der KZ-Eröffnung," *SZ/DN*, 22 Mar. 1983.

9 Details such as this suggest that Reitmeier may have studied Schwalber's November 1945 speech while writing his own. Reitmeier's suggestion that the Dante quote "lasciate ogni speranza, voi, ch'entrate!" would have been an appropriate motto for the camp gate was made previously both by Schwalber and in Neuhäusler's 1960 publication *Wie war das im KZ Dachau?* Other passages indicate that Reitmeier was aware of criticism leveled at one of his predecessors as mayor of Dachau, Hans Zauner, who remarked to a reporter in 1960 that the inmates had "illegally" resisted the legitimate Hitler government. Such close parallels indicate that a file on the camp and memorial site is kept in city hall, although officials there have repeatedly denied its existence.

10 See Judith Miller, *One, by One, by One: Facing the Holocaust* (New York: Simon and Schuster, 1990), 46. Miller translates *Gnade der späten Geburt* as "grace of having been late born." My translation follows Maier, *Unmasterable Past*, 167. Timothy Ryback, "Report from Dachau," *New Yorker* (Aug. 1992), 43–61, 49, calls it the "blessing of being born late."

On Kohl's visit to Israel, see *Bulletin des Presse- und Informationsamtes der Bundesregierung*, no. 13 (2 Feb. 1984), 113. Kohl made the remark in a discussion with members of the Israeli parliament on 24 January.

11 See Anita Eckstaedt, *Nationalsozialismus in der "zweiten Generation": Psychoanalyse von Hörigkeitsverhältnissen* (Frankfurt: Suhrkamp, 1989); Werner Bohleber, "Das Fortwirken des Nationalsozialismus in der zweiten und dritten Generation nach Auschwitz," *Babylon*, no. 7 (1990), 70–83.

12 "Dachau streckt die Hand zur Freundschaft aus – aber niemand will sie haben," *MM/DN*, 24 Sept. 1969; "Eine Stadt im Schatten der Vergangenheit," *Mitteilungen LGD*, Dec. 1969.

13 Lorenz Reitmeier (ed.), *Dachau: Ansichten und Zeugnisse aus 12 Jahrhunderten* (Dachau: Stadt Dachau, 1976–82), 3 vols. with volume of addenda: *Dachau: Der berühmte Malerort: Kunst und Zeugnisse aus 1200 Jahren Geschichte* (Munich: Süddeutscher, 1990). A short catalog accompanying an exhibition in Dachau castle was also published in 1990. It has the same title as the addendum volume.

14 Reitmeier, *Dachau*, vol. III, 7.

15 For another example, when Georg Englhard gave the "Ansichten" to US Rabbi Cooper, see Rainer Rutz, "Morde aus der NS-Zeit sollen nicht verjähren / Delegation von US-Politikern und Rabbinern im ehemaligen KZ / Simon Wiesenthal in Dachau," *SZ/DN*, 14 Mar. 1979. The set held by the Denver, Colorado, Public Library is inscribed to a delegation of Rainbow Division liberators.

16 Anecdote told to me by Barbara Distel and summarized in a letter of 3 Aug. 1992.

17 "Lorenz Reitmeier schreibt an Ronald Reagan, Helmut Kohl und Franz Josef Strauss," *SZ/DN*, 19 Apr. 1985.

18 The 1990s plateau may actually be 20 or more percent higher, as the previous head

counts as visitors enter the museum have given way to hourly estimates. My personal observation of the museum personnel doing the counting suggests that in the busy summer months actual numbers may be as much as 20 percent higher. Additionally, during the most crowded times both individual and group visitors are more likely not to enter the museum at all, and are thus not included in the counts. In personal communications, memorial site director Barbara Distel has confirmed that in recent years the statistics for individual visitors have become very unreliable. (But see also ill. 72.)

19 The proportion of Germans in school and youth groups: total German visitors was calculated using an average of twenty-seven persons per group.

13 The 1970s: redefining the three myths and ending ignorance

1 The original was: "Ein Volk, das diese wirtschaftlichen Leistungen erbracht hat, hat ein Recht darauf, von Auschwitz nichts mehr hören zu wollen." Quoted in *Die Zeit*, 43:41 (7 Oct. 1988), 2.

2 In his bill to close the crematory in 1955 Landrat Junker mentioned Dachau buses that were damaged or defaced when driven abroad (*SZ*, 21 Sept. 1955). Junker's exact words were: "Der Name Dachau ist so verrufen, dass sich ein Omnibus aus unserer Stadt im Ausland nicht mehr sehen [lassen] kann ohne verschmiert zu werden oder die Fenster eingeworfen zu bekommen." See also Wilhelm Maschner, "Im KZ Dachau wohnen auch heute noch Menschen," *Die Welt*, 24 May 1960; Hans-Ulrich Engel, 1 Nov. 1968; *MM/DN*, 22 Mar. 1983; Hans-Günter Richardi, *SZ/DN*, 20 Apr. 1985. I have not, however, been able to find a documented case where cars or buses were actually damaged.

3 The film was produced by Ernst-Ludwig Freisewinkel at the Westdeutscher Rundfunk. A summary and selection of the articles and letters were published in the *Mitteilungen LGD*, July 1971, 1–3; I was only able to examine copies of the articles in this exchange because the Bavarian State Library's copy of the *MM/DN* for 1971 was being rebound while I was doing my research. The newspapers also reported about and quoted letters written to the mayor of Dachau; I was not allowed access to those letters, which are presumably preserved in city hall.

4 Wolfgang Spreitler, "Stellungnahme des SPD-Ortsvereins zur Sendung des Ersten Deutschen Fernsehens vom 23.5.1971," *Dachauer Volksbote*, 11/12 June 1971. It should be noted that the youth group of the Dachau SPD represented a vanguard of the younger generation at odds with the older SPD members; in April 1970 the Jusos had presented a seven-point plan to improve the relationship between the camp and the memorial site. See pp. 324f.

5 See "Rote Omnibusfarbe ärgert KZ-Besucher," *MM/DN*, 2 Mar. 1972; eighteen letters to the editor, *MM/DN*, 11/12 Mar. 1972, 2–4. Thirteen of the letters were reprinted as a special two-page offprint.

6 The street was given that name in the late 1930s, in reference to an SS division from the Sudetenland stationed at the Dachau barracks. The name can be found on a 1938 map in the collection of the DaA.

7 All ten of the following letters were printed in the *MM/DN*: Dieter Hentzschel, "'Bereitet dem unwürdigen Schauspiel ein Ende,'" 11 Jan. 1975; Jakob Lamp, "'. . . können ihre Vergangenheit nicht bewältigen,'" 22 Jan. 1975; A. Kuhnigk,

"Gedenkstätte und überzeitlicher Charakter," 28 Jan. 1975; Edmund Kuna, "Es ist schlimm, wenn man mit Kerker bestraft wird, ohne Verbrecher zu sein," 31 Jan. 1975; Eugen Kessler/Lagergemeinschaft Dachau, "Beschimpfung der Museums-Besucher?," G. Kautsch, "Erinnerung an eine grausige Vergangenheit lebendig mit der Gegenwart verbinden," Louis Köckert, "Sind die Ermordeten so schuldig wie die Mörder?," all 4 Feb. 1975; Bund der Opfer des politischen Freiheitskampfes in Tirol, "Ringen um richtiges Verständnis der KZ-Gedenkstätten," Michael Höck, "'Richtigstellung und Ergänzung,'" both 13 Feb. 1975; Mayor Dr. Reitmeier, "Beseitigung der Gedenkstätte Anlass zu Missverständnissen: Stellungnahme des Stadtrats auf Antrag der Lagergemeinschaft," *MM/DN*, 22/23 Feb. 1975.

It should be noted that the headlines were selected by the editor and do not always accurately reflect the content or main emphasis of the letters (e.g., Kuna entitled his letter "The Truth about KZ Dachau"; the question mark in the headline of Eugen Kessler's letter reflects the skepticism of the editor). A summary report about the debate was published in *Die Tat*, 22 Mar. 1975, p. 14, reprinted in *Mitteilungen LGD*, Apr. 1975. Although more letters were printed in the Morton Frank exchange, they were written simultaneously and thus did not constitute an ongoing debate.

8 The farm wagons used to haul corpses to the graves under the SS (known in prisoners' jargon as the "Moor Express") were pulled by men, not horses or other draft animals. See Paul Hussarek, "Der Berg der Toten: Eine dokumentarisch-kritische Betrachtung über das Massengrab bei Dachau," *Dachauer Stimmen*, no. 1, Leiten notebook, DaA.

9 Edmund Kuna (b. 1907) was a German–Czech refugee who had been interned in Dachau by the US army, for whom he later worked. He was a personal acquaintance of Kurat Roth. See his letter to the editor later that year: Edmund Kuna, "'Von Wahrheit besessen,'" *MM/DN*, 28 Aug. 1975.

10 The term used was *Grundrecht der freien Meinungsäusserung*, which I have translated literally because it has different connotations than the simpler term for "freedom of speech," *Redefreiheit*.

11 The *Dachauer Nachrichten* seems never to have tired of revisiting the debate. See, for example, the full page of letters commenting on the demand "Einfach abreissen und Wohnungen hinbauen," *MM/DN*, 22 Mar. 1983, 19. The six readers calling for removal or reduction of the memorial site were born in 1915, 1922, 1943, 1953, 1955, and 1965.

In contrast, members of the second postwar generation (1979ers) debated the issue of closing the Dachau memorial site in the national press in 1973 and came to the conclusion that the site did not evoke "bitterness and hatred" in foreign visitors, but served an important educational function. See Thomas Mösler, "Besser totschweigen?" and Philip v. Randow and Eckhard Pohl, "Schweigen ist . . . keine Lösung," *Die Zeit*, 1 Mar. and 15 Mar. 1973 (nos. 9 and 11). Reprinted in *Mitteilungen LGD*, Apr. 1973.

12 *Mitteilungen LGD*, July 1983.

13 This occurred in the fall of 1985; see articles in the clippings collection, DaA.

14 *Mitteilungen LGD*, Dec. 1987.

15 Photo report, *SZ/DN*, 23 May 1987; "Spuren wurden vernichtet" (joint letter to the editor), *SZ/DN*, 3 June 1987. These and other relevant articles can be found in the notebook "Alte Römerstrasse," DaA.

16 I walked through those houses in 1985, when they were (illegally) inhabited by homeless persons. At that time they were clearly structurally sound. By the fall of 1988 they had been torn down.

17 Hans Holzhaider, "Trotz Wohnungsmangels: Häuser mit wechselvoller Geschichte stehen leer / Zehn Gebäude . . . angeblich nicht mehr zu renovieren," *SZ/DN*, 12 Aug. 1980.

18 Thomas Soyer, "Die Stadt sträubt sich gegen Denkmalschutz / Bauamt gibt Bauvorhaben Vorrang / Schutz für den Kräutergarten fraglich / Landesamt für Denkmalpflege will den gesamten historischen Umgriff des KZ Dachau als Ensemble schützen," *SZ/DN*, 25/26 July 1998.

19 The criticism was leveled in a letter to the editor by Nikolaus Fischer, "Nur ein Gesicht Dachaus?," *SZ/DN*, 2 June 1977. The responses were: Bernd Sondermann, "'Nur Bemühen um objektives Dachaubild,'" *SZ/DN*, 4 June 1977; Ernst Metzner, "KZ-Gedenkstätte zeigt nur eine Seite der Medaille," *SZ/DN*, 15 June 1977; Lorenz Reitmeier, "Mehr als Aufklärungsschrift nicht möglich," *SZ/DN*, 24 June 1977.

20 Council member Bernd Sondermann was one of the Jusos who drafted a "seven-point plan" for the city to integrate the memorial site into its self-image in April 1970. In the Morton Frank exchange he wrote that he thought it would be better to ignore such criticism (*MM/DN*, 11 Feb. 1972). In 1989 he suggested improvements in the infrastructure connecting the city and the former concentration camp (e.g. validity of Eurail passes on the buses from the Dachau train station to the memorial site) ("Hinweise auf Gedenkstätte sollen verbessert werden: Sondermann für Veränderungen am Dachauer Bahnhof," *SZ/DN*, 5 Sept. 1989). This example shows how locally pervasive the local "mythical" perceptions discussed here were and are: they cut across political and ideological lines, affecting even proponents of less mythologized historical recollection.

21 See Martin Broszat, "'Holocaust' und die Geschichtswissenschaft," reprinted in Hermann Graml and Klaus-Dietmar Henke (eds.), *Nach Hitler: Der schwierige Umgang mit unserer Geschichte* (Munich: Oldenbourg, 1987), 271–86, 282f.

22 Joachim Fest, *Hitler: Eine Biographie* (Berlin: Propylaen, 1973; New York: Harcourt, Brace, Jovanovitch, 1974); Walter Kempowski, *"Haben Sie Hitler gesehen?" Deutsche Antworten* (Munich: Hanser, 1973; Hamburg: Knaur, 1979), *Did You Ever See Hitler?* (New York: Avon, 1975).

23 For an excellent discussion of the film, see Anton Kaes, *From Hitler to Heimat: The Return of History as Film* (Cambridge, Mass.: Harvard University Press, 1989), 5f. In response to Fest's "seduction" thesis Sebastian Haffner wrote his *Anmerkungen zu Hitler* (Munich: Kindler, 1978) (Engl.: *The Meaning of Hitler*, 1979).

24 See Robert Harris, *Selling Hitler* (New York: Pantheon, 1986), and Charles Hamilton, *The Hitler Diaries: Fakes that Fooled the World* (Lexington: University Press of Kentucky, 1991). On the content of the diaries, see esp. Hamilton, *Hitler Diaries*, 60–5. See also Helmut Dietl's 1991 satirical film *Schtonk!*

25 Dieter Bossmann (ed.), *"Was ich über Adolf Hitler gehört habe . . ." Folgen eines Tabus: Auszüge aus Schüler-Aufsätzen von heute* (Frankfurt: Fischer, 1977); Anneliese Mannzmann (ed.) *Hitlerwelle und historische Fakten* (Königstein: Scriptor, 1979). On the reception of the studies by the educational establishment, see Bundeszentrale für politische Bildung (ed.), *Der Nationalsozialismus als didaktisches Problem: Beiträge zur Behandlung des NS-Systems und des deutschen*

Widerstands im Unterricht (Bonn: Bundeszentrale, 1980), 107, 182; Rainer Geissler and Jürgen Delitz, *Junge Deutsche und Hitler: Eine empirische Studie zur historisch-politischen Sozialisation* (Stuttgart: Klett, 1981). Slightly later a national poll about right-wing attitudes sparked another public discussion of education about Hitler: SINUS Institut (ed.), *Fünf Millionen Deutsche: "Wir sollten wieder einen Führer haben. . ."* (Hamburg: Rowohlt, 1981).

26 Reprinted in Sekretariat der Ständigen Konferenz der Kultusminister der Länder in der Bundesrepublik Deutschland, *Zur Auseinandersetzung mit dem Holocaust in der Schule* (Bonn: KMK, 1991), 37. The publication contains an English translation.

27 The resolution reads: "The Ministers of Education and Cultural Affairs will draw the attention of schools . . . to the resolutions adopted by the KMK in this regard [i.e. 1960 on the 'recent past' and 1964 on 'totalitarianism']. They will direct the schools to take up this matter with particular intensity in accordance with the guidelines and syllabuses."

28 See, for example, Günter van Norden, "Nationalsozialistische Judenverfolgung: didaktische und methodische Überlegungen zu einem Unterrichtsproblem," *Geschichte in Wissenschaft und Unterricht*, 21 (1970), 660–71; Joachim Leuschner, *Geschichte an Universitäten und Schulen: Materialien, Kommentar, Empfehlungen* (Stuttgart: Klett, 1973); Axel Böing, *Auschwitz: Unterrichtseinheiten für den Schulgebrauch, erprobt im Deutschunterricht einer 10. Hauptschulklasse* (Frankfurt: Röderberg, 1976); Thomas Berger and Alf Lüdke, "Überlegungen und Vorschläge für eine Unterrichtseinheit 'Faschismus in Deutschland' in der Hauptschule," *Geschichtsdidaktik*, 1 (1978), 39–61.

The first truly comprehensive study of the Holocaust in West German textbooks was conducted at this time, albeit by non-Germans. See Martin and Eva Kolinsky, "The Treatment of the Holocaust in West German Textbooks," *Yad Vashem Studies*, 10 (1974), 149–216.

29 There were earlier examples of what in German is called *Alltagsgeschichte* of the Nazi period, for example William Sheridan Allen's *The Nazi Seizure of Power: The Experience of a Single German Town, 1930–1935* (New York: Franklin Watts, 1965), and Franz Josef Heyen (ed.), *Nationalsozialismus im Alltag: Quellen zur Geschichte des Nationalsozialismus vornehmlich im Raum Mainz-Koblenz-Trier* (Boppard: Boldt, 1967), but they did not include (or explicitly avoided) the most derealized and incomprehensible aspect of National Socialism, the brown-collar crimes.

30 The project was originally named "Resistance and Persecution in Bavaria." Publication of its results began in 1977. See Martin Broszat et al. (eds.), *Bayern in der NS-Zeit*, 6 vols. (Munich: Oldenbourg, 1977–83). The other major academic project on the Nazi era, headed by Lutz Niethammer at the University of Essen, focused on workers' culture in the Ruhr area. Publication of the results as *Lebensgeschichte und Sozialkultur im Ruhrgebiet, 1930–1960*, 3 vols. (Bonn: Dietz, 1983, 1983, 1985). On the origins of *Alltagsgeschichte* in the student movement of the late 1960s, see Geoff Eley, "Labor History, Social History, Alltagsgeschichte," *Journal of Modern History*, 61 (1989), 297–343.

31 Günther Kimmel, "Das Konzentrationslager Dachau: Eine Studie zu den national-sozialistischen Gewaltverbrechen," in *Bayern in der NS-Zeit*, vol. II (1979), 349–413.

32 See the student's report in *SZ/DN*, 11 Feb. 1978, and the response: Wilhelm Horkel, "Dachau war ein Haftlager," *SZ/DN*, 29 Mar. 1978.

33 Letters to the editor by Präsidium der Lagergemeinschaft/Eugen Kessler: "Die Wahrheit über Dachau"; Herbert Asam, "Wie in Dachau gefoltert und gemordet wurde"; Mariane Gräfin Schwerin, "Vergiftungstechnik sabotiert"; and Hildegard and Ulrich Burzinski, "Exekutionen und medizinische Versuche," all *SZ/DN*, 8 Apr. 1978.

34 See Sabine Lietzmann, "Die Judenvernichtung als Seifenoper: 'Holocaust' – eine Serie im amerikanischen Fernsehen," *FAZ*, 20 Apr. 1978, reprinted in Peter Märthesheimer and Ivo Frenzel, *Im Kreuzfeuer: Der Fernsehfilm "Holocaust": Eine Nation ist betroffen* (Frankfurt: Fischer, 1979), 35–9. The English book version released three weeks before the American broadcast sold 1.25 million copies before the evening of the premiere: Gerald Green, *Holocaust* (New York: Bantam, 1978). Although the book was published in several languages, it was never translated into German. The 450-minute TV series was produced by R. Berger and directed by Marvin Chomsky; it was released on video by World Home Video in 1988. For more background on the film, see Jeffrey Shandler, *While America Watches: Televising the Holocaust* (New York: Oxford University Press, 1999), 159–78.

35 Siegfried Zielinski, "History as Entertainment and Provocation: The TV Series 'Holocaust' in West Germany," *New German Critique* 19 (winter 1980), 81–96, 87. See also "Tele Biss," *Die Zeit*, 2 June 1978, on the role of the SPD government in bringing the film to Germany (reprinted in Märthesheimer and Frenzel, *Im Kreuzfeuer*, 42ff).

36 See Wilhelm van Kampen, *Holocaust: Materialien zu einer amerikanischen Fernsehserie über die Judenverfolgung im "Dritten Reich"* (Düsseldorf: Landeszentrale für politische Bildung, 1978). See also Josef Hackforth, "Nationalsozialismus und Fernsehen: 'Holocaust,' die Funktionen der Massenmedien und Erkenntnisse der publizistischen Wirkungsforschung," in Anneliese Mannzmann (ed.), *Hitlerwelle und historische Fakten* (Königstein: Scriptor, 1979), 95–104.

37 See Y. Michael Bodemann, "Reconstructions of History: From Jewish Memory to Nationalized Commemoration of Kristallnacht in Germany," in Bodemann, *Jews, Germans, Memory: Reconstructions of Jewish Life in Germany* (Ann Arbor: University of Michigan Press, 1996), 191; Jeffrey Herf, *Divided Memory: The Nazi Past* (Cambridge, Mass.: Harvard University Press, 1997), 346f.

38 See Ivo Frenzel (preface) in Märthesheimer and Frenzel, *Im Kreuzfeuer*, 21.

39 See the perceptive and detailed essay by Jeffrey Herf, "The 'Holocaust' Reception in West Germany: Right, Center, Left," *New German Critique*, 19 (1980), 30–52.

40 See Frenzel in Märthesheimer and Frenzel, *Im Kreuzfeuer*, 21.

41 Uwe Magnus, "Die Einschaltquoten und Sehbeteiligungen," in Märthesheimer and Frenzel, *Im Kreuzfeuer*, 221–4.

42 For example, Frenzel in Märthesheimer and Frenzel, *Im Kreuzfeuer*, 18f, and Andreas Huyssen, "The Politics of Identification: 'Holocaust' and West German Drama," *New German Critique*, 19 (winter 1980), 117–36, 123, 128f.

43 See Tilman Ernst, "'Holocaust' in der Bundesrepublik: Impulse, Reaktionen und Konsequenzen der Fernsehserie aus der Sicht politischer Bildung," *Rundfunk und Fernsehen*, 28:4 (1980), 509–33. This essay includes data collected fourteen weeks after the broadcast. See also Andrei Markovits and Rebecca Hayden, "'Holocaust' before and after the Event: Reactions in West Germany and Austria," *New German Critique* 19 (1980), 53–80, 80, and Zielinski, "History as Entertainment," 93f.

541

44 Herf, "'Holocaust' Reception," 51.

45 In addition to the sources cited below, there are numerous other monographic studies. The most important are: Heiner Lichtenstein and Michael Schmid-Ospach, *Holocaust: Briefe an den WDR* (Wuppertal: P. Hammer, 1982); Yizhak Ahren, *Das Lehrstück "Holocaust": Zur Wirkungspsychologie eines Medienereignisses* (Opladen: Westdeutscher, 1982); Friedrich Knilli and Siegfried Zielinski, *Holocaust zur Unterhaltung: Anatomie eines internationalen Bestsellers: Fakten, Fotos, Forschungsreportagen* (Berlin: Verlag für Ausbildung und Studium, 1982); Erwin Gundelsheimer et al., *Betrifft "Holocaust": Zuschauer schreiben an den WDR, ein Projektbericht* (Berlin: V. Spiess, 1983); Joachim Siedler, *"Holocaust": Die Fernsehserie in der deutschen Presse: Eine Inhalts- und Verlaufsanalyse am Beispiel ausgewählter Printmedien* (Münster: Lit, 1984).

46 I am assuming that these critics meant German resistance and not Jewish, which does play a role in the film. It is unlikely that left-wing critics at that time would have emphasized the passive behavior of many Jews caught in the Nazis' genocidal net. The emphasis on the lack of Jewish resistance is usually a preserve of the right wing. The first major publication to challenge this claim was Hermann Langbein, *Nicht wie die Schafe zur Schlachtbank: Widerstand in den nationalsozialistischen Konzentrationslagern 1938–1945* (Frankfurt: Fischer, 1980), translated by Harry Zohn as *Against all Hope* (New York: Paragon House, 1994).

47 See Märthesheimer and Frenzel, *Im Kreuzfeuer*, 228, 242–8, 277–80, 293f; also Zielinski, "History as Entertainment," 91f; Moishe Postone, "Anti-Semitism and National Socialism: Notes on the German Reaction to 'Holocaust,'" *New German Critique*, 19 (1980), 97–115, 99 with n. 4.

48 Henri Nannen, "Ja, ich war zu feige," *Stern*, 1 Feb. 1979, quoted after Zielinski, "History as Entertainment," 91, reprinted in Märthesheimer and Frenzel, *Im Kreuzfeuer*, 277–80. See also the half-confession by Rudolf Augstein in *Spiegel*, 29 Jan. 1979.

49 See also Günther Anders, *Besuch im Hades: Auschwitz und Breslau 1966; Nach "Holocaust" 1979* (Munich: Beck, 1979), 179–203.

50 Märthesheimer in Märthesheimer and Frenzel, *Im Kreuzfeuer*, 15.

51 See "Suche nach der verlorenen Zeit," *Die Zeit*, 8 Feb. 1980, and the detailed discussion of some of these books by Michael Schneider (b. 1943), "Väter und Söhne, posthum: Das beschädigte Verhältnis zweier Generationen," in Schneider, *Den Kopf verkehrt aufgesetzt* (Neuwied: Luchterhand, 1981), 8–64; translated as: "Fathers and Sons, Retrospectively: The Damaged Relationship between Two Generations," *New German Critique*, 31 (winter 1984), 3–52.

Some of the individual titles were: Sigfrid Gauch (b. 1945), *Vaterspuren* (Königstein: Athenäum, 1979, 1990, 1997); Peter Härtling (b. 1933), *Nachgetragene Liebe* (Darmstadt: Luchterhand, 1980, 1982); Paul Kersten (b. 1943), *Der alltägliche Tod meines Vaters* (Cologne: Kiepenhauer und Witsch, 1978); Christoph Meckel (b. 1935), *Suchbild: Über meinen Vater* (Düsseldorf: Claassen, 1980); Ernst Rauter, *Brief an meine Erzieher* (Munich: Weismann, 1979, 1980); Ruth Rehmann (b. 1922), *Der Mann auf der Kanzel: Fragen an einen Vater* (Munich: Hanser, 1979); *The Man in the Pulpit* (Lincoln: University of Nebraska, 1997); Brigitte Schwaiger (b. 1949), *Lange Abwesenheit* (Hamburg: Zsolnay, 1980; Rowohlt, 1982); Bernward Vesper (1938–71), *Die Reise* (Frankfurt: Zweitausendeins, 1979); and Heinrich Wiesner (b. 1925), *Der Riese am Tisch* (Basel: Lenos, 1979).

52 Axel Eggebrecht (ed.), *Die zornigen alten Männer* (Reinbek: Rowohlt, 1979).
53 This "encounter" is based on my interview with Jürgen Z., 19 May 1991, and a 6 Sept. 1996 letter to me, as well as various conversations. For some of his publications see Jürgen Zarusky, "Dachau fürchtet um sein Image," *Tribüne*, 95 (1985), 122–4; "Jugendbegegnungsstätte Dachau," *Das Baugerüst*, no. 1 (1989), 63–7; "Die KZ-Gedenkstätte Dachau: Anmerkungen zur Geschichte eines umstrittenen historischen Ortes," in Jürgen Danyel (ed.), *Die geteilte Vergangenheit: Zum Umgang mit Nationalsozialismus und Widerstand in beiden deutschen Staaten* (Berlin: Akademie, 1995), 187–96.

14 The 1980s: relinquishing victimization

 1 See Bergmann, *Antisemitismus in öffentlichen Konflikten*, 369f; Peter Reichel, "Vergangenheitsbewältigung als Problem unserer politischen Kultur: Einstellungen zum Dritten Reich und seine Folgen," in Jürgen Weber and Peter Steinbach (eds.), *Vergangenheitsbewältigung durch Strafverfahren? NS-Prozesse in der Bundesrepublik Deutschland* (Munich: Olzog, 1984), 158; Christa Hoffmann, *Stunden Null? Vergangenheitsbewältigung in Deutschland 1945 und 1989* (Bonn: Bouvier, 1992), 167–9.
 2 Dieter Weichert, "'Holocaust' in der Bundesrepublik: Design, Methode und zentrale Ergebnisse der Begleituntersuchung," *Rundfunk und Fernsehen*, 28 (1980), 488–508, 505.
 3 See the special report "20 Jahre Schülerwettbewerb," *Spuren Suchen*, 7 (1993), 48–62. This journal is published by the Körber Foundation in Hamburg-Bergedorf. See also Körber Foundation (ed.), *Remembering the Holocaust: Some Experiences of the German President's History Competition for Young People* (Hamburg: Körber, 1995), 58f, on the selection of themes and the impact of *Holocaust*. The late industrialist Kurt Körber co-founded the history competition with his close friend Federal President Heinemann in 1973. Entries to the 1980 competition were published in Dieter Galinski and Ulla Lachauer (eds.), *Alltag im Nationalsozialismus, 1933–1939* (Braunschweig: Westerman, 1982), and D. Galinski, Ulrich Herbert, and U. Lachauer (eds.), *Nazis und Nachbarn: Schüler erforschen den Alltag im Nationalsozialismus* (Reinbek: Rowohlt, 1982).
 4 Körber Foundation (ed.), *Remembering*, 60.
 5 Other examples would be Edith Raim, who went on to write a Munich dissertation on a series of huge Dachau branch camps: Edith Raim, *Die Dachauer KZ-Aussenkommandos Kaufering und Muehldorf, Rüstungsbauten und Zwangsarbeit im letzten Kriegsjahr 1944/45* (Landsberg: Neumeyer, 1992). See also Martin Paulus (b. 1959), Edith Raim, and Gerhard Zelger (b. 1961), *Ein Ort wie jeder andere: Bilder aus einer deutschen Kleinstadt, Landsberg 1923–1958* (Hamburg: Rowohlt, 1995).
    Mathias Heyl (b. 1965), who won a prize in the first competition for a project about the Jews in the Hamburg suburb of Harburg, has emerged as one of West Germany's leading experts on the didactics of the Holocaust. On a 1990 return visit of eighteen former Harburg Jews that he organized, see Reta Barsam et al., *Schalom, Harburg? Nicht nur ein Besuch* (Hamburg: Christians, 1992). For examples of Heyl's work: Mathias Heyl and Helmut Schreier (eds.), *Dass Auschwitz nicht noch einmal sei: Zur Erziehung nach Auschwitz* (Hamburg: Kramer, 1995); Mathias Heyl and Ido

Abram, *Thema Holocaust: Ein Buch für die Schule* (Reinbek: Rowohlt, 1996), 61–332; also his dissertation *Erziehung nach Auschwitz, eine Bestandsaufnahme: Deutschland, Niederlande, Israel, USA* (Hamburg: Krämer, 1997).

    Frank Brandenburg's (b. 1963) *Holocaust*-inspired quest to find out about the Holocaust fills an entire monograph: Frank Brandenburg and Ib Melchior, *Quest: Searching for Germany's Nazi Past, a Young Man's Story* (Novato, Calif.: Presidio, 1990). See also the documentation of another prize-winning project: Geert Platner and Schüler der Gerhart-Hauptmann-Schule in Kassel (eds.), *Schule im Dritten Reich: Erziehung zum Tod* (Cologne: Pahl-Rügenstein, 4th augmented edn, 1998). The authors appeared on television, organized symposia in Kassel, and traveled to Israel, Japan, and Vietnam.

6 Michael Verhoeven, *Das schreckliche Mädchen* (1989); *The Nasty Girl* (New York: HBO video, 1990).

7 See Hans-Dieter Schütt, *Anna Rosmus, die "Hexe" von Passau* (Berlin: Dietz, 1994); also Körber Foundation (ed.), *Remembering*, 37f; *Die Zeit*, 6 Aug. 1993, 36, and *Emma* (Sept./Oct. 1993), 24.

8 The original publication was Anja Rosmus-Wenninger, *Widerstand und Verfolgung am Beispiel Passaus, 1933–1939* (Passau: Andreas Haller, 1983). See also Rosmus's later publications: *Exodus – im Schatten der Gnade: Aspekte zur Geschichte der Juden im Raum Passau* (Tittling: Dorfmeister, 1988); "Gedenkstätten für die Opfer des Nationalsozialismus in der Region Passau" (MA thesis, University of Passau, 1993).

9 Anna Rosmus, *Wintergrün: Verdrangte Morde* (Constance: Labhard, 1993).

10 Körber Foundation (ed.), *Remembering*, 31f.

11 Sven Siedenberg, "Über die Opfer reden – aber nicht nur: Michael Brenner lehrt jüdische Geschichte und Kultur an der Münchner Universität," *SZ*, 25 July 1997. Brenner's main publications are: *Nach dem Holocaust: Juden in Deutschland 1945–1950* (Munich: Beck, 1995); *The Renaissance of Jewish Culture in Weimar Germany* (New Haven: Yale University Press, 1996); *Rebuilding Jewish Lives in Postwar Germany*, trans. Barbara Harshav (Princeton: Princeton University Press, 1997).

12 For the activities of Brenner's Institute of Jewish History and Culture, see its web site: http://www.lrz-muenchen.de/~jgk/.

13 See Monica Richarz, "Luftaufnahme – oder die Schwierigkeiten der Heimatforscher mit der jüdischen Geschichte," *Babylon*, no. 8 (1991), 27–33, 29. The 270 studies were reviewed by Ernst Lowenthal in the *Leo Baeck Yearbook* from 1966 to 1984; the Cologne "Germania Judaica" Institute's collection of local publications about German–Jewish history cataloged about 2,000 studies published between 1965 and 1990.

14 The numbers, available from DaA, were 2,242 German classes and groups in 1977, 3,261 in 1978, and 5,070 in 1979. The highest previous increases were 96 percent, from 471 in 1968 to 922 in 1969, and 38 percent, from 606 in 1972 to 836 in 1973. The numbers leveled off after 1979. The highest subsequent increase was 18 percent, from 5,237 in 1988 to 6,191 in 1989.

15 The number of German visitors of all ages (the memorial site personnel guesses according to appearance) went from 187,500 in 1977 to 249,500 in 1978 (a 33 percent increase) to 311,000 in 1979 (25 percent). The official count peaked at 376,000 in 1982 and 380,000 in 1987.

16 The count of foreigners went from 379,500 in 1978 to 453,000 in 1979, foreign groups from 395 to 483.

17 Dirk Rumberg, "Alltag in Dachau 1933," ms. available in DaA. See also Dirk Rumberg, "Alltag in Dachau," in Galinski, Herbert, and Lachauer (eds.), *Nazis und Nachbarn*, 223–33. Rumberg also participated in the next competition with a paper on the "Evangelische Kirche in Dachau" (DaA).

18 No systematic study or bibliography of these works exists, although they are conveniently collected in DaA. Especially noteworthy is a third-prize-winning project submitted by seven students at the Pestalozzi gymnasium to the 1992–3 competition on "Monuments": Arbeitskreis Politik und Zeitgeschichte, "Geschichte der KZ-Gedenkstätte Dachau, 1945–1992," DaA. See also Jürgen Zarusky, "Mehr als ein historischer Ort: Das Archiv der KZ-Gedenkstätte Dachau," *Freiheit und Recht* (Jan. 1988), which lists some of the titles.

19 In 1998 Richardi published a detailed guide about the history of the town that was subsidized by the city administration: Hans-Günter Richardi, Eleonore Philipp, and Monika Lücking, *Dachauer Zeitgeschichtsführer: Die Geschichte der Stadt im 20. Jahrhundert* (Dachau: Stadt Dachau, 1998).

20 Richardi related this story to me in a 1983 interview. The article was presumably: "Wen kümmert's, dass hier 30,000 starben?," *Quick*, 15 Sept. 1962.

21 Hans-Günter Richardi, *Dachau: Schule der Gewalt* (Munich: Beck, 1983, 1995).

22 Hans-Günter Richardi, *Dachau: Führer durch die Altstadt, die Künstlerkolonie und die KZ-Gedenkstätte* (Passau: Passavia, 1979). A tour by Richardi is also available on the internet at http://members.aol.com/zbdachau/index_e.htm.

23 Hans Holzhaider, "Neue Akzente bei Volkshochschule und Forum: Man spricht wieder über die Nazizeit," *SZ/DN*, 28 Jan. 1981.

24 Hans Holzhaider, "CSU-Stammtisch zum Thema KZ: Gutes und weniger Gutes über die Dachauer. Hans-Günter Richardi berichtet von seinen Forschungsergebnissen / Heinrich Rauffers Erinnerungen," *SZ/DN*, 22 Oct. 1981. See also Richardi, *Von der Roten Armee*, 43.

25 The booklet was Richardi, *Von der Roten Armee*, esp. 50–6. Many of Richardi's fifteen examples were taken from Louis Köckert's book *Dachau, und das Gras wächst* (Munich: Freies Volk, 1980), esp. 59–63. The exhibition catalog was Hans-Günter Richardi et al., *Die Stadt und das Lager: Nationalsozialismus und Widerstand in Dachau* (Munich: Süddeutscher, 1983), esp. 13, 17, 23, 25.

26 Aside from the gypsies and homosexuals discussed below, slave laborers and Jehovah's Witnesses have been researched in the greatest detail. Very little is known about prostitutes and deserters. On the various individual groups, see Detlef Garbe, *Zwischen Widerstand und Martyrium: Die Zeugen Jehovas im "Dritten Reich"* (Munich: Oldenbourg, 1993); Gisela Bock, *Zwangssterilisation im Nationalsozialismus: Studien zur Rassenpolitik und Frauenpolitik* (Opladen: Westdeutscher, 1986); Christa Paul, *Zwangsprostitution: Staatlich errichtete Bordelle im Nationalsozialismus* (Hamburg: Edition Hentrich, 1994); Wolfram Wette (ed.), *Deserteure der Wehrmacht: Feiglinge, Opfer, Hoffnungsträger: Dokumentation eines Meinungswandels* (Essen: Klartext, 1995).

27 Viola Roggenkamp, "In der KZ-Gedenkstätte Bergen-Belsen forderten Zigeuner Wiedergutmachung," *Die Zeit*, 2 Nov. 1979, 13.

28 See especially Tilman Zülch, *In Auschwitz vergast, bis heute verfolgt: Zur Situation*

der Roma in Deutschland und Europa (Reinbek: Rowohlt, 1979); George von Soest, *Zigeuner zwischen Verfolgung und Integration: Geschichte, Lebensbedingungen und Eingliederungsversuche* (Weinheim: Beltz, 1979); and Anita Geigges and Bernhard Wette, *Zigeuner heute: Verfolgung und Diskriminierung in der BRD* (Bornheim-Merten: Lamuv, 1979).

29 On the week-long hunger strike in early April 1980 in Dachau, see Kurt Kister, "Parteien wollen Abbruch des Hungerstreiks im ehemaligen KZ Dachau / Die SPD zollt den Sinti Respekt / Landtagsfraktion bedauert moralisches Unrecht und Diskriminierung / Forderungen als berechtigt bezeichnet," *SZ,* 11 Apr. 1980.

30 See Gerd Kummet, "Was für eine Möglichkeit," *SZ/DN,* 19 Apr. 1980; Hans Holzhaider, "Reitmeier fordert: Kulturzentrum der Sinti soll nicht nach Dachau," *SZ/DN,* 7 May 1980. On a pseudo-poll of mail-in postcards conducted by the conservative *MM/DN,* see "96 Prozent der Bevölkerung lehnen Zigeuner-Standort ab," 10 June 1980.

31 See Kurt Kister, "Begegnung soll Blickwinkel ändern / Reitmeier: 'Die Stadt ist glücklich über diese Veranstaltung' / Hunderte Besucher," *SZ/DN,* 24 Nov. 1980.

32 See dpa reports of 18 May, 25 June, and 3 July 1993.

33 "Nackter 'Homo' demonstriert im KZ: Auf schnellen Beinen durch das Gelände," *MM/DN,* 6 June 1976.

34 A folder containing the correspondence between Eckart Prinz of the Nationale Arbeitsgruppe Repression gegen Schwule, the memorial site, and the CID can be found in the uncataloged CID papers at DaA. The correspondence dates from Aug. 1977 to Feb. 1978.

35 On the rising awareness of the Nazi persecution of homosexuals, especially in comparison to the usual emphasis on Jewish victims, see Paul Parin, "Die Homosexuellen und die Juden," *Psyche* (1986).

36 See Kaes, *Hitler to Heimat,* 163–92, esp. 183ff. The following portrayal follows Kaes. See also Dagmar Stern, "A German History Lesson: Edgar Reitz's *Heimat,*" *Film and History,* 17:1 (1987), 9ff.

37 James Markham, "West German TV Specials Spark Debate on Reconciliation with Nazi Era," *NYT,* 24 Apr. 1985.

38 Timothy Garton Ash, "The Life of Death," *New York Review of Books,* 19 Dec. 1985.

39 Reinhard Kühnl, *Das Dritte Reich in der Presse der Bundesrepublik: Kritik eines Geschichtsbildes* (Frankfurt: EVA, 1966). Kühnl examined the three anniversaries mentioned here, but not *Kristallnacht.*

40 See Bodemann, "Reconstructions of History," 185, 191, 211. Bodemann explicitly attributes the change in tone in the late 1970s to the departure of the politicians born before 1915 (i.e., the 1933er cohort) from positions of power. For the text of Schmidt's speech, "A Plea for Honesty and Tolerance," see Werner Nachman, Nahum Goldmann, and Helmut Schmidt, *An Exhortation and an Obligation: Speeches Delivered on the Occasion of the Memorial Celebration in Remembrance of 9 November 1938 in the Cologne Synagogue on 9 November 1978* (Bonn: Press and Information Office of the Federal Republic, 1979).

41 Quoted after Herf, *Divided Memory,* 347.

42 The following is after Bark and Gress, *History of West Germany,* vol. II, 376ff.

43 The conference is documented in *Deutschlands Weg in die Diktatur: Internationale Konferenz zur nationalsozialistischen Machtübernahme im Reichstagsgebäude zu*

Berlin, Referate und Diskussionen, ein Protokoll (Berlin: Siedler, 1983). For Lübbe's talk, see "Der Nationalsozialismus im politischen Bewusstsein der Gegenwart," 329–79 (with responses); reprinted in *Historische Zeitschrift*, 236:3 (June 1983), 579–99.

44 See Charles Maier, *The Unmasterable Past: History, Holocaust, and German National Identity* (Cambridge, Mass.: Harvard University Press, 1988), 121–39. References to the relevant literature can be found in Richard Evans, *In Hitler's Shadow: West German Historians and the Attempt to Escape from the Nazi Past* (New York: Pantheon, 1989), 147 n. 42.

45 See Bund deutscher Architekten (ed.), "Denk-Mal: Gedenken-Denken-Erinnern," *Der Architekt*, no. 12 (Dec. 1984), 541–71. This special issue includes the text of the Volksbund's "Aide mémoire" and numerous commentaries.

46 Die Grünen (eds.), *Wider die Entsorgung der deutschen Geschichte: Streitschrift gegen die geplanten historischen Museen in Berlin (W) und Bonn* (Bonn: Die Grünen, 1986).

47 See "Einen schönen Salat hat man euch serviert," *Spiegel*, 30 Jan. 1984, 27f. The slang of the original German is difficult to translate: "Die Juden sollten den Deutschen nicht immer mit Auschwitz kommen."

48 "Besuch der Peinlichkeiten," *FAZ*, 10 Feb. 1984.

49 See Kohl's 25 Apr. 1985 explanation to the Bundestag, reprinted in Ilya Levkov (ed.), *Bitburg and Beyond: Encounters in American, German and Jewish History* (New York: Shapolsky, 1987), 105–9. Given the situation, I find this more plausible than Kohl's "deep hurt" at being excluded, which was later alleged in retrospective accounts. See Hilberg in Geoffrey Hartmann (ed.), *Bitburg in Moral and Political Perspective* (Bloomington: Indiana University Press, 1986), 16; *Spiegel*, 39:18 (29 Apr. 1985), 20; Andrei Markovits and Beth Simone Novek, "West Germany," in David S. Wyman and Charles Rosenzveig (eds.), *The World Reacts to the Holocaust* (Baltimore: Johns Hopkins University Press, 1990), 433; Miller, *One, by One*, 47. The *Spiegel* article contains photographs of the Normandy and Verdun events.

50 Foreign Office, confidential paper, 27 Nov. 1984, quoted in *Der Spiegel*, 4 Feb. 1985, 14.

51 A detailed chronology can be found in Hartmann (ed.), *Bitburg*, xiii–xvi. Levkov, *Bitburg and Beyond*, 22–8, offers a narrative portrayal.

52 "Kohl will im Mai 1985 in einem früheren KZ eine Rede halten / . . . / Kanzler verliess USA," *FR*, 3 Dec. 1984, 1.

53 "Ronald Reagan im Mai nach Dachau? Noch keine Bestätigung aus Washington," *MM/DN*, 16 Jan. 1985.

54 "Reagan-Visite im KZ Dachau," *Spiegel*, 21 Jan. 1985, 14.

55 dpa, "Reagan will das ehemalige KZ Dachau besichtigen," *SZ*, 21 Jan. 1985, 1.

56 See below, note 69.

57 Reinhard Zrenner, "Noch steht's nicht absolut sicher fest, aber auf jeden Fall: Reagan ist uns hier in Dachau jederzeit herzlich willkommen," *MM/DN*, 21 Jan. 1985.

58 Beate Frommhold, "Dachauer wollen Reagan nicht / 'KZ-Besuch schadet uns,'" *Bild-München*, 22 Jan. 1985, 1.

59 Hans Holzhaider, "CSU-Fraktion und Reitmeier einig: Reagan soll auch die Stadt Dachau besuchen / Der OB hat schon in diesem Sinn an Strauss geschrieben," *SZ/DN*, 22 Jan. 1985.

60 Reuters, "Reagan: Kein Besuch in Dachau, *SZ*, 25 Jan. 1985; dpa, "Reagan nicht nach Dachau," *SZ*, 26/27 Jan. 1985. My retranslation into English.

61 "Ronald Reagan verzichtet auf Abstecher nach Dachau / 'Rückkehr der Deutschen zur Demokratie wichtiger,'" *MM*, 26/27 Jan. 1985.

62 Hans-Herbert Gaebel, "Reagan in Dachau," *FR*, 22 Jan. 1985; *Spiegel*, 29 Apr. 1985, 19.

63 Levkov, *Bitburg and Beyond*, 23; see also Barbara Distel to Reitmeier, correspondence file, DaA.

64 Levkov, *Bitburg and Beyond*, 23, after *Washington Post* interview with Reagan, 1 Apr. 1985.

65 The manhunt for Mengele was the title story of *Der Spiegel* on 22 Apr. 1985. On Barbie, see Alain Finkielkraut, *Remembering in Vain: The Klaus Barbie Trial and Crimes Against Humanity*, trans. Roxanne Lapidus (New York: Columbia University Press, 1992).

66 Helmut Löhlöffel, "Reagan soll jüdischer Opfer gedenken / Kohl bedauerte Absage des Präsidenten, das ehemalige KZ Dachau zu besuchen," *FR*, 17 Apr. 1985, 1; Hartmann, *Bitburg*, xiv; Levkov, *Bitburg and Beyond*, 24; Richard Cohen, "Kohl: The Balsa Wood Chancellor," *Washington Post*, 11 June 1993, A21.

67 "Lorenz Reitmeier schreibt an Ronald Reagan, Helmut Kohl und Franz Josef Strauss," *SZ/DN*, 19 Apr. 1985. At that time, although Reagan had added a former camp to his agenda, it was still unclear whether that camp would be Dachau.

68 "DGB attackiert den Oberbürgermeister," *SZ/DN*, 22 Apr. 1985; "Missdeutung von Gutgemeintem," *SZ/DN*, 24 Apr. 1985.

69 Given Kohl's announcement in the US in December that he himself would speak at a camp, and the Foreign Office's pre-24 Jan. announcement that Kohl would accompany Reagan to Dachau, I find it highly unlikely that Kohl ever openly tried to dissuade Reagan from visiting a former concentration camp. In late April, when Reagan was in the midst of what had become the worst crisis of his term in office and his advisers were seeking a way out, one of them told the press that Reagan had decided not to visit a camp because the German diplomats working out the detailed agenda had used "signs, body language and hesitations" to show their US counterparts "that they really didn't want Dachau" on the president's agenda (*Spiegel*, 29 Apr. 1985, 23). Since it is unlikely that Reagan himself ever saw those undersecretaries, if they had indeed behaved that way, and because Speakes' 24 January announcement was so unequivocal, it seems that the decision to omit a camp was truly his own. After he had received Kohl's second invitation on 15 April, Reagan told the press that he had not considered Kohl's first invitation "official" and had thus not accepted it, "perhaps because of my own confusion or because of the way in which it was expressed" (ibid., 28). This phraseology smacks of subterfuge.

70 Hartmann, *Bitburg*, xiv.

71 See "A Troubling Time over Nazis and Their Victims," *NYT*, 21 Apr. 1985, 1. See also Alvin Rosenfeld, "Another Revisionism," in Hartmann (ed.), *Bitburg*, 92f.

72 Interview with Elie Wiesel, *Spiegel*, 29 Apr. 1985, 27, translated in Levkov, *Bitburg and Beyond*, 385.

73 See Georg Bauer, "Kohl in Bergen-Belsen: Es war Abfall von Gott / Der Kanzler mahnt im ehemaligen Konzentrationslager zur Versöhnung," *Welt*, 22 Apr. 1985, 1, 3.

74 See Ulrich Schiller, "Reagan in der Bundesrepublik / 'Die Schuld hat ihr Kanzler,'" *Die Zeit*, 19 Apr. 1985, 2.
75 James Markham, "House Fails to Sway Kohl on Bitburg," *NYT*, 27 Apr. 1985, A4; "US-Abgeordnete beschwören Kohl / Kongressmehrheit gegen Bitburg-Besuch," *FR*, 27 Apr. 1985, 1.
76 This is based on my viewing of the contemporary newscasts of German channels One and Two, which followed the motorcade. One channel had turned off the live sound, but the continuous jeering was clearly audible on the other. The newspaper reports are more ambivalent, perhaps due to the location of the individual reporters. For example, both 6 May reports in the *Washington Post* note the dearth of protestors: Bernard Weinraub, "Reagan Joins Kohl in Brief Memorial at Bitburg Graves" (A1, A9); Michael Dobbs, "Camp Survivors, Protest Groups Absent at Visit" (A1, on Belsen). Compare Eckart Spoo, "'Eine Geste der Versöhnung wurde zum Schauspiel': Viele Absagen für die Gedenkfeiern im Konzentrationslager Bergen-Belsen," *FR*, 6 May 1985, 3, and dpa, "Keine Zwischenfälle in Bergen-Belsen und Bitburg," *SZ*, 6 May 1985, 1, which reported that "The applause for Reagan was mixed with the hissing and raised fists of protesting demonstrators."
77 The speech is reprinted in Hartmann (ed.), *Bitburg*, 258–61. Interesting documents about the development of the speech are available at the Reagan Library.
78 For a nuanced examination of the German reception, see Werner Bergmann, "Die Bitburg-Affäre in der deutschen Presse: Rechtskonservative und linksliberale Interpretationen," in Werner Bergmann, Rainer Erb, and Albert Lichtblau (eds.), *Schwieriges Erbe* (Frankfurt: Campus, 1995), 408–28; and Bergmann, *Antisemitismus in öffentlichen Konflikten*, 419–24. For an excellent compendium of responses from around the world, see Levkov, *Bitburg and Beyond*, 318–689.
79 Two other events not discussed here deserve particular mention. The first was the passage of a so-called Auschwitz Lie Law in June 1985. On 14 March, under the pressure of the impending Bitburg debacle, the SPD under Hans-Jochen Vogel forced Chancellor Kohl to express his support for the amendment of the law criminalizing defamation to make the denial of the Holocaust a punishable offense, even if a member of the defamed group did not press charges. As a concession to conservative opponents, denying the postwar expulsion of Germans from Eastern Europe was added to the text – an offense that had never created a public problem.
   The other event underscoring the competitive victimization between Germans and Jews was the second controversy surrounding left-wing German author Rainer Fassbinder's play *Garbage, the City, and Death*. Because the play cast Jews as stereotypical exploitative landlords, Jews – for the first time in the history of West Germany – protested publicly by occupying the stage and preventing the premiere. They, too, began to transcend the role as victims. The 1976 and November 1985 controversies are documented in Heiner Lichtenstein (ed.), *Die Fassbinder-Kontroverse oder das Ende der Schonzeit* (Frankfurt: Athenäum, 1986). For an English-language discussion, see Andrei Markovits et al., "Rainer Werner Fassbinder's *Garbage, the City, and Death*: Renewed Antagonisms in the Complex Relationship between Jews and Germans in the Federal Republic of Germany," *New German Critique* 38 (fall 1986), 3–27.
80 For the text of the speech, see Hartmann (ed.), *Bitburg*, 262–73. The quotations

below are from 263, 264f, and 267. For detailed discussions of the speech, see Herf, *Divided Memory*, 355–9, and Helmut Dubiel, *Niemand ist frei von der Geschichte: Die nationalsozialistische Herrschaft in den Debatten des Deutschen Bundestages* (Munich: Hanser, 1999), 207–15. See also Ian Buruma, *Wages of Guilt*, 142ff, Bernd Weisbrot, "Der 8. Mai in der deutschen Geschichte," *Werkstatt Geschichte*, 13 (June 1996), 72–81, and the brief autobiographical sketch: Richard von Weizsäcker, "Nobody Could Foresee the Horrors," *Newsweek* (international edn), 15 Mar. 1999.

81 The full version of Habermas's original essay was translated as "A Kind of Settlement of Damages (Apologetic Tendencies)," in *New German Critique*, 44 (spr./sum. 1988), 25–39; the abridged version was first published in *Die Zeit*, 11 July 1986. There is a vast literature on this debate. For a solid contextual discussion including broader philosophical issues, see Charles Maier, *The Unmasterable Past: History, Holocaust, and German National Identity* (Cambridge, Mass.: Harvard University Press, 1988). Richard Evans, *In Hitler's Shadow: West German Historians and the Attempt to Escape from the Nazi Past* (New York: Pantheon, 1989) offers a monographic interpretation; Peter Baldwin (ed.), *Reworking the Past: Hitler, the Holocaust, and the Historians' Debate* (Boston: Beacon, 1990), is a collection of interpretative essays.

82 Michael Stürmer, "Geschichte im geschichtslosen Land" ("History in a Land without History"), *FAZ*, 25 Apr. 1986; "Suche nach der verlorenen Erinnerung," *Parlament*, 17–24 May 1986. Stürmer did not allow the complete text of his essay to be published in the original German collection of documents. On its genesis, see Evans, *In Hitler's Shadow*, 173 n. 14.

83 The conference is documented in Hilmar Hoffmann (ed.), *Gegen den Versuch, die Vergangenheit zu verbiegen: Eine Diskussion um politische Kultur in der Bundesrepublik aus Anlass der Frankfurter Römerberggespräche* (Frankfurt: Athenäum, 1986).

84 For a discussion of Hillgruber himself, see Omer Bartov, *Murder in our Midst: The Holocaust, Industrial Killing, and Representation* (New York: Oxford University Press, 1996), 71–89; also Hans-Ulrich Wehler, *Entsorgung der deutschen Vergangenheit? Ein polemischer Essay zum "Historikerstreit"* (Munich: Beck, 1988), 20–4.

85 The original contributions have been translated into English by James Knowlton and Truett Cates as *Forever in the Shadow of Hitler* (Atlantic Highlands: Humanities, 1993). This translation is not reliable and should always be checked against the German originals, collected in Rudolf Piper (ed.), *"Historikerstreit": Die Dokumentation der Kontroverse um die Einzigartigkeit der nationalsozialistischen Judenvernichtung* (Munich: Piper, 1987). The ages of many of the participants can be found in Knowlton and Cates (eds.), *Forever*, 270f. See also Maier, *Unmasterable Past*, 7, 175 n. 4.

86 Baldwin (ed.), *Reworking*, 295–304, and Evans, *In Hitler's Shadow*, 186–89, contain bibliographies of the secondary interpretations.

87 See Immanuel Geiss, *Die Habermas-Kontroverse: Ein deutscher Streit* (Berlin: Siedler, 1988); Wehler, *Entsorgung*, with further references on 212f.

88 I am referring here not only to the "revisionists" who took an active part in the debate (see, for example, Geiss, *Die Habermas-Kontroverse*), but also to historians

such as Uwe Backes (b. 1960), Eckhard Jesse (b. 1948), Manfred Kittel (b. 1962), Michael Wolffsohn (b. 1947), and Rainer Zitelmann (b. ca. 1959), who later stylized themselves as the "generation of 1989" (in my terminology, they are 1979ers). See Uwe Backes, Eckhard Jesse, and Rainer Zitelmann (eds.), *Die Schatten der Vergangenheit: Impulse zur Historisierung des Nationalsozialismus* (Berlin: Propyläen, 1990). A number of their works are cited in Peter Dudek, "'Vergangenheitsbewältigung': Zur Problematik eines umstrittenen Begriffs," *Aus Politik und Zeitgeschichte*, 3 Jan. 1992, 44–53, esp. nn. 18–21.

For a more recent example of the Zitelmann circle's position on resistance and victimization, see the 5 May 1995 *FAZ* and 6 May 1995 *SZ* articles cited by Thomas Schmitz at: gopher://h-net2.msu.edu:70/00/lists/H-GERMAN/discuss/ve/schmitz. For a discussion of this group of 1979ers as "89ers," see Jacob Heilbrunn, "Germany's New Right," *Foreign Affairs*, 75 (Nov./Dec. 1996), 80–98.

89 The development of *Kristallnacht* commemorations since 1945 is portrayed by Bodemann, "Reconstructions of History," 179–223. Richarz, "Luftaufnahme," 29, notes that the number of publications about German Jewish history peaked in 1988.

On the commemorative changes after the 1989 "fall of the Wall," see Elizabeth Domansky, "'Kristallnacht,' the Holocaust and German Unity: The Meaning of November 9 as an Anniversary in Germany," *History and Memory*, 4:1 (spring/summer 1992), 60–87.

90 For a sampling of special events in Munich, see Anna-Jutta Pietsch (ed.), *Im Schatten der Vergangenheit: Deutsch-Jüdischer Dialog / Semesterschwerpunkt 1988/89* (Munich: Volkshochschule, 1988).

91 Arbeitskreis "Reichskristallnacht," *"Dachau ist somit judenfrei"* (Augsburg: Pröll, 1988). See also Hans Holzhaider, *Vor Sonnenaufgang: Das Schicksal der jüdischen Bürger Dachaus* (Munich: Süddeutscher, 1984).

92 The speech and reactions are documented in Armin Laschet and Heinz Malangré (eds.), *Philipp Jenninger: Rede und Reaktion* (Koblenz: Rheinischer Merkur, 1989). See also Lutz Niethammer, "Jenninger: Vorzeitiges Exposé zur Erforschung eines ungewöhnlich schnellen Rücktritts," *Babylon*, 5 (1989), 40–6.

93 Laschet and Malangré (eds.), *Philipp Jenninger*, 17f.

94 Ibid., 33.

95 For a good summary of the longer-term development of West German policies regarding foreigners, see Peter O'Brien, *Beyond the Swastika* (New York: Routledge, 1996), 43–128. More recently, in the fall of 1998 the CSU carried out a petition drive that succeeded in thwarting the new SPD–Green government coalition from liberalizing the citizenship laws.

96 Laschet and Malangré (eds.), *Philipp Jenninger*, 15. Jenninger repeated the claim again near the end of his speech, see 24: "It is also true that everyone knew . . . that everyone could see what happened in Germany 50 years ago today."

97 The following is based on a telephone interview with Kurt Piller, 28 August 1997; notes in my possession. Piller confirmed the accuracy of this portrayal in a fax of 17 Sept. 1998.

98 Interview with Silke Schuster, Dachau, 23 July 1997, notes in my possession.

99 See Thomas Soyer, "Authentischer Zugang: Neue Ausstellung in KZ-Gedenkstätte Dachau 2001 fertig," *SZ*, 24 Apr. 1999.

15 The 1990s: resistance vs. education

1 For an discussion and overview of this phenomenon, see J. David Case, "The Politics of Memorial Representation: The Controversy over the German Resistance Museum in 1994," *German Politics and Society*, 16:1 (spr. 1998), 58–81.

2 In general, see Hans-Peter Rouette, "Die Widerstandslegende: Produktion und Funktion der Legende vom Widerstand im Kontext der gesellschaftlichen Auseinandersetzungen in Deutschland nach dem Zweiten Weltkrieg" (Ph.D. dissertation, Free University of Berlin, 1983). One of the seminal works of the revival of interest in everyday resistance was Detlev Peukert and Jürgen Reulecke (eds.), *Die Reihen fast geschlossen* (Wuppertal: Peter Hammer, 1981).

   On the changing reception of the "White Rose," especially through Michael Verhoeven's 1983 film about the group, see Harold Marcuse, "Remembering the White Rose: (West) German Assessments, 1943–1993," *Soundings*, 25:31 (1994), 25–38, 34f. The revival of interest in resistance by women, which had already been a subject of research in East Germany, can be traced in Gerda Zorn's work, e.g., Gerda Zorn and Gertrud Meyer (eds.), *Frauen gegen Hitler: Berichte aus dem Widerstand, 1933–1945* (Frankfurt: Röderberg, 1974). The literature on the changing reception of the 20 July movement is voluminous. See David Large, "'A Beacon in the German Darkness': The Anti-Nazi Resistance Legacy in West German Politics," in Michael Geyer and John Boyer (eds.), *Resistance against the Third Reich, 1933–1990* (Chicago: University of Chicago Press, 1994), 243–56, and Gerd Ueberschär (ed.), *Der 20. Juli 1944: Bewertung und Rezeption des deutschen Widerstandes gegen das NS-Regime* (Cologne: Bund, 1994).

3 See Martin Broszat, "Resistenz und Widerstand: Eine Zwischenbilanz des Forschungsprojekts 'Widerstand und Verfolgung in Bayern 1933–1945,'" in Martin Broszat, Elke Fröhlich, and Anton Grossmann (eds.), *Bayern in der NS-Zeit*, vol. IV (Munich: Oldenbourg, 1981), 691–709. For a trenchant criticism of the term, see Saul Friedländer, "Some Reflections on the Historicization of National Socialism," in Baldwin (ed.), *Reworking the Past*, 88–101, 96f.

4 Josef Schwalber, speech manuscript for 9 Nov. 1946, BayHsta, JS01. The resolution of 5 Nov. 1946 was published in the *Dachauer Amtsblatt*, 27 Nov. 1946. The six streets are on the south side of Dachau, east of the main road leading to Munich.

   In 1990 a group of streets adjacent to the memorial site were also named after prominent former KZ prisoners. The naming was initiated by Heinrich Rauffer; see Ferdl Miedaner, "Ehrung des Dachau-Häftlings Pater Roth?," *Informationen der Lagergemeinschaft Dachau*, no. 1 (Jan. 1987), 10f.

5 Kurt Kister, "Peinliches Verschwinden eines Strassenschildes: 'Widerstandsplatz' in Dachau unbekannt / Namensgebung erinnerte an Aufstand während der letzten Kriegstage / Nachforschungen der SZ erfolgreich," *SZ/DN*, 15 Jan. 1981.

6 For a summary of that initiative, see *Stimmen aus Dachau*, Apr. 1960. The debate about erecting the monument was part of the larger conflict between Leonhard Roth and Mayor Zauner (see pp. 231, 233).

7 Ralph Giordano, *Die zweite Schuld, oder: Von der Last, Deutscher zu sein* (Hamburg: Rasch und Röhring, 1987). See also Ralph Giordano (ed.), *"Wie kann diese Generation eigentlich noch atmen?" Briefe zu dem Buch: Die zweite Schuld* (Hamburg: Rasch und Röhring, 1990), and Ralph Giordano, *Erfahrungen mit*

einem Buch: Die zweite Schuld oder von der Last, Deutscher zu sein (Passau: Rothe, 1989).

8 Peter Sichrovsky (b. 1947), *Schuldig geboren: Kinder aus Nazifamilien* (Cologne: Kiepenheuer und Witsch, 1987); *Born Guilty: Children of Nazi Families*, trans. Jean Steinberg (New York: Basic, 1988); and Dörte von Westernhagen (b. 1943), *Die Kinder der Täter: Das Dritte Reich und die Generation danach* (Munich: Kösel, 1987). On the discussion provoked by Sichrovsky's book, parts of which were serialized in *Der Spiegel* in Feb. 1987, see the postscript to the English edition, 159–74.

9 Sabine Reichel (b. 1946), *What Did You Do in the War, Daddy? Growing up German* (New York: Hill and Wang, 1989); Gabriele von Arnim (b. 1946), *Das grosse Schweigen: Von der Schwierigkeit, mit den Schatten der Vergangenheit zu leben* (Munich: Kindler, 1989; Knaur, 1991). See also von Arnim's "Immer noch eine schmerzende Wunde: Nachkriegskinder befragen ihre Eltern," *Zeit*, no. 17 (24 Apr. 1992), 19, and Stefan Liebert, *Denn du trägst meinen Namen* (Munich: Blessing, 2000).

10 Dan Bar-On (b. 1938), *Legacy of Silence: Encounters with Children of the Third Reich* (Cambridge, Mass.: Harvard University Press, 1989); Gerald Posener, *Hitler's Children: Sons and Daughters of Leaders of the Third Reich Talk about their Fathers and Themselves* (New York: Random House, 1991).

11 For a summary of this project, see Brian Ladd, *Ghosts of Berlin* (Chicago: University of Chicago, 1997), 217–24.

12 See Laurenz Demps, *Die Neue Wache: Enstehung und Geschichte eines Bauwerkes* (Berlin: Militärverlag der Deutschen Demokratischen Republik, 1988); Daniela Büchten and Anja Frey, *Im Irrgarten deutscher Geschichte: Die Neue Wache, 1818 bis 1993* (Berlin: Aktives Museum Faschismus und Widerstand, 1993).

13 The Bundestag debate is documented in Christoph Stölzl and Jürgen Tietz, *Die Neue Wache unter den Linden: Ein deutsches Denkmal im Wandel der Geschichte* (Berlin: Koehler und Amelang, 1993).

14 Actually, Weizsäcker's text was modified to remove precisely those taboo-breaking elements that had electrified the nation in 1985: naming the Jews first, mentioning the communist victims, and using the word "unsäglich" (unspeakable) to describe the Germans' behavior.

15 The various debates about this monument are documented in a 1,248-page collection: Ute Heimrod, Günter Schlusche, and Horst Seferens (eds.), *Der Denkmalstreit – Das Denkmal? Die Debatte um das "Denkmal für die ermordeten Juden Europas": Eine Dokumentation* (Berlin: Philo, 1999). I was not able to consult this work. See Ladd, *Ghosts of Berlin*, 168–72; Jane Kramer, *The Politics of Memory: Looking for Germany in the New Germany* (New York: Random House, 1996), 257–93 (originally published in the *New Yorker*, 14 Aug. 1995); also Richard Chaim Schneider, *Fetisch Holocaust: Die Judenvernichtung – verdrängt und vermarktet* (Munich: Kindler, 1997), 115–32, 163–9; Hans-Ernst Mittig, "Künstler in Schuldgefühlen: 'Denkmal für die ermordeten Juden Europas,'" in Johannes Heil and Rainer Erb (eds.), *Geschichtswissenschaft und Öffentlichkeit: Der Streit um Daniel J. Goldhagen* (Frankfurt: Fischer, 1998), 279–94. Detailed documentation of the project and its various stages of development can be found at the web site of the Berlin Senator for Wissenschaft, Forschung, und Kultur: http://www.berlin.de/home/Land/ SenWissKult/kult/mahnmal/index.html.

16 The series in talk-show format is documented in Eberhard Jäckel and Lea Rosh, *Der Tod ist ein Meister aus Deutschland* (Hamburg: Hoffmann und Campe, 1990).

17 For a detailed discussion of Rosh's involvement in the project, see Uta Andresen, "Allein unter Tätern," *taz*, 12 Oct. 1999.

18 At the time observers predicted that the project would be dropped if Kohl was defeated. See Ignaz Bubis, "'Der Antisemitismus braucht keine Juden': Warum es das Holocaust-Mahnmal nur mit einem Kanzler Kohl gibt," *SZ*, 21 Sept. 1998.

19 The budget of the memorial as proposed by Lea Rosh's organization was originally DM15 million, which Naumann increased to DM150 and then 180 million in early 1999, in order to incorporate a "house of memory" or "documentation center" with a library and archive. By mid-June 1999 Naumann, negotiating with the parliamentary budget committee, had come down to DM80 and then 25 million. See "Der Bundestag für ein Holocaust-Mahnmal: Nach zehn Jahren wohl noch kein Ende der Diskussion," *Neue Züricher Zeitung* (*NZZ*), 26 June 1999.

  In the various rounds of voting on 25 June 1999, 439 of 559 delegates present voted for a monument; then the text monument was rejected by a vote of 354:188. See Christof Siemes, "Noch Fragen? Das Holocaust-Denkmal wird gebaut / Rückblicke, Prognosen, Seitenhiebe," *Die Zeit*, 1 July 1999.

  By way of comparison, the Berlin Jewish Museum by Daniel Libeskind, which was built at the same time, cost DM120 million to build, and an estimated DM18 million annually to run. See "Shoah-Archiv soll ins Jüdische Museum: Naumann greift Spielbergs Angebot auf – Mahnmal-Diskussion bekommt neuen Akzent," *Welt*, 19 Nov. 1998. In 1999, a planned documentation center in the former Nazi Party parade grounds in Nuremberg was to cost DM18 million. See Dietrich Mittler, "NS-Pomp soll entlarvt werden: Sechs Millionen für Nürnberger Dokumentationszentrum," *SZ*, 4 Aug. 1999. In April 1967 the central monument in Auschwitz-Birkenau was to cost DM3.5 million (about DM7.7 million in 1998 marks). The West German government contributed DM200,000 (about DM440,000 in 1998 marks).

20 See Renate Schostack, "Umdenken in Dachau: Die Gedenkstätte wird saniert, die Ausstellung erneuert," *FAZ*, 29 Jan. 1998, 33.

21 See Christian Krügel, "Im August sollen die Bauarbeiten beginnen / Jetzt wird der Umbau umgebaut: KZ-Gedenkstätte bleibt für Besucher geöffnet / Keine neuen Kinosäle im Westflügel," *SZ/DN*, 11 Feb. 1998; Thomas Soyer, "Bonn löst die Ankündigung vom vergangenen November nun konkret ein: Bund gibt 500 000 Mark für das 'Jourhaus'" *SZ/DN*, 19 June 1998.

22 See Reuters, "Denkmalschutz für das KZ Sachsenhausen," *NZZ*, 23 Sept. 1998.

23 Another example not discussed here is the publication of Victor Klemperer's diaries in 1995. This 1,800-page book immediately became a runaway success (the best-selling Holocaust-era memoir since Anne Frank), indicating that many Germans were now willing to read documents showing that most Germans had indeed been informed about the Holocaust. At the same time, the diaries were comforting in that they featured a Jew who loved Germany, and his non-Jewish German wife who stood faithfully by him. On their popular reception see Amos Elon, "The Jew who Fought to Stay German," *New York Times Magazine*, 24 Mar. 1996, 52–5; Schneider, *Fetisch Holocaust*, 237–49, 254–67; Martin Walser, "Laudatio auf Victor Klemperer," in Walser, *Literatur als Weltverständnis* (Eggingen: Isele, 1996), 19–58; Hannes Heer

(ed.), *Im Herzen der Finsternis: Victor Klemperer als Chronist der NS-Zeit* (Berlin: Aufbau, 1997); Cornelia Essner, "Die Tagebücher von Victor Klemperer, 1933–1945," *Geschichte in Wissenschaft und Unterricht*, 49 (1998), 440–6; Alexandra Przyrembel, "Die Tagebücher Victor Klemperers und ihre Wirkung in der deutschen Öffentlichkeit," in Heil and Erb (eds.), *Geschichtswissenschaft und Öffentlichkeit* 312–27.

An example of the persistance of mythic resistance is the massive public support for Hava Kohav Beller's 1991 film *The Restless Conscience*. The film uses present-day interviews to suggest that the prime motivation for the 20 July 1944 *putsch* attempt was to rescue Jews.

24 On the German reception of *Schindler's List*, see Schneider, *Fetisch Holocaust*, 207–36; "Der Holocaust aus Hollywood?" *Deutsches Allgemeines Sonntagsblatt*, 25 Mar. 1994, 3; Leopold Glaser, "Die Zumutung des Erinnerns: Zur deutschen Rezeption von 'Schindlers Liste,'" *Neue Gesellschaft/Frankfurter Hefte*, 41 (May 1994), 400–2; Eike Geisel, "E.T. bei den Deutschen oder Nationalsozialismus mit menschlichem Antlitz," in Initiative Sozialistisches Forum (ed.), *Schindlerdeutsche: Ein Kinotraum vom Dritten Reich* (Freiburg: Ca Ira, 1994), 107–33, cited in Geoff Eley and Atina Grossmann, "Watching *Schindler's List*: Not the Last Word," *New German Critique*, 71 (spr.–sum. 1997), 41–62.

25 Herbert Schultze, *Schindlers Liste: Materialien zum Film* (Loccum: Religionspädagogisches Institut, 1994); Christine Hesse et al., *Zum Film Schindlers Liste* (Bonn: Bundeszentrale für Politische Bildung, 1995); Wolf-Rüdiger Wagner and Matthias Günther, *Schindlers Liste* (Hannover: Landesmedienstelle, 1995).

26 This phenomenon is discussed in Schneider, *Fetisch Holocaust*, 222–33.

27 See Michael Naumann (b. 1949), *Der Krieg als Text: Das Jahr 1945 im kulturellen Gedächtnis der Presse* (Hamburg: Hamburger Edition, 1998).

28 See "Kohl: Auschwitz a Permanent Obligation to Protect the Life, Dignity, and Rights of Every Human Being," *The Week in Germany*, 3 Feb. 1995, 1.

29 Helmut Kohl, "Jedem einzelnen Schicksal schulden wir Achtung," *FAZ*, 27 Apr. 1995.

30 On the absolute peak in the number of articles published in 1995, see James Carroll, "Shoah in the News: Patterns and Meanings of News Coverage of the Holocaust," discussion paper D-27, John F. Kennedy School of Government, Oct. 1997.

31 "Gedenken an die Befreiung des Konzentrationslagers vor 50 Jahren," *SZ*, 2 May 1995. When Minister President Edmund Stoiber told his audience that "there is no way a line can be drawn under this darkest chapter of German history," he was speaking from experience. His 1988 warning that Germany's problems stemmed from its "racially mixed society" (*durchrasste Gesellschaft*) followed him throughout his later career. See *Stern*, no. 50 (8 Dec. 1988), 6.

32 The exhibition was shown in March 1995 in Hamburg, then Berlin, Potsdam, Stuttgart, and Vienna; see Karl-Heinz Janssen, "Als Soldaten Mörder wurden," *Die Zeit*, 24 Mar. 1995, 13f. It is accompanied by a catalog: Hamburger Institut für Sozialforschung (ed.), *Vernichtungskrieg: Verbrechen der Wehrmacht 1941 bis 1944* (Hamburg: Hamburger Edition, 1996), 222pp.; translated by Scott Abbott with a foreword by Omer Bartov as: Hannes Heer, *The German Army and Genocide: Crimes against War Prisoners, Jews, and other Civilians in the East, 1939–1944* (New York: New Press, 1999).

See also the volume of essays: Hannes Heer and Klaus Naumann (eds.),

Vernichtungskrieg: Verbrechen der Wehrmacht 1941 bis 1944 (Hamburg: Hamburger Edition, 1995), 685pp. An additional volume of essays about the reception of the exhibition has also been published: Hamburger Institut für Sozialforschung (ed.), *Eine Ausstellung und ihre Folgen: Zur Rezeption der Ausstellung "Vernichtungskrieg: Verbrechen der Wehrmacht 1941 bis 1944"* (Hamburg: Hamburger Edition, 1999).

The Hamburg Institute maintains a large web site about the exhibition: http://www.his-online.de/veranst/austell/vernicht.htm. The Shoah Foundation in Munich also maintains a web page with links to current exhibition sites: http://www.shoahproject.org/daten/wehrmacht/ausstellung/index.html.

For background on the exhibition's relationship to the myth of resistance, see Klaus Naumann, "Die 'saubere' Wehrmacht: Gesellschaftsgeschichte einer Legende," *Mittelweg 36*, 7:4 (1998), 8–18.

33 "'Sühne am Untermenschen': Die Ausstellung über die 'Verbrechen der Wehrmacht' löst in München Empörung aus," *Spiegel*, no. 10 (3 Mar. 1997), 54–62. The Munich reception is documented in Landeshauptstadt Munich, Kulturreferat (ed.), *Bilanz einer Ausstellung: Dokumentation der Kontroverse um die Ausstellung "Vernichtungskrieg: Verbrechen der Wehrmacht 1941 bis 1944" in München, Galerie im Rathaus, 25.2.–6.4.1997* (Munich: Knaur, 1998).

34 Angelika Königseder, "Streitkulturen und Gefühlslagen: Die Goldhagen-Debatte und der Streit um die Wehrmachtsausstellung," in Heil and Erb (eds.), *Geschichtswissenschaft und Öffentlichkeit*, 295–311, 308.

35 See Helmut Lölhöffel, "Persönliche Töne zur Wehrmacht: Bundestag debattierte über umstrittene Dokumentation," *FR*, 15 Mar. 1997. The plenary protocol containing the March debate can be downloaded from http://www.bundestag.de/ftp/13163a.zip. The second debate took place on 24 Apr. 1997.

36 Information from http://www.his-online.de/presse/war/war1.htm.

37 In October 1999, shortly before the exhibition was to open in the United States, historian Bogdan Musial showed that about nine of the 800 photographs in the exhibition depicted crimes committed by the Soviet army, not the German Wehrmacht. The exhibition was withdrawn from circulation until a panel of experts could certify that all remaining pictures were correctly identified. See Volker Ullrich, "Von Bildern und Legenden: Der neue Streit um die Wehrmachtsausstellung zeigt, wie sorgfältig mit Fotodokumenten gearbeitet werden muss," *Die Zeit*, 28 Oct. 1999.

38 On the reception, see Hans-Günther Thiele (ed.), *Die Wehrmachtsausstellung: Dokumentation einer Kontroverse: Dokumentation der Fachtagung in Bremen am 26. Februar 1997 und der Bundestagsdebatten am 13. März und 24. April 1997* (Bremen: Temmen, 1997; Bonn: Bundeszentrale für Politische Bildung, 1997); Hannes Heer, "Von der Schwierigkeit, einen Krieg zu beenden: Reaktionen auf die Ausstellung 'Vernichtungskrieg: Verbrechen der Wehrmacht, 1941 bis 1944,'" *Zeitschrift für Geschichtswissenschaft*, 45 (1997), 1086–1100; Hans Arnold, "Das Ende einer Legende: Anmerkungen zur Wehrmachtsausstellung," *Neue Gesellschaft/Frankfurter Hefte*, 44 (May 1997), 399–403; Omer Bartov, "German Soldiers and the Holocaust," in Arad (ed.), *Passing into History*, 162–88; Reinhard Kannonier and Brigitte Kepplinger, *"Irritationen": Wehrmachtsausstellung in Linz* (Grünbach: Franz Steinmassl, 1997); Heribert Prantl (ed.), *"Wehrmachtsverbrechen": Eine deuts-*

che Kontroverse (Hamburg: Hoffmann und Campe, 1997); Hamburger Institut für Sozialforschung (ed.), *Besucher einer Ausstellung: Die Ausstellung "Vernichtungskrieg: Verbrechen der Wehrmacht 1941 bis 1944" in Interview und Gespräch* (Hamburg: Hamburger Edition, 1998).

39 Daniel Goldhagen, *Hitler's Willing Executioners: Ordinary Germans and the Holocaust* (New York: Knopf, [Mar.] 1996); *Hitlers willige Vollstrecker: Ganz gewöhnliche Deutsche und der Holocaust*, trans. Klaus Kochmann (Berlin: Siedler, [Aug.] 1996).

40 Matthias Heyl, "Die Goldhagen-Debatte im Spiegel der englisch- und deutschsprachigen Rezensionen von Februar bis Juli 1996: Ein Überblick," *Mittelweg 36*, 5:4 (1996/7), 41–56.

41 These and other reviews are reprinted in Julius Schoeps (ed.), *Ein Volk von Mördern? Die Dokumentation zur Goldhagen-Kontroverse um die Rolle der Deutschen im Holocaust* (Hamburg: Hoffmann und Campe, 1996). Some of these reviews are published in translation in Robert Shandley (ed.), *Unwilling Germans?: The Goldhagen Debate* (Minneapolis: University of Minnesota Press, 1998).

A scholarly discussion of these reviews on the internet discussion forum H-German is archived at: http://www.h-net.msu.edu/~german/discuss/goldhagen/index.html.

42 On the reception in Germany, see Josef Joffe, "Goldhagen in Germany," *New York Review of Books*, 43:19 (28 Nov. 1996), 18–21; Amos Elon, "The Antagonist as Liberator," *New York Times Magazine* (26 Jan. 1997), 40–4; Michael Schneider, "Die 'Goldhagen-Debatte': Ein Historikerstreit in der Mediengesellschaft," *Archiv für Sozialgeschichte* 37 (1997); Schneider, *Fetisch Holocaust*, 19–98.

43 Daniel Goldhagen, *Briefe an Goldhagen* (Berlin: Siedler, 1997). Several writers admitted that they had only seen one of the TV appearances, while numerous others were prompted to buy the book after seeing the author on TV.

44 For examples of the scholarly criticism of the book, see Norman Finkelstein and Ruth Bettina Birn, *A Nation on Trial: The Goldhagen Thesis and Historical Truth* (New York: Henry Holt, 1998); Franklin Littell (ed.), *Hyping the Holocaust: Scholars Answer Goldhagen* (East Rockaway, N.Y.: Cummings and Hathaway, 1997); also Dieter Pohl, "Die Holocaustforschung und Goldhagens Thesen," *VfZ*, 45:1 (Jan. 1997), 1–48.

45 Published in translation as Jürgen Habermas, "On the Public Use of History: Why a 'Democracy Prize' for Daniel Goldhagen?" in Karl Bredthauer and Arthur Heinrich (eds.), *Aus der Geschichte Lernen: Verleihung des Blätter-Demokratiepreises 1997* (Bonn: Blätter für deutsche und internationale Politik, 1997), 14–36.

46 Ibid., 34, 16. Others, such as Hans-Ulrich Wehler and Ulrich Herbert, also noted their discomfort with the vehemence of the German scholarly rejection.

47 Werner Bergmann, "Im falschen System: Die Goldhagen-Debatte in Wissenschaft und Öffentlichkeit," in Heil and Erb (eds.), *Geschichtswissenschaft und Öffentlichkeit*, 131–47, 143f.

48 A fall 1998 attempt by author Martin Walser to "resist" the use of "Auschwitz as a moral club" against the resurrected post-unification Germany provoked a heated debate among the older cohorts that was dispassionately observed by the younger cohorts. On Walser's 11 Oct. 1998 speech and the reactions, see the essays in *Universitas*, 12 (1998), and *FAZ*, 14 Dec. 1998. See also pp. 433f n. 6, above.

49 Bernd Greiner, in an article about the reception of the *Vernichtungskrieg* exhibition ("Bruch-Stücke: Sechs westdeutsche Beobachtungen nebst unfertigen Deutungen," in Hamburger Institut für Sozialforschung (ed.), *Eine Ausstellung und ihre Folgen*, 40), put it succinctly: "Wir sehen eine zur Akzeptanz ihrer Erblast bereite Gesellschaft vor uns: willens, das Unüberbrückbare zwischen Opfern und Tätern, aber auch zwischen den Generationen von Tätern, Kindern und Enkeln als unüberbrückbar zu akzeptieren."

50 For these two examples, see Gernot Facius, "Gemeinsame Wurzeln erkennen: Die Kirchen in Deutschland versuchen, ihr Verhältnis zum Judentum neu zu bestimmen," *Welt*, 27 Nov. 1998; "Kinderärzte bekennen sich zu NS-Schuld," *FR*, 5 Oct. 1998.

51 See *SZ* (Landkreis edn), 6 Sept. 1955. On Graubard, see also Baruch Graubard, "In den Fängen des Todes," reprinted in *Dachauer Hefte*, 6 (1990), 118ff.

52 The proposal was presented to Minister of Culture Maier on 24 July 1970. A parliamentary inquiry in May 1972 revealed that in the interim nothing had been done. See *Verhandlungen* (17 May 1972), vol. 2, 2093.

53 "Steigende Besucherzahlen in der KZ-Gedenkstätte: Braucht Dachau eine Jugendherberge?" *SZ*, 26 May 1978.

54 Cited after Hans Holzhaider, "'Ein diffuses Unbehagen': Widerstände gegen die Errichtung einer Jugendbegegnungsstätte in Dachau," in Förderverein Internationale Jugendbegegnungsstätte (ed.), *Erinnern-Begegnen-Verstehen: Ein Zwischenbericht* (Dachau: n.p., 1986), 26.

55 See "Musealer Charakter der Gedenkstätte bedrückend ideenlos: KZ, den Verpflichtungen aus der Vergangenheit nicht entsprechend," *MM/DN*, 27 Feb. 1982; "Auch die SPD will Friedensinstitut in Dachau," *SZ/DN*, 3 Mar. 1982; "Friedensforschung stösst auf zurückhaltendes Interesse: Stadt zeigt wenig Neigung, sich um das Institut zu bewerben," *SZ/DN*, 12 Mar. 1982.

56 See Hannes Otter, "Chronik des Dachau e.V.," in Förderverein (ed.), *Erinnern*, 29–32; Timothy Ryback, "Report from Dachau," *New Yorker* (Aug. 1992), 43–61, 45f.

57 Jürgen Zarusky, "Förderverein für Jugendbegegnungsstätte: ... auf der Gründungsversammlung bereits 108 Mitglieder," *SZ/DN*, 26 Nov. 1984.

58 See Förderverein Internationale Jugendbegegnungsstätte (ed.), *1984–1989: Ein Zwischenbericht* (Dachau: n.p., 1989); also Stefan Stadler, "Das Internationale Jugendbegegnungszeltlager in Dachau," in Annegret Ehmann et al. (eds.), *Praxis der Gedenkstättenpädagogik: Erfahrungen und Perspektiven* (Opladen: Leske und Budrich, 1995), 186–93.

59 Jürgen Zarusky, "Jugendbegegnungsstätte unerwünscht: CSU lässt das Visier herunter: Dachauer Spitzenfunktionäre bekunden geschlossene Ablehnung des Projekts," *SZ/DN*, 26 Mar. 1985; Eva Klimt, "In Bonn spontane Unterstützung gefunden: Drei Mitglieder des Vereins internationale Jugendbegegnungsstätte beim Empfang des Bundespräsidenten," *SZ/DN*, 25–7 May 1985.

60 The 5–6 March 1987 conference is documented in the volume: Bayerischer Jugendring (ed.), *Lernort Dachau: Protokoll einer Fachtagung im Institut für Jugendarbeit des Bayerischen Jugendrings* (Munich: BJR, 1988). See also Peter Steinbach, *Modell Dachau: Das Konzentrationslager und die Stadt Dachau in der Zeit des Nationalsozialismus und ihre Bedeutung für die Gegenwart* (Passau: Andreas Haller, 1987).

61 Wolfgang Eitler, "Jugendbegegnungsstätte: Englhard lässt abstimmen / Überraschender Auftakt zur Wahlveranstaltung mit Lothar Späth," *SZ/DN*, 21 Aug. 1986. Späth (CDU) was the minister president of Baden-Württemberg.

62 Ulrike Steinbacher, "CSU Dachau fordert 'nationale Lösung' / Jugendbegegnungsstätte nach München, Berlin oder Nürnberg / Georg Englhard gegen 'Kainszeichen' für nachfolgende Generationen," *SZ/DN*, 23 Mar. 1987. See also Walter Gierlich, "Jugendbegegnungsstätte am Konzentrationslager: 'Wir werden uns mit aller Kraft wehren' / Dachauer CSU gegen das Projekt," *Die Zeit*, 22 May 1987.

63 "Keine Vergangenheits-Bewältigungsstätte," *Dachauer Woche*, 26 Mar. 1987; Rolf Hanusch, "'So werden Gespräche sinnlos,' Förderverein Jugendbegegnungsstätte zu CSU-Äusserungen," *SZ/DN*, 4 Apr. 1987; Ralph Giordano, "Fearful of History? Commemorative Work in Dachau and Other Places," *Dachau Review*, 2 (1990), 143–55, 150.

64 "Leserumfrage soll Lücke im Informationsgehalt der KZ-Gedenkstätte schliessen helfen / Heimatzeitung will Dokumentation über das Verhalten der Dachauer," *Dachauer Woche*, 10 Sept. 1987.

65 "Leserumfrage könnte dazu beitragen, dokumentarische Lücke zu schliessen: Abgeordnete, Landrat und Bürgermeister vom Ergebnis beeindruckt: Über 1700mal Ja," *MM/DN*, 8 Oct. 1987.

66 This vote and the reaction to it are vividly described by Ryback, "Report," 46.

67 See "Die Deutschstunde," *Stern*, no. 47 (17 Nov. 1988), and "Unsere unendliche Geschichte," *Stern*, no. 48 (24 Nov. 1988).

68 am, "Leiter des Stadtbauamtes weist Bedenken der zukünftigen Nachbarn zurück: 'Geordnetes Miteinander' garantiert," *SZ/DN*, 11 Aug. 1994.

69 Adalbert Zehnder, "Gestern früh um 8.07 Uhr: Die Bauarbeiten an der Rosswachtstrasse beginnen / 235 PS Schubkraft fürs Jugendgästehaus / Was die Nachbarn sagen und was die Bauleitung vorhat / Offizieller Festakt am 25. März," *SZ/DN*, 5 Mar. 1996.

70 Unofficially, it was in use since March. See Hilmar Klute, "Der Dachau-Überlebende und Schriftsteller Solly Ganor aus Israel eröffnet das Jugendgästehaus mit einer Lesung," *SZ/DN*, 24 Mar. 1998.

71 The German and English editions of the catalog were published in May 1978. See *Mitteilungen LGD*, Nov. 1978.

72 Initially only three teachers could be found to fill the four slots (one each for *Haupt, Real-, Berufsschule*, and *Gymnasium*). See *Mitteilungen LGD*, Apr. 1981; Erwin Kottermeier, "22. März 1933 – Dachau und das KZ," *MM/DN*, 22 Mar. 1983. For the original announcement, see Kurt Kister, "Damit die Schüler besser begreifen: Eigene Lehrer für KZ-Führungen / In Dachau werden vier Pädagogen Klassen beim Besuch der Gedenkstätte betreuen," *SZ*, 4/5 Oct. 1980.

73 See, e.g., Akademie für Lehrerfortbildung, Dillingen (ed.), *KZ-Gedenkstätte Dachau: Unterrichtshilfen und Materialien zum Besuch mit Schulklassen* (Dillingen: Akademie, 1983); also A. Kreuzkam, "Broschüre über die Betreuungsarbeit von Gruppen und Initiativen in der KZ-Gedenkstätte Dachau," 3 Nov. 1988, DaA. For the studies of visitors, see Sven Gareis and Malte von Vultejus, *Lernort Dachau? Eine empirische Einstellungsuntersuchung bei Besuchern der KZ-Gedenkstätte Dachau* (Munich: University of the Bundeswehr, 1986); Sven Gareis,

Didaktik der Begegnung: Zur Organisation historischer Lernprozesse im Lernort Dachau (Frankfurt: Peter Lang, 1989).

74 For information on the Scholl Prize, see: http://www.buchhandel-bayern.de/ geschw-scholl/index.html. The reprint edition was published by dtv in 1994.

75 Using a conservative estimate of 700,000 annual visitors, with 5–10 percent coming on Mondays (weekends have the highest visitor numbers), even if half of them know of the closing and come on other days instead, that would leave 17,000–35,000 people annually who attempt to come on Mondays. On the closing and the initiatives to end it, see gn, "SPD im Landtag: KZ-Gedenkstätte auch montags öffnen," *SZ/DN*, 3 Feb. 1988.

76 Even when the ministry's own advisory board recommended ending the Monday closing in its 1996 report, the ministry issued no response. For a more recent call to end the Monday closure, see Achim Sing, "Lernort und 'Ort der Stille': Kolloquium zur Neugestaltung der KZ-Gedenkstätte Dachau," *Bayerische Staatszeitung*, 3 July 1998.

77 See Helmut Rez, "Es geht um die Neubelebung der Gedenkstätte," *SZ/DN*, 22 Sept. 1993, 7.

78 Statistics available at DaA.

79 See Rez, "Es geht um die Neubelebung." For the explanation of Delpeche's reaction, see Jürgen Zarusky, "Was gilt bei Ihnen nun eigentlich, Herr Richardi?," *SZ/DN*, 22 Sept. 1993. Zarusky notes that without the work of the CID there would be no memorial site at all in which books could be sold.

80 See Wolfgang Eitler and Thomas Soyer, "Die aktuelle Diskussion um die Zukunft der Gedenkstätte und ihre Hintergründe: Wie ein Dachauer Arbeitskreis ehemalige Häftlinge brüskiert," *SZ/DN*, 30/31 Oct. 1993.

81 See the joint letter to the editor from twelve members of the working group: "Kolumnist der Dachauer Neuesten oder inoffizieller Gedenkstättensprecher?" *SZ/DN*, ca. 20 Oct. 1993.

82 Hans Lacker (high school teacher in Dachau), letter to the editor, *SZ/DN*, 2/3 Oct. 1993.

83 Zarusky, "Was gilt bei Ihnen."

84 With roughly 61,000 catalogs sold and 812,000 counted visitors in 1988, and 46,000 catalogs and 633,000 visitors in 1995, about 7–8 percent of visitors purchase catalogs. Statistics available at DaA.

85 Norbert Reck, "Gut gemeint . . . Ein Plädoyer gegen den moralischen Imperialismus bei der Arbeit mit Jugendlichen in Gedenkstätten," *Gedenkstättenrundbrief*, no. 33 (Nov. 1989), 3–6, 4.

86 Quoted in Julie Salamon, "Walls that Echo of the Unspeakable," *New York Times*, 7 Sept. 1997, 84. University of Chicago historian Peter Novick, who studies Holocaust museums in the United States, said it another way: "The notion of coming to any kind of historical understanding of what was going on there on the basis of spending a couple of hours looking at displays is nutsy." He was quoted by Geraldine Baum, "Do Holocaust Museums Make Us Better People?" *Los Angeles Times*, 11 Dec. 1997, E1,4.

87 Alison Landsberg, "America, the Holocaust, and the Mass Culture of Memory: Toward a Radical Politics of Empathy," *New German Critique*, 71 (1997), 63–86, 66. The following quotation is taken from p. 85.

For a much earlier discussion of this position, see Gerhard Schneider, "Mehr Affektivität im Geschichtsunterricht? Die Darstellung des Zweiten Weltkriegs in der trivialen und populärwissenschaftlichen Literatur und ihre Verwendung im Unterricht," *Aus Politik und Zeitgeschichte*, B45 (1980), 16–38.

88 For critiques of too much emotional appeal in Holocaust education, see Sebastian Fetscher, "Das Dritte Reich und die Moral der Nachgeborenen: Vom Dünkel der Betroffenheit," *Neue Sammlung*, 29 (1989), 161–85; also Dietfried Krause-Vilmar, "Überlegungen zum Verständnis des Lehrens und Lernens," in Doron Kiesel et al. (eds.), *Pädagogik der Erinnerung: Didaktische Aspekte der Gedenkstättenarbeit* (Frankfurt: Haag und Herchen, 1997), 79–88; Annegret Ehmann, "Über Sprache, Begriffe und Deutungen des nationalsozialistischen Massen- und Völkermords," in Ehmann et al. (eds.), *Praxis der Gedenkstättenpädagogik*, 86.

89 Quoted in Achim Sing, "Zwischen Gedenkstätte und Lernort – eine neue Ausstellung über das KZ Dachau: Das Haus der Bayerischen Geschichte gestaltet die Gedenkstätte des Konzentrationslagers Dachau neu," *Bayerische Staatszeitung*, 17 Apr. 1998.

90 This has been confirmed by empirical research. See, for example, Richard Meng, "In Gedenkstätten spüren Jugendliche oft nur 'Reiz des Grauens' / Studie belegt: Besuch von Orten, an denen nationalsozialistische Verbrechen verübt wurden, führt noch nicht zu Lernprozessen," *FR*, 9 June 1992. The study in question is Cornelia Fischer and Hubert Anton, *Auswirkungen der Besuche von Gedenkstätten auf Schülerinnen und Schüler: Bericht über 40 Explorationen in Hessen und Thüringen* (Wiesbaden: Hessische Landeszentrale für politische Bildung, 1992).

91 The Heidelberg center did not officially open until March 1997. See http://www.cvb-heidelberg.de/deutsch/Museum12.html.

92 See "KZ-Gedenkstätte Dachau: Empfehlungen für eine Neukonzeption vorgelegt vom wissenschaftlichen Fachbeirat," 23 May 1996, 60pp., DaA. Hereafter cited as: Fachbeirat, "Empfehlungen." The guidelines can be found on 6f. To improve readability I have paraphrased slightly, except for the principles set out under point 5.

93 Once experts realized the important role the rooms in the west wing played in the experience of arriving inmates, they decided not to install the movie theater there. See p. 562 n. 109, below.

94 See Dwork and van Pelt, *Auschwitz, 1270–Present*, 363f.

95 This is definition 7b of "authentic" in the 1986 edition of the Merriam-Webster Third New International Dictionary. For thought-provoking reflections on the effects of reconstructions, see Günther Anders, *Die Schrift an der Wand: Tagebücher 1941–1966* (Munich: Beck, 1967), 223–8.

96 Mannheimer is cited in Sing, "Zwischen Gedenkstätte und Lernort," 1f.

97 For photographs of the late 1960s' condition, see John Mitchell, *Dachau Museum and Memorial Grounds* (Marceline, Mo.: Walsworth, 1968).

98 In 1998 the advisory council decided that *every* room should contain documentation of its original purpose. The scope of that documentation would be "commensurate with the historical importance [of the room]."

99 For a discussion of this issue in the recent reconstruction of the Buchenwald memorial site, see Roger Cohen, "The Germans Want Their History Back / Many American Visitors Are Surprised that Buchenwald Had No Gas Chambers," *New York Times*, 12 Sept. 1999, 4.

100 Fachbeirat, "Empfehlungen," 9.
101 For example, in November 1999 the semi-annual memorial site seminar took place in Dachau to discuss these very issues. See "Didaktische Zugänge zu historischen Orten – Das Beispiel KZ-Gedenkstätte Dachau: Bundesweites Gedenkstätten-seminar in Dachau," *Gedenkstättenrundbrief*, no. 89 (June 1999), 21–5.
102 See Sichrovsky, *Born Guilty*, 30f, and p. 313, above.
103 This reasoning was also reported in Thomas Soyer, "Bund gibt 500,000 Mark für das 'Jourhaus': Als Teil des Sanierungskonzepts wird das Eingangsgebäude nun doch restauriert," *SZ/DN*, 19 June 1998. On exhibiting the perpetrators in general, see Wulff Brebeck, "Zur Darstellung der Täter in Ausstellungen von Gedenkstätten der Bundesrepublik," in Ehmann et al. (eds.), *Praxis der Gedenkstättenpädagogik*, 296–300.
104 Fachbeirat, "Empfehlungen," 16.
105 Hockerts is cited in Sing, "Zwischen Gedenkstätte und Lernort." For a more detailed discussion of reasons not to stage past events, see Günter Morsch, "Überlegungen zur Ausstellungskonzeption in der Gedenkstätte Sachsenhausen," in Bernd Faulenbach and Franz-Josef Jelich (eds.), *Reaktionäre Modernität und Völkermord: Probleme des Umgangs mit der NS-Zeit in Museen, Ausstellungen und Gedenkstätten* (Essen: Klartext, 1994), 91–4.
106 See "Ausstellungskonzept für die Neugestaltung der KZ-Gedenkstätte Dachau," 19pp., 28 May 1998, DaA, and http://www.bayern.de/HDBG/projekt-kz/index.htm.
107 See Felicitas Amler, "Neue Recherchen für eine moderne Ausstellung: Kolloquium macht Anforderungen des Denkmalschutzes und der historischen Forschung deutlich / Forderung nach Besucherzentrum," *SZ/DN*, 4/5 July 1998, 11.
108 See Dietrich Mittler, "KZ-Gedenkstätte Dachau erhält ein neues Gesicht: Besucher sollen den 'Weg der Häftlinge bei ihrer Einlieferung' nachvollziehen können," *SZ*, 18 Dec. 1998; Felicitas Amler, "Die KZ-Gedenkstätte des Jahres 2001: Haus der Bayerischen Geschichte erläutert Ausstellungskonzept / Eingang durchs Jourhaus, Zufahrt noch unklar," *SZ/DN*, 18 Dec. 1998; also Felicitas Amler, "'Neuralgischer Punkt': die Zufahrt: Neugestaltung der KZ-Gedenkstätte / 'Keine Konfrontation mit den Bürgern,'" *SZ/DN*, 29 Mar. 1999.
109 See Christian Krügel, "Jetzt wird der Umbau umgebaut: KZ-Gedenkstätte bleibt für Besucher geöffnet / Keine neuen Kinosäle im Westflügel," *SZ/DN*, 11 Feb. 1998; Renate Schostack, "Umdenken in Dachau: Die Gedenkstätte wird saniert, die Ausstellung erneuert," *FAZ*, 29 Jan. 1998, p. 33.
110 Although Krügel's February 1998 article (cited in the previous note) implies that the murals would be preserved as well, the exhibition designs being discussed in the summer of 2000 presumed their removal.
111 See especially Detlef Hoffmann's June 1998 presentation "Konservieren – Restaurieren – Rekonstruieren: Das Baudenkmal 'KZ Dachau' zwischen 'historischer Quelle' und 'Erlebnisort'", in Haus der Bayerischen Geschichte (ed.), *Räume – Medien – Pädagogik: Kolloquium zur Neugestaltung der KZ-Gedenkstätte Dachau* (Augsburg: Haus der Bayerischen Geschichte, 1999), 15–17. On Sachsen-hausen: Martina Madner, "Comics im Konzentrationslager: Die Wandmalereien in Sachsenhausen werden restauriert, einige entstanden nach 1945," *taz*, 27 July 1999; on Buchenwald: Jens Schneider, "Neue Ausstellung in Buchenwald: Gezeigt wird die Manipulation des Gedenkens durch die DDR," *SZ*, 25 Oct. 1999.

112 See Thomas Soyer, "Authentischer Zugang: Neue Ausstellung in KZ-Gedenkstätte Dachau 2001 fertig," *SZ*, 24 Apr. 1999; Barbara Distel, "Der Weg der Häftlinge ins Konzentrationslager: Ein Plädoyer für die Wiederherstellung des ursprünglichen Zugangs," *SZ/DN*, 11 May 1999; Christian Krügel, "Neue Verwirrung um Konzeption und Zufahrt: Staatsminister Naumann fordert rasche Einigung," *SZ/DN*, 1 Dec. 1999; Felicitas Amler, "Im 'Bunker' leiden die Besucher mit / 14 Millionen Mark für authentische Darstellung," *SZ*, 28. Jan 2000.

113 For brief sketches of three 1979er cohort teachers' personal connections to National Socialism, see Helmut Schreier, "The Holocaust: Consequences for Education," in Schreier and Matthias Heyl (eds.), *Never Again? The Holocaust's Challenge for Educators* (Hamburg: Krämer, 1997), 189–98, 196ff.

114 This obsession with controlling the reception of memorials was highlighted by a discussion regarding Germany's central Holocaust memorial in Berlin in 1999. Asked about people who would "misuse" the memorial to lie in the sun or spray graffiti, Jewish-American architect Peter Eisenmann replied: "There will also be graffiti, the more the better. Every graffito shows that someone was there who thought about something. It would be awful if people ignored the memorial. Let them picnic between the concrete blocks." The (1968er) German authorities, in contrast, wanted to erect a fence around the memorial. See "Kein Wort an einer Stele: Ein Gespräch mit dem Architekten Peter Eisenmann," *SZ*, 21 May 1999; "Des Mahnmals Schwarzer Peter," *SZ*, 19 July 1999.

115 My results are similar to the conclusions of Peter Schneider, who interviewed some 300 young Germans born between 1973 and 1980. See Peter Schneider, "The Sins of the Grandfathers: How German Teen-Agers Confront the Holocaust, and How They Don't," *New York Times Magazine*, 3 Dec. 1995, 74–80. Schneider also discusses the implausibility of the 1943er grandparents' accounts for this cohort.

 For additional discussions of this cohort, see Stiftung für die Rechte zukünftiger Generationen (ed.), *Was bleibt von der Vergangenheit? Die junge Generation im Dialog über den Holocaust* (Berlin: Christian Links, 1999); Björn Krondorfer, *Remembrance and Reconciliation: Encounters between Young Jews and Germans* (New Haven: Yale University Press, 1995).

116 Interviews with Tanja K. and Klaudia K., conducted during a bus trip in Poland, 24–6 June 1997. Notes in my possession. See also my interviews with Sybille Steinbacher (b. 1966), Dachau, 23 July 1997, and Marijke Oidtmann (b. 1976), Freiburg, 9 Aug. 1993.

117 Interview in Cracow, 27 June 1997. Notes in my possession. Other relevant interviews were Hartmut L. (b. 1966), Freiburg, 8 Aug. 1993; Kevin W. (b. 1967), Santa Barbara, 12 Mar. 1993; Markus F. (b. 1967), Plön, 22 Aug. 1993; Jens G. (b. 1967), Weimar, 3 Aug. 1995; Carolyn Bronstein (b. 1968), 10 Sept. 1998 (see also p. 275, above); Sascha P. (b. 1971), Cracow, 27 June 1997; Diana S. (b. 1971), Santa Barbara, 10 May 1993; Justin M. (b. 1976), Santa Barbara, 7 Oct. 1998.

118 One of my teaching assistants noted that proportionally more women enrolled in my Holocaust course emphasizing common people and daily life in Nazi Germany (the ratio was about 2:1), while in another professor's course, entitled "Hitler and Nazi Germany" with a concomitant emphasis on "great men" and high politics, the proportion was reversed. That might be an expression of the same phenomenon.

Index

Note 1: since many of the names in this book are relatively unknown, most have been indexed under the person's occupation or role, such as architect, artist, historian, or journalist. Some politicians can be found under headings such as Bavaria, minister presidents, or Dachau town, mayors. Other important categories are: comparisons, films, research topics, and terms. However, within these categories, names and terms marked with an asterisk (*) are listed as main entries.

Note 2: The term "Dachau" has been broken down into the subcategories: concentration camp, county, memorial site, internment camp, and town. Certain terms that cross the concentration camp and the memorials site have been indexed separately: for example, barracks, crematorium, gatehouse, inscriptions, roll-call square, signs, and watchtowers. These, too, are marked with an asterisk (*).

Index

Index